UNLEASHED

BORIS JOHNSON

UNLEASHED

WILLIAM
COLLINS

William Collins
An imprint of HarperCollins*Publishers*
1 London Bridge Street
London SE1 9GF

WilliamCollinsBooks.com

HarperCollins*Publishers*
Macken House, 39/40 Mayor Street Upper
Dublin 1, D01 C9W8, Ireland

First published in Great Britain in 2024 by William Collins

1

A catalogue record for this book is
available from the British Library

HB ISBN 978-0-00-861820-9
TPB ISBN 978-0-00-873345-2

Set in Adobe Caslon Pro
Printed and bound in the UK using 100%
renewable electricity at CPI Group (UK) Ltd

This book contains FSC™ certified paper and other controlled
sources to ensure responsible forest management.

For more information visit: www.harpercollins.co.uk/green

To Carrie

and to the memory of my mother, Charlotte

Hasta la Vista, Baby

– Arnold Schwarzenegger,
Terminator 2: Judgment Day (1991)

Contents

Part Three – Confessions of a Eurosceptic

Part Four – Global Britain

Part Five – Crunch Time

Part Six – A Great Plan for Britain

Part Ten – Last Months

Part One
Trapped

Chapter 1

The Curse
of Spiderwoman

In which I am apparently skewered
by the Supreme Court

They say the hour is darkest before dawn. Well, my watch said dawn was hours ago and it was still dark. What the hell was wrong? Oh yes. I was in New York.

I was in a not very flashy hotel, to judge by the size of the room; and as consciousness returned, I remembered the other key data.

I had come to New York with my wife-to-be, who was lying asleep next to me. She was pregnant. And, that's right, I was prime minister of the United Kingdom, and first lord of the Treasury, minister for the civil service and the Union; and before I could reflect any further on the position I saw the light that had woken me up.

It was Martin Reynolds, my brilliant private secretary, whose name was flashing up from London on my iPhone.

'Morning, PM,' said Martin, in his characteristically bouncy tones. You could almost hear his tail thrashing the carpet.

'Sorry to wake you so early, but I think you need to turn on your TV. It's bad news I am afraid.' Bad news? I thought. I wasn't sure how my political position could possibly get worse.

Yes, I was the leader of a G7 country, and yes, I had supposedly enormous executive powers. I had heavily armed and highly trained detectives who physically protected my person. Yesterday one of them had actually crossed from one side of the New York pavement to the other, to push some unsuspecting pedestrian from my path. He gave a startled cry.

I had cars and planes and helicopters and a trillion-pound budget. But politically I was trapped. My grip on power was already tenuous, and after sixty-three increasingly turbulent days in the job, I felt I was clinging to the rain-slicked window ledge of office.

My parliamentary majority was zero and sinking the whole time. I had sustained the fastest by-election defeat of any PM in history. Three weeks ago I was on my feet in the House when one of my colleagues – actually a rather thoughtful GP from Bracknell – had stood up as if to intervene in my speech, but rather than catch my eye, he had then sauntered across the floor, as I burbled on, to join the Lib Dem benches, where he was received with rapturous acclaim.

I had no real electoral mandate, having become PM solely thanks to the votes of 160,000 Tory members, all of them no doubt estimable and responsible people, but only a tiny fraction of the wider electorate. I had not won a single vote in Parliament; and I was stuck, as in one of those suffocating dreams where your legs won't do as you order them.

I could not do the one thing that I had promised my Tory selectorate I would do. I could not deliver on the mandate of the people. I was unable to execute the promise we had made to 17.4 million people and to honour their vote to leave the European Union. We were hurtling towards the October 31 deadline by which we were due to leave the EU, and I had sworn to make it happen, 'do or die'. But the result was looking much more like die than do.

I couldn't see a way through. Parliament was refusing to vote through a deal that would allow us to leave. The EU was refusing to give us a new deal. The UK negotiating position, already pretty weak, had been more or less destroyed by the 'Surrender Act', a parliamentary bill that meant the UK could not just walk away from the talks and would have to sign up to whatever the EU would give us. And the EU was not going to give us anything that Parliament would accept.

I could go neither forwards nor backwards. The crowning indignity of my situation was that I was not even allowed the final remedy of the despairing prime minister. Under the terms of the Fixed-term Parliaments Act, I could not call a general election.

I was stymied, stuck, stumped, and as I switched on the TV – to Carrie's protests – I wondered what new disaster was unfolding. I found the BBC News channel, and saw that it was all about the Supreme Court.

Whoa, I said to myself. I was aware that some court judgment impended today, but then I was well used to crackpot legal actions about Brexit. Ever since the UK had voted to leave the EU on June 23, 2016, the courts had been clogged with furious petitioners. The gist of their complaints was that the people had been duped, that the Vote Leave campaign had cheated, and that in helping to lead that campaign I was guilty of some malfeasance in public office. All such vexatious cases had been rightly chucked out, and I had put them in the same category as the man in the blue top hat with the European flag, dressed like Mr Bumble the beadle, who used to bawl unpleasantness at me through a megaphone and even bare his buttocks at my motorcade.

They were all a symptom of the national fever. They showed how fired up they were, on the losing side. But I had assumed they were just an irrelevance, just noise, and that they would not in themselves be any kind of impediment to Brexit.

This, on the other hand, looked serious.

A grey-haired woman appeared on the screen. She had a severe expression and a silver brooch that looked like Shelob the giant spider from *Lord of the Rings*. She was Baroness Brenda Hale, president of the UK Supreme Court, and she was delivering the unanimous judgment of the court in a case that had been brought against me by Gina Miller, a businesswoman who believed that the UK was wrong to leave the EU.

It was hard to follow exactly what Baroness Hale was saying because by now Carrie was getting up, and people were constantly on the phone, and I was trying to get my running kit on. By the time I tuned in to her judgment (I suppose it must have been around 10.30 a.m. in London and 5.30 a.m. in New York), Hale had got about halfway through and – this was no doubt why Martin had rung – it was not going well.

She and her colleagues had already decided one crucial question, which was that they had the right to opine on the matter in hand. This was in itself a pretty extraordinary step.

The issue was whether I was within my rights, as prime minister, to prorogue Parliament: that is, to bring an end to a parliamentary sitting and start a new one, with a new Queen's Speech. None of my legal advice had suggested there was any problem with this. I was doing what every PM has always done.

In fact, you could argue that in this case proroguing – or prorogation – was long overdue. This parliamentary session had been going on for 348 sitting days, that is excluding weekends and holidays. It was the longest since the English civil war of the seventeenth century, and as Cromwell told them at the time, this one had sat too long for any good they were doing.

We were a new government with a new agenda. We had big plans for building more hospitals and putting more police on the streets; for skills and infrastructure and planning. We needed new bills and a new parliamentary session, and all we were doing, in sending MPs home, was losing a handful of sitting days – between four and seven.

What on earth was the problem? This was a decision for the PM, not for the courts.

Spiderwoman was now coming to the climax of her remarks and she was being increasingly critical of someone – it must be me. She seemed to be saying that I was trying to stop Parliament from debating Brexit.

Her argument was that Parliament needed to be integrally involved in the process of leaving the EU, and that by proroguing Parliament I was stopping MPs from doing their job. At this point eyewitnesses say that I erupted with anger. Stopping Parliament debate Brexit?

I wasn't stopping Parliament debate Brexit. MPs had been gassing on about the subject for more than three years, and they had totally failed to deliver on their promises to the people.

They didn't want to debate Brexit. They wanted to block Brexit.

So did many powerful and consequential people – doubtless nice, kind, good people – and so, I was increasingly beginning to suspect, did this judge. She dealt the final blow, saying that what I had done was unlawful, that I had not in fact prorogued Parliament, and that as far as she was concerned MPs should hot-foot it back to Westminster to get on with talking about Brexit.

As soon as she got to her denouement, about Johnson the law-breaker, the internet exploded in a twittergasm of delight. 'Boom! Boris Johnson's position has collapsed,' said a BBC correspondent. At the Labour Party conference, which was going on at the same time, the leader of the opposition, Jeremy Corbyn, interrupted his speech to give them the news, and Labour activists responded with a howling ovation.

Within seconds I was facing calls to resign, from Labour, Scots Nats, Liberals and from Conservative colleagues such as Dominic Grieve, the former attorney general and MP for Beaconsfield (electoral slogan: Grieve for Beaconsfield), who said that I needed to 'consider my position', by which he meant resign.

So as I showered and flung on my suit I considered my position, and I was still considering it throughout an emergency meeting of my officials in one of the hotel rooms, and as we drove through New York to my first engagement, breakfast with big US investors.

I considered the position as I looked at the sun striking the tops of the skyscrapers, the delis opening, the steam coming from the grates. I felt the fundamental energy and optimism of my native city. Yes, I considered my position, and found it on the whole not too bad.

I found myself unshaken in the belief – which I still hold – that the judges were wrong. Baroness Hale and her colleagues were not only contradicting the legal advice. They were overturning the opinions of the Lord Chief Justice, the Master of the Rolls and the President of the Queen's Bench Division. Even if we left on October 31, 2019, as planned, there would be plenty of time for parliamentary debate, if that was really what they wanted.

I meant no disrespect to any of them in the Supreme Court, but I felt I could see the psychological pressures that had driven them to this piece of legal adventurism. You have to understand that in 2019 the country was still split over Brexit and, if anything, the divisions were getting worse. The UK had voted to leave the EU by a majority of 52 to 48 per cent. That was a narrow margin, but still astonishing given the balance of forces in the debate.

All the main political parties were in favour of remaining in the EU. The entire engine of government propaganda campaigned for Remain, and it would be fair to say that most members of the British establishment were overwhelmingly hostile to leaving the EU: most readers of *The Times* (more than 70 per cent, some said); most BBC journalists; most university lecturers; most members of the Confederation of British Industry; most MPs, by quite a long way; and most members of the great British legal profession.

For decades a lot of these people had regarded me (in so far as they were conscious of the subject) with a vague but amused disapproval. They knew me as a TV game show host, a newspaper columnist who said scandalous things, a prize gaffe-merchant. It had never occurred to them that I would actually become PM and take Britain out of the EU.

Now some of them were borderline hysterical. My opponents in Parliament – in all parties – claimed to fear a 'no-deal Brexit', an economic calamity in which the UK abruptly fell out of the EU legal order. They prophesied stock market panic, shortage of medicines, planes refusing to obey their autopilots, that kind of thing.

In reality, that was never going to happen. It was never my plan; neither side would have allowed such chaos; and my opponents knew it.

What they really wanted was no Brexit at all: to trap me in the EU, like my predecessor Theresa May; to keep using parliamentary devices to drain me of my authority, to force me to break my promise to leave the EU, to rob me day by day of my credibility with my Tory MP colleagues – a famously ruthless bunch – until I threw in the sponge and resigned over Europe, like May, like Cameron, like Thatcher herself.

Already some of my predecessors were calling for a second referendum. Should I give in? Should I resign? I thought back to a speeding fine of almost forty years ago, the last and only time I had been found guilty, by a court, of breaking the law. I remembered my indignation at the offence. I was clocked doing 34 in a 30-mile-an-hour zone in Headington, Oxford, and I was so outraged – my Fiat 128 was barely capable of forward movement, let alone speeding – that I actually went down to the magistrates' court to challenge the decision.

I arrived just too late and remember watching through the door as a prim-looking grey-haired woman, the spiritual forerunner of Baroness Hale, pronounced my doom and ruthlessly ordered me to be fined. I felt the same sort of exasperation today.

Resign? I would no more resign than I would have given up driving in 1985. As the day went on, my confidence grew. I gave a speech at the big breakfast for major investors in the UK, and it went well. I had an enjoyable bilateral with Donald Trump and his giant inflatable personality. He gave me his enthusiastic endorsement, and in UK politics if you can survive the endorsement of Donald Trump then you can survive anything.

I had meetings with the leaders of Egypt, Afghanistan, Iran, Rwanda. I talked to Tayyip Erdoğan of Turkey and Leo Varadkar of Ireland. They had all observed the Supreme Court decision, and it occurred to me that in going for Brexit, it was as if the UK had tip-toed to the edge of the ten-metre diving board, and the whole world was watching.

We were about to launch ourselves off into a glorious and exhilarating adventure. We were going to show that we could once again be an independent country; and then, amid global consternation, hilarity, embarrassment, confusion – we had sustained some kind of dramatic swimsuit malfunction.

We were visibly wobbling on the edge of the board. Well, we couldn't allow that. We had to go through with it, and show what we were made of.

At about 6.30 London time, I rang the Queen to discuss the position and give her my view. I cannot tell you what she said, but in all my time she was never less than encouraging and supportive. I briefed the cabinet, who were quietly resolute (at least I think they were resolute: it was one of those conference calls where they were on mute). I made two more speeches, one to the Commonwealth representatives and one jumbo speech, to the entire UN Assembly, about the future of data.

By this time it was 9 p.m. in New York and 2 a.m. in London, and the audience for my data speech was appreciative but pretty select. Then I flew back on the Voyager for my reckoning in Parliament. By the time I got to my feet in the late afternoon, the place was in uproar.

John Bercow, the speaker, was in an ecstasy of pomposity and self-righteousness, since he had never approved of the prorogation and was delighted to see me humiliated. The opposition benches were a writhing sea of angry faces, and the shouts of 'Resign' went on for well over two hours. If there was one thing they hated, they told me, it was my insouciance, my brass neck.

It did not help that in her judgment Baroness Hale had quoted a box note of mine, in which I noted that the practice of holding a parliamentary sitting in September had only been recently introduced.

It was just 'girly swot' David Cameron, I scribbled, trying 'to show that MPs were earning their crust'. This was not judiciously phrased, even if you don't normally expect such documents to surface for thirty years. I noted a while later (after she had retired) that the good Baroness Hale herself was sporting a T-shirt saying 'Girly Swot', so I can assume the words somehow irritated her.

But what really enraged my opponents, they said, was not just my reckless behaviour and attitude. It was my dangerous language. A Labour MP called Paula Sherriff challenged me: 'Why do you use words like surrender, betrayal, traitor?' she demanded. It was the kind of thing, she implied, that had led to the murder of Jo Cox – an MP who was tragically murdered by a right-wing nutter during the referendum campaign.

Well, I wasn't having that. I had never called anyone a traitor, and I thought it was perfectly fair to describe the Surrender Act as the Surrender Act, since it demolished the UK's ability to negotiate and forced us to surrender to EU terms.

'I have never heard such humbug in all my life,' I said.

There was total fury opposite, and repeated calls for me to retract and to apologise. Sometimes it is when you are on the stickiest wicket that you hit the most runs or feel that you have. That evening I generally tonked it around the park, duffed up the opposition and came out feeling well pleased with my performance.

My staff were anxious – because the BBC coverage was pretty grim and Twitter was in meltdown. I was being accused of arrogance, insensitivity and even sexism. There were many now saying that I might be the shortest-serving prime minister in history. But the debate itself had proved my point. In well over two hours, Parliament had offered not a single new idea about the negotiations, or about Brexit. Nor did MPs do so in all the weeks that followed. The court was wrong. There was no need for more time to debate.

The truth was that the Supreme Court judgment was painful, but made no practical difference to my position, since Parliament already had me trapped.

There is, moreover, a sense in which Brenda Hale and her colleagues played into our hands. Whatever else it did, the judgment confirmed the general impression of the public that this government – and I – would stop at nothing to get Brexit done. After three years of misery and paralysis, that was what people wanted.

Chapter 2

Poisoned Chalice

How and why I became Tory leader – and the beginnings of levelling up

But wait a mo. Before we surge on with this narrative, let us draw breath. There are some preliminary questions that need to be addressed.

I can imagine that many readers are still vaguely mystified about how I came to be prime minister – what possessed the Tory Party to choose me. Remember: to the prune-lipped Pharisees of the UK establishment, I was the guy from some satirical TV game show (*Have I Got News for You*).

I was the gaffe-prone scandal-magnet who should have long since been excised, like some benign but irritating polyp, from the body politic. It was almost twenty years since the former defence secretary and media star Michael Portillo had written a column in the *Sunday Times* that announced – following one of my regular career disasters – that 'his political career is over'.

As a piece of political prophecy, this turned out to be premature by at least two decades, but it showed what people were thinking. I still treasure a piece by Simon Carr, then the *Independent*'s sketch writer, who concluded at about the same time that the Tories 'will never recover until Boris Johnson leaves the stage'. I expect that there were many Tories who agreed, secretly or openly.

So what the hell happened?

They say politics is all about timing, and of course that is true. But it is also about what you do to make your own luck, to try to script the movie in which you vainly believe you are starring.

Some people have a knack for being in the right place at the right time. They just happen to be under the tree when the apple plops into their lap. Some people have to bash and butt at the base of the tree for an awfully long time until the exhausted apple stalk can bear the weight no longer.

I am definitely in the second category.

To understand how I came to be PM, it helps to remember how grisly it all seemed in the years after the EU referendum. It is too much to say that the country was in shock, but the ruling classes were certainly at sixes and sevens.

They were struggling to adjust to the reality that they appeared to have lost an argument to those that they considered their intellectual inferiors. In the snooty phrase of Jeremy Clarkson (who for some reason was an ardent Remainer), they felt they had been cheated of their European citizenship by a bunch of 'coffin-dodging idiots' in places like Sunderland.

I am afraid that people started mentally to divide the terrain. There were the places that had voted to remain in the EU – the lush, sensible, civilised places: London, the London commuter belt, the university towns, and of course the Scots, whose sense of identity and separateness was sedulously coddled and funded by the EU.

Then there were what one female columnist called the 'Brexity' places. I can almost hear her spitting the syllables. She seemed to mean the Midlands, the north, the seaside towns, the less fashionable and less affluent places, the places that later came to be called the left-behind places, where getting a degree was not thought to be so essential to success or to enjoyment of life; not forgetting Wales, which heroically voted Leave by 52 per cent.

People began to formulate a clear (if stereotyped and exaggerated) vision of the difference between the two groups. Suddenly, for the first time in living memory, the wishes of the ruling liberal establishment had been not just ignored but overwhelmed. It wasn't like a general election, where the powers-that-be invisibly transfer their allegiance from Labour to Conservative and back again.

It was more fundamental than that. The Brexity places of Britain had been threatened with all sorts of consequences. They had been warned that it would be a disaster if they voted to leave the EU. George Osborne's emergency tax-raising budget. Mass unemployment. Remember all that?

Then they had gone right ahead and flicked the most colossal V-sign at all the experts of the Remain establishment – and the ruling classes were utterly furious. They ran the country, not the Brexity places, and they would show it.

On the morning after that referendum, Friday June 24, 2016, a group of Eurosceptic Tory MPs met in the Boothroyd Room in Portcullis House. Some were simply jubilant. Some were struggling to assess what it meant. Everyone seemed to assume that the argument was over. So I stood up and gave a warning.

Every time this happens, I said, every time there is a referendum that goes against the general direction of EU integration – and I cited examples from Denmark, France, Ireland, the Netherlands – the EU establishment always finds a way of overturning that popular decision and forcing people to think again. They will try it here too, I said.

That is exactly what happened. In the months that followed, the establishment in Britain combined with the EU to try to make a nonsense of Brexit and to make it impossible to deliver. By the spring of 2019, we had been in a state of Brexchosis for almost three years. We had promised the people that this was a once-in-a-lifetime moment, that if they voted Leave, then we would leave the EU, no ifs no buts. And yet when it came to it – when it came to delivering on that promise – the MPs shied away, again and again.

We were becoming so stuck, as a nation, that word was getting around the global campfire. People were starting to sneer. In Paris the French president Emmanuel Macron, a former London banker, openly derided the Brexit experiment as a disaster that was based on a pack of lies.

Across the continent, from *Le Monde* to the *Süddeutsche Zeitung*, the EU commentariat slated the leadership of the UK as a bunch of demagogic dilettantes who were leading a great country to ruin. We were stewing in a vat of xenophobia, they said. It was all falling apart, and the Eurosceptics (they often singled me out) were getting their intellectual comeuppance.

We were like the dog that chases a car every day until one day we catch it – and don't have a clue what to do next. The public could see all this very clearly, and the effect on the Tory Party, as you might expect, was verging on the catastrophic.

By May 23, 2019, we reached what must have been the all-time nadir in our two-hundred-year history as 'the oldest and most successful political party in the world'. Since we had failed, time and again, to get Brexit done, we were forced into the utterly ludicrous position of contesting the Euro-elections. Yes, in 2019 we actually fielded a whole army of candidates for a body that we had voted to leave three years previously.

It was humiliating. Never in history has a major party so pathetically and so abjectly pointed its wobbly chin at the electorate and invited them to give it a pasting. Never has the electorate so cheerfully obliged.

We had an inkling of what was coming on May 2, 2019, when our councillors – through absolutely no fault of their own – were badly mauled at the local elections, and we lost 1,300 seats. On Thursday May 23 we managed to get only 9 per cent of the vote in the Euro-elections. The Conservative and Unionist Party came fifth – fifth! – in a national election.

In fact, we hardly beat anyone except a fronde movement called Change UK, whose plan was to rejoin the EU and which included such luminaries as former Labour MP Chuka Umunna and my sister Rachel, whose undoubted rabble-rousing talents – as I tried in vain to explain to her – were wasted in that party. Whatever the voters were signalling in that election, it was not a lust to rejoin the EU.

So that is the frame of mind in which Tory MPs were considering the position in the summer of 2019. In the face of these results, Theresa May had announced she was standing down. Even if you made allowances for the peculiarity of those Euro-elections, and the emptiness of the vote, they could see that they were staring down the barrel. On this maths, the next election was going to bring a complete annihilation.

My MP colleagues started to turn to me that summer – for the same reason that anyone ever turns to any MP.

They were pretty desperate, and they had run out of better ideas.

They knew I had been at least a moderately successful mayor of London (even my worst enemies conceded that). They knew that I instinctively wanted to cut taxes, and set people free, and that I wanted to make use of Brexit freedoms – and they were right about that. The one big advantage of Brexit, for me, was that it would enable us to do things differently from our competitors, and faster; and I knew that idea – what people sometimes called Singapore-on-Thames – is what Angela Merkel and Emmanuel Macron really feared.

I knew that there was no earthly point in Brexit if you stayed in the single market and customs union – accepting EU rules but unable to set them. My colleagues got all that, and I was certainly winning that argument. But I believed I had something else to offer. De Gaulle once said that he had a certain idea of France. Well, at the risk of being pretentious about my political convictions – and I think, after all this time, I have earned the right to be at least a bit pretentious – I also had an idea about the future of the UK. It was connected to Brexit. But it was also bigger and wider than Brexit.

It was about how we could address the problems that the Brexit vote expressed. It was about how Britain could be, and it was based on all I had observed and done in journalism and politics. For years I struggled to articulate it. Then I hit on a phrase. It was all about levelling up.

What? You don't understand what I mean by levelling up? You have heard the phrase, but you weren't sure what it meant? Don't worry. I don't blame you. Perhaps it would help if I gave some illustrations, a few snapshots from my levelling-up album. Let's start with school.

As many people know, I went to the same school as the party leader. We were both lucky enough to find our way into its hallowed and ancient red-brick confines, not far from the Thames.

Yes, I went to Primrose Hill primary school, Princess Road, Camden – the alma mater of Ed Miliband, former leader of the UK Labour Party, and his brother David.

It must have been when I was about seven or eight years old that I went out into that playground at break and, like all of us, I learned some of life's hard lessons: about what seem to be the differences between human beings, about what I was good at and what I was less good at.

I was hopeless at football – couldn't dribble for toffee. I wasn't much use at the recorder. I could draw a bit, but other kids were much more accomplished (I think of Matthew Bakewell, son of Joan Bakewell the famous broadcaster).

What COULD I do? I was quite good at piggyback fights, and carried my friend Joel Harris into battle against other pairs, easily knocking them over. Maybe I was strong? That's it. I concluded, without any firm evidence, that I was a kind of pre-pubescent Chuck Norris, with a flair for the martial arts.

I decided, insanely, that I was going to challenge all-comers to a fight. Come on and have some, then, I said as I went into the knee-scabbing tarmac playground. Come on, I said, or words to that general effect, if you think you are hard enough. Most of them just laughed, but eventually an older child turned in my direction.

She was called Tracy and she must have been a good head taller than me. I didn't have time to get ready, to form my hands into a tiger claw or perform my kung fu routine. I didn't even dance around her like my then hero Muhammad Ali.

All I can remember is noticing how large and knobbly Tracy's fists seemed to be, and then – this is picture one of my levelling-up album – I am lying on my back, legs waving feebly in the air. Looming above me are Tracy and all her friends, silhouetted like a laughing spinney against the grey London sky.

In that instant I am learning an important truth about life: that we are not as good as we think we are, and that other people often turn out to be better at something than you predict. Above all – here's the key point – you don't know who that person is going to be. Hold that picture, and then spool forward five or six years.

Having spent a few years abroad, I am now at another Thames-side pile of ancient privilege. I am in the Farrer Theatre of Eton College, Windsor, Berks, SL4 6AU, and at the age of thirteen or fourteen I should be feeling much more confident. I have won an academic scholarship, worth an awful lot of money in those days, from the foundation endowed by Henry VI.

I am what they call a Colleger, because I live in a special super-swot hothouse called College, or a Tug, because unlike the 1,200 other kids we wear gowns, hence *gens togata*, or 'toga'ed race'. But now my heart is thudding because I am being tested again, in a terrifying ritual called 'Reading Over'.

It is the end of the term (or 'half') and all 250 boys have been assembled to be publicly informed how they have done in the exams (or 'Trials'). The results are read out in reverse order, start-ing with whoever has come bottom. A hush falls as the master takes the stage. He is a tall, thin, pale man – probably perfectly nice, but I remember him as an inveterate flagellator, and I thought that beating adolescents was a pretty grim system of punishment.

'Number 250,' he begins, 'and a general total failure …' Imagine that! Is there any school nowadays where they would tell a boy, in front of all his contemporaries, that he was a general total failure? He names the general total failure – a genial chap who goes on to be a highly successful luxury travel agent and make more money than most of the rest of us.

He takes a bow, amid general acclaim. The master continues his tormenting recitation of names and numbers, and for a hundred places, two hundred, my heart beats faster.

I can't remember exactly where I came in those early years. Since you ask, since you absolutely insist on knowing, I think I ended up fourth in the final sixth-form rankings, which I know that many readers will rightly assume was something of a fluke. But that's not the point of this story.

As the names and numbers are read out, you are able to observe genetics in action. This is still a time when the Eton admissions system is sentimental about the history of the school. There are names being read out in that theatre that have been names at the school for hundreds of years, names that appeared among the dead of Waterloo and the Somme, names that are carved on the oak panels of the pre-Tudor classrooms.

As you listen, you notice something about the distribution of those names in the binomial curve of academic performance. It is true that there are unquestionably some sprigs of the aristocracy who are brilliant. Lightning does indeed strike twice in the same place. Sometimes. But you also notice that there are quite a few who are not. It really doesn't seem to matter how illustrious your genes, you could just as easily end up average – or below average – as somebody from any other family.

As I close my eyes and wait for the judgement of the examiners on myself, I feel I am in the presence of some ineluctable biological-historical process. I have read somewhere that intelligence, like other human qualities, reverts to the mean. (Was it H.J. Eysenck who gave me that idea? Eysenck it was.)

Well, here it is. Like David Attenborough breathlessly observing some law of evolution exemplified by a tribe of baboons, I can hear the genes for intelligence being expressed in some of the most powerful and successful families in Britain, and it is surely reverting to the mean.

Slowly and amateurishly – real biologists and real experts please avert your eyes – I start to form some kind of theory about human potential, and the inchoate beginnings of a levelling-up campaign. Of course I didn't really believe that this brutal numerical hierarchy was a real guide to intelligence.

Nor did I think that those on the left of the exam binomial – the left-hand brim of the bowler hat – were necessarily fated to be less able, or less talented, or to achieve less, than those on the right. We all know that human intelligence is a complex and multifaceted thing, and that it develops in different ways and at different speeds. No one wants some chill Darwinian meritocracy, where alphas are picked and promoted on the basis of their IQ.

I just couldn't help wondering what the world would be like if so many others had the chance that I had at that wonderful school: the chance to listen to such life-changing teachers, to enjoy the green vastness of the playing fields, to sit in the light and space of the drawing schools, to fool around with the school Gutenberg Bible, the school racquets court, the school cyclotron.

Maybe I am exaggerating about the cyclotron, but you get my drift.

Before winning my scholarship, I had spent four terms at an English prep school, where I had gulped down Latin and Greek like a python swallowing an egg. I had also learned by heart Thomas Gray's famous 'Elegy Written in a Country Churchyard'. You know that one.

The poet is standing at dusk in the churchyard, in what is now the affluent Buckinghamshire commuter-belt village of Stoke Poges, and he meditates in iambic pentameters on the lot of the rural poor. The curfew has tolled the knell of passing day. The lowing herd has wound slowly o'er the lea. It's 1750, and there is no compulsory primary education, let alone secondary education.

These people all died illiterate, he says as he looks at their mouldering graves. They could have been poets. They could have been politicians or great military leaders. They could have been contenders. They never had the chance.

> Full many a gem of purest ray serene,
> The dark unfathom'd caves of ocean bear:
> Full many a flow'r is born to blush unseen,
> And waste its sweetness on the desert air.

So says Thomas Gray, and I am with him. It's the job of teachers, politicians, leaders to excavate those dark undersea caves and allow that talent to shine. We all know instinctively that it is there.

We all know people who have risen to the top, miraculously, through sheer ability.

*   *   *

The last snapshot from my album of levelling up is a smiling geezer with a shock of grey hair. He's called Frank Johnson, and I first heard of him at about the time that I was sitting palpitating in that school theatre. I must have been in my early teens, and for my Sunday essay I had written some meritless spoof or other.

Clearly puzzled, but wanting to sound encouraging, the teacher scrawled at the bottom of the page, 'Frank Johnson of the Daily Telegraph?'. I dug around for old *Telegraph*s and managed to find a couple of pieces. He was very funny, brilliantly capturing the atmosphere of the House of Commons. He made it sound exciting but also faintly demonic. Norman Tebbit was the 'Chingford Skinhead' and Dennis Skinner – a famously caustic Old Labour MP – was the 'Beast of Bolsover'. (He really was a beast. I was once clearing my throat in the Chamber when he called out something so unmentionable that I completely lost my train of thought.)

I met Frank later, when I was about to leave university, and I will always love him for his personal kindness and the advice he gave me at a critical stage; but much more importantly, he was a shining gem-like example of the point I am trying to make.

As he said in his *Who's Who* entry, Frank was the son of a pastry chef and confectioner. He failed his 11-plus, went to a secondary modern in Shoreditch, left with one O-level. And yet through sheer power of verbal invention he rose to the top of journalism: foreign correspondent for *The Times*, deputy editor of the *Sunday Telegraph*, editor of the *Spectator*, and by common consent the master of the parliamentary sketch.

He was a lover of ballet and opera, an autodidact who was constantly carrying some learned book or other, and his deepest wish – so he told me often – was to be able to read Thucydides in the original Greek. 'Thucydides!' he would say, in his tense East End whisper, tapping his copy of the text, 'He's the man!'

Frank used to badger me to talk about the debate on Mytilene, when the Athenians proposed and then regretted a massacre – and what it meant for democracy. I would ransack my memory, wishing I could satisfy his thirst for knowledge.

I'd call up some dusty old quote or half-remembered fact, and he would fall on it as if finding an Old Master in a car boot sale. To me they were lumber; to Frank they were gold. It seemed so unfair. The attic of my mind was stuffed with desiccated heirlooms, once lovingly bequeathed by my teachers, now covered with cobwebs.

No one had done the same for Frank. No one had told him at Shoreditch secondary modern that he had the potential to study Greats at Oxford, which – so he now told me – he so desperately wished that he had. So when I later became spokesman for the opposition for higher education, I became obsessed with this idea of talent-finding – to put it simply, spreading opportunity.

I didn't want to bully the universities into admitting kids that did not have the right academic qualifications. Nor did I want them to discriminate against parents who scrimped and saved to pay for tutors. Nor did I want to put up barriers against those who had been to fee-paying schools.

That wasn't levelling up; that was levelling down. That's what Labour did, that's what lefties got off on. Abolishing grammar schools, banning academic selection, taxing fee-paying schools (as we are now under Labour), punishing effort, punishing investment, punishing aspiration, insisting that all must have prizes. That was the agenda of the left, and the exact opposite of what I wanted.

I wanted to create ladders, springboards, trampolines, catapults – anything to help kids with energy and talent. By the late 1990s and early 2000s there were parts of London where not a single pupil – I mean no one in the maintained sector – was doing advanced mathematics for A-level.

There were schools where physics A-level had more or less died out, where German was a distant memory. As for the Latin and

Greek Classics, the subject that pole-vaulted me to university – you might as well ask to study Sumerian or Akkadian. It was gone. And so, naturally, was the kind of social mobility that we saw in the post-war period, when grammar schools leavened society with talent. When Frank Johnson lost his life, far too early, to cancer, the *Evening Standard* billboards said: 'Fleet Street genius dies'.

He was a genius. But it was still a kind of miracle that he emerged. He happened to become a tea-boy in a trade, journalism, that is – or used to be – porous to talent, where you could rise to the top by spotting the story in a morass of fact, by writing a sharper intro, striking a more mordant paradox, telling a better joke.

My political aim for the last thirty years has been to do what I can to give a leg-up to every potential Frank Johnson, and to every kid who has even half the potential of Frank Johnson.

There are some who are pessimistic about all this. I remember having long conversations with my friend David Willetts, himself said to be blessed with two brains, who doubted my continual assertion that Britain was one great Klondike of undiscovered talent.

In his view there are complex reasons for the drying up of social mobility, not least the habit of 'assortative mating', by which female graduates tend only to marry men who are themselves graduates. This habit of exclusive inter-graduate mating tends to deepen the divide, they say, between those who have been to university and those who have not.

The only way to break the cycle of assortative mating, if I understand Two Brains correctly, is for more female graduates to be encouraged to marry more hod-carriers and dustbin men, which sounds deeply romantic but which doesn't seem to be happening, or not enough, not yet.

As the Sutton Trust continually informs us, all the top professions continue to be colonised by the children of the rapacious university-educated middle classes, who are so expert in passing on their privileges. But does this mean we should all give up? Of course not.

To repeat: I am a proud member of the pushy bourgeoisie. I am right behind their values. But I also believe that there really is gold in them thar hills, not to mention gems of purest ray serene, and in colossal quantities.

Levelling up is about extracting or unleashing that potential. By 2019 I believed pretty messianically in that project and I felt sure it could be done. For eight years I had been mayor of London and engaged flat out on a transformational plan to regenerate huge tracts of the city.

Again, this is why I am not a socialist or even a social democrat. I hate words like 'deprived' or 'disadvantaged', because they encourage a sense of inevitability. I remember being told, before I became mayor, that there were parts of inner London that were just doomed to economic decay. I was told that whole communities, whole estates, were locked in a cycle of underachievement from one generation to the next, with one jobless household giving birth – at the expense of the taxpayer – to the next. I was told that there was nothing much you could do about the poverty of these places. It was just a fact of life.

Well, I am here to tell you that this is all rubbish. Yes, of course there are places that get locked in a cycle of decline, and of course there are left-wing politicians who get elected time and again by fostering a culture of resentment and entitlement and dependency on the state. But it is just nonsense to say that there is something fated or inevitable about this kind of urban decay. I saw how London changed. I saw it with my own eyes and I played my own part in the regeneration.

There was the change in the culture of London schools, and by the time I became mayor in 2008 those crunchy subjects – advanced maths, physics, languages – were catching on again. Thanks partly to the energy and ambition of immigrant families, 'disadvantaged' London schools were suddenly outperforming the schools of the surrounding 'leafy' Home Counties.

Everything we did – massive transport projects, cracking down on crime, apprenticeships – was intended to spread opportunity, to level up the boroughs that people believed were fated to be left behind. But it was not, repeat not, just a question of state spending (when I was mayor, City Hall actually cut our share of council tax).

Government money, in the end, cannot hope to make the difference on its own. It was all about creating the conditions – safer streets, better transport – for the private sector to invest. Governments have billions, or tens of billions. The private sector has trillions. That money flooded into London, across the city, in growing quantities, from around the world.

Above all, levelling up is about leadership. You need teachers who believe in the potential of their kids, the inspirational figures (we have all had them) who keep alive the flame of our interest and aptitude. You need the local leaders who will bang the drum for their city or town or community and tell its special story, who will champion talent and opportunity and who don't just moan about deprivation. And you need a government that sees the potential of the whole country.

Which takes me to a moment of epiphany, when I decide that the skills and ideas I am acquiring in London might well have a more general application. It is May 2014. I have been mayor for six years. The Tories are campaigning to hold the Newark constituency in a by-election, and I am in the back of David Cameron's prime ministerial Jag.

This beast is so thickly plated with armour that the mobile signal is dodgy. So we chat away. I have no idea why Dave has done me this honour – inviting me to campaign with him – but I am happy to be there.

He is on the whole a good-natured and friendly sort of chap, and we tend to speak pretty freely to each other. By this stage I think we have left Newark and we are gliding through some East Midlands suburb, I can't remember exactly where. Today, for whatever reason, the place is not looking its best. There are boarded-up windows, there is buddleia growing through the cracks in the brickwork, and the local economic activity seems to consist of tattoo parlours and kebab shops.

Dave taps the reinforced window of the Jag and gestures languidly outside. 'The trouble with the UK economy,' he says, 'is that outside London and the south-east, there really isn't much.' I want to stress that he is not being dismissive.

He does not mean to disparage. He is being elegiac. He is lamenting, like the poet Gray at the graveside, what he sees as a giant socio-economic fact, against which we all struggle in vain. His remark encapsulates, it seems to me, the attitude of the Treasury for the last few decades. It is one of those remarks that really lodges in your head. I think about it as we go, and I think that even if it is true, it doesn't have to be true.

Dave is right, in the sense that the UK is the most imbalanced major economy in the world, certainly in the G7. London is about 56 per cent more productive than Wales. Go to the great provincial cities of continental Europe, and of course you will find here and there all sorts of signs of urban blight: graffiti, dereliction and so on. But on the whole these cities are rich places that lift the average wealth of the country.

Go to the US, and even though there are such huge and famous inequalities of wealth, you will also find a rich and varied sameness, a homogeneity from state to state.

The UK is different. For decades London and the rest of the south-east have been way out in front, and too much of the rest of the country has been treated as a kind of economic afterthought, a long comet's tail of underproductive streets and businesses like the one we were looking at.

So I look at the streetscape and I think, Is this inevitable? Is this our nation's doom? And I think, No: this is the Midlands, this is the birthplace of the industrial revolution that first gave Britain its position of world leadership. It was here or hereabouts that people invented the forges and foundries and mills and looms that were to change the fortunes of humanity. Are you telling me that the descendants of these inventors are somehow less naturally gifted?

I know it's not true, and I think we are making a huge mistake. It's morally wrong to be fatalistic about the shape of the UK economy, but that's not the point. It's madness.

Look at the economic map of Britain, and the story of our development in the last 150 years. Go to our great provincial cities and you will see the architectural legacies of previous urban leaders: proud city halls, corn exchanges and wool exchanges, beautiful stone-colonnaded museums, soaring red-brick station hotels. These Core Cities – Belfast, Birmingham, Bristol, Cardiff, Glasgow, Leeds, Liverpool, Manchester, Newcastle, Nottingham, Sheffield – were once the pumping pistons of the UK economy.

They were not just great centres of population growth; they were the homes of technological innovation that changed the world. And yet the story of those cities, in the last century, has been one of relative – and in some cases absolute – population decline and massive relative decline in productivity.

Londoners now produce about £90,700 per year in gross value added. In Core Cities outside London, that figure is down to £45,000–£60,000; and nowhere comes near the capital.

London and the south-east are just about the most productive regions in the whole of Europe. But the UK Core Cities are way, way less productive than their European counterparts. Take the secondary cities of Germany – Munich, Dusseldorf, Stuttgart, Cologne, and so on. Workers in those cities are about 30 per cent more productive than in the UK's secondary cities.

Or take the inhabitants of Marseille, Lyon, Bordeaux, Toulon: they are about 22 per cent more productive than their British equivalents. The workers of secondary cities in the Netherlands are 26 per cent more productive, and in Italy they are 17 per cent more productive.

Why is this? Having run a great city (the greatest) for eight years, I can tell you there is nothing fated about any of this – as we shall see. Cities rise and fall overwhelmingly, I am afraid, because of politics and leadership.

When a city thrives, it is almost always because of 'agglomeration effects', the critical mass of talent that encourages other talented people to move there. To make that happen, you need safe streets, good education, efficient transport, and you need ambitious civic leadership that can tell the story of the place and why people should be proud to live there.

If you can pull that off, the chances are that you will level up; and you will get those young professional families moving back to enjoy all the buzz and benefits of urban life. It happened across London, even in the areas people said were irremediable.

It can and will happen across the UK, if we level up. Andy Haldane and his colleagues have calculated that if we could bring UK Core Cities up to par with their European comparators, we would easily add £100 billion a year to national GDP, or 5 per cent in perpetuity. You would drive growth not only in the Core Cities, but in the peri-urban areas – provided the transport was good. You would also reduce some of the intense pressure to develop the Home Counties.

If we levelled up Britain – closed the gap between the least productive and most productive regions, so that it was no more pronounced than in the rest of Europe – we would achieve a total transformation. We could actually become the richest economy in Europe. It can be done.

Look at what the people of East Germany have done. East Germany still has problems, but it is a stunning fact that the productivity differentials between parts of the UK are now bigger than the differentials between the old East and West Germany. How in heaven's name can that be? How can we waste so much potential?

I also happen to think that this imbalance – and the chronic toleration of this imbalance – is political folly. It was two years after Dave and I slipped through those shuttered streets in our armour-plated Jag that the revolt finally happened. Those left-behind places rebelled against an economic model that plainly was not working for them.

They rebelled against the fatalism of the Treasury orthodoxy. I believed and I believe that they were right. By voting to leave the EU, they revolted against the idea that Britain was just a territory of a vast Euro-empire, where levelling up (or convergence, as they call it in Brussels) was a matter for the EU Commission's directo-rate general for regional policy.

No matter how well-intentioned those EU officials, no matter how kind and how clever, the people of the Midlands did not feel it was working for them, and nor did 52 per cent of the entire population. Yes, it was partly about immigration. But I don't believe that the people of the UK are hostile to immigrants; far from it.

It was more that they were fed up with a system that seemed to undervalue their own skills, and their children's skills, because business could always supplant those skills with talent from abroad. They wanted the thought and the care and the love to be directed at their country, our country.

They thought it wasn't good enough to wheeze elegiacally and say that things couldn't change. They wanted change, and on June

23, 2016 they voted for change in greater numbers than any British population has ever voted for any proposition or any government.

Three years later, with Brexit still undone, I finally found myself in a position to deliver that change, and to make a serious and determined run for the Tory leadership.

The contest began, as is customary these days, with a kind of Grand National of contestants. But it wasn't long before the Tory MPs had whittled it down. Then for weeks it was just Jeremy Hunt and me, in what I think the media found to be a disappointingly gentlemanly campaign, slugging it out in debates around the country. Jeremy had many things going for him: decent, very able, son of an admiral. But he had voted to remain in the EU, and it was obvious, after three years of stasis, that the government should be led by someone who actually believed in the project.

I had the advantage of knowing exactly what I wanted to do. I had the ideas, and the slogans to capture them. I wanted to level up and unleash the potential of the whole UK, and I wanted Britain to be stronger and more confident abroad – what I called Global Britain.

I wanted to show them all how wrong they were, those who thought that Brexit somehow marked a retreat from the world stage. After the appalling Salisbury poisonings of March 2018, when Vladimir Putin used chemical weapons in the UK and murdered an innocent member of the public, I wanted to show that we would stick up for our values around the world.

Both ideas depended on getting Brexit done; that is, properly taking back control of our legislative and regulatory system; and the reason I was in the race was because a lot of people now seemed to believe that I was the only person with the force of personality to do it; to do the necessary and get Brexit done.

Of course I wasn't always sure that they were right, and of course I was worried about my own abilities. Any sane person has those worries. I was also worried about the vast and glorious roll-call of enemies I now had, after many years in journalism and politics in which I had been far from cautious about what I said or did.

Jeremy put up a strong fight, but in the end I was able to muster just under two-thirds of the vote. I had a plan. I had the job. But time was very, very short, and the sharks were out there beneath the waves – far more numerous than I ever imagined.

Chapter 3

Locked-in Syndrome

Northern Ireland and the plot to stymy Brexit

I had only been PM for about a week when they told me that I was facing my first natural disaster. It was early August, and the rains had been heavy in the Peak District. The waters had been pouring off the moors into an elderly piece of infrastructure called Toddbrook Reservoir. Suddenly a great gash had appeared in the side of the dam.

Some concrete slabs had slipped, exposing mud and rubble beneath. It didn't look good. If this thing burst, I was told, then 1.2 million cubic metres of water were going to engulf the town of Whaley Bridge, home to 6,000 souls, including famed Tory ex-minister Edwina Currie.

By the time I got there, in the late Sunday afternoon, a state of emergency had been declared, with 'imminent risk to life', and 1,500 people had already been evacuated.

Some were refusing to move. I remember marvelling at what seemed then to be the limits of the coercive power of the state. If a freeborn Englishman or woman chose to drown like a rat in his or her own home – then there was not a damn thing the government could do. I thought it rather splendid. (Little did I imagine, of course, that I would soon be taking such vast powers, in the name of public health, not so much to evacuate as compulsorily to intern the entire population.)

I watched as a big double-rotor Chinook helicopter appeared in the evening sky, with a huge hessian sack of aggregate suspended below it. The sappers expertly dropped the load, with a *thwok*, onto the hole in the dam. Would it hold? It looked pretty make-shift, and more rain was said to be on the way.

It was clearly a race against time and a metaphor – you saw this one coming – for my own political position.

Day by day the pressure was building. The Tory Party had hired me to get Brexit done and it was now only three short months until we were meant to leave on October 31, 2019. If we failed yet again, if we delayed again – then I would look ridiculous, nothing but Theresa May in a blond wig – and I would be swept aside in a torrent of public indignation.

Some people on the opposite side were already starting to claim that the 2016 referendum was losing its valence. It was more than three years ago. Many of those elderly Brexiteers were probably now pushing up the daisies, they said. The whole thing should be rerun. It was time for a 'People's Vote', they said, as though the People had not been consulted the first time. As for the Leavers – the 52 per cent – this kind of talk was just infuriating.

They had been told that this was a once-in-a-lifetime decision and that their votes really mattered. Now, yet again, it looked as though their wishes were about to be ignored. So I was like some boastful motorcycle stuntman who had claimed he could do an impossible trick; and now they were holding me to my promise.

Like Evel Knievel, I was revving my bike and preparing to hurl myself up the ramp, in the gulping knowledge that I had to clear two giant double-decker buses parked end to end. I had to get the EU to give us a new deal and then I had to get Parliament to vote for whatever they gave us, and frankly I wasn't sure I could get over the first, let alone both.

By the third week of August 2019, we were getting nowhere. The UK now had a new chief negotiator in David Frost, a former don and diplomat, an aesthete and expert on medieval German poetry, whose mobile phone screensaver, for some reason, is the *Adoration of the Blessed Lamb* by Jan van Eyck.

Frosty had been my adviser at the Foreign and Commonwealth Office for years. On Brexit, on what it meant and what it could mean, he was and is one of my closest allies. He saw very clearly what we needed to do and how Brexit was nothing unless we truly took back control.

Frosty presented his case to the EU with clarity and logic; and, yes, he got a frosty reception.

The EU chief negotiator was Michel Barnier, the former French finance minister, and the Brussels view was that the British had already signed up to a withdrawal agreement and that we should jolly well stick with what we were given. As many commentators pointed out, both in the UK and abroad, it was hard to see why they should make any special effort to help me, of all people.

I was the monstrous Johnson, the beast of Brexit and the big bullshitting bus, the Pied Piper who played the devil's tunes and led the people to perdition. Why would they unbend and make difficult legal compromises – just because I was in a bit of a political mess? Why should they make concessions if I could be carried away at any moment, to be replaced by yet another ephemeral Tory leader?

As Barnier continually told Frosty, he had no mandate to change the agreement, and there was nothing he could do. So by August 21, we had decided that it was time to stop talking to the monkeys and start on the organ-grinders.

The EU is ultimately the creation of the Franco-German axis. We needed to go to Berlin, and then Paris, and quickly.

*   *   *

I was amazed at the formality of the reception in Berlin. There was a vast red carpet running to the door of Angela Merkel's Kanzleramt and a military band that gamely played our national anthems, almost drowning out the crowds of anti-Brexit protesters that had gathered at the gates.

For some reason (I think she was worried about fainting in the heat) Angela had to sit down during the ceremony, but once we had reached her office upstairs, she was full of beans – and her usual chirpy and slightly pointed humour. She and I were poured flutes of crémant d'Alsace and ushered out onto her roof terrace in the hope that we would bond.

We looked out over Berlin, where the parks and avenues are so thick with leaves that it appears from above almost like a great umbrageous forest interspersed with buildings.

I told her we had to change the withdrawal agreement. She needed to give the orders to the Commission, I said.

She gestured at the Bundestag, whose Norman Foster glass dome was twinkling in the sun, a perfect symbol of post-war Anglo-German friendship.

'I can control my parliament,' she said. 'Can you control yours?'

There didn't seem any point in sounding hesitant. There are times when you can pour out your troubles to your international friends, and times when you certainly can't.

No worries, I said: '*Wir schaffen das!*' We can do it.

It was not perhaps a supremely tactful choice of phrase.

Those were Angela's words at the beginning of the 2015 refugee crisis, and I thought it showed that I shared her positive can-do spirit. It was later explained to me that her enemies had tried to turn them against her and she was a bit sick of hearing them.

Oh well, I thought: never mind. Let's try Macron.

It was swelteringly hot the following day, and we sat for ages in the garden of the Élysée Palace trying to cook up new plans for Anglo-French unity. I suggested all kinds of wheezes: a second fixed link across the Channel, a new hydrogen-fuelled Concorde aircraft, a new nuclear pact. Macron was warm, and I liked him a lot. But I could sense his deep reserve.

He had been working in London for Rothschild when I was mayor, and I knew he felt that Brexit was a terrible snub to the EU and to his view of the world. He had been on record many times already, to the effect that Brexit could not be a success – politically or economically.

The British, said Macron, had to be seen to be penalised for their decision – if only *pour encourager les autres*. Why should he help Johnson, *menteur* and *tricheur extraordinaire*?

I drank more white wine and the perspiration trickled down the brows of Macron's military advisers, in full braid and epaulettes, as I extemporised more plans for cross-Channel cooperation. It was no use. It was clear that we were stuck until Brexit was fixed.

Eventually Emmanuel and I went inside for a tête-à-tête. He showed me a curious steel stool in the shape of an African drum. To test how heavy it was I lifted my foot and briefly rested it on the stool, a moment that was unfortunately captured by the cameras.

Emmanuel was leaning forwards as if peering at my foot, and I was leaning back. It looked as though I was inviting him to shine my shoes, which was emphatically not the message we were trying to convey.

If anything, we were trying to lick his boots, not the other way round.

By the time we got back to London, it was clear that we were no further forwards. The EU was not moving. It was no use trying to build support in other capitals. I knew from long experience that the Franco-German motor drives the EU. Other countries may occasionally make helpful noises; other countries may sympathise. But if the French and the Germans are united on something, they tend to get what they want. In this case, they wanted to make us sweat.

They wanted to rope-a-dope us, to see how long I could last. They were in an immensely strong position, and they knew it. They had managed electrically to cross-wire the ambition of Brexit with the cause of peace in Northern Ireland; and anyone who disagreed with them – anyone who wanted to take the whole of the UK out of the EU – was at risk of being electrocuted, *pssssscht*, on a charge (however exaggerated) of putting that Northern Irish peace at risk. No one wanted to do that.

Back in 1996 I had been in my office at the *Daily Telegraph* in the Docklands when there was an almighty bang. I happened to be talking to my old friend Chris Lockwood – a veteran of Balkan war zones – and with characteristic presence of mind Lockers dived under the desk.

It was an IRA bomb, and as well as blowing out a lot of windows I am afraid that they murdered two more innocent people, men working in a local newsagents. They injured hundreds more.

I had hated and feared the IRA since I was a child in 1970s London; hated their indiscriminate bombings of pubs and shopping centres; hated their bogus 'warnings' and their synthetic 'regrets'.

So of course I rejoiced, two years later, at the 1998 Belfast Good Friday Agreement. It was an act of great statesmanship, the culmination of work by successive British and Irish governments, with the help of the Americans, and no UK PM would want to put it at risk.

It was that fear – let us be blunt, the fear of renewed IRA activity – that was being used to trap the UK in the EU. The argument was that once the UK had left, there would be a new land border with the EU, along the border between Northern Ireland and the Republic. The EU would have no choice, we were told, but to have checks at that border – customs posts to stop the smuggling of goods. That would be a calamity.

As members of Theresa May's government, we were given ever more bloodcurdling warnings about what the terrorists would do. I was shown pictures of border infrastructure (I think they were security cameras) that had been torn down and smashed by Republicans.

There were about three hundred crossing points. There would have to be customs posts everywhere, we were told, and the IRA would be merciless. They were implacably opposed to the very notion of a border.

They would blow up the customs posts. They would kill whoever was there, including innocent members of the Garda.

Of course I didn't accept any of this, and for years, as Theresa's foreign secretary, I argued that this threat was chimerical. The UK government would never have border checks with the Republic of Ireland; we had all made that clear. As for free movement of people – well, the Common Travel Area had existed since 1922. It was nothing to do with the EU.

And there was simply no need for the EU to have border checks at all. There already was a fair bit of cross-border smuggling, as people took advantage of differentials in excise duty on fuel. You didn't need border checks for that.

You just had cooperation between police forces, between Irish customs and excise and UK customs and excise. It was telling that in the months before the Brexit vote, in early 2016, the Irish government had very smartly foreseen the problem and set about solving it with commonsensical remedies.

They were going to have trusted-trader schemes, or checks by customs officers or trading standards officers, in the unlikely event that UK goods went south of the border without paying duty, or without complying with some EU norm. None of these remedies involved checks at the border; all the so-called problems were capable of being solved.

But the whole point of these problems – essentially theological – was that they were not meant to be solved.

In the months after the Brexit vote there were an increasing number of people in London and Brussels who started to see how the Northern Ireland issue was the perfect excuse to do what they had wanted to do all along – what I had prophesied they would try to do.

They escalated the problem, sacralised it and instrumentalised it: to stop Brexit. Their objective was to keep the UK in the customs union, and in the single market. I got an inkling of what was happening in September 2017, when half the cabinet was flown, for some reason, to Florence for another of Theresa May's speeches on Brexit.

She had begun her premiership vowing to take Britain out properly. Now – as I looked at the text on the way to Florence – it was clear that she was caving in. Britain was going to accept EU regulations and laws, even if we weren't there to make them.

I protested bitterly to the chancellor, Philip Hammond, an amusing cynic with floppy grey hair and a general air of disdain. In fact, we had a long row in the back of the Italian government Lancia, all the way from Florence airport to the speech. It was infamous, I said. It was totally anti-democratic for the people of the UK to be rule-takers from Brussels. We would be a vassal state, a satellite, a colony. And anyway, people had voted for freedom. There was no point in Brexit if we couldn't do things differently.

Brexit gave us a chance to get out ahead of the rest of the world: on data-sharing, on biosciences, AI, medicines, you name it.

Look, said Hammond, a little wearily. I was being naive, he said.

All this talk of divergence was nonsensical. Britain was a European nation, with a European economic model.

'We get our foreign policy from America and we get our economic policy from the EU,' he said.

I said that I found both ideas equally repulsive.

*   *   *

By the end of the year I found that I had been completely outgeneralled. On December 8, 2017, I was summoned across to Number Ten to look at what was called the 'Joint Report', a new agreement between Britain and the EU. The document contained a new clause that I had never seen before, let alone agreed.

It was designed to protect the Good Friday peace process, I was told. It was all about stopping violence in Northern Ireland. It came to be known as the 'backstop'. It was a single paragraph and it said that until we could sort out the problem of the Northern Irish border – and ensure that there were no checks at all – the UK would remain 'in full alignment' with the EU.

We would follow EU laws, even though we had left the EU. We would levy the same tariffs as the EU at our borders, even though it meant we could no longer do free-trade deals. We would remain in such EU bodies as the European Medicines Agency (a restriction that – had it remained in place – would later have had momentous implications). Whatever this document entailed, it clearly wasn't Brexit.

It was Brexit in Name Only. It was BRINO. It was a moral and political disaster. Of course the largely Remain establishment liked it (and I apologise for using this faintly conspiratorial shorthand, but it is a fact that the overwhelming majority of the people who were tasked with delivering the details of Brexit had actually voted Remain, including, of course, Hammond and May).

The Northern Ireland backstop fulfilled two functions very well. It mollified the anxieties of the CBI and the Treasury about trade frictions. There should be no frictions, since Britain was to remain in the regulatory orbit of the EU. And by stopping divergence, by ending the prospect of independent free-trade deals, it meant that under a different PM the whole Brexit experiment could be Breversed and the Brits could vote to Brejoin.

The backstop was deeply sinister, and the worst of it was that once we signed it, and once we had ratified it, we couldn't even get out unless the EU allowed us. We were locking ourselves into the customs union and the single market – with no say on either – and handing the key to our jailors.

No wonder Brexiteer MPs opposed it so bitterly. We were turning ourselves into the punk of Brussels, the orange-ball-chomping gimp of the EU.

That was the deal I had to work with in the autumn of 2019. Parliament wouldn't pass it. The EU wouldn't change it. I had only one card in my hand, only one way of making them take me seriously. As we trundled remorselessly towards the October 31 deadline – and what looked like the end of my political career – I had to make them believe that we would leave without an agreement. It was generally agreed that this option – a no-deal exit – was unthinkable.

The papers were full of the usual horrors of what would happen. There would be panics and queues and runs on the currency, they said, and Millennium Bug-style computer disasters. There would be restrictions on the movement of vital drugs, and the Mars Bar factory in Slough would run out of milk solids and whey. Even if it was all greatly exaggerated (where there's a will there's a whey, I often said), I could see that there would be a period of dislocation and that the government would be blamed.

I really, truly, deeply did not want a no-deal exit from the EU. But as you know if you have conducted ANY type of negotiation, you simply have to be able to walk away. I could see that there was only one way to persuade Merkel and Macron to give us a better deal, only one way to burst out of the slavery of the backstop, and thereby get an agreement that would actually pass through the House of Commons.

We had to be able to bluff, to show that we were at least willing to do a no-deal Brexit. I had a curious advantage, as PMs go, in that our partners thought that I might actually be mad enough to do it. They listened to my 'do or die' rhetoric. They saw the proroguing of Parliament – and they heard the crazed revving of a man who might really be prepared to drive the car off the cliff.

In reality, I wasn't going to do any such thing. But I needed them to believe that I might well (and that's why I was so impatient with Spiderwoman Hale and believed that the Supreme Court was so misguided: they were interfering with the prerogative power of the executive to negotiate with other countries, as well as to prorogue Parliament).

And, of course, if the EU could see that no-deal exit was the last desperate card in my hand, then so could all my Remainer colleagues in Parliament. They came up with a most ingenious plan, whose details I am afraid I simply had not foreseen. With the active connivance of Speaker Bercow, whose car boasted a sticker saying 'Bollocks to Brexit', the MPs took control of the House of Commons order paper, like cruise ship passengers suddenly storming the bridge and taking the wheel.

On September 4, 2019, they passed the Surrender Act – or the European Union (Withdrawal) (No. 2) Act, or Benn Act, after one of its instigators, Hilary Benn. Under the terms of this extraordinary piece of legislation, they effectively took over the negotiations and bound me, by law, to rule out any possibility of a no-deal Brexit.

The Surrender Act said that I had to reach a deal with the EU by October 19 – then about six weeks away – and get that deal through Parliament; or else I would have to write to the EU (and they set out the terms of the letter) requesting another extension, forcing me to break my promise to come out of the EU by October 31, and wounding me politically – probably fatally.

They weren't really worried about a no-deal Brexit. Unlike the EU, they knew me, and they knew I wouldn't want to inflict that kind of commotion on the country. It was more cunning than that. By forcing me to take no-deal off the table, they wanted to weaken my negotiating position so badly that in the end I couldn't even get a better deal or a deal that would go through the Commons. Let us be clear: these people wanted to humiliate their own country, by destroying our ability to negotiate properly on behalf of the British people. They had promised in the 2017 election to take Britain out of the EU. They were shamelessly breaking their word.

They wanted us to stay in the EU for month after month, paying our exorbitant tithes, unable to leave, until the dam of public patience finally burst and the Johnson government was sent roaring down the valley in a foaming tide of destruction.

Then they could begin the campaign to rejoin. It was monstrous, but it was effective. We were trapped.

Chapter 4

The Madder Hulk Gets ...

... the stronger Hulk gets

On the Sunday before the vote on the Surrender Act, September 1, 2019, I thought it would be a good idea to take the temperature of the parliamentary party. Our move to prorogue Parliament had been hailed by some; others were appalled.

We knew from our intelligence that the Remainers were hatching a plot, and we broadly understood what they were trying to do: to seize the wheel and stop Brexit. But it was far from clear that they would succeed. How many would dare to defy their constituents and join the revolt?

The entire whips' office turned up for lunch at Chequers, led by Mark Spencer, the chief – a Nottinghamshire farmer with enormous pheasant-strangling hands. Everyone was very jolly, and we stood on the terrace drinking Balfour English sparkling wine (otherwise known as Brexit juice), and I asked each whip to predict how many would rebel.

I don't suppose that in my parliamentary career I have always endeared myself to the whips, but now I needed them, and I needed them to tell me the truth.

The party would be solid, they said. Everyone could see what was at stake. If you voted to take a no-deal Brexit off the table, you were voting at a crucial moment to weaken the UK in the councils of the nations. You were voting to undermine our ability to get a good deal out of the EU. It was obvious, therefore, that if you voted with the rebels, you were also voting to terminate my premiership. So it had to be a confidence vote, and the MPs had all been told of the automatic consequence – time-hallowed – of voting against the government on a matter of confidence. You would lose the whip. You would not be able to stand as a Tory candidate.

Stripping an MP of the whip is the most savage utensil of punishment in the armoury. It is the ultimate tool of parliamentary correction, the last to be brought out clanking from the chest. I asked how many times de-whipping had actually been used since 1979, when Margaret Thatcher came to power. It turned out that it was on fewer than twenty occasions.

To lose the whip, you need to do something pretty amazing. You need to be caught bang to rights engaged in a giant tax fraud or running a sex-slave ring, or selling nuclear secrets to the Chinese. Voting against the government, on a confidence motion, was worse than all of them put together.

Maybe it was the port, or the carbohydrate-fuelled sticky toffee torpor, but the whips were virtually as one in insisting that we were safe. The one exception was Mike Freer, MP for Finchley and Golders Green, whom I had known and liked since my London days. He had been talking to some of his flock, he said, and he didn't like the mood. Two days later, it was clear that Mike was right.

On Tuesday September 3, 2019, Sir Oliver Letwin, the Professor Branestawm of Tory politics, unveiled his lethal government-trussing contraption. He managed to propose and pass a bill allowing backbench MPs to seize control of the agenda from the government, and on Wednesday 4th MPs outraged all precedent by using his motion to pass the Benn-Burt Surrender Bill.

They did it with Tory votes. Not one or two, but twenty-one of them. I looked at the list with stone-cold disbelief.

I was now going to take the Tory whip away from Ken Clarke, the Father of the House, and one of my political heroes – the man I had actually voted for to be party leader in 2001. Talking of former chancellors, I was being asked to kick Philip Hammond out of the party he had joined forty-five years ago.

I was going to have to expel Nick Soames, grandson of Winston Churchill, a man who had only twice voted against the party in his entire thirty-seven-year career as an MP. I felt like Octavian – that chill and subtle tyrant – ordering the proscription of names from the grandest senatorial families.

The door of my office swung open and the chief whip came in. He was pale – even for a man who was well used to scenes from the abattoir – but he was resolute. They had been warned. They knew the price they would pay. He just wanted to check that I had not been overwhelmed by a sudden squeamishness. I looked at those names. Stephen Hammond. Ed Vaizey. Richard Benyon. I thought how Soames was so funny, when it came to telling stories, that he could make me almost retch with laughter. I remembered how when I first got into Parliament, he had encouraged me and told me to take no notice of the whips. 'They are mice auditioning to be rats,' he said.

Was I really going to do this to my political allies, my friends? The authority of the government, and the chief whip, was at stake.

We gotta do it, I told Mark, and we did it. We sacked more Tory MPs, in one go, than had been sacked in the previous four decades. It would be fair to say that the political reaction bordered on the hysterical.

John Major denounced me for turning the Tories into a narrow-minded sect. Nick Boles, my former chief of staff, announced that there was nothing and no one I would not slaughter on the blood-drenched altar of my ambition. As the week went on, the muttering grew.

I was now being forced to negotiate with one hand tied behind my back, and the EU could see that my political position was crumbling. So could others. At a meeting of the political cabinet, Michael Gove said something a bit ambiguous about how we had lost many valued and respected colleagues. Incurably fond as I am of Michael, I think I speak for several Tory ex-PMs if I say it is always a good idea to watch him in the wing mirror.

There were a couple of others who were not notably steady on parade. The position was so obviously dire that on the Wednesday evening I did something no PM does in a hurry. I tried for the first time to press the button on the ejector seat. If I couldn't get a deal through this Parliament, I would try and get a new mandate and a new Parliament. That night I dared Jeremy Corbyn to join me in the lobbies and vote for a general election. He refused, and I have to say that he looked pretty damn ridiculous.

The right honourable gentleman, I told him, was paid by the taxpayer to try to remove me from office at a general election. That was his job. That was what he was there for. Now he was the first opposition leader in history to refuse to give battle; in fact, he was the first opposition leader to express his effective confidence in Her Majesty's government.

It was no use. We won the vote, but we were miles under the two-thirds threshold required under the Fixed-term Parliaments Act. Labour wouldn't play ball, and my exquisite torment continued.

The following day my brother Jo resigned from the cabinet. I really don't blame him at all. I was proud to have him there, given how strongly we disagreed over Brexit. Blood in our family is a lot thicker than water. But I have to admit that it didn't look brilliant.

Later that day I made a speech at a police college in Wakefield, Yorkshire, to emphasise one of our most important commitments

– getting another 20,000 police officers out on the street. By the time I got there, I had spent too long on the phone, faffing about the cabinet – and the recruits had been standing for a while in the sun. One of them – poor thing – actually fainted while I was talking. She disappeared from the ranks behind me like a soldier shot in battle.

My speech was meant to be a few uplifting phrases about the importance and interest of a career in policing. It turned into a rambling political rant (for which I was later and properly criticised), in which I became increasingly hysterical about my determination to leave the EU. I would rather be 'dead in a ditch', I told the slightly stunned police cadets, than extend British EU membership beyond October 31.

The media concluded, perhaps not unreasonably, that I was showing signs of strain. So it was balm to the soul, the following day, to go to another universe, a place where party politics is actively banned. On Friday, Carrie and I went to Balmoral, to stay with the Queen.

I think there had been the gentlest suggestion in some of the papers that Her Majesty might look askance at an unmarried PM arriving to stay with his girlfriend. Would we be allowed to sleep in the same bedroom? they asked.

As anyone could have predicted, from a study of a thousand years of the British royal family, the Queen did not give a monkey's about any of this. (Though we were advised against bringing Dilyn the dog. It seemed that Princess Anne had once brought some dogs and they killed a corgi.)

Balmoral was a curiously calming experience, mainly because it was so surreal. It wasn't just this great Gormenghast of a castle, with its endless antlered corridors. It was the fact that we were in the monarch's home and she was treating us as her guest, looking after us and making sure we had a good time.

That evening the ninety-three-year-old Queen of England drove us at top speed in her Range Rover, bouncing up an unmade road with the moon shining on the moors. I had to pinch myself. We reached a bothy, once a favourite of Queen Victoria, and it felt so paradoxical, so topsy-turvy, to watch the Queen bustle around and make her special vinaigrette and lay out the elements of the picnic in their Tupperware boxes.

The Duke of Edinburgh fired up his enormous steel barbecue – which he had designed and made himself – and after supper he and I talked for a while by the fire, about the disasters of human demography and the loss of the natural world. Finally, we were summoned outside, because a torchlit procession of pipers had appeared, and I will never forget the sparks of the torches flying upwards into the night sky, and Her Majesty watching her piper intently, and beaming, and tapping time with her foot.

The following day we were – bump – back down to earth. That Saturday night Amber Rudd rang me to say that she was resigning as secretary of state for work and pensions. Again, I can't say that I was much surprised. She was never, to put it mildly, much of an enthusiast for Brexit. I felt that her resignation was a blow from which I could plausibly recover, and we soon had an excellent replacement in Thérèse Coffey. But how many more such blows could I take?

The following Monday – September 9, 2019 – we tried again to go for an election. I had decided to punch this bruise until Corbyn recognised the absurdity of his position. We tabled another motion in Parliament. We failed again. It was now barely five weeks until the crucial European summit of October 17, our last chance to get the EU to agree a deal.

Everyone could see that I was being squeezed as if by a gigantic nutcracker, with an obdurate Parliament as one of the pincers and the implacable EU as the other. My notional parliamentary majority had gone down from about minus one to about minus forty-three.

I continued to insist that it was all just a flesh wound, like the maimed knight in Monty Python, and that we would still leave the EU on October 31; and people started to become a bit impatient with my claims. Yeah, right, they said, or words to that effect. How are you going to do that? A suspicion was forming, in some parts, that I would not actually write the famous Benn-Burt letter asking for yet another extension of UK membership; that I might actually be so reckless as to disobey parliamentary statute and refuse to comply with the Surrender Act.

Some cabinet colleagues started to say that this was too much, that they could not accept this and that the law must be obeyed. Of course I would obey the law, I said, and stuck ever more crazily to my line that we would leave on October 31. Inwardly, I really wasn't sure what to do.

I recoiled at the idea of writing the Surrender letter. I was damned if I was going to be turned into some automaton, the powerless amanuensis of Hilary Benn. I started pondering various manoeuvres. Perhaps the letter should contain an acrostic so that the capital letters of every sentence – LET BRITAIN GO! – contradicted the sense of the letter. Perhaps I should try a palimpsest or code.

Perhaps I could nullify the letter's effect if I wrote it in Greek hexameters, or perhaps I should write two letters, one contradicting the other, or a letter on special self-combusting paper. I tried all sorts of ideas, but none of them cut much ice with the lawyers. The Benn-Burt Act was watertight. The law was the law, and if I failed to comply with the law I would be sent to prison.

I seemed so outwardly serene that people started to surmise that I must have some trick up my sleeve, some Houdini-like greased piglet ruse for getting us out.

I didn't. What I had, rather, was an instinctive belief that it would not be possible for parliamentary pranks, no matter how ingenious, to stop Britain from leaving the EU. The people had voted for it. The people would prevail.

When journalists asked how the hell it was actually supposed to happen, I was Delphic. I compared the UK to the mild-mannered physicist Dr Bruce Banner, who wakes up in the Marvel comics to find that hostile forces have bound him in shackles. As Banner struggles with his chains, he begins to get angry at the injustice of his position, and as rage takes him over he morphs into the great green goliath, the Incredible Hulk.

The longer they tried our patience, I explained, and the more unreasonable the demands of our captors, the more fiercely we would fight to break free. Or, as the Incredible Hulk used to put it, delighting my eight-year-old soul, 'The madder Hulk gets, the stronger Hulk gets.'

As September wore on, and we got ever more desperate, we also got more creative. Perhaps there was some idea to solve the problem of the Northern Ireland border, something extra to throw in the mix.

I was and am a Unionist. When in 1990 the Tory Northern Ireland secretary Peter Brooke declared that Britain had no 'selfish strategic or economic interest' in Northern Ireland, I saw what he was driving at and why he said it. It was the first step on the way to the end of that miserable conflict and the beginning of the Good Friday Agreement.

I also thought it was a slightly dispiriting turn of phrase. It sounded as though we didn't care about Northern Ireland, or as if we were not interested in preserving the boundaries of our own country. I did care.

I disliked the echoes from Brussels, where the German secretary-general of the EU Commission, Martin Selmayr, was quoted as saying that 'the loss of Northern Ireland is the price the British must pay for Brexit'. Selmayr, in fact, denied that he had said any such thing, but it chimed with the generally punitive sentiment from some in the EU. I thought there was probably no smoke without fire.

It enraged me that anyone in the EU Commission might even think this way. That was why it was my objective to get the UK out of the EU, whole and entire, with complete restoration of national control. But you can be a Unionist without being an unreconstructed Unionist, or a blinkered Unionist.

I recognise that Northern Ireland is highly complex and bruise-easy. There are different traditions and different aspirations. Though I abominated the IRA, I also understood – as any UK PM must – the history and strength of nationalist feeling. There must be a balance in Northern Irish politics, and the secret of that balance, and the principle at the heart of the Good Friday peace process, is the principle of consent.

Perhaps one way to solve this was to give agency and responsibility to the people who were most directly affected – the people of Northern Ireland. I started to think about a time-limited solution to the problem of the border with Ireland, which would depend on the principle of consent.

On October 2, 2019, the last day of the Tory Party conference, David Frost tabled a new proposal from the UK side. It was radically different from the Theresa May deal. Under these plans, Britain was fully leaving the EU. We would come out of the customs union and the single market. We would take back control of everything – money, borders, laws.

We would reflect the particular circumstances and needs of Northern Ireland – and the need to avoid any checks at the border – by keeping Northern Ireland aligned with at least some EU standards, such as for food and manufactured goods. But this alignment would be time-limited and it would have to be actively reaffirmed by the people of Northern Ireland.

The EU didn't like this at all. They didn't like the time limit, and they didn't like the idea of consent. But the Irish did. That was the essence of the deal we did with the Irish Taoiseach Leo Varadkar at Thornton Manor near Liverpool, a rather nice wedding venue once used for the birthday party of Coleen Rooney, wife of footballer Wayne.

I thought it was, on the face of it, a very good agreement. It was clear from the text that Northern Ireland was leaving the EU with the rest of the UK. It was explicitly stated that Northern Ireland was part of the UK customs area, and envisaged that Northern Ireland would be able to take part in UK free-trade deals with the rest of the world.

It was made clear that Northern Ireland was part of the UK internal market, and that there should be minimal interference in trade from GB to NI. Yes, there were objections, especially from Unionist parties in Northern Ireland.

They pointed out that it was anti-democratic to ask the people of Northern Ireland to accept rules and regulations made in Brussels when they had no say in them. They were worried about new barriers to trade down the Irish Sea, since under the protocol we had agreed that UK customs would check on goods coming into Northern Ireland which were deemed to be 'at risk' of going on into the Republic of Ireland.

I did not believe that these checks would or should be onerous; and in the case of every objection, I was able to point to the consent mechanism. Unless the Northern Ireland Assembly expressly voted to maintain these arrangements in 2024, they would lapse automatically. Northern Ireland would become as economically indistinguishable from the rest of the UK as Hampshire, and totally outside the EU.

I am afraid, looking back, that I allowed the wish to be the father to the thought. In allowing the EU the continued right to adjudicate over customs controls in Northern Ireland, I imagined that they would be reasonable. I did not think that they would be so petty and vindictive as to ban British sausages, or British bacon, or potted plants, from entering Northern Ireland.

I was wrong. As for the consent mechanism, it did not fairly reflect the Good Friday Agreement's principles. Instead of majority support, in the assembly, for continuing with the protocol, I should have insisted on cross-community support, so that Unionist feeling could not be ignored.

The trouble was that by the time I became PM the UK negotiating position had been so badly enfeebled. We had endured three years of surrenderism. Given a blank slate, I would never have agreed to the backstop or the Northern Ireland protocol. I would have done the obvious thing – for which I always argued in cabinet – and negotiated our exit and the new free-trade deal at the same time.

But for now all that was secondary. All that was ignored in the excitement of getting a deal. I had found a way out and I knew Parliament would vote for it, and that I would be able to sell it to the people of the UK. And if there were problems down the line, well, we were finally out, and we were about to be a sovereign independent country.

If there were problems, in our own country, then – like any other country – we would pass a bill to fix those problems. That was the point of taking back control.

On October 19, after the deal had been agreed by the EU, we had a special Saturday session of Parliament, for the first time since the Falklands War. We voted the deal through, because there was simply no good argument against it.

The people had voted for Brexit, and now finally we were delivering it.

My enemies still had a little ambush to spring. Amazed (and secretly chagrined) that I had got a deal with the EU after all they had done to spike my tyres, my colleagues tried one last time to finish me off.

Having voted with gritted teeth to deliver Brexit, they immediately voted against the 'programme motion', holding the bill up in Parliament so that technically we could not pass it by October 31.

They claimed, completely spuriously, that they needed 'more time' to consider the agreement.

They neither needed more time, nor took it. They were just trying to mess with my head. They wanted the consolation prize of forcing me to break my promise – and forcing me to eat my words, in public, and to write that wretched letter.

In the end I wrote not one but two. One was unsigned, and just a copy of the pro forma letter in the Benn-Burt Act. The other was a personal letter that I wrote and signed to Donald Tusk, president of the EU Council of Ministers, saying that I could see no conceivable case for delay in allowing Britain to leave the EU.

Alas, as our lawyers had predicted, the EU decided that the first letter was the operative text, and for another three months they kept us in. But politically it didn't matter. We had defied all the predictions by removing the backstop and getting a new deal. We had routed the sceptics by getting that deal through Parliament, or at least through its second reading in the Commons.

Now Jeremy Corbyn was the one in the trap. He had said he would not have an election without a deal – and now he was cornered. He tried to hold out for a few days, but we kept up an unrelenting clamour. In the end the Lib Dems and the SNP deserted him, and he was forced to fold his tents. On October 29, he agreed to an election. Of course, there were plenty who said I was mad. Danny Finkelstein, a Conservative columnist and all-round sage, said Corbyn could well end up PM; the great polling guru John Curtice said we would lose twenty seats and make way for a Corbyn-led coalition.

But unlike Labour we had a plan to take to the people. After three and a half years, we had shown we could get Brexit done. We had a deal in time for a pre-Christmas election, and it was oven-ready.

Oven-ready! I can hear some of my opponents say. It wasn't oven-ready!

It is true that we had not yet negotiated the new relationship with the EU, because the May government had agreed, alas, that the withdrawal would have to come first. But we had finally found a way out of the EU that ensured our constitutional independence – and that would make the shape of the new deal obvious.

What was absolutely ready to bang in the oven was our plan to leave the EU. Now it was up to the public to vote on it.

Chapter 5

Earthquake

The biggest realignment in
UK politics for decades

Now it was only seconds until the bongs went bong at 10 p.m. and we heard the results of the exit poll. We were up in the Thatcher Room – Margaret Thatcher's old study on the first floor, looking out over the Number Ten garden.

There was beer. There were crisps. There was the ubiquitous Andy Parsons taking photographs of the moment – and I mentally tried to prepare my features.

Defeat? That meant looking defiant, and I rehearsed a lantern-jawed resolution. Victory? Hmm – that would entail a kind of noble-browed beam, but without being smug.

Hung Parliament?

'Why are you making that face?' said Carrie, and I gave up. In my head, I was back to one of those school 'Reading Over' moments, back to those seconds before you know whether or not you have won some academic prize, and my pulse was sloshing in my ears, *lup-dup lup-dup*, with a vigour to delight any cardiologist.

I stared at the faces of the BBC's election night broadcasters – Huw Edwards, the lot of them. They had a strained, sallow, costive look, as though troubled by some digestive complaint.

They knew the results of the exit poll. They must have known it for about half an hour at least.

Why did they look so stricken? It was true that we Conservatives began the election with a poll lead – but then so did Theresa May. It was only a couple of years ago that she had launched herself at the electorate with a vast twenty-point cushion. She had assumed that she was going to get a landslide – and she managed to blow our majority.

I knew that a general election is a gamble, a crapshoot. The public were feeling frankly over-consulted. They were fed up with being constantly asked to give their opinion of us politicians in this needy does-my-bum-look-big-in-this way. They wanted us all to shut up and get on with it.

Now I was asking them to vote for a fourth consecutive Conservative government, with the third consecutive Conservative leader – and maybe I was just trying them too high. Jeremy Corbyn was still a cult hero to millions of younger voters. 'Oooh Jeremy Corbyn', they would chant outside the studios during the TV debates to the tune of 'Seven Nation Army' by the White Stripes.

Not many hip young people were chanting anything about me. Nothing printable, anyway.

It is in the molten crucible of an election campaign that you separate the base from the true metal. What if I was somehow rumbled? What if the nation peered into my soul and decided that it was time for a change? In the last few days, the tension had been rising, and I had been starting to lose discipline.

It began to go wrong three days before polling day, on Monday December 9, 2019. We were at a fish market in Grimsby, and I had spent about an hour holding and posing with cod – huge, slimy, gape-jawed monsters of the deep – and pretending to auction them off. It was fun, and I sensed a lot of support for our candidate, Lia Nici, from the fish market folk. Then it was time to do my media interviews, and the man in the fish market was ITV's aptly named Joe Pike.

I thought Pike would like to talk about taking back control of our waters and how our oven-ready deal would allow us to end the iniquities of the Common Fisheries Policy. Pike cut me off. He wanted to talk about Labour's main campaign theme – the state of the NHS. In particular he was exercised by the treatment of a four-year-old called Jack, who had apparently spent the night on the floor – lying on a coat – at Leeds General Infirmary.

Well, it so happened that I was right up to speed on Leeds General Infirmary. I had been there only recently and seen its dusty aspidistras in its ancient Victorian halls. It was one of the forty hospitals that we were going to rebuild, and I knew that we were going to give the amazing staff at Leeds General Infirmary exactly the facilities they needed to help them deal with sad cases like the young boy in question.

I had begun a long and passionate and fact-filled answer to this effect when Pike shut me up again. He held out his phone and asked me to look – if I could bear it – at the image on the screen. I knew what he was up to.

I was familiar with this technique. You are gassing away in a TV interview and the reporter suddenly hands you something incriminating – a leaked document that purportedly contradicts whatever you are saying – and they film your befuddled reaction. It had happened quite a lot with a particular ITV journalist when I was mayor of London, and I had devised a cunning solution.

I just took the offending document, folded it up, put it in my pocket – and carried on talking about whatever I wanted to talk about. OK – it looked a bit bonkers, but at least you remained in control of the interview.

Applying the same principle, I took Pike's phone and slid it invisibly (so I thought) into my pocket, saying that I would study it later. This looked deranged. Pike rightly pointed out to the viewers that I was not only refusing to look at a heart-rending picture of a young boy suffering on an NHS ward. I seemed to be stealing his property. 'You have taken my phone and put it in your pocket, Prime Minister,' he said.

I paused. He was right. I fished it out of my pocket, looked at the picture of Jack asleep on the coats – and of course apologised. I apologised to the child, to his family, to anyone who had a bad experience of the NHS, and, a bit tetchily, I apologised to Joe Pike for briefly confiscating his phone.

It was not an easy day. According to Laura Kuenssberg, the episode showed, for some reason, that I was at least potentially indifferent to the north of England, while Paul Brand of ITV wondered which bad aspect of my character had come out more clearly – my callousness or my blatant inability to distinguish, when it came to mobile phones, between *meum et tuum*.

Labour's Jonathan Ashworth said my refusal to look at an image of a suffering child was a 'new low' and that it showed exactly why voters should not give 'this disgrace of a man' another five years in office. The Lib Dem guy said that I had shown 'a shocking lack of empathy'.

In my defence I would say that the material of these journalistic ambushes often turns out to be misleading, especially NHS horror stories. Remember the 1992 election and the war of Jennifer's ear, when Labour's claims about a little girl's grommet misery did not survive scrutiny.

I think the story of little Jack was also more complicated than it first appeared, and that the staff at Leeds had certainly done their best. But Labour had succeeded, in the last week, in getting the story on to their territory. Of course I was worried. You would have been worried, in my shoes.

By the eve of the poll – Wednesday December 11 – I was getting very jumpy indeed. The day began well enough. I had a simple mission – to symbolise our determination to 'deliver' by delivering some milk to an address in Leeds. So I got up shatteringly early, went to the dairy, got the milk and rang the doorbell at 8 Jacquard Gardens, where the family seemed happy to get the delivery and even moderately pleased to see me. I then had to be 'prepped' for my media interviews and went back to the dairy.

As I got out of the car, all sorts of media folk with cameras were inviting me to come on their show, like hawkers in a bazaar. Someone representing the broadcaster Piers Morgan was particularly insistent. I assured him that I would be with him in a minute.

But where was the briefing room? I needed to be 'prepped'. We had to avoid another NHS horror story ambush. Over here, said someone from the media team, I think the excellent Rosie Bate-Williams. We scrambled through a door, pursued by the journalists, and shut it gratefully behind us.

It was a large fridge used by the dairy company and, like all fridges with the door shut, it was cold inside. And pitch-black. Someone had the wit to turn on the flashlight on their mobile, and we assessed the situation.

There was no other way out but through the front door of the fridge. We were surrounded, like Butch Cassidy and the Sundance Kid at the end of the movie. The cameras of the nation's breakfast TV shows were trained on our fridge, like the rifles of the Bolivian army.

There was nothing for it. Anyway, it was getting cold. We emerged from our refrigerated refuge amid national derision, and an incontinent Piers Morgan denounced me as a coward and a fridge hider. One of the de-whipped Tory rebels, David Gauke, even went to the trouble of tweeting a picture of himself in a fridge.

Unlike me, said Gauke, he was willing to talk to Piers Morgan any time. You may think I am making heavy weather of these inconsequential media teapot tempests. But they stick in my mind partly because I was so paranoid but also because – for the most part – that campaign was a model of message discipline.

I was the mouthpiece; I was the messenger. But the real heroes of the 2019 election campaign were the people – from campaign director Isaac Levido to head of operations Shelley Williams-Walker – who came up with the stunts and the gimmicks to get our message across.

A few years later I happened to be swimming in a lake in Slovenia. Two locals came by on a kind of kayak. From some distance away they spotted my head in the water, then hailed me by my name and shouted, 'Get Brexit Done!'

That's what you want in an election campaign – a three-word slogan with global cut-through. At a traditional Jewish bakery in north London, I iced Chanukah doughnuts with the legend 'Get Brexit Done' and distributed them to a roaring crowd. At the John Smedley knitwear factory in Derbyshire, I helped to make a 'Get Brexit Done' headscarf.

I baked a giant meat pie, with 'Get Brexit Done' spelled out in pastry letters on the crust, and slammed it in the oven, to show we had an oven-ready deal. The crowning moment, the pièce de résistance – of which Isaac was so proud that he concealed it from me until the day itself – came two days before polling day.

We went to the JCB factory at Uttoxeter. I mounted the cab of a 4CX backhoe loader decked out in gorgeous Union Jack livery. I revved it up and then drove it at a fair lick through a wall of giant Styrofoam bricks.

The wall said 'GRIDLOCK' – and guess what words were emblazoned on the shovel of that JCB digger as I blasted through that wall. It was corny. It was plonking. But it certainly obliterated my remaining embarrassment at having snaffled Joe Pike's mobile phone.

As a visual expression of what we were trying to say – about unblocking a gridlocked Parliament – it was also brilliantly effective. Of course, the media scoffed and sniffed. But we got that message through and past them, disintermediating the media as if they were a bunch of unresisting polystyrene blocks.

All my stump speeches were an elaboration of that central metaphor. Parliament was like a broken-down bendy bus, jack-knifed over the yellow box junction of our national life. The voters had the tow-truck to move it aside.

Parliament was a great fatberg of delay, blocking the pipes of the nation. Now was the time for the electorate to send up the cleansing dynorod and blast the obstruction aside.

By the 2019 election I was a pretty seasoned political campaigner. There were moments – amid my general anxiety – when I started to feel the political ground shifting beneath us. I noticed it in the cheery responses of the steelworkers in Scunthorpe, the mid-afternoon enthusiasm of the drinkers at a JD Wetherspoon in Walsall. It certainly wasn't conclusive; it could have been a tremor; it could have been nothing.

If you have done a lot of walkabouts, you develop a kind of instinctive bat-squeak sensitivity to people's body language. Are they avoiding your eye? Are they actively asking for a selfie, or asking to shake your hand? What percentage is asking you to f--- off?

You start doing guesstimates, and in the good areas I felt that we had well over 40 per cent support – surely enough to form a government.

So when Huw Edwards fixed the nation with his eye and prepared to tell us the result of the exit poll – effectively, these days, such is the accuracy of the poll, the result of the election – the truth is that I genuinely had not the faintest idea what he was going to say.

I was braced for bad news, but I was willing to believe that things had gone well. I certainly wasn't prepared for what he said. If this poll was right, it looked as though the 2019 election was a seismic event. After almost ten years in office, and four elections

– it looked as though the Conservative Party was headed for a massively increased majority. Eighty-six seats, said Huw. No wonder the funereal mood in the BBC studio.

The live audience for the Channel 4 election night show was so shocked that they gasped – and then booed. I am afraid I was so exultant that I leaped up like a lottery winner, fists clenched and eyes bulging in a thoroughly undignified way. Andy Parsons caught the moment, and we later released the photo; which I thought was a mistake, since it looked so triumphalist. Soon the BBC politics team were spitting out the rest of the statistics – fourteen million Tory votes, the second-biggest ever poll by a political party; terrible night for Labour, etc., etc. – and we tried to work out what had happened.

We had won the biggest share of the vote since Margaret Thatcher in 1979, bigger even than Tony Blair in 1997.

Where had we won? What was going on? As the night wore on, it was obvious that an earthquake was underway. It wasn't so much the size of the Tory victory – it was the social and geographical composition of that victory.

At 11.33 p.m. we had the first sign of what was happening. Ian Levy won Blyth Valley for the Conservatives, the first time the Teesside seat had gone to us since 1950.

At 1.23 a.m. Mark Jenkinson, a former steelworks apprentice, won Workington, for the first time since 1979.

At 1.50 a.m. Sarah Atherton won Wrexham from Labour. Wrexham! Wrexham had never ever returned a Conservative MP. It wasn't a bellwether. It wasn't a seat to watch. It was a result that no one expected.

I knew Wrexham, a bit. I had fought the neighbouring seat of Clwyd South in the 1997 election – and been duly thrashed – and Wrexham was spoken of by my activists in hushed tones, a place so viscerally anti-Tory that a former candidate (Owen Paterson, as it happened) had been set upon and beaten in the street by an elderly man. Now Wrexham had gone blue, and, good Lord, we had won Clwyd South as well.

It was clear that we were producing a double whammy – routing Labour in their ancient heartlands and also holding on to our traditional territory in London and the south-east.

At 2.33 a.m. I was relieved to hear that Iain Duncan Smith had hung on in Chingford and Woodford Green.

At 2.54 a.m. we retained the Cities of London and Westminster, as Nickie Aiken beat Chuka Umunna, who had switched horses from Labour to Change UK to the Independent Group to the Lib Dems.

3.32 a.m.: we took Don Valley – the first time Labour had lost the seat since 1922.

3.38 a.m.: we won Wakefield, Labour since 1932, and Bassetlaw, Labour since 1935.

On it went through the night. We were toppling the bricks of what had once been described as Labour's red wall, the invincible fastnesses that have traditionally provided a route to a majority.

At 3.44 a.m. the blue bulldozer took Rother Valley, Labour since 1918, and Sedgefield, formerly the seat of Tony Blair. Yes, to cap it all, we reversed the humiliation of 1997 and took the seat of Labour's three-time election winner.

A couple of minutes earlier I had held my own seat of Uxbridge and South Ruislip with a substantially increased majority. I thanked my team and had a few quick words with the other candidates. Lord Buckethead seemed a nice enough chap, though it was hard to hear what he was saying inside the bucket. He appeared to be asking after Dilyn the dog.

Then I raced to CCHQ and thanked everyone there – Isaac, James Cleverly, who had done a great job of rousing the troops, Ben Elliot, Dom Cummings and others. At 7.23 a.m. I made a speech at an impromptu rally in the QEII Centre, which I might as well reproduce here because it captures the flavour of the night and the sense of mission. I stood on a podium proclaiming that this was now 'The people's government' ...

Good morning, everybody – well, we did it – we pulled it off, didn't we?

We broke the deadlock, we ended the gridlock, we smashed the roadblock and in this glorious, glorious pre-breakfast moment, before a new dawn rises on a new day and a new government, I want first of all to pay tribute to good colleagues who lost their seats through no fault of their own in the election just gone by. And of course I want to congratulate absolutely everybody involved in securing the biggest Conservative majority since the 1980s. Literally, literally – as I look around – literally before many of you were born.

And with this mandate and this majority we will at last be able to do what? [Crowd shouts, 'Get Brexit done.']

You've been paying attention. Because this election means that getting Brexit done is now the irrefutable, irresistible, unarguable decision of the British people. And with this election, I think we've put an end to all those miserable threats of a second referendum.

And I say respectfully, I say respectfully to our stentorian friend in the blue twelve-star hat [Steve Bray], 'That's it, time to put a sock in the megaphone and give everybody some peace.' [He didn't.]

I have a message to all those who voted for us yesterday, especially those who voted for us Conservatives, One Nation Conservatives for the first time. You may only have lent us your vote and you may not think of yourself as a natural Tory. And, as I think I said eleven years ago to the people of London when I was elected in what was thought of as a Labour city, your hand may have quivered over the ballot paper before you put your cross in the Conservative box and you may intend to return to Labour next time round. And if that is the case, I am humbled that you have put your trust in me, and that you have put your trust in us. And I, and we, will never take your support for granted.

And I will make it my mission to work night and day, flat out, to prove you right in voting for me this time, and to earn your support in the future. And I say to you that in this election your voice has been heard and about time too. Because we politicians have squandered the last three years, three and a half years, in squabbles about Brexit – we've even been arguing about arguing, and about the tone of our arguments.

And I will put an end to all that nonsense, and we will get Brexit done on time by the 31st of January, no ifs, no buts, no maybes. Leaving the European Union as one United Kingdom, taking back control of our laws, borders, money, our trade, immigration system, delivering on the democratic mandate of the people.

And at the same time, this One Nation Conservative government will massively increase our investment in the NHS, the health service that represents the very best of our country, with a single, beautiful idea that whoever we are – rich, poor, young, old – the NHS is there for us when we are sick, and every day that service performs miracles.

And that is why the NHS is this One Nation Conservative government's top priority. And so we will deliver 50,000 more nurses, and 50 million more GP surgery appointments and how many new hospitals? [Crowd shouts, 'Forty.'] Correct.

And we will deliver a long-term NHS budget enshrined in law, £650 million extra every week, Health Secretary.

And all the other priorities that you the people of this country voted for. Record spending on schools, an Australian-style points-based immigration system, more police, how many? [Crowd shouts, 'Twenty thousand.'] Colossal new investments in infrastructure, in science, using our incredible technological advantages to make this country the cleanest, greenest on earth with the most far-reaching environmental programme.

And you the people of this country voted to be carbon-neutral in this election. You voted to be carbon-neutral by 2050 and we will do it. You also voted to be Corbyn-neutral by Christmas by the way and we'll do that too.

You voted for all these things and it is now this government, this people's government, it's our solemn duty to deliver on each and every one of those commitments and it is a great and a heavy responsibility, a sacred trust for me, for every newly elected Conservative MP, for everyone in this room and everyone in this party.

And I repeat that in winning this election we have won votes and the trust of people who have never voted Conservative before and people who have always voted for other parties. Those people want change. We cannot, must not, must not, let them down.

And in delivering change we must change too. We must recognise the incredible reality that we now speak as a One Nation Conservative Party literally for everyone from Woking to Workington, from Kensington, I'm proud to say, to Clwyd South, from Surrey Heath to Sedgefield, from Wimbledon to Wolverhampton.

And as the nation hands us this historic mandate we must rise to the challenge and to the level of expectations. And Parliament must change so that we in Parliament are working for you the British people.

And that is what we will now do, isn't it? That is what we will now do. Let's go out, let's go out and get on with it.

Let's unite this country, let's spread opportunity to every corner of the UK, with superb education, superb infrastructure and technology.

Let's get Brexit done.

But first, my friends, let's get breakfast done too.

Thank you all, thank you all very much for coming, thank you all very much, thank you all, thank you, thank you.

Andrew Marr sniffed afterwards that it all sounded a bit totalitarian, this talk of the people's government, but I meant what I said.

There were all sorts of reasons for the earthquake and what looked like – at least then, in that glorious moment – a realignment of British politics.

There was Corbyn, a far-left extremist, who had done nowhere near enough to purge his party of the taint of antisemitism. He was also hopeless on the central issue of the campaign. His policy on Brexit was to say he would have a second referendum – but he wouldn't say whether he would campaign for Remain or Leave!

I suspect that Jeremy was really an old anti-EU Bennite but didn't dare say so because his party was so full of angry Remainers. So he looked vapid and irresolute. Whatever else you said about us in the people's government, we did not look irresolute.

All those things that drove them nuts in SW1 – proroguing Parliament, de-whipping the rebels; all the things that had the left-wing media reaching for the smelling salts – these were the very things that showed the wider public that we were serious and that we would deliver.

They saw us not as continuity Conservatives but as radicals, a change government. I think they liked what we were saying about the direction of the country – that it was time for growth, time for an increase in wages, time for levelling up. I felt it keenly – this vast weight of expectations. I said over and over again to my team, to Tory MPs, that this decision by millions of people to change the voting habits of generations was not just miraculous. It was entirely contingent.

People had trusted us. People had given us the benefit of the doubt. But they would only trust us again if we showed we could get things done. I knew how difficult it was, in a modern democracy, to deliver – to get things done.

But I comforted myself with this thought – that unlike many other new occupants of Number Ten, I had done a decade of hands-on delivery across almost every area of public policy.

Part Two

London

Chapter 6

The Greatest City on Earth

Taking on Red Ken

It was the poet Dante who had a shattering experience *nel mezzo del cammin di nostra vita* – at the midway point of life's journey. I must have been about forty years old when I, too, had a life-changing moment. I was literally *nel mezzo del cammin* – in the middle of High Holborn – and a new and incomprehensible force was pushing me remorselessly into the oncoming traffic.

It was about 2004 and I was coming to the end of my time as editor of the *Spectator*. I was MP for Henley-on-Thames, and I think I must have been late for some parliamentary engagement, so I was puffing along on my pushbike when I got to that bit where the traffic all turns left before heading down Shaftesbury Avenue.

I needed to make progress, but my path was blocked. I had come up against the rear of a red single-decker bus, operated by Transport for London. I considered my options. I could squeeze past it on the left, but there were railings and I didn't fancy being ground to a paste as the bus moved off. I decided to swing out past the bus on the right.

I don't normally favour this manoeuvre, since there is always a risk that the bus will accelerate – and you find yourself surrounded by fast-moving vehicles, some coming at you from behind, some heading towards you. No cyclist enjoys that. But things were pretty gummed up in Holborn that day and I reckoned I would have the time.

I stood up on the pedals and gave it some grunt. I was overhauling the bus when I started to feel that something was awry. This bus had no end. It just went on and on. It seemed to be two buses articulated by a giant rubber concertina.

Now the bastard contraption was picking up speed, and I had to respond. I pedalled harder and harder, but it was keeping me stranded on its right; and now it was turning left and as it turned the leviathan lazily swayed its hips and – whoa – I was being sent out into the oncoming taxis, parping at me, and cursing and telling me what I already knew – that this was getting dangerous.

'Hey!' I yelled at the bus, and saw the passengers look down apathetically at this man in a suit, panting with terror and exertion. They gazed bleakly and went back to their papers.

Avoiding the cars, I made a superhuman effort to overtake this double-tailed diplodocus, but now I had come up against a traffic island. The bus was so huge that its tyres were scrunching over the kerb. I was going to get minced. I knew I was beat. I got off the bike and pressed myself up against the railings of the traffic island until the monster was past.

Who the hell put that thing on the road? I asked myself. And by what authority? I later established that this was an eighteen-metre Mercedes-Benz Citaro bendy bus, capable of carrying about 144 people and their assorted pushchairs and luggage. The man who put it on the streets of London was the mayor, Ken Livingstone, and he had done it on the authority of the Greater London Act of 1998.

I vowed there and then to do whatever I could to remove him from office.

It would be an exaggeration to say that I spent the next two or three years plotting the political assassination of the mayor; but the seed had been planted in a crevice of my brain, and slowly began to germinate.

It must have been back in 1996 – when it had become clear that Labour were going to win the next election – that I saw something on the news about new parliaments in Scotland and Wales, and a new mayor for London. Wow, I thought – mayor of London. That sounds interesting.

So ten years later, when Tory friends started to mention the possibility – I think they were Howard Leigh and Hugo Swire – my ears pricked up. I liked the sound of the job. It was basically monarchical. You didn't have to worry about cabinet mutinies or backbench unrest. You didn't have to understand the difference between the second and third reading of a bill. You had your powers and your budgets, and you just got good things done. So I didn't exactly dismiss these kind suggestions. I probably muttered something non-committal, and vaguely wondered if I would hear more about it.

For a while, at least, the Tory Party leadership had other ideas. Mayor of London was already one of the most powerful jobs in the country. This was to be a flagship campaign – a dry-run for the all-important general election campaign of 2010. All eyes would be on the capital. Was I really the best they could find? I had plenty of supporters, but I also had a lot of powerful critics.

When I was chosen to succeed Michael Heseltine as MP for Henley, the *Evening Standard* carried a leading article on July 14, 2000, as follows:

The selection of Boris Johnson, the *Spectator* editor, as the Tory candidate for Michael Heseltine's Henley constituency confirms the Tory Party's increasing weakness for celebrity personalities over the dreary exigencies of politics. One might have expected the selectors to have gone for someone more in the Heseltine mould: a high-flying politician of a Euro-friendly disposition, but that is not how selection committees work.

Johnson is a noisy Euro-sceptic who, for all his gifts, is unlikely to grace any future Tory cabinet. Indeed, he is not known for his excessive interest in serious policy matters, and it is hard to see him grubbing away at administrative detail as an obscure, hardworking junior minister for social security.

And so on. Snootsville, Arizona, eh?

I think I detected the hand of Max Hastings, my former editor at the *Daily Telegraph*, whose early pride at my reporting from Brussels had evolved into a Dr Frankenstein-like horror at the monster he had created.

It looked for a long time as though he would be proved correct. When my friend Zac Goldsmith suggested to David Cameron that I would be a good candidate for the mayoralty, Cameron snapped: 'He has completely the wrong profile.' I am not sure exactly what he meant by that, but they asked virtually everyone else. An invitation to be the Tory candidate was extended to former PM John Major; to Nick Ferrari, the LBC radio show host, who would have been excellent but claimed he had too much alimony to pay; to Sir Greg Dyke, the former director general of the BBC who had once promoted a character called Roland Rat.

Greg wasn't even a Conservative, and insisted that he would have to serve as a kind of cross-bench mayor before eventually saying no. Finally they picked Nick Boles, who then had to withdraw because of ill-health. So by the summer of 2007, the Tory Party had run out of alternatives, and they were running out of time. Which is probably why they ended up with me (a position that may sound familiar to attentive readers of this narrative). I wasn't at all sure that I should do it.

I had a wonderful constituency in Henley-on-Thames and at last I had a political job – shadow spokesman for higher education

– that I found absorbing and rewarding. And there was a good reason why all those potential Tory mayoral candidates had, in the end, declined the blandishments of Cameron.

The job might sound great, but it was likely to be a thoroughly nasty campaign and to end in defeat.

Ken Livingstone was the five-hundred-pound gorilla of London politics. He had become leader of the Greater London Council in 1981, when I was seventeen years old, and he had a way of demolishing his opponents, and of being proved right. If you look at all those causes he championed in the eighties – when he was being demonised as the leader of London's loony left – they included gay rights, feminism, anti-racism; and they had all become mainstream, indeed they were what marked out Cameron's 'modernised' Conservative Party. He had championed the IRA and now the former terrorists had been brought in by the Good Friday Agreement. They were part of the government of the country.

He was not just a victorious culture warrior; he was also an original and effective administrator. He had come up with a plan to discourage people from using their cars by charging them for driving in central London and then using the cash to invest in public transport. It was audacious and it was actually popular with Londoners.

I didn't see his dark side: his occasional crapulous outbursts, or the way – as with so many others on the Corbynite left of the Labour Party – his views on Israel would shade into something so close to antisemitism as to make no difference. What I saw was a cockney cheeky chappy who had failed his 11-plus but through sheer political energy and intelligence had taken on the entire British political establishment – from Margaret Thatcher to Tony Blair – and won the top job in the city he plainly loved.

Livingstone was ruthless and unscrupulous. He had a weird fascination with newts. He spoke in a nasal south London drone. But I admired him and frankly – like everyone else – I was apprehensive about taking him on. Why would I waste almost a year of my life being publicly beaten up by Red Ken? The odds were against me winning. Was the job worth the risk?

It was clear, the more I looked at it, that it was.

You see, that bus that almost squashed my career – it was, in one sense, an offence against nature. A thing that size should never have been put on the ancient winding streets of London.

The bendy buses not only scared the cyclists, they blocked the roads when they broke down or caught fire – as they often did – jack-knifed across the yellow box junctions like beached whales. But there was also a very good reason why Livingstone had decided that they were necessary.

He needed a bigger bus because more and more people were using the buses, just as more and more people were using the Tube. That was because the population of London had started rising again, and that was because London was booming – after decades of decline, a decline that I vividly remembered.

There is no subject more fascinating or more melancholy than the rise and fall of the great civilisations, by which we mean the great cities. Think of Edward Gibbon back in 1776 as he sat in the ruins of the Roman forum, while the barefoot monks sang vespers, and came up with his idea for a book on the decline and fall of the Roman Empire. He quotes a sixteenth-century Italian scholar called Poggio Bracciolini: 'The benches of the senators are obscured by a dunghill … The forum of the Roman people where they assembled to enact their laws and elect their magistrates is now enclosed for the cultivation of pot-herbs or thrown open for the reception of swine and buffaloes.'

Rome had been the greatest city on earth – with probably a million people in the age of Augustus – and for centuries this once marshy malarial site on the banks of the Tiber was the home of the biggest, roughest, toughest power on earth. Then Rome fell, in a revolution that as Gibbon says is still felt by the peoples

of the earth, overcome by a combination of war, disease, inflation, taxation, excessive bureaucracy and uncontrolled waves of
immigration.

Out of this epic trajectory, this vast parabola of rise and fall,
there is one searing lesson. There is nothing predestined in any
story of urban success. There is no intrinsic reason why any city
should or should not triumph; no intrinsic reason why it should
not collapse.

It all depends on the people who run it and the decisions they
take. Collapse can happen fast and it can happen today. *Iam seges
est ubi Troia fuit*, says Ovid: 'cornfields grow on the site of Troy'
– and for decades the vegetation has been returning to the heart of
some American cities. Look at the creepers ravaging the buildings
of St Louis, Missouri, the trees punching through the roofs. The
population has fallen by more than 60 per cent since 1950. When
government fails, when crime is too high, when taxes are too
much – the jobs disappear and the people flee.

Which was the greatest city on earth in AD 800? Probably
Baghdad. Look at poor Baghdad today. Which was the greatest
city on earth in 1800, the heart of a new European culture of
global exploration and trade? Yes, it was already London.

Which was the world's greatest city in 1900? Still London – the
centre, by then, of an empire seven times the size of the Roman
Empire at its greatest extent under Trajan. By 1939, on the eve of
the Second World War, the population of London had reached
8.6 million.

But by 1964 – the year I was born – it had lost two million
people, almost a quarter of the population. Across the rest of the
country the population was rising; it was still the baby boom. Yet
London was falling; London was failing.

It went on into the seventies, a tumbling population and a sense
of decline. You don't remember London in the seventies? I do. I
was there.

I remember the smell of the beer-splashed pavements outside the shuttered pubs, the parks full of dogshit and spangles wrappers, the carious teeth of the children. I see a poor Pakistani bus conductor, the leather lanyard of his ticket machine soaked with sweat, and I remember admiring his masterful calm in the face of the rudeness of the largely white-skinned passengers.

The food was globally satirised. I must have been seven or eight when I read *Asterix* and realised that British food – boiled beef, boiled lamb, boiled cabbage – was mocked across Europe. They were right, those French cartoonists. I could have taken you to restaurants, back then, where they seriously offered you tinned grapefruit as an hors d'oeuvre.

I remember the news: endless strikes, race riots, inflation. It wasn't the people's fault. There was genius everywhere: in the 1960s and 1970s, the London suburbs produced some of the greatest rock and pop music ever heard – tunes that still form part of the soundtrack of the world. London wasn't suffering from a lack of native talent or enterprise.

It was a failure of politics. It was a failure of leadership, of planning, of vision. The docks collapsed, and London lost the greatest source of employment in the East End; not just because no one had the guts to take on the unions (though that was a large part of it), but because London's infrastructure was too small and too outdated, and could not cope with containerisation.

So the jobs went to the Netherlands, or Felixstowe. With the best possible intentions, the post-war planners had tried to clear the slums – and so they sent people to big purpose-built estates outside London, from Crawley to Hemel Hempstead. They tried to 'spread the jam', to create employment in these peri-urban areas; and they put crimping restrictions on office and factory space in the capital.

The result was a downward spiral. It was harder to run a business in London because you couldn't get planning permission, and so people moved out in search of jobs, and as the population fell it became even harder to find the staff in London, and harder to set up a business. This decline did not stop in the 1980s; it went on, and the population kept falling.

But something changed in the 1980s – and that was the political leadership. Margaret Thatcher refused to accept that Britain was fated to decline, and she did some remarkable things – things that got London moving again and turned the city once more into a magnet for talent. She did things that were decidedly free-market and revolutionary. She deregulated financial services in the so-called big bang and allowed people to buy their own homes, and encouraged them to own shares.

She also did some things that were decidedly not free-market, interventions that could only have been performed by the state. She drove forward colossal – some would say grandiose – plans for transport infrastructure, from the Channel Tunnel rail link to a new light railway in the Docklands and the completion of the M25 London orbital with a vast bridge over the Thames at Dartford. She not only stimulated the private sector; she helped people move to the jobs.

In 1988 I was sitting at my desk in Brussels when I read a brilliant *Sunday Telegraph* piece by my old colleague Simon Heffer, who put his finger on what was happening. The whole point about Essex Man – the sociological phenomenon he identified – was that he not only had a good and lucrative job as a trader in the City, but was able quickly and conveniently to take the train from Liverpool Street Station to his Essex home.

Never mind that he was often so pissed after work that he chundered in the carriage (the service was known as the vomit comet). It was this combination of good jobs and good transport that made his life possible and earned his undying devotion to Maggie.

By the time I was almost killed by that bendy bus, these two political philosophies – laissez-faire economics and state intervention in infrastructure – had been working side by side for almost twenty years, and London was rapidly recovering. The population was back up to eight million, some said eight and a half – and dynamic municipal action was responding to demand.

With the help of central government, Ken was investing in the bus and the Tube, and planning Crossrail. He was intent on building hundreds of thousands more homes. He was by now a very different ideological beast from the old ultra-leftist Livingstone of the 1980s. He was consorting with property developers and capitalists of all kinds. He was doing sensible things, like banging the drum for London on trips to China and India. He went to Davos and to MIPIM – the giant property fair in Cannes – and advertised the incomparable investment and development opportunities of London.

The city was once again becoming a huge global magnet for talent and money. Personal taxation was relatively low under Tony Blair (lower, I am sad to say, than under the fourteen years of Tory rule that have just ended) and there were attractive inducements for non-doms. There were more languages spoken on the streets of London than in any city on earth, and more French people than in the entire city of Bordeaux (or so I was later to claim, without contradiction).

There was still poverty in those inner London estates, and glaring inequality. If you took the Jubilee Line eight stops from Westminster to Canning Town, it was said that you lost a year of life expectancy with every stop. I don't mean that taking the Tube was a life-shortening experience, just that the ambient health and prosperity of the population diminished as you went east. There was also too much knife crime; too many young kids dying on the streets. The problem needed grip.

As I wrestled with my decision, I could see the makings of a campaign. Ken was formidable, but he was asking Londoners for a third term and that is always a big ask. If you put on some rosy spectacles and squinted at some of the polls, you could just about see a way of beating him. If it comes to a choice between doing something exciting and not doing it, I am one of those people who generally decide to do it. I decided to take Ken on.

By July 2007 I was the official Tory candidate and cycled down to City Hall to make my announcement – in what I hoped was an intimidating fashion – right by Ken's Great Glass Testicle head-quarters. There was a mob of reporters and hecklers. The BBC man was Guto Harri.

'This is a joke, isn't it?' said the man who was to go on to be my official City Hall spokesman.

Watching from Australia was Lynton Crosby, the political strategist who had propelled John Howard to several victories. He turned to his wife Dawn and said: 'That man will never be mayor of London.' Six months later, he was masterminding what would turn out to be a successful campaign.

That afternoon I went back to the Commons tea room. Bill Cash said he had seen some commotion on the news: what was that about? I said that I was going to try to be mayor of London.

Ah, said the veteran Eurosceptic. He considered the matter. 'London,' he said. 'Big place, isn't it?'

It was, and is, enormous – the biggest city in Europe by geographical extent, over six hundred square miles, and its peculi-arities required a taxi driver's knowledge of detail.

That summer we went on a family camping trip to America and I took with me four heavy lever arch files containing the collected recent press releases of Ken Livingstone. I leafed through them in amazement. There was no aspect of life that this modern Augustus did not touch; nothing he touched that he did not adorn with taxpayers' gold. The arts, the environment, transport, housing, crime – he was everywhere at once. How the hell could I compete?

I was terrified that I would be exposed as a rootless cosmopolitan, not a proper Londoner, who had been born in New

York and lived much of his childhood in Washington and Brussels. If you had asked me then which was the more easterly borough, Havering or Hillingdon, I would have frozen in panic.

There were times when I was simply skating over the intricacies of the job and, I am afraid, in those early months of the campaign it showed. By the end of 2007 I was lagging conspicuously in the polls. People were writing us off. An anonymous briefing appeared from someone close to the Tory leadership – Cameron and Osborne – suggesting that my campaign was a shambles, and that they were braced for embarrassment.

I spent a miserable Christmas wondering what the hell to do – and then in January, things began to improve. Lynton Crosby had run the Tories' 2005 campaign, and though we had not won, he had come away with rave reviews: pugnacious, with an occasional brutal Australian frankness – but also a rare gift for motivating the troops. Someone told me he might be persuaded to become campaign director.

So one night I rang him from a wintry Thame, while he dangled his feet in the warm seas of South Australia. I talked up my chances, and he said he would think about it.

To my intense relief, he rang me back and came on board. He told me I had to focus, and I did.

I started to beat Ken up for wasting taxpayers' money on fripperies: his personal supplies of Châteauneuf-du-Pape, his 'Londoner' newspaper, a Pyongyang-style free-sheet in which he regaled the citizenry with his doings. I belaboured him for his bizarre friendship with the Venezuelan Marxist dictator Hugo Chavez, and above all for his failure to stop kids bleeding to death in fights between gangs. I pledged to tackle knife crime and challenged him to take it more seriously.

Ken made the mistake of blaming the media. The problem was exaggerated, he said. 'If it bleeds it leads,' he said, quoting an

American newspaper axiom, and I hammered him for his complacency.

Of course, he hit back. His officials combed my back articles for evidence that I was – as they claimed – the most right-wing, racist, sexist, xenophobic, homophobic candidate ever to stand for high office in Britain. In one televised debate he finally drove me off the edge. He tried to undermine my assertion that I was – like so many millions of Londoners – the descendant of immigrants by attacking the patriotism of my Turkish great-grandfather, Ali Kemal.

I was sensitive about this because I am very proud of my ancestor, but he was (and remains) controversial in Turkey.

I cornered Livingstone in the green room afterwards, got him in a Vulcan nerve pinch at the back of the neck.

'You fucker,' I said. 'Don't ever say anything like that again.' He didn't.

On the day of the election the *Guardian* ran one of those supplements in which various left-wing notables promised to leave the country if I was elected. (Of course, none of them did, any more than dear old Max Hastings ever fulfilled his vow to live in Argentina during my premiership.)

That night London did something that John Ross, Ken's economic adviser, said was mathematically impossible. The city voted Tory.

When they saw the sheer numbers who had turned out to vote in Bexley and Bromley, I am told that Ken's team were stunned into silence. By the morning, I had almost 54 per cent of the vote and the biggest personal mandate in British politics. I had made all kinds of pledges in my manifesto, but one thing was morally and politically imperative: I had to stop the teenage murders.

It just took time to work out how to do it, and my first few months in London government were, I am afraid, as shambolic as my enemies had predicted.

Chapter 7

Crisis in London

In the City and City Hall

One of the great things about democracy in the UK is that when you win – *whoomph* – that's it: the mantle of office instantly descends.

One minute I was ambling along as a low-to-middle-ranking shadow minister, whose experience of hiring and firing did not go much beyond the *Spectator* magazine (and I am afraid there were times, even then, when I would take someone out to lunch with the intention of sacking them and they would leave – after a couple of bottles – with the vague impression that they had been promoted). The next moment I ran every bus, every Tube train, every tram, every fire engine and every one of the 52,000 men and women of the Metropolitan Police. I was responsible for the environment, for skills, for housing, for planning, for the entire spatial development of a city that already comprised 23 per cent of the UK economy and was probably – therefore – about the eighth or ninth biggest economy in Europe.

On Saturday May 3, 2008, at 9 a.m., there was nothing for it. I had to go down to City Hall to take charge. All seemed quiet as I arrived in a snazzy granite-paved precinct owned by a private consortium called More London. As I got off my bike, I looked up at the beetling profile of the building, a Norman Foster sphe-roid like a sinister helmet from *Star Wars*.

I could feel the dark force within: the force of Livingstone. This was an institution that my defeated opponent had fought for years to create; that had been to a large extent framed in his image. As I walked into City Hall, I noted the funky colour schemes – yellow and purple – and the modernistic sans serif font of the signs. There were no flags, no portraits of the Queen (I added one later), and I felt the contrast with Westminster. This was all about cool twenty-first-century metropolitan socialism and I wondered whether I really fitted in.

What was going on in all these curvy corridors and meeting rooms? I had a vision of brilliant young lefties with tattoos and face jewellery – and first-class degrees from Wadham – all of them muttering indignation at my victory and plotting my removal.

I reached the eighth floor and was shown my office – Livingstone's office – and again I caught that Vader-like whiff, the presence of the dark lord. He had been here only hours ago. The shredders were still hot from throbbing and panting all night, as Ken and his team destroyed documents.

I opened his drinks cabinet and – my God – there they were, glinting in the gloom like a Pharaoh's tomb, just as I had told the people of London: the taxpayer-funded bottles of Châteauneuf-du-Pape!

I think there were only about a dozen of them left. It was enough to make the point.

Then I was whisked upstairs to talk to the staff, my staff – in the big reception room at the top of City Hall that is known as London's Living Room. I looked out at the audience: the heads of police and the emergency services, the heads of quangos whose functions I barely understood. All these people had been given their jobs by Ken. Most of them had been presuming – or hoping – that I would fail.

I felt a twinge of impostor syndrome as I mounted the rostrum, and because I was so nervous I had actually yielded to my team and bought a new pair of shoes, with leather soles so shiny and slippery that I skidded and almost fell flat on my face. Which was a metaphor, pretty much, for the first year in office.

At the very moment I was trying to learn my trade, the job of running London suddenly became a lot harder.

In the spring of 2008, the whole city had a seizure, a spectacular and catastrophic crash that sent shockwaves through the economy and put millions out of work. Almost no one saw it coming.

At the tail end of 2007 I had taken my sputtering mayoral election campaign to the City of London and I sat round a lunch table with some masters of the universe – led by ICAP's Michael Spencer. I eagerly gave them my pitch (conscious that the markets were pretty sceptical, then, about my chances).

We were going to cut crime, cut City Hall waste, cut council tax, cut barriers to investment and growth, I told them. We were going to invest in mass transit and make it easier for their workforce to get a home within striking distance of their job. It was gonna be great, I told them. In fact, we were going to make London the greatest city on earth. The man on my right stirred.

'This all sounds good,' he said languidly, 'but what have you actually run before? I mean, what have you been in charge of?'

It was cruel, but I knew what he was driving at. I went into a mental defensive crouch and tried to work out what the hell to say. It was true that under my leadership the *Spectator* magazine had earned record sales and profits (long since exceeded, of course). We had a turnover of well over £20 million and we must have had twenty-five employees. Call it thirty. Maybe forty. It didn't sound very impressive.

It was true that I had been in charge of all sorts of things in the course of my life. I had been captain of the, um, school and keeper of the – er – College wall and president of the, ahem, Union …

This sounded desperate. I couldn't say that …

If I'd had my wits about me, I would have said that Margaret Thatcher was never in charge of anything much, before she became a minister and then prime minister. As for Tony Blair, he wasn't even a minister and hadn't run anything in his life. But I am afraid I didn't think of it. I was a bit intimidated by this suave and nattily dressed fellow, who wielded billions every day. He was called Johnny Cameron and I have a feeling he was wearing tartan trousers, as though he were off shooting or barn-dancing. He was in charge of equities at the Royal Bank of Scotland.

Remember him? Remember what happened to the Royal Bank of Scotland? I will give you the gist.

The rot seems to have started in America during the Clinton administration, when there was a lot of lending to low-income people with the excellent intention of encouraging them to buy their own homes. The trouble was that many of these poor folk then failed to make the payments on their mortgages. But before they all defaulted the banks had done something very clever.

They had taken all this mortgage debt, good and bad, and packaged it up and sold it on to other financial institutions. They used complicated names like collateralised debt obligations and credit default swaps to conceal the reality of what they were doing. They were compared to meat pie manufacturers who thought they could pass off some meat that was past its sell-by date by chucking it in with the good stuff and hoping that no one would notice. As with meat pies, however, the bad contaminated the good.

The truth was that these packages of debt – in which they traded and speculated and whose price they drove higher and higher – were actually getting more and more toxic; and still they traded in them and span the plates faster and faster, even though many of them had started to rumble the problem.

Goldman Sachs famously persuaded the market to buy a load of CDOs – and then shorted the market. They took a bet that they would fall in value, which of course they did.

It was like selling you a car with faulty brakes, and then taking a bet that you would crash. It was monstrous.

The whole thing blew up. The pastry lids flew off those rotten pies with a great gaseous explosion. The banks were shown to have wildly inflated their balance sheets by speculating in assets that turned out to be less than worthless – and the banking crash soon spread to the wider economy. People couldn't get loans. Mortgage lending dried up. By October 2008 the deputy governor of the Bank of England, Charlie Bean, said it was 'the biggest financial crisis in history'. Businesses started to go under – but not the banks, not the big ones.

Everybody knew who the culprits were. Everyone could see what the banks had been up to – the shameless flogging of dodgy debt. But no one could work out how to punish them. By rights, we should have let them fail, as Mervyn King, governor of the Bank of England, at first seemed to suggest. Didn't we believe in Schumpeterian destruction?

The trouble was that we just couldn't take the risk.

If people couldn't get access to finance, then the whole global economy would have a heart attack. So instead the banks were kept alive, with huge transfusions of cash; and to make sure that credit would keep flowing, the UK and other countries started to print money, in a process known as quantitative easing – the inflationary consequences of which we are still feeling today.

It is worth dwelling on this crisis, and the great depression that followed, because it is crucial to an understanding of the revolt eight years later – the Brexit vote of 2016. It was in 2008 that UK living standards stopped rising and UK productivity began to flatline. Everyone started to feel the pinch; everyone, that is, except the bankers – who were buoyed up by government largesse and who (as my sister Rachel has chronicled) started to dig ever deeper and more Neronian Sensurround cinema-cum-swimming pool complexes in the basements of their Notting Hill palazzos, whose values were, of course, inflated by the quantitative easing cash being poured into the system.

This was the beginning of that sense of the gap between London and the rest of the country, the deepening sense of alienation; though at the time, frankly, we weren't even confident that London would make it through.

One afternoon I was standing on the roof of City Hall, being interviewed by a woman from US TV. 'Mr Mayor!' she interrupted me. 'Look behind you!' I whirled round.

'The cranes,' she yipped. 'The cranes have stopped moving. No one is building anything in your city any more!'

She was right. The credit crunch had walloped the property market and the developers were drawing in their horns. That summer the cover of *Time* magazine showed a tidal wave crashing over the city, with the headline 'London's Sinking'. People were talking about an exodus of talent and investment – to Shanghai, Dubai, Mumbai, and bye-bye London. It started to look as though I was jinxed, as though Ken had taken the eight fat years of boom and I was coming in for the downturn, and – to add to my worries – things at City Hall were about as chaotic as they were in the financial markets.

I lost a string of advisers in more or less embarrassing circumstances. In fact, *The Times* hired a special City Hall correspondent, whose job seemed to be to delight her readers with accounts of my pratfalls.

She had a stock intro.

'In a fresh blow to the Mayor ...' she would begin, rubbing her hands.

Here are some of those blows, more or less in order ...

POW! First to go was a political adviser, James McGrath, who was asked a pretty absurd question – whether my election would trigger an exodus of older Caribbean residents – and James replied that, of course, anyone who didn't like London was free to leave.

This was crass. I felt an apology would have been enough but was persuaded that we had to show complete intolerance of anything that sounded remotely like discrimination. Poor James fell on his sword, and went on to great things in Australia, where he is now a senator.

The trouble with resignations, of course, is that as soon as the media get one scalp, they start hunting for more. And soon …

POW! POW! POW! they started raining more blows; first on my deputy mayor for education, Ray Lewis, a charismatic barrel-chested Guyana-born Londoner who has now died, far too young, but who then ran a school in Hackney called Eastside. Ray took young black kids, gave them discipline and self-belief – and sent them to some of the best schools and universities in the country. I was a believer in him and a passionate believer still in what he was trying to do. It was levelling up in action.

But the London lefties were after him. They didn't like his disciplinarian methods. They didn't like the way he got his kids into fee-paying schools. They didn't approve at all of his outrageous political incorrectness. (If it is untrue that he once told a woman that he could imagine parking his bike between her buttocks, then I am afraid it is the sort of thing he could easily have said.)

Above all, they didn't like the way he hung out with me and other Conservatives. And there were some peculiarities in his CV that we struggled to sort out. Was he really a JP? Was he a vicar? In what sense was he a prison governor?

What happened to that raffle money all those years ago? It enraged me to see the way the lefties hounded Ray. What difference did it make to his ability to change the lives of kids in London?

It was no use. I tried to defend him in a joint press conference, an event so chaotic that 'joint press conference' became a City Hall euphemism for some new disaster or resignation.

I was able, happily, to bring him back later, but by July 4 there was so much confusion that Ray had to step down, and now the blows were coming fast as …

BIFF! the media claimed that I had 'lost' another adviser when my acting chief of staff, Nick Boles, moved on (in fact he had never intended to stay long) and

SOCKO! I also 'lost' the top civil servant in City Hall, a genial and cultivated man called Anthony Meyer, though the reality is that he too had been planning to step down but by now the media had what we love most of all – a 'narrative'.

On it went as

DOOOF! I lost my first deputy mayor, a top businessman and turnaround king called Tim Parker. Tim had gallantly agreed to do a stint in local government, perhaps as a prelude to a political career, but by August he had decided that it really wasn't for him, and the final blow of this series –

THUDDEROO! – was the departure of my deputy mayor for government relations, a small if combative former leader of Bexley Council called Ian Clement.

Ian outdid all his predecessors in the manner of his exit, first by being caught in a honeytrap in Beijing in which a beautiful Chinese woman drugged him, took him to bed and then downloaded the contents of his City Hall BlackBerry (containing, he claimed, top-secret information about his planning decisions); and then by using his City Hall credit card to buy such essentials as nights in a hotel with his girlfriend and his Blaupunkt car stereo.

I am afraid Ian was convicted of embezzlement; and the joy of the media was more or less unconfined.

*   *   *

Did I mind about any of this? Was I dazed by these fresh blows? Not really. Beneath the media narrative we were beginning to find our feet. Some people left the team, but new and brilliant people soon replaced them: Sir Simon Milton replacing Tim Parker, and Isabel Dedring arriving as deputy mayor for the environment.

Of course, the media were yearning to say that Johnson's City Hall was a shambles. ('Boris: The wheels come off already!' exulted the *Daily Mail*'s front page on the day Ray Lewis resigned.) But my polls were surprisingly good. I was beginning to enjoy the work; and my experience is that I go through quite a bit of chaos in any new job before the triumphs begin.

It just takes patience.

As for Johnny Cameron, the tartan-trousered fellow who enquired what exactly I had ever run: his investments collapsed, his bank was nationalised and he himself was told formally that he could never work in the City again; and I expect he is out there somewhere, like the rest of us, giving motivational speeches about what life has taught him.

The high point of that summer in 2008 was my first trip to Beijing, where I was tasked on behalf of London with accepting the Olympic flag. This was a purely ceremonial role, the sort of thing that should go without a hitch.

I was standing in the bowels of the Bird's Nest stadium, waiting for my cue like a perspiring gladiator in the Colosseum. My instructions were simple.

Walk on. Take flag. Wave flag twice in figure of eight, using both hands and making broad sweeps so as not to tangle the fabric. Walk off.

But billions were watching and the noise was terrific. The Chinese seemed to have spent more than our defence budget on fireworks alone (how were we going to match this in 2012?), and I was worried that I was missing my cue. The man opposite me grunted and pointed at my midriff, with what I took to be cheerful Confucian frankness. I grinned and grunted back – as if to say, too late to lose weight now!

He grunted again and then to my surprise he lunged at me and grabbed the sides of my jacket and tried to draw them together.

Ah! I got it. He wanted me to do up my buttons. I was just about to comply when I suddenly thought: Sod it. I am the mayor of London, with the largest personal mandate in British political history. I am not some stooge of the Chinese system. I am going to take a stand for freedom, for democracy, for the inalienable right of the freeborn Englishman to decide when and where to do up his own buttons.

So I batted him aside and went out into the seething superdome and waved the flag with what I hoped was appropriate vigour – and was duly attacked by viewers and readers across Britain for looking dishevelled and unbuttoned and generally letting the side down.

That evening we enjoyed ourselves in London House, a villa that we had requisitioned in the ancient grey-sausage-roof-tiled Hutong district of Beijing, with the general purpose of promoting the UK.

Since they began in the eighth century BC, the Olympic Games have been commercial as well as sporting bonanzas. Countries come to tout their wares, vying for investment as well as athletic victory. On that closing night in Beijing, the place was heaving. There were athletes, businesspeople, politicians, camp-followers of all kinds, many of them well refreshed.

In a mood of some euphoria, I hailed Team GB's medal haul and pointed ahead to what I said would be even greater success in London in four years' time. The Chinese had put on a great show, I said, but so would London. As my jingo spirit climbed – and unaware that I was being watched on UK TV, as well as by Marina and the children (who almost fainted with embarrassment) at a 'live site' in Hyde Park – I claimed British paternity for just about every sport in the Olympics.

Yes, I said to the exultant and intoxicated crowd, 'I congratulate our Chinese friends on their success in the ping pong. But where was ping pong invented? It was first played on the dining tables of Victorian England and it was called whiff-whaff!

'The French looked at a dining table and saw an opportunity to have dinner. The British looked at a dining table and saw an opportunity to play whiff-whaff.' That was why we had won so many medals, I argued. That was why a country with 0.7 per cent of the global population seemed to be so good at sport, I told the crowd, who were baying assent.

All these games, all these athletic events, all these forms of exertion – we invented them! And now they were coming home. Whiff-whaff was coming home, ping pong was coming home, sport was coming home, and London would put on an Olympic Games to do the world proud.

My detractors, of course, leaped on this stuff (all true, by the way) and said it was just the kind of chauvinistic codswallop to expect from Johnson, and accused me of again being disrespectful to our Chinese hosts.

Frankly, I felt it caught the mood of the moment, near enough.

You have to understand how it felt, in those early days in London, as the banking crisis took hold.

It felt as if the air was coming out of a gigantic bouncy castle that was folding and collapsing before our eyes; and my job was to go around and insert the nozzle of my patent morale pump into every orifice I could find.

I had to keep people's spirits up. Whatever I privately thought about what the bankers (or a small minority of them) had done, I knew that they were essential to the economic future of the country. The tax yield from the City of London alone was about £65 billion.

As the crisis deepened, so did the national rage about the risks those bankers had taken – and the nauseating size of the bonuses that had persuaded them to take those risks. Of course, the banker-bashers had a point, but only a point.

Someone needed to stand up for financial services. It's not just that they are vital for London and the UK economy. They are vital for the world. It is by lending money, at risk, that you enable people to develop and market the innovations that will save our lives and our planet. How do we make the cancer-curing drugs and vaccines, the disease-resistant crops, the carbon-neutral cars? How do we finance the colossal cost of these enterprises? Banking, banking, banking.

Someone had to stand up to the brainless banker-bashers. Someone had to stand up for London, and that job fell to me.

When the Treasury started to feel the effects of the recession, it was not long before they began to look for savings. As ever, infrastructure was the first target; and London offered some juicy opportunities to hack back.

We were told that we could either have the £20 billion Tube upgrades, or else we could have a vast new underground railway called Crossrail. We could not have both.

I rejected these bogus alternatives, and decided that any such choice would be disastrous. My approach to cake, as noted elsewhere, is pro having it and pro eating it.

London's Tube system was the oldest in the world, and it was now hot, dirty and subject to infuriating delays. We had to do better. We had a huge plan to put in new signalling and new track across the network. We had to increase average speeds and reduce average journey times. Londoners had been promised it. They were expecting it. If we failed, we would be lynched.

As for Crossrail – well, fifteen years later it is now the Elizabeth Line. You may have taken it yourself. It is a beautiful 108-mile railway system by which people are transported in air-conditioned, purple-liveried comfort from Berkshire to Kent and Essex through a series of colossal subterranean vaults and cathedrals under the heart of London. It is a massive and crucial addition to London's network. The Elizabeth Line will be driving jobs and prosperity for generations to come.

But then it was just a drawing on a map, and a huge potential saving. By 2009 or so, everyone could see that a change of government was coming. George Osborne, the chancellor-to-be, was looking for big things he could cut, and cut painlessly. Even in those days, Crossrail was going to cost £16.9 billion.

One Saturday the Osbornes came for a family lunch in our back garden in Islington.

'Why is it called Crossrail?' asked Frances, George's wife. 'Is it because it makes so many people cross?'

I tried to explain the massive advantages for UK GDP, the jobs that the scheme would create.

'Which way does it go?' Frances went on. 'Up and down or left to right?'

I didn't blame her. It wasn't so long since I might have asked the same sort of question.

'Look,' said George, after we had argued about it for a while. 'Why don't you just stop talking about it?'

I knew what he meant and what he was trying to do. The reason governments so often cut future infrastructure projects – short-sighted though that is – is that people never miss what they cannot see.

Here was a chance to save the thick end of £20 billion on what Ken Clarke – then shadow business secretary – at the time denounced as a 'giant trench under London'.

I couldn't afford to give George that option. So I redoubled my rhetoric about both – about the Tube and Crossrail – because we had to show confidence in London, in the future of London. We had to keep the capital moving and working, and these projects were already creating thousands of jobs. Those big investments – Crossrail, the Olympic site, the Westfield Centre at Shepherd's Bush – were fortuitously timed for London: vast counter-cyclical programmes that kept the spades going into the ground and people in work across the city.

As I said at the launch of Crossrail in 2009 – with the Labour transport minister Andrew Adonis – you can sometimes find yourself in a hole so big (and Crossrail was a very big hole) that the only answer is to keep digging.

All these projects – or so I desperately hoped – would get the UK's capital city through the recession. We launched huge investment drives overseas, urging businesses and tourists to take advantage of the weakness of the pound.

I believe that eventually it worked. As time went on, we would see something different happening – that for the first time since the Second World War, London would be less hard hit by a big recession than the rest of the country.

In fact, you could say that London – where the banking crisis had originated – seemed comparatively insulated. Unemployment in the capital would barely take a hit – ending up perhaps 0.2 per cent higher as a result of the crash. The rest of the country had it far worse, with a 2.5 per cent rise in unemployment.

People in the end noticed what was happening – the way the metropolis and its guilty bankers just seemed to power on. I am sure that this phenomenon sharpened the sense of apartness and – I would argue – made levelling up more essential than ever.

But we couldn't see that yet, in those first couple of years. All we could see was the spectre of economic disaster; and every conventional analysis says that when the economy turns down, crime goes up.

Chapter 8

The Cult of the Knife

Tackling the gangs – and misplaced liberal squeamishness

The sun was beating down on the dusty, curvy windows of my cabin at the top of the City Hall spaceship. You couldn't open these windows, for some no doubt excellent environmental reason, but it wasn't just the heat that was causing a prickle down my neck.

It was shame. To cope with the grief of your constituents: it's one of the things we have to do, as elected politicians. In the face of the anguish of Barry and Margaret Mizen, I was reduced to incoherence.

It was now the early summer of 2008, and any trace of a honeymoon had long since waned. I had to deliver. There was no doubt that I had won the mayoralty partly by hammering my opponent, Ken Livingstone, for his failure to tackle crime, or more particularly knife crime.

Week in, week out, the mayoral campaign had been interrupted as if by a bell, tolling the death of another young kid on the streets of London. Teenagers were being stabbed to death, one after the other, and no one seemed to be able to control it or to explain it.

As a crime, as a method of killing, there is something hideously intimate about using a knife, yerking someone beneath the ribs. It makes pulling a trigger look impersonal. As Tim Godwin, the deputy commissioner of the Metropolitan Police, put it to me: 'You have to get so close you can smell the other person, feel their breath on you.'

The media were understandably fixated with the offence. The *Evening Standard* began to run a tally of teenage deaths, as a reproach to political failure, and every teenager tragically exsanguinating on the pavement became a political event, and properly so.

I didn't believe that the police were doing enough to stop it. It didn't seem to me that Ken Livingstone had been serious enough about the issue. For every death, there were dozens if not hundreds who were injured, often very seriously, or stabbed in the buttocks as a favoured gesture of humiliation. The gangs were seemingly on top; ruling by fear – using the threat of their horrible weapons, from Kitchen Devils to great gap-toothed zombie knives, to command allegiance and to claim their territory. It seemed that in our whole response, as a society, to this type of crime there was a soft and unspoken racism.

Who, overwhelmingly, were the perpetrators? Young black kids. Who, overwhelmingly, were the victims? Young black kids.

Let's be frank. It wasn't a crime type that had much impact on the lives of white middle-class Londoners, and it was an issue on which Livingstone seemed unusually tone deaf. In the middle of the election campaign, we were sitting in some church hall in Edgware and he tried to explain the phenomenon by saying it was really a cultural import, from the machete-wielding tribal wars of central Africa. It wasn't a home-grown London problem, he seemed to be saying.

I watched the stirring in the audience of largely black Londoners. They clearly felt he was missing the point. You couldn't blame the conflict between Hutu and Tutsi. You couldn't blame the Interahamwe.

The spores of this plague were seeded in London, and it required a dynamic mayoral response. That, as I had boasted repeatedly at the hustings, was what I was going to provide. I was going to 'grip' the issue. I was going to 'drive the numbers down'. I wasn't quite sure how, but I felt that somehow I could.

Now I was actually doing the job and I felt my powerlessness.

Jimmy Mizen – the son of the couple in my office – was only sixteen. He was standing at a bakery counter in Lee when another kid, known to him and his family, had come in and started a fight, finally hurling a glass hotplate that shattered on Jimmy's chin and sent a shard of glass through his carotid artery. He bled to death in the shop. Jimmy was utterly innocent; he had his life before him, with all its potential – and now it had been taken, in another senseless squabble between teenagers.

As we sat there, several weeks later, Barry and Margaret didn't berate me as some parents might have done. They didn't blame me, or the police, for the culture of street violence that had cost them their son. But their very sweetness and gentleness was almost excruciating.

They just wanted to help, to stop it happening to someone else's child; and I felt that prickling sense of fraudulence. I had taken on this huge problem, raised Londoners' hopes that I could fix it; and now I was going to fail, because frankly I wasn't sure what to do.

As the weeks went by, the number of kids killed kept ticking up. It looked like a frenzy. In one twenty-four-hour period in July, six people were stabbed to death and the media were appalled. They called it 'Blade Britain'. They said it was an epidemic. Kit Malthouse, my deputy mayor for policing and crime, was as anxious as I was.

We would literally lie awake at night, worrying about what might be happening in Haringey or Ealing or Croydon. As soon as dawn broke, Kit would roll over and look at his phone for the overnight digest from the police and then send me the bad news.

We urgently tried to understand what was going on, to think ourselves into the lives of these teenagers and to imagine why they were doing it. Was it video nasties – that perennial source of conservative moral panic? Was it computer games? It seemed unlikely. Some said it was about the status and prestige of going around in a gang and being a person of consequence. Others said it was all about the loss of family, the absence of fathers. The gangs gave young people that sense of security, of belonging to a family unit. In tough economic times, drugs money was important.

As for the knives, I was told, the kids only carried them because they were afraid. They didn't dare walk the streets unarmed and they didn't trust the police to protect them.

People took various positions, depending on their view of crime. Is crime a function of multiple underlying socio-economic causes? Or is crime mainly caused by criminals?

Sensing my difficulties, people started to flock to City Hall and offer solutions. The pop star Lily Allen came and said that we should pay to have special knife blunters on street corners. Perhaps they could put corks on the end, she suggested. Lily Allen is a brilliant creative mind, but I wasn't sure I could make sense of a knife-blunting strategy.

Others came up with schemes for specially designated 'safe spaces', shops and cafés where kids could go without the fear of knives – perhaps identified by some sort of plaque or sign, like a Michelin rosette. I said that sounded all very well – but we had to make the whole city safe, not just a few cafés. I set up a group of experts, called the Mayoral Expert Advisory Group, or MEAG. They were professors and criminologists and social workers and reformed gang members both male and female, and we had endless knife crime summits and seminars and teach-ins. We tried to learn from other cities and their wars on gangs, from Boston to Bogotá.

I wish I could say that the MEAG genuinely elucidated the problem. After a while, it felt as if we were going round in circles.

It was the same old ideas, and as with so many issues that become suddenly politically salient, and where public money may be available, I had a feeling that people were starting to talk their own book. There was a kind of implicit shakedown in the conversations.

People would come up to me at the end of meetings and say, in effect, 'You've got a problem with gangs and knives. I've got a project that tries to sort these kids out. Give me some cash and I'll say you are doing a good job.'

I was sure that some of these projects were worthy, but times were tight, and how was I to know which were any good? One former gang member (wholly reformed, he told me) came to see me to make his pitch. He had a musical act that was intended to discourage kids from shooting each other. It was called Bra-ka-ka.

'What's Bra-ka-ka?' I asked.

It was the noise of a gun, he said, and he had turned it into a rap song. I was a bit dubious, but I was also desperate. A few days later I attended a school morning assembly, watching as he performed Bra-ka-ka. He acted out the shooting and dying very convincingly, but I found myself asking what effect it was having on the kids. Were they really going to be discouraged from using knives and guns?

If anything, we seemed to be glamourising this crime – infusing these ghastly and humdrum murders with a spurious melodrama. I began to regret the way we had politically escalated the whole issue. If knife crime was partly about fashion, and mimicry, and kids daring to do something forbidden, then the risk was that we had unintentionally made it more fashionable.

The more panicked the grown-ups sounded, the more hushed-tone discussions of knife crime there were on TV, the more interested the kids became; and bear in mind that some of the kids who got caught up in knife crime were not even teenagers.

I started to fear that our admonitions were psychologically counter-productive. If you walk out of your house in the morning and you say, 'Whatever you do, kids, don't stick a baked bean up your nose', what do you think they are going to do?

We needed to end the mystique and treat it for what it was – a banal and stupid way to die. We needed a mixed approach. In the immortal phrase, we needed to be tough on crime and tough on the causes of crime.

After a few months, Kit (with editorial help from his wife Juliana) produced a plan to defeat knife crime. It was called 'Time for Action', and it was pretty comprehensive. We began by addressing the underlying causes – the disaffection and vulnerability of young people – and took all sorts of steps to win kids away from the cult of knives and gangs. We backed Ray Lewis's school in east London. We backed mentoring schemes, and I think we found a thousand mentors, whose task it was to sit down on the bed with young kids and have manly, from-the-shoulder chats about how crazy it was to carry a knife.

We sponsored a special unit in Feltham Young Offenders Institute, called the Heron Wing, tasked with rehabilitating young people through education and reducing the otherwise appalling rate of reoffending. We sponsored an excellent Christian outreach group called XLP, who took a double-decker bus around some of the toughest estates as a safe space where kids could escape the gangs and play on computers.

I am sure that some of these interventions were effective, some of them less effective. But they were nowhere near enough. After months of study and thought, and talking to young kids in London, I decided that I was not getting a complete account from the lefty criminologists and Labour councillors who decided to gravitate towards City Hall and the MEAG.

Knife crime, I concluded, was not a public health problem. It was not a mere epiphenomenon of social and economic disadvantage. No, my friends, that was all largely baloney.

It was a criminal problem. It was caused by criminals and criminal gangs, and what was needed was a criminal justice solution. We needed to start enforcing the law.

Like many other UK politicians in those days, I had been much influenced by the 'broken windows' theory of crime: namely, that if you tolerate small signs of incivility, like broken glass or graffiti, then your neighbourhood will be more likely to be hit by more serious crime, including robberies and street violence.

So as soon as I was elected, I sent some signals about the kind of city I wanted us all to live in. On day one, I banned alcohol on London transport. It was a suggestion from a friend, David Ross, who had done it on National Express coaches, with good results. It sounds illiberal, but it was instantly popular, especially with women who were fed up with drunken comments or behaviour on the bus or Tube. We had a scheme called Payback London, in which people caught spraying graffiti were made to wash it off in hi-vis tabards.

We got tough with kids for misbehaving on buses. Livingstone had given them all free travel, and they would take the bus – often for perfectly walkable distances – and cause a terrific kerfuffle at the end of the school day, shouting and fighting and alarming the elderly passengers. Again, you may say it is trivial stuff, and indeed Livingstone downplayed it as 'kids letting off steam'. But we started to take away their Zip cards (free travel cards) and never mind if they had to walk to school for a while.

Some kids whinged; the left protested; but it was popular with the pensioners of Bexley and Bromley who had elected me to do precisely this. More important, it worked. The buses became quieter and calmer, and because we weren't tolerating any kind of argy-bargy at all, crime on buses began to fall quite sharply.

Most important of all, we started a massive campaign of stop and search. This was, and is, deeply controversial. In London and across the UK, there are memories of the old 'sus' laws, whereby the police had extensive powers to stop someone on suspicion that they might be about to commit an offence.

In the late 1970s and early 1980s, it was true that this law had been abused. The police had stopped and searched far too many young black men, on 'sus', in a way they felt was discriminatory, and the sense of injustice helped to trigger the Brixton riots of 1981. Following the Scarman Report into those riots, the sus laws had been scrapped, and though in 2008 the law did allow for stop and search, its use was heavily circumscribed.

Under section 60 of the Public Order Act, the police were allowed to deem that an area was one in which an offence was likely to be committed, and that stop and search could be carried out. But they were reluctant to use these powers, not without explicit political cover and support.

I didn't see what else we could do.

We all knew – I had talked to the families, to the gang members themselves – that the kids were walking the streets armed to the teeth. They would make appointments to meet, gang on gang, so that knife fights became knife battles. I needed the police to have the confidence to take the knives off them.

By the time I became mayor, the police had reached something like the same conclusion themselves. They had launched a stop and search drive called Operation Blunt. It was relatively modest in scale, and plainly had not worked, and critically it was not being actively promoted by the Livingstone City Hall.

The police under the commissioner of the day, Ian Blair, seemed to be taking a pretty softly-softly psychological approach. They had posters on the Tube of a man in a great big fluffy pink chicken suit with the caption, 'Carrying a Knife – it's not a good look'. It seemed as baffling and ineffective as Bra-ka-ka.

I was becoming impatient with what I thought was general squeamishness about stop and search. I didn't believe that kids carried knives because they were 'scared', as all the lefty criminologists had been telling me for so many months. I didn't believe that it was all about 'self-defence'.

What do all criminals say, when they carry an illegal gun or knife? What do they all say, when they shoot or stab someone? They say it's self-defence.

It's almost always rubbish. These people might be young, but in 'going equipped with a bladed weapon' – as the law puts it – they knew what they were doing. They were massively increasing their chances of killing or being killed in a disastrous encounter that would blight the lives of London families forever.

So we embarked upon Operation Blunt 2, which was like the first – but this time bigger, and with conviction. We had knife arches in the Tube, knife 'wands' or metal detectors on the streets, and we told the police that provided they used their powers sensitively and in accordance with the law, we would give them complete political top cover to do as much stop and search as they needed.

It would be fair to say that after a few months in City Hall, and after the agony of so many deaths, we became pretty directional in our approach. We insisted that the budgets should go on frontline policing, so that we had as many officers as possible out on the street; and by a great deal of juggling we kept the number of police officers at or near 32,000 throughout my time in office.

In October I decided to change the Metropolitan Police commissioner, by using my right to be chair of the Metropolitan Police Authority. Ian Blair was a talented and intelligent man, and had in many ways done a decent job – but he was part of the old guard, and in the struggle against knife crime we needed a new energy and a new zap.

We needed what they call an old-fashioned copper, someone who was metaphorically thudding the beat in his size twelve boots, hammering down doors and reaching out the long arm of the law to feel the collar of the criminals. That is more or less what we got with Blair's successor, his deputy Paul Stephenson, and then with Bernard Hogan-Howe.

In the first few months of Operation Blunt 2 we took 10,000 knives off the streets. The lefty criminologists, of course, said it was all mad and that the stock of knives would be instantly replenished – if not from kitchen drawers then from the internet, where you could buy the most obscene-looking blades. They said that the policy was basically racist, because – inevitably – so many of the people stopped were young black men, and so many of them were stopped again and again. For the first few months, I of course feared that our critics were right.

Maybe it was delusional to confiscate knives. Maybe it was like trying to tackle obesity by taking away people's forks. The number of dead kids continued to rise, miserably and seemingly ineluctably.

Kit tried to reassure me. It was to some extent a function of the way the statistics were reported. Knife crime numbers were going up partly because there was so much more police activity in that area, and so many knives were being confiscated. It was true (and is a paradox of many crime statistics: the mere fact of trying to fight a particular type of crime seems to produce more of it, as more is reported).

And then, after about a year of effort – and we really strained at this – it all seemed to begin to pay off. Young people started to get the message. If they went out with a knife – regardless of whether they believed they were doing it in self-defence – there was quite a good chance that they would be caught, and that if they were caught several times they would go to prison.

Lo, the numbers of knife offences started to fall, quite steeply. As the overall volume of offences diminished, the number of kids being killed began to decrease, down from about thirty a year to about ten a year or fewer.

It wasn't just teenagers. The murder rate tumbled overall, so that for several years in a row we had a hundred murders a year or fewer, an astonishingly low number for a city as huge and diverse as London. As Paul Stephenson would say to me when he brought in the latest statistics – 'If we had done this in New York, we would be getting a ticker-tape parade.' It became one of the staples of my speeches – to the slight irritation of Mayor Bloomberg – that if you lived in London you were five times less likely to be murdered than if you lived in New York.

And it wasn't just the murder rate that fell. Overall neighbourhood crime went down by 20 per cent. Bus crime (that's crime on buses rather than by buses, I used to tell the audience; crime by buses being already very low) was down by 40 per cent. It is one of my proudest achievements that during my time as mayor, London got a deserved reputation as one of the safest big cities in the world.

It was, of course, deeply frustrating that – for whatever reason – not all politicians agreed with my approach. In 2014, after six years of slog, the Conservative home secretary Theresa May decided that she didn't approve of my support of stop and search; and she changed the law so as to make it more difficult – again.

Because the Metropolitan Police is a kind of condominium between the mayor and the home secretary, the police in London had no choice but to comply. It was infuriating, and I thought that Theresa and her advisers were probably motivated not so much by a dislike of stop and search as by a general desire to clip the wings of the mayor.

It was also a great shame, because crime – including knife crime – has risen again since I left City Hall, and it became one of my most important jobs, on becoming PM in 2019, to try and get the city and the country back on track.

Knife crime – the killing of kids by kids – is a horrendous and chilling phenomenon. But we showed that it is not intractable, that it can be beaten. You need to use every possible lever to get the kids out of the grip of the gangs, to inspire them with hope of a better life (and above all a job). You need mentors and coaches and volunteers, so with the help of the Reuben Foundation I set up 'Team London' – to recruit volunteer youth workers from across the city. And you need to give our broadly superb police the powers and the encouragement to do what they signed up to do.

Don't tell me that it is discriminatory or racist to support stop and search. The people who most strongly support the searching of those kids – in my experience – are the mothers of the kids who carry the knives.

I'll tell you what's racist – it's letting young black kids die on the streets and not do enough, out of liberal squeamishness, to turn it around and stop the killing.

Tackling crime is fundamental for levelling up. If crime goes down, confidence goes up, investment goes up, property values go up. I wanted a healthier, happier London, where people felt safe on the streets, even on two wheels.

Chapter 9

The Cycling Revolution

How we made it quicker and safer by bike

You must have sometimes had that choking feeling when your car is totally jammed, when your train is held at signals for no reason that you can understand, when your bus is immobilised in a sea of fuming traffic.

You must – if you are anything like me – have sometimes had this overpowering urge to get out of the car, to bust out of the train and down the siding or along the tunnel; anything to recover your sense of autonomy.

Have you ever felt like that? Have you ever wished you could magically whizz to the front of a queue of overheating cars?

Have you ever wished that you had a speedy and reliable means of personal propulsion – some way of getting from a to b that cannot be thwarted by sheer weight of traffic or the leadership of the Rail, Maritime and Transport Union or the failure of the train driver (how amazingly often this seems to happen) to set his alarm clock correctly and to turn up for work on time?

You have? You know what I am talking about? Then I have the answer for you.

It's the bicycle, one of the most beautiful and ergonomically efficient inventions ever to emanate from the human brain. It is a machine that is all upside. It's fun; it's clean; it's green; it's easy; it's fast; it's great exercise; and in the space of only twenty minutes, it will take you anywhere in central London without let or hindrance; oh, and I almost forgot to say: unlike any other form of mechanised transport it costs absolutely nothing to run.

By the time I became mayor, I had been cycling in London for about ten years. I had had a couple of harmless tumbles (I went over the handlebars in Trafalgar Square when a taxi braked sharply in front of me; and I had boinged off the Michelin Man belly of a French tourist who looked the wrong way before stepping off a pavement in Knightsbridge – he was fine; I sustained a slight sprain of the wrist). But I had learned to be wily.

I knew the danger spots. I had worked out where to station myself at traffic lights (out in front). I knew the everyday hazards – the unexpected opening of a car door, the lorries turning left – and I loved it. It was the freedom, the fresh air, the sunlight dappling the street through the plane tree canopy. It was that sense of boundless choice that goes with watching your front tyre before you, nosing its way like a ten-inch rubber missile through the backstreets of London, and nobody knowing exactly where you were or when you would arrive. Of course it rained from time to time, but I got used to it; I dried off in no time, and if anybody detected an aroma of wet Labrador, they were good enough not to mention it.

As I tootled along – and one of the secrets of safety is to go at onion-seller speed – I was able to drink in fragments of conversation floating from the pubs and cafés, to sample snatches of life in London's vast network of town and village centres. Your cares melt away on a bike. You lose your aggro and your impatience. The endorphins start to course through your system and you arrive in a state of quasi-euphoria, maddeningly full of ideas and initiatives.

I loved cycling so much that I wanted others to share my love. I couldn't understand why so many people wasted their lives in cars or trains, when they could be active and enjoying themselves. So among the things I promised Londoners in that first manifesto in 2008 was a bike hire scheme, a bigger and better version of the idea that had been born in Lyon and then taken to Paris, where it was known as the Velib. As the incumbent mayor, Livingstone had been promising such a thing for ages, but he had done nothing.

When I arrived in City Hall there was no plan for it, no budget, and certainly no agreement with the London boroughs that would have to station the docking apparatus on their pavements. The truth is that London's Labour mayor didn't really like cycling as a transport mode. Like so many socialist tyrants, he wanted people on buses and trains: collectivised systems where he was in control.

I think the main problem was that he had no personal psychological investment in cycling – because he couldn't actually ride a bike (no more than he could drive a car, that other individualistic mode of getting around). He sometimes said that this was because he was afraid of being pushed off by an irate Londoner, sometimes that he had problems with his inner ear that made it hard for him to balance.

For whatever reason, Ken just wasn't into bicycles, not in the way that I was; and nor, at least to begin with, was TfL – Transport for London – the otherwise superb body, then run by Peter Hendy, that keeps Londoners moving. TfL could see immediately that a bike hire scheme would be a massive extension of their responsibilities. Suddenly they would be providing a whole new transport mode, in addition to trains, buses, trams and Tubes.

They saw the trap. My plans involved a new breed of public bicycle. They believed that it would cost them money – and they were right.

I had bragged in the election campaign that the scheme would be self-funding, like the Velib in Paris. But there was a hitch. On closer inspection, it turned out that the Velib scheme was self-funding because the Paris mayoralty had done an unrepeatable deal with JC Decaux, the billboards company, which provided the bike hire scheme free in return for the use of all the advertising hoardings on the cycle hire stations.

I tried to do the same trick in London, but it was clear, after extensive talks with JC Decaux, that it wouldn't add up. We didn't own the hoardings, not in the same way. We were adrift by tens of millions. We had to pay for thousands of bikes and hundreds of docking stations, and for armies of people to move the bikes around and make sure they were serviced and in the right docking station.

People were starting to mutter about a mayoral vanity project. They were saying that money should be going on the Tube, not on bicycles – which tended to be used, anyway, by middle-class white males. I was insistent. I had promised the scheme. It was part of my dream for London.

I had grown up partly in Belgium, where they are if anything as velocipedophile as the Dutch. I had spent many happy days cycling around places like Amsterdam and Copenhagen. I was absolutely sure – religiously convinced – that a cycling revolution would be good for London, for people's mood.

When talking to Conservative audiences (who could sometimes be a bit anti-bicycle, to put it mildly), I would remind them that in London in 1904, 40 per cent of journeys were made by bicycle, and the city was then the heart of the greatest empire the world had ever seen. I wanted to turn the clock back to 1904, I said, and if that wasn't Conservatism, I didn't know what was.

TfL – Peter Hendy, and the excellent head of surface transport, David Brown – started to warm to the idea. They wanted motor cars off the road; they wanted less pollution, and they agreed that it was a good idea to promote walking and cycling. They just wanted a sponsor. I tried Jaguar Land Rover, who almost did it (we were going to have lovely bikes in British racing green), but they then decided that it didn't fit in with their key mission in life, which was to sell more cars.

Who else? I wondered. Who had pots of money? Who might think that they had something to expiate? Who might want to win the good opinion of Londoners?

You've got it!

The banks! For months I had been just about the only politician in Britain with a good word for the bankers. Surely it was time for them to make some gigantic act of corporate social responsibility. Never mind greenwash or sportswash.

I decided that we were going to bikewash the whole sector: they were going to be called bankers' bikes. Every time a Londoner used one of these banker-funded machines, he or she would feel a little less hostile to the whole financial services industry. Genius!

I needed someone to assemble the consortium of bike-backing banks and called Bob Diamond, who was then the energetic head of investment banking at Barclays. He put me on to the chairman of Barclays, Marcus Agius, and Marcus agreed to do his best.

For months we got nowhere, mainly because my idea was pretty terrible. The banks didn't want to be lumped together with other banks, not for the purposes of sponsorship. They didn't see what was in it for them.

In January 2009, you would have seen me tramping through the snows of Davos, in a state of some gloom, for a meeting with Marcus. I was fully expecting him to tell me that my idea was a dud – and he did.

'This consortium idea won't work,' he said.

I nodded dumbly.

'So why don't we do it?' said Marcus.

'What do you mean, "we"?' I said.

'I mean Barclays,' he said. 'We will give you £25 million.'

Put it there, pal, I said, or words to that effect. It wasn't enough, but it was a whole lot better than nothing, and it made a big dent in the cost of the scheme.

Within a couple of years, by July 2010 (two and a half years ahead of the original timetable), the hire bikes were operational. They were a roaring success. The bikes were so obviously sturdy and stately, with big well-padded saddles, that you felt safe – that you really occupied the road as of right. The motorists could see them from afar, with their bright blue Barclays livery, and gave them a wide berth. I decided that people should be able to ride them without a helmet, so that you could pick one up whatever you were doing, whatever you were wearing. It worked.

Everyone started to use them. There were hardly any accidents, and hardly any were stolen. After a year in which thousands of bikes were taken on millions of journeys, only eighteen were missing (one of them turning up at Base Camp on Everest), and I could not resist comparison with the Paris Velib, thousands of which were stolen every year, because instead of forcing users to put them back in the docking stations they gave them useless little flimsy bike locks, a policy TfL viewed as insane (or in-Seine, since so many ended up in the river).

The Barclays cycle hire scheme was so successful that soon we were planning to extend it to east London – because it was imperative that it should comprise the Olympic Park. We needed more money.

I went back to Barclays. They looked thoughtful. They loved their sponsorship, they said. They were proud to be associated with a scheme that had won the hearts of Londoners. They had just noticed one thing.

A lot of people seemed for some reason to call them 'Boris bikes', rather than Barclays bikes.

Was there anything I could do?

'I tell you what,' I said, 'if you give us another £25 million, I will change my name by deed poll to Barclays Johnson.'

They gave us another £25 million.

But for a real cycling revolution, it wasn't good enough just to get people tottering around on the hire bikes. If we were to turn London into a proper cycle city, we needed to go further – to show the motorists that the urban environment had changed. We simultaneously rushed out a network of 'cycle superhighways', where bikes were somehow to have priority.

Here, to be frank, our ideas were not quite so well formed. Under huge pressure of time – and with a desperate shortage of road space – we decided that it would be enough just to paint these routes in with long ribbons of blue tarmac running down the left-hand side of the carriageway. In one of my less successful attempts at cake-ism (pro having it and pro eating it), we didn't exactly ban cars from these blue havens; they could stray into the lanes if they wanted to. We were just trying to signal that this was a space mainly intended for bicycles.

As the cycling world was quick to point out, the message was a bit confusing – and perhaps not very safe.

At the time I was becoming entranced by the ideology of 'shared space', championed by such great urban designers as Denmark's Jan Gehl. I was persuaded by Daniel Moylan, a Kensington councillor with a highly developed aesthetic sense, that we had made a terrible mistake in trying always to deconflict car traffic from walking and cycling.

Ever since Colin Buchanan's famous 1963 report, 'Traffic in Towns', we had tended to build urban clearways and bypasses fringed by heavy railings, and a few vomit-splashed pedestrian precincts in town centres. In other countries they tried other tactics: not banning cars but forcing them to be respectful to other more vulnerable road users – hence the concept of shared space.

We tried it on Exhibition Road, where Moylan went into a kind of interior-designer frenzy. He ripped out all the kerb stones – laid, he pointed out, for an age when horse dung would pile six inches high in the street – and created a beautiful piazza, stretching down from Hyde Park to the Cromwell Road, where cars could mingle with bikes and people.

The original cycle superhighways were based on the same sort of idea: that cars would negotiate with cyclists, like lions and wildebeest at the evening waterhole – but keeping their distance and avoiding conflict.

The idea plainly has its limits. As Jan Gehl said to me when I met him a year or so later in Copenhagen, 'There can be no negotiation between a toddler and a juggernaut.'

Nor could there be any negotiation between a cyclist and a tipper truck, or a cyclist and a cement mixer. I knew that our superhighways were not perfect. On the day we launched cycle superhighway two, from Tower Hill to the Isle of Dogs, I assembled a peloton of politicians and officials to ride the route in triumph.

There was Andrew Adonis, the Labour transport minister, my cycling adviser Kulveer Ranger, and several others. We had just reached Limehouse when I heard a loud rumble behind us. A van was thundering down the middle of the street, bouncing over a bridge so fast that its back doors swung open – and in a freak accident the handle of one of the doors somehow caught the bumper of a parked car, so that the whole car was hoisted into the air and waved around like a giant club as the van roared past us.

This terrifying episode was caught on camera: the City Hall cycling posse almost decapitated as they cowered on their defence-less stretch of blue paint. The enemies of cycling were cock-a-hoop. Cycle superhighway? Shared space? Huh. It was what they said all along. Cycling was just too dangerous.

By now a backlash was beginning. Taxi drivers who had broadly preferred me to Ken were infuriated to find all these novice cyclists wobbling in their path. Tory donors were incensed to find cycle hire docking stations outside their Knightsbridge flats.

As so often when people don't like something, they started invoking health and safety. I had manoeuvred myself into a politically exposed position. I was the one who had encouraged people to cycle with nothing but blue paint to protect them (we put the woad on the road, I said); and I was responsible therefore for each and every cycling fatality.

Soon the media had started to fasten on the deaths of cyclists, and it wasn't long – to my horror – when one of them was killed on a cycle superhighway; then another, and another.

One widow insisted on coming to see me in City Hall and I listened, with my heart in my boots, as she described in awful detail what had happened to her husband. In the summer of 2013 we had nine deaths in quick succession, and suddenly it was like the media frenzy over knife crime.

I rang the editor of the *Evening Standard* and tried to reason with him. The number of deaths was no higher than previous years, I pointed out, and yet many more people were getting on their bikes – tens of thousands more cycling journeys every day. Why did he have to treat every incident as if it were a shark attack?

The editor was unmoved, quite reasonably. People were wound up about cycling fatalities. The subject was very emotive. It was his job to reflect public emotion. It was my job to sort out the problem. In my frustration I made the mistake of going on the radio and saying what I knew to be true – I saw it every day – that some cyclists, including, sadly, some of those who were involved in accidents, appeared to be in the habit of jumping the traffic lights.

Brzzzzzzt! I had touched the electrified wire. I was victim-blaming. I was being insensitive to the bereaved and their families.

There was a huge outcry from cycling groups, and they started to stage die-ins outside City Hall. They all lay down, with their bicycles, and pretended to have been run over.

It was effective. Polls showed that people were being put off cycling. We had to act.

First we put the police on to it, issuing fixed penalty notices (25,000 of them) to anyone, motorist or cyclist, who was caught breaking the laws of the road. We began to rebuild the most dangerous roundabouts, with special advanced traffic lights for cyclists and Trixi mirrors on the poles. We paid for 75,000 cycle courses in schools.

We made lorry drivers take cyclist awareness lessons, so that they had to cycle around before they got their HGV licence. We had to deal with the most prevalent and most obstinate problem: what happens when there is, as we traffic engineers say, a conflict of desire lines – when the cyclist wants to go straight and the lorry wants to turn left?

What happens when the driver fails to spot the cyclist on his inside flank? Time after time, the cyclists were being caught and dragged under the wheels, and the injuries were horrific, with heads and bodies so flattened as to be almost unrecognisable. All too often, as the media quickly realised, the victims of these dreadful crushings were female; who knows why – perhaps because they tended to hang back in the lee of the HGVs, so that the drivers could not see them.

We launched a big campaign to educate all cyclists about where to station yourself, how to catch the attention of the truck driver (wave at them, if necessary, like Simon Rattle bringing in the percussion). But that wasn't enough. We realised we had to change the design of the lorries themselves. We forced all HGVs to put special side-guards under the chassis, to stop cyclists from being dragged under; but still we were worried.

The driver was so high up, so obscured from life at road level, that we needed to put windows in the lower part of the cabin doors as well as the upper part – so that the drivers could actually see the vulnerable human beings around them, whether cyclists or pedestrians.

To my frustration, we had no luck with this reform, not in my time as mayor. I was told that the Department for Transport would not let us impose cycle-friendly truck windows – because (you guessed it) truck cab design was an EU competence, and the EU Commission for some reason was being slow in coming up with a new directive. It seemed that the Brussels officials were waiting for Renault and DAF to be sure they could comply.

Until then the lorries would continue to blunder blindly through city centres. As you can imagine, this prohibition incensed me so much that it was one of the reasons I later decided that single market membership was not everything it was cracked up to be.

Finally, and as a last resort, we started to rebuild and fortify the superhighways. Where we reasonably could, we tried to protect cyclists by actually segregating them from motor vehicles. I am afraid that this drove some of my Tory friends utterly nuts. Nigel Lawson, the great former chancellor, said that the cycle lane along the Embankment had done more damage to the London economy than the Luftwaffe.

Much later the Tory chancellor Philip Hammond tried to bribe my successor Sadiq Khan to rip it out. But I have to tell you: I look at that cycle lane, now carrying more traffic, in the peak, than the other three vehicular lanes put together, and I think it is a triumph. I wish I could have done more.

By the end of my second term, cycling had gone up by 50 per cent, with hundreds of thousands more cycling journeys per day, and in the last two years of my mayoralty we had fewer than ten cycling deaths per year – in both cases the lowest tally for well over a decade. In other words, cycling had increased enormously in popularity and the numbers of those being killed or seriously injured had fallen – both absolutely and, even more sharply, as a proportion of journeys made.

By 2016, my last year as mayor, 20 per cent of all vehicles in central London were bicycles. I didn't quite turn the clock back to 1904, but we went a long way. Cycling was no longer confined to bad-tempered white middle-class males in Lycra. Everyone was doing it, both sexes and all ethnic groups. The politics – looking back – were illuminating and should guide future policy.

Some Tory MPs and Tory councillors intensely disliked what we were doing, and sometimes they campaigned actively against our plans. But the interesting thing was that these campaigns never really prospered with the wider electorate. The anti-cyclists certainly had the support of the taxi drivers and people like Philip Hammond – the modern equivalent (as I told him to his face) of J. Bonington Jagsworth, the crazed petrolhead leader of the Motorists' Liberation Front. But the wider electorate was more thoughtful. They could see that cycling was basically good; for the environment, for traffic flow, for human vitality.

We sometimes had public protests against our schemes – like Ride London, where we closed the streets to stage a massive circular route from the Olympic Park, via the Surrey hills; or our 'mini-Hollands', where we tried to make some boroughs as cycle-friendly as the Netherlands. But the public overwhelmingly approved, and wherever we encouraged a culture of cycling, property values rose dramatically.

As for my left-wing critics, I am pleased to say that my love of cycling slightly fried their brains. Here I was, a Tory, absolutely rampaging across the territory of the soft metropolitan liberals, winning support (and no doubt votes) from people who would otherwise never have dreamed of backing me.

Like all the best things, the things that really work, I didn't do it because I thought it would be popular, but because I knew with utter certainty that it was the right thing to do. And did the motorist suffer? Not really. Not at all. Thanks to some nifty work with traffic lights called SCOOT (split cycle offset optimisation technique) and a few other measures, not least cracking down on roadworks, we actually increased average car speeds in London.

How much? From 9.3 to 9.4 mph. Not quite supersonic, I admit, but still.

Chapter 10

Hop On, Hop Off

A beautiful new bus

My mother once explained a secret of painting. Every picture needs a hero, she said. Every canvas needs a focal point – some interesting object or splash of colour, to draw the viewer's eye before it roves around the rest of the composition.

In a Vermeer it might be a pearl earring. In a Turner seascape it might be a red buoy in the surf, or in a Titian it might be a rosy left nipple.

Look at any picture of the London cityscape – postcards, photos, film stills: anything that is supposed to sum up the metropolis, that tries to say 'London'. Look at that picture for half a second and then tell me who is the hero.

It's the bus! It's the great panting pachyderm, the dome-browed double-decker, the wonderful curvilinear crimson cuboid. No visual portrait of London would dare omit the Routemaster bus, and in any such image that bus is always the star – simply the most charismatic and eye-catching object in the scene.

When Japanese consumers buy British biscuits (and they buy a lot), they buy them in tins shaped like a red double-decker. For decades film directors across the world have known how to tell the audience, in a flash, that the action has moved to London. Just show them a glimpse of that AEC Routemaster with the lovely red aluminium monocoque shell, the rivets like a Second World War plane's, the half-cabin at the front and the open platform – the immortal hop-on, hop-off platform – at the back.

The Routemaster is (or was) a landmark of our culture, a key part of the UK's global brand; and yet by the time I became mayor in 2008, something dreadful was happening. They were vanishing. They were too old – built between 1954 and 1968 – and they were knackered.

You used to see them at the side of the road, the driver looking apathetically at the blackened innards through a hatch under the back staircase, with the reddish moquette rear-seat bench stacked upright against the machine – to show, as if there could be any doubt, that the bus had broken down. They were no longer in compliance with the laws on disabled access: their floors were too high; they had no ramps.

They were on the verge of becoming extinct, plying just a couple of 'heritage' routes. They had made way for Volvos and Scanias and Mercedes-Benzes. These foreign substitutes might be red, they might be double-decker – but they had nothing like the character and grace of the old Routemaster, and they weren't even British. The great big red bus, the symbol of our country, was no longer being made here. Oh, I know you will say that I was being irrational.

The royal family is largely from Germany, the Crown Jewels are from India, the very stones of the Tower of London were imported from Caen in France (as for the plane trees of London, they turn out to be a Spanish breed and the saplings are imported from Belgium). Why did it matter to me where our buses were made?

I don't know why, but it did. The new ones were perfectly comfortable and efficient. They were smooth and clean, and air-conditioned. But I am afraid they just looked wrong. All the great twentieth-century pieces of British transport design rely on the curve, from the Mini to the great wide rump of the nuptial Rolls-Royces. Why is the design of the Spitfire so much more pleasing than that of any other fighter plane? It's that elliptical wing. These new buses were just boxes on wheels, all right angles and huge plate-glass windows. They could be from any city. They didn't say 'London'. And anyway, they didn't have the open platform.

As soon as you got on, you were trapped – until the driver let you off. Who knows when you might need to make a break for it? For a time – before I discovered the joys of the bicycle – I used to take the 277 all the way from Highbury Corner to Canary Wharf. I was then a leader writer on the *Daily Telegraph* and I would sit in the front row of the top deck, with a panoramic view of Hackney, arguing about politics with a brilliant, elfin twenty-something leader writer on the *Independent* called Yvette Cooper. These were the days before the Blair victory in 1997, and I was warning her of the risks of the minimum wage.

What about small businesses? I said. What if they just can't afford the extra wages?

Well, snapped Yvette, who was to go on to be Labour home secretary, in that case they would just have to go bust. People deserved to be paid more, she said, and that was that.

I was startled by her lefty brutality towards business, but later concluded that she had a point. It was one of the features of modern capitalism that the wealth gap was relentlessly growing, and the difference in the pay packets between the boardroom and the shopfloor was getting bigger every year. People on lower incomes did deserve to be paid more – and part of my campaign to level up London, ten years later, was greatly to expand the London Living Wage.

Businesses didn't collapse; they just paid their workers more, and saw greater productivity and commitment as a result. That argument with Yvette was important. It was the kind of in-depth conversation you cannot have on a bike, or a Tube train, or even in a car – since someone has to concentrate on the road.

It was the bus that encouraged our debate and forced me to think. But what if our conversation about wages policy had been so acrimonious that we just couldn't take it any more? What if I (or Yvette) had felt so desperate to escape the crazed ideology of the other person that we wanted to get off the bus?

In the old days you could. If it really looked as though we were about to come to blows, I (or Yvette) could have suddenly made my excuses and run down the stairs to the platform. We could have leaped out at the traffic lights, like POWs escaping a train, and lost ourselves in the wilds of Dalston.

I yearned for that old freedom. What was wrong with us, as a country? Why had we allowed it to be taken away? In one of the periods when I was growing up in London, we had a flat on the corner of Elgin Crescent and Ladbroke Grove. All day and much of the night my siblings and I would hear the Routemasters outside, the Number 52. We would hear their flanks literally heaving in and out, *ka-chugga, ka-chugga, ka-chugga*, wheezing like great beasts of the Serengeti. We learned how to get off right outside our house – even if the lights were going green and the bus was starting to pull away.

You have never got off a moving vehicle? It's easy. The key thing is to get out at the side of the platform – never the back – extending the left foot and going briskly in the same direction as the bus as it moves.

Do NOT just jump off the back. As we discovered, you will combine your velocity with that of the bus, so that 5 mph becomes 10 or 12 mph. You stumble, you whang into the parked cars. You fall. If the worst comes to the worst, you brain yourself, and some people no doubt did. Yes, it was a risk – but was it so much of a risk that we had to ban it? Think of what we asked our grandparents to do in the war, constantly jumping off all kinds of moving vehicles: tanks, planes, landing-craft.

Were we all so feeble that we couldn't get off a bus, even in the glacial traffic speeds of London?

Then there was the unparalleled thrill of chasing that moving platform and trying to get on – beautifully captured towards the end of Kingsley Amis's *Lucky Jim*, published in 1954. The hero, Jim Dixon, is pursuing his bus through the traffic of the university town, knowing that it will take him to the arms of the beautiful Christine, and knowing that if he misses the bus, he may lose the girl.

The bus slows, and dawdles, and then Jim stages a great lung-igniting sprint until he is almost able to jump on the open platform, at which point the conductor – who has been watching him expressionlessly – pings his bell and the bus moves off again. It is only when the exhausted and defeated Jim throws him a V-sign that the conductor pulls the bell again and stops the bus and lets him aboard, with the deathless words, 'Well run, wacker.'

I thought of that scene every time I charged down the pavement as a young man. That was how Dixon got the girl, and there was a lesson: because the prizes in life go not necessarily to the swift or the strong, but to those who are willing to bust a gut and mount a moving bus from the rear, just to make an appointment.

Why was it now forbidden to give people that option? Why were all the doors shut and locked with a hiss, as soon as you got on board? We were losing our national mojo, our willingness to take a risk. In fact, that exhilarating experience – leaping aboard a vehicle – was being stifled by 'elf and safety across the western world. The only other vehicles still to have an open moving plat-form, as far as I know, are the old-time trams in San Francisco.

So in early 2008, as I prepared my campaign, I was casting around for pledges to make to Londoners, and I came across an idea in an abandoned manifesto of Nick Boles. We would build a new Routemaster, a New Bus for London, designed specifically, like its great forebear, for the needs of the city. I would be both conservative and modernising at once. The new Routemaster would stand in relation to the old one as the new Mini (bigger, bulgier, more muscular) to the old Alec Issigonis Mini of the 1960s.

It was going to be a design masterpiece, a new emblem of the greatest city on earth, and it was going to be made in the UK. I put it in my manifesto, mentioned it a couple of times in my speeches (to no special acclaim), and then more or less forgot about it; until I was elected. As with knife crime and the cycle hire scheme, I then found that I had to deliver.

There were plenty of left-wing commentators and self-styled bus gurus who began, predictably, by saying that I was insane.

They said that my new bus was impractical, uneconomical, and that I would be ejected from office long before it ever hit the streets. Most cars, they pointed out, took at least six years and hundreds of millions of pounds to develop. TfL were also dubious, at least at first.

If they understood what I was saying correctly, they told me, this new Routemaster presented insuperable problems of design. If I really insisted on an open platform at the back – and I did, vehemently – then it was going to need a conductor. You couldn't have an open platform, floating through the streets of London, with people hopping off and on and no one to supervise. It was just too dangerous – and expensive in lost fare revenue. People would scoot upstairs without paying and the driver would not have a clue what was going on.

And on the other hand, if you had a conductor as well as a driver you were doubling the wage bill of the bus. I was asking the impossible. Could I think again?

I could see that these were serious objections, but I fought back. Wasn't it important to teach our children risk? The country was then in the grip of a mild panic about the loss of outdoor adventure.

Kids were glued to electronic machines. They were mollycoddled, airbagged, swaddled to oblivion in cotton wool – and people had had enough of it. The number-one bestseller was called *The Dangerous Book for Boys*, which taught the younger generation the skills their parents allegedly knew – how to climb a rope, skin a rabbit, fashion a dug-out pirogue from stinkwood with a pen-knife; that kind of thing.

Surely it was a good idea, I argued, if young people could make rapid calculations about time, distance and speed from the open platform of a new-generation Routemaster. Think of the Greek hoplites, I told the transport experts of TfL. They were *anabates* and *apobates*, leaping up and down from their chariots in the middle of battle. They were the hop-on, hop-off hoplites. From the depths of my memory there floated a snatch of Homer – the bit in *Iliad* V where Diomedes goes berserk and starts attacking the gods themselves.

I reminded them how Athena leaped up into the chariot of Diomedes and how the platform groaned with the weight of the goddess. The bus men from TfL looked at me bleakly.

They didn't care about Homer, or middle-class paranoia about the loss of adventure. They were in charge of thousands of heavy machines, including 8,000 buses, each one capable of causing mayhem on the streets of London. Their job – one of their main jobs – was to make transport safe.

OK, I said, if we absolutely must have conductors, perhaps we could save money by employing volunteers, tour guides, out-of-work actors. The words died on my lips. It was absurd. We were Transport for London – we weren't going to staff our buses with volunteers. I had to face the reality. One of the reasons we got rid of the old Routemasters was precisely because modern buses were OMO or OPO – one-man or one-person operated.

You got on at the front, as the driver swished open the electric front doors, and you paid with your Oyster card (now your bank card, phone, watch, etc.) and then found your seat and eventually left by the doors at the back, which, again, were controlled by the driver.

I groaned as I wrestled with the problem. How the hell were we going to create a new bus, with an open platform at the back, and with only one person to operate it?

We needed a designer of genius. We found one.

'It has to be Heatherwick,' said Daniel Moylan, then deputy chairman of TfL. 'He's the only person who can do this.' Thomas Heatherwick certainly looks like a designer. He has flashing eyes and floating hair, and strange tweedy suits, and he is constantly whipping out a little pad to sketch ideas.

But he is also – as Moylan had told me – intensely practical, obsessed with the technical details of what a bus will actually require, what the passengers will experience. We solved the problem of the open platform with a piece of classic cake-ism.

It was going to be both open and not open. It was going to be liberating for passengers dawdling in the city centre, and safe for longer and faster journeys. Heatherwick designed a gorgeous curved rump for the bus, with a stunning diagonal window – somehow recalling the external spiral staircases of the very first omnibuses. And there was a curved electric door, a bit like the door of some large posh hotel shower, that could expose the platform at will.

If you were meandering down Oxford Street and you wanted the passengers to have the hop-on, hop-off experience, then you went with a conductor and in open-platform mode.

If you were whizzing up Shooter's Hill, or the Edgware Road, then you could have one-person operation and the platform closed. Brilliant!

We had an open platform – or enough of an open platform to satisfy my lust for risk. But the revolutionary feature of the bus is the way we managed the flow of human beings. The problem with the old London buses was that there was only one way on and off – the back platform. Everyone had to queue up until the passengers got off, with the inevitable argy-bargy between those hasty to get on and those slow to get off. These delays increased what we call 'dwell time' – the time spent at stops – and reduced punctuality.

More modern double-deckers had two doors, one at the front and one at the back, ingesting and expelling passengers like a more conventional alimentary system. This speeded things up a bit. We went further and had three sets of doors – the front, the middle and the back. To cap it all, we had two staircases, so that passengers were continuously flowing through the vehicle, reducing dwell times and increasing punctuality.

Have you ever seen another double-decker with two staircases? The result was a beast – three metres longer than the old Routemaster. If that great bus was an Indian elephant, this was a vast African bull elephant, and I felt a surge of pride whenever I saw its noble brow on the horizon. To produce a new bus in less than four years – we had five of them on the streets by the 2012 Olympics – was a pretty stunning achievement. How did we do it?

The truth is that after their initial scepticism, the TfL supremos became total enthusiasts. Peter Hendy, David Brown, Leon Daniels – they were all busmen to the core. You may wonder why so many males like driving around in great big red throbbing machines – but whatever the Freudian roots of their fascination, it worked. They believed that London deserved a new bus and they made it happen.

When it did happen, against all the odds, my enemies were aghast – and then determined to find fault. They claimed that it overheated in summer. They called it the sauna bus. The papers were full of people describing how they almost passed out, had panic attacks, etc.

The TfL team were adamant that this was nonsense. They sent people with thermometers to sit in the back seat, under the full glare of the sun, and then showed me readings seeming to prove it was no hotter than an ordinary bus. Still the people complained. I decided that the customer was always right and we solved the problem by the revolutionary expedient of opening the windows.

I am sure that some people did start to feel hot in the new bus; I don't think they were making it up, and we were right to fix the problem. But I am also sure that in many cases that stifling, choking feeling was intensified by sheer irritation with the person (me) who had so blatantly and so personally insisted on creating the new bus.

What they disliked, I think, was the way my ego was so obviously engaged. People called it the 'Boris bus', like the 'Boris bikes', and frankly I am not surprised that many people started to feel a bit put upon. They were literally being forced to travel in a public conveyance that bore my name – and I wasn't even dead. And I was a Tory.

No wonder they fumed, and perspired, and undid the top buttons of their shirts.

Of course they had a point. It was, inevitably, about me. Once I had promised it to Londoners, I just had to get it done. If the charge is egomania in driving forward a project with which I had become personally obsessed, then I am guilty. Yes, it was a vanity project, in that my pride and political future were at stake – but then so is every other great human advance: the Parthenon, the Eiffel Tower, the sewers of Bazalgette; all of them vanity projects.

The new bus for London did what I had promised it would do. It was beautiful throughout – elegantly styled by Heatherwick – and rapidly became an icon. We had hardly finished the prototype when the Bond film producers wanted it for *Skyfall*. You see it in Whitehall, just as Bond is racing to save Judi Dench from Javier Bardem, and since then it has gone global as an emblem of the city.

The new Routemaster cost only £7.8 million to develop and was barely 10 per cent more expensive than a normal diesel bus; and yet it was a hybrid, with 40 per cent lower emissions. It was and is the embodiment of levelling up – getting Londoners to work in style and simultaneously driving job creation around the whole of the UK. Heatherwick's whorly seat coverings were fabricated in Huddersfield. The engine came from Darlington. The destination blinds came from Middleton in Greater Manchester, the seats from Telford, the wheelchair ramps from Hoddesdon in Hertfordshire and the heavy-duty cork-based Treadmaster flooring from Liskeard in Cornwall.

The whole thing was assembled by Wrightbus of Ballymena, County Antrim, in Northern Ireland, and Wrightbus provided the chassis and the bodywork. The bus personified the Union of the United Kingdom, and indeed the Wrightbus workforce was solidly Unionist.

I went to Ballymena when they had finished the first bus, and made a speech from the open platform. The octogenarian Billy Wright clapped me on the back as I stepped down. 'No surrender!' he said.

Like that great Northern Irish entrepreneur, I am chuffed to the core that we built a truly British bus, chuffed that so many people (except the minority who claimed that we boiled them alive) seemed to love it and to love travelling on it.

I learned some important things in driving that project. If you don't chop and change your plans, and if you have a great team, and if that team really believes in the project – then you can still get big things done with enormous speed, even in the UK.

In spite of the economic shocks, and in spite of the fare rises I imposed, bus ridership increased – and so did Tube ridership.

We got ourselves into a virtuous cycle. As the fare revenue increased, we were able to pump billions into Tube upgrades –

improving the signalling and improving the speed and reliability of the trains. That in turn encouraged more people to take public transport – increasing our revenues and taking cars off the streets.

Safe and reliable mass transit is the great equaliser. It gets people on low incomes to the high-wage jobs they need. Every day in London I was learning the connections between housing and transport and education, the link between safer streets and economic growth. I was learning about levelling up.

But after three years of recession – and when not a single banker had been jailed for the banking crash – there was a simmering magma of resentment in some parts of the city. One night in August 2011, it blew.

Chapter 11

London Burning

A contagion of violence and greed

There have been many embarrassments in my life but on only a very few occasions have I felt such a cowering sense of shame that I actually wanted to disappear. This was one of those moments.

It was early evening on Monday, August 8, 2011, and I was in the departure lounge at Calgary Airport. There was still an hour until boarding, and I was going mad with impatience. I had stationed myself in what I hoped was an unobtrusive corner, head down, collar up, but I could somehow feel that people were glancing at me nonetheless.

'They know!' said my conscience. 'They know who you are. They know your dreadful secret.' There was a large TV screen suspended from the ceiling and people were standing around it, their faces bathed in the hellish orange glow of fires that were blazing 4,500 miles away. Even from where I was sitting, I could see that there were mobs torching buildings and breaking into shops; and, *whoosh*, what appeared to be a department store went up in a great phlegethontean fireball.

My need to know overcame my caution. I got up and walked towards the screen, and at once I could see exactly where it was. That was Croydon. That was Reeves Corner, a furniture store that had stood on that spot (as all the papers chronicled the following day) since 1867.

Oh God, I breathed. Oh almighty God, what on earth are they doing? I watched with horror and disgust, and a plentiful admixture of self-loathing. This was my city. These were my electorate. I was the mayor – and I was thousands of miles away, and the situation was getting worse with every minute.

It was later established that there were more fires burning in London that night than on any evening since the Blitz of 1940. I was still stuck at Calgary, on the other side of the world, and wouldn't be back until breakfast time the following day. I must have emitted a whimper of frustration, because another passenger turned to look at me.

'Hey,' he said. 'Aren't you the mayor? Shouldn't you be there?' and his words went through my heart like a skewer.

To hold a major political office in the UK is an immense privilege. You have all the excitement and interest of taking decisions at the highest level, of painting on the broadest possible canvas. But you have to understand that you are now – literally – a servant of the people. You are their hireling.

Your time is their time, twenty-four hours a day; and sometimes that fact is hard to remember – especially when you are on holiday. I love work as much as the next fellow, perhaps a bit more, but after a few months of solid effort I start to yearn for that cold glass of retsina in the beachside taverna and the feeling of the sand scrunching between your toes.

What happens, as a politician, is that you count down the days until you can get away, and then, *wham*, after only a few days – when you have barely sussed out the way to the beach – something happens, an event of sufficient magnitude that your opponents can suggest it needs your personal attention, and then the calls begin, at first sporadic, and then mounting in frequency until they become a single yammering cry: where is the mayor?

Where is the foreign secretary? Where is the prime minister? Why is he still on holiday, the idle bum, and when is he coming back? The art is to know when you are beat. It is precisely because you are abroad – unable to feel the pulse directly, with no advisers on hand – that this can be so hard to gauge.

You see the headlines from home; and then you see the happy faces of the kids, and you hear the anxious questions of your wife, and you know with an aching heart that if you give in, it is going to mean yet another wrecked holiday and even more toil for her; and so you shut a Nelsonian eye to the problem, and you say to yourself, Is this really so bad? Can't someone else manage it? Is my journey truly necessary?

And so a psychic arm-wrestle begins, between pleasure and guilt, between family and duty, between your desire to sit on the beach and the media's desire to bring you home. As soon as that struggle begins, believe me, you have lost.

You may not realise it at first, but you are going back.

I heard the first cheep of alarm from London on Saturday August 6, round about lunchtime Canada time. We were on the road from Vancouver to the Rockies – Marina and me and our children Lara, Milo, Cassia, Theo – and we were all in very high spirits. We had a huge recreational vehicle, a proper *Meet the Fockers* mobile home, well over thirty feet long. We had a well-stocked fridge and the music on, and we were winding ever higher up into the mountains, away from civilisation and away from any mobile signal.

My little Nokia got a last message to call Kit Malthouse, my deputy mayor for policing and crime, and then the signal cone went totally blank. Hmm, I thought, what would Kit want on a Saturday?

Luckily Lara was getting an intermittent connection and I put Kit on speaker as we drove up through the maples and pines.

There had been a protest at Tottenham, he said, and it had got a bit out of hand.

It concerned the shooting of Mark Duggan, he said.

Oh yes, I said. I was aware of this shooting, which had taken place a couple of days before, on August 4, when I was already out of the country, but I was puzzled.

It was awful that Duggan had been shot. It was doubly awful that he had been shot by the police – but wasn't Duggan on the way to kill someone? Didn't he have a gun in the car?

Why were the people of Tottenham so inflamed by the death of this obvious gangster?

Kit agreed: Duggan was a wrong 'un. But there were questions. Where was Duggan's gun at the moment he was shot? Had he fired it, as the police initially claimed, or was he unarmed when he got out of his taxi? It seemed that the Met had said some contra-dictory things.

Ah, I said, one of those, eh? Every so often – and it is amazingly rare by comparison with other big cities – the police CO19 armed response unit makes a mistake. They shoot someone who does not really represent a threat to the public; like Jean-Charles de Menezes, who was sadly killed on the Tube in the belief that he was a terrorist, and who turned out to be a wholly innocent Brazilian plumber.

No, no, said Kit: Duggan was definitely a baddie, but he was a good-looking twenty-nine-year-old father of six, and he seemed to be popular in Tottenham.

At this point Lara's phone also lost signal, and we drove on and up through the majestic glens of British Columbia. By now the splendour of the landscape was being driven out of my head and I was starting to imagine things in Tottenham: fists and placards waving outside the police station, and then, as dusk fell, the first hail of bottles and bollards.

By mid-afternoon we were at our campsite, a lovely round lake called Clearwater, and I had a signal. I called Kit. It was worse than I had thought. Cars had been burned, shops looted.

Look at the TV, he said. I don't have a TV, I said.

And, er, a bus had been burned, he said, and a post office reduced to ashes.

Wha—?? I said.

I was starting to feel like the French marquise in the old song, who rings her butler from Cannes, to find that her grey mare is dead, because the stables caught fire, because her husband has decided to destroy the château before committing suicide.

What else has happened? I asked. Well, twenty-six police officers have been injured, he said, one of them quite seriously.

Jeez, I said.

Now you, the reader, can see that the position is irretrievable. You know, with the advantage of hindsight, that a full-scale disaster is unfolding. But at both ends of these types of conversations, there is an overwhelming urge to minimise the problem. The holidaying politician is desperate to persuade himself that he can somehow stay on holiday; the person minding the shop is naturally keen to show that he has things under control.

'It's under control,' said Kit, and we agreed to talk as soon as we could the next day.

I had been talking to Kit in the moonlight, from a half-submerged jetty leading out into the lake, the only place I could find a signal. As I walked back through the darkened campsite, I could have sworn I heard someone whispering my name. Maybe I was imagining it, but it sounded like they were saying I should be in London.

When dawn broke in Canada, it was lunchtime in London, and things seemed calmer. Opposition politicians were certainly clamouring for me to come back from holiday, but at least Tottenham was no longer ablaze. Perhaps I could tip-toe through it. Maybe it was just one bad evening. I would take a hit, politically, if I stayed away. I would ship some water. But if I was lucky there would be no more aggro. Most of my City Hall team were off at a wedding in Spain, but Guto Harri organised for me to go on Sky News, so that I could show that I was at least abreast of the situation.

I walked out onto the submerged jetty, up to my ankles in water, and fulminated against the rioters. We would bang them up, I told Sky News over my mobile phone; we were flooding the streets with police, I said. We were going to come down hard on the criminals.

All the while I could hear lake water lapping by the shore and hoped that it was not audible to the viewers.

No, I said scornfully, I certainly would not be coming back. The rioters wanted to cause maximum chaos. They wanted to disrupt people's lives.

Well, I wasn't going to give them that satisfaction, I burbled.

But surely you have to come back? said the slightly incredulous newscaster.

No, I said scornfully – coming back now would be, er, to reward bad behaviour!

Even as I spoke, I knew that it sounded like a pretty hopeless defence. I was now in some political difficulty; up to my ankles if not the knees. But what could I do? I was 4,500 miles from home and hundreds of miles from the nearest airport. Marina could not drive the RV, which was a real beast and far bigger than anything she had driven before. If I fled Canada, we would need to hire two more cars – one for her and the kids, and one for me – and we would need to ditch this enormous mobile home in the wilderness. The whole operation would cost a fortune. Plus I was going to be in the doghouse for mucking up yet another holiday.

There was nothing for it. We had to keep going. I got through to home secretary Theresa May, who was on a walking holiday in Switzerland. We agreed that we would both stay abroad – but we would warn each other if we changed our minds.

So we crossed our fingers, packed up our camp – and drove on: higher and higher, further and further into the mountains. We

passed bear, and elk and other types of deer; we saw high lakes
with that icy pale-blue snowmelt colour. It was all so lovely that I
began to hope that somehow it would all be OK. I looked at the
Nokia screen. I had no messages. I had no signal.

Perhaps we would get to the town – a place called Jasper – and
find that I still had no messages, even when I got a signal.
Wouldn't that be just blissful? By late afternoon we reached the
outskirts of Jasper in British Columbia, and my machine suddenly
throbbed into life.

Brzzt-brzzt, brzzt-brzzt, the pent-up messages pumped in
from the stricken British capital.

I dragged Kit and the deputy Met commissioner Tim Godwin
from their beds and discovered that things were worse than I had
feared, worse than I could have imagined. It wasn't just that
Tottenham was still under curfew. There had been disorder in
Brixton, Wood Green, Dalston, Enfield, Woolwich, Shepherd's
Bush, Oxford Circus, Islington – just about all over the place.

Young people seemed to have developed a new and contagious
mania for raiding sports shops and electric goods shops, smashing
the windows and carrying off their booty with a brazen impudence
that was encouraging a general free-for-all. I don't know whether
any of them heard the ranting threats of the mayor, delivered from
his vantage point in a Canadian lake. I don't know if they gave a
damn; but they certainly didn't behave as though they did.

I know when I am licked. The following day I hired two more
cars, parked the RV, and we said emotional farewells before I
drove like the wind to Calgary Airport. The flight was terrible,
bolt upright as we flew up towards the Pole over endless desolate
tracts of lakes and swamps – God, Canada was big – and all the
while I was wondering what the hell was happening in the city I
was meant to represent.

Arriving in London at dawn, I showered and jumped on my
bike. It was now Tuesday morning and the place was in a state of

shock. It was like the description of London in John Wyndham's *The Day of the Triffids*, the morning after a meteorite explodes.

I cycled from Islington to Southwark, and saw that there was no one around, and an awful hush – except for the distant wailing of sirens.

When they gave me my briefing in City Hall, I could not believe the scale of the violence. Town centres had been pillaged across the city, from Croydon to Enfield, from Ealing to Barking. The rioters had used petrol bombs. The bill for the damage was going to run to hundreds of millions.

In some places, such as Eltham, groups of vigilantes had turned out with clubs and staves to defend the community. In Ealing a sixty-eight-year-old man had come out to remonstrate with a mob and to extinguish a fire in a bin. He was set upon and died of his injuries three days later.

There are times when things are so bad that you don't need to think what to do. I had only one option. I had to get out on the streets, show my face, bring the disorder to an immediate halt, thank the heroes and jail the villains.

First I went down to Clapham, where public-spirited people had come out with brooms to sweep up the mess of broken glass. I tried to rally the crowd, hailing them for what they had done and heaping obloquy on the rioters. It went OK for about thirty seconds, until they started heckling.

Why had I taken so long to come back? Why didn't I resign? What about Mark Duggan?

There is some fine footage of me trying to pacify the mob, flanked by a stony-faced Theresa May. As the good people of Clapham start to cut up rough, you can see how Theresa's instinct for self-preservation kicks in and she drifts gently out of shot.

I thanked firefighters and police officers and ambulance workers. I reassured shopkeepers and businesspeople of all kinds. That night the virus spread to other cities. In fact, the mania afflicted the whole country, with shops being trashed by young people in search of big white sneakers and other consumer goods (the one shop they didn't attack was Waterstones the booksellers); but London – from Tuesday on – was relatively quiet.

In three or four days of tramping the streets, apologising, sympathising, thanking, reassuring, I think I picked up a fair idea of what had happened and what we got wrong. I am afraid that it all goes back to those first few hours in Tottenham.

Of course the death of Mark Duggan was a tragedy, but the plain fact is that he was carrying a reconditioned Beretta 92 pistol that had been given to him fifteen minutes earlier. He wasn't going to use it on pigeons. He wasn't going to be the starter in a 1920s school sports day.

He was on his way to kill someone. Yes, he was shot as he was getting out of his taxi – because those officers had an entirely reasonable anxiety that he might kill them. One of the bullets passed through him and lodged in the radio of a police officer, giving rise to the myth that there had been an exchange of fire. That was not true.

Duggan did not fire his weapon; but it was typical (and human) of the police that they seized prematurely on a piece of evidence that seemed to justify their actions, even if it wasn't necessary to their case – because the officers were manifestly doing their duty.

It was that initial confusion about what happened, and doubts over the police account, which provoked the protests at Tottenham police station. There were some good people at that scene, friends of mine who worked with me to help fight knife crime.

I believe that unfortunately they managed to whip things up when they should have calmed them down. But the biggest mistake of all was in that hour, when the first missiles were thrown.

In the weeks and months that followed, there were endless attempts to 'read the riots', to offer the deep underlying sociological causes for what had gone wrong. The lefty criminologists were consulted, and they produced the kind of guff you would expect. It was all the fault of the recession; it was Tory cuts; it was the police; it was the relationship between the police and young black men; it was family breakdown; the absence of good male role models; and yadda yadda yadda for yards in the pages of the *Guardian*.

Well, in all the interviews I personally conducted, I didn't meet anyone who said anything of the kind. It was sheer criminality, people told me. The young people were hot, they were bored, it was August – and the impression they had from the TV was that the police had lost control; and so they all got on their electronic communications – from Twitter to BlackBerry Messenger – and they went amok.

The thing that intoxicated them was those first broadcasts from Tottenham: of the police retreating and the rioters in charge. To understand why the police proceeded so gingerly in those early moments, you have to go back to the Tottenham riots of 1985 and the horror of Broadwater Farm.

It was there, on the very estate where Duggan had been born a few years earlier, that PC Keith Blakelock found himself isolated by a group of rioters. He tripped and fell, and was set upon by a mob who attempted literally to decapitate him. When his fellow officers recovered his body, hours later, they found forty wounds – inflicted by everything from a machete to a screwdriver – and a six-inch knife buried to the hilt in his neck. I used to talk to PC Blakelock's family every year, at a ceremony in Hendon to mark the sacrifice of Metropolitan Police officers killed in the line of duty.

I know how engrained was that horror – of letting a PC get isolated – in the culture of London policing, and I would not be surprised if that memory, conscious or unconscious, affected the way the police handled those crucial first few hours.

It is arguable that they showed too much restraint, too much reluctance to come down hard and to nip things in the bud. It was in the face of that apparent tentativeness that the rioters grew even bolder.

They saw from the TV that the police wouldn't stop them, and the virus of disorder roared through London and on through England to almost all the major cities. By the end, five people had died, three of them in Birmingham, and about 180 police officers had been injured (and five police dogs). Afterwards, the Met Police requested to be able to use water cannon and I went to great trouble to secure some ancient German machines – only to be blocked by Theresa May, still doing her liberal thing.

In truth, I don't think water cannon would have made much difference. What was needed was decisive and robust action on that first night, before the public got the impression that the police would vacate the street.

By Wednesday August 10, things were much quieter in London, not least because we now had 16,000 officers on the streets and we were arresting literally thousands of miscreants. Still, I lay awake, listening to the wail of the sirens, hoping that they would soon die away, praying that it was not another conflagration. Eventually they did die away and – partly because we had put so many of the usual suspects behind bars – the crime level fell still further.

One of the smartest things David Cameron did was to refuse to hold some spine-cracking public inquiry into the riots. No one really wanted one, because everyone could see broadly what happened. A large group of kids – some of them otherwise well behaved – had succumbed to a kind of social media-driven hysteria and given way to felonious temptation; and now they were paying the price.

It taught me how thin is the integument of civilisation, and how frail the instruments of control. Ian Blair, the former police commissioner, told me in our very first conversation that I would one day 'lose the streets'. In a sense that is obvious. You can't hold down a city of nine million people with only 32,000 police officers. There are tides that move beneath the surface of a city that can suddenly swing in a dangerous direction – and then move back again.

It was only a year later, after the worst riots for a generation, that London was experiencing one of its greatest and most golden moments of optimism and unity.

Chapter 12

A Summer Like No Other

How London triumphed at the Olympics

Mitt Romney seemed a decent sort of cove, but I am afraid there was no case for mercy. He had screwed up. I was, regretfully, going to have to slot him in the slats.

Romney was in London, several days before the start of the Olympic and Paralympic Games, and he had made the cardinal mistake of giving an entirely candid opinion. He was asked about the host city's preparations for the Games.

Well, said the square-jawed senator from Utah, who had successfully run the Olympic Games in Salt Lake City, there were some things that were 'disconcerting'. There were some other things that were 'discouraging'. In fact, he wasn't sure how it was going to turn out. It so happened that I was that evening in front of a crowd in Hyde Park – 60,000 people who had come to celebrate the arrival of the Olympic torch in London. The sun was beating down, they were waving bottles of Corona, and the air was full of the golden glow I remember from that summer – as though someone had already begun steadily pumping serotonin into the national water supply.

I hadn't been expecting to make a speech, but on the way there my brilliant adviser Neale Coleman suggested that – from the sounds of things in Hyde Park – a few words might go down well. They shoved me onto that famous stage, where Mick Jagger had sung 'Sympathy for the Devil' in 1968. I could see a vast rabble just waiting to be roused.

I told them that this was one of the most amazing sights I had ever seen in my life. They ululated their approval. I sensed that they were not a difficult crowd.

I told them that 'the Geiger counter of Olympomania was about to go – *zoink!* – off the scale', and they agreed.

People were coming from all around the world to see London, I said. They were coming to the greatest city on earth (loud acclaim), and to see the preparations we were making.

'I hear there is a guy called Mitt Romney, who wants to know whether we are ready. He wants to know whether we are ready. Are we ready? Yes we are! [deafening assent]

'The venues are ready, the stadium is ready, the aquatics centre is ready, the police are ready, the transport system is ready, the security is ready' – and I went on to list all the things that were allegedly ready, above all the athletes, Team GB, who were about to produce such a rich golden haul of medals that we would be able to bail out Greece! And Spain! (It was now the height of the European debt crisis.) As for the rowers, they were going to deliver the greatest aquatic triumph since Trafalgar, and I ended with a crescendo of pure jingo.

We were going to beat Australia (Yee-arrgh! said the audience). We were going to beat France, we were going to beat Germany (Yeee-aargh!!! they said).

I am told that Barack Obama happened to watch this speech and was delighted by the embarrassment of Romney, his presidential rival. Today, I look back with a touch of queasiness, because the truth is that things were far more touch and go than I felt able to say.

Mitt Romney was not wholly wrong. There was plenty to worry

about. Until that evening, I didn't have any real evidence that these Olympic and Paralympic Games would be any kind of popular success. They had been seven years in preparation and there were a great many people who hated the whole thing.

In so far as we were 'on budget', as I constantly claimed, it was only because we had trebled the original bid budget from £3.2 billion to £9.3 billion; and at a time when the public finances had been badly hit by the banking crisis, this was felt keenly. People loathed the 'Olympic Route Network' of Soviet-style Zil lanes on the roads of London, reserved for the use of the so-called 'Olympic family', mainly made up of a vast group of more or less corrupt international sporting bureaucrats. They hated the general disruption, all for the sake – as the Olympo-sceptics saw it – of watching a few people in singlets scampering about a stadium in east London.

Indeed, before I became joint chairman of the London Organising Committee of the Olympic Games, I hadn't taken much interest in athletics as a spectator sport, and I wasn't at all sure that it was really prime-time stuff. London had not hosted the Games since 1948 and memories were faint. We knew that it had gone well, but it was the era of post-war rationing and it had been a frugal affair. At one stage Prime Minister Cameron suggested that perhaps we should borrow from history. 'How about the austerity Olympics?' he suggested.

No, I said. I didn't like austerity, as a slogan or as a strategy. The public didn't want Stafford Cripps-style drinking our own urine. They wanted economic growth, and confidence. As for the rest of the world, they didn't want a 1940s experience of Spam fritters and jumpers for goalposts. This was London, hub of the universe. To hell with austerity, we were going to put on a fantastic show, I said. I was in a strong position.

The Olympic and Paralympic Games are not awarded to a country but to the host city, and as mayor of the host city I was the closest thing to the actual host, even if the whole colossal project was very largely run by others. The real heroes of the Olympic and Paralympic organisation were people like Seb Coe, Paul Deighton, David Higgins and John Armitt. But I had a titular status, as well as some real responsibilities – and this gave me terrific clout to get things done, at top speed.

It also put me in the firing line for when things went wrong. For a long time, it seemed as if nothing could go right.

When we unveiled our Olympic logo, a jazzy asymmetrical magenta splodge, it was denounced by the Epilepsy Society. When we produced a lovable pair of mascots called Wenlock and Mandeville (named after Much Wenlock, the Shropshire village that originated the modern Olympics, and Stoke Mandeville, whose hospital was the birthplace of the Paralympics), they were derided as un-cuddly and sinister; and it is true that for some reason they only had one eye each.

When the first athletes arrived in the middle of July, it looked as though everyone's anxieties about the transport network were going to be fulfilled. The Australian team got lost, because the bus driver had never been to London before and didn't know how to use a sat-nav. The American team took four hours to get from Heathrow to Stratford in east London and arrived thoroughly out of sorts – because our driver seemed to have confused Stratford with Southend.

It was mortifying. We had put squillions into the transport network, upgrading the Tube and the Docklands Light Railway, and desperately trussing together the pillars of the M4 flyover at Hammersmith (which had chosen this year to reveal that they were about as structurally sound as a freshly dunked Hobnob). And now the whole operation was being let down by some poor bus drivers from out of town.

As the day of the opening ceremony approached – Friday July 27, 2012 – we were becoming increasingly alarmed at the prospect of rain. It was a staple of my speeches that it is not raining in London 94 per cent of the time. There were some days, that July, when the ratio seemed the other way around. It was bucketing down.

In order to save money on the stadium, we had built it with a very short-brimmed roof (a decision I had taken and for which, reasonably, I would be blamed), and if it rained on the night of the opening ceremony – and the forecast was getting more and more menacing – then a lot of very important people were going to get very wet.

By now Jeremy Hunt had taken over from Tessa Jowell as my government counterpart, and he and I conferred on the subject of ponchos. He was in favour of buying 10,000 pac-a-mac plastic ponchos; I thought they were probably a waste of money. In the end, he persuaded me – though we never worked out what would happen to the un-ponchoed remainder of the crowd.

All these anxieties were nothing, however, compared to our problems with security. Ever since 1972, when the Olympic village in Munich was taken over by some PLO murderers, the organisers of the Games had been rightly paranoid about terrorism. London seemed especially vulnerable.

The very day after we won the right to host the games – in July 2005 – our city suffered the 7/7 bombings, a concerted series of Islamist attacks on public transport in which thirty-six people were killed. So we had decided that we were going to screen every Games site with airline-like vigilance. In fact, you wouldn't even be able to bring your own liquids into the venues.

With two weeks to go, we had the X-ray machines. We had the screening systems. We had a US aircraft carrier off the coast and we had a Starstreak ABM system on a housing block in Hackney. We had vast concrete chicanes to stop suicide bombers driving cars into the crowds. Then, suddenly and bewilderingly, it appeared that we were missing one crucial thing: we had no staff to do the checks.

I was lying on the office floor at home at 7 a.m., on one of our early morning conference calls, when they broke the news. I thought it was some kind of nightmare. I had to get them to repeat the numbers – because they were staggering. The whole security staffing operation had been contracted out to a private company, G4S, and there had been a massive no-show; not a few hundred missing, but thousands and thousands – perhaps 14,000 all told, though they couldn't be sure.

Whaaa? I croaked. How could a company simply lose track of 14,000 employees? It was the biggest, most intergalactic cock-up I had ever heard of.

It seemed that G4S had received over 100,000 apparently enthusiastic applications and bought thousands of jazzy magenta London 2012 uniforms, and prepared all the necessary training sessions – but had somehow failed to ensure that they had locked them in.

So, in the way of young people (and this was a sign of the economic resilience of London), they had just vamoosed to pursue other and perhaps more lucrative job opportunities – short order chefs in Acapulco, bodyguards to Russian oligarchs, whatever.

We were facing disaster. Of the G4S staff who did turn up, two were instantly involved – I kid you not – in bomb hoaxes. Where could we find 14,000 reliable people?

The only way to get the Games underway was to call in the armed services. We did, and they were superb. They jumped to it. We found berths and bivouacs for them in the East End, and soon 11,000 servicemen and women, in uniform, had become one of the most cheering and popular features of the London Games. It was as if we had planned it all along.

They allowed us to go ahead with the opening ceremony, on time, without a hitch. There was a bit of rain, but more of a Scotch mist than a downpour, and we didn't need the ponchos.

Danny Boyle, the director of *Slumdog Millionaire*, had produced a stirring pageant of all that is great about Britain, with quite a long section about the splendours of the NHS (strange how no other countries have adopted the same model, wonderful though it is); but the show was stolen by Her Majesty the Queen, who appeared – through Boyle's trickery – to have been summoned from her desk at Buckingham Palace by Daniel Craig, aka James Bond 007, and then flown across London in a helicopter to hover above us, and then, to the joy and shock of the heads of state and government around me, to leap from the helicopter in her pink dress and parachute down to join us.

The following morning it was my happy duty to show her around the rest of the Olympic Park, and she was very keen to know if people had enjoyed the performance.

'Did they think it was funny?' she asked.

'Ma'am,' I said, 'the reviews have been uniformly terrific.'

A few moments later I showed her the ArcelorMittal Orbit, a structure which she professed to find 'fascinating'. It was one of the proudest moments of my life.

It felt as though some things were perhaps starting to go well. Transport for London was conveying people smoothly, and in huge numbers, to all parts of the capital. Everyone had fallen in love with the 'Gamesmakers' – the volunteers who were helping people get around. The city looked great, with the Olympic bunting everywhere and the bridges adorned with special illuminations.

If anything, though, my tension was growing. It still didn't feel like a real party. For all my talk of Olympomania, there were some gaps in the stadium (caused entirely by guests of sponsors who couldn't be arsed to use their freebie tickets, when others would have given their right arm to be there) and this had attracted some BBC comment. We soon fixed it by making sure that if you failed to claim your seat in time, you simply lost it. But that still didn't really lift my mood.

There was one gigantic fact that was now looming oppressively in all our conversations, one unmentionable truth – that Team GB had yet to win any goddamn gold medals.

When I was first thinking about running for the mayoralty, Colin (Lord) Moynihan of the Olympic Committee had come to brief me. We were going to do brilliantly in London 2012, he said. We had fantastic talent coming on, in rowing, horse-riding, cycling, sailing – 'all the sports that involve sitting down,' as he put it.

That is why I told the Hyde Park crowd to be so confident about our medal haul – and now it looked as though I might have been wrong. We had misfired on that crucial first Saturday, July 28, when our theoretically all-conquering cycling team failed to win the road race around Surrey. Then Sunday came and went and still no British golds.

Then Monday July 30, and no end to the drought, and Tuesday July 31. France, China, USA, Australia – every other country in the world was starting to rack up the top gongs – but not the hosts!

Not us! Time after time I would hear the *Chariots of Fire* theme tune in the distance, indicating that a medal ceremony was being carried out, and it was always someone else's anthem, never 'God Save the Queen'.

What the hell was happening? I thought of my mad promise in Hyde Park that we would win enough gold bullion to bail out Greece. Talk about hubris. To make matters worse, my team were anxious about the 'vibe' in London. In order to keep the traffic flowing smoothly – and to clear the roads for the all-important 'Olympic family' of athletes and officials – I had issued some pretty blood-curdling stay-at-home warnings over the Tube Tannoy. These had been, if anything, too successful.

In those first few days – it is hard to remember this now – the place felt a bit quiet. To encourage the festival atmosphere, we had set up 'live sites' in the parks, with big screens, hot dogs, hog roasts and so on, so that Londoners who didn't have tickets could still watch in a crowd. People were certainly turning up and enjoying themselves, but the atmosphere was not yet electric. So on Wednesday August 1, I went down to Victoria Park in Hackney, where I had decided the live site should be made particularly exciting by the addition of a zipwire.

I had been obsessed with zipwires ever since taking something called the Flying Fox over the crenelations of Jodhpur in India. I was sure it would be a hit with the crowds. For some reason it had taken some time – five days into the Games – to erect this diversion in Victoria Park. So I was going to inaugurate it.

I climbed to the top of the scaffolding tower, connected by a steel hauser to another tower about a hundred yards away. It all looked a bit ramshackle.

'Am I really the first person to try this?' I asked.

'You are!' they beamed. They pointed to a chap with a clipboard just going down the other side of the tower. 'That's the council health and safety guy. He has just approved it.'

'Great!' I said.

I strapped on the harness, put on a blue helmet and, waving two plastic Union Jacks, I launched myself into space.

Beneath and around me was a scattered and apathetic crowd of Londoners. My plan was to try to rouse and excite them with my derring-do. This immediately went wrong in that I swivelled round and found myself travelling backwards, so that I couldn't see where I was going.

Having begun by going worryingly fast, I now found that I was going rather slowly – slower and slower, in fact, until I came to a stop, suspended in mid-air, about three-quarters of the way along. I shifted in my harness so as to try to alleviate some pretty extreme discomfort in my groin. I waved the Union Jacks and tried to jolly along the crowd. There was no disguising the truth.

It was obvious that I was stuck, forty feet up, and no one had a clue how to get me down. Some of my children, and their cousins, had come along to try the zipwire. I saw them try to slink away. Then I saw Carl, a Metropolitan Police protection officer who had been assigned to me for the Games.

'Carl,' I said, 'can you get me down?' Slowly he reached into his breast pocket, as if preparing to draw a gun and shoot the wire in two; and then took out his mobile to take a photo of my humiliation.

About half an hour later, after they had found a rope to drag me to the far tower, I was driving away with my political adviser, Ben Gascoigne. It did not seem that the episode would burnish my credentials as an all-round *homme serieux* and world statesman, and I wanted some reassurance.

'I shouldn't think the media will make much of that, will they?' I asked Ben. 'I mean, I don't think they will have any pictures, will they?'

'No', said Ben, 'I am sure it will be fine.' He was already looking at his mobile phone, where the news was popping up, and laughing.

By teatime that day, thank heavens, my clowning was wiped away. The drought was over. It was raining gold and silver and bronze. Cyclist Bradley Wiggins of Team GB won the road time trial. Helen Glover and Heather Stanning won the women's coxless pair, and on it went, for day after glorious day, in a wild crescendo of excitement.

The next day we won the canoeing and the double sculls, and then came that Mo-Mentous Saturday, when Mo Farah won the 10,000 metres and Greg Rutherford won the long jump and Jess Ennis won the women's heptathlon. Who says we only win the sports that involve sitting down?

You should have been there that Saturday night when Mo, this young Somaliland-born Briton, brought us weeping and cheering to our feet as he did the triumphant 'Mobot', a gesture he invented that involves making an M with his elbows by putting his hands on his head.

There we are – I thought: a country and city that feared another Islamist attack; and instead we were coming together in an outpouring of pride, and I mean deep national pride, in a young Londoner called Mohammed, and we seemed more happy and united and harmonious than I can remember.

John Major, the former prime minister, used to talk about his vision of Britain as a 'nation at ease with itself'. Well, this was it.

And then Andy Murray won gold in the tennis, and Nicola Adams won gold in the boxing, and on it continued. In the end we came third in the medal table, and the national euphoria actually seemed to grow, as the Olympics turned into the Paralympics, and two more golden weeks of sport.

People look back at that moment and wish we could return, and so do I. But don't forget the key lesson of that amazing national experience. It's not just about togetherness and rejoicing in our beautiful multiracial identity – important though that is. It is about an utterly ruthless individual determination to excel, to beat others and to get on that podium. It's about the brutal subordination of everything else to winning and the blindingly hard work that entails. It's about competition.

Those Olympians and Paralympians had grace and humour and dignity in defeat. But they also had the grit to succeed against the best of the rest of the world. That, in the end, is why we all felt suffused with that golden glow – with pride in their efforts.

In this epoch of slight post-Covid, post-lockdown languor, it is perhaps that spirit of effort that we really need to recapture.

Chapter 13

Miracle in Battersea

And a lesson in levelling up London

'Really?' I said to Roisha Hughes, my private secretary. 'I have got to go and see Prince Andrew? What on earth for?' I am all in favour of the royal family, but I couldn't see what use I could be to the Queen's second son.

Sorry, said Roisha: you've got to go.

Roisha was my private secretary for eight years in City Hall, a young Northern Irish woman with a first in German from Cambridge. She was one of the big reasons things went well.

It was not long before I was drinking tea with His Royal Highness (as he then was) in what I assumed was his apartment, a dark and cluttered room in Buckingham Palace. Things gradually became clearer.

It seemed that the prince wanted to talk about investment into London, in his capacity as a global champion for UK business and trade ambassador – a job he actually did rather well. So I had brought my deputy mayor and chief of staff, Sir Simon Milton. No one knew more than Simon about planning and the built environment. Whatever was in His Royal Highness's mind, I wanted to show that we were taking it seriously. We talked about all the things that might put off investors – the pressure at Heathrow, what to do about the traffic, etc. Then the prince mentioned Battersea Power Station. It was 2009, and this vast brick cathedral had loomed uselessly for decades over the London skyline. Its famous chimneys were crumbling. Its roof was gone. Its interior was derelict, dank, dripping.

It was fit for nothing but the final shoot-out-and-torture scene in noir-ish British gangster movies, and the last useful thing it had done was to feature on the cover of a Pink Floyd album, with a giant inflatable pig hovering symbolically above it. Now it was totally abandoned, like some bloated dead quadruped stuck upside down in the mudflats on the banks of the Thames, blighting a huge forty-two-acre site around it. The whole shambles was just a stone's throw from Westminster. It was a disgrace, a reproach to the imaginative failure of politicians, of all parties, who had tried and failed for thirty years to regenerate the site. They had tried to turn it into a theme park, cinemas, offices, ice rinks, zoos, homes, circuses. Nothing worked.

Shortly after I was elected in 2008, a Uruguayan architect called Rafael Viñoly came to see me with a truly deranged plan to create a kind of eco-dome, with a three-hundred-metre chimney erupting from the middle – like a super-colossal bog-roll tube – and the whole thing encased in a kind of polythene canopy full of birds and foliage. It was mad, as I told him.

The prince had another idea. 'Why don't you just tear it down?' he said.

Simon Milton looked at him and grinned his cheerful grin. Simon was a small, dapper, slightly rotund man, with unflappable good manners. He was also a bit of a killer. 'Well,' he said, 'why don't we just knock down Buckingham Palace? There is a huge old space here. We could build loads of affordable housing.'

The duke/prince/Randy Andy goggled at Simon; but my deputy was right. It would have been sacrilege to knock down the old power station. We had all grown up with it, and Londoners broadly loved it. The power station was in many ways an architectural masterpiece, a modern ziggurat with six million bricks, designed in the 1920s by Giles Gilbert Scott, who also did the red telephone box, for which sentimental affection had also long outlasted its practical use.

In any case, even if we wanted to destroy it, we couldn't. As environment secretary in the 1980s, Michael Heseltine had listed it Grade II. We couldn't touch that famous silhouette – and nor could we develop it. The local borough, Wandsworth, had long since had a plan to build 2,500 homes. But it was going to cost hundreds and hundreds of millions – maybe more than a billion – to make the site remotely habitable, to say nothing of restoring the battered fabric of the power station.

You couldn't possibly justify that expenditure if you were only going to build 2,500 flats – and you couldn't hope to build more than 2,500 flats because the transport links were so poor that there was no way of getting to the site. As we urban planners put it, the PTAL – public transport access level – was way too low. To make the whole project work, you needed one and probably two more Tube stations.

You needed to extend the Northern Line – and that would itself cost billions. We were already stretched to bust building Crossrail and upgrading the signalling on the Jubilee and District and Circle Lines and across the network. How were we going to pay for new Tube stations?

There the problem rested, as it had done for decades, and the power station decayed.

A year or so later I was sitting by Simon's hospital bed in St Mary's Paddington, with his partner Robert Davis. We were both in tears. I was talking to my unconscious friend, trying to comfort him, saying all the things that you say in these situations – that he needed to hang on, that everyone loved him.

It was no use. He slipped away as we watched. Simon died at

only forty-nine, his life cut short, as he knew it might be, by the residual damage to his lungs from an earlier bout of leukaemia. I think there are now five statues or memorials of him in London, more than most prime ministers. Quite rightly.

He was one of those politicians who get on and do things, in the most self-effacing way. As leader of Westminster Council he had been instrumental in driving forward the new academy programme, and it was a measure of the general respect in which he was held that he was knighted – though a Tory – by the Blair government.

He had helped me stabilise things in City Hall, after that rocky first few months. He tempered some of my crazier ideas, and helped deliver many others. In my grief, I wondered how we would cope without him – and so did many observers. It was perhaps part of his administrative legacy that, as things turned out, we were fine.

We were coming towards the end of my first term, and the mayoralty was really humming. The team was very strong – stronger, person for person, than Ken's – and we loved our jobs. Every day we came to work knowing that we were engaged in dozens, maybe hundreds, of projects to improve the lives of Londoners. We could see the progress we were making in the crime stats, the housing figures, the reduction in Tube delays, the air quality numbers. For all of us, I think the satisfaction and the fascination were intense.

Even though I sprinkled things with my usual quota of gaffes and goofs, that impression – of a frenzy of determined activity – must have somehow communicated itself to Londoners, because in May 2012 I was re-elected as mayor, to serve a second four-year term: not bad going, considering the Tories were then about fifteen points behind in London, and the national political context was an 'omnishambles' budget whose most memorable measure was a bitterly resented tax on Cornish pasties.

A few months later, we had overseen one of the most successful Olympic and Paralympic Games, and on billions of screens around the world that summer we were able to dramatise our message. This was the world's greatest city, a cheerful, welcoming multi-ethnic place where crime was low and falling, where the air was getting cleaner and where you would find a fast and affordable mass-transit system.

It is the job of any mayor to sell his or her city, but now we went stratospheric, criss-crossing the world on post-Olympic afterburners. In championing London to the global audience, I was blessed above all with a brilliant new deputy, Sir Edward Lister, silver-locked former veteran leader of Wandsworth Council, whose cost-cutting, tax-cutting approach had earned the admiration of Margaret Thatcher.

Eddie had all Simon's calm and tact, and an encyclopedic understanding of planning. He was also a trout-tickling master of the art of wooing investors. In the months after the Olympics we fared forth like Elizabethan navigators, with a very simple mission – to bring back booty to our city.

We went to Hong Kong and Australia, to India, the Gulf, America, Malaysia and wherever, frankly, we thought we would find an audience. We went to the top of Shanghai skyscrapers and toasted our generous hosts – *Kampai!* – with great tureens of Château Margaux. We went to camel races in Arabia and found ourselves then eating camel for dinner (one hump or two, as the waiter is supposed to have said).

The money rolled into London in a great unstoppable Nazaré-like wave of dosh, slooshing into the furthest reaches of the city. Within a year of the Games, we calculated that we had attracted a further £4 billion of commitments, in Croydon, the Royal Docks, the Olympic Park and every point of the compass. It was in this fulfilling and fertile period that I refined my thoughts about levelling up.

I believed in the market, of course; I believed in letting businesses and people decide how they were going to spend their money. But I also believed that in a globally competitive economy, when capital could go anywhere, you needed to hustle. You needed leadership. You needed someone who could tell the story about London, about Britain, about where we were going and exactly what our ambitions were – and Eddie and I found that we were good at it.

We knew that people had a short attention span. They wanted the elevator pitch. They wanted to know – why London? Why now? We had the answers. We also knew that when it comes to clinching a deal, the titans of the private sector will want to know one key thing: that you, the government, are also committed.

They want to know that you will use your levers, planning law, power supply, transport infrastructure to make the whole thing work, and we could show that, vividly. The biggest and most gripping example was the Olympic Park.

Modern history is full of post-Olympic disasters – buddleia-infested swimming pools, deserted stadiums, athletes' villages colonised by drug addicts and squatters. I was determined to make London the exception, and we did – on a scale that far exceeded even my own expectations.

In the years leading up to the Games, I was obsessed with this problem of 'legacy' – that after spending £9.3 billion on an athletics competition, we would actually leave something behind. We needed to show that we believed in the rhetoric about the transformation of east London; and that the post-Olympic Park would be a truly special new zone of the city – a magnet for the curious in Britain and across the world.

One cold Saturday morning in January 2009 I was sitting at home, staring at the plans for the park, and it hit me: this was all too functional, too sport-obsessed. There was nothing to bring the tourists, nothing to make you say, Cor, Doris, look at that – let's go to the Olympic Park. I remembered that in my childhood in Brussels, we had gone quite often to a swimming pool on the site of the 1958 World Fair, where for reasons best known to themselves the Belgians had constructed a giant steel model of a carbon molecule called the Atomium.

Whatever your views about the Atomium (I doubt it is accurate, as far as carbon molecules go), it put that part of Brussels on the map. What this vast Stratford site needed, I decided, was something similarly preposterous, something vertical. We needed a landmark – an exclamation mark! – to draw the eye. I talked it over with Tessa Jowell, one of those Labour ministers with whom it was possible to have a warm and friendly relationship, and soon she was confederate in my schemes.

The following week I was in a gents in Davos, and I spotted Lakshmi Mittal washing his hands. We had never met before, but I knew who he was and he knew who I was, and within seconds – I mean about forty-five seconds – he had agreed to provide the steel for a structure of some kind, something big.

But what? We held a competition. We formed committees. We looked at modern versions of Trajan's Column, Tatlin's Tower, a colossus of Stratford. Antony Gormley came within an ace of persuading us to give him untold millions to construct yet another public effigy of himself, a Gormley so vast that it would take you about an hour to tramp up Gormley's leg via Gormley's abdomen to Gormley's head, from which you would have a good view of everything from the Chilterns to the South Downs.

In the end we came up with the ArcelorMittal Orbit – which is a kind of exclamation mark with a question mark superimposed. This is now the largest piece of public art in Britain, and though it has its detractors it also has its fans, of whom, you will not be surprised to know, I am one.

It is a weird 120-metre fantasy in red steel, twisting and writhing asymmetrically above the site. After the Games we added a long silver curly-wurly slide, the longest tubular slide in the world. If you want to know what it feels like to be the bolus in the alimentary system of a gigantic red mutant trombone, go and zoom down the Orbit slide, which goes slightly faster than you really want to go.

The slide actually makes money, these days, but that wasn't the point of the ArcelorMittal Orbit. The point was to say: this is a destination. This is a new and different way of looking at what had been one of the most rundown parts of the city. We added a giant new cultural centre, which I grandly christened Olympicopolis. We got the Victoria & Albert Museum to build a V & A East; we imported Sadlers Wells, the great ballet company. The University of the Arts set up a campus, and so did Loughborough, the great sports university.

The BBC set up studios. The former media centre of the Games became a tech hub called Here East. Success bred success. There was no tumbleweed in the Olympic village – adorned at my behest with Periclean friezes. Every flat was sold and more and more were built as the Qataris piled in. A stone's throw from the stadium – a javelin's throw – a new academy was opened which was to have stunning success in getting local kids into Oxbridge.

Property values rose faster in those Olympic boroughs – Hackney, Newham, Waltham Forest – than anywhere else in London. Even as I write, more than ten years later, this project continues to accrete thousands more jobs and thousands more homes. Stratford Station has gone from being a backwater to being one of the busiest stations in Britain, because it brings together the Elizabeth Line, the Jubilee Line, the Central Line, the DLR and the Channel Tunnel rail link.

It was because we put in those fluid transport connections that the whole thing became viable, and the private sector felt confident to invest in the housing and the museums and the university campuses. And that – to get to the punchline of the sermon – was how we solved Battersea and other regeneration conundrums.

It was in that euphoric post-Olympic surge that Eddie and I got on a plane to Kuala Lumpur and did the deal with Prime Minister Najib of Malaysia. We did the trick that gave the Malaysian sovereign wealth fund the confidence to invest.

You remember the problem of the derelict power station, the vicious circle. You couldn't knock it down and yet you couldn't build enough homes to justify the expense of restoring it because there was no transport, and you couldn't justify spending billions on new Tube stations because there were no homes and no people.

Suddenly we had an idea, or rather, someone gave me an idea and we ran with it. It was called tax increment financing, and the gist is that you borrow against future tax revenues – council tax, business rates, stamp duties – from the properties that will be created as a result of the new transport links.

Of course it was speculative; it was taking a risk. But it was the heart of London, greatest city on earth. Surely it would work?

We went to the chancellor, George Osborne, and to his eternal credit he immediately said yes (whatever our other differences, our collaboration in London was both fun and hugely productive) – and that is why Battersea is now transformed.

Transport for London was given permission to borrow to extend the Northern Line, and it has worked. The power station has risen again and the dynamo is turning, and rather than producing sulphurous black smoke it is generating jobs and growth and homes; not 2,500 homes, as Wandsworth initially envisaged, but 25,000 and tens of thousands of jobs, including the UK HQ of Apple.

Already the tax income generated by those homes and offices is amply repaying the Treasury for the cost of the Northern Line Tube stations. The chimneys have been rebuilt; the art deco interiors lovingly restored. It is a phoenix-like rebirth, a triumph of cake-ism: both keeping a historic building AND allowing vast quantities of new development to go ahead.

As I came to the end of my time as mayor, there were all kinds of statistical data to show that we had levelled up. Across the city we had given 2,300 planning permissions, including for two hundred tall buildings, many of them taller than the tower at Canary Wharf.

In spite of the crash, we had kept the London economy moving along at a fair old lick and youth unemployment was the lowest for twenty-five years. In so many ways the things we did were disproportionately beneficial to the lower socio-economic deciles.

In bringing crime down by 20 per cent, and the murder rate down by 50 per cent, we helped the poor, because it is the poor who are disproportionately affected by crime. In reducing the numbers of people killed and seriously injured on the roads, we helped the poor – because it is the children of the poor who tend to die on the streets.

In reducing deaths by fire by 50 per cent as we did (this was before the terrible fire in the Grenfell flats), we helped the poor and the needy because statistically it is overwhelmingly those on low incomes who die in such domestic disasters as chip pan fires. Indeed, we made tragedies such as Grenfell much less likely in the future because we promoted high-quality materials in what was to be known as the New London Vernacular style.

Look around London and you will see the New London Vernacular in virtually every good new development since about 2011. The style consists of classically proportioned (or portrait-shaped) recessed windows and front doors opening to the street, and above all – like the Georgian and Victorian terraces – we insisted on brick. We set our faces against the horrible cladding that had been so ubiquitous hitherto, and so helped to make London more beautiful and less combustible.

By cutting air pollution, we helped the poor – because it is always the children of the poor who grow up near the heaviest traffic and the most polluted streets.

By the end of my eight years, the population of London had grown by about a million, but the whole city was richer. We started with four of the six poorest boroughs in the whole of the UK. We ended up with none of the bottom twenty. Life expectancy had increased by eighteen months for women and nineteen months for men, and there were parts of the Harrow Road where life expectancy at birth was ninety-seven years old.

What did they eat on the Harrow Road? I asked myself. Royal jelly and monkey glands? They were living longer than Caucasian hermits.

By the end, thanks in part to those successful Olympics, London was not just the most productive region in Europe; it was also the most visited city on earth, with 18.8 million visitors.

I loved the job, and had certainly improved as I went along. In my rational moments I thought that it would probably be better for everyone – self, family – if it was the last major job I did in UK politics. The trouble is that politics is addictive, and as the 2015 general election approached, there were suddenly people popping up in my office – kindly and well-meaning Tory MPs – who were saying I should have a crack at getting back into Westminster.

Eddie Lister agreed. He had just the place, said the supreme fixer. How about Uxbridge? he said.

I was tempted. The job in London had changed me. I had become far more serious, more fascinated by the intricacies of policy. In at least one important field, I had begun to change my mind.

Chapter 14

Copping Out in Copenhagen

From climate sceptic to believing in net zero

If you are one of those people who has never been troubled with doubts about climate change …

If you have been filled for the last thirty years with an adamantine certainty about the science …

If you have never once wondered whether it might all be a bit exaggerated …

If you have never looked at the falling snow, or slipped on the ice, and thought, Eh, what about global warming …

If you have never once been the teensiest bit irritated by the moralising of some of the eco-warriors …

If you have never cursed under your breath when stuck in traffic caused by Extinction Rebellion or Just Stop Oil supergluing their cheeks to the road …

… Then, my friends, this chapter is not really for you.

But if you have ears for a tale of scepticism and repentance; of how a cynic became an evangelist; of how I joined that now crowded thoroughfare of former doubters on the road to Damascus – then here it is.

This is how I found a way of reconciling my natural heretical instincts with the campaign to save the planet from disaster. It begins with the COP 15 summit in Copenhagen. I was there that fateful evening when it all went tits up.

My duties at the summit were light – I was ostensibly there to speak at a meeting of global cities. In reality I was there because the bright and idealistic young officials at City Hall were all determined that I should be there, because they all believed – I mean really BELIEVED – that this summit was essential for the future of our planet, that if it went wrong we were all guilty of a vast collective crime against posterity.

They were convinced in a way that I am afraid I wasn't – not in my heart, not yet.

So quite late in the evening on December 15, 2009, I wandered back into the Bella conference centre, well refreshed after dinner with the crown prince of Denmark, an excellent fellow – Hamlet without the dithering – and I could tell that something was up.

I am a veteran of summit cock-ups. I had been there in Rome in 1990, when the other European Community leaders had ambushed Margaret Thatcher with their plans for a European Monetary Union. I was there in The Hague when talks broke down between Milošević the Serb and Tudjman the Croat, and the war for Bosnia began.

You name it, I saw it: the juddering climax of the GATT world trade talks, John Major's ill-fated beef war with the rest of the EEC. I have covered them all.

I have seen the panicked look on the faces of the officials when they know that they can no longer paper over the cracks. I have chased them down the corridors with their compromises and their communiqués, full of language still in square brackets.

'What's going on?' I asked – with languid detachment. It was a disaster, I was told.

After a year of global negotiations, we seemed to have achieved nothing. The developing world was crying betrayal. The small island states were, it seemed, about to be dissolved like sugar cubes in rising warming waters.

The EU was blaming the Americans; the Americans were blaming the Chinese. I passed a room in which Barack Obama was said to be talking to the Chinese, and you could almost hear the blame bouncing back and forth like ping pong.

It was no use; it was after 11 p.m. The Conference of the Parties (COP) of the UN Convention on Climate Change was ending its fifteenth summit in chaos and disagreement. The only output was a vague statement to the effect that it would, on the whole, be a bad thing if the world continued on its current trajectory.

We deplored the fact that temperatures seemed set to rise another two degrees Celsius by the end of the twenty-first century. But what did we actually do about it? Zilch.

The world came to Copenhagen in the run-up to Christmas 2009 and twiddled its thumbs. We made no legally binding commitments to cut CO_2 by so much as a pint. We consigned future generations to disaster – ice-melt, habitat loss, desertification, mass movement of people.

Thousands of politicians and officials had enjoyed themselves on their expense accounts in that famously liberal capital, and for all they had actually done the earth was still on course to be sizzled up like a sausage; flash-fried, for all they cared, like a giant juicy steak in a plush Copenhagen restaurant.

Outside the summit there were tens of thousands of more or less crusty protesters, living in makeshift bivouacs and encampments, begging us to get our act together. Across the world there were millions, if not billions, of environmentalists young and old hoping, praying, that we would show some leadership.

We failed.

All sorts of people were responsible for the failure. The Americans should certainly have done more (imagine the vitriol from the world's liberal media if the US delegation had been led by, say, Donald Trump rather than Barack Obama). I am sure the Chinese could have offered more. And as for me, what did I do?

When the world stood on the brink of climate apocalypse – I went to the Thorvaldsens Museum to look at the sculptures. When the Copenhagen summit collapsed in acrimony, I just went to bed.

In explaining our failure, and my unforgivable apathy, I urge you not to ignore the obvious: the one big thing you would have noticed about Copenhagen that December. It was the weather. Snow had fallen, snow on snow, snow-ho-ho on snow, settling even on the green copper turrets of City Hall, made famous by *Borgen* and other great Danish TV shows. You didn't need a female detective in a sweater to tell you who killed the climate deal in 2009. It was staring us in the face.

Snow whirled in eddies through the tent flaps of the conference marquees. The snowmelt got into the welts of the delegates' shoes and chilled their toes, and when you looked at their shivering blue-lipped faces you could see that their hearts were not in it. We were holding a summit on global warming in what seemed like a mini-Ice Age. It was absurd. As for me, frankly, I was already politically traumatised by snow, and the awful power of cold weather.

It was only eleven months earlier that I had been sitting at my desk at home in Islington, quite late, on Sunday February 1, 2009. Hmmm, I thought to myself, staring out of the window – that's quite a dump. It was coming down in big asymmetrical flakes like shredded cotton wool. It was piling up in vertical crusts on the twigs and the rose bushes. When I woke up there was that wonderful muffled brightness that tells you today is going to be a special day, a snow day.

I slalomed off to the office on my bike, veering between icy compacted snow and slush, in what felt like an increasingly fool-hardy journey. When I arrived, exhausted by the effort of staying upright, I found that I was already under political attack. We had taken eight inches of snow in London, the most for twenty years, and at 4.32 in the morning the TfL controllers at Centre Comm had thrown in the towel.

The buses had been skidding and banging into cars with such regularity that they were all sent back to the garage; and there they stayed for the rest of the day. As my enemies were not slow to point out, this was almost unprecedented. It had not happened since before the Second World War. Ken Livingstone, my once and future opponent, was out on the airwaves, cachinnating away. 'Not even the Luftwaffe were able to stop London's buses,' he gloated. 'Boris Johnson has done it within a year of taking office.'

The general implication was that London's busmen, and their mayor, were themselves a bunch of snowflakes. As it happens, I think that was unfair, and that the decision to stop the buses was completely right. In the first few hours of the blizzard there had been thirty accidents involving buses alone. What were they supposed to do – wait for a bunch of kids to get mown down at a bus stop?

That week the snow paralysed the entire country. It shut 4,500 schools; it shut universities, and millions of people decided that on the whole they were going to stay at home.

Now if you were to tell me that when confronting a few inches of snow the Brits seemed a bit feeble by comparison with, say, a Scandinavian country, I would be forced to agree. We make a big fat fuss, when other countries take it in their stride. But if you accused Londoners – or the London mayoralty – of being abnormally pathetic by comparison with the rest of the UK, well, then I would take umbrage.

What were we supposed to do? We had covered the roads in beachfuls of grit. We had gritted (grat? grut?) again and again. As I told the House of Commons Transport Select Committee a few weeks later, it was absurd to expect me to stand on the top of City Hall and wave my arms, as if to repel the snowflakes.

I explained how our manic gritting and re-gritting had actually become counter-productive, as successive layers of snow and grit turned into a lethal icy lasagne. It was no reproach to TfL that they had stopped the buses, I said. They had taken the right operational decision and it would have been ridiculous of me to countermand it.

I then left the committee, having exceeded the forty-five minutes they requested, in what was described as an 'angry walk-out' but which was, of course, intended to be nothing of the kind. So I hope the reader will understand why in those first months and years of the mayoralty I was not yet perfectly conditioned, psychologically, to wage war on global warming.

I had been worried about the climate, all right; but I had been looking at the other end of the thermometer. I am afraid that the whole experience of 2009, from white hell in London to the farce of Copenhagen, had triggered my natural tendency to heresy. Global warming, I muttered as I clutched the handlebars and cycle-skated down an ice-bound City Road. Really?

Please don't misunderstand me. I am and always have been a fervent environmentalist, and like many of my generation I have been filled since childhood with horror and dread about what humanity is doing to the natural world. From the age of about eight – like so many others – I was a votary of Gerald Durrell. I wondered if I too, like the author, might become a naturalist. I spent one summer laboriously drawing pictures of life forms I found in the fields and streams of Somerset – caddisfly larvae and what have you. I truly mourned the loss of whales and all the other species being edged out of existence by humanity, and I strongly supported my father's maximalist approach to conservation.

My grandmother Bice once challenged him and asked him whether he would really sacrifice his own children to save the last breeding pair of tigers. I felt proud – if a bit sobered – when he said he would. Lose a few kids to save an irreplaceable species? Quite right.

In 1975 we all went to see *Jaws*, in one of the cinemas on the Avenue Louise in Brussels. When the house lights came up, my father (then an official in the EEC Commission's environment directorate) said loudly, 'I think it's terrible what they did to that shark.'

I laughed, but I could also see the point. As undergraduates, my sister Rachel and I drove around Spain as volunteers for the International Fund for Animal Welfare. We documented instances of cruelty to animals – drugged lions and chimps in the fairgrounds, ghastly carousels where fat children were plonked on tiny miniature ponies, the animals' backs bowed with the weight and their penises knotted so as to stop them urinating.

When I first met Michael Gove at Oxford, he claims that he asked me what political party I supported and I replied, 'I am a green Conservative.' It seems highly likely.

I was a green, I am a green – and yet I strayed, my friends. On the Big Science of Global Warming, I became at least temporarily a bit unsound.

To the embarrassment of my team at City Hall, I started listening to the sceptics. I found as ever that the devil had all the best tunes. Somehow I got on friendly terms with the Marxist conspiracist Piers Corbyn (long before his brother Jeremy became leader of the Labour Party), and even visited his Weather Action meteorological unit in Bermondsey.

According to Piers, who had a first-class degree in physics from Imperial, it was all to do with sunspots. Anthropogenic climate change was a hoax, he said, showing how often there is a confluence of conspiracy theories on the extreme left and right.

It was quite reasonable of me to worry about the snow, he said, and there was every chance of a new Ice Age. I didn't exactly endorse Piers, since my common sense told me he was a bit of a crank; but I gave him airtime in my *Telegraph* columns. And I went further. I actively collaborated with some of the sceptics and climate deniers in making fun of green power – comments that have not aged at all well. These windmills, I said in an article for the *Sun*: they wouldn't pull the skin off a rice pudding.

I likened them to 'some hideous Venusian invasion, marching over the moors and destroying the dales, colossal seaside toys plonked erratically across our landscape, an endless parade of waving white-armed old lunatics, gesticulating feebly at each other ...'

How could I have said it? How could I have been so wrong?

These days you will hear me championing the UK as the Saudi Arabia of wind power. Why was I so off-beam?

It was cussedness, really. I was impatient with the semi-religious aspect of the climate change thesis. I didn't like the howls of disapproval that greeted people like Matt Ridley or Nigel Lawson when they dared to differ. I was suspicious of the dogmatism and the zealotry of the climate change argument. I needed someone to take me to one side, calm me down, run through the science again and help me to a better understanding of the issue. Luckily, I had that person in Isabel Dedring.

Isabel is an American of German descent, a former McKinsey analyst and a brilliant eliminator of bullshit. She was the City Hall environmental adviser, and she rescued me from madness. She never really protested at my antics. She didn't object in meetings when I started quoting Piers Corbyn and ranting about a new Ice Age. She would sympathise; she would say she understood the doubts I was wrestling with, and she would go over it again – the effect of building up carbon in the atmosphere, the unprecedented speed with which it was happening, and the risk that we were creating a kind of lethal tea cosy around the world.

By this stage I was spending more time in planes looking down on the world, and I could see the ubiquitous impact of humanity. The risk of a man-made catastrophe seemed more and more plausible. We discussed for hours how the right environmental policies could actually add to economic growth – boost GDP, lift life chances, help levelling up. She understood my anxieties – my worry that it was all driven by middle-class angst and that it just meant higher bills for people on low incomes.

It didn't have to be that way, she argued. You could go green and actually cut costs.

I decided to take a Pascal's wager – and believe in global warming. You remember that the great French philosopher decides that the most sensible course for him is to believe in the Almighty. If I am wrong, he reasons, I lose nothing. If I am right, then I gain eternal bliss. And if I fail to believe, and it turns out that God does exist, then I am damned for eternity.

Over the years I have tried to construct a similar no-lose outcome for believing in global warming and campaigning against climate change. If we are wrong, we lose nothing. On the contrary, we reduce pollution, we encourage clean and sustainable technology and we create huge numbers of well-paid jobs in green industries.

If we are right, and we take the right measures, then we are also ensuring the salvation of much of the human race and the natural world as we know it. If we fail to believe, and we fail to act – then the risk is that we are damned.

Slowly, beneath the carapace of cynicism, I was pupating into a green evangelist. We campaigned for (and delivered) a cleaner, greener London, with hundreds of thousands if not millions more trees, more cycling, less pollution.

We hired Rosie Boycott – founder editor of the feminist magazine *Spare Rib* – as our food tsarina, and she launched a campaign to get Londoners to grow stuff. Soon hundreds of odd places – rooftops and roundabouts – were sprouting asparagus and runner beans. She set out to create 2,012 such spaces by 2012 – and succeeded.

I became a zealot for electric cars, long before they were really practicable. In 2009 we launched a campaign to give London 25,000 electric vehicle charging points, so as to banish range anxiety. I am afraid that by 2015 we had just 1,400, and most of them were unused or broken, like forgotten totem poles of a defunct religion.

I announced that London would have at least 100,000 electric vehicles – and yet by 2015 we had only 3,000. But I look at the traffic today – Tesla after Tesla – and I know that we at least made the start. I went to Beijing in 2008 and did a deal with Geely to create a spanking new electric black cab for London. Those cabs are now made in Coventry; they are on the street, and very good they look.

Over the eight years of the mayoralty we not only cut pollution, we massively cut greenhouse gases. The population of London rose. The GDP rose. The per capita GDP rose – and CO_2 output fell by about 24 per cent, almost entirely because of new and better technology. Having been a cynic, I became a believer, because I could see a way of going green that encouraged economic growth, that didn't mean a load of hair-shirt moralising, and that allowed levelling up.

It was twelve years after the Copenhagen summit collapsed around my dull and apathetic ears that I was actually the host of another make-or-break global powwow – the COP 26 in Glasgow. This time, though I failed to spot it, I faced a different political risk: not failure, but that the very measures we adopted – legally binding and radical – would alienate the increasingly vociferous climate sceptics in my own party.

Though I had moved in my views, many others had not.

There was one area where I disagreed with the eco-fundamentalists, and that was aviation. We are living in a globalised economy, where more and more freight goes by air, and where ever more people want to fly. There are still probably billions of people who have never even been on a plane.

The answer to the problem of CO_2 from planes is not to put air travel out of the reach of ordinary people, or to cut the number of flights. The answer is sustainable aviation fuel, and electric planes, and in places like London we needed more slots, not fewer.

Chapter 15

Some More
Radical Solutions

That are sadly still on the drawing board

Good morning, everyone, says the plane captain, sounding chipper. The good news is that we have made up some time, and in fact we are early.

You are on the red-eye coming in from New York and it seems the wind gods have puffed you ahead of schedule, carrying your jet so high and so fast on the Gulf Stream that a still-snoring England is already beneath you.

Down there is Oxfordshire, and a few minutes more and you will be in Slough – and then, *whooom*, down to Heathrow. No more time watch movie! No time brush teeth! Get act together!

You put your seat into the upright position, you do up your shoes and you think, Great. It's only 6.30 a.m. Maybe I will surprise my wife in bed. Maybe I will get to see the kids before they set off to school. Maybe I will have some extra time to prepare for that crucial meeting, and you sit, ears popping, jaw working, waiting to land; and after a while you look at your watch and you think, That's funny. When did he say we were landing?

You look out of the window. Surely those are the same reservoirs that we passed a few minutes ago; and as the plane banks and turns you realise, yet again, that you are in a holding pattern above

Heathrow. All your earliness is melting away as the Rolls-Royce engines spew pointless CO_2 and fumes into the upper air; and when you finally touch down, what do you find? That there isn't a stand ready! So you taxi around the apron, as it starts to get hot on board and the cabin is full of muffled exclamations and curses: connections being missed, appointments scrapped. That morning meeting, that breakfast with the kids – forget it.

You stormed over the Atlantic at virtually supersonic speed, so fast that you gained almost half an hour, and with this unexpected advantage you were going to attack the day, surprise your enemies and delight your friends. Instead, grrr, you are stuck in one of the greatest productivity bottlenecks in London and the whole UK – the shortage of runway space at LHR.

It's not the fault of the Heathrow staff. They do a phenomenal job with the slots they have. The problem is that the place is already operating at 98.5 per cent capacity, and it only has two runways. Paris has four. Frankfurt and Madrid also have four. The the last time I looked, Istanbul had five and Schiphol has six.

I was in the middle of my first mayoral campaign, back in 2008, when I hit on the solution. It was then the official position of the Conservative Party that there should never be a third runway at Heathrow. No ifs, no buts, said David Cameron. He even planted a tree, in his name, in the land where the third runway had been due – for decades – to be built; and in my view he was correct.

It was and is never going to happen, and it was the wrong place to build new capacity. It is not that I am, personally, allergic to aircraft noise. I went to school virtually under the flight path, in the days when 747s made a hell of a racket, and I don't remember it once affecting my concentration. It was just another part of the noise of the school day, like the clanging of Lupton's Tower or the barking of the master in College's dog.

There are plenty of other people who do mind, intensely. I had constituents in Henley-on-Thames – round about Binfield Heath

– who were driven crackers by early morning flights. Noise pollution is subjective, but it is also real.

I long ago recognised the truth: people who live in the general
neighbourhood of Heathrow are very happy with the logistical
advantage it gives them. They like to get there quickly in a taxi.
They are not averse to the extra soupçon it gives to the value of
their home. But they emphatically don't want more noise; they
don't want more planes.

It wasn't just west London. If you built a third runway, you
would be waking people up across the city – Camden, Islington,
Southwark, you name it: the casements would be rattling across
parts of London where people fondly imagine they are nowhere
near the flight paths. To build a third runway, you would not only
be knocking down a Norman village church, at Sipson, with all
the attendant hoo-hah.

You would be doing something that no other city would
contemplate – bringing more and more planes in to land in a route
directly above the main conurbation, because the prevailing winds
are westerly, from west to east, and planes fly into the wind to
land.

It would also be hopelessly short-term, since the third runway
would immediately be full and the clamour would begin for a
fourth.

It was madness, I decided, and since it was never going to
happen, I had to find the solution. I did. It was, and is, a beautiful
idea.

Across the world great cities have moved their main airport to
gain space and to minimise noise and congestion, and they have
often, like Hong Kong and Singapore, solved the problem of noise
pollution by building where no one lives at all – on reclaimed land
on the edge of the sea.

The solution to the chronic problem of Heathrow – obvious
once it hit me – was to revisit the plan that the incoming Labour

government had wrongly dumped in 1974. It was time to revive the Thames Estuary Airport. The advantages were overwhelming. You could have multiple runways. You could land around the clock.

You would create a vast multi-mode transport hub to the east of London, sea port and airport combined – with a tidal barrage to develop your green power – and you would enable fantastic development in some of the most rundown parts of east London, Kent and Essex, a region that had long been known as the Thames Gateway. With a high-speed rail line, you could be in central London in half an hour – far quicker than taking a taxi from Heathrow to Westminster.

To cap it all, you would be able to release the entire site of Heathrow Airport – an area bigger than the Royal Borough of Kensington and Chelsea that already had some of the best transport connections and infrastructure in the south-east. Think of the housing you could build! Think of the hope you could give to young people currently locked out of the London market.

It was one of those campaigns that began as a slow burn. I got Doug Oakervee, a craggy and distinguished engineer in his seventies, to look at the options, and one day in early 2009 we all found ourselves on a dredger, going slightly green about the gills, somewhere off the coast of Kent.

The sea was grey and choppy. Strange rusted structures, looking a bit like Martians, prodded from the waves – some relic of 1940s counter-invasion measures, I was told. What would we do about them? Not far off was the wreck of the SS *Richard Montgomery*, a Liberty ship that ran aground and broke up in the Second World War and still contained 1,400 tonnes of high explosive.

If that went off, I was told, we would shatter every window from Sheppey to Southend. What would we do about that? The whole thing looked pretty unpromising and the BBC transport correspondent, an otherwise fair-minded chap, was able gently to satirise our plans. They called it 'Boris Island'. They said it was fanciful, even delusional. But among Tory MPs, the idea was starting to catch on.

London MPs disliked the third runway at Heathrow, because of the noise and the fumes and the extra traffic it would bring. Some Essex MPs could see the potential for growth in the Thames Gateway. Bernard Jenkin, then the MP for Colchester, rang with encouragement, and I simply crooned to him, down the line, the great Dolly Parton-Kenny Rogers duet.

> Islands in the stream
> That is what we are
> No one in between
> How could we be wrong?
> Sail away with me
> To another world, etc.

How could we be wrong? I asked my team. No one had a better solution. The new Tory-led coalition government was still against the third runway. What else were we going to do?

No one wanted more planes over any inland site. My campaign sputtered along for a while, and then we had the 2012 Olympics, and suddenly people had a new confidence, a sense that perhaps we really were a can-do kind of place. Other countries were all building colossal new airports away from city centres. Why were we being held back by this ancient planning dispute over Heathrow?

The Olympics had shown that we could build on a big scale and whatever else people thought of me, they had the impression that I could get things done – and fast. New bikes, new bus, Crossrail on the way. I had even built a new cable car across the Thames, from Greenwich to the Royal Albert Docks.

Like so many of my projects, this had its detractors. But I say phooey. It's beautiful, it's perfect for romantic assignations. It's used by about 1.5 million people a year, and the numbers are climbing steeply again after the pandemic, up 200,000 year on year. The key feature of the cable car, for me, is that it was built in such record time. It was conceived in 2010 and opened in time for the Olympics – perfectly linking two sets of venues, at Greenwich and the ExCel Centre. In the first week of the Games, I took Arnold Schwarzenegger up for a ride and we surveyed the glories of Canning Town beneath us.

'Very naaice,' he said.

It was in that moment of post-Olympic confidence that people really began to pursue the idea of a knock-out new airport, and precisely because it had started to catch on, and because they could not think of a viable alternative, the government came up with a brilliant plan to kill it.

They formed a committee. George Osborne asked Sir Howard Davies, one of this country's great all-purpose Balliol panjan-drums, to study the question of airport capacity in the south-east and to come up with a solution AFTER the 2015 general election.

Howard had sustained a minor ding on the bonnet when it was discovered that the London School of Economics, which he was then running, had been taking money from Muammar al-Gadd-afi, the Libyan dictator and sponsor of terror. I thought at the time that it was most unfair to blame him for this, since the British government had been pursuing a pretty craven policy towards Gaddafi's Libya; but he had stepped down from the LSE none-theless, and I reckon he probably took on the Airports Commission as a kind of penitential act.

He was always decent and thorough, and went through the motions of considering the options. But his purpose was simple – to come down in favour of the solution the Treasury wanted in the first place, viz. the third runway at Heathrow.

Howard Davies was there to help Cameron execute a graceful U-turn, and it was really naive of me to believe otherwise. In the course of an enjoyable lunch early in his deliberations (which took about three years), he told me the trouble with my idea.

'It's just not British,' he said. 'It's not the way we do things.'

I asked him to explain.

When you look at the way we develop things, he said, whether towns, roads, rail, airports, whatever, we don't do a big bang. We do things piecemeal, bit by bit. We don't like taking giant steps. That's what they do in places like France, where things are more *dirigiste*.

There is a deep truth in what he says. It is both a great national strength: a tendency to be cautious, incremental, empirical, to build only where the market shows there is an interest or a need. It is also a grave potential hindrance.

Sometimes, when it comes to solving massive problems of spatial development, you really do need to be bold. To build Crossrail – to connect Berkshire and Essex and Kent – you really do need to build a giant tunnel under London. To deliver the Olympics, you really did need to clear a giant site in east London.

When Bazalgette built the sewers in the nineteenth century, he took the diameter of the tunnels that they asked him to dig – and doubled them; because he was thinking about the future, and he was right. Sometimes we need that approach in UK infrastructure today.

When I left City Hall in 2016, I had far exceeded the record of my predecessor in home-building, in spite of the recession, and that housing was made possible at least partly by our frenzied investment in transport links.

As the time drew near for me to go, I saw more and more clearly what needed to be done and the scale of the solutions required. If London was going to remain the greatest city on earth, and to lengthen its lead, we needed to sort out the traffic, without further clobbering of the motorist. I had a beautiful plan to take between 10 and 20 per cent of the cars off the surface roads.

We were going to use new tunnelling techniques to bury the north and south circular roads, massively improving journey times in London, creating new parks and new homes in the space released above ground, and sending electric vehicles through the tunnels.

I had launched Crossrail Two, or the Churchill Line as I hoped it would one day be called. It was going to be even bigger than the Elizabeth Line, a new underground railway that went from Chelsea to Hackney. At a stroke it would solve all the congestion on the trains coming into Waterloo from the south-west, and it would allow the development of hundreds of thousands of good homes on the brownfield sites of the Lee Valley corridor.

It was only when I was looking at the detail that I noticed the main bore of one of the tunnels went directly beneath 20 Colebrooke Row, which was my home. I think this was an accident rather than some joke at my expense by the TfL planner, but it did make the house rather more difficult to sell.

Among the many other things I was forced to leave on the drawing board in those last few months was the Garden Bridge, on which my successor was to spend another £17 million before cancelling it. It was a pity, because it was a truly beautiful scheme, and every city must keep doing new and interesting things. But never mind.

To solve the problem of aviation capacity, to fix Heathrow – that was a massive prize, and there we were thwarted. To regenerate the Thames Gateway, to create the greatest logistics hub in Europe, and to deliver jobs and growth to an area that had never recovered since the collapse of the London docks – that would have been levelling up on a huge scale. Think of it, next time you are hovering above London like a disconsolate condor –

circling and circling in the hope of a slot, like a car in the Waitrose car park on a Saturday morning.

We are being left behind. We need those direct flights to cities in Latin America and Africa, because it is the access to direct flights that can make all the difference to trade and investment decisions. Why come to London if you are going to have to change at Frankfurt or Madrid or Amsterdam? Global Britain needs those direct connections to the rest of the world, and the only way to be sure of those connections is to have enough runway space in the same place; and the only way to do that is to have a great global hub.

I expect that Labour will have another crack at the third runway at Heathrow. I doubt they will succeed. There is only one place with the potential to be a truly environmentally friendly long-term hub for the UK – and that is in the estuary.

The idea will come back, as with Crossrail and the Channel Tunnel and the M25, all of which took many decades, if not (in the case of the Channel Tunnel) centuries; and time, logic and geography will one day make it happen.

So in 2015 I fought the general election in Uxbridge, and thanks partly to things I had been able to do for outer London, and also thanks to the high reputation of the local Conservative Council, led by Sir Ray Puddifoot, I was comfortably elected. By this stage it would be fair to say that I had a good political reputation.

We had done an awful lot in London, and as a municipal government were leading the country in all sorts of areas, from cutting homelessness to promoting music in schools. I was thought to be a pretty liberal kind of Tory, and indeed I had championed such controversial reforms as gay marriage.

At one Pride Dinner at Brown's Hotel I announced that we would be hosting these new ceremonies in the Olympic Park, so that the registrar would be able to bring the service to a climax by informing the happy couple: 'You may now take your partner up the ArcelorMittal Orbit' (at which I am afraid some Labour MPs, led by Angela Eagle, walked out).

At any rate, there was a time when I could have gone to a north London dinner party and not have been pelted with focaccia. I wouldn't say that polite metropolitan opinion loved me, but they thought on the whole that I wasn't too bad.

What they had not been reading, of course, was my vast twenty-year back catalogue of articles about the European Union.

Part Three

Confessions of a Eurosceptic

Chapter 16

Prawn Cocktail Flavour Crisps

And their part in the debate on UK sovereignty

At a certain moment in our call, I detected a note of asperity in the voice of the Commission official – a dash of impatience. It was getting on for going home time, and she probably yearned to be elsewhere.

She didn't want to spend another second being pumped by some thuggish British journalist. She tried to bring the conversation to a close with what she perhaps imagined was the decisive argument. I could almost see her finger wagging as she sat in her office in the Berlaymont building, Brussels, HQ of the EEC (as it then was) Commission.

'But it's not good for children to eat those crisps,' she said; and at that moment I admit that I saw red – as red as the erythrosine dye that goes in a Danish frankfurter, which the Commission was also in the process of banning. I started to get mildly cross.

I really couldn't believe it was true, but from what this official in the single market directorate was saying, there was no getting round it. They were actually going to ban the prawn cocktail flavour crisp. It was a national delicacy, I told her. For decades, I explained, it was what you ate – either that or pork scratchings – with a pint of bitter in the pub.

Now this health-conscious nanny-figure in Brussels had decided that British children were quite spherical enough already – and, pow, that was it. She had substituted her own discretion for that of the UK government. She had ignored the British Food Standards Agency, which could find no scientific basis for her concerns.

She had overruled the various UK government ministers – including David Maclean, a very nice man who went on to be the Tory chief whip – even though they were elected members of Parliament who expressed the sovereign will of the British people. With a snap of her fingers, she had prohibited an entire class of comestibles – eliminating a harmless British tradition with the random senselessness of a poppy felled by a passing scythe.

It wasn't just crisps. It was everything produced with a certain kind of sweetener. They had all fallen foul of single market directive 91/71/EEC. They were getting rid of the sweeteners in Worcestershire Sauce. They were getting rid of the sweeteners in traditional British sweet and sour pork.

They were attacking our takeaways! And our bloody Marys! It was a wholesale assault on our culture. I was nettled, partly because it seemed so unnecessary and also – though it still pains me to admit it – because I had been scooped. Someone else, probably the legendary Geoff Meade of the Press Association, had broken the story of the assault on the prawn cocktail flavour crisp. I was in the humbling position – in which no journalist likes to find themself – of being asked by the foreign desk in London to 'stand it up'; to check whether or not it was true, and so I had no particular motive to believe it.

Really? I said to myself, when I read that the Commission was planning to ban this vinegary pinkish staple of the national diet. Surely they wouldn't be so crazy.

It was May 1991 and I was sitting at my desk in Square Marie-Louise, looking out at an ornamental lake and some of the finest art nouveau houses in Europe. I was the European Community Correspondent (or sometimes Common Market Correspondent) of the *Daily Telegraph*, a position I had held, with an ever-tighter grip, since the age of twenty-four.

I was, by now, quite experienced in the doings of the Commission, and this prawn cocktail crisp story – well, it should have been mine. I took pride in reading the small print of the euro-bumf and working out the implications. Already, thanks to me, *Telegraph* readers had learned of Brussels' madcap plans to harmonise everything in our mortal passage through this world, from the euro-condom, where the Italians were offended by what we in the media gleefully presented as Brussels strictures over the inadequacy of the dimensions of their prophylactics (too narrow), to the euro-coffin, where the Commission was sensibly trying to formulate minimum standards for the trans-frontier shipment of human remains.

I had revealed some of the barmier logic of the EU's Common Agricultural Policy, according to which every food product had to be categorised and fitted into a regime. Snails were fish, I told the marmalade-dropping *Telegraph* readers, and carrots were fruit, because they could be made into jam. I discovered that Brussels was trying to harmonise standards for manure, with a ruling on 'the maximum permissible odours for farmyard compounds'.

It all sounds pretty innocuous stuff, and it was. These stories were just the logical by-product of a gigantic effort to create a single European market, so that across the whole territory of the EEC, with 340 million citizens, goods, people, services and capital could move freely and with the assistance of common or mutually recognised standards. It was in many ways a practical, business-friendly ambition, or should have been.

So why, apart from the professional embarrassment of being scooped, was I indignant about the fate of the prawn cocktail flavour crisp? Let me explain.

In the two years I had been in Brussels, the story had changed and grown. When I arrived in March 1989, the Belgian capital was felt to be a bit of a journalistic backwater. The general view among my colleagues was that I would have some fine lunches, but that my despatches were unlikely to make it to the front page. My predecessor as *Telegraph* correspondent was an amiable man who actually contrived to live in Southend – or at least he returned there every weekend – and I found the pace of Brussels life, to begin with, by no means pressured.

There was no mobile phone, no internet. I had a wonderful Flemish secretary called Therese, who shielded me from my employers while I 'made contacts', or had long lunches, at the expense of Conrad Black, our generous proprietor. At one stage the *Telegraph* foreign desk got so fed up with my general elusiveness that they demanded I should have a pager.

Therese brilliantly prevaricated, eventually killing the plan by showing that Belgacom would have to construct a thirty-foot mast on top of the office. Then history speeded up, and I found I was trying to drink from the spouting hydrant of the biggest running story in politics.

It seems hard to believe nowadays, but when I went to Brussels there were horrendous rules that prevented east Europeans from leaving their own countries. In the middle of Berlin there was still a wall, with barbed wire and machine gun nests, which stopped Berliners from moving around their own city. There was a vast and bitter ideological confrontation between the two halves of the continent.

On one side were the western European countries that tended to be members of the EU or Nato or both, and on the other side was the communist bloc, and the difference between the two, in quality of life, was becoming more and more painfully evident.

Our shops sold things we wanted to buy; theirs didn't. We had BMWs; they had the foul old two-stroke Trabants. We had the

Lavazza coffee; they had weird ersatz potions made of chicory. We had soft bog roll; they had that greasy tracing paper you used to get at school.

It couldn't last, but in the way of these things, no one expected it to collapse like it did. In the summer of 1989, a great picnic was staged at the border of Austria and Hungary; and suddenly the crowds were ignoring the shouts of the guards and moving over the frontier – East Germans going west in a great unstoppable tide of freedom.

A few months later, in November, they attacked the wall itself, and I watched the TV footage of these joyful Germans tearing it apart and felt a surge of pure gladness. It was over – all that horrible spine-prickling Soviet threat, the fear of a nuclear holocaust that had loomed over my childhood.

We had won! And without firing a shot. Freedom, capitalism, democracy – they appeared to have won. At once, far sooner than anyone had predicted, we faced the logical consequence. If German friends and family could be united, then Germany must be reunited, whatever the wartime generation might think. If you had asked my grandfather James, who had fought in the war, he would have told you bluntly: Germany must never be reunited (and he went on to become president of the European Commission for Human Rights, so he was hardly illiberal). His apprehensions were widely – and in my view quite wrongly – shared around Europe.

West Germany was already the most populous and economically powerful country in Europe. A reunited Germany would be even stronger, people said, and it would resume its old dominance of central and eastern Europe. There had to be an answer.

The French had one. The solution was 'Europe', they said, and everyone started adapting the old Thomas Mann dictum – that you either had a European Germany or a German Europe. The answer was to create a European Germany by rapidly accelerating and intensifying the hitherto somnolent process of European integration.

The plan was to lock Germany up, tie Germany down, and generally bind Germany in with the great web of EU legislation. The first and most important goal was to take away Germany's monetary dominance of Europe by abolishing the Deutschmark in favour of a single European currency – then thought likely to be called the Ecu, which was both an acronym for European currency unit and also (conveniently) a medieval French coin.

Under the inspirational leadership – by any standards – of a former French finance minister called Jacques Delors, the Commission came up with a three-stage plan, culminating with the creation of a European central bank and the extinction of the DM, the franc, the lira, the guilder and every other participating currency, including the pound sterling. At the same time the old plan for creating a single market was given new political urgency and a new treaty was planned, what was to become the Maastricht Treaty – later souped up at Lisbon and Amsterdam – in which national vetoes would be done away with for most areas of legislation, and by which European countries would embark not just on economic and monetary unification, but political union as well.

The old gold-on-blue twelve-star flag (nicked by the EEC from the Council of Europe) became more and more prevalent in the general agitprop; there was a new mauve European passport, and the concept of European citizenship was born. Brussels bumper stickers started to carry the slogan 'Europe – mon pays'.

Of the twelve members of the European Economic Community (as it still was – it only became the European Union by the Treaty of Maastricht in December 1991), most were more or less enthusiastic for this programme. The French liked it, because they saw it as a sensible response to a potentially recrudescent German dominance, and they were confident that their skilled international bureaucrats could manage the EU institutions – as Delors was doing with such genius – in the interests of France.

The Benelux countries – Belgium, the Netherlands, Luxembourg – were keen for more or less the same reasons. They had bitter memories of the wartime Reich, and they certainly wanted a European Germany rather than a German Europe. The Italians were fervently enthusiastic for anything that was presented as European integration, mainly because their own post-war political history had been so chaotic.

The Spanish, the Portuguese and the Irish were still at the stage when they were heavily dependent on European structural or regional funding, and in so far as 'more Europe' meant more money, they were certainly in the market.

The Danish population was basically heroically sceptical and independence-loving; but they were only six million, and their politicians tended to go with the European flow.

As for the Germans themselves, some of them were a bit anxious, to begin with, about the idea of a single currency. How could you do it without a single fiscal policy? they asked. What if people (the Italians, the French) borrowed and spent too much? They didn't want to be responsible for all of Europe's debts. But fundamentally Chancellor Kohl – that vast tripe-eating Rhinelander – was all for it. He could see that he had been called by history to make a giant bargain. Germany would be permitted to unite, but as a final act of expiation for the nationalist horrors of the Second World War the Germans would simultaneously abandon their proudest post-war possession, that symbol of their post-war economic stability and success – the almighty Deutschmark – and enter joyfully into this great multiple marriage.

There were also plenty of Germans who saw the large economic advantage to Germany of being generally the most effective manufacturing power in a single currency zone, where other countries could no longer devalue their way back into a competitive position (and if you want proof that these German single currency enthusiasts were right, then look at what has happened to the Italian car industry – blitzed, at least partly, because they now priced in euros and could no longer sell with a falling lira).

Of the twelve countries round the table at those great foundational summits, from 1989 to 1991 – from Strasbourg to Maastricht – there was only one that had serious reservations. There was only one that felt a bit queasy about the birth of a federal Europe. There was only one leader at Strasbourg who was not remotely stirred by the idealism of a single European currency; indeed who viscerally disliked it. She had a handbag and pineapple-coloured hair, and her position had not shifted by the time of the Rome summit of October 28, 1990.

'No, no, no,' said Margaret Thatcher to the Delors vision for a federal Europe. Within days of this outburst she was gone, felled by MPs who had long been plotting to remove her and for whom her 'obduracy over Europe' was as good a pretext as any.

On the day she resigned, it is said (by Marina) that I was to be seen stumbling tearfully down Rue Stevin, in the neighbourhood of the Commission, protesting bitterly at the cowardice and treachery of her MPs. I am not sure about the tears, but I did think it was an injustice.

Thatcher had campaigned to join the EEC in the 1970s, but now I thought broadly that she was right to be sceptical. In that extraordinary period, when the political map of Europe had changed so fast, I read and thought a lot about the history of our continent: about nations, and nationalism, and national feeling; and more particularly about whether Britain was cut out to be part of a United States of Europe.

I concluded that there was much to admire and to love about all other European countries and cultures, and that there was plenty that was noble about the European project, but that in the end this federal vocation – especially the single currency – was not for us.

We just did not share the end goal, what they call the *finalité politique*, of a perfect European Union. We forget – years after voting to leave – that being in the EU is not like being in a club with a load of fixed rules. It is dynamic, a one-way ratchet always clicking forwards.

It is being in a club of nations that are constantly changing the rules of their association so as to resemble something more and more like a single state, with ever more powerful centralised political institutions and an all-pervasive legal system enforced by an incontrovertible European court whose very purpose is teleological – to create a European Union.

I couldn't see how this was really compatible with British independence, or with democracy. We had our own political institutions and, unlike those of many European countries, they had stood the test of time. They had lasted a thousand years, more or less, and they had not been destroyed or humiliated by the events of the twentieth century.

As a people, the Brits did not conspicuously burn with Euro-enthusiasm. There was no hunger that I could see to be part of a great supranational enterprise. And why were we in Britain supposed to be especially cognate with this particular group of eleven countries on the end of the Eurasian landmass?

What about the Commonwealth? What about America and Australia and Canada and New Zealand? Surely we aspired to be citizens of the world, not just citizens of Europe. It felt a bit culturally supremacist, a bit surreptitiously racist. As for the logic of 'locking in' Germany – the main justification, given by Delors and the French, for the hysterical acceleration of EEC integration – I suspected that it was all baloney.

I didn't really believe in the 'threat' from modern Germany, and still don't; and it seemed perverse to try to solve one potential problem, of undemocratic German influence on the rest of Europe, by creating another and much greater problem – the undemocratic influence of EU institutions on everyone in Europe.

Of course, there were plenty of others who secretly or openly shared our doubts; but it was only Thatcher who really had the courage to challenge it all. So the UK became the backmarker. We became the bad guys, the party poopers, the people holding the project back. We always seemed to be saying no, and I disliked the way our objections were turned into some kind of moral and political failing.

Our beaches were dirty, our drinking water was substandard, our employees were slave-driven, our chocolate should really be called vegelate – and now I was being told that our prawn cocktail flavour crisps were so unhealthy that they should be banned; and whether or not the directive was a cock-up (as the Commission now likes to claim), the fact is that I know they wanted to ban them, and frankly they would have gone ahead and done it if there had not been such a fuss in the UK media.

Most journalists and politicians go to Brussels from the UK and find that they 'go native'. They get caught up in the great campaign to build a European future. I drifted in the opposite direction. I deeply disliked, and still do, the idea that this country can be systematically told what to do by other countries in a process that is neither transparent nor democratic.

I came to believe that the quest for European Union was basically a Freudian wish-fulfilment dream, a continuous attempt to rediscover the lost childhood of our continent – the great peaceful unity of the Roman Empire, when goods, people, services and capital certainly did move freely and there was a single citizenship from Portugal to Iraq, from Denmark to Algeria.

Years later I wrote a book on the various attempts to recreate the Dream of Rome. I concluded that it certainly can work, but only if you have an all-powerful central authority. Rome's success depended, among other things, on the use of systematic military violence, common taxation, common languages and a cult of emperor worship.

The European Union was obviously very different and much less ferocious. But it was still trying to create a single political identity in a way, I decided, that was not for us; and so, in reality, did all the UK prime ministers who followed Mrs Thatcher. John Major fought tooth and nail to keep Britain out of the euro and was very proud that he had fended off UK participation in the 'social chapter' of workers' rights.

We were always the reluctant Europeans, always half-in, half-out, always claiming that we could get the 'benefits' of the single market while abjuring the federalist ideology. It was a chronic incoherence – and resolving that incoherence would be painful. To a degree that I had not foreseen, many British people had become quietly and perhaps even subconsciously Europeanised.

When I first heard Jacques Delors' ideas for European citizenship I thought it was ridiculous, a gimmick. But many people liked it, just as they liked the idea of 'dividing their time' between Scotland and the Dordogne, or Norfolk and Greece.

They liked the idea of an identity that was bigger and somehow more generous than being narrowly British. I underestimated all that.

I write these words in a lovely Oxfordshire village, where the European flag flies over some of the homesteads, like despairing fifth-century owners of Romano-British villas still paying lip-service to their bust of the emperor, long after the legions have sailed back to Rome (come to think of it, the twelve-star flag has sometimes been thought to be a nod to the old necklace of the twelve Caesars that was worn by some ultra-loyal citizens).

The truth is that then as now we were a divided people, and then as now elite Romano-British opinion was very different from the popular prejudice.

I never imagined how fractious it would all become if we were forced to make a binary choice, or how much obsessive importance would be attached to my own view on the matter.

So that's how I became a prey to doubts about Britain and the EU. It was a scepticism hardened and tempered by watching British ministers come out to Brussels, time after time, and claiming to have won some kind of 'victory', while all the time we knew that EU integration was continuing unabated and that the UK was being dragged remorselessly along.

As an EU diplomat put it at the time, 'Great Britain protests, but in the end she always signs up.' I became convinced that most British officials were complicit in what the journalist Hugo Young called 'This Blessed Plot' – the covert campaign to keep the UK locked in the EEC, whatever the expostulations of British MPs or the UK public.

As my pieces became more provocative, I began to be identified by the rest of my friends in the UK press corps as a bit of a renegade. At one point the secretary-general of the EEC Commission, a UK national called Sir David Williamson, announced that they were boycotting me. 'Sorry,' he said, 'we don't talk to the *Telegraph*.'

The UK minister for Europe, Tristan Garel-Jones, said that I was a 'thug'. Douglas Hurd, the foreign secretary, complained in fairly strenuous terms – I later gathered – to Max Hastings, editor of the *Telegraph*.

In about 1993 I was summoned back to see my esteemed editor, who had batted away Hurd's protests. I was still, then, a protégé. Max had his feet on the desk and was smoking a cigar.

'I don't want you to become – phwah – you know – like one of those people with small feet.' I wasn't sure exactly who he meant, but I got the gist. He didn't want me to become a Eurosceptic. It was a bit late.

So when it came to making a choice about Britain's EU membership, I had a very long record of illuminating – sometimes quite caustically – the fundamental problem, which is the lack of democracy.

Chapter 17

Voting Leave

The fork in the road

It was Saturday February 20, 2016, and I was sitting on my own in our farmhouse near Thame, trying to think. The sun was going down; the cold was starting to seep through the old timbers of the building. The fire had gone out and stubbornly refused to reignite. My spirits were sinking with the thermometer.

Come on, I said, trying to cudgel myself into action. I had to write the goddamn piece, to be published on Monday, in the *Telegraph*, and above all I had to make my so-called mind up.

Get on with it, brain, I said. No more pussy-footing, shilly-shallying and generally dickering around. For years and years, I had flirted with the idea that Britain could leave the EU. I had batted my eyes at what was now increasingly known as Brexit, and now, finally, the moment of consummation was upon us. Did I have the guts? I had sat on the fence for so long, as the saying goes, that the iron had entered my soul.

I was choked, stuck, blocked – and it didn't help that my phone was ringing every other minute, with people urging me, begging me and cajoling me to come out for Remain. So many people that I loved and cared about seemed to have been tasked with lobbying me that weekend.

Don't do it, said Hugo Dixon, one of my oldest and dearest friends. We had known each other since the age of about eleven; had been in College together at Eton, and then at Balliol. Don't go for Brexit, he said. You'll be signing up with Farage and the xenophobes. You might as well tender your resignation from the human race.

Don't go for Brexit, said Ben Wallace, a close political friend and ally. It's just not you. Don't do it, Al, said Rachel, Leo, Jo and my father Stanley. Let's stay in! Nicholas Soames – whose father had been the UK's first Brussels commissioner – pleaded with me to see sense.

'If you vote Remain, I promise I will be your campaign manager for party leader,' he said.

It's not like that, Nick, I groaned.

And then there were my friends on the Eurosceptic side of the argument, ringing to check that my nerve was holding firm.

In the end I got so badgered and bothered that I switched my phone off. Before boiling it all down to about a thousand words, I tried to tabulate the pros and cons of EU membership – as many of us do with big choices. It felt weirdly as though it wasn't just my decision, because there were so many readers whose thinking I could help.

If anybody knew the answer to this bloody question, I told myself, it might well be me. I had lived a long time in Brussels – two stretches, as a child and a journalist. I knew it all inside out, had seen it change and grow. I knew the arguments and the facts. Plus I had my instincts about what to do – so come on!

I marshalled my points, for and against, and had soon built an overwhelming case for Leave. There was the economics. Never mind the cost of the UK contributions – about £20 billion net per year. No one could say that the process of European integration was a triumph for growth and jobs.

We sceptics had been proved right about the euro. Even if it had been helpful for Germany, the single currency had been little short of disastrous for many other European countries. The Greeks had been forced into all kinds of humiliations – selling off their assets at knockdown prices to the Germans; and I had been appalled, when I took the family on a New Year holiday to Granada, to see the level of youth unemployment in Spain.

It was true that the UK was outside the euro, but we were still part of the giant regulatory project – and those high non-wage costs were surely one of the reasons for the anaemic growth in the entire continent.

Why did we need to be part of an economic government of Europe? It was absurd that EU Commission officials should be using our own money to fund roads and bridges in Wales. It was mad that a mayor of London should be able to build a cable car with an £8 million contribution from the EU's 'regional funds'. I mean, I was very grateful to Commissioner Hahn, the twinkly-eyed Austrian politician who had approved the donation on a visit to City Hall. But it was still mad.

It wasn't the job of Brussels to care about regional development in Britain. It was the job of British politicians. It was our job to bring our society together, to level up.

Who is my brother? the Bible asks us. I suppose that the answer is the whole of the rest of humanity. But for British voters and British taxpayers our first duties are to the rest of the sixty-seven million, and the ideology of the European Union seemed to be that no, there was a new polity, a new loyalty, a new citizenship of 510 million people – and our duty was to all of them.

In so far as some people did buy into this concept of European citizenship, I felt that it was a weakening of the ties that should bind the nation; a weakening of the Union of the parts of the United Kingdom (as we saw, perhaps, during the Scottish referendum in 2014), a weakening of the basic solidarity that should exist between all of us as British people.

I didn't see how in the long run it could make sense. At some stage it would blow up; better for Britain to quit before it was too late.

In the course of that evening I rang Marina, my wife in 2016. I had known her longer than I had known any other contemporary. I had known her in Washington when I was four years old. She had been with me at the European School in Uccle. There are few people less xenophobic or more sensible. I am not sure that she has ever voted Conservative, except possibly for me as mayor, though I never had the courage to ask.

She had told me that she was also inclining towards Leave. I took this very seriously. She had a degree in European law; she had practised law in Brussels. For her, as for me, there was this sense of – if not now, when?

We were faced with the endless judicial activism of the European Court, the continual expansion of the empire of EU law – a special type of law that could never be repealed or amended by the UK Parliament. In a democracy, the people in charge – the people who make the laws – must be able to answer the old Tony Benn question: Who elected you? Who put you in authority over me, and how can I remove you from office?

Under the EU system there was no way UK voters could really choose their lawmakers, and no way they could remove them from office; and they frankly didn't have a clue who most of them were. It was becoming too remote, too centralised. Fortified by Marina, I began to write.

I must ask you to accept what my opponents have so often disputed: that my arguments, that evening, were not somehow manufactured out of narrow considerations of political advantage. In fact, the truly opportunistic thing would have been to go for Remain. You have to remember that the Remain campaign had the support of all the main political parties; it had the support of virtually the entire British establishment, the broadcasters, the CBI, the business world, and so on.

It was also thought overwhelmingly likely to win, and the Remain campaign was ahead in the large majority of the 168 polls that were taken during the campaign. The bookies were all for Remain.

So, come to that, was a large majority of Conservative MPs. In so far as I cared about my political future, it looked much brighter and happier if I backed the government. Back in the previous autumn, I had played a game of tennis with David Cameron at Winfield House, the US ambassador's residence in London. He won, as usual (he's a left-hander, and very hard to outfox).

Afterwards he said magnanimously, 'Come on – go with the campaign to stay in and I'll make sure you get a top-five job in the Cabinet.' Wow, I said, that sounds great – and tried swiftly to work out what 'top-five' might mean.

Hmmm ... 1 PM; 2 Chancellor; 3 Home Sec; 4 Fgn Sec; 5 ... er ... Defence? Health?

Whatever it was, it sounded great. But still I hesitated and havered.

Then, only a few weeks back, the PM had rung me one evening at City Hall, urging me to make up my mind. I was torn, I said. I wanted to back him, but over the years I had written hundreds if not thousands of articles attacking the undemocratic features of the EU. I felt I had to be consistent.

'This isn't about articles!' he spluttered. 'It's about ... the future of the country!'

Well, I said, we were agreed on that but I was still thinking of voting Leave.

'If you do that,' he said – and these were his exact words – 'I will fuck you up forever.'

I relayed the conversation to the family when I got back home to Islington that evening. 'You've got no choice,' said Milo instantly. 'You'll have to vote Leave.'

But I had to admit that the threat sounded serious. Did I want to be fucked up? Forever? By a prime minister equipped with all the fucking-up tools available to a modern government, and thousands of fucker-uppers just waiting to do his bidding?

It looked as though we were going to lose, and once we lost the failed and defeated Leavers would of course be crushed like bugs: cranks and misfits who had been rejected by the people.

The smart thing to do was stick with Dave, knuckle under, take the 'top-five' job, avoid the grief, and vote cravenly for Remain.

But how could I?

As Marina and I had agreed, this was the moment of truth. The UK would never again have a chance to be free, to be truly democratic, to make its own laws.

By 7 p.m. or so, the piece was done. I had made the key points, laying particular emphasis on the corrosive effect of chronic British half-heartedness on our influence in Brussels. Of the many thousands of energetic officials in the EU Commission, I noted, only 4 per cent were British – even though the UK contributed 12 per cent of the EU's population.

I noted the volume and immutability of EU law. I got up, stretched, walked in the garden, had a tin of tuna fish, lit the fire – and wondered. I thought about the idealism of Monnet, Schuman, De Gasperi, Spaak, the founders of the EEC; how they hoped to make something that would render a European conflict psychologically and politically impossible.

I thought about my own happy childhood in Brussels, the merry polyphonous chaos of the playground at the European School, Uccle, and my excellent teacher, Colin Black. How could I turn my back on all that? Should I not, in the words of the Beach Boys, be true to my school? And frankly, I didn't like the anti-foreigner feeling that was inevitably (if wrongly) associated with leaving the EU.

Perhaps, I brooded, it was the DUTY of the UK to remain in the EU – never mind our selfish national interest – to argue for common sense and free markets, to make sure that it did not turn into something worse. What would I say, I wondered, if I had to put the alternative case? It is easy, when you have already been writing and thinking for a while, to write more. The flywheel of the mind is already turning and needs no cranking. I will give myself forty-five mins, I said.

I sat down and thundered out what reads like a really hasty and half-baked pastiche of a column. The gist of the argument was that David Cameron's attempt to reform the EU might have been a failure, but it was better than nothing, and that it might be worth backing the government, staying in the EU and generally having a quiet life.

I wasn't trying to persuade anyone. I was red-teaming my thinking. I was being a devil's advocate. I was mounting both sides of the argument, like an ancient suasoria, and the very weakness and triviality of the second piece was intended, in my mind, to show why the arguments of the first were correct.

The following day Rachel and Ivo came to play tennis, and Ivo (a passionate Remainer) thought that the second piece was much better than the first. I sent it to Ben Wallace, hoping that the two sets of arguments, side by side, would prove to him conclusively why he was wrong.

Fat chance. He thought the second column much more enjoyable; and he passed it – for reasons never quite explained – to Tim Shipman of the *Sunday Times*, which is how it emerged, much later and much to my embarrassment, in the public domain.

At that stage the second piece was wholly redundant. I had made my mind up.

It was time to head for London, where – this was Sunday afternoon – a crowd was growing outside our house in Colebrooke
Row. There were dozens of reporters and cameramen, said Will
Walden, the City Hall communications chief, plus some rubber-
necking Islingtonians.

I needed to get going, he said, since the journey was over an
hour. Before I got in the car, I rang my father Stanley, who had
come to Brussels in the early 1970s as one of the first wave of Brits
to go to the Commission.

There was a pause. He coughed.

'Well,' he said, 'I suppose you'll get some brickbats for that, but
I suppose you might also get some plaudits as well.' It can't have
been exactly what he had been hoping to hear, given everything he
had done in his own career, and the corpus of European environmental law that he had personally helped to produce.

But you know what – from that day to this, he never once
complained, moaned, whinged; far from it. Nor has he been
anything less than completely personally supportive. He may have
campaigned for Remain, and he may go around on his bike wearing a Bollocks to Brexit bobble hat. That is entirely his prerogative.
But he has been relentlessly good-humoured and backed me up in
every other conceivable way. No son could ask for more.

As I got closer to Islington, I could feel my tension rising again.
It was gone 5.30, and I hadn't yet filed the piece for the *Telegraph*.
They were expecting it within the next twenty minutes. I had my
friend and former spin doctor Guto Harri on the mobile – hands-
free – and he was in a state of high emotion. He had left City Hall
after the first term, purely because he needed to charge the family
coffers, and we remained close. He was harrying me, for the good
of the country, for my own political health, to go for Remain.

And just as I got him off the line his successor, Will Walden,
would come on, calming me down and urging me to stick with my
decision. I parked the car, forced my way through the mob, filed

the piece, told Number Ten of my decision – then, to clear my head, decided to do some press-ups on the bathroom floor.

Then I went out to explain to the crowd of journalists why I had come out for Leave. I was so wired that Hugo Rifkind, of *The Times*, said that he could scarcely understand a word. But, of course, the media weren't interested in my arguments.

They had decided to play the man, not the ball. It was as if the Remain side were so concerned at my persuasive powers, and my knowledge of the subject, that they had to discredit me.

The first question was from the BBC, and it wasn't about my views, which I had just gabbled out, on the vast legal penumbra of the European Court – of course not.

It was all about me: why I was saying this, whether I was sincere, whether I could be trusted, and so on, so that the whole thing sounded like a referendum not on the EU but on my intellectual good faith.

It was to become rather oppressive and hysterical. It started to make me quite impatient, and more determined to win. Above all, it didn't work.

Chapter 18

Inside the Bus

The referendum campaign

Right, I thought, as soon as I heard the news. That's it. That's the end of this campaign. The whole thing was just too horrific. It was June 16, 2016, and we were sitting in the great big red bus – the Vote Leave battlewagon.

It was one of those colossal swish machines designed for Premier League football players, and possibly their WAGs, and there was a super-deluxe curtained section at the back, with comfy black leatherette sofas and a TV screen and drinks cabinets and whatnot.

I was sitting there with Penny Mordaunt MP, my Conservative colleague, and Gisela Stuart, a Labour MP whose beam – as she won Birmingham Edgbaston – had lit up Tony Blair's election night victory of 1997.

We were all in pretty high spirits. We had just come from a sunny seaside event in Norfolk, where we had banged on about the infamy of the Common Fisheries Policy and I had done a knockabout interview on the pier with John Pienaar of the BBC.

It was early afternoon, and we were on our way to a rally at a digger factory in the East Midlands, when Rob Oxley stuck his head through the curtains. Rob was our media guy – the highly effective operator that readers may remember from an earlier chapter on the siege of the fridge. Rob looked grave.

He had bad news – that a Labour MP had been attacked, and that it might be fatal. Then the news got worse.

Her name was Jo Cox, and she had been brutally murdered. I didn't know her, but she seemed to have been universally liked, a kind and popular campaigning MP. She had been on her way to a constituency event in Birstall when someone had shot her with a reconstituted .22 gun and then stabbed her many times.

She and her husband had two children, aged five and three. I listened with a sick feeling in the pit of my stomach. It was appalling, and there was no getting round it.

We had to ask ourselves if our campaign – the campaign to leave the EU – had played any part. The details were sketchy, but it sounded as if the killer had shouted something political, like 'freedom for Britain', or 'death to traitors'.

My God, we were all thinking, have WE triggered this? A few days earlier my brother Jo had relayed, with amusement, a message he had received from Tristram Hunt MP who was campaigning for Remain in his home seat of Stoke-on-Trent. It was no use, Hunt told Jo. The people of Stoke were deaf to his pleas. 'Pfeffel has unleashed the beast,' he said.

His words came back to me now. Had I (de Pfeffel being my much piss-taken-out-of middle name) unleashed something awful in the national psyche? Had I inadvertently potentiated the latent virus of racism and extremism? As the details of Jo Cox's murder became clearer, the shock spread through the bus. Penny was in tears, and members of the press corps were visibly upset.

It was clear what we had to do. We scrapped the rally that afternoon, and campaigning was suspended for three days. We dropped off half the press corps, who needed somewhere to write, and we went straight back to London. Even if this was the purely incidental work of a maniac, and the murder had nothing to do with the current referendum campaign, I knew that – openly or by implication – our campaign would be blamed.

It was the Thursday before polling day. We had exactly a week to go, and in a tight campaign – even one that had sometimes seemed to be swinging our way – this must be the decisive event; and I was not alone in that analysis.

Most people thought that we were done, and that we would now lose. Never forget the disparity of the forces in the debate. Of the 650 MPs sitting with me in the House of Commons, 479 were for Remain – almost three-quarters – and only 158 for Leave. Of the cabinet – and I stress that this was the nominally Eurosceptic Conservative cabinet – 25 were for Remain and 6 were for Leave.

That was about the balance across the whole of the political world. The Remain campaign had the big battalions. They had the money, the experience, the endless carefully gridded announcements, the marrow-freezing press releases from big business. They had lined up foreign worthies who could be relied upon, at the right moment, to wag their finger at the British public and tell them not to be so mad as to vote Leave.

The Remain campaign had everything except the one thing you really need in a campaign. They lacked conviction.

They lacked enthusiasm, and so what they had to say, inevitably, lacked interest. None of them had anything truly positive to say about the dream of European integration. None of them – not even Ken Clarke or Anna Soubry – seemed to yearn, or at least not in public, for Britain to be part of a United States of Europe.

This problem went to the very top of government, because in truth David Cameron – at least by political formation – was a bit of a Eurosceptic. Consult the media coverage on Black Wednesday, September 16, 1992, when the pound was expelled from the Exchange Rate Mechanism of the European Monetary System, because the markets no longer believed that John Major's government could maintain an exchange rate of 2.95 Deutschmarks to the pound.

It was the total humiliation of the government's European strategy (to be 'at the heart' of Europe), and it was the implosion of its economic policy. The public never forgave the Major government for the interest rate hikes that day – to an astonishing 15 per cent – that were deemed necessary to try to protect the Deutschmark parity, or the impression of a government that was suddenly and involuntarily rudderless.

Black Wednesday was an utter disaster. It led directly to the rout of 1997 and the Blair landslide. It sent the iron of Euroscepticism deep into the Tory soul. I wrote the splash of the *Daily Telegraph* that day, and there in some of the photos you can see a young whippersnapper at the side of Norman Lamont, so smooth and fresh-faced he might have been carved from a block of Sunlight soap.

David Cameron had begun as the special adviser of Lamont, the Tory chancellor who had (if unwillingly) presided over John Major's catastrophic policy. Cameron was supposed to have been so psychologically scorched by the experience that he was eternally opposed to UK membership of the euro.

He was against the federal vocation of the EU ('ever closer union'). He had told the Tory Party that he was against handing any more powers to Brussels. He had bragged that he was a Eurosceptic.

He was therefore a captive of his previous rhetoric, and unable to be really evangelical about the EU. The task of trying to nudge us all into being more enthusiastic was accordingly deputed, over the years, to George Osborne, his chancellor and yokemate, who prided himself – sometimes justifiably – on his Florentine political cunning.

When we three had just been elected, in 2001, we were politically in the doldrums. Tony Blair was at the height of his powers, and scoring boundaries with every shot. From time to time the three of us would have discussions about how to rescue the Tory Party – how could we fight Blair, who had stolen so many of our Tory clothes?

It was George who suggested that we should imitate 'the Master', as he called Blair. We should position a modernised Tory Party as the 'heirs to Blair', and as part of our 'modernisation' we should junk the tired old backward-looking attitudes, including attitudes towards sexuality and Euroscepticism.

What did I think? they asked me. I goggled at them.

Yes, we should be a kinder and more progressive and more generous Tory Party, I said (and I think Dave, George and I were the only three Tory MPs to rebel against our party, on a three-line whip, over gay adoption).

But scrapping Euroscepticism: surely we didn't believe in that?

Come off it, I said, and Dave, I think, agreed. The idea was dropped, and when Cameron became leader in 2005, the official Tory position remained resolutely Eurosceptic. We were opposed to any new Euro treaties; we were against any more majority voting in Brussels. We were fiercely against any further erosion of UK democratic control.

Then, in 2009, it was clear that the Osborne way of thinking was starting to prevail. One evening, I got a summons for dinner in Oxford Gardens, Dave and Samantha Cameron's house in Notting Hill. I arrived, late and puffed out, to find that it was just George and Dave and me – Pompey, Caesar and Crassus – so clearly something was up.

Sam Cam had whipped up something delicious and Notting Hill-ish and left us to it, and since it had been a long bike ride from City Hall, and thirsty work, I set to the red wine. After the usual rivalrous but basically good-natured banter, it was George, again, who was tasked with delivering the message.

By now the Tories were closing in on government; there was an election expected the following year, 2010, and they were expected to win. It was time to get the barnacles off the boat, said George.

You know the pledge we have made to hold a referendum on the Lisbon Treaty, he said.

I did.

I knew all about it. The Lisbon Treaty on the European Constitution was the latest evolution of the process of European integration, and it was the biggest since Maastricht in 1991. The treaty was also a classic example of the way the European elites have tended to bulldoze popular opinion.

Lisbon was basically a rehash of proposals for a new 'European Constitution', drawn up by French ex-president Giscard d'Estaing and which the voters of France and the Netherlands had embarrassingly rejected in national referendums (the British people were not consulted). Rather than take the hint and abandon these federalist plans, EU leaders had simply repackaged them as the Treaty of Lisbon.

This gigantic fraud had understandably caused consternation among Conservative MPs and activists.

The Lisbon Treaty more or less abolished national rights of veto in matters of EU competence, moving to majority voting in about forty-five areas – so that UK ministers could find themselves outvoted over all sorts of social, cultural, educational and economic policy decisions. It created more Euro-panjandrums and presidents, including a kind of European foreign minister.

Tories in opposition had raged about this treaty. William Hague, shadow foreign secretary, had been particularly blood-curdling, calling it the end of the nation state as we knew it. David Cameron had given a 'cast-iron' pledge that the people of Britain would have their say on this treaty, in the form of a referendum – and at once my purpose at this merry gathering was clear.

They were going to do a U-turn, and I was there to give my blessing. There was no point in having a referendum any more, said Dave 'n' George. The incumbent Labour government had already ratified the Lisbon Treaty. If we won the election next year, as seemed likely, we would be the first Tory government for thirteen years. We didn't want to get snarled up in some endless wrangle over Europe.

Well, I could see the logic. Better to do a U-turn now than to break a promise after an election. I could see why they wanted to clear the decks. But it struck me nonetheless as a massive goof. I didn't see how, after all we had said, we could just swallow the Treaty of Lisbon.

'I think it will go down very badly with the troops,' I said, and weaved off into the night. I am afraid I was right.

After thirteen years of Labour rule, we didn't win an overall majority in 2010; at least partly because we were vulnerable to the UK Independence Party (UKIP), who made much of the 'betrayal' over Lisbon; and so we were forced into coalition with the Lib Dems (who DID, absurdly, offer a referendum on the EU).

By 2013 Cameron felt so concerned about his Eurosceptic flank, and so fearful of what Nigel Farage and co. might pull off at the next general election, expected in 2015, that he decided to blow them all out of the water. He was going to silence his Eurosceptic tormentors (including me, I suppose) once and for all. He was going to end their muttering and whingeing about betrayal over the Lisbon Treaty with a single devastating rejoinder. He was going to wheel out the biggest gun of all, light the fuse and hope for the best.

For the first time in forty-one years, the British people were going to have a referendum on their relations with the EU – but not on Maastricht, or Nice, or Lisbon or some other amendment to the Treaty of Rome. They were going to be asked to pronounce on the whole damn thing – in or out, in a binary choice.

I thought it made sense. I saw the Farage problem, and believed that UKIP was fundamentally a nuisance – a party that could achieve nothing except take Tory votes and keep us from power. I could see why Dave wanted to squeeze them out.

There are some who now believe that Cameron made this pledge cynically, calculating that it might never have to be delivered. It seemed unlikely, back in 2013, that the Tories would win an outright majority at the next election, and more than likely that they would be forced to do another deal with the Lib Dems, in the course of which the referendum pledge could be more or less honourably scrapped (because the Lib Dems had now, typically, switched positions on referendums).

Instead – and no doubt in part because of that stunning pledge to hold an in-out referendum – the Tories had won outright. We had a small absolute majority over all other parties, and this time there was no option. We had to do the right thing and finally ask the British people what they thought about it all.

Dave 'n' George decided to go early in the parliament, to get it out of the way; and so the referendum was called for June 23, 2016. It was NOT called because of massive public demand for an in-out referendum. It was NOT called because lots of people thought that was the right thing for the country. It was NOT called because either Dave or George particularly wanted it to happen.

It was called because they had broken their promise on Lisbon and didn't see how they could break another. In other words, it was all a total mess – and so was their strategy for winning. Unable to be positive about a United Europe, the Remain campaign had no choice but to be negative: to hammer the Brexiteers and try to scare the pants off anybody thinking of voting Leave.

Donald Tusk, the Polish president of the European Council, was one of many foreign dignitaries invited to make our flesh creep. Brexit, he said, might be the 'beginning of the unravelling of western civilisation'. A letter was produced from eight former US secretaries of state, all calling for Remain.

On April 22, David Cameron had invoked the aid of Barack Obama, who flew in on Air Force One like a kind of deus ex machina and obligingly poured scorn on the idea – dear to many

Brexit-backing hearts – that we might get a post-Brexit free-trade deal with the US. Britain would be 'at the back of the queue', said Obama, his choice of words ('queue' being British English for what Americans call the 'line') revealing that he had been fed the script by Number Ten.

The IMF, the OECD, the World Bank – just about every global organisation you can think of – was given the same drill, and they all played up loyally, mindful as ever of the funding they receive from the UK government.

The Treasury itself was utterly disgraceful in its manipulation of statistics. They produced a whole seventy-page paper, with a preface by George, claiming that Brexit would lead to mass unemployment – of between 500,000 and 1 million. In London alone, they said, with the precision of the epic bullshitter, there would be 73,000 job losses, and a further 74,000 in the rest of the south-east.

Property prices would fall by 18 per cent, said George, and tax yields would fall so dramatically that there would be a £30 billion hole in the public finances. If the people of Britain were so temerarious as to vote for Brexit, they were warned, they would be punished by an emergency tax-raising budget.

To rub it all in, the government spent £9.3 million of taxpayers' money to send a pro-Remain leaflet to every household in the country. This vast exercise in misinformation they proudly called 'Project Fear'.

It wasn't that Project Fear didn't work. The sad thing is that for millions of people it probably did, in that it was scary enough to stop them voting Leave. But the incredible thing – and this is really a testimony to the lion-hearted courage of the British people – is that it still wasn't enough to defeat us, or the arguments we were making.

The Remain side chose to use fear. We had hope. They said Britain wasn't good enough to go it alone. We said it was. They had vague threats. We had a brilliant clarity of message, and we thumped it home, every day, at every press conference, every bus stop.

We were going to 'take back control' of our money, our borders and our laws. They were offering more of the same; we were offering something different, our version of the change that people craved.

Every big electoral contest turns on who 'owns' the future, and there is no doubt that we owned the future in this debate. We had a vision of a dynamic free-trading Britain, able to exploit Brexit freedoms and to unleash the potential of the whole country. They had no real alternative; and the reality of what was likely to happen if we remained, a Britain ever more tightly enmeshed in a federal Europe, was not one that the Remain side were even prepared to discuss, let alone (avowedly) support.

We were a movement for freedom, for independence. What were they? A campaign for the gradual erosion of UK independence?

No wonder they gave up arguing and tried to hammer us personally – to undermine us and erode trust in what we were saying. It was all they had left.

I was a liar, they said; Gove was a liar; our big red bus was a great big fat liar, because of the slogan on its side. It was a message that had been exhaustively tested by our campaign director, the banzai-spirited Cummings. It had been shown to drive people potty with indignation.

The red bus said, in enormous white letters, 'We send Brussels £350m a week – let's fund the NHS instead'. It was a brilliant slogan because it had what they call cut-through. It became the subject of discussion up and down the country, and it was the Remain campaign that did our work for us – by massively intensifying the impact of what we were saying. As soon as they realised just how potent the slogan was, and how furiously it was driving the national conversation, they tried to fight back. They made the cardinal mistake, in any campaign, of playing on our turf.

No, no, no, they said: that was all wrong. They pointed out that £350 million was the gross figure, and that when you factored in the EU's investments in the UK – agriculture, regional policy, etc. – as well as the UK budget abatement, the real number was about half that, maybe £175 million.

What they never understood, in all their pop-eyed indignation about the bus, was that as soon as they engaged in debate on the detail they began to lose the public, because the facts always turned out to be on our side.

Yes, it was true that some of the money was spent in the UK, but not in a way that was democratically controlled by the British people; and even if the net figure was only £175 million, that was still a hell of a lot of money – enough for a cottage hospital a week.

Actually, when you dug into the figures, the UK's contributions were due to rise so steeply that by 2020 we would be paying £420 million per week.

The Remain campaign were finding as the weeks went by that they couldn't deny the essential facts of the case. They couldn't deny the meaning of the EU treaties, or the supremacy of EU law, or the way it had flowed in – as Lord Denning said so many years ago – like an incoming tide, up every creek and inlet in Britain.

It wasn't long before they started to get impatient, then angry, then desperate. If they couldn't defeat the message, they would savage the messengers, in particular yours truly.

One evening in May our bus rolled into Stafford, and I got off, with Gisela, to find a large and happy throng who were hoping for a speech. I stood on a platform and began some extempore remarks. Why, I asked them, did we need the EU to tell us how powerful our vacuum cleaners should be? If Dyson said they were safe, and our trading standards people said they were safe, then what possible business was it of Brussels to tell the British people that there was too much sucking power in a British vacuum cleaner?

At this point I generally digressed with an account of some of the grievous and unmentionable injuries that had been sustained by some people – men, I am afraid – in the course of vacuum cleaner abuse. But was it not the right of every freeborn Englishman to use a vacuum cleaner as he chose?

Did we need Brussels to tell us how to use a vacuum cleaner? I would ask them – and by now the crowd was generally in a mood of delighted assent. It was at that moment, having done my vacuum cleaner point, when I slipped up.

Someone had mentioned something to me about bunches of bananas – and in repeating it I got it slightly wrong (the vacuum cleaner stuff was all absolutely true).

Why, I raved to the Stafford crowd, should Brussels forbid a freeborn British greengrocer from selling bananas in bunches of more than three?

Pzzzt – I had boobed. The speech was being carried more or less live on the 6 p.m. news, and soon a great Remain pile-on was underway.

Liar! they shrieked. He's wrong about bananas, and he's wrong about everything.

They wheeled out Lord Heseltine, assassin of Margaret Thatcher and my illustrious predecessor in Henley-on-Thames. He and I had previously enjoyed a relationship of cautious cordiality – but now he went for my vitals with his New and Lingwood loafers.

He was clearly under instructions, from the Remain campaign, to take me out – personally. He went on the news to comment on bananagate.

Hezza limbered up by saying that I was being 'completely reckless and irresponsible' in my language, that I was 'obscene and preposterous and near racist' in my (totally innocuous) remarks about Barack Obama and his intervention.

He claimed that I had likened Brussels to Adolf Hitler, when I had done no such thing.

'His judgement is going,' he said. 'The strain of the campaign is beginning to tell.'

His noble lordship then came to the issue of substance – what Brussels says about bananas, and EU law on the size of a bunch.

'It's a complete fabrication,' said Michael Heseltine on the TV news. 'I know. My wife and I eat bananas,' said the great man with magnificent authority.

'I have bought bunches of bananas,' he said, as though that clinched the matter. But even as they tried to trash me, Remain were missing the point.

Everyone rushed off to look up the directive – and they found that though I may have got the detail wrong in an off-the-cuff stump speech, I was far from spiritually wrong. Here, for your enjoyment, is what the 2011 regulation 'on the presentation of bananas' actually says:

The bananas must be presented in hands or clusters (parts of hands) of at least four fingers.

Bananas may also be presented as single fingers.

Clusters with not more than two missing fingers are allowed, provided that the stalk is not torn but cleanly cut, without damage to the neighbouring fingers.

Not more than one cluster of three fingers with the same characteristics as the other fruit in the package may be present per row.

In the producing regions, bananas may be marketed by the stem.

Give me a break, folks!

So I got it the wrong way round – in my haste and fatigue. It wasn't the maximum size of a bunch of bananas that was being prescribed in this insane piece of legislation. It was the minimum size. And why? Why shouldn't a greengrocer in Stafford be able to sell a bunch of three bananas?

Why on earth did Brussels think it worth prohibiting him – or any banana vendor across the whole vast 510 million-strong territory – from selling two bunches of three bananas in the same row?

Why should this be European law, the law of the Medes and the Persians, the law from which no national parliament or court or citizen could dare to deviate? The point I am making is that whenever they got into the actual arguments, Remain started losing, and so their strategy from the outset (and I am proud to say that they have kept it up more or less ever since) has been to attack me *ad hominem*; and it didn't work.

I loved much of that campaign. Like all British political campaigns, it was all about food and gags for the photographers. When I wasn't waving bananas, I was eating Cornish pasties, or licking ice creams, or hefting huge slimy fishes in markets. Whenever we were outside London, away from the condescension of the metropolis, I felt that we might just win. And then came the tragic murder of Jo Cox.

We went into the last few days with our heads down, our confidence gone. Our own final rally in Fishmongers Hall – two days before polling – was actually a half-hearted and thinly attended affair; partly because we all felt winded, and partly because we didn't think the public was in a mood for anything else.

The funny thing was that it turned out the voters didn't actually see it that way. When the polling came in, it showed that neither Remainers nor Leavers believed that we had caused the killing of Jo Cox; they thought the murderer was just a nutter, and I think they were probably right.

He did turn out to be a neo-Nazi with a history of mental illness; and as it happens the public were right to be generally sanguine about the effect of Brexit on the national psyche. As study after study has shown – and despite all the predictions to the contrary – it did not actually lead to a rise in racism. It did not provoke more xenophobic attacks. If anything, the evidence shows that it did something to defuse some racist feeling.

Above all, as things were to transpire, the great British public were completely and utterly right to ignore Project Fear. They were told by George Osborne and Mark Carney that they were going to plunge themselves into recession. They stuck up two fingers to the experts, and they were proved resoundingly right.

The pound recovered. The property market barely skipped a beat. As for unemployment – huh. They were told that jobless rolls would increase by at least 7,000 in the July after the vote. You know what, in July that year the UK ADDED 9,000 jobs.

At the time of writing, the UK has still not seen any surge in unemployment more than eight years after the vote; indeed unemployment is at about the lowest level since 1974 (and they still have the cheek to moan about our bus).

In their vast and collective wisdom, the great British public instinctively knew it was all balls, and were preparing to vote accordingly. In the last few days our supporters, frankly, were therefore more confident than we were. I started to feel a surge two days before the vote, walking the streets in Wolverhampton and Leicestershire. People were coming across the road to shake hands, slapping us on the back, honking with approval as they passed – and I got an inkling of what might happen. Then on the evening of Wednesday June 22, there was the final TV debate, a huge hustings before a crowd of thousands at White City.

I wound up the debate and stared down the barrel of the camera to tell the country that if they voted for freedom, and took back control, then Thursday would be our independence day; and you could tell something from that audience, which had been carefully picked by the BBC so as to represent both sides equally.

Though the cheers of the Remainers were loud, the cheers of the Leavers were louder still.

Chapter 19

Triumph – and Disaster

How Cameron's flouncerama triggered chaos

After all that effort, I almost failed to cast my own vote in the EU referendum. On polling day afternoon, Marina and I were at Lara's graduation ceremony in St Andrews in Scotland. We flew back down in some haste to find that London had been inundated by a freak summer storm.

Every taxi was occupied, and it took ages to get to the polling station in Islington. We sneaked in just before polls closed, and then went back to Colebrooke Row to watch the results.

You would not have been especially confident of victory if you were in my shoes, after our experiences in Scotland. I suppose there might be somewhere in the British Isles where there is a higher concentration of Remain voters than the faculty of St Andrews University, Fife, but I can't think where.

They were liberal-minded, they were academics, they were Scottish, and they viewed me as a traitor to my class and educational background. As we stood on some grassy quadrangle waiting for the ceremony to begin, I was conscious of how many were looking at me like the turd in the punchbowl – and adjusting their subfusc so I could see the Remain sticker on their lapels.

We breezed through it – mainly because we were so proud of Lara, who had done well in her degree; and the last thing I wanted was aggro of any kind. But the anti-Brexit sentiment seemed to be everywhere.

'You'll lose!' shouted a man at Edinburgh Airport, with what seemed to be general assent from other passengers. So when I sat down in London that night to watch the results, I was feeling pretty wound up, and utterly determined to prove that man wrong.

By this stage I had taken a hell of a lot of flak. I had stopped watching or listening to most of it, but was amazed by the ferocity of it all.

One day I was in a TV studio waiting to go on, and John Major was there. He was perfectly charming in person (as he always is) and so I was astonished to watch him go on and tear chunks out of me. I would attack the NHS, he said, like a python swallowing a hamster. I mean, really. Where did he get that from?

I will tell you where: it was the Remain campaign script. They were still obsessing about the bus and the £350 million for the NHS. I don't really blame them for their tactics. It is a sad and eternal truth of politics that people become proxies for the ideas and programmes they advance. So if you want to undermine the message – and you are finding that difficult – you have to beat up the messenger.

I can understand why Remain did it; it was what their polling and focus groups would have suggested they do (though we on the other side were nothing like as personal in our rhetoric). I am just trying to explain my feelings at the time.

By the evening of June 23, I had been so goaded and derided and (as I saw it) traduced that my dander was thoroughly up. When the first results started to go our way, and especially when there was that huge early vote for Leave in Sunderland, I could feel a surge of excitement. I was watching it with Ben Wallace, and he was not quite so cheery – being a natural Europhile and

Ken Clarke Tory. But Will Walden shared my excitement, and so did Marina. We stayed up all night eating cold lasagne and bacon sandwiches, and watching the most extraordinary event in British psephological history.

The polls were wrong. The bookmakers were wrong. The markets were wrong. Even Nigel Farage, the leader of an unofficial (and unconnected) campaign called Leave.UK, was wrong. He for some reason had conceded defeat earlier in the evening, on the basis of some rumour that swept the City.

It turned out that there was a pool of people – a vast pool – who had been touched by this debate in a way that they were never touched by normal politics. How often, in the years that I was writing editorials for the *Daily Telegraph*, had I quoted those old lines of G.K. Chesterton?

> Smile at us, pay us, pass us; but do not quite forget;
> For we are the people of England that never have
>   spoken yet.

Now they had spoken, 2.3 million of them that the pollsters were not expecting to go to the polls. They were the voices of people who felt excluded from the current consensus, who genuinely wanted change, a government that would properly heed them and their interests.

More people voted Leave – 17.4 million – than have voted for any government in British history. More people voted Leave than have voted for any person or proposition in our history. By 7 a.m. it was clear that we had won, and in my elation I must have allowed my eyelids to close, because when I woke again, at about 8.30 a.m. the cameras were trained on Downing Street.

David Cameron was expected to speak to the nation; yes, there he was, with Sam Cam by his side, and my God, he was actually stepping down. Forthwith.

He wasn't going to oversee the implementation of the people's will – even though he had asked them to decide. He was off.

He was walking back inside the black door and whistling some jaunty air, as though to say to us, the victors – right, you tossers, you've made this mess. Now you sort it out.

I thought it was the wrong thing to do, and a bit petulant. Plenty of other European leaders sustain referendum defeats and carry on with their duties.

Now what the hell were we supposed to do?

Some people have claimed that neither Michael Gove nor I really intended to win that campaign, which is transparent rubbish, as I hope I have explained. Others say that we did intend to win, but that we – more particularly I – were not really motivated by the arguments over the EU but by a desire to overthrow the Cameron government and take over.

Again, that is patent rubbish. Any such claim is readily disproved by what actually happened.

I had known Michael Gove since he was about eighteen, and I was about three years older. We came across each other at the Oxford Union, and I admired his brilliantly improvised Scottish orotundity. He was owlish, tweedy, often quite drunk, and then as now wonderfully polite. He had hung around at my college, and from time to time we would go to the same preposterous debating club dinners.

He was an important part (I don't think he would deny it) of my all-conquering Balliol-New College machine, before taking it over and going on to victory himself. He seemed kind, and libertarian, and I am certain he was sincere in what he said about Brexit.

His father had been in the fish processing business in Aberdeen; and fishing was one of the industries – thanks to Edward Heath – that had been worst clobbered by EU membership. He seemed to see the democratic deficit in the EU in exactly the way I did.

The point I am making is that Michael and I had been friends and collaborators for decades, but we didn't once put our heads together to discuss the possible aftermath. Never at any point in that campaign did we discuss a future Leave-based government, because we did not imagine that there would have to be a change of government. The government's stated policy was to implement the referendum result. It was a referendum, not an election. It was a popular consultation, and not a moment for the transfer of power.

I was not fighting that referendum campaign thinking, Cor – this is going well: in a month's time I could be prime minister; and nor, I am pretty sure, was Michael Gove.

So when David Cameron flounced off the stage, we were wrong-footed. Of course we were. We had no plan for government, no plan for the negotiations, because it was not our job, and in so far as the next few days were chaotic, which they were, it is utterly infuriating that we should be blamed.

It was up to the government to announce its plan for withdrawal. It was up to the government to begin the negotiations. It was up to the government of David Cameron to deliver the result of the referendum they had called. It was up to the government immediately to bring forward a White Paper (which they should have prepared) on how they were to implement a vote to Leave. Why didn't they? Probably because they thought, in some clever-clever way, that the best way to deal with the result was to let the Brexiteers 'own' the chaos.

The PM had just flounced out, whistling, rather than deal with the logical consequences of the events he had set in motion.

So if we looked pretty whey-faced and shell-shocked a few hours later, when we finally stood up – at about 11 a.m. – to claim victory, it was not, as everyone on Twitter immediately pronounced, because we were downcast at having won (we weren't). It was because we suddenly had a lot on our plates.

Nothing except a battle lost can be half so melancholy as a battle won, said the Duke of Wellington after winning at Waterloo – and I saw what he meant. We had to show appropriate respect to David Cameron, our departed leader.

We had Remainers shrieking at us outside our houses, calling us cunts and banging on our cars. We had to deal with the anger and bewilderment of our colleagues in Parliament. It was barely a year since Cameron had won an absolute majority, and now he had thrown himself spectacularly on the funeral pyre of UK membership of the EU.

Parliament, the City, the media, the foreign exchange markets were all clamouring for us to own this result – to step up and answer the question: now what?

And now who?

Cameron having gone, the general consensus was that the next prime minister should be someone from the Leave team – someone with the mandate of the 17.4 million. That meant either Gove or me, since we had been the most prominent Tory campaigners.

Michael had undoubtedly been brilliant in the campaign, but there were plenty who asserted (on what basis I am not sure) that I had been reaching an even wider group of voters, and there was a view that I might be even more successful than Michael when it came to fighting and winning any future general election campaign. That at any rate seemed to be the view of Dom Cummings, the campaign director who was also a great friend and close colleague of Gove.

So at a certain point that Friday morning Gove and I went into a tiny office – perhaps even a broom cupboard or other janitorial facility – to try to thrash it out. We emerged with a tentative deal, and the following day – Saturday – he rang to confirm it 100 per cent.

He would be my chancellor and effective number two. We would form a joint ticket. We would fuse the angry Cameroons with the jubilant Eurosceptics and bring peace to our party. We would form a great government.

I was so exhausted, and so relieved to have something like a plan – even the beginnings – that I underestimated the perils of the days ahead, and the immense complexities entailed in trying to become prime minister of the UK.

As soon as he announced he was off, Cameron fired the starting gun on a vast orgy, across Westminster, of plotting and machination. Offices were being rented, phone lines put in, lists of supporters drawn up. Hostile briefings were being pumped out to the media, and friendly journalists repeatedly canvassed.

What was I doing, that all-important Saturday?

I went off to play cricket. For years Charlie Spencer, Earl of, has invited the Johnson family to field an XI, and every year we have turned to the most ridiculously talented ringers – one year we had Kevin Pietersen; another year we had Brian Lara – and even so we always lose. I really didn't want to cancel.

It would have been rude, and Charlie always provides a magnificent lunch and tea; and I thought of the spirit of Drake at Plymouth, completing his game of bowls even though the Armada was in sight.

I can see in retrospect how frivolous it looked. The country was in tumult; we had voted to embark on a massive geo-strategic realignment and constitutional change, which I had encouraged, and I was at my old mucker's stately home, larking about in cricket whites and knocking back the Pimm's.

It didn't look like much of a leadership campaign, and it must have irritated some of my supporters; and yet it didn't feel that bad to me. If we could just hold together until nominations opened, I felt we were very likely to win.

For the next few days, the Johnson-Gove alliance bashed on. We had a barbecue at my house in Thame on the Sunday, and it became clear that there would be some difficulties melding our various teams of followers. There were tensions and rivalries, naturally enough, between the City Hall team, and the talented young Govies, and the Vote Leave team – but nothing that seemed fatal, at least to me.

We were a good fit, we enjoyed working together, we had the mandate to deliver a full Brexit. We could have been unstoppable.

Alas, it was not to be. On Thursday morning – just as I was due to go out and launch my campaign at the Stakis St Ermin's Hotel in Victoria – Michael decided to blow me up on the launchpad.

He was my campaign chair and effectively my running mate, and now in a position of great power and trust. So I was taken aback when Lynton Crosby rang me at the crack of dawn and tersely brought the bad news.

'Gove's running, mate,' he said. (I didn't hear from Michael himself at all, I think.)

Now if I had been preparing to run for months, if I had a list of supporters and a well-oiled machine of my own, I suppose I might have pushed on.

Some people thought I should, and it was a nightmare to have to let my supporters down.

I remember Andrew Mitchell standing at the back and noisily punctuating my speech with shouts of 'WINNER!' – until I reached the peroration and announced that I wasn't running after all; and then I saw that some of my closest friends and supporters were actually in tears.

Gove had chosen the perfect moment to strike – to throw me off my balance. I knew it was essential that my team should look strong from the outset, and should present a united front. Gove scuppered that completely.

To this day I don't know exactly why he did me in. He had all sorts of voices in his ear. George Osborne was certainly urging him to run.

It so happened that Michael, as campaign chair, had appointed a bright young Brexiteer MP to be my minder; to sit with me in Parliament as I made my pitch to colleagues and to make a note of what was said. He was called Rishi Sunak. Much later Rishi told me, 'You were far too trusting of those people. A lot of them really weren't on your side.' Six years later I was to remember that remark – and the historical irony it contains.

I of course was sad at Michael's behaviour. I particularly disapproved of the way he started slating me publicly in order to justify his own decision. What I resented most was the sheer stupidity of what he had done.

I felt that he had been used by Osborne and co., who had wound him up and radicalised him to do the dirty on me, when I didn't really think he would win himself; and he had made it much less likely, therefore, that Brexit would be delivered by someone who actually understood or cared about what we were trying to do; and there was a real possibility that Brexit would not be delivered at all.

My fears were well founded. Gove himself blew up shortly thereafter, as he failed to get enough votes from MPs to stay in the race – and Cameron texted me, saying, 'I bet that felt sweet.'

Actually, it didn't: it just made me even gloomier. The last Leaver in the race, Andrea Leadsom, also managed to implode, for some reason, and the home secretary Theresa May – who had campaigned for the UK to remain in the EU – was elected leader unopposed.

Oh well, I thought. I hadn't ever hit it off with Theresa, and we had locked horns over stop and search and water cannon, and other things. Back to the drawing board, I thought, and I resumed my vast and happy labours on a book about William Shakespeare (that unjustly neglected author), which was one of the projects I owed to my publishers.

One evening that July I was working in the Commons, and had just nipped off to the gents, when I heard my phone go in my pocket. It is quite difficult to stand at a urinal while talking on your mobile, but I thought I would check who it was.

Blow me down – it was the Number Ten switch. Would I come and see the PM, they said. You bet, I said, spraying away.

I was even more amazed, and thrilled, to discover that she wanted me to serve as foreign secretary.

Part Four
Global Britain

Chapter 20

Soft Power Superpower

'More swagger, Foreign Secretary?'

The following morning at 9.30 I was in the Durbar Court, a vast glass-roofed atrium in the heart of the Italianate palazzo that is the Foreign and Commonwealth Office. It was populated by hundreds of busts of dead imperialists and thousands of young officials – jammed on the marble floor, craning their necks round the pillars and crowded on to the three floors of balconies, like the crowd of jailbirds in *The Shawshank Redemption*.

These were some of the very best that the UK system has to offer – and now I was in charge of the whole lot of them. As I looked out, I saw familiar faces, people who had helped the London mayoralty on trips abroad. They were good people, amusing and interesting brains that I liked and got on with; and, much to my relief, they were not scowling.

They had that reassuring eye-contact-full look – presumably one of the first things you learn as a diplomat – of being simply fascinated to know what I was going to say.

It was hot, under the glass. I did not want to keep them long. Though I hadn't much time to cobble together a script, I knew what I wanted to say. I gave them the gospel.

We might be leaving the EU, but we were not leaving Europe.

In fact, now was the time actively to rebuild bilateral relations with many European countries, since I felt that they had become atrophied in the centralised Brussels-based system. We needed to show our European friends and partners, the whole world, that Brexit did not mean that the UK was turning in on itself. It was not a vote for some kind of isolationism. It was the very opposite.

It was time for us to be more ambitious, more confident, more engaged with the world. It was time to revive old alliances and friendships, to rediscover old muscles – and develop new ones: challenge orthodoxies, do things differently.

We had done decades of Britain trying and generally failing to be at the heart of Europe. Now it was time for GLOBAL BRITAIN™ to demonstrate the spirit that made this country great and made it rich.

The diplomats listened carefully to what I had to say. Then Sir Simon McDonald, the permanent pecretary, asked if there were any questions. (Simon was my Sir Humphrey figure, a tall, pale fellow who always looked, for some reason, as though he was wearing mascara.)

There was a pause, and then one man put up his hand.

Would I overturn the ruling of the last foreign secretary (Philip Hammond) and restore the right of UK embassies to fly the rainbow LGBTQI flag?

Of course, I said. I had once worn a pink Stetson the entire length of the Pride march. I was totally cool with that.

I wanted us to be proud of our values, and not cringe in the face of 'local sensitivities'. We believed (I believe) that people should have the freedom to love whomsoever they choose – provided they do no harm; and we should use our considerable moral weight to stick up for oppressed gay people everywhere. But I wanted to go further.

As I saw it, we needed to be more confident in all sorts of ways. If you looked back at the last thirty years, it felt like we had generally lost our mojo, our ambition, our willingness to assert ourselves abroad. In the 1990s and early 2000s, Britain had regularly been willing to use force overseas – in the defence of democracy, freedom and human rights.

Under the governments of Thatcher, and Major, and Blair, we had stuck up for the rules-based international order. We had expelled Saddam from Kuwait; we had defended the Kosovars; we had helped topple the Taliban in Afghanistan and helped give millions of women the benefits of education.

Then in 2003 we had joined our American allies and invaded Iraq, and it felt as if that disaster – and it was a disaster, even if I voted for it – had been a climacteric, the beginning of the end of the American-led unipolar world. Our confidence had started to deflate. Our troops had a very tough time, in Basra in Iraq and in Helmand in Afghanistan, where we sustained quite heavy casualties; and we had ended up leaving both provinces. We had helped to get rid of Gaddafi in Libya. But you could not say that chaotic country was now a conspicuous advertisement for foreign intervention. In the last few years, before my arrival in the FCO, it felt as though we were shying away from confrontation.

In 2013 the Syrian leader Bashar al-Assad used chemical weapons to poison completely innocent Syrian civilians, terrible weapons that burned the lungs and destroyed the nervous system. In spite of repeated promises to punish this barbarism I am afraid we did nothing about it. In 2014 Putin invaded the east of Ukraine, and took the Crimea, in complete defiance of international law; and again, the western response was feeble. Slowly the west was losing prestige, and so when I got to the Foreign Office it wasn't clear what UK foreign policy really was.

We moaned about the rise of the 'autocracies', Russia, China, Iran. But what was our posture today? In the days of Blair and Clinton, and then Blair and Bush, we had been willing to risk lives, and to go to war, and to use high explosive to impose our values from 30,000 feet. Those days were now gone, for good or ill. But what was the replacement doctrine?

Did we still believe in exporting democracy? What about human rights? The Russians clearly had no inhibitions about using violence, whether in Syria or in Africa. How could we compete? Above all, what was our attitude to China – in many ways Russia's enabler, and the world's great emergent power? Were we still in the Cameron-Osborne 'Golden Era' of China– UK relations? If not, what was our strategy?

Many years ago I had heard a previous foreign secretary, Douglas Hurd, give a speech in which he claimed that the UK was 'punching above its weight'. Now it felt as though we were actually punching below our weight. It was absurd.

As I sat down behind my desk in the office of Lord Palmerston – gilt, mirrored, the size of two squash courts – I tried to add it all up. On any realistic assessment, British influence, or potential influence, is huge.

Take our 'hard' power (number-two defence spend in Nato, nuclear weapons, two vast new aircraft carriers, more heavy lift than the rest of Europe combined).

Combine that with our 'soft' power (the Premier League football competition, watched all over the world, the world's best universities, the scientific research, the tech, the ubiquitous British music – from the Beatles to Adele – that gives us a claim to have written the playlist of the modern world, and on and on).

Then chuck in the vast network of historic relationships, which has left the UK with a bigger overseas diaspora than almost any other OECD country. Remember that we still have an economy about twice the size of Russia's, and we are the world's fourth-biggest exporter, the second-biggest exporter of services, and the number-one financial centre in our hemisphere, etc., etc.

Military superpower – no longer. Soft power superpower –

certainly. And we unquestionably had the ability to give more political leadership around the world.

'I can see you want us to have more swagger, Foreign Secretary,' said Simon McDonald, making one of his Alvin Stardust hand movements.

Not swagger, I said, if you mean pointless swanking around.

How about confidence? I wanted us to recover our spunk, zap and drive.

The wonderful thing about the FCO is that even though the majority had almost certainly voted Remain (though a fair few were quietly for Leave), they all did their best to make it work; and I believe that for the two years I was there, they – for the main part – threw themselves into the project.

They really had to remake British foreign policy, from top to bottom; to stop thinking about how to position us in the EU, rather how to position us globally. I know they sometimes thought I was a bit of a barbarian (and I would merrily play to their prejudices) but I have nothing but praise for the FCO. They worked exceptionally hard, and it was a pleasure, and an honour, to serve with them.

At the end of those years in the Foreign Office, we had some fairly distinguished achievements. Among other things, we had helped biff Assad so hard on the nose that he never again used chemical weapons, against his own people or anyone else. We had persuaded most of our friends and allies to adopt a much tougher line on Russia, expelling a total of 153 diplomats, from twenty-nine countries, after Putin used novichok in Salisbury. We had launched a campaign, of which I was especially proud, to make sure every girl in the world gets twelve years of quality education, and so on.

But the first and most important task was to explain what I meant about Brexit, and Global Britain, to the rest of the world; above all to our number-one friends and partners in the United

States. It was a slight handicap, of course, that until the sudden disappearance of the Cameron administration the official and downright hysterical position of the UK government was that Brexit would be a disaster. We needed to clear that up, and as fast as possible. We needed to get to Washington.

Chapter 21

Brexit in America

Debunking the bogus analogy between
the EU and the USA

It was September 2016, and a lovely day to be out on the water at Boston Harbour. I had been foreign secretary for a couple of months, and I was starting to enjoy myself hugely. For reasons that now escape me, the US secretary of state, John Kerry, had decided to have an informal meeting in his home town with his closest European buddies; and for reasons that are now vaguer still, he had decided that we should go out on a boat and view Boston from the sea.

So there I was, leaning on the taffrail of this touristic pleasure boat, with our most powerful European allies: the French, the Germans and the Italians. The warm breeze was riffling our hair and we all felt (no doubt this was the desired effect) pretty special, and pretty loved by the US.

We felt we were the inner court, the intimates of the most powerful country on earth – and our host was the steward of that country's entire foreign policy.

John Kerry is lean and craggy and Wasp-looking, with an iron-grey thatch of hair, piercing blue eyes, a stonkingly rich wife (Teresa Heinz, no wonder he's full of beans) and seemingly every other advantage in life, including a remarkable memory for the details of foreign policy.

It must have been about 5 p.m.; the sun was beginning a gentle descent; the light was twinkling off the buildings of Boston, and our conversation roved. We did Afghanistan, we did Syria, and then the subject of Brexit came up. Kerry turned to look at me and said, with a sudden air of conspiracy, 'Can't you walk that thing back?'

All eyes were on me; not just those of the US secretary of state, but the pleading, anxious eyes of our European friends; and it occurred to me that this might in fact be the purpose of the gathering.

We were called the Quint; not after Quint the fisherman from *Jaws*, who gets eaten somewhere in these waters, but because there were five countries represented. In diplomacy, three is a troika, four is a quartet and five is a quint. It would be fair to say – in fact it would be a vast understatement – that I was the only member of that Quint who was in favour of Brexit.

There was Jean-Marc Ayrault, the former French prime minister who had once taught German for a living. Indeed his German was better than his English, and for a while I tried my French on him, which he endured with great fortitude.

Jean-Marc was pretty much inseparable from his German counterpart, the equally earnest and white-haired Frank-Walter Steinmeier. Frank-Walter was to go on to become president of the Federal Republic of Germany, and like so many Germans of his generation he found Brexit painful. According to the *Guardian*, it was an ordeal for Frank-Walter just to be in the same room as me – though he was perfectly civil to my face. Like Jean-Marc, he was essentially a man of the centre-left, and we tended to be quite a long way apart on Russia, where – in my view – he cut Putin far too much slack.

Then there was Paolo Gentiloni, the Italian, who was an impossibly aristocratic former journalist and the incarnation of

Italian charm and good manners. I always cheered up when Paolo was in the room, though he too was pretty bleak about Brexit.

And then – how could I forget – there was the EU's own 'foreign minister', the so-called high representative for foreign affairs, an Italian called Federica Mogherini. She was young, smart, socialist, competent, fragrant; but she was also, in my view, the incarnation of what was going wrong with the EU.

Her office had been called into being by the Treaty of Lisbon (see above) and it had been decided that as high representative and vice president of the Commission (or HRVP as she styled herself), she was the permanent chair of the EU Council of foreign ministers.

Having by now attended a couple of these events, I was already fed up with the emetic fawning with which she was treated by my peers. 'Thank you, Federica,' they would gush as she gave them the floor, as though they were contributing by the grace of the Commission rather than by their right as member states.

Mogherini was the queen bee, the ranking officer, the person who got to sum up the mood of the meeting and whose officials drafted the conclusions. I basically thought that she – or her office – should not exist, and that we shouldn't have a federal EU spokesperson for foreign policy, when it should plainly be reserved for national governments; and she probably wished I didn't exist, either.

So there we were, three months after the referendum, on this boat in Boston Harbour, and the challenge from my fellow Europeans was clear. Look, Johnson, they were saying: so much for your precious vision of an outward-looking free-trading Global Britain.

So much for your precious special relationship with the US! So much for your vaunted US–UK free-trade deal!

Listen to what Kerry just said. Not even the Americans want you to do Brexit. The whole thing is paralysed (which it was).

Theresa May does not know what to do, or how to interpret the result (which she didn't).

Can't you walk this thing back?

I saw what I had to do. I had to make it absolutely clear to John Kerry that he was deluded if he thought we were going to reverse the decision, and to get that point across in a way that made sense to an American.

'See that over there,' I said, and all eyes swivelled as I gestured in the direction of Boston harbourfront. 'Remember what happened on that quayside in 1776,' I said (actually it was 1773, but the point was still good). 'You guys threw our tea into the sea.' It was the Boston Tea Party, and the beginning of the American Revolution, I said, because you guys – I meant the Americans – decided that you did not want to be ruled from overseas by a government over which you had no control.

'That's what it was all about, and that's what Brexit is all about,' I said; and I thought it was a pretty sizzling return of serve.

Did they take the point? I dunno. They goggled at me with that speculative look.

What I had come up against that afternoon was the orthodox view of the US foreign policy establishment. Never forget that the EEC was born with the explicit and fervent support of the United States. It was no coincidence that the brilliant Frenchman Jean Monnet – cognac heir and visionary founding father of the Common Market – had spent the war in Washington, working in the UK mission and helping to procure equipment for the Allies.

As he watched the degradation of his continent, the moral humiliation of Europe, he decided that the only way to prevent another war was to create a European Union out of France, Germany and Benelux.

The Americans backed him all the way. Of course they did. They had twice been forced to settle world wars, both started in Europe, and the cost in American lives had been huge. They wanted the problem fixed, and a European Union sounded like a great and logical idea. Monnet played on the Americans' well-earned pride in their own nation-building achievement, forging this extraordinary federation of states into one – *e pluribus unum* – and creating the greatest power on earth.

There are many Americans who assume that the process of European Union is essentially imitative of American genius, and that it is entirely natural that the countries of Europe should eventually fuse – just as the American states had been through their own appalling civil war to form the great star-spangled republic of today. Anybody who has lived in Europe or watched the process of European integration will know that this analogy is simply bogus, and that type of integration will never happen on the European continent.

These are ancient countries, with ancient parliaments and other institutions, and whatever blessed unity may once have been imposed – with extreme violence (see *The Dream of Rome, passim*) – there is now no emperor, or single source of charismatic authority; and in so far as power is centralised in Brussels, and in so far as there is a twelve-star flag, it does not command the allegiance of the people in the way that Old Glory helps to unify the states of America.

It is that constant attempt to create such a unity, top down, and in advance of what people want, that helped to drive Brexit.

All of that, though, is essentially irrelevant to American concerns. The traditional State Department view is that it is a good and logical thing for Europe to unite, and if Europe is going to unite then it is a good and above all a convenient thing to have their closest Nato ally – us, the Brits – around the table in the EEC, able to tell them what is going on and pipe up for common sense. And for the British foreign policy establishment this sense of the American interest became, in turn, one of the key selling points of EEC membership.

It was the INFLUENCE, they always claimed, and that INFLUENCE of the UK in the EU was invaluable, because it helped to make us SPECIAL in Washington. Yes, it was the cornerstone of the 'special relationship' and without that influence Britain would be just … and they would go all glassy and wistful … just a little island, adrift, lost in our fogs and pounded into irrelevance by the Atlantic billows.

It is at this point in the argument – when it is claimed UK membership of the EU is somehow essential for the special relationship – that my bullshit-o-meter starts beeping like an overloaded washing machine.

The United States was born out of war with Britain. We burned down the White House in 1812, and when I once went to visit senate majority leader Mitch McConnell, he showed me a great crack in his fireplace – a legacy of the British attack on the Capitol. As America waxed and Britain waned, the US lost few opportunities to get one over on the old imperial power. When Britain was gasping for life in 1940, Roosevelt did give us some fifty obsolete destroyers – in exchange for American rights to British bases all over the Caribbean. Even when they finally joined the war against Hitler, they charged the earth for Lend-Lease (the last repayments for America's wartime generosity were made under the government of Tony Blair).

So it is important to be realistic about US–UK relations. You have to recognise that they are essentially transactional. And yet that relationship – whether you use the word 'special' or not – is a giant geopolitical reality. When Bismarck was asked at the end of the nineteenth century to name the single most important political fact of his time, he replied, 'The inherent and permanent fact that North America speaks English.'

Those were prophetic words, because in the century that followed the transatlantic alliance was essential to the defeat of Germany in two world wars, and after the Second World War it was the Americans and the Brits (very largely) who set up institutions – the UN, Nato, IMF, World Bank – that were grounded in Anglo-Saxon ideas of liberty and democracy; and in all the intervening years the organic strength of that alliance has survived and, if anything, intensified. There is the sharing of nuclear and other defence technology, on a scale that the US permits with no other ally. There is the sharing of intelligence, the reflexive assumption that we are on the same side that holds as true today as it did for James Bond and Felix Leiter of the CIA.

There is the basic willingness, time after time, to back each other up in war. The US was quietly indispensable during the Falklands conflict; and with the notable exception of Vietnam, Britain has been the *fidus Achates* of America, always loyal, always at its shoulder. We were there in the first Gulf War, when the Belgians wouldn't even sell us ammunition.

Why DID Tony Blair decide to go to war in Iraq, when there was no good evidence that Saddam possessed weapons of mass destruction? It was basically because he believed that when the chips were down, it was in the UK's long-term strategic interest to support America.

The war, alas, was a mistake. But the UK motive – backing the Americans – was sensible and right. This is an alliance that has survived and prospered because a strategic community of interest is endlessly reinforced by social and cultural exchange.

At its most basic, as Bismarck foresaw, there is the language, 500,000 words – more than twice as many as either French or German – daily evolving in the mouths of Americans and Brits. There is the economic inter-penetration, the million Brits who work for American companies, the million Americans who work for British companies.

There is the great invisible two-way travelator between London and New York, where Brits have for so long been a feature of the US media that they were satirised by Tom Wolfe in *Bonfire of the*

Vanities – remember Peter Fallow and Caroline Heftshank coming up with wheezes to get the Americans to buy them drinks? One of the problems I had in explaining Brexit to American audiences was the sheer number of British journalists who had established themselves in lofty eyries in the US media, and who were only too happy – in the time-honoured fashion of liberal England – to pour scorn on the pretensions of the Brexiteers.

Of course, there are innumerable American-made films and TV programmes that fill our global imaginations and conversations, but it is amazing how many of them seem to have British actors, and no one turns a hair. Good Lord, there's old Damian Lewis, whose brother was in my rugby team at school, sustaining a perfectly convincing American accent through umpteen episodes of *Homeland* before finally copping it, and now again in something about hedge funds called *Billions*.

There are British comedians who star in late-night US chat shows – and comedy is the toughest export of all. There was a time when Peppa Pig was so popular among pre-school New Yorkers that they started saying tomarto rather than tomayto, to the disgust of their parents; or so I am told.

I stress this cultural continuum, and this abiding strategic alliance, because I did not for one moment believe that Brexit would imperil that relationship. It was a community of ideas and values and interests that long pre-dated UK membership of the EEC, and that would comfortably outlast it.

I suppose I should add that my thinking and instincts were formed by my own personal love and admiration for America. I was born in New York City, where my parents were students, in 1964, the year after Charles de Gaulle first rejected Britain's application to join the EEC. I spent the first five years of my life in the US, and whenever I go back I have flashbacks to things I must have noticed as a child: everything bigger except the squirrels, which for some reason are slightly smaller.

I even retained dual citizenship, until the ruthless extra-territoriality of the US tax system made this impossible.

So it was all the more galling, as a convinced and sentimental Atlanticist, to be told by our number-one ally that we had made a mistake and that we should 'walk this thing back': have another referendum, presumably, like all the other European countries that had been so impertinent as to vote against EU integration. Kerry was asking us to change our minds and fold ourselves back into the bosomy embrace of Brussels.

I was indignant, and later tried to explain my feelings in more detail. It was the hypocrisy that got me. Think of those Sons of Liberty, the great tea chuckers of Boston in the eighteenth century. That spirit – the flame of freedom – still burns in America.

Of all the great western democracies, the United States is the most ruthless and the most absolute in the protection of its constitutional independence. The United States will neither share nor compromise its sovereignty with any other power or institution. The United States – unlike the UK and virtually every other European country – does not accept the jurisdiction of the International Criminal Court. The United States – unlike the UK and virtually every European country – has never ratified the UN Convention on the Law of the Sea.

Unlike the rest of us, the US has never even deigned to ratify the UN Convention on the Rights of the Child. And here was John Kerry telling the UK, the mother of parliaments, that we had to snap back into line and get used to being run by a court that we could not control and that was based in another country; and to get used to being told, forever, how many bananas you could have in a bunch, or on a shelf, or how many hours you could work per week, and how much paternity leave you had to give to a part-time worker, and so on for millions of pages of euro-bumf, all of it enforced by this international court with an explicit teleological mission to create a United States of Europe.

The Obama administration was asking us to accept something that America would NEVER accept for herself – precisely because (and here was the crowning irony) America was founded by us, by British people, on Anglo-Saxon ideas of liberty and popular sovereignty.

That evening our delegation went out for dinner at a seafood restaurant, and as I looked around Boston, this successful hub of innovation in everything from banking to bioscience, it occurred to me that the position of the Obama administration wasn't just hypocritical. It was also unfair.

They were asking us to bow down to a constitutional servitude of a kind that America would never endure. They were also asking us to accept an economic and regulatory model which – at least by comparison with America – was manifestly failing.

Compare the growth rates achieved, in the period that concerns us, by the Eurozone and the United States of America. In 2008, when the crash came, the two economies were of roughly the same size – even though the Eurozone was a bit bigger in population. The Eurozone's GDP was about $14.2 trillion, while US GDP was about $14.8 trillion.

By September 2023 – fifteen years later – the difference was staggering. The Eurozone had inched up to $15 trillion; the US had soared to $26 trillion; and British growth rates, of course, had followed the European and not the American path. Yes, China has grown too – vastly – but more at the expense of the EU than the US, and it is European jobs that are now more at risk from Chinese manufacturing.

The poorest people in America – the people of rural Mississippi – are now richer, on average, than the people of France. In Brussels they recognise this embarrassment, and they draw exactly the wrong conclusion.

Yes, they say: the US is richer than us – but that is because they have a gigantic single market. That's why you have all those Teslas silently nosing round the lanes of Oxfordshire; that's why you have an iPhone in your pocket and a MacBook on your desk. For decades the EU Commission has decided that we need an American-style single market in Europe, with vast European champion businesses to take on the Americans – in the way that Airbus has successfully challenged Boeing.

It is clear, after so many years of trying to 'complete' the EU single market, that this is very far from being the real answer.

Why are American businesses kicking European ass? Is it really because we are lacking in regulation from Brussels? Of course not. We need much less of it – and in the case of the UK we need none at all. The solution is not to hope that a European single market will miraculously incubate European versions of Apple and Tesla and Microsoft.

We need to recognise that if we want economic growth, and productivity growth, of the kind we see in America – then we need, bluntly, to be more American: in our attitudes to wealth creation, and enterprise, and personal and business taxation, and hours of work – on which Brussels keeps such a beady eye. We need to STOP imposing ever more non-wage costs of a kind that the EU is so fertile in devising.

How dare the Americans tell us to keep limping along in the slow lane, with the EU, when they have taken a wholly different approach?

Was there no one in the US who supported Brexit, on democratic grounds? Was there no one who saw the economic opportunities, both for the US and the UK?

Was there no one who wanted to do a free-trade deal?

Well, there was at least one person. A strange phenomenon was now dominating the American political landscape, like an orange-hued dirigible exuberantly buoyed aloft by the inexhaustible Primus stove of his own ego. He was provocative, he was polemical and he was profusely complimentary about Brexit Britain.

It was time to talk to the Trump campaign.

Trump and Brexit – another loose analogy

We were in the elevator in Trump Tower, a tiny group from the UK Foreign Office on an ultra-hush-hush mission. I wasn't sure exactly whom we were going to meet, and I wasn't sure what reception we would get. It was only a few months ago that Donald Trump had launched one of his casual broadsides against London – the city I had been proud to lead – and claimed, on what basis I have no idea, that parts of the UK capital were so dangerous that they were no-go areas for the police.

Law and order was maintained, he said, by groups of Muslim vigilantes. It is true that his criticism seemed to be aimed at my successor, Sadiq Khan, rather than me – but I wasn't having him say that about London.

I tweeted that London was a very safe city, and the only reason I wouldn't visit parts of New York was the risk of meeting Donald Trump. I meant it to sting.

I am not sure he even noticed. Then came Brexit in June, and the US media began drawing a read-across between the two phenomena – Brexit and the Trump campaign. According to the anti-Trump, anti-Brexit media (on both sides of the Atlantic), both of them were ugly, nativist, anti-immigrant, playing on people's basest feelings, and so on.

I did not like this loose analogising. I didn't see Brexit as a platform for the alt-right. You couldn't say that David Owen or Gisela Stuart were xenophobes. Support for Brexit was drawn from across the political spectrum. We even had some Lib Dems. So I was keen to meet the Trump team, but I was also wary.

The door opened and in came Steve Bannon, looking like a serious hangover. He was unshaven and wearing a frowsty black T-shirt, with rheumy red-rimmed eyes. He was absolutely thrilled by Brexit; and the Trump team clearly believed that our victory was to be the harbinger of their own.

I was fascinated by Steve, and liked him. I enjoyed his faint air of mania and his obvious conviction that things needed to change. We sat for a while in a strange, white, unfurnished room and tried to work out how much congruence there really was between our two movements.

We both seemed to dislike political correctness, and we both thought there were millions of people who felt left out of the current debate. So far so good – but then these things are easy to say. We got on to the economy, and I was struck by his eagerness to reopen coal mines. Why do that? I asked. They are dirty, they are uneconomic, they contribute massively to CO_2, and it really isn't that much fun being a coal miner. He grew visibly impatient.

Good jobs were being sacrificed, he said, just to appease the green movement. It was all nonsense.

Hang on, I said. In my country Margaret Thatcher went to a great deal of trouble to close the coal mines. She had to face down militant unions who went on strike illegally, without a ballot, and now we were far less dependent on coal.

Her battle with Scargill was one of the reasons, as a student, I first became even vaguely Conservative.

Was she really wrong to close those pits? I challenged Steve Bannon.

'I think it was one of the worst things she ever did,' he said.

We stared at each other across a gulf of incomprehension.

It is always treacherous to analogise between politics in the US and the UK, and the reality is that the partisans of Brexit and Trump certainly had some things in common, but also many differences.

The media were not much interested in any subtleties, and nor was Donald Trump. As far as he was concerned, Brexit was the anticipatory bow-wave of his arrival, and it just happened to have broken first in the UK.

He surfed it enthusiastically. 'It's gonna be Brexit plus plus plus,' he said on the eve of the US election in November 2016.

That night I lay awake in a hotel in Zagreb, watching the results come in. I had stayed up talking to my officials, and to a man and a woman they seemed to want Hillary Clinton to win. They were probably being careful in my company, but it was pretty clear that Trump was very far from their cup of tea.

As for me, I rather admired Hillary. She seemed a pretty no-nonsense sort and had a good sense of humour. I once met her on a mayoral trip to New York, and when a member of the British press corps pointed out that I had previously compared her to Nurse Ratched, the sadistic psychiatric nurse in *One Flew Over the Cuckoo's Nest*, she was graciously amused.

But as the counting went on into the night, and Trump started making surprising gains in odd places, I became aware that my own psyche was playing a curious trick. I was lying flat out on the bed, with the TV on, and following through half-closed eyes. Consciousness was slowly seeping away. The mammalian parts of my brain closed down, and only the lizard cortex remained functioning.

Some subconscious instinct took over. Every time the predictions of the pundits were fulfilled, and things went well for Hillary, I drifted closer to final oblivion. But every time Trump did well, and took an unexpected district or state, it was as though some hormone or neuro-transmitter was switched on, and I felt a little surge of interest and realised that some part of me – maybe just the lizard part – really wanted Trump to win.

We are all human and it is hard not to be sympathetic to those who are openly sympathetic towards you. It was hard not to like a man who was willing – in defiance of so much polite opinion – to stick up for Brexit, the great project on which Britain was then engaged, if still with too much nervousness.

And it was hard not to chuckle when prime minister Theresa May arrived in the Oval Office a few weeks later, on her first visit to see the new president, only for Donald to ask her – in front of the reporters – why Boris Johnson was not prime minister.

Reader, I confess it: the more they bashed Donald Trump, the more disdainfully they spoke of him, the more inclined I was – whatever the differences between us – to sympathise.

When he won, of course, it was wonderful to see how vastly more important and interesting I became to all our European friends. Suddenly Brexit Britain had an ally and a champion – the most powerful of all – and they wanted to know us.

They were all paranoid about Trump – terrified that he would inaugurate a new era of populist America-first politics and show no interest in the wider world. Well: you will shortly discover that the prejudices of the anti-Trump Europeans were (at least in my view) very largely misplaced.

It would be fairer to say that by 2016 US politicians on all sides were much more leery of foreign entanglements, much more worried about the loss of American life and treasure, than they had been two decades previously. To understand what had happened, we need to go back to that post-Cold War moment when the USA was the unchallenged hyperpower and we seemed to carry all before us.

We need to go back to the moment in 1999 when Tony Blair felt so confident that he actually made a speech in Chicago proclaiming the doctrine of 'liberal interventionism'; by which he meant the right of the west to use force in the name of democracy. For a while, you see, it worked.

Chapter 22

Britain Abroad

How success in Kosovo helped to breed complacency

I could see why it had all gone to Tony Blair's head. It was November 2016, on one of my first trips as foreign secretary. I stood in that little parliament in Kosovo – breasting the applause from Albanian Kosovar MPs – and I understood why our former PM had gone the teensiest bit mad.

How would you feel if you had helped to liberate a nation and grateful mothers actually named their babies in your honour? When Caesar conquered Gaul (and slaughtered about a million people in the process), there was many an ambitious new provincial who changed his forenames to Gaius Julius. When US president Andrew Johnson helped to liberate the slaves, there were plenty of African-American families who took that great surname – synonymous with freedom – and made it their own.

Today, dotted across the tiny Balkan state of Kosovo, with a population of only 1.8 million, there are eight young men, in their mid-twenties, whose parents were rendered so ecstatic at Blair's bombing of Serbia that they now bear his name. Or rather, they have a version of his name.

They are not called Tony. They are not called Blair. They are called Tonibler – a strong name for a boy.

Looking back a quarter of a century on, you can see why those Kosovar Albanians were so thrilled with the UK (and the US: there is a ten-foot statue of Bill Clinton, on Bill Clinton Boulevard). What we did, as the west, was audacious. We did not have a UN resolution with which to justify our intervention. We bombed a sovereign and independent European country, probably killing several hundred civilians within Serbia itself, and probably about a thousand members of the JNA, the Yugoslav People's Army. We pulverised bridges, roads, gas refineries, car factories.

We even took out a giant cigarette factory in Nis, as though to deprive the Serbs of the tobacco to steady their nerves.

We paved the way for a popular uprising against the iron-quiffed Russian-backed strongman Slobodan Milošević – who eventually died behind bars, while awaiting trial in The Hague.

We became one of the first countries in the world to grant official recognition to Kosovo, and to allow the overwhelmingly ethnic Albanian province to seek its own destiny. We rejected Milošević's claim that Kosovo was somehow spiritually integral to Serbia, just as we reject Putin's pseudo-religious claim to Ukraine.

I had strayed into Belgrade in the spring, before Nato really began to bomb the bejeesus out of the Serbs. My plan was to write a column or two and then get out – but once I arrived, things somehow got hairier. Alastair Campbell, the Number Ten press spokesman, later joked that as soon as Blair heard I was in Belgrade, he told SACEUR – Nato's Supreme Allied Commander in Europe – to step up the bombing.

As the Nato sorties intensified, my permission to travel was withdrawn by the Serb authorities, and so I stayed at the Hyatt hotel, for night after night, as distant explosions lit up the landscape outside. I lay in bed, sleepless, and watched that stirring movie *Face/Off* starring Nicolas Cage and John Travolta. It was tough to decide which had the more plausible plotline, the pyro-technics on screen or the events outside. By day I filed colour pieces about what it was like to be bombed by Nato.

I interviewed a family in a Nato-wrecked house, and recorded their indignation (though I did not see mass casualties, and tend to believe Nato claims about the precision of the strikes). I wandered the streets of Belgrade, browsing in the bookshops of Knez Mihailova Street and drinking beer while watching strange Serb techno-funk concerts, with suntanned women in boots and furry bikinis belting out nationalist Serb anthems. Since the whole world seemed to deplore the Serbs, I found myself, naturally, feeling some sympathy for them, as people; though not for their leadership.

After seventy-eight days of the Nato air war the Serbs decided they could take it no more, and Milošević agreed to western demands that he should pull his troops out of Kosovo. We were about to witness the triumph of Nato. So I hired a car with a Serb driver.

His name was Vuk. He was a basketball player with a neck about as thick as his head, and he drank prodigious quantities of Coca-Cola to which he attributed astonishing medical properties.

'Vuk,' I said, 'let's get the Vuk out of Belgrade.'

The British land forces were about to roll into Kosovo. It was clearly crucial that I – as the only *Daily Telegraph* reporter in the vicinity – should be on the spot to see our boys come in on their tanks. As we roared off southwards in that turbo-charged Fiat, it would be fair to say that neither Vuk nor I, nor Nato, nor the Serbs, nor anyone in Number Ten or the White House, really had a clue what was going to happen next.

It was estimated that about 800,000 Kosovo Albanians had been purged from their homes in Kosovo – in Serb-led pogroms that had begun before the Nato bombing started. The Muslims had fled to Albania and other parts of the region. Presumably they would come back. But what would happen to the Serbs?

Who would run Kosovo? All I knew was that British armed forces were about to arrive and that we British were about to make our mark, yet again, on the history and boundaries of another part of the world – a place, let's be honest, that before 1999 the average member of the British public would have struggled to find on a map.

It wasn't that I thought we were doing the wrong thing – not at all. Milošević was a commie thug, and he treated the Albanian minority appallingly. The Serbs had committed terrible atrocities in Bosnia, from 1992 to 1995. Egged on by Belgrade, the Bosnian Serb troops had engaged in slivovitz-fuelled orgies of violence and rape, ethnically cleansing villages and communities and massacring their opponents – Croats and Muslims – on a scale not seen since the Second World War.

In 1998 there was evidence that Milošević was doing the same again in Kosovo, fomenting sectarian violence against the Albanian Muslims, even though they formed the majority of the population; whipping up Serb nationalist feeling, just to shore up his own position.

I agreed that he must be stopped. I agreed that the west had been too weak in Bosnia and had intervened too late. But as I drove into Kosovo with Vuk, I wasn't at all sure what was meant to happen – and nor, I think, was anyone else. I knew that we were engaged in a novel project of humanitarian intervention. It just wasn't clear how it was supposed to work.

It did not occur to me that I would be coming back to Kosovo almost two decades later, not as a journalist but as foreign secretary, to inspect the results of what we had done.

When you become foreign secretary, you inherit all kinds of quite extraordinary things. You become the person whose instructions adorn the opening page of every British passport. You are His Britannic Majesty's Principal Secretary of State for Foreign and

Commonwealth Affairs, and you request and require of every official in the world, every unshaven border guard, every Kalashnikov-toting skunk-smoking sentry at every crossing or barricade on the planet, to permit the bearer to pass by without let or hindrance, in the name of the Crown.

You acquire the use of Chevening House, in Kent, whose beauty and luxury I scarcely dare describe for fear of provoking paroxysms of jealousy. For the purposes of travelling the world, you inherit the use of 32 Squadron of the RAF, who in those days still flew some vintage but serviceable BAe 146 jets, and whose wonderful RAF staff, uniforms pressed like knives, would serve you lavish and ruminative feasts, one hard upon the other: full English breakfasts, lunch and dinner with beer and wine, late-night canapés, and great teas – fruit cake, scones with jam and cream, and always three types of freshly cut sandwiches (ham, cheese, cucumber) – wherever you were in the world, all with RAF crockery and silver and well-ironed napkins.

All the while, on every flight, you had the gluttonous pleasure of talking to the men and women of the Foreign Office and harvesting their well-stocked minds. If you have been a foreign correspondent, as I had, and therefore come to treasure snatched conversations with these clever people, it was like being given the keys to the tuck shop.

It was heaven. You also realise, as foreign secretary, that you are the living heir of all previous British foreign policy. You are the modern legatee of former British plans, ambitions and, above all, military interventions that have – for better or worse – shaped much of the world today. The British and their armed forces have invaded, conquered, or at least partly governed, 171 of the 193 countries that make up the UN. I don't suggest that is necessarily a matter for pride, or necessarily a matter for shame and regret.

It is just a fact, and the world has to deal with it, and we have to deal with it. As foreign secretary, you go to country after country that has been created by your predecessors. You meet the modern representatives of dynasties that were put on the throne by the gunboats despatched by people who sat in the same great gilt-painted racquet-court-sized office in King Charles Street.

You have to deal with the same ethnic or religious tensions that your forebears had tried (and often failed) to solve, and across the world you scratch your head at the boundaries and borders they created. The more you travel – and in a couple of years, I visited 132 countries – the more you marvel at the global impact of the UK: the world language, the world sports, even the business suits worn by men in every government in the world, which have their origin in early nineteenth-century London.

You find that we are often blamed and resented; and you hang your head at some of the truly shocking things that were done in the name of empire. You also find that we did some good things. I am writing this on a plane from Brazil, where the curator of a gallery reminded me that theirs was the last country on earth officially to abolish slavery, and they did it thanks to the Royal Navy.

Everywhere I went I found that people wanted more Britain, not less. They wanted more British investment, more partnership, more commitment; and in many turbulent places there was one export – and this was certainly the case with the Kosovo Albanians – that they craved more than any other, and that was UK armed forces.

The great question for Brits of my generation is how to respond. Our means are now so limited, relatively speaking. We are dependent on our partnership with the US, for logistics and intel-ligence-sharing and so much else.

When was it right, morally and strategically, to intervene? For much of the post-war period – in the 1960s, 1970s and 1980s – the decades in which I was born and grew up – the British ruling classes were pretty leery of conflict abroad. The country's leaders felt reduced, exhausted by the Second World War, and then humiliated by Suez in 1956, when the Americans pulled the plug on us, and – quite sensibly – halted an Anglo-French operation to seize the Suez Canal. We were deterred from any traditional British adventurism, above all, by the logic of the Cold War, and the risk that any conflict would be turned into a Great Power conflict in which we would find ourselves ranged against the Soviet Union and its allies.

Yes, Margaret Thatcher retook the Falkland Islands in 1982, and yes, the UK played a big role in helping to kick Saddam Hussein out of Kuwait in 1991. But in the Falklands the UK had an unassailable legal right to self-defence, and the first Gulf War had a clear UN mandate; in other words, both ventures had Russian and Chinese acquiescence. They were about restoring sovereign borders, and rectifying gross and blatant violations of international law.

They were not advertised as interventions in the lives and domestic politics of other countries. Then came the collapse of the Soviet Union, and the dawn of a unipolar world in which the United States had more or less unchallenged military authority – with a navy, for instance, that was thirteen times bigger than the next-biggest navy in the world (no longer the case; the Chinese now have more ships, though far fewer aircraft carriers).

As the 1990s wore on, a new possibility emerged: that the west could use a kind of morally sanitised violence to effect change in other countries and to export our values by force, just as we had once been powerful enough to ban suttee in India. Western publics had been scandalised by the massacres in Bosnia and Rwanda and their inescapable echoes of the genocide of the Second World War. By the time Tony Blair came to power in 1997, there was a liberal internationalist consensus that it must not happen again. The Clinton administration was determined to stop it in Kosovo, and so was Blair.

So that warm June day I drove into Kosovo, my eyes peeled for the effects of what we were doing: liberal interventionism – bombing or invading a country because we disapproved of something being done, within its own borders, by the rulers of that country.

We were in a kind of Wacky Races convoy of international journalists, and though Vuk was driving like a maniac, it was slow-going. We kept pulling off the road to avoid getting crushed. Roaring towards us, sitting on their tanks and waving bottles of beer and plum brandy, was the Yugoslav army: drunk, cheering, elated, I suppose, that they had escaped the Nato bombs. I saw tanks and rocket launchers still covered with foliage; and sinister units whose armoured personnel carriers (APCs) were painted black with white skull and crossbones, or with black and orange stripes and giant fanged mouths. These, I was told, were the dreaded 'Tigers' of Arkan, the swaggering track-suited Serb war criminal – real name Željko Ražnatović – who hung around the lobby of my hotel and gave blood-curdling interviews about the reprisals he would inflict on the Kosovar Muslims.

As they passed, I could tell that Vuk was distressed to see his country's army in retreat. He parped his horn in support of the vanquished Serbs and cursed under his breath. It was increasingly clear that he was worried about what might happen to him in Kosovo.

I, Johnson, would be all right, but he was a young Serb male.

'They will shoot me,' he said, meaning the Albanians. 'They are kinds of stinky monkeys.' Vuk was expressing the classic dehumanising language that is the prelude to ethnic cleansing or murder – the sort of atrocities that were committed by all sides in the Balkans. He was right to be fearful about what could happen next.

When Number Ten was trying to articulate the Nato objectives in Kosovo, they came up with a typical verbless Blairite slogan: 'The Serbs out, Nato in, the Refugees back home'. I suppose they meant the Serb ARMY out, rather than the Serb population. The distinction was lost on the vengeful Muslims.

Now the boot was on the other foot, and for the next few days it was the Serbs' turn to flee their farms and villages. I watched a long convoy of Serb families as they wound slowly through the dust from a town in the south called Suva Reka, their little red tractors pulling carts piled high with mattresses and saucepans.

It was a humiliation for the Serbs, a disaster, and it was no consolation that the blame lay largely with Milošević. It was also a humiliation for their sponsors, the Russians. In the old days, Milošević would have had the protection of being a Soviet client. Not any more. We were living in a unipolar world, and we didn't really care much what Russia thought about it all.

I was there at Pristina Airport when – or so everyone claimed afterwards – we almost had World War Three. Vuk and I had got to Kosovo before the Americans, and before the Brits. But so did the Russians.

A group of about thirty Russian APCs – curious, squat, purple-painted vehicles – had torn down the road from Bosnia. They had hastily daubed the letters 'KFOR' on their sides, meaning that they were now part of a UN-led Kosovo Protection Force; and they occupied Slatina Airport.

Their plan was to hold the runway and allow Russian Ilyushins to land, and fill Kosovo with enough Russian troops to provide sanctuary for the Serbs – the beginning of a partition of the province. The Nato commander was an American general, Wes Clark – a slightly messianic figure.

He went crackers at the news. This was a Nato operation, and the Russians were plainly trying to stuff it up. He told Mike Jackson, the British general, to clear the Russians out of the airport – by force. I saw a stand-off in which an eminently reasonable young British officer tried to get the Russians to budge.

Washington, DC
aged about 4

With Marina at
the *Spectator*

Opposite, top left: First
school, aged about 4,
Washington, DC

Opposite, top right: With
Leo and Rachel in the
early 1970s, Primrose Hill

Opposite, centre left:
Swotting aged about 16

Opposite, centre right:
Becoming a Eurosceptic:
EEC Correspondent of the
Daily Telegraph c.1989

Opposite, bottom: *Spectator*
editor about 1999

Waving the Olympic flag
in the Bird's Nest stadium,
Beijing, after refusing to do up
my jacket buttons, 2008

Above: Walking with police superintendent Jo Oakley near burnt-out Reeves Corner furniture store in Croydon on August 9, 2011. Overcome with shame, I watched it burn while at an airport in Canada

Left: Thanking Clapham residents for sweeping up the glass – just before the crowd turned hostile

Below: Marina and the kids waiting to hear the 2012 mayoral election results at City Hall – we won, even though the Tories were 15 points behind in London

Above: With Lara, Milo, Marina, Cassia and Theo on our way to see Miley Cyrus

Right: Squeaky bum time. With Eddie Lister, Lynton Crosby, Sam Lyon and Kit Malthouse on mayoral election night, 2012

Below: With my old adversary Ken Livingstone, a brilliantly creative politician and a great disruptor

Launching the new-generation
Routemaster in 2012

With Leo, Rachel, my father and Jo – out in Orpington campaigning for Jo, 2015

Cycling down Whitehall – I cycled miles every day as mayor and never fell off

Phoenix from the ashes
– a new powerhouse
at Battersea: a model
for infrastructure-led
regeneration

Launching the
ArcelorMittal Orbit

Showing Arnie
the hire bikes

Shooting backwards, basketball, April 8, 2013

Above: At the Olympics, with Tessa Sanderson, Kelly Holmes and Jayne Torvill

Above: Honouring Usain Bolt with volunteers and Gamesmakers, London Olympics 2012

With Milo and Theo at the cycling in 2012

Successfully promoting the
Zipwire at the Olympic Live
Site in Victoria Park, 2012

Vote Leave, with Gisela
Stuart, May 11, 2016

Let's Take
Back Control

Arriving at the Foreign Office

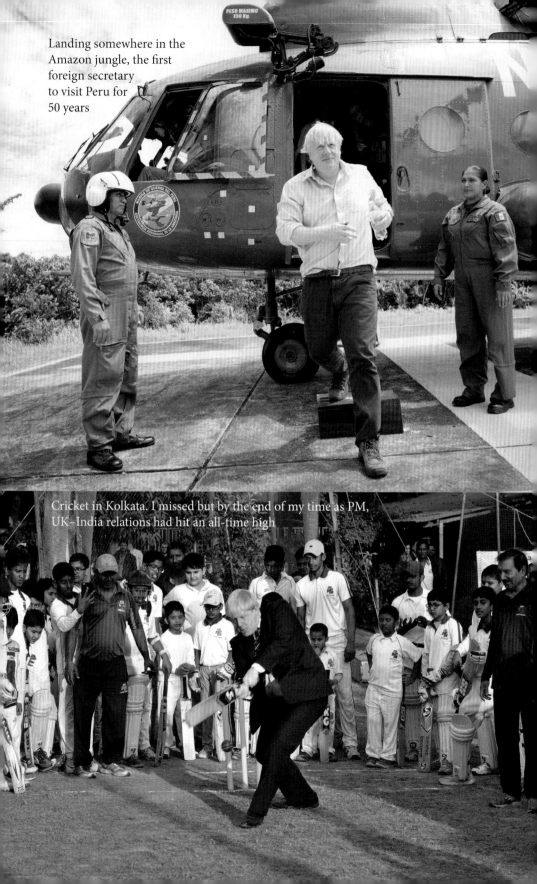

Landing somewhere in the Amazon jungle, the first foreign secretary to visit Peru for 50 years

Cricket in Kolkata. I missed but by the end of my time as PM, UK–India relations had hit an all-time high

In the charred remains of a Rohingya village, Burma, and finding the clearest possible evidence of genocide

Laying flowers for Boris Nemtsov on a bridge by the Kremlin in Moscow, December 22, 2017, having outwitted the Russian security team to do this. Their revenge was to take me on a long detour around Moscow, making me late for my next meeting

Winning the Tory leadership, July 2019. Jeremy
Hunt was competitive but gracious throughout

I wasn't exactly sure how I was going
to punch through and get Brexit
done – but I always knew we would

The Russian commander was one of those high-cheekboned Slavic types, with steel-capped teeth and pink Yuri Gagarin gums, and wrestler's forearms. He looked pretty scary. He wasn't moving, he said. In the end Gen. Jackson told Clark, 'I am not going to start World War Three for you', and conflict was averted.

The Russians had nowhere else to go, and nothing much to do. They were not invited to be part of the coalition effort. They were not given a sector to patrol. After a while they left, along with the Serbs.

Yes, I suppose it was psychologically tough for the Russians to come to terms with the new reality, that they no longer had a 'sphere of interest'. But the whole point of the end of the Cold War was that we had a 'Europe whole and free', in which peoples and nations were free to choose their destiny; and the Kosovars were choosing their own.

Of course Nato expansion was on the agenda of many of those former Soviet-dominated countries, and rightly so. They had made their choice. They didn't want to be the satellites of Moscow, effectively under imperial Russian rule. They wanted to join the great western clubs. They wanted to be free market democracies, and they were perfectly entitled to ask for Nato protection and membership, and we were quite right to give it.

That was the year, 1999, when Poland, Hungary and the Czech Republic became the first central Europeans to join the Nato alliance. They wanted to join partly, of course, because in the last fifty years they had ALL been invaded brutally by the Russians (which is why the case for Ukrainian membership is now unanswerable). So began the steady expansion that has so fuelled Russian paranoia; a paranoia that is much more about Russian pride and *amour-propre* than any real strategic threat.

We helped to protect the Kosovars because it was morally justified; but also because we could, because we felt that the west was now unchallengeable. We even bombed the Chinese embassy in Belgrade and killed three Chinese reporters.

So I walked around a dank and drizzly Pristina seventeen years later, and I asked myself: did it work? What did we achieve by our ethical bombing?

Well, it certainly worked for the Kosovo Albanians, who had faced chronic persecution and discrimination from the Serbs, and for the 800,000 Kosovar refugees who did indeed return home. They now have their own state, recognised by over half the UN countries.

Did it work out for the Serbs in Kosovo? I am afraid not.

As I nosed around the town it still looked a bit drab, a bit sludgy, a bit socialist. They had fixed the bombed-out windows of the Grand Hotel, where I had stayed – but it wasn't exactly the Ritz. You could not say that Kosovo today, for all that we have done, is a model of free-market democracy. I had a very warm welcome from the president, Hashim Thaçi, and have always maintained the friendliest relations with him. It is a measure of how hard it is for Kosovo to escape the past that he has now been forced to resign, indicted for war crimes that include allegedly trafficking in the organs of Serb soldiers.

Kids in Kosovo don't spend long enough in school. The place is still far too dependent on remittances and the cash handouts of the western agencies. The few remaining Serbs, mainly in the north, face persecution, and Kosovo is continually vulnerable to economic manipulation by Serbia, its much bigger neighbour to the north.

What are the lessons? Number one: that you can't leave places in limbo. The really successful parts of the former Yugoslavia – Slovenia and Croatia – are the ones that have joined both Nato and the EU, and that have had a straightforward western vocation. There are still five EU countries, led by Spain, that won't even recognise Kosovo.

That is a mistake. It is a mistake we were to repeat in Ukraine. If countries and populations want to choose the west, we should help them come.

The other lesson is that you can change a regime, and you can inflict a military defeat, but you can't necessarily change a country for the better – not from outside, not just by bombing and invading.

In the end change must come from within, and it must come from the people themselves. Kosovo was therefore a partial success for the new triumphalist doctrine of liberal humanitarian intervention, and at any rate it was deemed a success at the time.

It was followed in 2000 by the Sierra Leone operation, where Blair successfully sent in troops to stop a murderous limb-chopping rebel army from overwhelming the capital. Then in 2001 there was the pushover war in Afghanistan, where the armies sent by Bush and Blair made short work of removing the Taliban.

Hubris was beginning to set in. It looked as though – after years of caution – we were starting to get an overweening confidence about our ability to use armed force to change the world for the better. In 2003 the doctrine of liberal humanitarian interventionism was invoked again – along with various patent falsehoods – to invade another sovereign and independent country.

This time the results were very largely disastrous.

Chapter 23

Mayhem in Mesopotamia

Where western hubris goes off the scale –
and I see the consequences

It was towards the end of April 2003. I was in the back of a taxi in Sadr City, a big Shia district of Baghdad with the wide, tank-friendly boulevards that are designed to help the regime put down rebellions. I had arrived just a few days after the end of the war – or just after the allied forces, led by the US, and with Britain in our loyal adjutant role, had biffed the Iraqi army to kingdom come, toppled Saddam like a ninepin and taken control of the Iraqi capital.

Control? Did I say control?

No one was in control. From the minute I arrived in Baghdad, it was clear that the sceptics were going to be proved right. The war had all the makings of a disaster. I tried to stay optimistic as I surveyed the damage – but the evidence was overwhelming.

I was then the editor of the *Spectator* and MP for Henley, as well as a weekly *Telegraph* columnist (those were the days, eh). With a total lack of battlefield training, I had bummed a ride overnight in a convoy of vehicles driven by those tough UK ex-special forces types (often from Belfast, for some reason) that tend to find jobs in war zones.

I checked into the Al-Rasheed Hotel in the small hours – looking pretty smashed about, but still the best in the city – and after a fine Iraqi breakfast of hummus and tabbouleh and whatnot I sauntered off, with my interpreter Isaac, to shove my notebook under some noses and get some 'colour' for my magazine.

It was a hair-raising day. Everywhere you could hear the *pop-pop-pop* of distant gunfire, like the tearing of a calico sheet. Almost immediately I chanced upon a serious misunderstanding between some US Marines and an Iraqi telecoms engineer. He was fiddling around with some wires on a pole, and they didn't like the look of it. The US soldiers kept shouting at him to get away from the pole and put his hands up, but he seemed oblivious.

I really think they might have shot him if I had not croakily intervened, at which point the Marines turned their carbines in my direction and stared through their wraparound sunglasses. Who the hell was I, they demanded, and what was I doing there?

The answer is that I was there to salve my conscience. As so often with those of us who are forced by our professions to take fast decisions on the basis of inadequate information, I had come in the nervous hope of being vindicated.

As an MP, I had voted for this war. As an editor, I had glumly leaderised in favour of going in. But the truth was that I had never liked it. In the weeks leading up to the invasion, in early 2003, I went to a political dinner at the home of Conrad and Barbara Black, Conrad being at the time the proprietor of the *Telegraph* (and one who was always unfailingly kind to me).

Some of my friends were there, young Tory MPs or would-be MPs: Gove, Boles, Godson, that kind of thing; and they competed as to who could strike the most stridently martial attitudes. It was a feast of neo-con belligerence. At the end Conrad summed up, semi-satirically, the mood of the meeting.

As far as he was concerned, he said, the war could not come soon enough.

'When,' he demanded, 'are we going to unleash the tide of hate?'

What's wrong with me? I wondered as I cycled moodily home. Why did I not share the bloodlust, the warlike spirit that burned with such magnesium brightness in the breasts of my comrades?

I was also struck by the scepticism of some of my Tory constituents, wise old birds who had seen a thing or two. 'Why are you lot backing this?' asked Bill Birch-Reynardson, a white-haired City lawyer, at an event in some beautifully tended Oxfordshire garden. He jabbed at my chest, and I noticed that he had a couple of joints missing from the middle fingers of his right hand.

No, I discovered later, it wasn't a lawnmower accident. He'd lost them on active service in the Second World War. He knew the horrors.

My answers seemed so feeble. Because my party leader, Iain Duncan-Smith, was backing it? Because British troops – some of them based in South Oxfordshire – were already being readied for battle, and it seemed unthinkable, as a Tory MP, not to back our boys?

There was to be a key vote in Parliament, and as the day drew nearer I found myself walking down the colonnade with Cameron and Osborne. I was loudly airing my doubts. Dave was also worried and had sceptics in his own association. But George was all for it (remember he thought that Blair was 'the Master').

He spotted William Hague, his chum and also then a bit of a neo-con, and hailed him.

Boris was being a wimp on the Iraq war, said George.

'Go on, Boris,' urged Hague, our former party leader, 'be a hawk.' Like a fool, I am afraid that I took his advice.

I made a tortured and unconvincing speech in the debate, voted for war; and now I was in Sadr City looking at what was, by extension, my handiwork. It wasn't just the destruction: the pancaked buildings; the charred Iraqi tanks, their turrets popped off like biscuit tin lids. It was the lawlessness.

There were gangs ripping the copper cabling from the streets and taking it off to be sold, and the resulting power failures were driving people crazy. In one bombed-out and deserted ministry I met a tall, grey-haired American in fatigues, wandering down the looted and paper-strewn corridors. He told me he was from the US government and that he was hoping to find some remnants of the Iraqi government.

Well, good luck with that, I said. We had destroyed the Iraqi government, and nothing was sprouting to replace it. The entire apparatus of state power had collapsed and scarpered. Anarchy reigned. It was like Thucydides on stasis in Corcyra, except with bombs and guns.

I went to the house of Tariq Aziz, the owlish and moustachioed foreign minister, deputy prime minister and close ally of Saddam Hussein (when does Saddam have his dinner? When Tariq Aziz). I found a detached villa, guarded by grinning Shia militiamen with AK-47s. Aziz was gone, they said, already held by the Americans. But I was welcome to go inside. I decided to rootle around, in an attempt to emulate my *Telegraph* colleague and friend David Blair, who had already found all sorts of fascinating stuff among the wreckage of Baghdad.

At the bottom of a disused indoor swimming pool I found the fellow's medical records (he had hypertension, not surprisingly) and a red leather cigar case, big enough for three cigars – one for him, one for Saddam and one for George Galloway, I imagine. I put it in my pocket, and later made the mistake of referring in print to my discovery. When I was campaigning to be mayor of London in 2008, the column was uncovered by Ken Livingstone's researchers, and he set up a great hue and cry, denouncing me as a thief of cultural artefacts; and even though the family of Tariq Aziz actually wrote to me to say that I could keep the damn thing, the Metropolitan Police have an extreme finickiness when it comes to political cases – as I was later to discover.

Scotland Yard sent me a let's-be-having-you letter, asking me to hand it over; so I did, and as far as I know it's still there, in some great vault of recovered stolen treasures. You can probably go and view it, the cigar case of the Iraqi deputy prime minister, looted by the future British PM, confiscated by the Met. I felt then, and feel now, that I wasn't stealing that cigar case.

Like Elgin rescuing the marbles from the Ottoman lime kiln, I was conserving it from the otherwise universal pillage.

What had we achieved, I wondered as I drove through that filthy market in Sadr City, full of yellowy dag-encrusted sheep. The crowd spotted me with my notebook. They started to complain about the blackouts and the failures of the sewage pumps. Who was in charge? they wanted to know, as I beat a retreat back to the taxi. They were jabbering at the window when a buzzard-like man thrust his face through and shouted that he had no money, no job, and that everyone was shooting the whole time.

'If this goes on,' he said, dramatically flapping open his waistcoat to reveal his skinny chest, 'I will become a suicide bomber.'

I shrank back. So would you. First people were pulling guns on me; now this chap was threatening to blow himself up. When Conrad Black talked about 'the tide of hate', I don't think he meant to be entirely serious – yet it seemed to be all too accurate. Whatever happened to that man in Sadr City, plenty of people did go on to be suicide bombers. How many people died in the inter-communal violence that followed the overthrow of Saddam Hussein? Estimates vary – from 200,000 to more than half a million.

Like Tariq Aziz, my interpreter Isaac was a Chaldean Catholic. Christianity was more or less protected under the Baathist regime of Saddam, and he was nervous – rightly as it turned out – about the persecution that would befall adherents of his own religion. When we got back to the Al-Rasheed that night, pretty drained, Isaac wagged his finger at me and rolled his eyes.

'As your William Shakespeare has written in his novel *Julius Caesar*,' he said, 'it is better to have a tyrant than no ruler at all.'

It is of course possible to argue that the west was not entirely to blame for the suffering and terrorism that followed the fall of the tyrant Saddam. The west didn't create the jihadi ideology, and it was obviously true that the worst Islamist atrocity against the west – 9/11 – had come before the war. We didn't create the Sunni–Shia division, and whatever the chaos we left, there had been plenty of sectarian murder in Iraq before we invaded.

Saddam had killed numberless Shia; he had gassed the Kurds; he had bombed the marsh Arabs and drained their homeland. The problem was that we in the west (I mean we who made the mistake of supporting the war) were rendered morally incapable of making any such arguments.

The war was supposed to have been fought to prevent Saddam Hussein from using his existing stocks of nuclear, chemical and biological weapons; and it was clear almost from the instant Baghdad fell that Tony Blair had lost all authority in the debate – because the war was patently based on a lie.

We may have found some fascinating objects in post-war Baghdad. But there were no weapons of mass destruction. We knew that Saddam had once had them. UK firms had even tried to supply them. In 1991 a company called Sheffield Forgemasters had been making huge round tubular segments for a vast intercontinental blunderbuss or supergun, 156 metres long with a bore of one metre, which would have allowed Saddam to fire a shell into the stratosphere.

What did they think they were making? A sewage pipe? A gin distillery? The project was only foiled when the gun's designer, a Canadian scientist called Gerald Bull, was shot at his flat in Brussels. I know, because as Brussels correspondent I reported the story, though I rather dully failed to grasp the implications.

Another company, Matrix Churchill, had been sending machine tools for making weapons, with the secret connivance of the Thatcher government. The French had not only supplied uranium. They supplied the Osirak nuclear reactor, later blown up by Israel. The Germans were at it, too.

It obviously suited the warmongers to claim that he still had WMD, or was still making them. I don't know what Tony Blair and Alastair Campbell actually believed, in the deepest recesses of their minds, when they claimed that Saddam possessed such weapons in 2003. But they surely knew enough, from the total failure of the UN weapons inspectors to find any proof in the months leading up to the war, to suspect that Saddam was actually telling the truth.

The pre-war searches had gone on and on. Hans Blix and his teams of UN inspectors found two-thirds of diddly squat. Many of us had already started to believe Saddam, rather than Blair, and to think that it was probably true to say that he had abandoned his programme of creating weapons of mass destruction after the first Gulf War in 1991. In fact, the one thing to be said in favour of my speech on the eve of the Iraq War is that I plainly did not swallow the Blair line on WMD.

I think Blair and Campbell also knew, or strongly suspected, that their claims were rubbish – and yet they claimed, and allowed the public to believe, that the Iraqi leader could at any moment equip fanatical Islamist terrorists with chemical or biological weapons. It turned out to be a great stinking heaving lie, and the fact of that lie, the fact that the war was based on a western false-hood, proved utterly poisonous.

The war did not create Islamist extremism; certainly not. But it handed to anyone preaching such hatred a powerful and seemingly unanswerable point: that the west was willing to attack Muslim countries and blatantly lie about the reason.

So of course the Iraq War helped to trigger the rash of terrorism that followed – the hideous bombings and stabbings and beheadings and crowd-rammings that were to become a tragic feature of life in so many western cities. And of course the Iraq War was responsible for the deaths of those hundreds of thousands of Iraqi civilians – and quite a few western troops – in the strife that followed.

I went back to Baghdad a couple of years later, with some parliamentary colleagues, and if anything things were even worse. The first time, in 2003, the whole place was still in a kind of shock – that was why I was able to wander around with a notebook, and no flak jacket and no protection of any kind. You certainly couldn't do that in 2005.

By now Baghdad was so bad that non-Iraqis hardly ever left the fortified green zone, and in Basra I didn't even leave the base. I slept in a kind of steel container surrounded by huge steel and concrete sacks called Hescos, and the following year UK forces were compelled, ignominiously, to flee the whole city.

Apart from getting rid of Saddam, I am afraid there is very little to be said in favour of what we did in Iraq in 2003. It was an arrogant, conceited and misbegotten venture. Blair joined the Bush mission partly because of a sound instinct – that it was always a good idea to stick close to the US – but partly out of hubris.

He felt that things had gone well in Sierra Leone and Kosovo. He felt he was a winner and that the laurels of victory would adorn his brow again. So we deposed a government and reduced a country to chaos, without a clue as to what would happen next. Then, oops, in 2011 we did it again.

Chapter 24

Killing Gaddafi

Was a lot easier than replacing him

When I first became conscious of Gaddafi – probably at school – he was partly a figure of comedy, a Sacha Baron Cohen parody of a Middle Eastern dictator, with his four-hour speeches, his braided epaulettes, his Amazon bodyguards in tight shirts and lipstick. He was also obviously evil.

He brutalised his population, tortured his opponents and extravagantly sponsored terrorist attacks on the west. He gave explosives and weapons to the IRA, and there are plenty who believe that it was Libyan Semtex that was used in the Hyde Park and Regent's Park bombings in 1982 – the first a particularly revolting nail bomb that maimed and killed horses as well as human beings.

There was no doubt at all that the Libyan government, and probably Gaddafi himself, were behind the cold-blooded shooting in St James's Square W1 of a twenty-five-year-old WPC called Yvonne Fletcher. As mayor of London, I used to meet her family every year; and I hung my head as I muttered my condolences, because her killers had still not been brought to justice, even though we knew perfectly well who had done it – in broad daylight, in central London.

I was sitting at my desk in Brussels in December 1988 when the news announced the bombing of Pan Am 103, and I listened in shock at the description of bodies raining from the sky over the town of Lockerbie, and how some of them were found almost unmarked, as if asleep, in the surrounding fields. Gaddafi was a monster, an egomaniac who was responsible for the biggest massacre in UK aviation history. How could the UK ever have anything to do with him?

Oh but we could, and we did. Somehow this egregious sponsor of terrorism persuaded the Blair government that he could be useful in the 'war on terror'. As an essentially military despot, 'Colonel' Gaddafi was none too keen on jihadis, and the Libyan security services were only too happy to identify members of al-Qaeda – whether they were really Islamists or just opponents of Gaddafi, or both.

British companies had already started to pile into Tripoli. Harrods proprietor Mohamed al-Fayed went out in 2000 to loll on the cushions with Gaddafi, and came back boasting of the £25 billion contracts he had secured for hotels and tourism – or so he told me in the pages of the *Spectator*. It seemed extraordinary that he should be allowed to do this; but it was more believable (and printable) than some of the things he told me.

This emetic love-in reached its zenith in 2004, when Tony Blair himself went to Tripoli and sat in the tent with Gaddafi. They did the deal in the desert. If Gaddafi admitted his crimes, paid compensation to his victims, and stopped his weapons programmes, then sanctions would be lifted and normal relations could be resumed.

In 2009 this glutinous détente finally went too far, when the Scottish government, then led by Labour, decided to release the one man convicted of the Lockerbie bombing, a former Libyan Airlines official called Abdelbaset al-Megrahi. It was a pretty remarkable decision.

This was the author of the biggest mass murder in British history. His Semtex bomb had killed 259 on the plane, and a further 11 inhabitants of Lockerbie on the ground. It was true that he was ill, and wanted to die in Libya – but was it really compassion that prompted us to let him go? He didn't show much compassion for the passengers of Pan Am 103.

What possessed us to send him back to Tripoli, where, of course, he received a hero's welcome? As I discovered when I became foreign secretary, Libya is basically a coastal road linking Tripoli and Benghazi, to the north of a huge hot desert, and its relative poverty and squalor are a total disgrace because it is sitting on phenomenal quantities of oil. We sucked up to Gaddafi because we wanted compensation for the Lockerbie victims, and we wanted him to stop his chemical and nuclear programme (which was sensible); but I am sure we were also thinking of commercial opportunities for UK companies.

That's why we tore up our principles and betrayed the memory of his victims. Then we switched sides again.

In 2011 we had the Arab Spring, a series of popular uprisings across the Middle East. First the Tunisian president was felled, then Hosni Mubarak of Egypt, and then Gaddafi was in the firing line. Now the Libyan strongman was facing a popular uprising, and threatening terrible reprisals against the people of Benghazi.

We didn't just turn our backs on him.

We launched air strikes against him, Nato air strikes led by the US, UK and France. In October 2011 we finished him off, as his convoy was driving out of his hiding place in Sirte, and Gaddafi and his entourage found themselves engaged from on high by an RAF Batavia Tornado. Look at the footage, if you can bear it, of Blair's buddy being dragged from a storm drain by the mob. They stab him in the buttocks, or sodomise him, according to some accounts, with a bayonet. They beat him. You can hear the former dictator begging for his life, pleading to know what he has ever done to hurt his captors. Then he is dead, his lolling face a mask of blood.

Gaddafi was a creep of intergalactic proportions. But you look at what we did in Libya and you can see why Putin is able to find an audience for his claim that the west is fickle, and liable to rat you out.

You look at post-Gaddafi Libya, and you ask yourself – was this really what we intended? I went several times, from 2016 to 2019, and my mission was to see if we could begin to bubblegum it all back together. It was pretty hopeless.

We had to go via Malta and then Tunisia (the elderly BAe 146s sometimes conking out en route, so that it took ages), and when we got there we found a total shambles.

Tripoli was flyblown and shell-scarred, with blue plastic bags and other detritus strewn over the landscape. Post-Gaddafi Libya was like post-Saddam Iraq in that it had collapsed into rival ethnic or tribal fiefdoms. There seemed to be about three separate parliaments and at least two rival seats of government, in Tripoli and Benghazi.

The nominal ruler of Libya was a charming gentleman called Fayez al-Sarraj, with whom I was on very cordial terms. I think he had a house in Wimbledon. He had the solid support of the British, the Americans and the Italians – but he didn't seem to control anything beyond the suburbs of Tripoli. There was a faction of Islamists in Misrata. Then there was a chap in Tobruk, a man of inveterate cunning called Agileh Saleh.

Libya had been shattered, and one ghastly glowering male ego had been replaced by a group of about half a dozen male egos all vying for mastery. Nothing we said or did, no blandishments we offered, would persuade them to grow up and unite and take the country forwards.

The result was that this vast country was, and remains, divided, chaotic, violent and a huge pulsing exporter of illegal immigrants from Africa to Europe. There was a brief flurry of excitement when a would-be strongman appeared on the scene, by the name of Field Marshal Haftar. This aged generalissimo had the backing of Emmanuel Macron, the Russians, the Egyptians. He seemed to have the requisite dark glasses and braid.

Perhaps he could be the new Gaddafi, bang heads, sort it all out? Some of my parliamentary colleagues went to see him in his headquarters near Benghazi.

Kwasi Kwarteng came back impressed. 'He's a bastard,' he said, 'but he could be our bastard.'

So I went to see for myself. I kind of loved Haftar for the effort he made. He did his best to look like a Middle Eastern strong-man. There was a band in ill-fitting uniforms that parped out a version of the British national anthem; a truly memorable noise. It was like a four-year-old's drawing of the Queen – you admired the effort.

There were ribbons of red carpet that crossed the yard of his headquarters, but the desert wind was blowing so hard that the carpet writhed ahead of us like a snake, and I kept having to jump on it to stop it blowing away.

He had acquired some of Gaddafi's legendary female body-guard, and as a visiting dignitary I was invited to inspect them, which of course I did. They were suitably statuesque and terrify-ing, and one of them stared at me imperiously through startling blue contact lenses.

He had the shades, he had the guns, he had the Amazons – but Haftar was no Gaddafi. The field marshal (he had elevated himself to the rank) seemed to be about eighty, and as we sat in his parlour we didn't really have a discussion. He simply read out, in Arabic, an interminable disquisition on the constitution of Libya – a pretty arbitrary concept at the best of times.

In the end Haftar failed to take Tripoli or unify the country, and the squabbling continued. I tried to reopen the British embassy, and hauled up the Union flag in a short and heavily guarded ceremony in Tripoli. But as far as I know the place is still a wreck, still burned out from the events of 2011. The only thing they hadn't looted was the pool table.

Our policy had slalomed across the piste. First we treated Gaddafi as a Mad Dog, in the words of Ronald Reagan: bombed him, shunned him, sanctioned him. Then we cravenly made peace with him, and chose to forget the crimes against Yvonne Fletcher and countless others, and in the process of genuflecting to the oil-rich fiend we even helped him crush his opponents, sending men like Abdel Hakim al-Belhaj back to Libya, where he was tortured by the regime.

And then, *whoosh*, we did a 180-degree turn and sent Nato warplanes to blitz Gaddafi and his family, and effectively collaborated in his torture and murder. Oh yes, we then apologised to Belhaj, in 2018, for sending him back to Libya to be tortured. The whole thing – a W-turn – was really pretty sinuous.

Saddam was a monster. Gaddafi was a monster. It was entirely reasonable to want them gone – but if and only if we had an idea of what would come next. In a way I sympathise with Tony Blair and Mohamed Al-Fayed, who wanted better commercial relations between Britain and Libya. The country is in a terrible state, but it has such potential: barely seven million people, a vast and underdeveloped coastline with wonderful beaches and some of the greatest sites of antiquity, most of them barely visited by western tourists, to say nothing of the natural wealth in hydrocarbons. As Herodotus put it, the world is divided into Europe, Asia and Libya.

I kept trying to help an enterprising British company that wanted to turn Sirte into a kind of Libyan Las Vegas, or Dubai, and I was attempting to explain their vision to an audience at Tory conference in 2017.

The only thing they had to do, I said, was clear away the dead bodies. It wasn't the most tactful way of making the point, and my enemies accused me of ghastly flippancy, etc. But the merit of jokes is of course that they wake up the audience and make them pay attention to what you are saying; and as with all my so-called gaffes, I was only telling the truth.

Sirte was then a nightmare landscape, where battles between Daesh and other fighters had only just ended; and there really were booby-trapped corpses in the ruins. The security situation was terrible, and remains so.

It isn't our fault that the Libyans can't get their act together; and you could argue that after forty-two years of Gaddafi's dictatorship, there was always going to be trouble replacing him. The problem is that we piled in on a popular uprising, helped to remove Gaddafi, and therefore cannot escape some responsibility for the chaos.

We broke it, we bought it, we own it; or that is certainly how it can be made to appear. That is why the Libyan failure really marked the end of the Blair doctrine of liberal humanitarian interventionism. As a doctrine, it lasted about a decade or slightly more.

It began with Kosovo. It reached its apogee in Iraq. When it finally collapsed in Libya, it was the end of hubris, the end of the swaggering self-confidence of the unipolar world.

We had been able to destroy regimes, but we had been signally unable to replace them. So when it came to Bashar al-Assad, the next Arab dictator to find himself in trouble, our confidence had melted away. As the Syrian civil war blew up and Assad tottered, we were willing to wound, but afraid to strike.

Chapter 25

The Butcher of Aleppo

Our indecision and confusion
give Putin his chance

I had been to Syria a couple of times before the war broke out: once with the BBC, making a documentary about the Roman Empire, and once with Milo and Cassia, when we went on the trail of a twelfth-century poet and diplomat called Usama ibn Munqidh, a sheikh who memorably satirised the Frankish crusaders – their primitive medicines and barbarous manners, the strange Brazilian waxes of their wives.

I was planning a book on ibn Munqidh and his world (contain your impatience: it's coming one day) and so we went to his family castle at Shayzar and picnicked on top of its soaring stone battlements, gazing down at the gurgling green Orontes far below.

We saw the wonders of Aleppo, where my great-grandfather Ali Kemal had been exiled, as a young man, by the sultan. We stayed in a bijou hotel that had once been the house of some noble, full of fountains and wonderful cooking, and talked to politicians and academics and journalists – going up to a rooftop restaurant so as not to be overheard.

We knew it was a police state, and a pretty nasty one at that. We knew what Assad did to his opponents. But the Syria I saw seemed peaceful and at least superficially civilised, a place where women had far more freedom than in much of the Arab world, where Damascus artists felt able to express themselves.

So it was gut-wrenching, as foreign secretary in 2016, to see what was happening to the places I had visited with the kids. Bashar al-Assad, that sometime west London optometrist, with his good-looking British-born wife, was using disgusting violence against his own people, and bit by bit he was blasting his opponents into submission.

With the help first of the Iranians, and then of the Russians, he had hauled himself back from what had seemed a hopeless position. In 2012 he had controlled just 16 per cent of the country, and the UK – along with the rest of the west – had begun to parrot the mantra that 'Assad must go'; because we assumed that a putsch was about to happen, just as it had happened in Tunisia and Egypt.

Only this time we did not have the nerve to make it happen – as we had done, so effortlessly, in Iraq and Libya. He was so weak in 2012 that we could have swatted him like a fly. We could have carbonised his armed forces, as we carbonised those tanks I saw in Baghdad. This time, however, we had lost strategic confidence – to the extent that we did not even carry out the limited threats that we made. The American president Barack Obama had said that if Assad used chemical weapons, he would 'cross a red line'; and though Obama did not spell out exactly what he would do in retaliation, we gathered that he would do such things that they would be the terrors of the earth.

Well, in August 2013, in the opposition-controlled Damascus suburb of Ghouta, Assad rained down missiles on his own population – and poisoned them with sarin gas. He killed perhaps 1,400 civilians with weapons that have been internationally banned since not long after the end of the First World War. Children died, breathless and frothing, their skin white and their pupils shrunken to dots. The west – having threatened explicitly to punish any such action – was duly outraged. We huffed. We puffed. We then did nothing.

The Cameron government had declared that the UK would join the US in attacking targets in Syria, but was amazed – and depressed – to be defeated in a parliamentary vote (in which I did not take part, since I was then still in City Hall). The vote was a mistake. It was constitutionally unnecessary; but once Parliament had voted against action, the plan was dead.

Barack 'no drama' Obama then seized on Britain's refusal to act – and decided that he did not need to make good his threat, and nothing was done to punish the dictator for using chemical weapons against his own people. Oh, we struck some unenforceable deal by which Assad promised to hand over his chemical weapons. But the message was disastrous.

The west had lost its nerve. We wouldn't even attack a thug like Assad when he had blatantly broken every law of war. That decision was a catastrophe, because it reeked of weakness and irresolution – and now Putin sensed his opportunity. The Russians had hated the actions of Nato in Kosovo but had been powerless to stop us. Putin had seethed at the steady expansion of Nato, to include most of eastern Europe and chunks of the former Soviet Union; yet at the time there was nothing he could do to prevent it.

He loathed the Nato strikes in Libya and the toppling of Gaddafi. But it was a fait accompli. Now the west had been tested by Assad, and we had blinked. Tired of our moral interventionism, with all the complexities and responsibilities it brings, the US and Britain had visibly wimped out. Putin drew his conclusions from that failure in 2013, and the following year he struck.

In 2014 he launched his first invasion of Ukraine, sending his military to capture much of the eastern Donbas and Crimea, a sizeable portion of what had been since 1991 a sovereign and independent European country. And what did we do, in defence of freedom and democracy?

We put some sanctions on Russia – but essentially Putin got away with it. We debarred him from the G8, which certainly rankled with him but hardly damaged Russia. So in 2015 Putin decided that he could go further. He sent his troops into Syria, along with the Wagner mercenary group – intervening where we had been too timid, and on the opposite side. By the time I became foreign secretary in July 2016, the position was very grim. Having failed to strike Assad, Obama had decided instead to pour large sums into backing the rebels. Yet who were they, really?

Who were Assad's enemies? I suppose they began by being vaguely democratic and secular in their credentials. But as time went on, in a process assisted by Assad's cunning strategy of releasing all the jihadi terrorists from jail, they became more and more Islamist and generally unappealing.

We chirruped our slogan that 'Assad must go'. We held endless conferences on the next Syrian government. But who did we think would form that government? We didn't have a clue. Early in my tenure as foreign secretary, we had a 'Friends of Syria' event in our magnificent Locarno Rooms to champion the cause of one Riad Hijab.

I met Hijab several times, and he seemed plausible enough. He had a good old Baathist moustache. He had once been a member of Assad's inner circle. He might well do as a replacement.

But I realised as we sat there – us, the Americans, the French, the Gulfies – that our proceedings were wholly irrelevant to what was happening in Syria itself. How many divisions had Riad Hijab?

Zero, and he had zero chance of taking over in Syria. As Assad and Putin had foreseen, and intended, the conflict was morphing into one in which we could see no good outcome. In 2014 a new Islamist movement had been born in the chaos of Iraq, one even more bestial than al-Qaeda. It was called Islamic State, and by the time I had become foreign secretary it had spread into Syria, with a capital at Raqqa.

It was a nightmare world of beheadings and immolations, which at its height claimed about twelve million people under its maniacal Wahhabi jurisdiction. Isis/Daesh were certainly no friends of Assad – but surely we didn't want Daesh to take over?

Then who? The Iranians? Hezbollah? The Russians? The Turks? The al-Nusra brigade, another bunch of jihadis? Syria was turning into an utter shambles and the Syrian people were suffering appalling casualties – at least 200,000 killed and millions displaced in the biggest humanitarian crisis of modern times.

Obama gave huge sums to support the Syrian opposition – who became steadily more unpleasant – with no real plan to help them win; and Assad became more and more ruthless in his suppression.

He was not just bombing his own people, with Russian help. He was using gas against them, liberally, on hundreds of occasions, while Sergei Lavrov, the Russian foreign minister, sneered at our protests. And he was winning.

The rebel stronghold of Aleppo was fully encircled by July 2016, and the world watched for months as Assad pounded away, with barrel bombs and missiles, on one of the oldest cities in the world. I am fairly sure that Assad is the only tyrant to have fired Scud missiles at his own people – not even Saddam did that.

I became obsessed with the notion that we had to do something, anything, to help. It was bad enough that he was destroying the souk, the great mosque, the citadel – the places I had strolled around with Milo and Cassia. As the autumn drew in, the people of Aleppo were cold and starving. Perhaps we couldn't raise the siege. But could we at least get them some supplies?

Could we stage a kind of Berlin airlift, with drones? I wish I could say that the Foreign Office sprang into action. We had the drones. We had the technology. We had the supplies. We just didn't seem to have the will. I hammered and hammered at the project, and David Blair – now my speechwriter and policy adviser in the FCO – worked heroically; but a certain defeatism seemed to have entered the bloodstream, a Pavlovian aversion to intervention, no matter how modest.

It probably didn't help that Number Ten was axiomatically uninterested in any project that was promoted by me. Finally we had the right plan; we had the money, and we had an apathetic sign-off from Number Ten. We all sat round the big table at the far end of the foreign secretary's office and a senior DFID official said, with a curl of his lip, 'Yes, I suppose it will give you something to talk about at north London dinner parties.'

I am not much of a hater, but at that moment I could have punched his blasted lights out. It just seemed pathetic that we were spending 0.7 per cent of our GDP on overseas aid, and we could do nothing to help the people of Aleppo; and anyway I hardly ever go to dinner parties, whether in north London or anywhere else.

In the end, the negative nellies got their way. We had the kit and we were confident we could drop supplies on Aleppo without flattening the besieged with well-meaning pallets of pineapple chunks. We just couldn't find, or so I was told, an adjacent country from which to launch the drones. Not Turkey, not Jordan, they said; and in the end I gave up, ground down by the system and by now timed out.

By December the last resistance in Aleppo was extinguished, and the siege was over. I later found out that DFID had in fact been funding food drops the whole time, into other besieged areas of Syria: areas besieged by Daesh and occupied, would you believe it, by the forces of Assad. The DFID people had given me the clear impression that they had an objection on principle to airdrops of food; and then I discovered they were paying for it all along – to the benefit of the Assad regime!

Go figure, as they say. I ground my teeth and resolved if ever I could to merge DFID with the FCO, and end the absurdity by which aid officials behaved as though they were some hoity-toity Scandiwegian agency, independent of UK government policy. Meanwhile the war went on. More and more people died or were displaced. Obama and the Americans kept feeding a futile rebellion, as did many others.

Emboldened and enabled by the Russians, Assad kept merrily gassing his people; until, at the beginning of 2017, we had a new US president, a man perhaps less cautious and more instinctive than his predecessor.

In April Assad dropped poison gas at Khan Sheikhoun, yet again burning the insides of children's lungs. Donald Trump seemed genuinely appalled. He hit back. It was about 2 a.m., and I was for some reason in the UK ambassador's residence in Athens when I was woken, as so often in this story, by Martin. Rex Tillerson was on the line, he said: the genial Texan oil man who served as Trump's first secretary of state.

As Rex explained what was about to happen, I felt suddenly embarrassed.

'We are right with you,' I said as I stared out of the open window into the cool Athens night. 'We back you all the way.'

As a pledge, it seemed a bit inadequate. That night the US struck the Shayrat airfield, knocking out about ten Syrian planes and killing several Syrian soldiers. Trump was acting precipitately, with barely any consultation. But we should have been there. We should have joined the operation. I said as much the following morning over the phone to Theresa May, and she was notably sniffy. She didn't think the Trump strikes would make much difference, she said, and she was right, in the sense that Assad was not really deterred, not enough.

He did it again – but by then I had made it my business to ensure that this time we would act too. Almost exactly a year later, he launched another horrendous chemical attack in the suburbs of Damascus.

Trump hit back, harder, and this time the UK and France were fully involved, and we at least partially atoned for the inertia of 2013. We really thumped Assad, firing about a hundred missiles, hitting three sites – two chemical weapons stores, and one factory where they were being made. We did a lot of damage. We weren't able to stop the slaughter in Syria; we weren't able to find a replacement for Assad.

But that was the last time – as far as I know – that Assad used chemical weapons against his people, or certainly the last time he used them to any effect. All those who criticise Donald Trump, or what is often seen as the isolationism and America-first-ism of the Republicans, should perhaps remember that irony from the war in Syria.

It was Barack Obama, the moralising liberal internationalist, who had let Assad get away with using chemical weapons. It was Trump, the cynic and dealmaker, who did the principled thing and retaliated in the name of humanity. I only point it out.

Still, it was fundamentally a gesture. Our limited strikes on Assad did not change the course of the war, nor, frankly, were they intended to do so. As I write, Syria is still a patchwork of feuding proxy armies, with different parts controlled by various outside powers. But having had only 16 per cent of the country, Assad now has the majority once more under his control, and he has been welcomed back into the Arab League.

Without exception, the leaders who demanded that 'Assad must go' have themselves departed the stage (including me). Assad, on the other hand, has remained in place.

Would it have been any better if we in the west had all launched an attack on him in 2013 and knocked him off his perch when he was most vulnerable? I don't see any reason for thinking so. Iraq was a disaster. So was Libya. I can tell you categorically that we were equally clueless about how we might have replaced Assad.

We should certainly have been tougher in 2013, having made those threats. We should have hit back hard after he used chemical weapons at Ghouta. We should have done what Trump did four years later – and we might, just might, have looked less feeble to the Kremlin, and, who knows, deterred the first attack on Ukraine.

That, I reckon, is the most we could reasonably have done. If there is a lesson from the chaos of the last twenty years in the Middle East and North Africa, it is that you can't simply invade a sovereign country without a plan, remove its government and hope that things will somehow turn out all right.

It was a mistake that Putin was to make himself, a few years later, with his catastrophic overreach in Ukraine. For now, though, it was we who had lost our oomph.

As western confidence sagged, the autocracies were starting to assert themselves: Iran all over the Middle East; China all over the world, and especially the South China seas; Russia wherever they could make mischief, often with their Wagner group janissaries.

But here was a paradox. This very rebalancing of the world – the end of unipolar western dominance – had actually created an opportunity for Global Britain.

Chapter 26

Gøing Gløbal

Finding friends everywhere

Not long after I became foreign secretary I happened to be spending a happy half-hour in the Pergamon Museum, Berlin, when a woman spotted me. She was British, fifties. Her face started working with fury.

'Why don't you go back to your ... your ... LITTLE ISLAND?!' she shouted.

I was of course very polite in return. But her language interested me: her view of what had become of Britain.

Because it really, truly wasn't the response we were getting from other governments. Far from shunning us, far from treating Brexit Britain as some kind of leper colony, our counterparts around the world seemed fascinated by Brexit (some of the Europeans secretly quite envious) – and keener than ever before to engage.

The appetite seemed inexhaustible, and I was pretty constantly strapping myself into that BAe 146, sucking in the kerosene vapour and heading somewhere new. Why did they want to see us? I am afraid it really wasn't the blue eyes of the new foreign secretary. The giant new geo-strategic fact was China.

Across the world China was building up obligations. With every port and debt-laden railway that the Chinese constructed, they were making other countries more and more beholden to Beijing. With America less engaged, and perhaps less dependable, than in the past, it is not surprising that these countries were becoming anxious. They wanted options.

They wanted to develop other friendships, other partnerships, and in many ways Britain is ideal. We have superb armed forces, special forces and intelligence agencies. We have the bankers of the City of London, with its vast pools of liquidity.

We have development economists and all the experts you could wish for, and we invest far more overseas than any other European country. Wherever I went, I found I was pushing at an open door.

So it was whoosh, cabin crew doors to manual and ho for the big wide blue bowl, fringed with economic dynamos. I went to the Pacific rim, future scene of so much of the world's growth and innovation. Here the UK has many historic friendships and alliances, all of which now need reinforcing.

On the left-hand side of the Indo-Pacific, I went to Pakistan, and marvelled at their Anglophilia and their expertise in Scotch. I deepened my friendship with India's Narendra Modi, which had begun when I was mayor; and we launched a discussion about UK–India military collaboration that was to bear fruit a few years later.

We talked about tech partnerships in Sing-app-ore, geddit; we talked about property developments in Malaysia (see above on Battersea). With Korea we began discussions on a new defence and security partnership, and in Japan – fuelled by draughts of Japanese whisky with my counterpart Fumio Kishida, and then Taro Kono – we began discussion of the amazing Future Combat Aircraft System, now known as Tempest.

Under this agreement – which I pray the current government upholds – the UK and Japan will collaborate on the building of the next generation of fighter aircraft, as well as all types of unmanned aviation. It is an astonishing thing that, eighty years after the war, Mitsubishi and Rolls-Royce will be working together to make the machines that will protect democracy.

We spent more time in Indonesia, where I had already made friends as mayor of London, and where there seemed to be a huge appetite for British goods. We went on down to Australia, where Michael Fallon, the defence secretary, joined me for four-way discussions with the Australian foreign and defence ministers, Julie Bishop and Marise Payne, and if you want to see where those conversations would lead – read on, and you will discover Aukus.

Then on another four hours to the last bus stop, New Zealand, which is already sending about a third of its goods – a lot of lamb – to China. That was the subtext of all the conversations.

Nobody wanted to be hostile to China (I certainly didn't); everybody had a huge commercial interest in China. But everyone wanted options, and they wanted partnerships with Britain.

So we opened new embassies in Vanuatu, Samoa and Tonga, and we began what was to become – under my premiership – the Indo-Pacific Tilt; a strategic decision to build up our economic, technological and military partnerships with our many friends in the region. They want us; they want to buy our stuff. Lean into the Tilt.

It was more or less the same story in Africa, where I visited more countries than any foreign secretary in living memory. They just wanted more Britain, especially in the places where Britain was already well known.

I spent happy hours talking to Uganda's Yoweri Museveni, that ancient bush fighter who is so important for the peace of the region, from Somalia to Congo to Sudan. He is crucial, and though we may disapprove of some of his prejudices (such as his 2014 ban on gay sex) we have to engage with him more; or else he will just talk to others instead.

In Kenya I went out to see BATUK, the UK army's training base in the Laikipia province, and saw how British troops are working with the Kenyans to foil the elephant poachers. In the capital Nairobi we talked to President Uhuru Kenyatta about what we could do to challenge the Chinese on transport infrastructure, and I am proud to say that the new Nairobi station will be British-designed.

I got on well with Uhuru, and we did a lot of work together on female education. He made an impassioned plea that BA should turn up the cabin temperature on its flights from Nairobi to London.

In Ghana I found the reason why those flights are so chilly – it's all the refrigerated fruit in the hold, sliced pineapple and paw-paw and mangos heading for the supermarkets of Britain. The Ghanaians wanted UK companies to help them go upstream, so that they weren't just harvesting the cocoa beans but making the chocolate.

Everywhere I found the same requests: more support with intelligence-sharing against the terrorists, in the Sahel and elsewhere; more investment. It wasn't development cash they wanted; or not simply the aid money. They wanted UK companies to come in.

They are right: the growth potential of Africa is huge, the youngest and fastest-growing consumer market in the world. Which is partly why one of the first events of my premiership in 2019 was a colossal UK–Africa investment summit.

In some places I was shocked by how much aid we were giving, and how little influence it was buying us. In Addis Ababa we have an embassy compound so vast that it has a nine-hole golf course and a leopard. One of our diplomats had the brilliant idea that I should run round the path with the great Ethiopian runner Haile Gebrselassie, at 2,355 metres in elevation and in fierce sunshine.

With ten metres to the finish, I pretended to have a heart attack (it looked pretty convincing) and as Haile stopped to look after me I got up and shot to victory.

That compound is an extraordinary statement of the British presence in Addis. But the Ethiopians knew where the real power was; not with the Foreign Office but with DFID, which was then giving them about £300 million a year, no questions asked.

So when we had a particularly difficult consular issue to resolve – the Ethiopians had a political prisoner whose family lived in London – I was very cheesed off to find that our munificence was buying us nothing (and I resolved, again, to bring DFID back into the FCO fold).

I was the first British foreign secretary EVER to visit Liberia, and the first to visit the Gambia. Why? We have links everywhere. Why not make more of them? Adama Barrow, the Gambian leader, actually worked in Argos while studying in the UK (so he told me) and regarded it as an invaluable preparation for life.

On our charter flight to Banjul there were at least some of those many mature British women who are apparently drawn to the Gambia's beaches in search of romance. It seems fairly harmless to me, provided no one gets excessively ripped off.

These British ladies probably stimulate more local economic activity than a lot of DFID spending.

In spite of the apathy of the UK political class, the UK is one of the biggest investors in Africa – so why not make more of the relationships? Why leave it to China, and Russia? We have huge natural advantages – and we don't make enough of them.

We opened a string of embassies and sovereign representations in Africa, including in Chad, Mali and Niger, and we should be doing more.

In South America I found relationships that were simply rusty from disuse. I was the first foreign secretary to visit Peru in fifty years, and yet I flew with President Martín Vizcarra far out over the Amazon jungle – until we reached a remote Indian village where, lo and behold, there was a revolutionary British clean-power plant that was providing electricity for the local school.

In Chile I heard people say that they owed their very freedom to Britain, because a man called Admiral Cochran had helped to liberate them from Spain; and that we are still one of the biggest international investors in and exporters to the country (the sixth).

And in Argentina (where no foreign secretary had been for twenty-five years) I stood high up in the great landmark in the port of Buenos Aires – the Torre Monumental – and learned that the British community built it in 1916, to say nothing of the railways and the ports.

My point is that Britain is far, far more global than we realise, and there are countries around the world that simply want more engagement, and are of course open to many more of our goods and services.

Now I know what you will be thinking, dear pro-EU reader – you will be thinking that all this exertion came at the expense of our engagement with the rest of the EU. That's nonsense.

In fact, we increased our representation in other European capitals, even though we were still members of the EU, and even though UK ministers, myself included, were still going to all EU meetings. By the end of my time as foreign secretary, we had more diplomats in Europe than ever before, and a bigger overseas representation than ever before.

Some EU friendships were really burgeoning – especially with the 'new Europeans' such as the Poles. I even did a joint trip to Ukraine with my Polish counterpart Witold Waszczykowski.

'Why don't I give you a lift in my plane?' I said grandly.

We picked him up in Warsaw, and as we took off – the old BAe 146 engines howling away – I watched a large piece of the wooden doorjamb slowly detach itself and fall into my guest's lap.

Ah well, I expect the British taxpayer would have approved. No one could say that we were not sweating the assets.

Of all the regions of the world, the one where we made the most progress – at least in my view – was in the Middle East, and generally with the Sunni Muslim countries.

In Egypt we began to unblock one of the worst problems in the relationship: the ban on British tourists travelling to the Sinai resort of Sharm-el-Sheikh that had been in place ever since terrorists blew up a Russian Metrojet passenger plane in 2015.

As the years went by, the Egyptians became more and more indignant. They had put all sorts of protections into Sharm, and soon it was no more dangerous than many other airports. They needed those hungry, thirsty British tourists. But they were faced with a classic case of political cowardice.

No home secretary wanted to take the risk, no matter how small, of approving flights – and then seeing another attack. So I told President Sisi that I would fix it, and I worked away at the system, and Number Ten, and finally (admittedly when I became PM) we got it done, and those Brits are back snorkelling at Sharm in the Red Sea.

The relationship with Egypt is historic and important. We are that country's biggest international investor; we are helping to build the Cairo monorail with trains made in Derby. Yes, the country has its problems, and of course I always raised the difficult questions of human rights and detentions.

But to get the best out of a relationship you cannot spend all your time being stand-offish and disapproving. You must engage, and accentuate whatever is positive. The same is abundantly true of that other regional powerhouse, Turkey.

Whatever people may say about the government of Recep Tayyip Erdoğan, I believe it was completely right that we became the biggest champions of the Turks in Europe. I ruthlessly played up my Ottoman heritage, and soon Erdoğan and I had a long list of projects we would discuss, from a joint fighter plane to aircraft carriers.

Turkey matters deeply. The Turks were in the frontline of the war in Syria, and coped heroically with the influx of refugees. They are running a much more assertive if not downright Ottoman foreign policy, with deployments in Libya, Somalia, Iraq.

When I flew into the airport in Mogadishu, I was amazed to find that it had been built not by the Chinese or the Americans but by the Turks. They are our Nato allies; they control access to the Black Sea; they are crucial for the war in Ukraine.

We need the Turks, and thanks at least partly to the efforts of a superb ambassador to Ankara, Richard Moore, later 'C', our relations with Turkey were as good, in my time, as they have ever been.

(As 'C', Richard would often travel to build intelligence partnerships, and when he went to Egypt I asked: 'Did "C" see Sisi?' In fact I might have said that a few times, alas.)

Above all we engaged, in the Muslim world, with the Gulf and Saudi Arabia. None of these countries show all the characteristics of liberal western democracies. But the changes are amazing, and fast.

The United Arab Emirates is probably punching further above its weight, per head of population, than any other country on earth. It has extraordinary ambitions, in science and technology, in space, in the cultural and academic world. Before he returned as foreign secretary, David Cameron was some kind of professor at a university in Dubai.

The same could be said of Qatar, and indeed of the whole Gulf region. In some of these places the British flag went down in the 1970s – in my lifetime; and my sense whenever I was there was that they wanted to do more with the UK: to buy more UK goods and services, and to invest more in Britain.

As one Gulf ruler once put it to me: 'Why did you leave us – to the French?' The Gulf countries are our fastest-growing market, by value, and we would be insane not to build that partnership.

Even more globally significant, perhaps, are the changes in Saudi Arabia. Tony Blair once told me that Mohammed bin Salman, the Crown Prince, was 'the hope of the region', and I can see why.

The Saudis play a pivotal role in Islam. They are the custodians of the two holiest sites. We all know that Wahhabi-inspired fanaticism caused the 9/11 massacre, and many other atrocities. But when did you last hear of a terrorist attack in Saudi Arabia? Whatever else he has done, MBS has made it safe to walk the streets of Jeddah and Riyadh.

Women can now drive (I know, I know, but think where they were). Tourism is being opened up. Projects like Neom, the new city in the desert, sound almost deranged in their grandeur. But the Saudis are serious, and there is nowhere else where so much is happening so fast.

It amazes me to hear lefties complain that Britain is close to Saudi Arabia. Yes we are, and it is a good thing. We have nothing for which to reproach ourselves.

Contrast the scruple and punctilio of the UK with the disgusting callousness of the Russians. Since the days of Mrs Thatcher we have had giant contracts to supply the Kingdom of Saudi Arabia with arms, contracts that create jobs across the UK (you won't hear the unions complaining about the al-Yamamah deal).

In 2015 the Saudis actually began to use those weapons in the course of an intervention in Yemen, against an Iran-backed tribal militia called the Houthis. There was a huge outcry in the UK – protest at the use of UK weaponry and the loss of Yemeni civilian life.

The war was bloody, and there was great suffering. But the intervention was part of a mission to restore the legitimate UN

Security Council-recognised government of Yemen, which the Houthis had deposed; and at every stage, when it came to using those British weapons, the UK insisted on the application of international humanitarian law to avoid or minimise civilian casualties.

We even had UK personnel working with the Saudis to understand the targeting and make sure that this was done, and the whole thing was regularly scrutinised in Parliament (I know; I did some of the statements).

Contrast Putin's Russia, which at the same time was actively encouraging the Assad regime to engage in the wholesale and indiscriminate slaughter of civilians – not minimising but maximising casualties – and the use of illegal chemical weapons.

No, the war in Yemen has not been a success, though it was never going to be easy. But if you look at what the Iran-backed Houthis are now doing in the Strait of Hormuz – targeting innocent shipping, forcing traffic to make huge detours round the Cape of Good Hope – you have to admit the Saudis were right to be concerned.

MBS is a changemaker in a region that has been crying out for changemakers; and among his many foreign policy ventures there is the whole process – spurred on by Trump and Jared Kushner – by which the Sunni Arab states have come to stand on the verge of a historic reconciliation with Israel.

That process has now been interrupted by the sickening Hamas massacre of Israeli civilians on October 7, 2023, and Israel's inevitable response. Exactly as the Iranian-backed terrorists intended, the Israelis have been driven to try to extirpate Hamas from Gaza, to make sure they can never mount such an attack again.

Exactly as Hamas intended, the scale and violence of the Israeli response has inflamed anti-Israeli and antisemitic feeling, not just in the Middle East but around the world.

I am firmly on the side of Israel, in that I believe the Israelis have a right to protect their population against the kind of orgy of sadism and violence that was perpetrated against innocent men, women and children on October 7.

I do not accept the equivalence between Hamas and the Israeli forces: on the contrary, the distinction, again, is that Hamas tries to maximise suffering, while I believe Israel has on the whole tried – if not always effectively – to minimise suffering.

But I also have to accept, as a former British foreign secretary, that we are dealing with a tragedy, and one of the many legacies of the British Empire, and the studied but fatal ambiguity of one of my predecessors.

Chapter 27

Selling the Same Camel Twice

The fatal incoherence of A.J. Balfour

'Here it is,' I said as I opened the door and ushered the Israeli prime minister into my office. I felt like Willy Wonka showing a child the ultimate secret of the chocolate factory – the room where they made the greatest diplomatic fudge of all time.

My guest was Bibi Netanyahu, and he claimed to be immensely impressed. He had never been here before, he said. What, never? No, never.

So it was a pleasure to walk with him from the ambassador's entrance, up the sweeping staircase, passing the oil-painted murals of a giant helmeted and tridented Britannia, each pose more imperialistic than the last. There is a tradition at the Foreign Office that if an ambassador comes for a friendly meeting, he or she will be taken to the stairs on the right of the red-carpeted landing, so that they arrive on the first floor under the gaze of Britannia Pacificatrix – Britannia the peacemaker.

If relations are frosty, or worse, we usher the ambassador to the left-hand flight of stairs to pass beneath Britannia Bellatrix – Britannia the warmaker. These murals date from just after the First World War, when fifty-eight countries comprising about a quarter of the globe were controlled from this Italianate palazzo-style building. They are exuberantly politically incorrect – Britannia accepting homage from less fortunate nations, Britannia offering her milky white breast to be suckled by a child, Britannia giving protection to a black kid with no clothes on, symbolising Africa.

One day some humourless lefty puritanical campaign will be launched to veil these treasures. We must be ready to fight it when it comes.

We came to the door to my outer office, beneath another mural, of another Junoesque woman with her finger to her lips and a sign beneath her reading 'Silence'.

As I showed Netanyahu into the gilt-mirrored splendour of the foreign secretary's office, I had an inspiration.

'This is it,' I said, marching over to the old walnut desk. 'This is where he wrote the Balfour Declaration.'

'Wow,' said Bibi reverentially, running his fingers over the polished timber.

'And this, er – this is probably the very blotter that he used,' I said, indicating the red leather blotter.

'Wow,' said Bibi. He seemed genuinely awestruck.

I was determined to keep the magic going. 'And this is the very pen that he used.'

I rootled around in the drawer of the desk and produced a Bic biro. Netanyahu looked at it uncertainly, and we both laughed.

Actually, I am not sure exactly how Arthur James Balfour came to compose his famous letter to Lord Rothschild on November 2, 1917. There is at least one of his desks in the Museum of Jewish History in Tel Aviv, and I must accept that I was probably wrong about that walnut desk.

There is no doubt that he wrote the letter, and there is no doubt what it says. The original document is kept in a fridge in the British Library – I once held it in my hands. The question is what it means. Even by the standards of diplomacy, it is a masterpiece of doublespeak, a prismatic gem whose words seem to mean different things in different lights.

He was a curious cove, was A.J. Balfour: tall, hooded-eyed, unmarried, a nephew of the great Victorian prime minister Robert Cecil, Marquess of Salisbury (whose nepotism in promoting Balfour in 1880 gave rise, so they say, to the expression 'Bob's your uncle'). He was a bit of an amateur philosopher of a sceptical sort of bent who once aphorised, 'Nothing matters very much, and few things matter at all.'

This is the sort of complacent twaddle you might come out with if you occupied the pinnacle of the British class system.

When Balfour wrote that letter, I bet he could think of a few things that mattered very much indeed: how to stop the seemingly endless slaughter in the trenches of the First World War; how to persuade other countries to join the fight against the Kaiser; how to save the British Empire. This was no time for philosophical detachment. It was time for the Foreign Office to come up with an idea, and Balfour's letter was the first official British expression of an idea that had been around since the middle of the nineteenth century.

Zionism was a project to create in Palestine a homeland for the Jews, to give a land without a people to a people without a land. It wasn't that Balfour had always been notably sympathetic to the Jewish people and their troubles: as prime minister in 1905, he had been pretty hostile to the waves of Jewish immigration that were generated by Russian pogroms, and even talked of an 'invasion' of Britain. But in 1917, as foreign secretary, he saw strategic reasons for playing the Zionist card.

To create a Zionist state in Palestine, under British protection – that could help produce a handy asset for the empire and secure the route to India. Balfour and his cabinet colleagues also calculated that by espousing Zionism they would excite the sympathy of the powerful Jewish lobby in Congress in America and encourage the Americans to engage more seriously in the war.

So this is what he wrote.

'His Majesty's government view with favour the establishment in Palestine of a national home for the Jewish people, and will use their best endeavours to facilitate the achievement of this object ...'

Whoa ... Wait a mo.

Let's just interrupt old Balfour halfway through this sentence and focus first on this bit: the bit for which he is venerated in Israel, and which explains why Bibi Netanyahu wanted to stroke his very desk. The declaration may or may not have encouraged the Americans to support the war against Germany – but it certainly paved the way for the creation of Israel.

Here was the foreign secretary of the greatest power on earth, then the British Empire, declaring in favour of Zionism, and actually pledging to bring it about. I have always instinctively believed that this act – creating the state of Israel – was a great and noble thing.

When Balfour sat down and scribbled his declaration, Russian and European Jewry had already suffered terribly; and after the horrors of the 1930s and 1940s the case was – and is – completely unanswerable. I feel as strongly about this, the inalienable right of Israel to exist and to offer refuge to the Jewish people, as I feel about almost any political proposition in history.

Why? Maybe it's partly because I have Jewish antecedents. (I took the precaution, before becoming foreign secretary, of stationing my ancestors widely around the world: Turks, French, Germans, Russians, Swiss – even Irish, according to my brother Leo.) When I was about five years old, I was taken with Rachel and Leo to meet my great-grandfather, then almost ninety, in his garden at the Institute for Advanced Study in Princeton.

He gave me chocolate money and told me there was a wolf at the bottom of the garden. He was called Elias Avery Lowe and he was a palaeographer. He had been born in Moscow in the 1880s, the son of a silk merchant called Loew (*sic*) and his wife, whose maiden name was Ragoler – a family, I am told, that numbers some distinguished rabbis.

Why was he there? Well, he was at Princeton because he was one of the world's great experts on the Latin handwriting of medieval monks and had written an anthology of the most important manuscripts, called *Codices Latini Antiquiores*; but the reason he was there in America at all was that his family had fled the vile persecution of the Jews conducted by Tsarist Russia.

He was there because antisemitism is a virus, a spore, which has lurked beneath the floorboards of European society for more than a thousand years, flaring up and subsiding from one generation to the next. It is out from the cracks again today, and spreading pestilence on the streets of many capitals, including London, I am sad to say. My great-grandfather knew all about it. My support for Israel was therefore possibly partly tribal, but also political.

From quite an early age I saw this country as a kind of miracle in the desert, a democracy surrounded by Arab monarchies or autocracies. By its very inventiveness and dynamism – in a region not much known for either virtue – Israel was living proof of my prejudice: that societies that are the most free will be the societies that are the happiest, and also the richest.

This naive enthusiasm survived a stint working on a kibbutz, when I was about nineteen. It was a place called Kfar Hanasi, in Galilee, and I must say that I found it hard yakka, as they say in Australia. My sister Rachel seemed very popular with the young male kibbutzniks, and they took her off for romantic horseback excursions around Lake Galilee.

I was ruthlessly stuck in the washing-up, standing for hours in a steam-filled pantry and desperately trying to scrape the yoghurt and falafel gunge off the plates and put them into the constantly gaping jaws of a rotating washing-up machine, while my supervisors shouted at me for my lackadaisical attitude; and when I wasn't washing up I was being berated for being too slow to pick the apples in the orchard – at 4 a.m. for heaven's sake – as though I was single-handedly impairing the productivity of the whole kibbutz.

I left that place with an even deeper admiration for the toughness and ruthless energy of the Israelis; and also a deep scepticism about any form of socialism. Whatever the idealism of the movement's founders, it does not seem to me that the kibbutz model was notably efficient. I have not been surprised, in the decades that have followed, to see the kibbutzim gently transformed into private enterprises.

It is capitalism that has flourished in Israel, not collectivism. It is the dynamic culture of individual risk and reward that has caused this tiny, arid country – with hardly any natural resources to speak of – to boast more billionaires per capita than any other country in the world.

That success has, of course, been so exorbitant that the contrast with the Palestinians – the Muslim Palestinian Arabs – is all the more painful. Things have not worked out for them, to put it mildly, in the way that the British – Balfour included – had intended or hoped. In so far as Balfour had a vision, it was that the incoming Jewish refugees would share their homeland with the existing population; or at least that is presumably what Balfour meant by the second half of his famous sentence. Having offered the world's Jews this miraculous solution, having put the British stamp on the Zionist cause, Balfour then tries to claw it back.

Having undertaken to use his best endeavours to bring about a home for the Jewish people in Palestine, Balfour coughs and enters the most colossal saving clause …

Ahem, he says … adding, 'it being clearly understood that nothing shall be done which may prejudice the civil and religious rights of existing non-Jewish communities in Palestine, or the rights and political status enjoyed by Jews in any other country.'

No one, looking at the Middle East today, could possibly claim that this proviso has been respected. For the Palestinians, the creation of the state of Israel has been a tragedy in which millions were dispossessed, or forced into exile, or into refugee camps. They call it the Nakba, the 'catastrophe'.

Fervent Israel-backer that I am, I also understand – who could not – the Palestinians' continuing grief and sense of displacement, their continuing dismay at the yet more Israeli settlements chomping into what they consider to be their land. Over the years I have been several times to the West Bank and seen the queues of Palestinians trying to get through piss-smelling Israeli turnstiles from one part of their land to another.

I have sat in Hebron and Ramallah and listened to Mahmoud Abbas and other Palestinian leaders, all of us knowing that their demands were hopelessly unrealistic. I have stood on high places in Judaea and Samaria and looked at the sprawling pseudopodia of the illegal Israeli settlements, growing inexorably and making any putative Palestinian state less and less viable.

Now, amid the violence in Gaza, I cannot help feeling the whole vast budget of pain and loss on both sides: the pain of the Israelis who have lost relatives, some of whom are still being held hostage; the agony and anger of the people of Gaza, most of whom cannot see that Hamas has brought this tragedy on them but who blame Israel.

That is why I have continued to psalm the Foreign Office line: that there must be a two-state solution, one for the Israelis and one for the Palestinians. I even wrote as much in the *Telegraph* in 2017, on the eve of Netanyahu's visit. The Balfour Declaration, I said, was only partly fulfilled. It was time to do justice to the second half of that sentence and honour our commitment to the Palestinians.

My words went down well in Ramallah, but seven years later we must be honest and confess that the prospect of symmetrically fulfilling Balfour's pledge seems more remote than ever. There is no realistic prospect of a two-state solution, not if by a state you mean a full-fledged Palestinian state, with their own army and their own foreign policy and their own security arrangements. That just isn't going to happen – not after what Hamas has done.

In 2004 I went to Israel on a parliamentary trip, at a time when there was a particular plague of suicide bombers on Tel Aviv and Jerusalem. We were taken to see a part of the wall that was being built to keep the bombers out and to keep the Israelis safe. We were being told about the sensitivity of the wall, and how its sensors could pick up intruders.

I walked towards it for a closer look.

'Don't touch it,' said the guide.

'What? Like this?' I said, and whacked it with my notebook; at which point an alarm went off and a jeep appeared from nowhere full of irritated Israeli soldiers.

Why did I do it? I asked myself when the panic had subsided. It was because I felt suddenly offended by the idea of this illegal wall, preventing Palestinian farmers from going from one part of the olive grove to another; and because something grated my nerves, and I felt like being bloody-minded – and of course I regret it now.

I was wrong. Unless you are an Israeli, it is difficult to understand the permanent sense of siege, of being in a tiny country surrounded by hostile neighbours; and if entirely innocent Jewish civilians are being blown up in buses or supermarkets, or tortured and killed in the gardens of their kibbutzim, then of course you have a right, if not a duty, to build a wall.

It is the tragedy of the Palestinians that they have never done any of the deals on offer, even when the terms have been much more favourable than they are today. As Abba Eban once said,

'The Palestinians never miss an opportunity to miss an opportunity.' Even if the Israeli government could be persuaded to agree, it is impossible to see how such an entity could now make geographical sense since the whole area is perforated, like Swiss cheese, with 150 Israeli settlements.

I pointed this out to Netanyahu, as a British foreign secretary always must. He replied, a bit casuistically, that there are some little Belgian enclaves in the Netherlands – a fact I am ashamed to say I did not know, but which hardly affects the point.

Belgium and the Netherlands are both still viable states; it will be hard to say the same of Palestine, on the current map.

Some people are now despairingly talking up the idea of a 'one-state' solution, a bi-national state of the kind that Balfour presumably envisaged, taking in Israel, the West Bank and Gaza combined. Again, there is no way the Israelis will allow that to happen – not if that means, as logically it must, that the new bi-national greater Israel contains an almost equal number of Jews and Muslim Arabs.

The whole point of Israel is that it is the place where Jews can never be persecuted, because it is unlike anywhere else in the world in that Jews are in the majority – and the risk of a one-state solution is that the Jewish people would once again become a minority in their own land.

Perhaps one day we will have some kind of two-state solution, but more of a federal one, whereby the Palestinians have their own territory with some but by no means all of the attributes of statehood, and certainly not the use of armed forces. Even so, there will have to be some movement of settlements.

But if that is to happen, then all the Palestinians, including Hamas, will have to abandon violence and recognise the fundamental right of Israel to exist. As long as Hamas is sworn to destroy Israel and murder the Jewish race, the Israelis will be perfectly right to protect themselves.

That is why the so-called Abraham Accords are so important, the process of reconciliation between Israel and the Arab world that was begun under the Trump administration. The Saudis have yet to sign up, and of course it was precisely to make it politically impossible for them to sign up that Iran triggered the Hamas attacks.

One day, however, I believe it will happen, and a changemaker like MBS can make it happen. When the Kingdom of Saudi Arabia officially recognises the state of Israel – with the rest of the Arab world – then there is a chance that we can change the whole economic geography of the region.

There could be and will be Arab-Israeli projects for clean energy, desalination, new transport infrastructure projects such as high-speed rail. Those young Palestinians now suffering such misery and privation would have the prospect of a place to call home. They would also have the prospect of a job.

At some point in the conversation the Israeli PM excused himself and asked for the washroom. It is a little-known fact that the foreign secretary, unlike the prime minister, has an entirely private and commodious convenience – a secret annex with a shower, shoe-shining stuff, wardrobe, maps, a bit like the gents in a posh London club.

Thither Bibi repaired for a while, and it may or may not be a coincidence but I am told that later, when they were doing a regular sweep for bugs, they found a listening device in the thunderbox.

There is one reason for thinking that the Abraham Accords will eventually succeed, in spite of what Hamas has done; and that is the basic and growing community of interest between Israel and its Sunni Arab neighbours.

They all face the challenge of Iran, the Shia theocracy that now (thanks partly to western mistakes) has its proxies in dominant positions across the region, in Lebanon, Yemen, Iraq and Syria.

The Iranians run their empire as their Hamas proxies run Gaza, with complete lack of scruple or respect for human life. As I was to discover as foreign secretary, they think nothing of jailing a completely innocent woman and using her as a pawn.

Chapter 28

Freeing Nazanin

And how petty UK politics helped to keep her in jail

A young mother arrives with her not-quite-two-year-old daughter at Tehran's Ayatollah Khomeini Airport. It is April 2016. She has taken Gabriella to meet her grandparents at Nowruz, the ancient festival of the New Year, and now it is time to go home.

The thirty-seven-year-old is wearing a white headscarf, as prescribed by Islamic law. The Tannoy bawls announcements. She pushes her heavily laden trolley towards passport control – unaware that she is already being secretly filmed by agents of the Iranian state.

Just then she is interrupted. Where are you going? asks a man. He takes her passport and says he's from the state prosecutor's office.

'London,' she says.

Is the child going with her?

Yes, she says.

What's your name? asks the man, and she replies 'Zaghari', which sounds in Farsi more like 'Zoggery' than the Za-gaari that has ever since become commonplace on the lips of so many western journalists and politicians.

By this stage the woman is clearly afraid. You can see her eyes widen with shock. The man asks her to take her backpack off the trolley, leave the rest of the luggage, and come with him.

So began almost six years of hell for Nazanin Zaghari-Ratcliffe, during which she was imprisoned in one of the most notorious jails in the world, with no idea when she might be released. She became at times so sick and so depressed that she had to go on hunger strike to get the medication she needed.

She despaired of seeing her family again, and the Iranian authorities never once explained what exactly it was that she had done to deserve this torment. Of course not. She was completely innocent of any crime whatever.

Nazanin was a pawn in the internal politics of the Iranian regime, between the hardliners and the moderates. She was a piece on the geopolitical chessboard, a victim of the suspicion and paranoia that has for so long existed between the British and Iranian governments; and I am afraid that for much of her sentence – which could have been years shorter – she suffered from pointless feuding at the heart of the government of Theresa May.

In snatching her at the airport and locking her up, the Iranians acted with total cynicism and cruelty. Their actions were straightforwardly immoral and illegal.

It is a measure of how febrile UK politics were in 2016 – and how controversial a figure I had become – that I managed somehow to blunder and to hand my critics the opportunity to blame me, not the Iranians, for keeping her in jail.

The plight of Nazanin had already become a cause célèbre before I became foreign secretary that July. The Iranians have long had a history of taking western hostages – going back to the US embassy staff in 1979 – and in recent years they have specialised in nabbing dual nationals, accusing them of being spies, and then ransoming them for cash or concessions from western governments. Barack Obama had recently sprung a batch of American-Iranians by sending a plane full of cash to Tehran. Since the UK government disliked paying ransoms, the advice from the Foreign Office to relatives of those who were taken was always the same.

Don't make a fuss, we would tell the distraught families. Don't inflate the issue; don't create a diplomatic storm. You will only encourage the Iranians and make it more difficult to get your loved ones out. Leave it to us, the FCO wallahs would say, tapping the side of their nose; and by and large they succeeded.

We had an excellent and wily consular team, and though the Iranians were monstrous in their behaviour, we had a good record of – eventually – getting people out.

It was clear, even before I got the FCO job, that Nazanin's family were not convinced by these reassurances. Richard Ratcliffe, her husband, was not going to be fobbed off – he wanted her back as fast as possible. He believed that the only way to achieve this was publicly to wring the withers of the British government; which he did, to very great effect.

He escalated the case of his missing wife, so as to encompass every outstanding issue between Britain and Iran; and who am I to say he was wrong? Sometimes you can only solve a problem by making it bigger.

So when on November 1, 2017 I appeared before the Foreign Affairs Select Committee, I had read a fair bit about Nazanin and I was aware of the vociferous public campaign for HMG to get a grip and get her out, and of course I sympathised. I knew that she was blameless.

When Ann Clwyd MP suggested that I should try to visit Nazanin in Evin jail, where she was being held, I said I would welcome the chance (we did try; the Iranians said no). I pointed out that I had regularly raised her case with my opposite number, the Iranian foreign minister, Javad Zarif.

I then made a mistake. In trying to emphasise Nazanin's innocence, I said: 'When we look at what Nazanin Zaghari-Ratcliffe was doing, she was simply teaching people journalism, as I understand it, at the very limit.' There I was wrong.

It was true that Nazanin was then an employee of the Thomson Reuters Foundation, and had formerly worked for the BBC World Service Trust; and it is true that both those organisations certainly have a role in educating journalists. But of course what I had forgotten was that this activity – which seems so right and so natural to us – sounded seditious to the Iranian ear.

Teaching journalists sounds to you and me like an activity essential to a free society. In the poisoned imaginations of Iran's Islamic Revolutionary Guard Corps (IRGC), the thugs who had detained her, teaching journalists was tantamount to trying to overthrow the Iranian state.

It was therefore crucial to Nazanin's defence that she was merely there on holiday – which she was. She was there to celebrate Nowruz with her family, to introduce twenty-two-month-old Gabriella to her grandparents.

I had somehow got hold of the wrong end of the stick; I made a slip of the tongue. Then, after I had repeated my condemnation of her detention, the conversation moved on to other questions about other countries. It is relevant to note that I was not alone in appearing before that committee.

I was flanked by two of the most senior and experienced officials in the Foreign Office. There was the excellent Karen Pierce, the first female ambassador to Washington, who was serving as my political director. Karen has a stylish dress sense, veering towards eccentricity, so that she sometimes looks a bit like a Quality Street wrapper. (Don't worry, I have said this to her face.)

She has a mind like a trap and doesn't miss things, let alone gaffes by the foreign secretary. On the other side was Sir Simon

McDonald, the permanent secretary to the Foreign Office, the most senior official of all and nothing if not a man for detail.

Neither interjected or corrected – as was their right and their job. Neither noticed anything awry, and nor did anyone on the committee. As we left we felt it had been a pretty dull affair, a no-score draw, and when it came to my public appearances the FCO officials were firmly of the view that dull was good.

In fact, the whole thing was forgotten for four or five days – until we heard some apparently awful news from Tehran.

In response to the noisy UK campaign for her release, the regime was already being cruel to Nazanin, toying with her like a cat with a mouse. They were threatening to bring unspecified new charges against her; and she had already been terrified to be told – before I gave evidence on November 1 – that she could face a further sixteen years in jail, on top of her five years for espionage.

So when she was taken to court again on November 5 she was appalled to hear that my words had 'shed new light' on her activities and proved that she was there for 'anything but a holiday'.

The news was relayed to her family, and thence to her employers in London – and Thomson Reuters decided to go public and to point the finger at me. Monique Villa, the chief executive of the Thompson Reuters Foundation, said that there was a 'direct correlation' between my remarks and Nazanin's appearance in court; and – *boom* – the British media had a story that seemed to bear out the prejudices of a large proportion of their audience.

My gaffe, said the *Guardian*, had effectively doubled Nazanin's jail sentence, and the BBC echoed the theme. It was thanks to me, and my ineptitude, that this young woman was going to languish in the squalor of Evin jail, Tehran. For my critics it was a heaven-sent vindication.

We told you he was too gaffe-prone, they said. We told you he was a blithering buffoon, a bull in a china shop who was basically unsuited to the role of the UK's top diplomat.

The story had what we call traction; people noticed it. If in the next few days you had asked the average punter who or what bore moral responsibility for the fact of Nazanin's incarceration, what do you they would have said?

The Iranian government? The Iranian judiciary? The Iranian Islamic Revolutionary Guard Corps – Quds Force? No, they would have said: it's that Boris Johnson, isn't it?

I usually sleep soundly – the sleep of the just. When my head hits the pillow, I am out. But this was one of those times when I was in a state of such anguish that I lay awake, berating myself for my stupidity.

Why had I rambled in that answer to Ann Clwyd? Why couldn't I have just shut up? Now an innocent woman was in jail, unable to see her daughter, and people genuinely thought it was my doing. It was ghastly.

My position was helped a few days later, when I received support from a completely unexpected quarter. The head of Tehran's revolutionary court, one Moussa Qasanfarabadi, said that western media accounts were inaccurate. There was no new trial, no new sentence, and my words had made absolutely no difference to Nazanin's position.

According to *Kayhan*, a regime-backing paper (I am not sure they have many non-regime-backing papers), 'The revolution court chief strongly rejected reports that Zaghari might stand a second trial and her jail term might be extended after Foreign Secretary Boris Johnson's gaffe about her, saying, "The western media release unreal reports." He said no new charges had been raised against her, and hence reports that her jail term might be extended are basically flawed.'

No one was really listening. It was one of those stories that feels instinctively right, that was too good to correct – that Johnson, the Beast of Brexit, had ballsed up badly. On November 12 the leader of the opposition, Jeremy Corbyn, called for me to be sacked for my incompetence and for my 'colonial throwback' attitude.

'It's time for him to go,' he told the *Observer*. As it happens, I was fortunate in that Iran was one of many areas where Corbyn's criticisms did not carry much weight. An arch-lefty from Islington North, he was one of the few MPs in Parliament willing to speak out in favour of the mullahs, and he had taken £20,000 for four appearances on Iran's propaganda channel, Press TV.

In fact, Corbyn's demand for me to be sacked probably helped to shore up what would otherwise have been a wobbly position. But the charge against me was sticking – that I had recklessly endangered Nazanin's freedom, if not her life.

She was now more emphatically my problem than ever, and I had to do something to get her out. Was there anything we could offer the Iranians?

There was, and Richard Ratcliffe, astutely, had been suggesting the solution from the beginning. The row over Nazanin was now so intense that the Iranians saw an opportunity to settle an old score with the British government, a grievance that went back more than forty years. Richard Ratcliffe was insistent on the point, and I started to think he was right.

The Iranians refer to Britain as the 'old Fox', and they traditionally ascribe to us a quite extraordinary guile and manipulative skill. It was the UK that had helped depose the Iranian leader Mohammad Mosaddegh in 1953, replacing him with the Shah (or king); and in 1979, when the Shah was in turn deposed, we performed an act, as Blackadder might put it, as cunning as a fox who is the Regius Professor of Cunning at Oxford University.

You may dimly remember that in 1914, on the eve of the First World War, Churchill – then first lord of the Admiralty – ruthlessly swiped two battleships that were being made for Turkey in UK shipyards, even though the Turks had already paid good money for them. That's more or less what happened to the Iranians.

Before his fall, the Shah had commissioned from Britain 1,500 Chieftain tanks and 450 armoured cars, doubtless to help him suppress his opposition. By the time he fled to Paris, leaving his country to the revolutionaries, the Iranians had paid the British, in today's money, about £400 million; and since the regime of Ayatollah Khomeini was immediately sanctioned by the west we trousered the cash, having sent them only a small fraction of the order.

We then shamelessly sold the rest of the tanks elsewhere. Some of them ended up in Jordan, and some of the armoured cars were eventually sold to – you guessed it, Saddam Hussein's Iraq.

For more than forty years that Iranian money had been sitting in an escrow account. Various international bodies and panels had ruled, over the years, that the money belonged to Iran, and we formally acknowledged the debt. But we always claimed that there was nothing we could do. Iran was sanctioned by the whole of the EU, and under the Common Foreign and Security Policy we had to play ball.

Hang on, I said: what about Brexit? Surely we could now do what we wanted? I went to see Philip Hammond, chancellor of the exchequer, whose support I would need to unlock the account containing the tank money. He was surprisingly sympathetic.

Nazanin had been seized when he was foreign secretary, and he was as keen as I was that she should be freed, along with the other UK-Iranian dual nationals. The trouble was logistics – how to move the cash.

The banks were terrified. In order to move £400 million from the UK to Iran you needed some form of wire transaction by a reputable western financial institution; and they were all fearful of the brutal extra-territoriality of the US sanctions regime.

If a US court deemed that the transaction was a breach of the sanctions against Iran, and if it touched any part of the vast American financial services network, then *pzzzzzt* – the bankers concerned could be extradited to Alcatraz. It seemed pathetic that we couldn't get round it, and an interesting comment on the continuing reality of US financial dominance. But there it was.

We were stuck, and so was poor Nazanin – now so sick, I was told, that her hair was falling out; the doctors were seriously worried.

Until one morning some bright spark at the Foreign Office worked out a solution. I won't say exactly what it was, only that it involved the Post Office savings bank. Suddenly I could see a deal.

I rang Javad Zarif, the Iranian foreign minister, with whom I was on good terms. He grasped immediately what I was trying to say.

There could be no question of ransom-paying. The two issues were not linked. But they could be solved, shall we say, in parallel. He invited me to Tehran.

By early December I was out in the Iranian capital, for the first time in my life. It was a strange old place, beautiful, with the snow on the surrounding mountains pink in the sunset – and it felt somehow sequestered from the modern world.

It was full of men in black leather jackets, and blue smoke coming out of the backs of their motorbikes, and women with their heads covered. It had the feel of 1980s eastern Europe, that black sludge in the streets and the ill-fitting green uniforms of the IRGC.

I went to see President Rouhani in his mirror-walled palace and we sat on little chairs facing each other, as if for a TV interview. He was a beaming, soft-spoken man who seemed to have fond memories of his time at university in Glasgow. We aired the usual mutual grievances.

He deplored western sanctions. I insisted that Iran must stop all efforts to construct a nuclear weapon, and prove it. We then spoke, in the oracular style of diplomacy, of the two issues that were the impediments to better relations.

It was quite wrong, I said, that his regime was detaining Nazanin and the other dual nationals, and we hoped for a speedy release. Well, he said, that was a matter for the courts.

The woman I had mentioned was Iranian, and Iranian law did not recognise dual nationality. But he understood that she was a mother of a young child, and he wished me to know that the government of Iran was merciful, and the people of Iran were merciful, even though – and he smiled at me through glittering spectacles – the sanctions were very cruel.

There were people who did not have enough bread, he said.

I saw my cue.

Well, I said, I knew of one particular issue that might be resolved, to the financial benefit of the people of Iran, though of course there could be no linkage – and I mentioned the tank money.

Yes, he said, nodding and smiling, there could be no linkage, but perhaps the consular cases could be resolved. I left the meeting elated. I was sure that Rouhani was sincere, and that we had an agreement.

I saw Nazanin's family at the embassy, her brother and parents and her daughter Gabriella. They were so kind to me, and so grateful for my efforts, that I felt quite overwhelmed, and of course the sight of the little girl was deeply affecting.

I vowed to them, to myself, to do everything I could to spring her mother. Without over-promising, I told them that we had begun the process – and I believed that we had.

I felt that the trip had gone so well that I celebrated by playing tennis with the ambassador, Nick Hopton, even though the embassy court was half covered with a sheet of ice. Nick had done a great job, and we both felt that we were on the verge of sorting it out; and then, rather like the tennis, I found myself going into a skid.

When I got back it was as though the Whitehall system had woken with a shock and discovered that I was about to end a chronic diplomatic problem that it had suited us, frankly, not to solve, in a way that no one expected. The Treasury remained in favour; the FCO was obviously in favour.

But Number Ten insisted that all relevant departments must sign off the deal. I absolutely required Gavin Williamson, secretary of state for defence, to say yes; and he just would not.

Come on, Gavin, I said over breakfast, we need to fix this thing.

No, he said, I won't send money to Hezbollah so they can buy weapons to kill our boys.

I wasn't sure which theatre of conflict he was talking about, but I let it pass and tried another tack.

Gavin, it's not our money, I insisted. We can't use it to build schools and hospitals. It's Iranian money.

It was no use. I have always been friendly with Gavin, who is a keen student of politics and power, and I could see what was really going on.

While Nazanin languished in Iranian captivity, with many blaming me, there were quite a few people who were savouring my moral torment – not least, I suspect, in Number Ten.

I cursed and strained, but for the rest of my time in the Foreign Office the Whitehall computer said no.

Poor Gabriella sent me tragic tokens, Christmas cards and messages begging me to help her mother. But I felt that I was now trapped, and Nazanin was therefore trapped, by one of those petty power plays that are part of British politics.

I had to become PM, and to wait several years, to achieve the executive authority required to Aquablast the blockage – which we finally did, with help of foreign secretaries Dom Raab and Liz Truss. Nazanin came out on March 16, 2022, and the tank money went back to Iran. By then she had been locked up, off and on, for almost six years.

Even then, at the last minute, the White House tried to stop us handing over the tank cash – which was pretty rich, frankly, when you consider the billions the Americans have spent to get their own hostages out.

Could we have done it more expeditiously and diplomatically, and without settling the IMS debt? Very possibly. We had done so with many others. But as I told the Foreign Affairs Committee in that infamous session in November 2017, the problem with these cases is publicity.

The bigger the row, the bigger the price the Iranians exact, and once Monique Villa of Thomson Reuters had pointed the finger at me and the media hoo-hah went critical, I am afraid the price on Nazanin's head was increased, so that it took years, and a big UK move, to sort it out; though clearly – and I will not mince my words – Nazanin would have been out years earlier, and she and her family would have been spared much misery, if Number Ten had allowed me to do the deal I struck with Rouhani in 2017.

As for their motives in Number Ten, ah well, who knows: I leave you to speculate.

Would we have settled that debt if Nazanin had not been unjustly detained in Tehran? Frankly, I doubt it.

We – and I – did it with great reluctance. I loathe the ideology of the Revolutionary government of Iran, the oppression of women, the prodigal public executions, and I am sure that one day it will change. It will take time, and change, as ever, must come from within.

We cannot write off this great and ancient country of eighty million people, with so many young people who want personal and political freedom but who don't want to make a choice between loving freedom and loving Iran.

In recent times we have seen changes that may or may not be hopeful – from huge protests against the mandatory headscarf to the rapprochement with Saudi Arabia, Iranian membership of the BRICS, and so on.

Which way will it go? I don't know, but we must be patient, and we must be clear-eyed about the threat.

When in January 2020 Donald Trump ordered the liquidation of Qasem Soleimani, commander of the IRGC Quds Force, I wept no tears. He and his organisation had jailed Nazanin, for no reason at all – and I am afraid he did much that was far worse.

At all costs we must stop the mullahs from obtaining a nuclear weapon, and it is worth engaging with Tehran just to make this point – that any such move would be a disaster for Iran and for the world.

You know when you are dealing with Iran that you are dealing with an autocracy, a place where power is not really in the hands of the people but ruthlessly guarded by an elite. You can tell by the sly contempt for the truth, by the bullying, by the shameless refusal to apply the most basic standards of decency.

If there is one regime, these days, that can match the Iranians for cynicism, it is their allies in Putin's Russia.

Chapter 29

Putin the Poisoner

And how we organised a fightback

It is not clear exactly how Dawn Sturgess responded when her partner Charlie Rowley gave her a present on June 30, 2018 in Charlie's home in Amesbury, Wiltshire. Was she amused? Was she touched? Perhaps it didn't matter that Charlie, who was unemployed, had found the present in a recycling bin in Salisbury, about seven miles away.

It didn't matter that the plastic tube was almost empty. It's the thought that counts. It was a plastic Nina Ricci perfume bottle with a nozzle like a soda syphon.

Dawn immediately squirted some of the oily mixture on her wrists and rubbed her hands together. Within moments Sturgess, a forty-four-year-old mother of three, was unconscious and mortally ill, and within days she was dead.

Scientists at the UK's defence laboratories in Porton Down later determined conclusively that the substance in the bottle was not French perfume. It was a 'novichok', a slang Russian expression for a newcomer, a new kid on the block – so called because when this class of poison was first concocted in the labs of the former Soviet Union it exceeded, in sheer nastiness, anything that the scientists had seen before.

Novichok could be used in liquid, solid or powder form, and was fatal in even the tiniest quantities. It was so potent that it could defeat Nato-issue protective gear, and yet Soviet agents could prepare it from precursors, or ingredients, that were themselves hard to detect.

Dawn and Charlie (who was also taken badly ill) were the latest victims of a brazen operation by President Vladimir Putin, whose purpose was twofold. The Kremlin authorities wanted to kill a man they regarded as a traitor. Perhaps more importantly, they wanted to show, by the grisliness of their methods, the contempt of the Russian state for international law and – I am afraid – for Britain.

The use of novichok on British soil was tantamount to a chemical weapons attack, in the sense that Putin didn't care who suffered. He knew that if you squirt stuff like novichok around a Wiltshire town, the chances are that you will kill and injure wholly blameless members of the British public – and that is what happened.

The attack itself was launched months earlier, on March 4, 2018, when Sergei and Yulia Skripal were seen lolling on a bench in the middle of Salisbury. Eyewitnesses said they looked frozen, like people on opioid drugs. Sergei Skripal, a bulky man in his sixties, had his hands raised in the air, as if shrugging, and his eyes fixed glassily on the building in front. His daughter Yulia was slumped against him, her eyes rolled back so that only the whites were showing. Both seemed to be frothing at the mouth.

As soon as the news was broken to the FCO, my officials knew exactly who had done it to Sergei and why. Skripal was a brave man, a UK agent in the Russian military intelligence (the GRU) who had been caught communing with the famous fake rock in Gorky Park. He had been spy-swapped out of Russia in 2010, and settled discreetly in Salisbury. Now he was almost dead, and Yulia – together with a police officer who attended the scene – was seriously ill.

In the days that followed, the Russians seemed to go out of their way to stoke the fires of British outrage. It wasn't so much the fact of the assassination attempt, or the callous disregard for innocent life. It was the ho-ho satirical gloating of the Russian 'denials'. They scarcely bothered to conceal what they had done. The two slab-faced Russian assassins were seen plainly, in multiple CCTV images, visiting Salisbury not once but twice in the days before the poisoning.

After months of work, the forensic evidence became overwhelming. When it was plain as a pikestaff that they had recklessly used the Nina Ricci bottle to daub novichok on Sergei's front door, the Russians had the gall to produce the two thugs, in Moscow, and put them on TV. In September the two assassins gave a kind of Derek-and-Clive deadpan double act while a female presenter lobbed them absurd softball questions.

Why did they go to Salisbury? asked the journalist from Russia Today.

Well, said one of them with a straight face, we wanted to see the famous cathedral which has a spire 123 metres tall and one of the oldest working clocks in the world.

And why did you need to go twice?

It was a bit snowy on the first day, said the Russians. There was a problem with the slush. They wanted to come back when it was less slushy. (One could imagine the Russian audience guffawing at the idea that a brace of GRU men would be put off by a spot of British slush.)

Wasn't it a bit odd, two men walking around together on holiday? asked the presenter. Were they homosexuals?

No, they weren't homosexuals, and by the way they could not have been carrying a perfume bottle, as alleged: only effeminate men would carry perfume bottles.

So what are your jobs?

To cut a long story short, they said, they were in the fitness business. They were sports nutritionists.

Sports nutritionists, eh. With novichok.

The whole thing was designed to be comically unconvincing – a gigantic V-sign flicked at the British criminal justice system. I could imagine the tears of laughter coursing down Putin's cheeks, and I imagine the Russian public – a lot of them – found it pretty funny too.

It was an insult to Britain, at a time when we were probably a bit sensitive to international insults. It was by now almost two years since the UK had voted to leave the EU, but we were still in a labyrinth of political pain, and struggling to find the exit. We had abandoned the comfort and support of EU membership – for what?

Perhaps Putin had used chemical weapons in Salisbury because he thought we were now a kind of Billy no-mates – the kid who gets their lunch money stolen by the playground bully.

Yup: they were already blaming Brexit, and of course I found that infuriating. There were all sorts of reasons why Putin might have chosen to lash out at Britain. We were by far his most aggressive critics, for instance, over the way he was conducting the war in Syria. But I could see that our response to Salisbury was all-important.

We had to look strong. We needed to dust ourselves down, push our spectacles back up our nose and give the bully what for.

We immediately announced the biggest expulsion of Russian diplomats since the depths of the Cold War and twenty-three spies were told to pack their bags, together with a package of slightly less than terrifying measures, including a ministerial and royal boycott of the forthcoming FIFA World Cup in Moscow. It plainly wasn't enough. We needed to prove that we were not on our own, and that the world agreed with us. We needed others to show that they joined us, on principle, in condemning the barbarism of the Kremlin. We decided to take a risk and to begin a Foreign Office campaign – to persuade all our friends around the world to show that they backed Britain and the rule of law.

The only way they could do that, I decided, was if they themselves were willing to incur the wrath of Putin and kick out a Russian spy from their own capitals.

Come on, we told our closest allies. We can't have the Russians spraying novichok around and getting away with it. Help us take a stand against chemical weapons. Expel a spook in the name of justice, we told them.

Whack a mole and show you care. It was a lot to ask – to get other countries to expend their own capital with Putin – and the campaign was slow to get underway. People were hesitant. Were we sure about this novichok? Where was the evidence? As the days ticked by, I fretted that we would fail – and then how would Global Britain look? Insulted by Russia, and jilted by our allies.

What else could we do? As is customary in the event of a serious diplomatic rupture, I summoned Alexander Yakovenko, the Russian ambassador, for a formal dressing down. He was marched up the naughty steps under the gaze of Britannia Bellatrix. He tried to give me a present – a book about the treasures of St Petersburg, intended, he said, for Marina. Well, we weren't having any of that.

Without preamble and certainly without any coffee, we sat him down and I read him the démarche. Though I say it myself, it was quite a steely performance. Yakovenko, a largish, pale-ish fellow, had the decency to look shocked as the tide of adjectives rolled over him. It wasn't just diplo-speak. I meant it. I hated what they had done. I hated their ghastly mixture of mendacity and insouciance. But I couldn't help feeling also appalled that it had come to this: two of the five permanent members of the UN Security Council, two great powers that had helped to defeat the Nazis, reduced to such pathetic and sordid squabbling.

Like many foreign secretaries before me, I wished that our relations could have been different. I wondered where it had gone wrong, and how we had squandered the hopes that soared at the end of the Cold War. Who lost Russia, as they say, and how?

My Russophilia went back a long way. It was a fascination that began with pretentious childhood reading of Dostoyevsky and was germinated by J.L.I. Fennell's superb Penguin Russian course, which I did for O-level; generously fertilised at sixteen by a school trip to Moscow, Leningrad (as it was) and the Baltic states, where we sat up getting blind on vodka and roaring the 'Volga Boat Song' and 'Kalinka' until the neighbours banged on the hotel walls.

Like all the best memories, those early Russian sights and sounds – and tastes, like that strange but delicious commie *morozhenoe* ice cream – are hormone-etched by my abortive efforts to win the heart of a girl from Swindon who was also on the trip. I loved Russia, in the sense that I loved Russian language, culture, literature, painting, landscape; and so ten years later, when the Berlin Wall came down and communism imploded, I just assumed that Russia – that great and blatantly European civilisation – would swiftly join the comity of democracies, and that seventy years of Leninist-Stalinist estrangement would be over. I think a lot of us thought, or hoped, the same.

So when, in 2000, the outgoing US president Bill Clinton gave a visionary speech, saying that he saw no reason why Russia should not join the EU, or indeed Nato (so incurring the indignation of the Little Europeans in the UK media; it wasn't for him to make such an offer, they sniffed), I wrote an editorial in the *Spectator* in which I yammered my assent. Was not St Petersburg a European city? Was not Chekhov a European author? These were high, heady days when the future was unwritten and it really seemed that Russia would come our way. In the late 1990s and early 2000s, I went a few times to Lena Nemirovskaya's Moscow School of

Political Studies, a birch-gladed retreat outside the capital where we sat up late with young Russian politicians and journalists.

It was so much easier to be a Russophile in those days – because Russia, as a power, seemed so greatly diminished. That chilling sense of nuclear threat had evaporated. The world had seen the chaos of the collapse of the Soviet Union, and Boris Yeltsin so trolleyed that he couldn't leave the plane at Shannon Airport.

As for his successor, the dapper little pointy-eared former KGB man Vladimir Putin, who took over in 1999, the UK began by misreading him completely; and for years we obstinately persisted in our delusion. Yes, we had disagreed over Kosovo, but the Blairites, with wonderful narcissism, interpreted him as a kind of Russian Blair, a reformer, a 'moderniser'.

We felt that we had won all the big intellectual and strategic arguments, and that it only remained now to do business together. In particular, of course, we were keen to get on with mainlining Russia's vast store of hydrocarbons. BP and other firms piled into Russia, drinking deep beneath the permafrost; and Russian oligarchs – approved of by the Kremlin or not – drank deep in the wine bars of Kensington.

In 2003 there was a state visit to the UK by Putin, the first and last time he was to be accorded such an honour. I was then only a junior MP, but for some reason I was invited to the dinner in the Guildhall. Putin appeared in an idiosyncratic version of evening dress, with a floppy ivory-coloured bow tie that didn't match his shirt and seemed too big for his head. As we all brayed our agreement with whatever it was he said, and toasted him in five different vodkas (one red, one green, one yellow), there was one word that summed up the attitude of the London audience: patronising.

Good old Vlad, was the message from British finance and industry and politics. Well done on not being a communist, keep the oil and gas flowing – and hard luck about the collapse of Soviet power. As the Queen herself had noted in her own speech the previous evening, we didn't agree about some details – minor matters like the war in Iraq (where Putin turned out to be closer to being right than we were) – but you know what, Vlad old boy, we thought, we don't really care what you think, not any more.

The following year we expanded Nato dramatically. Poland, Hungary and the Czech Republic had already joined in 1999. Now seven more members of the former Warsaw Pact decided, entirely reasonably, that their future belonged with the western democracies: Bulgaria, Estonia, Latvia, Lithuania, Romania, Slovakia, Slovenia. The west was now rightly absorbing some of the territories of the former Soviet Union itself – Russia's 'near abroad' – and that was inevitable.

The Russian empire was created by force, and as the British discovered so long ago, you cannot use force, indefinitely, to hold an empire together. If people want to be free, if they want a different destiny – then you have to let them go.

The Russians have nothing to fear from their Nato neighbours, and everything to gain from good relations; but the tragedy is that they just can't see it this way. Putin saw it as a humiliation, and he reacted poisonously.

Alexander Litvinenko was a former Russian GRU agent who had been employed by Boris Berezovsky, a London-based oligarch and now a foe of Putin. Litvinenko started revealing all kinds of discreditable things about the Putin regime – though some of what he said was probably a bit far-fetched. He claimed, for instance, that Putin was a paedophile, on the strength of a clip in which the Russian president stoops to kiss a five-year-old boy – a child athlete – on the stomach. It is a bit rum, I suppose, but you have to make allowances for cultural differences, and I know of no other evidence for Litvinenko's assertion.

Whatever it was, something about Litvinenko got in among Putin, and in a move that directly presaged the Skripal attack he caused him to be poisoned – executed with baroque savagery by pouring polonium, a rare nuclear isotope, into a teapot in a London hotel. Litvinenko died an awful, public death, visibly wasting in hospital, his body consumed by radiation sickness. The official British reaction, I am afraid, was pretty tepid.

We expelled four Russian diplomats, but that was about it. We knew exactly who had done it (as with Skripal), and though we demanded the extradition of the two killers from Moscow, Putin effectively laughed in our face. He even gave one of them a medal and he is now an MP in the Duma. When foreign secretary David Miliband addressed the Commons, he clung to the deflating life-raft of the old Blairite policy: that Russia was an important partner and that we must have a relationship. So it went on, even when the Tory coalition came in.

In 2012 Putin came to the London Olympics and watched the judo with David Cameron. I wasn't invited to the event, but suggested to the media that the Russian leader should live up to his hard-man reputation, strip to the waist and have a bout of judo himself. 'That's what the public want,' I said, 'a politicians' Olympics!'

Where was Litvinenko in all this tomfoolery? All but forgotten, I am afraid. Then in 2014 Putin took advantage of western lassi-tude to invade Ukraine. Our collective response, this time, was limp.

This was an absolutely critical moment – the first time that Russia had reacted to the humiliations of the end of the Cold War and changed the borders of Europe by force. What were we going to do? How were we going to support Ukraine? In 2008 we had grandly proclaimed – at the Bucharest Nato summit – that Georgia and Ukraine were going to join the North Atlantic alliance!

Now Putin's armies were in Ukraine, hacking hunks off the country, taking parts of the Donbas and Crimea. We were watching the dismemberment of a sovereign and independent European nation – and what did we do? We channelled the spirit of Neville Chamberlain.

We cobbled together some inadequate sanctions, but otherwise we did nothing. We forgot all about the Nato promises of 2008. The US and UK conveniently glossed over the 1994 Budapest Memorandum, by which we had solemnly committed to come to Ukraine's aid in the event of attack.

The Ukrainians had once possessed one of the world's biggest arsenals of nuclear weapons, and when they gave those weapons up we agreed, with the US and Russia, that we would 'assure' their security. What happened to that commitment? We had mentally ripped it up and thrown it away. Did I say Chamberlain? We were far more jelly-like than Chamberlain – who at least honoured Britain's promise to come to the defence of Poland.

It was as if the UK had decided that Ukraine was a faraway country of which we know little, in Chamberlain's deadly phrase, and, worst of all, we bizarrely subcontracted the management of Ukraine policy to the French and the Germans.

That June of 2014 was the seventieth anniversary of the Normandy landings. In the margins of the commemorations, Putin met François Hollande of France, Angela Merkel of Germany and Petro Poroshenko of Ukraine. At the initiative of France and Germany, the four of them established the 'Normandy process', a Franco-German-led forum for dealing with the consequences of Putin's invasion. As an exercise in diplomacy it was a moral abomination.

The French and Germans were trying to act as marriage guidance counsellors, helping the Ukrainians and Russians to patch things up – and ignoring the reality that this was a vicious invasion in which Putin had expropriated huge chunks of Ukrainian territory. Thousands of Ukrainians were already fighting and dying for their country, and the Franco-German axis was behaving as though both sides were to blame, six of one, as my mother used to say when her children were fighting, and half a dozen of the other.

Where was America, where was Britain when the infamous Normandy format was being set up?

By the time I became UK foreign secretary two years later, the position was grim. The war in the Donbas was grinding on, and Putin's tactic was continuously to weaken and destabilise Ukraine by twisting the knife in the country's eastern flank. Ukraine could never be secure, never be free to join the EU, for instance, as long as its eastern borders were in chaos. The Normandy process was getting nowhere – exactly as Putin intended.

You couldn't have elections in a war zone, and you couldn't have an end to the war without some sort of political solution involving elections; and Putin was determined to ensure that any new constitutional settlement would allow him to control the whole country through his control of the eastern cities of Lugansk and Donetsk.

In September 2016, only a few months after becoming foreign secretary, I made my first trip to Kyiv. We were by now trying to make up for our failures, and in 2015 Britain had despatched a few dozen soldiers to help 'train' the Ukrainians, in what was known as Operation Orbital. We claimed to have trained many thousands of Ukrainians. At least, unlike the French and the Germans, we were taking a side. But I could tell that our contribution was more symbolic than practical.

That trip to Ukraine was invaluable because I saw the memorials to the thousands of dead since 2014 and I talked to veterans of the Donbas conflict. I grasped how deeply the Ukrainians loved their country, and how determined they were to fight for its life. I went again as foreign secretary, and was confirmed in my view: Putin would be mad to invade.

Later, just before Christmas 2017, I made a long-delayed trip to Moscow. I went with no real confidence that any good would come of it, but because I thought it was peculiar that of all the P5 countries (the five permanent members of the UN Security Council), the UK was the only one not to have any consistent dialogue with Russia – no 'load-bearing relationship', as they say in diplomacy. It was a pretty futile exercise.

Sergei Lavrov is a tall, chain-smoking half-Armenian, swarthy and with a strange amused squint. He is the longest-serving Russian foreign minister since the Tsars, and he is the Gromyko *de nos jours* – the wearying personification of Russian foreign policy in all its sophistry, evasion and lies.

'I am not Sir Gay,' said Sergei as we shook hands. 'Sir Gay is what you have in the Foreign Office.'

After a platitudinous bilateral we had a literally torrid lunch, during which he made me sit in front of a blazing log fire so hot that the sweat ran down my face – as though he was a prefect torturing a fag at a Victorian public school. The meeting achieved nothing. We were nowhere near agreement on Syria or Ukraine, and when I mentioned Litvinenko he crossed himself – and smirked.

'The Jews killed Jesus,' he said. 'That does not mean we should refuse to have relations with the state of Israel.'

Which was at least an admission that they had murdered Litvinenko.

The fundamental fact was that Russia was a different place from twenty years ago; no longer just the vanquished power of the Cold War. Russian confidence was back, and Russian aggression was back. They were willing to use extreme violence, to send in their own regular troops or their Wagner proxies, in a way that had become politically prohibitive for us Brits.

We had been chased out of Iraq, pulled out of Helmand. There was no way we would put regular soldiers' boots on the ground in

Syria, let alone Ukraine – and Lavrov was gazing across the table at me with the slight insolence of someone who was fully aware of the contrast.

It was clear that the Russia hawks in the Foreign Office – men like Laurie Bristow – were right, and that the French and the Germans were wrong. We had to learn something from the courage of the Ukrainians and stand up to the Russians. It was only a few months later, in March of 2018, that Putin signalled his contempt for our relationship and launched the Salisbury attack.

This time I knew we had to do better than in the aftermath of Litvinenko. We couldn't get our friends to agree sanctions, so we needed another gesture of solidarity. We needed those mass expulsions of Russians. At first, it was hard.

The Russians engaged in a blizzard of disinformation. They demanded that we send them the novichok samples from Porton Down so that they could conduct their own analysis. It was absurd, but Jeremy Corbyn, the Labour leader, chose (pretty shabbily) to support Moscow in this request – and for a few days it really seemed as if people were prepared to question our assertions and the Porton Down analysis. 'We need the facts,' said one German politician, 'not just the British allegations.'

We hit the phones even harder and set up a big war room at the top of the Foreign Office, ably led by Philip Barton. By March 18, two weeks after the poisonings, we had our first breakthrough. The Polish foreign minister happened to be coming to my constituency of Uxbridge, to see the famous bunker from the Battle of Britain in which Polish pilots had performed with such gallantry and success. Once again Britain and Poland stood side by side, as Jacek Czaputowicz announced that Poland would indeed be acceding to our request and kicking out four Russian spies. Then things started to roll our way. We hit the phones harder still – and by the end we had done something pretty remarkable.

A total of 29 countries expelled 153 Russians in sympathy with

Britain. I will give you the figures: Albania 2, Australia 2, Belgium 1, Canada 4, Croatia 1, Czech Republic 3, Denmark 2, Estonia 1, Finland 1, France 4, Georgia 1, Germany 4, Hungary 1, Ireland 1, Italy 2, Latvia 1, Lithuania 3, Moldova 3, Montenegro 1, Nato 7, Netherlands 2, North Macedonia 1, Norway 1, Poland 4, Romania 1, Spain 2, Sweden 1, Ukraine 13, United Kingdom 23, United States 60.

It was an amazing feeling to come in morning after morning and to find that the global chorus of disapproval for Russia was growing louder and louder. You must bear in mind that all these countries stood to be punished by Russia – virtually all of them experienced symmetrical expulsions, at least, of their own diplomats.

You will also note that for all his alleged sympathy for Putin, the administration of Donald Trump surprised massively on the upside. To kick out sixty Russians from the United States – that was far beyond our wildest dreams. It was the biggest mass expulsion in diplomatic history. There had been nothing like it even in the Cold War – and yes, I was very proud of the Foreign Office and our teams.

You will notice, of course, that there are some lacunae in the list, in Europe, the Gulf and elsewhere around the world. There is no point in dwelling on them now; but already I was seeing the curious spell of Putin, and Russia, on the world's floating voters.

There was a time at the end of the Cold War when we would dismiss Russia as Upper Volta with rockets. Well, we were now being forced to modify our verdict. Yes, it was a kleptocracy, and true, its economy was about the size of Spain's, and certainly, for many Russians the quality of life – and life expectancy – continued to be abject.

But we had misunderstood Putin, and in some ways underestimated him. We had underestimated his appeal to the Russian public, his ability, with all his semi-camp chest-baring, spearfishing machismo, to incarnate the idea of Russian strength. We also underestimated his appeal to at least some people around the world, a peculiar and unfortunate attraction that we in the UK were to face and to challenge again when Putin came to launch his second attack on Ukraine.

It is a sad fact that Putin's aggression against Ukraine, which is a clear violation of UN principles, has been officially sanctioned, at every stage, by China. We have to ask ourselves why they have done this.

Why are they supporting a revanchist and imperialist attempt to change borders by force? What does it mean for Taiwan and the rest of the South China Sea?

Relations with Beijing seem very different from the time I first went there to pick up that Olympic flag; and that is also sad.

Chapter 30

Golden No More

The rise of China and how to deal with it

It seems incredible that it is now only a few years ago that Britain and China were in the grip of that breathless romance that was known – all too briefly – as the Golden Era. Do you remember it? I do.

It was that shining moment when the Conservative government decided that there should be 'no limits' (© Xi Jinping and Putin) on our friendship and no no-go areas in our commercial relations. Come on, China, we said: help us build our nuclear reactors. We will pay you top dollar!

Come on, Huawei, we said to the vast telecoms company. Show us how this 5G stuff works – and if you can't explain it, just land-mark all our lanes and hedgerows with your sexy little radio masts, and never mind the security implications. It's the Golden Era!

I suppose the ultimate golden moment was Xi's state visit to London in the autumn of 2015 – when Dave and George had finally won a Conservative majority. We signed ourselves up to Xi's grandiose One Belt One Road project to recreate the ancient silk routes – from the days when the Middle Kingdom was the centre of the world. There is now a 7,500-mile rail route, apparently, from somewhere called Yiwu to London.

That's right: you just go down to Victoria Station and ask for a ticket to Yiwu.

We kow-towed so abjectly to Xi, in the organisation of that visit, that we allowed his personal security guard to defeat all the equerries, to elude the royal protection squad and to scramble uninvited into the Gold State Coach, the first time this had happened in the 260-year history of that vehicle. Her Majesty the Queen, you will be pleased to know, was made of sterner stuff.

'Get orff,' she said, or words to that effect, and the goon was ejected; in a metaphor, you could say, for what was to happen to the Golden relationship itself.

There was to come a point when we suddenly realised that the Chinese state had infiltrated things that really mattered – the crown jewels of our critical national infrastructure – and the careless rapture was over.

My first sensations of enthusiasm for China began in 2008, when I flew out to take the Olympic flag – as mayor of the next host city. The day after the handover ceremony we were in a mood of some elation, and we went up on to the Great Wall: tall, misty, far bigger and more bonkers than the photos – ancient ribbons of perfectly dressed stone, swooping and soaring over the thickly wooded mountains. I slid down from one of the watchtowers on a long steel slide, of a kind the 'elf and safety maniacs would probably ban in the UK (and which I decided nevertheless I would copy in London: see earlier on the Orbit). I got some suits made in the Pearl Market, my brother Max – a fluent Chinese speaker – negotiating the price.

I started practising the script, with the help of a textbook. I could do Middle Kingdom, or Zhongguo: 中國. Everyone should be able to do that.

I could do the Chinese word for a woman: 女.

And the Chinese for a quarrel? You got it – two women: 女女.

The Chinese word for good? A woman and a child: 好. No wonder they had a population explosion, ho-ho.

The Chinese word for a mother: a woman and a horse: 妈, presumably a comment on the work involved, ha-ha-ha.

I enjoyed the brain ache of trying to learn the language – though I never got as far as my daughter Cassia. I ate a thousand-year-old egg, with no ill effects. I admired eighth-century Chinese painting – far more advanced than anything in Europe of the same period.

I was becoming a Sinophile, and never in that period did I feel spooked or intimidated by China, even when I was sitting up late one night in the hotel in Beijing, hammering out a column, and my laptop flashed up a message (which I have never seen before or since) saying, 'Other people are currently using this computer.'

Oh well, I thought, if the Chinese secret police want to read my *Telegraph* column before anyone else, who cares? Perhaps I would have to be more security-conscious with my electronic equipment in future (and I was); but that didn't diminish the potential of the relationship.

The Chinese not only hungered to read my *Telegraph* column, and to obtain the secrets of its composition; they wanted our Jaguar Land Rovers, our whisky, our rubberised Burberry raincoats, and with 1.3 billion people, and plenty of rain, that was a lot of potential raincoat sales.

It was one of my proudest boasts, as mayor of London, that we had more Chinese students in London (about 120,000) than any other city in the world – outside China, that is, where they have a lot of Chinese students. So when I went back in 2013 on a post-Olympic mayoral drive to sell London to the Chinese, I saw no need to restrain myself.

We enjoyed a fervid reception, possibly because Chinese state media had extensively covered the London Olympics and my recognition factor was high. In Shanghai I rode a Brompton bicycle, and in Hong Kong, so recently a British colony, I tried to sell them our new-generation hybrid Routemasters, and even shipped one out to show it off.

Hong Kong was unique – part of China since 1997, but still (just about) with its own democratic and legal institutions. As the slogan went, One Country, Two Systems! What the Hong Kongers needed were giant diesel-electric double-deckers, I announced from the open platform: One Bus, Two Systems!

I may have failed to flog the bus, which was a bit big for some of the Hong Kong streets; but when it came to London real estate the Chinese buyers were omnivorous. Over twelve-course banquets – complete with dry ice, live bands and the finest wines known to humanity – we did deals for sites that had lain vacant for years, if not decades.

It so happened that my old friend Chancellor George Osborne was knocking around China at the same time, and we agreed to team up. There was a certain amount of teenage sparring for media attention (including, I seem to remember, a ridiculous handbags-style fight in a lift).

But we enjoyed the double act, and over dinner in Hong Kong we agreed that we shared the same basically pro-China perspective. London should be the main centre for renminbi trades, and the UK should be China's natural commercial partner.

When I got back to City Hall, Eddie Lister and I found we had a long list of Chinese investments to take forward, from Vauxhall to Tower Hill to Greenwich. There was a prodigious plan to build a new commercial district in the Victoria and Albert docks – which we never quite got away.

The project that really gripped my imagination was an out-of-the-blue suggestion, from the Chinese side, that we should rebuild the old Crystal Palace. At first I couldn't believe that they were serious.

*   *   *

You must have seen pictures of this super-colossal greenhouse, once the greatest wonder of Victorian Britain. It was twice the size of St Paul's Cathedral, and was originally erected in Hyde Park as the centrepiece of the 1851 Great Exhibition, when the whole world came to gawp at Britain, heart of the biggest-ever global empire and workshop of the world.

Then the palace's vast wrought-iron frame was dismantled, together with its 60,000 panes of glass, and they were reassembled on the top of Sydenham Hill in south London, where the palace continued to sparkle until 1936 – when it was destroyed, somewhat mysteriously, by fire.

Now, with funding from the Bank of China, a Shanghai developer wanted to rebuild it, as a huge centre for the creative industries. It was going to have studios and offices and exhibition spaces; there would be nothing like it in Britain, in Europe. I boggled with excitement. I was also puzzled. I could see what was in it for young Londoners. I could see what was in it for the London creative economy. But what was in it for a state-backed developer from China? Where was the return?

We had worked on the project for almost a year, slowly accumulating the necessary approvals and support, before I understood what was really afoot. Look at the history, someone suggested.

In 1860 British armed forces in China had brought the Second Opium War to a decisive conclusion, with victory over the Chinese imperial troops. They forced the Chinese to change their own laws on drugs – compelling them, at gunpoint, to open their markets to opium grown in British imperial India and to consign countless Chinese to the spiritual degradation of addiction.

They then rounded off this shameful episode by destroying the Summer Palace of the Qing emperors; an act of which the average Brit may today be oblivious, but the Chinese certainly are not.

The footings of that palace are still visible in Beijing today, like the footings of the Crystal Palace; the difference being that the ruins in China are regularly visited by young Chinese still seething at what Britain did. So what was being proposed now was in fact an elaborate and veiled revenge.

They were going to rebuild that palace, but not in Beijing, not in China. They were going to erect it in the heart of the old oppressor's capital, and they were going to fill it with works of art – like the countless masterpieces looted from the Summer Palace by the 8th Earl of Elgin and his troops.

It was going to be a gigantic effulgent symbol of the new China, and how the tables had now been turned on Britain. The new Chinese Crystal Palace would show how it was now China's turn to reach abroad – but in a spirit of creation, not destruction.

When I finally twigged, I was no less enthusiastic for the scheme – though sadly it was one of those projects for which I just ran out of time. But I felt I had glimpsed something important about the Chinese mentality: their feelings towards Britain, and our imperial past, and the sheer scale of the ambition of Xi Jinping's China.

By the time I became foreign secretary in 2016 in the administration of Theresa May, the UK's attitude towards China had hardened. The Golden Era was associated with Osborne, and there didn't seem much love lost between George and the new PM.

In fact, Osborne went so far as to tell a newspaper that he would not be happy until Theresa was 'chopped up in a bag in my freezer' (a remark that provoked the inevitable scandal and disgust), while Theresa took the cleaver to the Golden Era.

First we reviewed the nuclear programme, one of the key outcomes from the Xi state visit. It was decided, after much deliberation, to winkle the Chinese out of the giant new Hinkley plant in Somerset, and eventually out of the entire civil nuclear construction programme – diplomatically painful and expensive though it might be.

I took part in a lot of these discussions and, even as a Sinophile, I could see the logic of what we were trying to do. China was not an enemy. We did not want to be overtly hostile to Beijing. But we had to accept the reality: that China was a communist country, with a one-party system and no great tradition of political, cultural or media freedom.

It was becoming more and more clear, to us and to the Americans, that China was a long-term strategic competitor, and that it therefore did not make sense to have the Chinese embedded in something as vulnerable (and risky) as the British nuclear industry. Chinese technology was excellent; Chinese finance was very helpful. But we would have to manage on our own. Slowly and painfully we began to unscramble the contracts.

Philip Hammond, the chancellor, would often argue for a balanced approach, and he pointed out, correctly, that we did huge amounts of business with China: trade that was already then worth about £50 billion per year, and which had grown far faster than trade, say, with India. It would be nuts, said Spreadsheet Phil, to cut ourselves off from Chinese markets – or to cut the Chinese off from our own.

I agreed; but I found that some of my fellow conservatives – on both sides of the Atlantic – were becoming almost boss-eyed with hysteria.

'It's China! China! China!' said Steve Bannon, Trump's strategist, when we first went to see him in New York and I asked him about the long-term strategic challenges.

Mike Pence, Trump's vice president, railed about China's debt-trap diplomacy, by which China would seek out vulnerable or impoverished countries and lend them billions to build 'Belt and Road' infrastructure – sometimes white elephants – and how China then trapped its debtors into political obedience; and though some of this was exaggerated, some of it was obviously true.

You could hear the anxiety in the voices of the Sri Lankans as they described their debts to China for the new port at Hambantota; or the Kenyan worries about the debts they were incurring for the Nairobi to Mombasa railway. Wherever I went, from the Horn of Africa to Pakistan to Latin America, I found Chinese-built ports, railways, roads, airports – and, of course, enormous Chinese investments in raw materials; and everywhere the plea was the same. Why are you leaving us to the Chinese? Where is the UK investment?

I felt increasingly frustrated that we – the west – were just vacating the field. It was all very well to complain about the Belt and Road initiative and to warn of growing Chinese influence. But where, frankly, was our counter-offer to the world?

When the Chinese started building huge steel and concrete bases on reefs and atolls in the South China Sea, everyone moaned. We all complained that these islands were in international waters, and that China – strictly speaking – had no right to convert them into a fleet of stationary Chinese aircraft carriers. But apart from complain, what did we do? I found one reef called Johnson's Reef. It is in international waters.

Come on, folks, I said to the Foreign Office: let's colonise this one. If the Chinese are going to claim the Spratlys and the Paracels, I claim Johnson's Reef.

Let's build a base!

I was trying to make a point: that it is no use just whingeing about the proliferation of China-backed infrastructure around the world.

We need to be making better offers, I said; and it was an idea I was to take up as PM, with Joe Biden, which we eventually called 'Build Back Better World'.

The Chinese have had such massive impact and do so many deals precisely because they ask no questions, and as representatives of an undemocratic regime they tend to favour stability over human rights, or the rule of law. You could see it in North Korea, for instance, where China theoretically opposes the nuclear escapades of that barmy dictatorship. But ultimately the Chinese also enable the regime.

When Donald Trump tried his great reset with Kim Jong-Un, we all played along loyally. I gave a speech about nuclear non-proliferation and urged Pyongyang to stop misbehaving.

We toughened our sanctions against Pyongyang, and tried to stop ship-to-ship transfers of oil. We sent naval vessels to the region to show solidarity with Japan, whose islands were being overflown by North Korean missiles with absurd names like No Dong – as if in unconscious revelation of the North Korean dictatorship's phallic anxiety.

We even closed our embassy in Pyongyang, one of the few remaining. Nothing made any difference; and though Donald Trump had great fun calling Kim 'Little Rocket Man', and then claiming that he was going to do a deal with him, a great deal, the greatest deal ever, it was pretty clear that it was all going nowhere.

North Korea was a tragedy, a place so badly run that its people sometimes starved, or ate grass. But its trade was 90 per cent controlled by China. It suited the Chinese that the North Koreans should remain in servitude. They would rather a communist ruler cult on their border than a vibrant, western-oriented liberal democracy – like South Korea – of a kind that might give their people ideas.

What China wants is strategic autonomy, the freedom to run its own affairs – even if that means keeping its neighbours frozen in tyranny.

*   *   *

Whoa, I said: stop. I want to get out. We were banging up through the jungle in Burma, in a convoy of people carriers, and on my right, in a gap in the foliage, I saw another ruined village. I could scarcely believe it.

Why were we being shown this? We were in the western Burmese province of Rakhine, which runs down the coast south of Bangladesh, and the Burmese military were taking us on the most bizarre and self-destructive PR exercise I have ever seen.

It was February 2018, and the whole world was outraged by what was happening. Since August of the previous year the mainly Muslim Rohingya people had been subject to yet another bout of persecution by the largely Buddhist majority.

More than 600,000 of them had been driven out of their homes, and even before I got to Burma I had heard pretty incontrovertible testimony: of people being killed in their thousands, of mass rapes, villagers being thrown alive into the blazing inferno of their homes. I had just come from the coastal town of Cox's Bazar, in Bangladesh, where about a million Rohingya were living in a vast cramped camp of shacks – too terrified to go back over the border to Burma, even if the Burmese troops had allowed them to enter.

This 2017–2018 pogrom was the latest bout of brutality in a pattern of persecution that had lasted decades, if not centuries. The Rohingya of Arakan, or Rakhine, are possibly the most put-upon people in the world: scorned, beaten, killed, disenfranchised and repeatedly expelled from Burma; and all because they are Muslim, not Buddhist, and because they look more Bengali than typically Burmese.

We had come to Sittwe, the capital of Rakhine, and the Burmese military – a hard-faced, flat-eyed bunch – had offered to give us a full inspection of the terrain. They took us up in an ancient Soviet M17 'Hip' helicopter so that we could see for ourselves.

Burma, or Myanmar, is a beautiful country, and from the air you see the golden Buddhas and pagodas gleaming amid the emerald vegetation. But when we reached the site of the Rohingya villages we gasped. It was horrific.

For mile after mile we looked down on places where all human habitation had been torched and then razed to the ground. We saw endless criss-crossing bulldozer tracks by which communities had been rubbed out. We had a big complement of journalists on that old Russian chopper, all staring in amazement through the open portholes; and Reeta Chakrabarti of the BBC was so stunned, as she tried to film the evidence on her mobile, that her iPhone fell into the jungle below.

Now we were heading back to Sittwe on a dirt track. I asked them to stop so that I could see the devastation up close. To my surprise they agreed.

I walked into the wreckage of the village, and over the ashes of the homesteads. Were these people really terrorists? Was it necessary to destroy the whole place, just because someone somewhere was said to belong to a terrorist group called the Arakan Rohingya Salvation Army? Was it really reasonable to torch and purge the entire village – just because someone somewhere had allegedly assaulted a border guard?

My minders just shrugged. In the ashes of one house I found the charred remnants of a kid's bike and held it up to the cameras. In another I found a broken coffee mug, decorated with a pink love heart. I kept it for a long time afterwards on my desk in Thame and wondered what family happiness that love heart represented, what world of joy the Burmese soldiers came and smashed.

This offence was rank; it cried to heaven. This was the violent attempt to extirpate a people – genocide, by any standard or definition. But why were we being shown this vileness?

Why were the Burmese military engaged in such blatant self-incrimination?

I think the answer is fairly simple. There was someone they

wanted to discredit, in western eyes, and she – not I – was their real political enemy.

She was the elected leader of Burma, or Myanmar, and for many years she was widely regarded by western commentators as a latter-day saint.

I had met Aung San Suu Kyi several times (this was now my second trip as foreign secretary), and we had talked for hours on the phone. It isn't quite right to say that I was enchanted. I just thought she had immense grace, intelligence, charisma, courage.

She had fought for years for the cause of Burmese democracy, and had already spent fifteen years under house arrest. Now she had been overwhelmingly elected state counsellor (effectively prime minister) since her party had swept the 2015 elections; and yet it was clear that her authority was heavily circumscribed.

She had to share power with the Tatmadaw – the thuggish generals who were the political heirs of Burma's military dictator Ne Win. Across the world her reputation, and the reputation of Burma, was being heavily tarnished by the massacres in Rakhine.

It was my job to try to get her to see the reality of her position and to act, with all her Nobel Prize-winning moral authority.

As my officials had spotted, we had a lot in common. We were both Oxford graduates, and we both had a habit of reciting poems. One night in Carlton Gardens we threw a splendid dinner for her, with sensational wine (little-known fact: while the French government tragically sold theirs off, the British government keeps an enormous cellar, the best in Europe, with underground racks so vast it looks like the archive scene at the end of *Raiders of the Lost Ark*).

We caused a piper to appear and march around the table. Daw Suu, as I was told to call her, seemed to love it, and we traded verses over the table from Kipling's 'Mandalay', in which an English soldier thinks wistfully of Burma.

The prime minister of Myanmar began, in the sweet low voice that is part Burmese, part St Hugh's.

'By the old Moulmein pagoda, looking lazy at the sea, There's a Burma girl a-sitting, and I know she thinks of me ...'

I volleyed the ball back.

'When the wind is in the palm trees, and the temple-bells they say, Come you back, you English soldier, come you back to Mandalay ...'

And so on.

I later got into terrible trouble when I was in the great Shwedagon temple in Yangon (Rangoon) and Channel 4 recorded me absently reciting the lines about a temple bell – because I had just been asked to sound a giant temple bell, with a kind of log.

Shock horror, said the *Guardian* and other outlets: cloth-eared Johnson recites politically incorrect colonialist poem – in a temple! It was most unfair. What they didn't know – and what I couldn't say in my defence – was that it was also one of the favourite poems of Burma's democratically elected leader; and anyway, the FCO had been delighted by our poetry recitals.

We were building a 'load-bearing relationship' that would enable me to deliver 'tough messages' (don't forget the tough messages, Foreign Secretary, they would murmur into my ear as I prepared to go into a meeting).

But whatever I said to her about Rakhine, it seemed to fall on deaf ears. We had another dinner in Naypyidaw, the old royal capital of Burma, where Daw Suu entertained us in her own residence.

Again, she was captivating company. We talked about the fabled white elephants of Naypyidaw, the sad albino (actually pink) beasts we had seen that morning, horribly hobbled with chains. They and their ancestors had belonged to the Burmese crown for centuries, and unlike other elephants they were not permitted to work – hence white elephant, something large and costly and of no practical value.

Were the Chinese building a lot of white elephants? I mused. Wouldn't it be sensible to encourage some British investment?

We talked about other unique Burmese creatures, pink dolphins in the Irrawaddy, and about the lovely but decaying colonial buildings of old Rangoon. What could we do to restore their faded grandeur? Perhaps we could have a charity concert with British bands – Showaddywaddy on the Irrawaddy?

We capped each other's recitation of Tennyson's 'Ulysses' – that perennial favourite of embattled politicians. In fact we talked of just about everything except the thing that really mattered – the brutal ethnic cleansing that was disgusting the world, appalling her fans and causing her halo to slip. Try as I might, I found it impossible to get her to acknowledge the horror of what was happening. Why not?

For all her wisdom and humanity, it struck me that she is also a Burmese nationalist, like her father before her, and it may be that she simply does not sympathise with the Rohingya in the way that we do – or at least that she attaches more weight to the threat of terrorism and separatism. It may be that she knows the Burmese people are, I am afraid, pretty badly prejudiced against the Rohingya, and she just doesn't feel she can dissent too strongly from public opinion.

More importantly, she was not – even then – really running the country, not properly. She hadn't been across to Rakhine to see the crimes being committed by the Tatmadaw; she hadn't seen what we saw. You could say she was sticking her head in the sand, but the reality is that the army – not Daw Suu – was responsible for the massacres. By their relentless brutality they were shoring up their own position, like all regimes that depend on an external threat, and discrediting her at the same time in the eyes of the west.

Three years later, having profoundly weakened her international position, they snuffed out democracy again. They arrested the seventy-five-year-old Daw Suu and jailed her once more, though this time in worse conditions.

As I write that fearless woman is in a small cinder-block cell – though her spirits remain apparently high. Burma has sunk backwards again. The Tatmadaw are unequivocally in charge. And who backs the Tatmadaw?

The same people who are building yet another giant Belt and Road project – a 268-mile roadway from the Chinese border to Mandalay, and then to the port of Kyaukphyu on the Rakhine coast. It's the Chinese, of course, and they want another convenient route for moving oil and other commodities up from the Bay of Bengal to the Middle Kingdom. Ultimately the Chinese want the stability provided by their clients in the military junta – and they are not much enthused by the prospect of democracy on their doorstep.

Or indeed anywhere else, come to that. They don't ask African states to comply with conventions on human rights, or environmental codes, or to have a good record on promoting the rights of LGBTQI communities.

They just want to be respected, to build up dependencies as lenders and customers and to extend their influence around the world and in the votes and elections of international bodies, from the UN to the International Telecommunication Union.

Everywhere I went I felt the impact of China, and the needs of 1.3 billion people – not just sucking in raw materials, but literally devouring – eating – some of the rarest creatures on earth.

I have already explained my slow-dawning enlightenment on climate change – but there was one aspect of my father's environmental work that I always fervently supported and that is his long and many-sided campaign to save the animals and plants of the world – and their habitats – from being wiped out.

As I flew over Africa at night, I could see the lava-like glow of human destruction: the endless bush fires that lit up the once-dark continent, from the Cape to the Sahara. I read with horror about species loss, the sheer weight of humanity that was crowding and crushing wild animals into oblivion.

Since 1970, less than my lifetime, we human beings have eradicated nearly 70 per cent of all the world's wild animal population, and three hundred species of mammal are literally being eaten to extinction.

The data enraged me, and I decided that Global Britain™ would launch a separate campaign, in addition to our campaign for twelve years of quality education for every girl. We would campaign to stop the trade in endangered species. Zac Goldsmith did an outstanding job, and so did Ben Gascoigne, and we worked up a big global summit for the second half of 2018.

The FCO officials came to realise that wherever I went I would ask about what was happening to wildlife populations – not hitherto a priority for British diplomacy – and deliver 'tough messages' about the fate of the animals.

All too often, I am afraid, we found that species were being hunted to extinction because of a totally groundless superstition in Asia – usually among people of Chinese heritage – that the claws or teeth or pelt or pancreas had some therapeutic property.

I became obsessed with pangolins, or scaly anteaters, whose scales are ground up for traditional medicine. Look at these beautiful little creatures, these walking artichokes, that can roll themselves into an armoured ball. Did you know that they are the only creatures in the world whose tongue is rooted in its pelvis? Why the hell should they be wiped out, so that middle-aged men can hope to get an erection?

Grinding up and eating pangolin scales will make no difference to your love life. Nor will it help you lactate, or cure cancer. It just means killing an increasingly rare species. Then there are the rhinos and the tigers …

I was wound up by China's attitude to the animal kingdom long before I had heard of the bat caves of Wuhan, or the possible role of the pangolin as a vector of Covid; and when I did, well, read on …

I hope I don't sound Sinophobic in saying any of this because I am not – far from it.

I don't think we should depend on China for our critical national infrastructure, or allow China to buy academic influence in places like Cambridge. We should accept that the gilt has more or less flaked off the Golden Era.

The Chinese engage in systematic industrial espionage and theft. They oppress the Uighur population and Tibet. They are squeezing Hong Kong. We must feel free to point all this out to the Chinese – not least because if we think it, but don't say it, they will decide we are just pathetic. But we would be totally wrong, and mad, to turn our backs on China and start a new Cold War, to cut ourselves off from trade and engagement and the basic business of understanding a fifth of humanity, with all the genius of that population. We must learn to love what there is to love about China – and there is a lot – and deal robustly with what we may fear.

I still think those fears may be overdone. It's fashionable these days to say the world is approaching a violent crisis – perhaps even World War Three. A few years ago we worried about the 'Clash of Civilisations' between Islam and the west. Now we worry about a vast schematic conflict of ideologies – democracies versus autocracies, like the followers of Athens against the followers of Sparta.

On one side we imagine the American-led west; on the other the North Koreans, the Iranians, the Russians, the Chinese. Well, it is always right to be worried about the possibility of conflict, and the infinite varieties of human folly. Read some of the journalism of the 1930s, and you will find plenty of people who woefully misunderstood Hitler and underestimated the chances of war.

All I can say is that I don't think such a conflict is by any means inevitable, let alone desirable. Are China and America really fated to go to war?

I had a wonderful time recently cycling around Bentonville, Arkansas, which is the headquarters of Walmart, the supermarket. Walmart is the biggest company in the world, with revenues of £460 billion and 2.1 million employees.

Yes, you read that right. This American store employs more people than the Chinese army (1.9 million) and more than the British NHS (1.7 million). It has 400 MILLION lines of products in its stores and is now expanding across Africa, India, Asia.

What is the secret of Walmart's success? In one word – China.

About 80 per cent of the manufactured goods sold in Walmart – that is, goods excluding food and beverages – are at least partly sourced from China. Take a Walmart vacuum cleaner or a Walmart bicycle or a Walmart laptop: chances are it's over 92 per cent Chinese.

Now what does that tell us? It tells us that the world is very different from the autarkic governments of the 1930s, and that there is already a huge economic symbiosis between the US and China. The success of Walmart is great for America, because it helps families to afford the things they need. The success of Walmart is great for China, because it creates jobs and feeds families in China.

To try to disentwine these economies, to cut the Siamese twins apart, would not only be virtually impossible. It would mean a colossal destruction of value that would impoverish people on all sides. I just don't think it is likely to happen.

Nor do I think, by the way, that China is even fated to replace America as the global hegemon, with the attendant risk of conflict that is sometimes referred to as the 'Thucydides trap'. If you spend a lot of time flying over America, as I do these days, you notice something remarkable.

The United States is huge, it's beautiful, it's temperate, it's overwhelmingly cultivable and habitable, and yet by comparison with Europe and Asia (certainly India and China) there's hardly anyone there. The Chinese population is older, poorer, and much more dense – with more than four times as many people per square mile. China, India – these are antique lands that have been for millennia the homes of large populations.

In America they already have very high per capita GDP, and in virtually every state you will find a tech hub or great university or hip and jiving centre of innovation. It is America that feels as if it's in its economic infancy, because it seems to have the space for ideas to grow. It is true that China has gained in its share of GDP, but at the expense of us slowcoaches in Europe, not the US.

So with the right leadership – and a willingness to stand up for the values of freedom and democracy – I reckon American hegemony could last the rest of my lifetime, and perhaps my children's lifetimes.

I might be wrong. Things can go bad, fast, and the war in Ukraine is plainly one of the biggest risks. The Russian invasion seems so clearly to symbolise the current global divide, in that it is a war between democracy and kleptocracy, between tyranny and freedom. If we fail to protect the Ukrainians, I do fear that worse will follow.

After two years as foreign secretary I had one idea for world peace and prosperity, one cure-all for just about every evil. We should set about righting one of the biggest injustices in the world – the literacy gap between boys and girls. What's stopping us? Political correctness, of course.

Chapter 31

Teach Her to Read

Level up the sexes, level up the world

The giant rotors of the Nigerian helicopter thwocked and thug-gered over the scrubby and impoverished landscape of the Borno province. It was August 2017. We were far off in the north-east of Nigeria, the top right-hand corner of that vast country, near places like Chad and Niger, a world of desiccated lakes where the soil is so bad that nothing much can put down deep roots – nothing much except Islamic extremism.

We were flying over what was until recently a war zone, and since we couldn't be entirely sure that the terrorists had been cleared out, we were scanning the ground with some apprehen-sion. It was so misty that we had to fly much lower than the pilot would have liked.

We were fully in range, and an ideal target, for a pot-shot from an AK-47. I kept thinking of the scene in *Apocalypse Now* when the GIs in the helicopter decide to sit on their helmets – the char-acteristic male choice between brain and balls.

Down there in the cinder-block farmsteads, among the straggly maize stalks, I could see goats – loads of goats. It was explained to me that we were coming up to the festival of Eid al-Kabir, which was a very big deal in this part of Nigeria.

No matter how poor you were, it was expected that you would slaughter a goat to show your devotion to God; and in a few days the goats would be comprehensively got. Yup, I thought, looking down at those poor goats in the mist – whatever risks we were running, goat life expectancy hereabouts was considerably shorter than ours.

Come to that, we were far safer and more comfortable than most of the human beings below – some of whose lives were in daily peril.

It was now over three years since Islamist militants had kidnapped 276 girls from a government secondary state school in Chibok – just to the south of where we were. They were aged sixteen to eighteen, and they had come back to their school that April, in spite of the security risks, to take their physics exams. They had tried to escape, some of them jumping from the trucks in which they were being transported, and a few had found freedom.

Overall the episode had been an epic of bungling, mainly by the government of Nigerian President Goodluck Jonathan. The UK RAF reported a sighting. An American eye in the sky apparently spotted some others. But the Nigerian government was reluctant to accept offers of help, and when I was flying over the territory there were still hundreds unaccounted for; at the time of writing there are still more than a hundred missing Chibok girls.

They were taken partly because they were Christian, but mainly because they were young women who had offended against their captors' twisted version of Islam, in that they were determined to be educated. Boko Haram, their kidnappers were called, from the pidgin Boko meaning book and haram meaning forbidden or sacrilegious.

The name was meant to be absurd. It was intended to satirise the girl-takers' bone-headed and nihilistic agenda. But the thugs had adopted it as their *nom de guerre*, and to teach girls that Boko was haram they thought it right, in the name of religion, to kidnap them, rape them, mutilate them, kill them, or, if they were lucky, to keep them as chattels or goat-minders somewhere in these arid wastes.

Or, as Boko Haram's maniacal leader Abubakar Shekau put it: 'I will sell them in the cattle market, by Allah.'

I know that Boko haram sound to you and me like nutters – egregious throwbacks to another age. Indeed, to call their views medieval is an insult to the relative tolerance and egalitarianism of the Middle Ages. But as I learned my job as foreign secretary, I started to think their basic gender-based prejudice was not in fact so rare, and that this disastrous hostility to female education was the biggest of all the impediments to human betterment.

In one of my very first trips I went to Pakistan, a country that traditionally receives hundreds of millions of pounds per year of British Official Development Assistance. We in the UK have deep and historic ties of kinship with Pakistan. That part of South Asia is also, sadly, one of the world's biggest breeding grounds for terror and one of the biggest exporters of Islamic extremists, both to the UK and to India, and elsewhere.

This was the country, never forget, that mysteriously found a home for Osama bin Laden – in a large detached villa in the old barracks town of Abbottabad – years after he committed mass murder in New York on 9/11.

I was encouraged to be told by UK officials in Lahore that we were doing a lot to help educate young people – including six million girls, they said. It was inspiring to go to the Kinnaird School and see the girls in their blue uniforms, full of confidence about their plans to go to university in the UK. But was this really enough? Could we hope to move the dial, even with these large sums of UK taxpayers' money?

The literacy numbers were terrifying. The population of Pakistan was approaching 231 million and female illiteracy was then about 60 per cent. It felt as if schools like Kinnaird were just a few bright lamps in the great ambient gloom of ignorance and prejudice, and around the world I found the story was even worse.

I went to Somalia, where the al-Shabaab terrorists – a kind of al-Qaeda in the Horn of Africa – are helping to keep that country permanently poor and chaotic, as well as exporting terrorism to Kenya and other parts of east Africa. How can Somalia ever escape this crazy macho cycle of clan violence and retribution when the men who rule the country think it somehow sensible, or tolerable, that only 26 per cent of Somali women can read?

We drove through Mogadishu, where people were walking around with Kalashnikovs – in the same way that Londoners might carry umbrellas. Finally we bounced through the potholes and the security checks, and arrived at a smallish white building that turned out to be the presidential palace.

I had a long conversation with President Farmajo, a soft-spoken and good-humoured former employee of the New York mass transit authority. He was interested, of course, in everything we could do to bring al-Shabaab to heel. He wanted us to help end the ghastly civil war – and I agreed with him. But I was not optimistic.

In the end groups like al-Shabaab can only flourish in a culture that enables their whacko sexism and bigotry. President Farmajo is a nice guy, and I am sure that he was doing his best. His name is a pidgin Italian *nom de guerre*, a throwback to the era when Somalia was a colony of Mussolini. He is Farmajo after Formaggio, the Italian for cheese – the idea being that he is a big cheese.

Well, my question was: what were the big cheeses of Somalia doing about the culture and attitudes of their fellow countrymen and women?

No quantity of foreign taxpayers' dosh can make a difference if the ruling classes of Somalia allow – as they do – the popular habit of mutilating little girls at birth by cutting off their clitorises. No amount of textbooks, no amount of ODA subsidies for teaching

– none of it will be worth a damn if the men, and it is (almost) always the men, think it is somehow acceptable to keep three-quarters of the female population in a grinding servitude of ignorance.

In every country that was backward, every country that suffered from civil war, famine, terrorism, destruction of habitat, infant mortality – you name it, I found the same underlying phenomenon. The levels of male literacy were bad, but the levels of female literacy were worse, sometimes far worse.

Take Niger, where an Islamist insurgency is now underway. Female illiteracy is running at 70 per cent. It is the same in Burkina Faso, Chad – across the whole of the Sahel region, that great incubator of instability that is driving so much of the migrant crisis across the Mediterranean and the rest of Europe. When I became the first foreign secretary to visit Liberia I found a country where 76 per cent of the women can't read.

I found myself getting furious, not just with the injustice but with the way we were always missing this glaring point – the primacy, in economic and political development, of reading and writing.

It is not difficult to teach a child to read. It takes a bit of patience, but once they are about four years old their minds are already vast and seemingly infinitely receptive data banks – echoing and rapidly understanding letters and sounds and words.

If a girl is illiterate, she will become an illiterate young mother, and the chances of her own children escaping her trap are greatly reduced. If young girls can't read, then the whole of a society will never escape the cycle of destitution and backwardness.

Teach her to read – and bingo, you change the odds. Teach her to read, and the chances massively increase that she can become economically successful herself.

Teach her to read, and she will have the confidence to control her own fertility; and the correlation now between female literacy and the stabilisation of population growth is irrefutable.

Teach her to read, therefore, and you reduce the scrabble for jobs among the unemployed youth; you improve the life chances of the whole population; you remove so many of the root causes of crime, and war, and terrorism, and religious discrimination.

Teach her to read, and, who knows, you may inspire in her male children a rejection of the crass chauvinism and sexism – which in truth should be no part of Islam – and weaken the grip of the Islamists.

And because reading is so easy, and learning to read is so relatively cheap, the transformation can be very fast. Look around the world and you will see places where the literacy rate has suddenly accelerated – the Indian state of Kerala, for instance, or some parts of the Middle East. It is all about attitude, and leadership, and that means – still – that it is very largely about what the men are willing to put up with.

As I pondered the problem I started to think that the whole aid budget – £14 billion every year, or 0.7 per cent of GDP – was topsy-turvy. We were spending prodigious quantities of money and intellectual and emotional effort trying to tackle the myriad symptoms of disaster – from childhood disease to terrorism. There was one thing we could do that was cheaper and more effective, and that was to tackle what was in so many cases the root problem and insist on the right of every girl in the world to have the same education as every boy; or at least twelve years of quality education for every girl.

I had become radicalised on the issue – not too strong a word – by meeting Malala Yousafzai. A friend of mine called Peter Rosengard persuaded me to invite her to City Hall in London, and I was glad I did. Some people seem to be bathed in a special, luminous otherworldly quality – a kind of modern saintliness. That was what I felt about Malala when she came to my mayoral office in 2014. She was so sweet, so charming, and so resolute in her convictions and so optimistic about the future of humanity. It was hard to believe what she had endured.

It was two years previously, in October 2012, that she had been riding on her school bus in the Swat region of Pakistan. A Taliban gunman got on board and shouted, 'Which one of you is Malala? Speak up or I will shoot you all.'

Malala was identified. He then shot her, and the bullet entered next to her left eye and travelled eighteen inches inside her, through her neck, before lodging in her shoulder. She was fifteen years old.

What was her crime? What made this rage and spite? She had protested against the decision of the Pakistani Taliban to close the girls' schools in Swat.

She had been so bold as to say that she had a right to an education, even though she was a girl; and just for saying that, just for claiming that she had a right to learn, these odious numbskulls in the Taliban decided – officially – that she had to be killed; and they almost succeeded. It was a miracle of modern medicine – much of it done in Birmingham – that she survived.

As I listened to her story in City Hall, it seemed so alien and incredible that grown men could behave in this way. The more I saw as foreign secretary, however, the more convinced I became that the actions of the Taliban, like the cruelty of Boko Haram, were just an extreme manifestation of the same syndrome that was holding back the world.

I went to Afghanistan, that other great breeding ground of terror where bin Laden had his camps. I saw the efforts we were making to shine the flashlight of literacy in the darkness. Some enterprising DFID officials took me to a performance of *Macbeth* in Dari, with both male and female actors (and I felt the Afghan audience responding strongly to the themes of treachery and gore).

I was introduced to Afghan female footballers and cricketers, and we played with bats and balls on a tiny patch of green, surrounded by the machine gun nests of the embassy compound. I marvelled at what our officials were pulling off, in gruelling conditions. But were they really lifting more than a few pounds of loose scree from the surrounding mountains of oppression?

Kabul, the capital, was already so dangerous that these hundreds of officials were virtually unable to leave the fortified compound. They were getting cabin fever. It was costing us more than £300 million to keep the embassy going – the most expensive of our overseas posts – and outside Kabul, things were going from bad to worse.

The Taliban were continuing to make advances – the same people, ideologically, as the Pakistani Taliban who had shot Malala. They wanted to close every girls' school in the country. Every time I saw poor Ashraf Ghani, the Afghan president, my instructions were to reassure him.

We were there for the long term, I was to tell him, and we had no intention of pulling out; and every time, having delivered this message, I would hope we could make good our promise.

And at the time I genuinely thought we could. I certainly did not foresee the complete and sudden US withdrawal that took place under Joe Biden, and the collapse that followed.

Today the state of female education in Afghanistan is so grim as to make you weep: proof, if ever it were needed, that the gains of civilisation can be lost, and that history really can go backwards and that darkness can return.

We learned that there are limits to our ability to force the Afghans to teach their girls. You can't bomb them or bribe them. You can't flood them with UK-funded laptops and teachers, even if the country were safe enough for British teachers to operate.

I began to think that there was one thing you might perhaps do – and that was make them understand that in this vital way they are the authors of their own misfortune, and that they have it in their hands – literally – to take up a book, put it under the noses of their daughters and sort it out.

I became pretty messianic about female education. In 2017 I staged a big event at UNGA in New York, to which – on the advice of my officials – I invited Emma Watson, the star of *Harry Potter*, who had expressed an interest in the subject. For some reason she turned me down. She later turned her wrath on J.K. Rowling herself, over the ridiculous issue of whether women can have penises, so I felt I was in good company.

Whatever any of us have done as politicians to stimulate young female interest in reading, it is dwarfed by the achievement of J.K. Rowling.

I made a big push at the London Commonwealth summit the next year, and we got all fifty-two countries to sign up to the ambition of twelve years of quality education for every girl (even though some Caribbean countries objected, very reasonably, that the real problem was often male underachievement). We did an event attended by Prince Harry and Meghan Markle, who both seemed well on top of it. I gave a keynote speech on the subject at the UN Human Rights Council in Geneva. It was received pretty enthusiastically.

The campaign grew. We had literature, pamphlets, stickers. I appointed a special envoy for female education. I felt it was a good campaign, the right campaign, and I would bring it into every problem that we were addressing.

I sat for hours in meetings on the intractable problems of Yemen. But what was really holding that country back? Was it the bombs of the Saudi-led coalition? Was it the Iranian-backed Houthi insurgents?

Or was it the chronic tragedy that Yemeni women were 30 per cent less likely to be able to read than Yemeni men? At one stage in the Commonwealth summit one of my team asked me to explain why I was so worked up about this issue.

'Why do you care about this so much?' she said, as if honestly trying to work out what was driving me.

I thought about it, and tried to answer the question for myself. I suppose the first answer is that this massive discrepancy is so cruel and stupid and wasteful of human potential. I grew up with a sister not much younger than me.

We played incessantly together. We remain exceptionally close. In so far as I have ever had any kind of urge to succeed in life, it is because I woke every day, as a child, realising that Rachel was at my heels.

The reality is that by the time I was five and she was four there were at least some words – so she claims my grandmother once said – that she could read faster than me (and some trees she now says she could climb higher).

My point is that from an early age I knew instinctively that talent and potential is evenly distributed between the sexes, as everywhere else (see above on levelling up), and in failing to promote female education it seemed to me that humanity is missing an enormous trick, because it is so obviously the multi-purpose Swiss army knife that will help us tackle so many other problems.

I became more and more evangelical because I started to suspect that my views were actually not that welcome, and perhaps not entirely fashionable with the experts in development.

Or at least they didn't like the primacy I attached to the issue. They saw female illiteracy as just another of the evils they were trying to address – all of which stemmed ultimately from poverty.

I disagree. I am with former UK PM Tony Blair. In solving the problems of global development it is education, education, education, in that order.

You say, how we can we teach girls to read when the civil war means the schools are all closed? I say, teach them to read and you greatly reduce the chances of civil war.

Illiteracy is different from so many of the other global ills in that it is relatively easy to fix. It shouldn't really need billions. It shouldn't need to be accompanied by a military intervention, or thousands of aid agency personnel going around in luxury taxpayer-funded air-conditioned white Toyota Land Cruisers.

It just takes the men in suits – the sweating corporeal men in suits who dominate the governments of these countries – to recognise the shame they are bringing on their own people by letting this ignorance continue.

I am sure you are asking yourself why, if it is such a silver bullet, this campaign for female education is not better known. Why is it not constantly on TV? Where are the endless full-page ads in the *Guardian*?

I think what the aid lobby didn't like about my campaign was the implicit suggestion that this was really the fault of the countries themselves.

Western liberals want to believe that the problem is always 'poverty', and that the poverty of the developing world is everywhere and always caused by the west – or the legacy of colonialism. It is always our fault for waging proxy wars, or failing to offer debt relief, or running unfair systems of agricultural subsidy (like the CAP of the EU, though you don't often hear that point); and above all it is our fault because we are never willing or able to spend enough on aid.

I am afraid I saw enough of our spending of ODA to become a bit jaundiced. Of course some of it works, and much good is done. But too often it is a question, as the development economist Peter Bauer immortally put it, of 'poor people in rich countries giving money to rich people in poor countries'.

How much better, cheaper and more morally excellent if the men in those countries could be persuaded by the global utensil of shame – electroconvulsive ridicule, at every international meeting – to stop allowing their nation's women to grow up illiterate.

If they wanted to do it, if they really cared, they could do it surprisingly fast. The world has made astonishing progress since the end of the last war, when 44 per cent of humanity was illiterate. We are now approaching only 10 per cent.

The tragedy is that so many countries are so far behind – and in some cases going backwards. But if we fix it, we level up the world.

The trouble with the aid industry is that they don't like the judgementalism of the literacy campaign – the suggestion that the problem may lie in the attitudes of the countries themselves. They are worried that they will be accused of Islamophobia – because both Boko Haram and the Taliban are united in their belief that their religion forbids them to teach their daughters to read, and that they will go to heaven if they keep them in ignorance.

They are worried that a global female literacy campaign smacks of paternalism or neo-colonialism; and I say to hell with that pathetic excuse.

There are too many (male-dominated) governments that are either actively conniving in or indifferent to female illiteracy; and the entire development industry, from top to bottom, is too drenched in political correctness to tell them so.

I wish I had been more successful in that campaign. With another year at the Foreign Office, I reckon I could have made much more of a noise, since it came to me pretty late on.

One of the problems was that it was my campaign, and our own female PM was not always in love with everything I did.

Part Five
Crunch Time

Chapter 32

The Road to Serfdom

Theresa May and the wrong type of Brexit

After eighteen months at the Foreign Office, I was now drifting into sniper's alley – the territory occupied by all cabinet ministers who do not command the undiluted affection of the prime minister. I was foreign secretary of the UK because I had helped to deliver Brexit; and my function was therefore to reassure 17.4 million Leave voters that the result of the 2016 referendum would be delivered – in full.

But let's face it: I did not hold this great office of state because Theresa May regarded me with any particular affection, nor was I there for my Kissingeresque diplomacy.

As the months go by, all cabinet ministers get at least theoretically vulnerable to the next reshuffle, or so they damn well should; and I started to become apprehensive, and realistic about my chances. If she chose to whack me, she already had the case against me: the gaffes.

There were the mis-speaks and mistakes, like the time I said that both Iran and Saudi Arabia were engaged in 'proxy wars' in the Middle East. This was, of course, true (see above on gaffes) but it seemed to suggest some kind of moral equivalence – in which we certainly did not believe – between the two of them; and that was deemed unhelpful to our deep and strategic friendship with Saudi Arabia. A lot of plaster came off the ceiling over that one.

Then there was the reality that Theresa and I were different kinds of people; we didn't always have the same sense of humour. One day we were holding a big state lunch for President Santos of Colombia. We had done a lot to help him fight off the FARC guerrillas and there was plenty to talk about as we sat in the pillared room upstairs in Number Ten, with the Chandos portrait of Shakespeare looking down. But Theresa said almost nothing, and the burden of conversation fell mainly on me.

President Santos was describing the wonders of his jungle-rich country, the many different types of amphibian.

'We have forty frogs!' he boasted.

'That's nothing,' I said. 'When I was mayor of London we had 400,000 frogs – in fact, we had more frogs in London than in the whole city of Bordeaux.'

There was a ghastly pause while Santos looked a bit bemused, and then got it – and laughed, just about.

Theresa goggled at her plate.

The bigger problem was that I wasn't sure we agreed on the basic mission and purpose of the government. When it came to Brexit, I just could not work her out.

I didn't dislike Theresa, not remotely. She was a highly intelligent and thoughtful woman, with a strong ethic of public service. I enjoyed her schoolmarmy self-righteousness and watching her roll her eyes when I said something outrageous. It seems weird, but I was particularly fixated upon her nostrils – immensely long and pointy black tadpole shapes, like a Gerald Scarfe cartoon, and the way she would twist her nose, as if to show them off.

What did it mean, this nose-twisting? Was it disgust? Or just reflection? What was she thinking?

She was presented by her handlers as a kick-ass bang-em-up chuck-em-out home secretary; and yet she seemed well to the left of me on law and order (and I am by no means a hanger and flogger). As the reader may remember, we disagreed on stop and search, and the use of water cannon. One Tuesday morning we were all sitting around the table and she announced, in breathy vicar's-daughter tones, that Penny Mordaunt had something very important to talk about.

At which point Penny began a long disquisition about gender recognition, and the problems of British transsexuals in changing sex. I didn't catch all the details, but it seemed fairly harrowing stuff, and at one point I heard Penny claim: 'This is the most important issue of our times.'

I didn't always agree with Phil Hammond, but I happened at that moment to catch his eye and to see that he – like me – was struggling to contain his amusement. I mean: I could see that this was an issue of huge importance to some people (though surely not that many?) and I could see that it needed to be handled with tact and sensitivity.

But 'the most important issue of our times'? Really?

There was Theresa, nodding away enthusiastically at what was clearly a presentation organised and approved by Number Ten. So was she a right-winger, or was she woke?

And as for Europe, to what extent – to borrow the language of Penny's presentation – had she transitioned? Was she still a Remainer, wrapped in Brexiteer clothes, or had she surgically altered her beliefs?

Was she some kind of cross-dresser – and could she switch back? I started to worry.

It mattered a great deal to me that we should deliver the right kind of Brexit – by which we would become a fully independent country again. As foreign secretary, I was exposed every week to the diplomatic costs of what we had done. Other European foreign ministers would gently tug my sleeve at the end of meetings and say how much they regretted our decision, and how much they would miss us in the councils of Europe.

Of course, I grieved inwardly when Anglophiles in other countries expressed their hurt and disappointment at Brexit. None of that made me for one moment repent or regret my decision.

None of it changed the arguments. But it made it all the more essential to get it right. There was no point in going through all of the psychic pain of Brexit if we ended up with none of the advantages – and I could tell, from the mutterings around Whitehall, that Brexit was in danger.

It looked as though we might stay in the customs union, someone said. Really? I said.

I instantly saw the flaw in that. If you stay in a customs union, your goods can circulate freely without attracting duties or tariffs. But if you have no checks at the border – which was the suggestion – there would be a natural pressure to ensure that goods conformed to the same standards, so that by staying in the customs union we would effectively be staying in the single market: following EU rules but without being able to shape them.

We would be rule-takers, satellites, colonials; a slave state; and anyway, if we stayed in the customs union we wouldn't have control of our own tariffs and duties and quotas.

We wouldn't be able to do free-trade deals – contrary to all the promises of the referendum campaign. So for two major reasons – because it would restrict regulatory divergence and prevent an independent trade policy – staying in the customs union was a total no-no.

We would look absurd, in the comity of free and independent nations, like some eighteen-year-old arriving at university but still wearing the old school uniform and following the old school rules, forbidden to stray from the old school diet and the old school timetable – while all the other students were free to do their own thing!

It would be a sham Brexit, a fraud on the electorate. I started to get hot under the collar. It was time to start shaping the narrative, time to nudge the steering wheel.

While Theresa remained publicly Delphic on the subject, I continued to tell everyone I met that we were indeed coming out of the customs union, and the single market, and every aspect of EU legal jurisdiction. We were properly taking back control, I said, oh yes, no doubt at all … and I waited to be contradicted by Number Ten.

Month after month went by. My glib assertions went unchallenged – but also unsupported. Then, on Tuesday November 15, 2016, when I had been in the job about five months, I found myself being interviewed by a Czech paper in Prague. They were good journalists, and they had spotted this vagueness in our plans. Were we leaving the customs union? What model of Brexit were we following?

It was a load of *hovadina* to say we were staying in the customs union, I said. Actually I don't know what word I used – probably bollocks – but *hovadina* was how they translated it, and it went up on the wires. Almost immediately my private secretary, Nick Wareham, was alerted: the *hovadina*/bollocks comment was not going down well in Whitehall.

'A bit forward-leaning on the customs union, Foreign Secretary,' said Nick a few hours later, as we prepared for some diplomatic soirée.

I was curious. Really? I said. Then I heard that I had been actually 'slapped down', and that the prime minister's official spokesperson had formally disowned my comments. It had not been decided, said Katie Perrior, whether or not we were leaving the customs union.

By now I was indignant. Eh, I said, what? It was a bit much to be rebuked by Katie Perrior, who had done such sterling service in City Hall; and anyway she was wrong. It blooming well had been

decided, in the referendum of June 23, 2016, the biggest democratic exercise this country had ever held. I rang Number Ten to
object, and later, in cabinet, Theresa raised the issue with me.

'Boris,' she said, as if I were a child caught eavesdropping on a
grown-up dinner party, 'I gather you are interested in the customs
union.' I was, I said, and gave her several paragraphs on why staying in the customs union was incompatible with any meaningful
version of Brexit.

She nose-twisted dubiously, and the matter was unresolved. I
found a solid ally in Nick Timothy, her Rasputin-bearded chief of
staff, who had campaigned for Leave and who understood the
issues. Come on, I said: we can't keep faffing around like this.

It wasn't good enough for Theresa to keep saying that 'Brexit
means Brexit'. She needed to explain what SHE meant by Brexit;
otherwise the other side, the EU, would not take us seriously in
the negotiations.

Don't worry, said Nick. She was going to do a big speech,
setting it all out.

Great! I said: let me contribute. So I sat down and thundered
out a draft.

Nick and his fellow speechwriter, Chris Wilkins, were very
polite about my efforts, and though I don't think a single sentence
of mine made the final cut, I was thrilled with the result – because
the overall sentiments were mine, and the arguments were clearly
accepted.

When Theresa had finished speaking at Lancaster House on
January 17, 2017 (her lectern branded 'Global Britain'), the EU
diplomats could all be seen jabbing on their phones and rushing
from the room.

What she had said was clear and consistent. We were going to
be out of the single market; we were not going to remain in regulatory alignment; we were no longer going to abide by the rulings
of the European Court of Justice; we were not going to pay the

EU for market access; we would take full control of our borders; we would be doing free-trade deals around the world; we were out of the customs union.

Phil Hammond looked a bit green, but I drummed my feet on the floor. We were there! We had a plan, a route map for Brexit.

Of course people complained and said it was a triumph of the Johnsonian head bangers – the hardest of hard Brexits. But Lancaster House was, and is, the only logical way to honour the democratic mandate of 2016; and three years later, those were more or less the terms on which we eventually came out.

I felt a deep sense of relief, as though I had won an important battle and done a large part of what I was there to do. It was a vision that I could sell, at home and abroad – and to myself. Then it all went wrong.

One morning in April 2017 we all turned up in cabinet to find that something was up. We were shut in the Cabinet Room, and we clustered around a TV set at the near end – by the blue baize doors into the PM's study – to watch Theresa as she delivered a speech in the street outside. To my surprise, and in contradiction of everything she had said in public, she was calling a general election.

We were all watching this, slack-jawed, when suddenly she appeared among us – because of the time lag on the broadcast – so that she came across as not only omnipotent but ubiquitous, a supreme being.

'Bravo!' we all cried. 'Brilliant move, PM!' 'Great generalship!' That kind of thing.

We could all see what this was about. Theresa was still trading off David Cameron's exiguous majority of 2015, and she was then riding very high in the polls – as much as 21 points ahead. If she could hold anything like that lead in an election, then she would have her own mandate, and in those circumstances she would be able to deliver the Brexit she wanted, and never mind the views of her pesky foreign secretary.

What would happen to Boris Johnson? What would happen to the Lancaster House vision for Brexit, once she had finished crushing Jeremy Corbyn like a toad beneath the harrow? Good question – but I wouldn't have given much for any of our chances.

Chapter 33

Chucking Chequers

Electoral disaster and how I was eventually driven to resign

The trouble was that this was now the third time the British public had been consulted in three years – first the 2015 election, then the 2016 referendum on the EU, and now this.

'What?' said Brenda of Bristol on the BBC. 'Another one?!'

We might have been all right, if we had somehow been able to hold the poll that April day – bundle people swiftly out to vote in an instant verdict. But that is not how elections work. They are designed to test your propositions – and we crumbled.

The polling all showed that Theresa was more popular than the Tory brand, and that she was widely held to be 'strong' and 'stable' – two words that apparently resonated with focus groups. So we plastered her name and image over the Tory battle bus, together with the words 'strong' and 'stable', and all might have been well if she had strongly, stably, staunchly, stoically stuck it to Labour from day one.

Instead she began by swerving the TV debates, and then performed a spectacular U-turn on social care in the middle of the election campaign. For some reason we had decided to announce – in the manifesto – that British people would be deprived of their home in order to pay for the cost of their care in old age. And we were going to lift the £72,000 cap on the costs of social care, so that if you had assets of more than £100,000 – even in property – there was no limit on what you could pay.

There was no hiding it: people were facing the loss of their family home to cover the cost of grandma going ga-ga. It was by any standards a pretty unpolishable turd, and a measure of the desperation in Number Ten that they sent me out to explain it all on the Sunday morning shows. I don't think I made much of a fist of it – though I thought that we were trying to do broadly the right thing in at least attempting to address the issue of social care, and was determined, if I got the chance, to sort it out myself.

All in, I played a moderately undistinguished and low-key part in the campaign – apart from two bizarre appearances in the TV debate spin room, where I seemed to be physically picking fights with Labour MPs: going nose to nose with Ian Lavery and getting Andrew Gwynne in my Vulcan nerve pinch. Very juvenile. I think I was just fed up.

They finally wheeled me on for Theresa May's eve-of-poll rally, where I did my best to gee up the troops for her stump speech.

I must say, as a punter, that I found her message a bit chilling. She stood above me on her platform, waving her pale arms heavenward like some priestess from the pages of Rider Haggard.

'Give meee the mandate!' she intoned. 'Give meee the power!'

Coo-er, I thought. Give her the power to do what? Screw up Brexit? Take away people's homes?

By the end of that campaign, it didn't feel as if we were surfing a wave of enthusiasm to give us the mandate to do anything much – and so it proved. Like many of my colleagues, I felt mildly cheesed off that election night in Uxbridge. My majority had been sawn in half, to no purpose whatever. As I told my troops, we were still alive, but like the Earl of Uxbridge himself I had seen one leg shot away in battle.

In a fit of almost superhuman electoral incompetence we had

managed to throw away our poll lead, lose the Conservative majority in Parliament. We had not only missed an open goal; we had made Jeremy Corbyn look like Diego Maradona.

Some time around four or five in the morning I got a message from Phil Hammond, the chancellor – dry as dust but with an excellent political brain. We talked while I drove back from Uxbridge to bed in Carlton Gardens.

He thought it was all very unfortunate, but Theresa's goose was cooked. She would have to go sooner or later, and it might as well be now. What he was proposing (I don't think he would deny it) was a Hammond-Johnson partnership, by which I would take the wheel at Number Ten and he continued to be my economic co-pilot.

I thought about it briefly, as dawn started to break, and then said no. Perhaps it was selfish of me. Perhaps I should have accepted the responsibility that morning and gone in with Phil to tell old grumpyknickers that her time was up. I hesitated partly because it all seemed so rancorous and febrile.

The media was already full of stuff about how I was 'on manoeuvres', and even though that was untrue I could see that if Phil and I launched some breakfast coup on Theresa, people's general fury would immediately be turned on me. And I continued to believe – perhaps naively – in the letter of what Theresa had said at Lancaster House.

She had finally come up with the right formula for Brexit. I believed that as a Remainer – transvestite or otherwise – she was in a powerful moral position to deliver that vision and keep our party together; even if she had ballsed up the election and shredded her own authority.

Well, I am afraid I was totally mistaken in that second calculation. The election fiasco had robbed Theresa of her mojo and also, it seemed, of any trace of a belief in Brexit.

*   *   *

One of the greatest things about Chequers is the chef, Graham, and one of the greatest of his masterpieces is the patent Chequers shortbread biscuit.

These are truly sensational: great pale roundels of sugar, butter and flour, teetering exquisitely between doughiness and crunchiness. Some of them were plain, some of them had chocolate chip – and by God I needed them after yet another three-hour session with my cabinet colleagues as we tried to sort out our position on Brexit.

We had at least two away days in the Grade I-listed Elizabethan house, where poor Lady Mary Grey had been interned, by the agents of Elizabeth, in a tiny bedroom upstairs and gone so mad that she wrote some weird Latin gibberish – still preserved – on the walls.

It was unintelligible, but it made far more sense than Theresa's Chequers plan: which was basically to leave the EU but remain run by the EU. She had lost her nerve. She had lost her two most important advisers, Nick Timothy and Fi Hill (sacrificed to appease Tory MPs – it never works), and she had lost the plot.

Ever since Lancaster House, in January 2017, I had been confidently peddling that script: we would be outside the customs union and the single market, completely free to do our own thing. In the year since the election, I had been zooming around the world – since I seemed to be surplus to Theresa's requirements in London – and whenever I was asked how Brexit was going I had been able to explain it all, in clear, bright, primary colours.

Of course, I told our European friends, we would remain committed to their security – but outside the main European architecture: like a flying buttress. This was for some reason translated in one European Council meeting as a 'flying bucket', but the gist was clear.

By the spring and summer of 2018 that clarity had gone, and we were drifting back towards the single market, the customs union and vassal statehood. Why couldn't Theresa have just stuck with her winning formula? Why couldn't she have forged ahead with Lancaster House? Heaven knows. Maybe she became fearful, after the election, that she would not be able to push a hard Brexit through a largely Remain-backing House of Commons.

Maybe she never really intended to go through with a proper Brexit, and called the election precisely so that SHEEE would have the mandate and SHEEE would have the power: to force recalcitrant Leavers – people like me – to accept a BRINO, a Brexit in Name Only. Who knows, and who cares. Whatever her motives, Brino was what we were getting and no quantity of Chequers biscuits would make it digestible.

It was obvious by 2018 that David Davis, the so-called Brexit secretary, was no longer really in charge of the negotiations – which were now entrusted to a former Home Office civil servant, Olly Robbins, in whom Theresa plainly had great confidence.

Robbins was excellent: infinitely patient with the PM, highly intelligent, and he knew his stuff. His problem was the Brussels negotiations, where they kept looking at him to explain the UK position and he found himself unable to speak – because two years after the vote the terminally divided UK cabinet was still unable to agree.

Now, at the second of our Chequers away days, we finally had Theresa's proposals for our negotiation on the 'future relationship' with the EU. They were uniformly ghastly. I kept asking Olly and Theresa a simple question: would we be able to do things differently from the EU? If not, why were we leaving?

I focused on the example from my time as mayor, when I had felt powerless to do what was necessary to avert the death of female cyclists. Would we be able to insist that juggernauts driving into London had cycle-friendly windows?

Nope.

OK, I said, and thought of some other examples off the top of my head.

Would we be able to change regulations on financial services, or genetic engineering, or AI, or cyber, or data-sharing?

Nope.

Would we be able to ban shark fin soup or the live export of animals?

Nope.

Would we be able to cut the tax on tampons?

Nope.

Would we be able to cut tariffs on things not grown in this country, like oranges?

Nope.

What about bananas?

Nope.

Olives?

Nope.

How about olive oil?

Nope.

Would we be able to diverge from the EU at all?

Not really.

Would we have any say in the making of all this law?

Nope. None.

So what was the point of leaving? I would ask, and Hammond would curl his lip and say, well, you voted for it. Gah, I would say. I didn't vote for this.

It was all rubbish. The question of the Northern Ireland border had been escalated and weaponised so as to keep us in the tractor beam of EU law. The talks concluded with a dinner, and at the end of the evening – more out of politeness than anything else – I raised a glass to us all, because I thought we had been commendably friendly, and serious, in at least trying to thrash it out.

The following day I was supposed to do a joint piece with Philip Hammond, hailing the Chequers deal. They sent over the text at about midday. I looked at it. My gorge rose. I couldn't put my name to this garbage.

The papers had all predicted that I would have to resign over Chequers, and now, much to my disappointment, they were going to be proved right. I loved, really loved, being foreign secretary; but in truth I had only one real duty, and that was to make sure that the government delivered Brexit. In that respect I was failing. It was time to go.

I talked to David Davis, who was also unhappy. We agreed to concert our resignations. He resigned late that evening, the Sunday. I went the following day.

There followed a year in the wilderness. I wrote torrential pieces for the *Telegraph*, lambasting the Chequers approach, and otherwise I led a kind of hillbilly existence by the pool in Thame, having barbecues with Carrie and sitting around in my shorts, drinking beer and shooting champagne bottles with my airguns. It was a happy and productive time.

I also realised I had no possible further excuse for political hesitancy. It was clear that Theresa was not going to deliver Brexit, not in any recognisable form. Her solution was so humiliating for the UK that not even the most ardent Remainer could support it. Sooner or later, as Phil Hammond had said, she would have to go, and then there was nothing for it: I would have my second shot at the top job.

This time, I said to myself as I squinted down the sights of my trusty .177 (bought at Elderkin's in Lincolnshire, with my old friend John Hayes), I am not going to miss.

Slowly I squeezed the trigger and ping-crack – I finally hit the champagne bottle.

* * *

All of which explains how I came to re-enter Number Ten, on December 13, 2019, with the biggest mandate for a generation; and if you have ears to hear, I will now relate how we worked to fulfil the pledges I had made, what we achieved, and the projects that I was forced to leave incomplete.

Part Six

A Great Plan for Britain

Chapter 34

Infrastructure Revolution

New homes, new roads, new rail,
new power stations, new broadband

On Monday December 16, 2019, the new Parliament descended on Westminster. The people of Britain sent Tory MPs from towns and cities where Conservative activists once hardly dared to set foot.

Streets where the mere sight of a blue rosette would have triggered a lynch mob, or at least a hail of eggs, had undergone a conversion and had come out en masse for the party of Disraeli and Thatcher – or in this case, as I liked to imagine, a subtle combination of them both.

After almost ten years in power, our share of the vote had not been eroded with time and ennui – but had actually risen to a forty-year high, and we had 109 new Tory MPs. They came from old coalfields, as well as the Surrey commuter belt; from urban Wales to Wakefield to Workington to the Wash to wherever. That afternoon we summoned this historic cohort of newbies to Westminster Hall for a photoshoot.

It was chilly in that great twelfth-century temple of democracy, where Charles I had been tried and Henry VIII had played tennis, and the alluvial damp of the Thames seeped up through the flagstones. As I looked at our troops I felt elated, like a revolutionary leader.

We had changed politics, broken the mould, in a realignment that saw fifty-four seats go straight from Labour to Conservative. As the new MPs ranged themselves over the grey stone steps, I briefly harangued them and reminded them of the sheer scale of what they had done. The Tory Party was now a gigantic coalition of people from every background and every region of Britain, from Ashford in Kent to Ashfield in Nottingham, from Abingdon to Aberdeen, I alliterated alphabetically, from Billericay to Bassetlaw to Bury to Bolton to Blyth Valley – we had about ten new ex-Labour seats beginning with B alone – to Blackpool to Bolsover!

Yes Bolsover, the seat formerly held by Dennis Skinner, the one-time 'Beast of Bolsover' (in the phrase of Frank Johnson), who had once unsettled me with an abusive heckle as I was about to open my mouth and make my debut as a junior shadow spokesman for something or other.

'You piece of shit,' said Skinner, just quietly enough for the speaker to miss it – and now the unthinkable had happened. Bolsover had gone blue, and it was Skinner's turn to be flushed, with a gurgling wail of disbelief, down the oubliette of history. Bolsover had a new MP, a hardworking and dedicated young Tory called Mark Fletcher. As I looked at their happy faces, I realised that many of them were not just thrilled but amazed to be there. Some of them were so new to national politics that they had hardly been to London before, never mind the House of Commons.

Some of them were just good public-spirited Tories who had obligingly allowed their local association to shove their name on the ballot – because someone had to do it – and who had been borne aloft by the blue blizzard. Some of them were still in their twenties. They beamed and they cheered my gags ('We turned Redcar Bluecar!'), and as I looked up at them all I felt overwhelmed by the message that was being communicated, through them, to me and to everyone involved in the government of the country.

Get on with it! the voters were saying. You wanted a working majority. Here it is – now get Brexit done, and get on with that plan to unite and level up Britain. As I had told the country that Friday morning after the poll from the Downing Street rostrum, I felt I knew the spirit in which the people had conferred their vote.

It was a landslide – but it was an elasticated landslide. It was conditional. We had to deliver or they would yank that support back like a yo-yo.

I knew from my time as mayor that your first term can fly by, and that delivery can be agonisingly hard; and over the next few weeks I roared around the country as if to prove our utter determination to deliver that manifesto. Together with home secretary Priti Patel, I went to police colleges where we congratulated the recruits – some of them so young that their new black uniforms seemed to flap around their skinny forms – on being part of the new crime-busting 20,000.

I went to schools, to illustrate the £14 billion we were putting into education, with a minimum starting salary of £30,000 for teachers. I hard-hatted and hi-vizzed my way up and down the country, staring appreciatively at muddy holes that would soon be new A & Es or paediatric units – part of our pledge to build forty more hospitals, including one in Uxbridge.

It was exhilarating; it was right. I had never been much of a fan of 'austerity' as a slogan, and we had to show our absolute commitment to public services – above all the NHS. But no Tory believes in public spending as an end in itself.

It had to be part of a plan for growth – for levelling up the country. The public had given us a once-in-a-generation mandate. If we worked hard, and delivered, as I knew we would – then it was very likely that we would be re-elected. In other words, this was now logically the beginning of a decade-long project. It was a mandate to crack the biggest problem of all, which was not our relations with the EU, difficult though that was.

It was and is the yawning productivity gap between different parts of the UK. If we could achieve the same rough economic uniformity as other western countries then the UK would become the most powerful economy in Europe. There was only one way to do that – to get the private sector to invest in those left-behind towns and cities.

The state cannot and must not try to replicate the private sector. You can't have the government owning or running businesses. We tried that after the war. It was a disaster. But the state can create the conditions for growth – using the billions of public sector investment to trigger the trillions of the market.

I was lucky in that I had a chancellor, Sajid Javid, who agreed completely with the agenda.

Javid was the son of a Muslim bus driver from the back streets of Bristol who had boinged his way from banking to the safe Tory seat of Bromsgrove. With his completely shaven head, he had decided that he looked a bit like a plasticine TV character called Morph, and he was charmingly free from self-doubt.

He referred to himself as 'the Saj'. It was amazing to discover, as you listened to him, how many advances the human race apparently owed to the Saj, from privatising the Post Office to – who knows – non-stick frying pans. One night early in my term we had dinner at Chequers – together with his wife Laura and Carrie.

The Saj arrived with two bottles of Tignanello and some cigars, and we sat up late in the garden, as the red kites above us gave way to the owls and the bats, and thrashed out the levelling-up agenda.

If we were going to transform the country, then we had to fix the skeleton. We had to upgrade the transport network.

As a Midlands MP, Saj agreed that it was an utter disgrace that the great cities of the north and Midlands did not have the kind of commuter rail networks that have existed in London and the south-east for the last 150 years, whooshing people back and forth between jobs and home; and it was a double disgrace that no major railway had been built north of Birmingham since Victorian times. Finally the country was taking steps to sort it out.

I could see why people were leery of HS2. This is the plan for a colossal Y-shaped high-speed rail line linking London to Birmingham and thence to the cities of the north-west and north-east. It had been cooked up by Andrew Adonis in the dying days of Gordon Brown's premiership, and then taken up zealously by George Osborne; possibly because he represented a Greater Manchester suburb.

The trains were going to be outlandishly fast (225 mph – far faster than the fastest Ferrari), and electric, and running on hundreds of miles of new track – and all along the route, as you would expect with a country as densely populated and cussed as Britain, there were armies of protesters.

They were particularly fierce in my own constituency of Uxbridge and South Ruislip. HS2 was going to erupt like a .44 magnum bullet through north-west London; and though as mayor I had succeeded in getting a lot of it put in a tunnel, the exit wound was still in my patch. My voters hated the disturbance involved, the lorry movements of spoil, the noise, the traffic. Their house prices were being blighted; the vibrations would be awful; the subsidence was going to cause cracks in their walls.

The supertrain was going to smash through local beauty spots, running on huge concrete stilts over a lake much used by kiddies' sailing clubs. I had every electoral motive, both as mayor and Uxbridge MP, to oppose the project flat out. All my Tory neighbours were against it ('Death to HS2,' Ruislip's Nick Hurd would whisper, drawing his finger across his throat) – and not surprisingly. The train was planned to howl through their patches without stopping, so that their constituents got all the grief and none of the benefits.

I could have gone for the votes, shored up my position in Uxbridge and bashed HS2. I never did; in fact, I always made the argument to my electors that what might be temporarily inconvenient for some of us would be good, in the end, for all of us.

It was crazy that this country – the birthplace of the railways – had no high-speed network. Japan, France, Germany, Italy, Korea – they have had high-speed rail for decades. They have a bigger high-speed rail network in Morocco than we do in the UK. They have more in Denmark. They have more in Belgium. And the Netherlands.

Some idiots say that Britain is 'too small' to need high-speed rail, and I would remind them that Denmark, Belgium and the Netherlands are not big countries, and that Holland is even more densely populated than we are. I felt it was a symbol of our national inertia – our chronic reluctance to do the big, bold things that can lift productivity and unleash potential.

It is now about sixteen years since we started discussing HS2 – in around 2008. How many miles of high-speed rail have they built in China since that date? The answer is 25,000 miles of completed track, with a Beijing–Shanghai train that is almost frighteningly fast. I once sat in the front cabin, watching the speedometer climb past 400 kmh, and it felt like being strapped to the tip of an ICBM. And how many miles of high-speed track have we built here in the UK in the same period?

The answer is zero. None.

It's pathetic. It's not a question of national prestige, or keeping up with our competitors. It's about basic fairness and opportunity in the UK.

Try taking a train across the Pennines, from Liverpool or Manchester to Sheffield or Leeds. It is a bone-jarring, bum-numbing exercise in tedium. Why is there still no proper metro service in the West Midlands? No wonder there is a productivity gap. In London and the south-east, commuters are using mass transit systems, hammering on their laptops or working their phones.

In the rest of the country they are bending their steering wheels, waiting for the traffic to move. Levelling up means valuing those people – and their time – in the same way that we value commuters in the south-east.

I saw that you could not make sense of Northern Powerhouse Rail (NPR) – linking the cities of the north, east to west across the Pennines – unless you also did HS2; because much of the putative new NPR line around Manchester is in fact the planned northern leg of the HS2 line.

You couldn't relieve the pressure on the other north–south lines, on the east and west coast, unless you built HS2; and then, of course, there were the environmental benefits. A new high-speed line would free up rail freight capacity and remove thousands of trucks that would otherwise thunder up and down the M1, always assuming the traffic would allow them to thunder. It would mount a serious challenge to air travel and cut emissions.

It had to be done. I knew the focus groups would hate it – because voters always put infrastructure way down their list of concerns. In fact, there are courses in Beijing universities where they teach the story of British chopping and changing on HS2 as an example of the flaws in democratic systems.

I knew that the Treasury would keep trying to kill it – just as they have tried to cut other big projects (the M25! Crossrail!) over the years. Some of my advisers were against it, but over dinner that July 2019, the Saj and I were as one. We worked out that the cost of borrowing was still so low that we could afford to be totally cake-ist: pro having it and pro eating it.

We could deliver on the manifesto promises AND we could inaugurate a vast infrastructure revolution; and by Christmas Saj sent me the plan – in a twenty-page summary. We could do the metro system for Leeds, and light rail in the West Midlands. We could do HS2 and NPR; we could start the construction of 4,000 more super-green British-built buses; and among many other things we could have hundreds of miles of new cycle lanes.

I saw HS2 and Northern Powerhouse Rail as a key part of our mission – to unite and level up the country. Together with my old friend and colleague Peter Hendy (then in charge of Network Rail, now a minister), we worked on plans to take HS2 – at speed – all the way to Scotland; and for a long time I was obsessed with the idea of building a fixed link to Northern Ireland. The Saj had the wit to stay out of this one.

The difficulties were immense – the sea was too rough for a bridge, it seemed, and there was a very long and very deep under-sea trench called Beaufort's Dyke, which meant a tunnel would either be exceedingly long to get round it or would have to descend and ascend at forty-five degrees.

But look at what the Norwegians are doing, or the Japanese, I said. The Norwegians were building hundreds of miles of undersea tunnel up their west coast, from fjord to fjord. Couldn't we do the same? The Americans had travelled 953,000 miles to the moon and back. It was only thirty miles of sea between two parts of the United Kingdom – were we really incapable of making a physical link?

Peter Hendy and I commissioned Doug Oakervee, the brilliant engineer and project manager, to look in detail at the issues; and together with Gordon Masterton, another former president of the Institute of Civil Engineers, he eventually produced a report. The project was, to say the least, ambitious. If you built a bridge, it would involve the longest suspension span of any bridge ever made – four kilometres across the Beaufort Dyke; and with the storms in the Irish Sea, a four-kilometre span was going to be a pretty stomach-churning drive. In fact, if the winds started gusting, there was a risk that the bridge would begin to sway so violently as to sling-shot your car into the sea.

If you dug a tunnel, you would have to go down about four hundred metres to avoid the Dyke, not to mention the million tonnes of wartime munitions that had been dumped there. To dig a road or rail tunnel to a depth of four hundred metres had never been tried before.

The world record for deepest tunnel is currently held by Japan, with a depth of 250 metres. The tunnel would cost about £209 billion. The bridge would cost £325 billion.

There was a silence at the end of Doug's presentation, and he wiggled his eyebrows at me. I know when I am beat. The project was patently bonkers – at least with the technology now available. One day, in an era of fully automated vehicles, and with better tunnelling equipment, we will do it. For now, we had more than enough to be going on with – because I believed that all our other projects had an excellent business case. We knew, though, that infrastructure alone is never enough.

The world is littered with redundant motorways and bridges to nowhere – the vanity projects of forgotten politicians. Roads, rail, bridges, buses, bikes: they are not enough, on their own, to encourage business to invest.

Far more important is the quality of the workforce, the skills and motivation they possess. Saj and I began working on a plan for skills, first by lifting literacy and numeracy rates at the age of eleven to 90 per cent – the absolute bedrock for increasing national productivity; then putting large sums into improving the fabric of further education colleges, and then on a way of breaking down the barrier between further and higher education, encouraging people to learn all their lives.

We tried to address all the causes of UK underproductivity. We needed better local leadership, to champion investment, to tell a story about why their town or city or region was the place to be. I started thinking about a programme of fiscal devolution, empowering local authorities, as I had once begged the government to empower me in City Hall.

We needed to work with local authorities to produce a much better housing supply and a much better planning system. No matter how good your transport systems or your skills base, you won't raise productivity if people can't afford to live near the jobs. The cost of housing in the UK was now becoming punitive – and it was a national disgrace that we, the Conservatives, the party of Thatcher and Macmillan, had been so lackadaisical. Rates of owner occupation for young people were now lower than in France and Germany; and all because our party was in thrall to the Nimbies.

As a country we were producing nothing like enough new homes. So we began work on a big planning bill so that young people would once again have the chance of owning their own property.

I could feel the erosion of opportunity, just in a single generation: the astonishing difference between what had seemed affordable to me in the 1980s and what seemed affordable to my children today.

We needed to fix it, or else, frankly, we might as well stop calling ourselves Conservatives. So Robert Jenrick, the housing secretary, launched himself at the project with a radical plan to build more homes on the brownfield sites where they are needed, declaring that on those buddleia-infested sites where nothing happens – especially in the cities – there was going to be a presumption in favour of development. The market responded to our lead.

I am proud to say that in our first year, 2019–20, we started to build more homes in the UK than in any year since 1987, when Mrs Thatcher was in power.

This is the right answer: building on brownfield. The opportunity for growth is in London (think of Barking Riverside, and all those areas that we still haven't developed), and in all the cities and towns outside London, because in some of those places the population actually fell over the twentieth century.

There is space, and by putting in good homes you encourage families to move back into these cities – and you level up. That is the way to close that productivity and wealth gap between the UK's second-tier cities and the capital.

That is how you add at least £100 billion a year to UK GDP and spread opportunity. It was frankly a tragedy that this planning bill was eventually to be junked by my successor Rishi Sunak, with so much else, and Labour's current plans make no sense at all … But we will come to that.

By putting in the transport infrastructure and fixing the planning system, we would make even more home-building possible. But how were we going to power all these homes and railways?

We were at risk of brown-outs, if not black-outs. We were the home of nuclear power, in the sense that in 1956 we opened the world's first civilian nuclear reactor at Calder Hall in Cumbria – and yet our nuclear power industry had been allowed to decay. We had at the same time been punctilious, to a fault, in closing our coal-fired power stations in a bid to reduce emissions.

In 1990, about 70 per cent of UK electricity came from coal; when I became PM it was less than 2 per cent. So we were heavily reliant on gas, much of it imported; and the supplies, as subsequent events were to confirm, were always less than 100 per cent secure.

There was one technology in which we excelled – and that was offshore wind. At one stage we were producing more offshore wind energy than any other country in the world, leading me to boast that we were the Saudi Arabia of wind.

Now, I had previously been sceptical about wind power. In the days when Piers Corbyn was the City Hall meteorologist, I may have allowed myself to scoff. As you'll remember, I even claimed that it 'wouldn't pull the skin off a rice pudding'.

I was wrong. Under the system known as 'contracts for difference', the government had triggered huge private sector investment in offshore windmills – many of them in the North Sea; and there were days when renewable energy of all kinds was producing well over 50 per cent of our energy needs. I became an enthusiast; a worshipper of the wind gods.

As I told Kwasi Kwarteng, I was going to change my name to Boreas Johnson, in honour of the ancient spirit of the North Wind. When I looked at the map of UK waters, the potential seemed limitless.

It was, after all, only 6,000 years ago that the area between Britain and the Netherlands was in fact habitable land – known as Doggerland.

For thousands of years the Dogger people had roamed the plashy meadows of Doggerland, doggedly eking out a living: hunting, fishing, water-fowling and, no doubt, dogging away in the great British tradition; until there was a catastrophe.

Far to the north off the west coast of Norway there was an undersea landslip called the Storegga, which in turn created a huge tsunami. The great surge rolled south and inundated Doggerland and the Dogger culture, traces of which are still dredged up by North Sea trawlers.

Now we were going to harvest that land again by planting 260-metre-high windmills in the shallows and producing a clean, green foison of energy. We made plans to forest the North Sea with windmills; and in the next three years I was thoroughly grateful that we had.

Skills, transport, housing, energy – and then there was one resource that was now deemed utterly indispensable and yet which, as a child, I had scarcely imagined.

*   *   *

I first became aware of the ravenous public demand for decent broadband when I was giving an after-dinner speech in Lincolnshire to a sodden marquee of farmers. It must have been about the time I was campaigning to be party leader.

They listened politely but apathetically as I reeled off the things I was going to do; and then as an afterthought I mentioned inter-net speeds. At which point they set up a great yammering cheer of assent.

They started banging the trestles with their horny fists; and I realised how callously we were leaving some areas behind.

How could we expect these people to run agri-businesses without decent broadband? It was obviously critical for the rural economy. It was critical for investment in the kind of decaying townscapes that Dave Cameron and I had once rolled through in his limo. Gigabit broadband was essential for levelling up, and I was appalled to find that only 7 per cent of UK households were connected.

In Spain the number was nearer 90 per cent. Again: what was wrong with us? Britain boasted one of the great pioneers of the web; we were way ahead of other European countries in the volume of goods bought online – and now our technology was letting us down. Spain was getting on with it, while we had the *mañana* culture. Oliver Dowden, the culture secretary, was tasked with organising the roll-out.

He would blench as I approached. 'How are we getting on with broadband, Olive?'

'Getting there, PM,' the honest fellow would say. 'We are up to 20 per cent!'

And indeed we started to make progress. The fiddly bit with gigabit was always the last mile – getting the fibre-optic filament into the home itself, penetrating every wainscot like glass vermicelli. We needed to encourage the councils to sort out the wayleaves – to allow the holes to be dug – and we needed to help the broadband companies to hire enough staff.

Oliver and I set up a task force, and soon BT Openreach and others were recruiting the necessary splicers – people with the skill to connect the main fibre-optic cable to the home. Many of them seemed to be female, so we called them splice girls, and soon it was a matter of pride for the diggers and splicers that they could bring speed-of-light internet to the remotest homesteads in the land.

BT Openreach even managed to run a cable over and down a precipitous hill to my father's farm on Exmoor, an undertaking so challenging that the BT van toppled into the Exe (easily done; my grandfather did it twice on the way back from the pub). But it was worth it. Now my father can watch about fifty-eight films at once, and broadcast to the nation, as he regularly does; and so can all the hill farmers of Exmoor.

Which is pretty extraordinary, when you consider that for most of my childhood we had no TV, no central heating and no mains electricity.

I saw levelling up partly as a moral mission, but also as a way to get the economy moving after years of tepid growth. Saj and I were agreed that we had the headroom to make the investments, and we also agreed that if we could increase growth and productivity, we would increase government revenues as well.

Then there was the final component of our plan to attract the private sector: we needed the right fiscal and regulatory framework. The burden of tax was far too high, on people and business, and that was at least partly because we were spending far too much money on the wrong things.

We needed to cut spending on everything that was not important to the core mission of the government; and I felt sure, after my experience as mayor of London, that we could do it.

What is government spending – now running at about a trillion pounds? It is overwhelmingly paying the salaries of people who are doing things that politicians have at some stage decided are or were important.

Every secretary of state inherits dozens of projects and priorities from his or her predecessor, and a huge quantity of government activity is therefore being carried out even if it is no longer necessary or relevant. In one of my very first cabinets, I told them all to go through their budget lines and cut at least 5 per cent. 'It's time to slaughter the sacred cows,' I said.

In London, Eddie Lister and I had abolished forty quangos and cut our share of the council tax by 20 per cent. I had sold off dozens of TfL buildings, and rationalised both the police and fire estate. We had substantially pruned the management.

I was sure that, on a big scale, we could do the same again – and put the savings either into tax cuts or the great investments we were making. It was hard going, but I enjoyed my work. We had the mandate, the momentum, and we had a great project in hand; or rather, two. We had levelling up and we had Global Britain – and I felt confident in explaining the mysteries of both.

Suppose you come into my office in the middle of January 2020, a month after I have won the election. You tell me that a total catastrophe is about to hit the world and derail my administration. You want me to guess what it is.

I struggle to answer. I can't imagine what you have in mind. Everything's good, I say.

Come on, you say, there must be something you are worried about.

I rack my brains further, but I am still stumped. We've got an eighty-seat majority, I say, we have a great mandate from the people, we are getting on with levelling up – the position seems uniformly excellent. We have weekends at Chequers, Carrie's about to have a baby. What's not to like?

OK, you say, I am going to give you five possible causes for the disaster. Number one is a no-deal Brexit.

Give me a break, I reply breezily. Of course we are going to get a deal. We are coming out officially at the end of the month, thanks to the oven-ready withdrawal agreement; and you can be absolutely sure that we will get a Canada-style free-trade deal at the end of the year, when the transition period is over. Look at that Africa summit, the one we just had in Greenwich. It was bursting with confidence and ideas. All the important African leaders were there. Everyone wants to do more business and more trade with the UK. Don't worry – Global Britain is gonna go gangbusters.

OK, you say. Risk number two is Trump. What if the US president does something crazy?

Rubbish, I say. He was terrific at the Nato summit in Watford in December, even if he calls Macron 'Li'l Emmanuel, ninety pounds of fury'; and actually he has played a blinder by liquidating Qasem Soleimani, the head of Iran's Islamic Revolutionary Guard Quds Force. The guy has been plaguing us for years, and Trump zapped him with a drone. The only thing left was his signet ring. People panicked at first but now they are all saying Trump did the right thing. The world needs a strong US, and a strong president. Trump continues to surprise on the upside.

Fair enough, you say. Risk number three is Putin. Aren't you scared of some kind of confrontation with Russia?

You must be joking, I say. Vladimir Putin and I saw each other only a few days ago in Berlin. We had a perfectly cordial conversation. I told him that we couldn't take our relationship out of the freezer as long as he went around poisoning people on UK soil, and he gave some platitudinous Kremlin reply. Yes, I think Putin is dangerous, and he's up to all sorts of mischief – but I don't think he is going to derail this government or stop us from delivering on our mandate.

Understood, you say. Risk four is the Queen or the royal family. Could something go wrong there?

Well, I say, it's true the Queen is now getting on but she is always in great form whenever I see her. I suppose it's a bit sad that Prince Harry and Meghan are off to California. There was a ridiculous business the other day when they made me try to persuade Harry to stay. Kind of manly pep talk. Totally hopeless, but it doesn't matter, really. Who cares if they go to California?

Right, you say, so let's just be clear about this. You see absolutely no clouds on the horizon. You see no political or geo-political crisis that is going to turn your world upside down?

Nope, I say, what have you got in mind?

Risk five, you tell me, is a kind of weird bat flu from China.

Really? I say, you mean that thing Matt Hancock is going on about. Are you serious?

Chapter 35

Zoonotic Nightmare

The slow mental progression
of the Mayor in *Jaws*

The man from the BBC was counting down with his fingers. I was stationed at a desk in the Terracotta Room, on the first floor of Number Ten, and I was about to go live to the nation. My message, by any standards, was one of the most desperate ever delivered to the British people.

From this building PMs had announced all manner of national humiliation, from Suez to the devaluation of sterling. Plenty of PMs had stared out pleadingly at the audience, prisoners of circumstances beyond their control.

Never in history, I think, had a prime minister been forced to go so completely against his instincts, his entire philosophy of life; and yet at the moment I prepared to gabble those crazy words, I had no doubt that I was right in what I was about to say.

The Beeb man made a chopping motion with his forefinger. 'And – live,' he said.

I folded my hands and leaned forwards over the brown Formica desk, composing my features into what I hoped was an expression both urgent and reassuring, but which probably looked a bit like a gasping codfish. Speaking rather too quickly, I summarised the recent progress of the Covid pandemic. Then I came to the crunch.

'From this evening, I must give the British people a simple instruction. You must stay at home.'

You must stay at home, I elaborated, until we decide that you can come out. In excruciating detail – a detail that was to become ever more baroque as the crisis went on – I spelled out the exceptions. You must stay at home unless you are going shopping for essentials; you must stay at home unless you are exercising, either alone or with someone else from your own household; you must stay at home unless you are suffering from a medical emergency, or need to report a crime. Other than that – you're gated, you're grounded, you're gaoled.

It was as though I had turned the whole country into a Victorian boarding school – and I was a mad headmaster who had decided to send the population to their dormitories until further notice. I knew that it was a disaster: for the UK economy, for the dreams of millions; and since I knew that the impact of these restrictions would fall most heavily on the left behind – those very areas that had dared to turn out and vote Tory, for the first time, in 2019 – I could already dimly sense that this would derail the whole levelling-up agenda, derail the government.

I had got to the point, however, where I could see no alternative. If a conservative is a liberal who has been mugged, I was a libertarian who had been mugged by Covid. In the last few weeks I had been on an exhausting mental journey, feet scrabbling as in a losing tug of war – from vague scepticism to slight unease to serious anxiety to that moment when you know that you have to smash the glass and sound the alarm.

By the time Matt mentioned his concerns about the new Chinese virus – as we were walking through the voting lobbies on January 7, 2020 – I had dimly clocked it; I had seen or heard something on the news. But if you had told me that within a few short weeks I would be compelling the incarceration of the entire population and asking the police to fine people for sticking their heads illicitly out of doors, I would have told you that you were barmy.

The problem wasn't that I was ignorant of zoonotic diseases; the problem was rather that I felt I knew all about them – and the risk of political overreaction. As a young teenager, I discussed species-jumping viruses with my father, who was then researching a prescient novel about a plague that is passed from green monkeys to human beings.

I am afraid I laughed like a drain as he explained the farce of the 1976 US swine flu epidemic. An army recruit at Fort Dix, New Jersey, had complained of feeling weak and tired; and when he succumbed to a new variant of swine flu – an influenza passed from pigs to human beings – the White House panicked. President Gerald Ford ordered a mass compulsory vaccination campaign of the entire American population, and it was later claimed (perhaps unfairly) that the vaccination campaign – which cost the lives of several elderly Americans – had done far more damage to public health than the swine flu itself.

Years later, as a leader writer for the *Daily Telegraph*, I had thundered against the junior health minister Edwina Currie for saying something unguarded about the presence of salmonella in UK eggs – so causing the British population to lay off eggs in such numbers that poultry farmers were driven to bankruptcy and four million hens were slaughtered.

Pointlessly. I doubt that Eggwina's warnings averted a single case of egg-borne salmonella in human beings. This was mild incompetence, however, by comparison with the government's mishandling of so-called mad cow disease in 1996. I saw the human cost myself, because in 1997, when I first campaigned for Parliament, I was seeking the votes of Welsh cattle farmers still reeling from the fiasco. They were furious – and rightly.

Scientists from what was then the Ministry of Agriculture, Fisheries and Food had determined that there was a small theoretical risk that meat from cattle infected with bovine spongiform encephalopathy (mad cow disease, in tabloid speak) could trigger an analogous disease in human beings. It seemed possible, they said, that certain 'prions' from the brains, spinal columns and other tissue of mad cows could leap into the brains of beef-eaters – and start a hideous wasting affliction called new-variant Creutzfeldt-Jakob disease.

The symptoms were said to be terrifying. It began with blanking people's names at parties – and ended with people staring and staggering and eventually dying, with Gruyère-like cavities in their brains. Some scientists were forecasting the deaths of millions. One famous professor said that the wave of mortality would be so huge that it would be necessary to build a new hospice on every street corner.

The media lapped it up, especially the suggestion that Britain's uniquely sordid agricultural practices were at fault. Mad cow disease was itself said to be a kind of cosmic retribution for our unholy habit of using cattle feed made from the remains of sheep who had themselves been suffering from scrapie – mad sheep disease – which also affects the brain and nervous system.

The British public was, understandably, appalled, and the roast beef of Old Englande dropped so low down the national menu that it was the turn of cattle farmers to go bankrupt. Then the government made things far, far worse. They should have stuck to the science – not the hysterics – and the scientific guidance was that there might be a theoretical link between eating beef and contracting a really nasty brain disease, but that the statistical likelihood was really very small indeed.

The trouble was that the Tory government's blundering announcement had stampeded the human herd. Rural Britain was in acute distress. They needed to show that beef was 'safe'. But how?

The Major government embarked on a great slaughter of cattle, killing and burning every bovine animal on every farm where BSE had been detected, and every cow more than thirty months old. A total of 4.4 million cattle lost their lives prematurely – innocent daisy-chewing milkers, prize bulls, each of them an investment of the farmer's love and money and care. Great tallow-fuelled plumes of black smoke rose from these hecatombs, night after night.

Did it have the desired effect? Did this gigantic bovicide reassure the public? Of course not. It had the opposite effect. It seemed to confirm what the government officially denied: that there was something wrong with British beef; and all Britain's beef-producing rivals slapped bans on British imports. The French kept their ban on illegally until 2002 – years after the EU Commission had officially lifted the embargo. The US ban was only lifted under Donald Trump. The whole thing was a shambles; the expense was colossal; and what was the result?

It turned out that the government's initial assessment was right: that there was perhaps a theoretical risk of cow-to-human transmission, but that it was very small. There were indeed a handful of cases of nv Creutzfeldt-Jakob disease, and though each of them was of course a tragedy, the link with beef was not always clear, and it was nothing like an epidemic.

There were no hospices constructed on street corners, there were no wards overflowing. The whole thing was essentially a false alarm, and government action – first the panic, then the cull – was to turn out to have been far, far more damaging than the zoonotic disease itself.

When I faced those Welsh farmers in 1997, I was dealing with the anger of people who had seen their livelihoods almost destroyed: not because their cattle were sick, not because their beef was dangerous – but because of a crazed and excessive government reaction to a public health panic.

So when Matt Hancock started talking about a new coronavirus – possibly from bats – and the risk that it would sweep the country, it was hardly surprising that I felt I had been here before. I even felt I knew about coronaviruses.

I remembered the SARS epidemic of 2002–3, a coronavirus that was supposed to have come from bats and had caused such consternation in Asia that everyone started the habit (which they have never lost) of wearing face masks – but that ended up killing fewer than a thousand people, and none, as far as I could remember, in the UK. I had been at the forefront of the bird flu scare of 2008, when as mayor of London I was challenged by my opponents to vaccinate the people of the city; and discovered that the City Hall stocks of Tamiflu, being egg-based, had unfortunately gone off.

So we waited in terror for the defenceless population to be ravaged by bird flu; which duly swept in and swept out again without doing any more damage than any other flu epidemic.

Then there was the swine flu pandemic of 2009 – remember that? – and though my daughter Cassia spent a couple of days in bed, it hardly amounted to a national disaster. There was MERS; there was Ebola; and though these had been very unpleasant for some parts of the world, it seemed as if they had become somehow depleted in their potency when they finally washed up on our shores.

After more than thirty years of writing about or dealing with new zoonotic diseases, I felt I knew my SARS from my Ebola, so to speak, and I had concluded two things: first, that these novel zoonotic plagues tended to sort themselves out – at least in the UK – with far less destruction than initially predicted; and second, that the greater risk of destruction was from the attempts, by politicians, to contain the disease.

In fact it was now about twenty years since I had first written a column announcing that my political hero was the mayor in *Jaws* – who tried to protect the economy of Amity Island and keep the beaches open, even though his electorate were being eaten by a giant fish. The mayor was not a particularly attractive character. He was a chain-smoking, sleazy sort of fellow with loud jackets.

He was also proved spectacularly wrong. The shark continued to eat his electorate – one after the other: first the naked girl, then the boy on the lilo, then the old fisherman, then the man in the lagoon, then Quint, and so on. But if you leave aside the requirements of the drama and you look at the cold, hard statistics – you can see that the mayor had a point.

It was really vanishingly unlikely, in the chilly New England waters, that a *Carcharodon carcharias*, or great white shark, would take and eat so many human beings. Nothing like it has ever happened in real life. So you could argue that the mayor was reasonable – on the basis of the data he first received – to think that things would sort themselves out.

In the narrative that follows, I try to explain how and why the penny dropped, and how our initial intuitions about Covid – not just mine, but the instincts of the whole government – were blown away by the facts. It was an agonising process. I know that there are millions of people in this country – and around the world – for whom the whole subject is still immensely painful. So I am going to set out the timetable of our collective revelation in some detail, and in chronological order.

Chapter 36

How the Crisis Began

The four steps to panic

1 – Vague scepticism

After Matt first alerted me to his concerns, I noted that he seemed to be on top of things and asked him to keep me posted. On Wednesday January 22, there had been 571 cases reported in China, and seventeen deaths, and the following day the Chinese authorities imposed a 'lockdown' in Wuhan and other cities – a novel measure that at first struck international observers as extreme and totalitarian.

A new Whitehall body – the Scientific Advisory Group for Emergencies, or SAGE – met to consider the matter, though I don't think their findings were ever raised with me. On Thursday January 23, Matt chaired a cross-Whitehall 'Cobra' meeting – so called because the Cabinet Office Briefing Room A is best suited to the rapid cross-departmental sharing of confidential briefings.

There was nothing remotely odd about a Cobra meeting being chaired by a secretary of state rather than the prime minister. All sorts of government business is done in Cobra. A PM-chaired Cobra is different. It is a signal to the public that a particular issue is now the number-one priority for the government – and no one

in January 2020 was claiming that this was our number-one priority.

It was a cloud no bigger than a man's hand – and at that stage
no one that I talked to believed it would turn into a typhoon.
When Matt made a statement to the House on Monday January
27 – announcing that anyone coming back from Wuhan, the
source of the outbreak, would have to be quarantined – the papers
hardly batted an eyelid.

Most of them chose to splash on some news about Prince
Andrew and allegations about his friendship with Jeffrey Epstein,
a dead millionaire who seemed to have trafficked in underage
girls. On Thursday January 30, the World Health Organization
declared that the new coronavirus was a PHEIC – a Public Health
Emergency of International Concern.

The WHO weren't even calling it a pandemic; it was hardly a
shrieking klaxon of alarm. On Friday January 31, the subject was
on our away day cabinet agenda at the National Glass Centre in
Sunderland.

We had come to Brexit city, the place whose 61 per cent vote to
leave the EU in June 2016 had amazed the pundits and proved to
be the harbinger of revolution. We were there to talk about levelling up – about all the things we intended to do beyond Brexit,
which legally fell that day – to deliver on our promises to the
people.

Covid was to do so much damage to all those plans, and yet it
only came up briefly at the end. Hancock, as ever, was full of
confidence. There was a chance that the Chinese could contain it,
and even if they didn't, we had a plan. The death rate, he noted,
was only 2 per cent.

If this had been a film, that would have been the moment – to
the accompaniment of some thumping chords by John Williams
– when we first glimpsed the shadow of the monster in the corner
of the screen. If we had known then how contagious Covid would

prove, we would have realised that we were staring at a potential disaster.

Of course 2 per cent sounds small, but a small percentage of a very large number is still a very large number. No one – then – made that point, and Covid was so low down the national political agenda that I wasn't even asked about it in PMQs, either in late January or early February.

When SAGE met again on Tuesday February 4, they had a first discussion about what might be done to contain the virus if it arrived on our shores. They decided that restricting gatherings or closing public transport would not work. Which shows, perhaps, how conceptually distant our best scientists still were from the measures we would soon have to apply.

It was not that British officials were doing nothing – far from it. A great deal of planning and preparation was by now under way. On Wednesday February 5, a Matt-chaired Cobra agreed the drafting of a bill to give the government the necessary powers to deal with a pandemic: ugly but vital things like how to speed up death certificates and handle large volumes of corpses. We were to get it through to royal assent by mid-March.

On Thursday February 6, cabinet met and briefly considered the outbreak, which was now popping up in ones and twos around the world, with twenty-five countries recording cases. Covid had infected 28,000 people in China, and around 600 Chinese had died, including Li Wenliang, one of the first doctors to raise the alarm about this new form of pneumonia.

2 – Slight Unease

By Friday February 14, we had nine cases in the UK, and the numbers in China were really starting to roar: 14,840 cases in the province of Hubei (where Wuhan is) on only one day. We held a cabinet that day – a new cabinet, since there had been an unexpectedly bloody and difficult reshuffle the previous day. Saj had resigned over a trivial row involving his spads, which I am afraid was confected by people who really didn't have my interests at heart.

I replaced him with Rishi, the obvious candidate. But I mourned the loss of Saj. He had shared my vision.

Today I warned colleagues that things were going to get worse. Two scientists joined us, of an equally brainy, balding and etiolated appearance. They were to go on to achieve vast national fame.

There was Chris Whitty, who was my contemporary at Oxford – though we didn't know each other – and who was now a professor of public health and the government's chief medical officer, and there was Sir Patrick Vallance, the government's chief scientific adviser. He, like Chris, was tall, ectomorphic and grave, and a highly distinguished academic clinician. He was also a pharmaceutical industry veteran with a deep understanding of the production of new medicines and vaccines.

Both men did incalculable service to their country. They helped explain the pandemic in ways everyone could understand. They showed great tact, over a very long period, in schooling a bunch of liberty-minded Tory politicians in the medical realities. They did not try to steer the government. They did what all good doctors do. They gave us the facts of our predicament, and they told us what types of actions, on the whole, would achieve what types of outcomes.

It was always clear that it was for us – which usually meant for me – to make the choices, to defend them, and to live with the consequences. That is because the trade-offs were so morally, politically, socially and economically complicated that only a democratically elected politician could really decide them.

We listened to Chris and Patrick, that day, like a class being told they could watch a nature film at the end of the morning: it was fascinating stuff, but somehow still not quite immediate to our concerns. Chris said that if it turned into a pandemic in this country, then 50 per cent of the population would be infected, and that it seemed to be a mild disease from which people would make a full recovery.

No one at that stage mentioned the 2 per cent death toll – or what that would mean if 50 per cent of the population were infected. For day after day – right until the end of February – we continued to think that this was still quite likely to be more of a problem for other countries than for the UK. So when I rang President Xi on February 18, it was partly to offer condolences for what China had been going through. At the time we were helping them with PPE (personal protective equipment) supplies and ventilators – an irony when you consider that in a few weeks we would be so massively dependent on Chinese supplies.

Xi praised British efforts. I tried to push him about the origins of the disease. What was happening, I asked, in these so-called wet markets, where all sorts of wild animals, some of them rare, were slaughtered for human consumption – so that the places were wet with blood and other fluids.

You will not be surprised to know that on the matter of the Chinese role in starting zoonotic diseases, Xi was not to be drawn. As for the possible role of the Wuhan lab, no one had so far mentioned it.

A couple of days later I talked to Donald Trump, who was less interested in the dangers posed by Covid than in the fact of Chinese embarrassment. It was 'wuflu', he said, meaning flu from Wuhan. China should acknowledge responsibility, he said.

Frankly, I thought that he had a point. It was interesting to note the gingerliness with which the UK scientific world – including our own advisers – approached the aetiology of the disease. I suppose that many good academic projects are partly funded by China, and I suspect that UK scientists shied away from the Sinophobia of some of the rhetoric.

They certainly didn't want to sound as if they agreed with Trump. As for the World Health Organization, they seemed to feel so dependent on the goodwill of Beijing that it took almost another month – until March 11, 2020 – before Tedros Ghebreyesus declared Covid to be a world pandemic.

Right until the end of February there was the same sort of phlegmatic attitude – or so it seemed to me – among UK public health officials. On Wednesday February 26, Public Health England said that there was no evidence that the virus was circulating in the community in England, and 'no change in risk' to the public.

We had, I was told, an excellent system for testing and tracing contacts; and yet by the end of the month, like the frog in the saucepan, I could finally feel the temperature rising around me.

Infected people were plainly coming into this country from abroad – skiers from the February half-term break. And yet the scientists said, emphatically and unanimously, that there was no point in closing borders.

Britain was a vast, open, free-trading economy. We depended on the outside world for food and medical supplies and much else besides. Closing the borders would cause colossal disruption, and it would only buy us a few days' grace, they said. The virus would find a way through.

The scientists changed their minds repeatedly throughout the pandemic on so many issues: on the banning of mass gatherings, on the efficacy of masks, on the timing of lockdowns, on the possibility of asymptomatic transmission, on whether or not to close schools, on the symptoms of Covid and many other crucial questions.

Of course they did. Our understanding of the virus kept changing. But on the uselessness of border closures they were consistent (whether they were right or not I don't know, though I am inclined to think they were).

So if we couldn't stop it coming in, I reasoned to myself, what was the plan, exactly? How were we going to stop the disease?

3 – Growing Alarm

For several days at the end of February, it had been clear to me that I had to take full political control and start chairing Cobra, and said so to my officials. Then, on Friday 28th, we had the moment I had been dreading, but which I had come to see was inevitable: the first British death, an elderly passenger aboard the *Diamond Princess* cruise ship in Yokohama, Japan.

The following day, Saturday 29th (it was a leap year), I sat down with Chris Whitty at the cabinet table to talk through what might be ahead. He sat diagonally across from me over the green baize, near the garden door, and told me something from his vast knowledge of pandemics. One thing history teaches us, said Chris, is that people expect the government to act. They will insist on measures to stop the spread of deadly communicable diseases. Even if they persuade themselves that they are themselves capable of acting responsibly and restricting transmission, they will not believe that other people can be so trusted.

They want rules, and they want government to enforce those rules. He explained that in order to stop or slow the spread of Covid, we would have to try to restrict human contact. He didn't use the word lockdown – that was still about ten days from entering widespread usage – but he clearly meant asking people somehow to seal themselves away from each other.

As I grappled with this miserable idea, he went on to say that you had to be careful with such measures. They would do considerable economic damage. They would have many other serious social and indeed medical disbenefits – depriving kids of education, depriving the elderly of company they badly needed.

There was a risk that public patience would wear thin, that compliance would fade – and therefore timeliness was crucial. It was important that these measures were not imposed too soon. On the other hand, you could not wait too long.

He wanted me to understand that in these crises there were no good options. At every stage the government – I – would have to decide which was the lesser of two evils; two giant but different evils. That was why the decisions had to be political.

I took it from Chris that things were very possibly about to get ghastly, but not quite yet. I did a clip for the news, in which I tried to summarise the advice I was getting. We were now completely focused on Covid, I said; it was the number-one priority. But at the moment the best advice I could give the public was still to wash your hands, regularly, with hot water and soap, for twenty seconds – and await further instructions.

That night I found a paper in my box from the Civil Contingencies Secretariat and fell upon it, hungry for facts. The author had done her best to paint a picture of the days ahead – but of course, through no fault of her own, it was maddeningly vague. It wasn't clear what we would do to restrict social contact, or how we would keep people from meeting. No wonder – these were entirely new concepts. No one then alive in Britain had tried anything like it.

Nor was it clear, from the paper, how bad we thought the disease would be. It might be like a bad outbreak of seasonal flu, she said, 'or it might be milder'. The reasonable worst-case scenario, the paper said, without any supporting argument, was 520,000 deaths.

Eh? I thought. I looked out of my window at the ducks in St James's Park. The crocuses were prodding through. The daffodils were on their way. Just as spring was upon us, it seemed we were about to enter a new kind of hell.

What was this thing? Was it like an annual winter flu, to which the NHS is well accustomed and which always carries off a few tens of thousands?

Or was it a Moloch that was going to kill half a million? None of my team seemed to know.

I believed we had a plan for pandemics. I had been told that we had a world-class system for testing and tracing people with the disease. I knew that we had put another £34 billion into the NHS, so it ought to be well stocked. But I could tell that people were increasingly anxious; and so I needed to show grip, and action.

The following day I went to see the headquarters of Public Health England in Colindale. This was the body that was theoretically responsible for containing the spread of Covid. It was only three days since they had said the virus was not circulating in the UK, and that the risk to the public remained low. I thanked them for what they were doing, and did another clip for the news in which I extolled the testing system. In truth I had been slightly taken aback by the Colindale visit.

Maybe it was because I talked to the wrong people as I walked around the office, but it wasn't clear that they knew that much about the disease or indeed how to track it. I then went to the Royal Free Hospital in north London, where a handful of patients were being treated after picking up Covid from abroad.

Having repeatedly washed or disinfected my hands, I shook hands with some of the staff. People later criticised me for this, and I wish, in retrospect, that I had not done it, or at least not spoken about it. At that stage I was still trying to strike a balance.

I wanted people to be cautious – to wash their hands – but I didn't think we had yet got to the stage of discouraging any kind of physical contact. Shaking hands is an ancient human gesture of goodwill. It's how you do deals. It seemed to me that if I told the British public that shaking hands was over,

well, that was a climacteric, an admission that the virus was starting to warp our behaviour, and I wasn't sure that we were there
yet.

By Monday March 2, when I chaired Cobra, there were forty
cases in the UK – all of them people who had caught it abroad.
Chris repeated his point about the need not to impose measures
too early, and over the next few days, even as the case numbers
ticked gently up, the scientific view remained the same: there was
no need to impose such restrictions as banning mass gatherings or
closing schools.

On Sunday March 8, I saw the TV news from Italy and was
fairly shocked. I knew the Italian health care system and had used
it several times. Once Marina's and my son Theo, aged two, had
wandered into a swimming pool at the deep end while we were all
having a lie-in – probably the single most frightening thing that
has ever happened to me.

I remembered the incredible speed with which the *pronto
soccorso* had roared to our remote farmhouse in Umbria, the noise
of the siren coming up the valley, as the child was lying blue and
apparently lifeless; and the way about a dozen young paramedics
sprang into action, covered him with electrodes and brought him
round.

I thought the Italian health care system was superb, and so I
could hardly bear to look at the scenes from Lombardy: people
gasping their last on trolleys in corridors and car parks. Something
was going badly wrong.

This thing was obviously nastier than we had bargained for, and
if it could happen in Italy, why not us?

It was from this moment on – I am fairly sure – that we started
to focus not just on Covid but on the impact of Covid on the
NHS. What if the numbers were so huge that our health care
system could not cope? What if we had scenes like those in Italy,
with people unable to get treatment – not just for coronavirus, but

for heart attack and strokes and all the thousand natural shocks that flesh is heir to?

We would be forced to break the fundamental pledge from the British state to the British people – that the NHS would always be there for them, free at the point of use. It would be an utter moral and political catastrophe.

That afternoon we had our third press conference, with a cast of Chris, Patrick and me. We had by now had four deaths of patients with Covid in the UK, and though they were all people of advanced years who had other conditions, I put the public on notice. We were going to have to reduce the spread of coronavirus by reducing human contact. On Monday March 9, I saw even more alarming data from Italy – seeming to suggest the mortality rate was not 2 per cent but 8 per cent.

My God, I thought, the UK population is at least as elderly as the Italians. Assuming 50 per cent of the population was infected in the UK, an 8 per cent mortality rate would mean a death toll in the millions. The following day, Tuesday March 10, it was announced that Nadine Dorries was the first MP to contract Covid – and yet we still underestimated the speed of spread in the UK. Matt repeated to cabinet what he had said from the beginning – that unless you had the symptoms, it was highly unlikely that you were suffering from Covid.

This was wrong – and it was one of our biggest collective mistakes in our early understanding of the disease. There were almost certainly far more people by that stage who not only had coronavirus asymptomatically, but were spreading it asymptomatically – so that its general circulation in the UK was already far bigger than we grasped.

On this basic fact, we were still ignorant. I summed up cabinet by saying we were going to have to do more – such as banning gatherings and closing schools – but not yet.

4 – Sounding the Alarm

By Thursday March 12, it was clear that the numbers were going to keep growing, and that I would have to level with people. We gave another press conference and I told the British public that many were going to die, that 'many families are going to lose loved ones before their time'.

When was the last time a British PM had to say anything half as grim? Even at this stage, the advice from SAGE was that we should hold our fire before imposing restrictions on contact, that closing schools would do more harm than good. We had a package of four measures ready to go, from self-isolation of those with symptoms to shielding the elderly and vulnerable – and yet SAGE still seemed to think that some of them could be postponed for weeks.

At this stage Chris, Patrick and the SAGE scientists had two basic arguments for delay. They can be described as the risk of 'bounceback' and the risk of 'behavioural fatigue'.

As Patrick had explained in Cobra: if we decided to imitate China and impose immediate and stringent measures, then there was a risk that the virus would simply come roaring back in the autumn and winter, when the NHS would be under greater pressure. The bounceback would be all the stronger, because the tough initial measures may have protected the population from infection – but they had also stopped them acquiring any immunity.

He also described how populations could suffer behavioural fatigue from measures that were imposed too early. If you go too early, said Patrick at the press conference, 'what happens then is that the effect wanes, and people get fed up with doing this, and you end up with not being able to do it time and time again'.

He even seemed to suggest that it might be desirable to let a proportion of the population get the virus, so as to build up what he called herd immunity – which some journalists misconstrued as a kind of laissez-faire strategy. I don't think Patrick meant anything of the kind.

The strategy was to suppress the virus and to protect the NHS, and a measure of herd immunity would be a happy by-product, not an objective. You couldn't let Covid rip. It was too contagious, too potent and too deadly for certain groups of people.

But I am afraid Patrick's point about bounceback was also right – as events were to prove later that year.

The following day, Friday March 13, SAGE looked again at the numbers, and all illusions finally melted away. It was clear to them there were far more cases than we had believed. We weren't four weeks behind Italy on the curve of the pandemic – we were two weeks, if that. Martin rang me that night to say that I needed to come back from Chequers first thing in the morning. We were up against it, he said.

Chris, Patrick and Ben Warner – a gifted mathematician working in Number Ten – showed me the graphs from the latest SAGE meeting. We had no choice. We had to lock down.

If that parabola continued on its current path, they said, then our hospital system would be completely overpowered, the dead would be cremated in the streets, and a mob would storm the gates of Downing Street and remove us from the building.

From then until March 23, the British state began an intensifying programme of removing ancient and hallowed liberties from the people. On Monday March 16, I told people to stay at home for fourteen days if a single member of their household had Covid symptoms, as well as outlining measures to protect the elderly and vulnerable.

I told people to stop all unnecessary travel, and to avoid pubs, clubs and restaurants. Many, many people were already taking such steps for themselves. It was now over a week since I had been mounting the rostrum in Number Ten and issuing fairly sepulchral warnings about Covid.

Many, of course, found the erosion of freedom outrageous. My father took to the airwaves and said, 'I'll go to the pub if I need to.'

So at cabinet on Tuesday March 17, we agreed that schools would have to close (with SAGE, slightly behind us, supporting the same measure the following day); and on Friday 20th we closed both schools and hospitality by law.

On Saturday 21st we decided that the public was not complying in sufficient numbers, and I said as much at the press conference. On Monday 23rd we went for full lockdown.

Was it right? Was it necessary? I will say a bit more about that later on. But let me put it this way. I was PM of a country where the number of daily deaths from Covid in the crucial period I have described – from March 11 to 23, 2020 – was ascending in the following rhythm: 6, 10, 15, 22, 27, 41, 38, 53, 50, 79, 71, 99, 102. That is an exponential curve, with a doubling time of about four days. I was advised that lockdown was the only way to stop this horror – and I had absolutely no option.

As it happens, the doubling continued. The daily death toll went on up: 120, 157, 214, and on March 27 we lost 231 people to Covid, having begun the month in single figures.

That day Chris Whitty took me aside after a meeting. He had noticed that I was coughing and spluttering a bit, and seemed red in the face. He thought I ought to have a test for the virus. I knew that tests, at that stage, were hard to come by. I didn't want it wasted on me when it could be used for an elderly or vulnerable person.

'Are you sure?' I said.

'Completely,' he said.

Later that afternoon I was told to go into the Cabinet Room, where a man appeared in a kind of nuclear waste hazmat suit (I later discovered he was Dr Nick Price), and stuck a probe down my throat.

A few hours later Chris called me on my mobile to say I had tested positive.

Oh well, I thought. It was a nuisance. It might slow me up. But as I kept telling everyone, it was generally a mild disease.

On the other hand, I also remembered my Athenian history. 'Pericles died of the plague,' I had earlier reminded Michael Gove, and his spectacles seemed to glitter at the thought.

Chapter 37

Intensive Care Unit

Where my life was saved by the
nurses of the NHS

OH boy, this was bad. It was *baaa-aad*. It was also worse than I had expected. It was Saturday April 4, 2020, and I was lying on my back on scratchy, crumpled, crumb-full bedclothes.

I couldn't read. I could hardly think. Music grated. All I wanted was for another hour to go by so that I could officially have another couple of paracetamols and that the throbbing in the skull would at least temporarily abate.

The curtains were shut, but outside I could tell that the sun shone. Balmy zephyrs riffled the blossom in the Number Ten garden. Little ducklings were hatching in the big lead seventeenth-century flower planters, and our gorgeous puppy Dilyn – omigod … Our dog Dilyn would be after those ducklings. I groaned. Or he could be drowning in that water feature – in fact a crater left by a German bomb. God knows what Dilyn was doing.

I should really get up and go down the – what? – one hundred spiral stairs from the flat to the garden and stop Dilyn persecuting the baby ducks – but the whole idea frankly made me feel faint. After a while Carrie came back in with the painkillers, and though I felt pathetically grateful, I also felt it was ridiculous. I should be ministering to her, not the other way round. Not only did she also have Covid, but she was more than eight months pregnant with our first child.

Ooof, I said, and tried to take a long breath through the nose.

No worst, there is none, said Gerard Manley Hopkins, but then he hadn't been banjaxed by Covid while trying to steer a G7 country through a pandemic. That was the trouble – that was why I think I felt so rotten. It wasn't just the physical distress; it was the guilt, the political embarrassment of it all.

I needed to *bee-oing-oing* back on to my feet like an India rubber ball. I needed to be out there, leading the country from the front, sorting the PPE, fixing the care homes, driving the quest for a cure.

As soon as I was diagnosed on March 27, I had gone into self-isolation in the Number Eleven flat. Carrie had sequestered herself away from me – since she had not yet tested positive – in the Number Ten flat, which still awaited the new chancellor, Rishi Sunak, and his family, and where camp beds had been laid out in rows in the expectation (correct) that people in the building would soon be working round the clock.

I had carried on doing my job, as best as I could. I had no choice. The country was facing the worst pandemic for a hundred years, and decision after decision was being funnelled all the way to the top. There was no way I could stop.

I began by issuing what I hoped was a fairly jaunty video bulletin. Since no one could stand near me, I made it myself, talking into my phone.

Hi folks, I said, I just wanted to let everyone know that – like so many others – I had tested positive for Covid and, like so many others, I was now working from home; but be in no doubt, I said, that I was continuing to lead the national effort against the disease – and that I was deeply grateful to everyone for what they were doing.

Together, I said, in the resolute tones of my recent press conferences, we would beat it. I looked bullish, rubicund, as though flushed from a good lunch. Perhaps I sounded a little short of breath, but only if you were listening for it.

Over the days that followed, as I waited for the disease to go away, I sat hunched over my laptop in my office – obsessively watching the data and trying to direct the UK response.

The next day the number of deaths was up again – to a horrifying 463. It was still doubling. When would our measures start to make a difference? When would the curve turn?

The news was getting to me – lowering my spirits, and perhaps lowering my resistance. Perhaps, I wondered blackly, it was some kind of cosmic judgement on me, on my whole worldview – founded as it was on a boosterish faith that our country could get through anything.

I cursed the day I had ever allowed myself to praise the mayor in *Jaws* – even if the essential point was still, statistically, a good one. By Wednesday April 1, the daily death toll had soared again, to 826, and when I went outside to clap for the NHS and social care workers, everyone looking after the sick, it was noted that I looked pretty groggy.

Next day Nick Price the doctor came round to see us both – me because I felt so grim, and Carrie because she was pregnant. He took one look at me and said that I should really get into hospital, as a precaution.

No, no, I said. I knew exactly what pressure the hospitals were under. It was ridiculous. I was sure I was on the mend.

By the following day – Friday 3rd – I should have been recovering, according to the usual pattern of the disease. I still had a temperature. So I composed another breezy video message. Slight hitch, folks, I said: I have still got Covid – but rest assured that the fight goes on. This time I was tie-less and had a face the colour of mayonnaise, and was slouching in an armchair.

The overall effect was a bit like that character by Paul Whitehouse – Rowley Birkin QC – who always concludes his incomprehensible clubland monologues with the pay-off line, 'I was vey, vey drunk'; except in this case I wasn't drunk.

By that weekend I was finding it exhausting even to walk, and was having some difficulty merely hauling myself downstairs to the chancellor's office, which they had cordoned off for my use. I started to wonder. At what stage should I seek further assistance?

I really didn't want to go into hospital. I knew my basic anthropology. I had read my J.G. Frazer. The tribe does not like it – to put it mildly – if the ruler is frail or sick. The tribe wants the ruler to be strong. Few things are more damaging, politically, than the spectacle of some physical infirmity. Think of the former US president Jimmy Carter, how he once conked out on a jog, wearing a pair of skimpy running shorts. Think of George H.W. Bush, interrupting a state banquet in Tokyo to vomit in the lap of the Japanese prime minister.

It is hard to come back from that kind of thing, and perhaps it is no surprise that they both turned out to be one-term presidents.

I tried for the rest of the Friday and Saturday to stick with it, to force myself back to wellness – though by now I was mainly lying on my back upstairs. By Sunday April 5, there were over a thousand daily fatalities across the country. I was still flat out, in the state in which you found me at the beginning of this chapter. I was floating in and out of consciousness, waiting for my fix of paracetamol, when Carrie came in like a ministering angel. 'Come on,' she said. 'You need to get something to eat.'

I said that the kitchen really felt a long way away.

So she brought up some apple and cheese. I looked at that cheese with such complete apathy that I knew – after a lifetime as a functioning cheese-o-holic – that something was definitely awry.

Carrie rang Dr Nick Price and explained things, and then passed the phone to me. I said I was sure I was fine, but the doctor cut me off. He wanted me to come in right away, to St Thomas's

Hospital. No, no, I said. There would surely be people who were far worse off than me – people who really needed the bed.

I'll be all right, I told him.

He wasn't having it. You have got to come in, he said. You have now spent too long getting worse, and it has got to the stage where it could go either way.

There are people who recover from your position, he said, but then there are also plenty who get suddenly and markedly worse. We need to get you into hospital, because we need to be able to get you oxygen if you need it.

Shortly thereafter Carrie and I were staggering out of the back entrance to Number Ten, trying to look inconspicuous. We got into a big blacked-out people mover, and within a few minutes we had crossed the river and were being wheeled – the doctors insisted on wheelchairs – into the bowels of St Thomas's.

As soon as I was upstairs and had an oxygen mask on, I started to feel better, though I was still worried about Carrie. At that stage we had no idea whether Covid could be harmful for an unborn child. But the doctors were confident. Her symptoms were much milder, and after a while she went back to Number Ten.

With the oximeter on my finger, we could see that my oxygen levels started slowly to creep up again, and I began to feel sleepy. Before I folded, there was one thing I had to do.

I rang Dominic Raab. 'First Secretary of State,' I said.

'PM,' he said.

'You know I said that you might have to deputise for me,' I said.

'Yes, PM.'

'Well, that moment has come.'

'No problem, PM,' he said. 'Get well soon.'

He didn't sound remotely rattled – in fact he was to go on to do an outstanding job.

The following morning, having been pumped with a lot of oxygen, I felt possibly slightly improved – and more guilty than ever about occupying NHS bed space. I looked out over the river to the Palace of Westminster. The view rang a bell, and I realised I was in the same ward – perhaps the same room – where my stepfather Nick Wahl had died in 1996. I had been with him right to the end.

I knew that view all right. I didn't want to stay there a second longer than I had to, but by the afternoon I seemed to be back to where I was. The oxygen levels kept sinking, and by the early evening I was conscious of a group of gowned and masked doctors, clustered around the doorway. They were lung experts, heart experts, zoonotic virus experts – some of the greatest leaders in their fields. On the whole, they said, they thought that I had better get down into intensive care.

Really? I said.

It was just a precaution, they said. My oxygen levels were looking more than a bit dodgy, and they wanted to be able to use the best possible kit to keep me topped up.

There was quite a lot of internet chatter, in the days and weeks that followed, about the exact severity of my illness. Some said that I was shamming, others that I was indeed ill but that I never needed to go to hospital, let alone occupy an intensive care bed.

All I can say is that I felt really lousy – anyone who has had bad Covid knows the feeling; that scratchy, breathless exhaustion. I also know that at one stage my oxygen levels had dropped to 72 per cent – and that below 70 per cent some nasty things start happening to your body; and that they were getting ready, that night, for the possibility that I might have to be intubated – that is, that they might have to spike a hole in my trachea and stuff a tube down my windpipe to forcefeed O_2 into my lungs.

Is that necessary? I said as they prepared to wheel me downstairs.

Oh yes, they said, and made it sound like a routine procedure. What they didn't explain is that patients who were intubated – at that stage in the pandemic – had about a 50 per cent chance of survival.

Before we could discuss the matter much further, I was in ICU – the intensive care unit.

The atmosphere was eerie, the light dim and yellow-greenish. As I was pushed to my section at the end of the ward, I glimpsed my fellow sufferers. It was like one of those sci-fi movies, where a complement of passengers is being transported cryogenically through space. Some of them had already been intubated, as far as I could see, and the place was very quiet apart from the wheezing and beeping of the machines.

There were about a dozen of us, and we all seemed to be middle-aged men. Some were black, some were Asian, and all, like me, were at least a touch overweight.

Then I was being manoeuvred off the gurney and on to the ICU bed – designed like a kind of dentist's chair, so that my back was at an angle of about forty-five degrees. I met the two nurses whose job it was, that night, to get enough oxygen into my lungs.

There was Jenny, from Invercargill in New Zealand, and Luis, from Porto in Portugal. They were both masked up, and it was hard to see their expressions, but they sounded a bit nervous. Which wasn't surprising, I suppose. Whatever your politics, no one wants to be the nurse in charge when your prime minister's vital signs monitor starts emitting that monotonous flatlining *beeeeep*.

Luis fiddled around with the oximeter, to check that the levels really were as low as they seemed. Then he instructed me exactly how to lie – slightly over to one side – and propped some cushions beneath me to get it right.

I concentrated, very hard, on breathing. By this stage Carrie had alerted my family that I was in the ICU. She was explaining things to my kids, and then I talked to them too, and to Marina.

Lara had resourcefully located some Tintin books – I think *Land of Black Gold*, still brilliant and entirely relevant to Gulf politics; but after a while even Tintin was too much. I started to doze, but didn't want to sleep – partly in case I never woke up, or in case they decided to perform some stealthy tracheotomy without letting me know.

So Jenny handed me an iPad full of films, and I watched a pretty gut-wrenching revenge movie called *The Revenant*, in which Leonardo DiCaprio is an eighteenth-century fur trapper in Canada who gets badly mauled by a bear, dunked in freezing rivers, thrown off cliffs – and survives.

Deep in my lungs, as the night went on, an allegorical struggle was taking place. Malign little creatures were wreaking havoc in the lining of my airways. I could visualise them: horrible purple or green spheres, with inverted bog-brushes of protein stuck all over them. They were burying themselves in the soft tissue, using my cells – as I understood it – to reproduce. But that night the bear wasn't Covid.

The bear was me.

My body, as it was later explained to me, had never encountered Covid before, and my immune system was so appalled by this alien life form that it went into a kind of frenzy.

I was having what was called a 'cytokine storm', in which the immune system fires ack-ack indiscriminately at friend or foe alike, so that the body is under attack from itself. That was the syndrome – the cytokine storm – that did a lot of harm to patients in those early days, before we had worked out that steroids could help.

One way or another, it was a rough night. But by daybreak it felt as if the storm had broken. Luis and Jenny had been at it more or less constantly – shifting me by a couple of inches, checking the oximeter, tilting me so that the oxygen could get where it needed.

Now my numbers were better – not exactly Olympic, but better. I was amazed by how weak I was – physically wrecked, as though

I had been in a car crash. I could hardly move, and the doctors were determined that I should stay another couple of days in ICU.

They turned the bed round so that I could look out of the window, and I saw that I was facing out on to a building site. Now I came to think of it, I was proud to have had a hand in the project. Part of this great and ancient hospital was being rebuilt with investment from the Gulf – which my indefatigable deputy mayor Eddie Lister had helped to secure. I stared down at this hole in the ground, where they seemed to have discovered the brick courses of some ancient Victorian ovens. I had come within an ace, I reflected, of having a hole dug for me. Why had I got so damn ill?

I expect that it is probably partly genetics – the way particular people can be badly affected by a new virus. It didn't help much that, like so many of us Brits, I was fat. I had also been exposed – I suspect – to a very large viral load: that is to say, I had been in many meetings with people who may have had Covid, but who did not necessarily have symptoms; and since I caught the disease right at the beginning, before we really understood Covid or how it is transmitted, I suppose it is possible that gust after gust of the virus had come my way.

It is also true that I was exhausted, emotionally shattered by watching the disease roll in, wave after wave, and knowing that there was relatively little I could do.

I didn't realise it, as I languished, but the fate of the UK PM was being watched with fascination around the world. Outside in the corridors of the hospital, though I never saw them, were representatives of the US pharmaceutical industry, despatched by Donald Trump to revive me with drugs not licensed or approved in the UK.

I am told that congregations were praying for my good health, and it may sound weird, but I am truly grateful for all such intercessions. I expect that some people were of course praying that one way or another the disease would mean the end of me – at least politically.

One thing is for certain: at the moment it was announced that I was going into ICU – when there was therefore believed to be a genuine chance that I was about to die – my popularity figures were the highest they had ever been, and higher than any PM in history.

Chapter 38

Silent Streets

Covid was awful – and so was lockdown

April is the cruellest month, said T.S. Eliot, and he was certainly right about April 2020. I left hospital on Easter Monday and drove with Carrie to Chequers – BBC helicopter overhead – for a two-week convalescence.

The privilege of the job of PM is to serve your country. The perk of the job is Chequers.

This Elizabethan house is framed by the Chilterns and surrounded by fields and deer-filled woods. The members of staff are uniformed and uniformly wonderful – some of them, by tradition, from the RAF, and the interiors are curated by Rodney Melville – a man with a refined eye for a Chinese pot or a Turkish kilim. Of all the rooms, the one I loved best is the Long Gallery. This runs cricket pitch-length down the north side of the house, on the upper floor, and it is so full of mullioned bay windows that it gets light all day. It is the room where the Chequers trustees keep some of the greatest treasures – from the pistols of Napoleon to the very ring that was on the finger of Queen Elizabeth I when she died.

The jewel flips open to show a miniature of her mother, Anne Boleyn, and was so prized by the queen that they took it off her finger and galloped it up to Scotland to show James I to prove that Elizabeth was really dead. That object alone is worth about £20 million, and there was a vague attempt when I was PM to sell it. I put my foot down.

Here I sat for much of the first few days, slumped in a chintzy armchair in front of a fire, going through my red box or asleep. Everything around me was vernal and beautiful. Outside I could dimly see the bluebells in the woods above the house. Beyond that were ancient pastures where my Coviddy eyes could just about see the lambs. Beyond this 3,000-acre estate was a country in agony.

On the day I was released, the virus had killed 737, and the daily toll was still rising. We were going to hit 10,000 fatalities and the gradient of the curve seemed steeper than that of France or Spain or Italy.

What could we have done? I asked myself as I looked helplessly at the daily 'dashboard' – the awful statistics of our suffering. Lock down earlier?

As I hope the previous chapters have made clear, that would have been absurd – since it would effectively have meant going against the advice I was getting. To have locked down faster than we did would have meant conducting a vast and novel social experiment of a kind that had never been done in living memory, and in advance of scientific opinion.

As April wore on, the costs of our action were becoming clearer. Twice I had warned the cabinet in March 2020 of the likely pattern of events: that the damage would be inflicted not just by Covid, but by government attempts to combat the disease. They nodded vigorous assent, especially, I think, Jacob Rees-Mogg. Now I was being proved right.

As therapies go, lockdown was devastating. In our preliminary discussions about these types of intervention – telling people not to go near each other – we had all assumed that we would have a problem persuading them to comply. Chris, Patrick and I had thought that if some Tory PM appeared on TV and told the British people not to go to the pub, and then not even to venture out of doors, their natural cussedness and libertarianism would encourage them to stick two fingers up to government.

Well, as it turned out, lockdown was an easy sell, and indeed my stay-at-home message was heeded so punctiliously by the workforce that the UK sustained the biggest fall in output since the Great Frost of 1709.

The trains were empty. Town centres were silent. The streets were deserted save for the cats – which we first believed, probably wrongly, not to be vectors of the disease. In that terrible April, new car sales fell by 97 per cent – not surprisingly, since I had shut the showrooms. National compliance was so total that we even desisted from some types of economic activity that were theoretically intended to continue – such as construction – and which did in fact continue in other countries like France and Germany.

With the traffic off the streets and the trains deserted, this could have been the ideal moment to accelerate that infrastructure roll-out: use Covid-secure protocols to build those bypasses, upgrade that track, send the fibre-optic cable sprouting through the national wainscot. Well, we missed that chance, and instead Crossrail was delayed, HS2 ground to a halt, and as the cost of it all exploded I felt as if the vast crenelated sandcastle of my plans was being washed away by the tide of the virus.

The frustration was appalling. I longed to be able to get back to my desk, to steer things – but my body had other ideas. On about the second or third day, I had tried to have a swim in the Chequers pool (donated by a former US ambassador, after President Richard Nixon paid a visit to Edward Heath and was horrified to discover that the British prime minister was expected to survive without one).

Margaret Thatcher had been so hostile to this luxury that she turned the heating off, but when I was there the water was generally pretty warm. Now it felt freezing. I am a strong swimmer, but I could barely manage a length, and had to haul myself out at the side. I lay there gasping like a grampus.

It was an effort to get up the stairs, and climbing the hill was impossible. So I walked along the flat ground, with Dilyn pulling like a husky, until I noticed to my horror that even Dilyn seemed suddenly to have succumbed. After a few hundred yards he would lie there all floppy, tongue lolling. I have never seen anything like it before or since, and Patrick Vallance later told me his dog had been the same.

It felt like a medieval chronicle of a pestilence so bad that even the dogs were struck down. It was not surprising, amid all the grimness, that the nation fastened on to anything remotely uplifting. While I was moping and wheezing, there were plenty of people who put me to shame.

There was Captain Tom Moore, a centenarian and British Army veteran who decided that he would raise money for the NHS by scooting up and down his lawn on his zimmer frame. He captured the national longing for a hero and raised so much money so fast that his family got into a muddle, sadly, about how to spend this unexpected meteorite of gold.

Then there was the ninety-three-year-old Queen, who gave a wonderful address to the nation about the importance of protecting the NHS, and reminded us of the astonishing power of the monarchy to touch the hearts of people; and then there were the NHS, the carers, the people who simply had to work – to put themselves day after day in the firing line of the virus.

Every Thursday evening the whole population – or a goodly chunk of us – would turn out to show their appreciation for these people working in health and social care by standing on their doorsteps and clapping and banging saucepans. Carrie and I turned out too, on the steps of Chequers, and I clapped with deep emotion because my lungs were telling me that I had been through something really pretty nasty, and that if it hadn't been for Jenny and Luis, fiddling with those oxygen tubes all night with all their skill and experience, I think I might have carked it.

Towards the end of the month, round about April 20, it started to look as though we had been through the crest of the wave. We had gone up over 1,000 deaths per day, but now the totals were falling – both for deaths and hospital admissions. They were still horrendous – 800, 700, 600 – but the trajectory was clear. It looked and felt to me as if the great national effort was beginning to work.

All that privation, all that seclusion – it was starting to deprive the virus of targets; we were protecting the NHS and saving lives. At that moment I believed completely in the correlation between the non-pharmaceutical interventions – the lockdown and other restrictions on human contact – and the shape of the epicurve.

I believed that we had bent that parabola by the strength of our collective will, like Uri Geller with a spoon.

It was only much later that I started to look at the curves of the pandemic around the world – the dromedary double hump that seemed to rise and fall irrespective of the different approaches taken by different governments. There were always two waves, whether you were in China, where lockdowns were ruthlessly enforced, or in Sweden, where they took a more voluntary approach.

Looking back, I wonder whether old King Cnut was right all along when he stationed his throne on the shore of the Thames and asked his courtiers to watch as he vainly ordered the tide to withdraw. Maybe there are limits to human agency; maybe it isn't possible for government action to repel the waves of a highly contagious disease, any more than it is possible to repel the tide of the Thames.

I am not saying that lockdowns achieved nothing; I am sure they had some effect. But were they completely decisive in beating back the disease, turning that wave down? All I can say is that I am less certain now than I was at the time – because then I believed that it was all down to us, and that government was responsible for both the rise and the fall.

That was certainly how our political opponents represented things, and so I hungered for anything – like all prime ministers – that looked like a success, to redeem my survivor guilt and to rebut the suggestion that we were somehow turning into 'plague island', worse afflicted by Covid than anywhere else in the world.

That was not true; it was always a lie. But some of the media made it feel as if it were true – and so I was inordinately proud of snatches of good news and the things that went well.

Covid may have been a nightmare, but it certainly brought us together. We had hundreds of thousands of volunteers – people who did such acts of kindness as delivering food parcels to those who were elderly or vulnerable. We managed somehow to protect the homeless and the rough sleepers, who I had feared would be among the most vulnerable to the disease.

Thanks to the hard work of the Prison Service, we did not see Covid rampage through our jails – as at one stage I had believed that it inevitably would. We certainly paid a lot of money for the furlough scheme – in fact the total bill for government support ranges in estimates from £310 billion to £410 billion; but Rishi Sunak and his team deserved great credit for the way they had put it together so fast and so decisively.

Even if we erred on the side of generosity – paying 80 per cent of people's wages up to £2,500 per month – we saved thousands and thousands of businesses from destruction. By a huge effort we built hospitals from scratch – the famous Nightingales, vast wards with oxygen beds, in places like the ExCel Centre; and it is a measure of how far the NHS was from being overwhelmed that they were never really used, or not for their original purpose as spillover wards for Covid patients who could not be accommodated elsewhere.

British manufacturers had responded heroically to my 'Ventilator Challenge' and had cobbled together all sorts of contraptions to deal with what we had believed, in the first few weeks, would be a desperate national shortage of machines to get oxygen into people's lungs. We had machines made by vacuum cleaner companies and Formula One racing car manufacturers – and though the effort was immense, I was glad that we didn't in the end have to use them, since none of them had been properly tested and approved, and I expect some of them were lethal.

That does not mean it was wrong to build the Nightingales, or wrong to cobble together the ventilators. The whole point was that this virus was new, and deadly, and we did not know which way the pandemic would turn.

British scientists were the first to come up with a genuinely useful treatment for the disease, by showing that the steroid dexamethasone could stop the nasty immune reaction – the cytokine storm. It came too late for me, but it was a chink of light, a hint that one day the cavalry would appear tootling over the hill, and medicine would come once again to the rescue of the human race. But when?

As I sat there reading and thinking, I could see the danger we were in. The disease was clearly now in retreat, whether through lockdown or because the weather was getting warmer, or because pandemics follow a natural curve – or a combination of all three. But everyone knew that it was likely to come back and that we were only in remission. If the evidence of the 1918 pandemic was anything to go by, the second wave would be nastier than the first.

This wasn't just a disease of the elderly and vulnerable, as some claimed; I knew that from my own experience, and I now read about poor Derek Draper, the husband of the broadcaster Kate Garraway. It was awful, and I could hardly believe it.

When I had first known Derek he was 'Dolly' Draper, an acolyte of Peter Mandelson and one of a group of New Labour thrusters that Frank Johnson had intelligently gathered around the *Spectator* after Blair came to power in 1997. The Derek I knew was smart, self-confident, unscrupulous, and above all he was young. Now he was in a coma, on life support, his organs riddled with damage from that internal civil war between the virus and his immune system; and after almost four years in which he never properly recovered, Derek has since died. If this could happen to Derek Draper, and me, it could happen to absolutely anyone – and what made me so anxious was that I couldn't see the answer.

On April 25, I felt able to have a general strategy discussion at Chequers, and the team came to see me. I explained my fears.

What is the way out, long-term? I asked. How do we beat this?

I was amazed when Patrick Vallance said, with every sign of confidence, 'Oh, we will get a vaccine.'

Chris seemed much less sure, and I shared his scepticism. We didn't have a vaccine for SARS, in spite of huge global efforts. We didn't have a vaccine for MERS. We certainly didn't have a vaccine for AIDS.

Why on earth would the Almighty choose now to smile on the human race and give us a vaccine for SARS-CoV-2? Was Patrick serious, or was he just whistling in the dark? Optimism, it seemed to me, was at a discount in this crisis.

I talked to Matt Hancock, the health secretary, about what else we could possibly do to prepare ourselves for the second wave. What about testing? we wondered. In the first few weeks of the pandemic, test kits had been few and hard to come by, and our diagnostics industry was not as strong as it should have been.

But what if you could test huge numbers of people every day? It seemed to me there were two advantages of mass testing. First, you could help to suppress the disease by spotting cases early and getting victims to isolate themselves.

Second, you might be able to use testing to allow people to have something like a normal life – to go to work, for instance, or to go to the movies, once they had tested negative. But to achieve anything like that outcome, a kind of ubiquitous test-and-release scheme, we needed to build a vast new testing industry, and we needed to do it with the speed of the Spitfire factories of the Second World War.

By April 27, I was still not fully back to normal. I felt far from tip-top. But I just did not see how I could spend any longer at Chequers and not at the helm in Number Ten. We had pledged to deliver 100,000 tests a day by the end of May.

We had to get ready for the next wave, and we had to deal with the damage done by the first. The exertion required was going to be enormous. I knew from all my political experience that – brilliant though the civil service is, wonderful though the NHS may be – when it comes to delivering any great project there is absolutely no substitute for daily drive and direction from the top.

When we went into lockdown, we had been frankly so scared about loss of life that we had barely had time to think of the social and economic consequences. It was only now, as the virus began to ebb, that the damage was becoming clear.

Lockdown was more or less OK for some – for the relatively affluent furlough-cocooned middle classes who could watch Netflix and make banana bread and drink rosé wine in the garden. But for millions of school kids – and we had eight million that year – it had been a total disaster. They had lost time in school, weeks and weeks that they would never get back; and the detriment had been greatest, of course, for the kids who needed school most and who were getting the least help from home.

It was the very opposite of levelling up, and we had to turn it around. I had at least one idea that I was determined to implement – but I had to be there.

Two days later, Carrie gave birth to Wilfred – and that cruel April came to an end, breeding, as T.S. Eliot puts it, lilacs out of the dead land.

Chapter 39

Closing Schools

A disaster and a new opportunity to level up

Let me take you back to your schooldays, and to one of those vacant moments – we have all had them – when you have mysteriously lost track of what the teacher was saying. Let's suppose you have been staring out of the window, and a fly enters your mouth; or you can't think about anything except the loveliness of the girl two desks down, and how she has no awareness of your existence.

For a crucial fifteen minutes your mind is elsewhere, and just as everyone else is learning Pythagoras or the causes of the American Revolution, your brain is tuned out – and the result is that for the rest of the school term you will have a very slight fog about something that everyone else understands.

Does that ring any bells?

Then imagine that you weren't even there that day, or even for the whole week, because you were off with appendicitis while everyone else was swotting up on percentages. The chances are that you will have a permanent weakness in your academic armoury, and that ever after you will become expert in weaving conversations so as not to be found out.

Yes? Then imagine that you have missed not a few hours or days, but weeks, even months, at the most impressionable age, when the brain can retain and regurgitate the most phenomenal detail – when you can remember not only what your teacher said, but the way he sat and the jokes he told when he was teaching you; and yet for this entire formative period you can't see your teacher, and you can't compete with your classmates, and there are great cooling carbonated springs of knowledge from which you are never allowed to drink – because the government has closed your school.

Covid hit the UK like a missile with multiple warheads. The pandemic struck at the elderly and infirm. It pounded the economy. It damaged the natural mental resilience of the population. It blitzed the educational system – and of all the disasters we triggered by locking down the country, this was the one I felt keenest of all.

We helped to protect our health care system – but there were eight million kids in full-time education who paid the price. What made it worse was that it was the most disadvantaged kids, the kids whose family backgrounds made them most in need of full-time educational support, who lost out the most.

In early June 2020 we began to get kids back into school – at the end of the first lockdown – and I found myself in a primary school in Kent, talking to teachers about the effects of the closure; and bear in mind that schools had already been closed for longer than at any time in living memory. We didn't even close schools during the Second World War and now, as we opened up, it was like taking off a bandage and seeing the pallid skin and half-healed wound beneath.

I tried to gee up the pupils, who were sitting double-spaced for disease control.

'Isn't it great to be back in school?' I asked, and they noisily assented. As we walked through the school corridors – full of yellow signs encouraging pupils to maintain social distancing – the head told me that many of them had been very resilient; but a few had taken it hard.

They had missed their friends. They had fallen further behind, she said.

Even by that stage some government figures already showed the disproportionate social impact of lockdown. During the first schools closure, from March to June, the average study period slumped to one or two hours per day – rather than a minimum of five. In the haste and panic of it all, some schools had been better than others in providing some form of online learning, and though we sent out about 1.4 million laptops, it was always likely that the more affluent families would do better than others.

The kids who suffered the most might have a government laptop – but then they might not have a desk, or a kitchen table, or even a quiet space to use it. When it came to the second lockdown, later in the year, we mandated a minimum of five hours a day of online teaching for every pupil. This was, of course, almost impossible to enforce, and the differentials in learning yawned wider and wider.

The overall effect was catastrophic, the very opposite of levelling up – a complete reversal of everything the government was supposed to be doing, and I hated it. What could we do?

Well – the first thing was to get kids back in school after the first lockdown. Education secretary Gavin Williamson and I shifted heaven and earth to do so. By this stage virtually every parent and most teachers wanted kids back in school; but there were objections, and they were coming from the left of the teaching unions, who were complaining about safety – a complaint that Keir Starmer, the new Labour leader, incautiously took up.

I was able to hammer him in the Commons. He would stand up and point out – quite rightly – that lockdown had been hardest for the poorest and greatly damaged their academic chances. He is right, I would tell him.

We both agree that the best place for kids is in school. So why won't he go against his masters in the teaching unions and say what the country needs to hear from him – that schools are safe?

At this point Starmer would do his puzzled/irritable face, like a bullock having a thermometer unexpectedly shoved in its rectum, and I would bash him again and again.

He won't say it, Mr Speaker, he can't say it. A great ox has stood on his tongue, etc., etc.

I think I belaboured this point for several weeks in a row. Starmer failed to stick up for parents, kids and common sense (never mind the scientific evidence, which also said schools were safe), and his mistake blunted his attack on the government – in what might otherwise have been a thoroughly wobbly period.

In fact, our most formidable opponent was not the new Labour leader but a football player called Marcus Rashford. This young Manchester striker had galactic gifts on the pitch, and he ran rings round us on the issue of free school meals. Raised in poverty by a single mum, he had been the beneficiary of free school meals himself, and with the assistance of an expert PR campaign he called for all eligible kids to be fed for free, by the state, even during the summer holidays.

Que? said the Treasury. Free school meals in the holidays? You don't have school meals in the holidays, said the Treasury: that's why they are called school meals. The clue is in the name.

The trouble was that the difference between school time and holidays had been obscured by the pandemic; and soon the government was being made to seem cheese-paring and horrible, snatching food from kids when household finances had been whacked by Covid.

Tory MPs started to get rattled by the Rashford campaign and their offices were daubed with angry slogans. By the end of that disordered year, Rashford was able to get us to back down – and extend free school meals into the holidays – not once, but twice. It was two-nil to Rashford.

Emboldened by his success, he and his supporters later tried to make us go further, so that more and more otherwise well-fed (and often frankly rotund, by European and world standards) British children would get free school meals, until finally I said enough.

The Labour government decided in 1946 that parents should be charged 6d for school meals – except for the quite small minority of families then classed as destitute; and I saw no reason to abandon the fundamental principle that on the whole it is the responsibility of parents, not the state, to feed their young. But when it came to providing education itself, it was a different story.

It has been agreed in this country since 1870, if not earlier, that education is something universal to which every child must have access – and Covid had grievously breached that principle of universality. Some kids had been pretty well home-schooled in lockdown, and many had not.

At this point I should doff my cap to the millions of parents and teachers who coped with what we had done to schools; who sat reading with their kids, or who ploughed on with online lessons. They were – as I said many times over those ghastly months – among the heroes of the pandemic, right up there with the NHS and social care.

I also knew something about home-schooling, which I had enjoyed at the age of about seven. When my parents moved back to the UK from America we first lived in Somerset, and then with my maternal grandparents in London. For some reason we couldn't find a school, so Rachel and I received instruction from my mother for about nine months.

We had exercise books, and we learned all sorts of useful stuff – how to tie our shoelaces and the names of the inert gases of the air, which I have retained ever since. We were lucky. My mother worked mainly from home, being a painter. She had the time and the energy to devise a curriculum.

Plainly, in the Britain of 2020 there were millions of kids who had a very different experience and whose parents felt suddenly abandoned by the educational system. We needed a strategy to help them, and I had long been nursing an idea about how we might do it.

Education, or the release of a child's creative potential, is the single most important part of levelling up. I am an avowed Blairite in that I believe that education, education, education are the first, second and third priorities of government. As soon as we got to power in 2019, I did some basic things to show we were on the side of the teachers – and, having briefly tried to be a teacher myself, I knew how hard it was, the skill and preparation you need to get a child to understand and remember something.

We had immediately put more money into schools, and increased the starting salary of every teacher in the country to £30,000. We put a big wodge – about £200 million – into further education, and especially the improvement of the buildings. I decided on the whole that we would give the teaching world a break from the revolutions of the last decade.

It was totally right to create the academies – largely the brain-child of Andrew Adonis – and I approved thoroughly of the reforms of Michael Gove: the changes to the exams and to the syllabus. But now was the time to let it all bed down a bit; give the teachers the chance to make it work properly.

I wanted to turn things around and look at the problems of education not from the standpoint of teachers, or even parents – but the child. I thought back to my own childhood, and the first time a teacher took even a desultory interest in my own academic performance.

It was at Princess Road primary school – the rough place by the canal with the knee-scabbing playground. I loved it there. I loved the food. ('Give this one a big helping,' the dinner ladies would say. 'He always eats it', and they ladled enough knobbly green liver and mashed potato on to my plate to make Rashford boggle.) I enjoyed the classwork, which was not onerous. We made Roman army uniforms out of bog roll and mosaics out of pasta, and we had a genial and thoroughly relaxed teacher.

He would sit with his feet up on the table, reading the *Daily Telegraph*, and organise our activities effectively but with a light touch. He had a dark beard and I think he was called Mr Fox.

One afternoon we were all going home when he tapped me on the shoulder and asked me to go with him. We went down into the basement, where there was a small swimming pool and a library of approved books.

'Here,' said Mr Fox, handing me about ten of them, including some of the C.S. Lewis Narnia stories. 'Why don't you take these and read them over the holidays.'

To this day I have no idea why he did it – whether he thought that this adenoidal kid needed remedial help, or whether he saw some kind of promise.

Someone was taking a particular interest in my development and it filled me with pride and with confidence, and so of course I read those books, and many more.

What, I wondered, many years later, if we could do that across the whole system – so that every child had the chance of the kind of one-on-one engagement that can make all the difference. What if we could give every kid access to the same sort of leg-up?

In the early 2000s some of my kids had been at an Islington primary school, and I had noticed that a kind of academic arms race was underway. In the afternoons and evenings, my kids' friends would go home and instead of slumping – like ours – in front of the telly they would be tutored. They would get extra coaching in maths, or English, or whatever it happened to be.

It wasn't always the richer parents who went for tutors; it was often the ambitious parents from ethnic minorities, and the results were very impressive. As has been extensively documented, London schools have shown phenomenal improvements, outstripping the performance of schools in the Home Counties. Partly this may be down to such government initiatives as the 'London Challenge', which I had helped support as mayor; but it was also a function of the energy of the aspirant immigrants in London and the widespread use of tutors. So, of course, I wondered about the kids – like our own – who didn't get tutoring, or whose parents couldn't afford it.

Education was starting to resemble a 1970s weightlifting competition – with the Soviet bloc all taking steroids. Was it fair?

It struck me that there were two groups who stood to benefit from some tuition: there were those who were a long way behind and needed to catch up, and then there were those who might be outstanding – but whose talents had never been brought to light because, as that previously quoted poet puts it, knowledge to their eyes her ample page, rich with the spoils of time did ne'er unroll. Chill penury repressed their noble rage, and froze the genial current of the soul.

Now was the time, I reckoned, to unleash that noble rage and unfreeze that genial current. Covid had given us the chance to put my ideas into practice – and to level up: with tutors.

With huge effort, and with some Treasury resistance, we launched a National Tutoring Programme. I won't pretend it was easy, and in the early days I am not sure that the state got value from some of the tutoring companies. It is very difficult, in the UK, to do anything fast and at scale.

Some of the tutors, at least to begin with, may have been more proficient than others. But I was determined that we should not turn our noses up at those who had qualified in another era – elderly Mr Chips characters, who knew so much and had so much to give.

We kept going, doggedly; not just because it was a prime minis-terial priority (though it certainly was) but because tutoring was one of the very few interventions that was shown in the academic literature to be effective and that was supported by all the top educationalists – probably for the very good reason that they used tutors themselves.

Over the years of my premiership, about three million pupils benefited from the programme – and though I believe we should have done more, and had another struggle with the Treasury the following year when I wanted to expand the scheme, it was a crucial part of our effort to recover from the educational damage of Covid.

Labour never really liked it, because socialists are (crazily) against most forms of academic pump-priming and discrimination. But they never had the guts to oppose the tutoring programme – mainly, I suspect, because they were also using tutors for their kids.

It is time to go further, and use the tutoring programme to tackle the biggest problem of all – the problem that lies at the root of the UK's relative lack of productivity. It is absolutely criminal (indeed it is probably a key driver of later criminality) that we allow so many children to leave primary school at eleven without being able to read or write properly, or to do basic mathematics.

As I write, fully a quarter of these children are still failing to meet the expected standard, and the expected standard is not frankly that demanding. Imagine the long-term benefits if we could raise that percentage – from 76 per cent to 90 per cent. Think of the effort and expense we would avoid in trying to provide remedial education later on, when it is so much more difficult to make an impression on the young mind.

Over the years we did a lot to try to level up education. Gavin Williamson was successful, for instance, in getting fee-paying schools such as Eton to open satellite schools; and we launched a big programme to integrate further and higher education – by funding adults to get skills qualifications which they could use as part of a university degree.

I am all in favour of our universities, the best in the world per capita and one of the great economic assets of the country. As shadow spokesman for HE, I had made many a speech about the role of universities in levelling up – how it was our job to widen access and get Jude the Obscure to Christminster. But I had also come to recognise that by the time you get to university entrance it is almost certainly too late – and in trying to widen access, to get kids from deprived backgrounds into Russell Group universities, you have to remedy disadvantages that have occurred much earlier in life.

I was amazed, in going round some of our best FE colleges, to find how many of them were doing remedial mathematics, and how fed up some of the teachers were with doing remedial English.

'I've got to tell you,' one engineering student exploded at me, 'I can't stand *Macbeth*.'

Why are they doing it? Because government requires it, and because UK business has been so chronically dismayed at the illiteracy and innumeracy of the products of the British educational system.

Imagine the boon – all round – if we could fix those problems, not at 16–18 but at 9–11. Ask yourself why the UK economy has been mainlining immigration for so long. It's partly because UK employers fear that indigenous talent is not so skilled in the basic maths and literacy they need.

That's why we need more tutoring. Fix it early. Find the kids who are falling behind, and the kids with under-recognised potential (and I bet they often turn out to be the same), and use tutoring to level up. It works. It breeds confidence in the under-confident.

We should also recognise that whatever merit the intervention may have had in controlling the spread of the virus – and I remain, I am afraid, not entirely certain about that – we underestimated the detriment to young minds of closing schools for weeks on end, and we should at all costs avoid doing it again.

Part Seven

The Fightback Begins

Chapter 40

Build Back Better

The struggle to get things moving

By the end of June 2020, we were finally daring to open up; not just shops, but cafés, restaurants, bingo halls, galleries, hairdressers. The British people slowly poked their noses out of their hibernacula, podgy with lockdown alcohol and carbohydrates.

As I surveyed the economic damage, I was in a state of deep anxiety and frustration. We had seen the biggest fall in sterling for decades, a 20 per cent loss of national output, and the national debt to GDP ratio had gone over 100 per cent for the first time in decades.

I called the July 4 openings 'independence day', with an attempt at cheerfulness; but already Covid had killed about 50,000 people in a few weeks – far more than our country lost in the first year of the Second World War – and people were still dying.

When I gathered a group of economists in the Cabinet Room (mostly on Zoom), their prognostications were awful. This was a turning point, they said, an economic watershed. Ever since the crash of 2008, the UK had been the home of zombie firms, full of underproductive people – and now there was going to be a reckoning. People were ordering stuff online, working from home, and they weren't going to stop.

All those shuttered shops, all that tumbleweed blowing through the city centres – well, I had better get used to it. These jobs were not coming back.

Over the Zoom call one economist predicted that unemployment would go up by four million by the end of the year. My blood ran cold. That would mean a jobless total of Thatcherian proportions; a huge chunk of the working population effectively told that they were surplus to economic requirements, that they had nothing to contribute.

And who had done it to them? The awful thing about the whole Covid catastrophe is that it appears to have been entirely man-made, in all its aspects. It now looks overwhelmingly likely that the mutation was the result of some botched experiment in a Chinese lab.

Some scientists were clearly splicing bits of virus together like the witches in *Macbeth* – eye of bat and toe of frog – and oops, the frisky little critter jumped out of the test tube and started replicating all over the world; and we all fought this anthropogenic disease with an ever-growing panoply of restrictions that were literally medieval in their savagery and their consequences.

In locking down our societies, we showed that we had barely progressed since early modern England, when Shakespeare and his colleagues were repeatedly compelled by law to shutter the Globe Theatre, and when they had rules on human contact – no more than six to a funeral, for instance – that eerily prefigured some of the arcane stuff we came up with, week after week, in the Cabinet Room.

Remember the 'rule of six'? We tied ourselves, and the public, into appalling knots as we tried to micromanage behaviour. If it was OK to meet in gardens, was it OK to go inside in order to visit the loo?

What if you met someone in the corridor? We banned pubs from serving meals – but what was a meal? A Scotch egg? Pork scratchings?

It was my team in Number Ten, against all my previous instincts, that had promulgated these weird restrictions on human contact, like something out of Leviticus. Since government was the culprit, since it was we who had auto-napalmed our own economy like a suicidal Buddhist monk, it did not seem to me that we could shrug and pretend that the recovery was something that could be left to market forces.

Unless we acted, I was being told, the dole queues would stretch round the corners – always assuming that the rules would allow people to queue – and the scarring would be worst in those parts of the country where the disease had proved the hardest to stamp out. As the summer dragged on, it became clear that the north-west, especially Manchester, and parts of the West and East Midlands were having an especially tough time. They had large ethnic minority populations who were often living in multi-generational families in what they call homes of multiple occupation.

In some of these places the blasted bug was so hard to shift that they barely came out of lockdown at all; and it made me weep inwardly – because these were the very places that had come over to us, as Conservatives, in that great election victory of 2019, only a few months before.

These were the places that had listened to my message about hope for post-Brexit Britain, that had taken a chance on us. They were the areas where families were becoming more confident, more aspirational. They were getting fed up with Labour and its endless clientelism and its ingrained hostility to home ownership (a hostility not shared, of course, by senior Labour figures, who almost always turned out to have pricey stuccoed homes in Camden or Islington).

These people didn't want to be told that their neighbourhoods were permanently blighted or disadvantaged. They wanted to hear about opportunity, and how great public services would enable the creation of more affordable good-quality homes for sale, and better private sector jobs. Just after the 2019 election, the *Economist* had published an excellent piece in which it tried to anatomise this phenomenon – the new peri-urban and suburban aspirant middle class that was springing up across the north and the Midlands.

The *Economist* rather snootily called them 'Barratt Man and Woman', after the nice boxy brick homes associated with Barratt the developer – the kind of homes that are mildly satirised by J.K. Rowling in the Harry Potter books, in the sense that they are where you might find the Dursley family, the defiantly prosaic tabloid-reading relatives of the teenage wizard.

The Dursleys live in a boxy brick cul-de-sac called Privet Drive, and though the house is not huge (doesn't Potter live under the stairs?), it is all theirs. I felt instinctively that the *Economist* piece was right; it corresponded to what I was seeing across the country. I knew that these were – or should be – our people, my people, and that if we could hold on to them, and continue to help them with their dreams – above all home ownership – then we would turn that coalition of 2019 into an unstoppable political force and complete the realignment that had begun. This is what I meant by levelling up – extending opportunity across the whole country; and it felt that my campaigning slogan had the merit of going with the grain of what was actually happening.

Now, to my horror, all that appeared to be going backwards – thanks to this goddamn virus. If these economists were right (a big if, I knew), then these areas might again become zones of high unemployment, and another generation would have their hopes blighted, and – aaargh. I stared through the bulletproof windows of my Number Ten flat at the near-empty park, where for months two people hardly dared to settle on the same bench for fear of being broken up by the police.

I thought back to the last time I had been through a big economic crisis: when the world economy had gone into spasm in the banking crash of 2008, described as the worst recession for fifty years. I remembered that in fact London had powered through the crash, and that in spite of all our apprehension we had not seen a serious spike in unemployment; and one of the reasons for the relative robustness of the London economy was that activity was buoyed by gigantic job-rich, state-backed construction projects.

There was Crossrail, the Olympic sites, the Westfield Centre at Shepherd's Bush – all of them involving colossal quantities of steel and concrete and architects and quantity surveyors and project managers and lawyers. So even as the cranes temporarily froze over the City of London, the cement mixers kept trundling around the whole of the greater London area and there was enough investment to keep the flywheel going; and my conclusion was clear.

We had to use this terrifying moment to our advantage – to try to fix the long-term problems of the UK economy, above all our low productivity, by driving on full-pelt with our investments in everything from HS2 to hospitals to broadband, so that with the billions of the state we could then entice the trillions of the market to choose the UK and create the jobs of the future, all over Britain.

We weren't going to retard our programme because of Covid; we were going to accelerate. We were going to double down on levelling up. I was increasingly itchy to explain all this to the public, to try to paint them a picture of the way ahead.

On June 30, 2020, I went to Dudley to make a speech at a further education college. Not all of my team were ecstatic at the idea. Wasn't it a bit early for all this boosterism? they said. The people of Britain had barely stuck their noses out of their burrows. Their whiskers were still trembling with apprehension.

The polls said that 49 per cent of the public now identified themselves as 'anxious' or 'very anxious'. Wouldn't it just cheese people off, they said, if I started raving about our great economic future – when we all knew that Covid was just waiting round the corner with its spiky knuckledusters, ready to whack us in the face a second time.

I considered. There is indeed nothing more irritating than unrelenting optimism. On the other hand, there are some moments so grim, and so uncertain, that people crave a plan – any plan – and it is the job of politicians to sketch the way ahead. There is just no point, in life or in politics, in allowing people to get their heads down, or to become fatalistic or apathetic. Sometimes in City Hall we would be enveloped by a disaster – some terrible poll or some scandal involving a deputy mayor – and you could almost feel the wind going out of people.

On days like this I would walk the corridors shouting, 'Morale pump coming round! Morale pump coming round!' – the idea being that I was carrying some invisible patent morale pump, and if anyone was feeling a bit flat I would offer to insert the nozzle into the appropriate orifice and pump them up again. Nobody ever volunteered, of course, to submit to this fantastical procedure; and I am not sure that I entirely succeeded in cheering people up.

But sometimes leadership is performative. You have to show that you are unbowed by events, and it was in that morale-pumping spirit that I went to Dudley.

I was still looking pretty jaundiced from my illness. My hair was more than usually scarecrowish, mainly because Covid rules still made it hard to get a haircut.

My audience was one of those tiny groups of FE students, apprentice electricians, brickies and plumbers in blue boiler suits – about six of them – and they sat silently as I orated, each properly socially distanced from the other.

I am not sure that they were exactly morale-pumped. But looking back at that speech – you know I was going to say this – I find myself nodding in fervent agreement. I talked about all the things we were doing to unite and level up: the £96 billion rail programme; the upgrading of crucial roads that had been neglected for decades, the A1 or the A303; the broadband roll-out; the schools, hospitals, FE colleges we were either building or rebuilding; the seven low-tax freeports we were inaugurating, making use of new freedoms obtained under Brexit.

We weren't going to be content, I said, with the old lackadaisical pre-Covid rate of construction. I promised that the chancellor, Rishi Sunak, and I were going to apply the cattle prod to the sluggish hindquarters of UK government projects and get things moving. We were going to call it 'Project Speed'.

Why, I asked the boggling apprentices, does UK public procurement take 50 per cent longer than in Germany? Why are UK capital costs between 10 and 20 per cent higher than comparable projects in the rest of Europe?

Why are we so slow in building homes, even by comparison with other highly regulated economies? In 2018 we built 2.25 homes per 1,000 people; in Germany they managed 3.6, in the Netherlands 3.8 and in France 6.8.

At this point I caught their eyes and realised that I might sound as if I were criticising – heaven forfend – the work rate of British builders and electricians. I swerved. It wasn't their fault, I said. It was nothing to do with their natural industriousness. They were being held back by the whole newt-counting, bat-house-building madness of the British planning system; they were being held back by the craven Nimbyism of local government, the land-banking of the developers, and we weren't going to put up with it any more.

I concluded with a peroration in which I invoked the psychic energy and determination with which the nation had come together to fight Covid, the spirit that built the Nightingale hospitals in record time, the spirit that produced all those patent new ventilators, the spirit of Captain Tom bounding around his garden.

We were going to take that spirit, distil, bottle and swig it like the magic potion of Asterix and use it to solve not just the problems of Covid but the immanent and structural problems of the UK economy.

We were going to build back faster, build back greener, build back better – and so was born the Build Back Better slogan that was to be emblazoned on Tory T-shirts for the next two years, and which Joe Biden was to borrow (quite rightly).

I finally came to a quivering halt, almost breathless from my exertions, and luckily someone gave the poor students the cue for a smattering of applause.

Whatever its faults, the speech created the framework for a lot of our post-Covid economic programme. As the year went on, I worked away at the agenda, and by the end of the year I had spliced together the infrastructure programme with the green industrial revolution. By this we would use new green technology (a) to tackle climate change and (b) to give the UK the lead in key strategic sectors of the twenty-first-century economy, from electric vehicles to clean power, so as to create hundreds of thousands of good-quality jobs.

In this Dudley speech I started to pull it all together: the Jet Zero plan for clean aviation, the plan for hydrogen of both green and blue varieties, carbon capture and storage, the development of nuclear power, with small modular reactors, and so on. As a vision for the country it certainly enthused me, and I couldn't understand how anyone could reasonably dissent from my objectives. But, as my team had predicted, the speech got only half a cheer from the media.

For the left-wing papers and the BBC, it didn't go far enough. For all my talk of New Deal economics and the biggest infrastructure programme since Victorian times, they claimed that it wasn't quite Rooseveltian enough in its ambition; but then I suppose that criticism was inevitable from the left.

The more serious challenge was from the Treasury. They had already spent hundreds of billions supporting UK business with the (exceedingly generous) furlough scheme and others; and there was resistance to my plan. I suppose that there may be readers who still wonder why I – supposedly a right-wing Thatcherite – was being so prodigal, so interventionist.

Is this really Tory, you may be asking yourself. Is it CONSERVATIVE? And I say, of course it is.

Whatever you say about Thatcher's vision of Conservatism, she understood that the state must take the lead when it comes to infrastructure. Yes, you could argue that the Channel Tunnel and Canary Wharf were examples of colossal private sector investment; but neither would have been remotely possible without the activism of government – stepping in to bail out the Channel Tunnel, and putting in the Docklands Light Railway and other infrastructure that made Canary Wharf viable.

As for the privatised utilities, they were given extraordinary rights by Margaret Thatcher – not least the right to blight the traffic by perpetually digging up the roads to put in their pipes and cables.

I saw the levelling-up agenda as a continuation of that Thatcherite agenda – a Tory marriage between a pro-business activist government and a confident private sector. As I had been saying in speeches for the last twenty years, the two went together: you needed the state to put in the public goods and create the conditions – the bedrock, the platform, the flowerbed, pick your metaphor – for business to thrive; and you needed profit-hungry capitalists to grow the economy and create the tax yield to invest in great public services.

It's a virtuous circle. It frustrated me that young people didn't seem to grasp the circularity, the absolute need for capitalism; and it seemed to me that one of the main reasons was that – unlike my generation – they didn't actually have access to capital themselves, because they found it so much harder to get homes, to get on the property ladder.

That was why house-building, kick-starting the developers, has always been such a key part of my programme and all successful Conservative governments, from Macmillan to Thatcher. The cost of housing, the difficulties young people faced in getting a mortgage or finding a deposit – these should be the key priorities of a Tory government, and that was why we needed to build build build.

Our planning bill had been warmly welcomed by the housing sector; now we had to get on with it.

I disagreed with the Treasury about the scale of ambition required by the position in which our country found itself, and I disagreed about our fiscal scope for intervention. In fact, I reckoned that if we could stimulate a new culture of confidence and investment, we would see not only more growth – which had been almost wholly lacking for the last decade or more – but also more tax revenues, and we would therefore be in a position actually to cut tax rates as well.

In the next few months I was fortified by my regular conversations with John Redwood, the MP for Wokingham and a friend for many years. It has long been fashionable for wettish Tories to roll their eyes at Redwood. They used to call him the 'Vulcan', as if he were some space-brain from another planet. They acknowledge his intellectual brilliance (he was a Prize Fellow at All Souls), but suggest that he is somehow lacking in common sense.

They are completely wrong. Before I became mayor in 2008, he used to drift into my room in Parliament, in Norman Shaw North, and we would talk economics.

You can take it from me: he forecast the financial crash perfectly, and uniquely.

The Queen famously asked, 'Why did no one see this coming?', and she was right that almost everyone missed it – except Redders. So I took him seriously, and I instinctively agreed with him, both about Brexit and about why the Treasury was wrong about Britain.

GET BREXIT DONE

Above: Bulldozing to victory with a three-word plan, December 10, 2019

Right: A kiss from Lucky the dog

Below: Cry Haddock! Marvelling at the marine wealth now back under UK control, December 9, 2019

Cornering some
Tory voters in a pub,
June 2019

Undignified exit poll
ecstasy, December 12, 2019

Asking HM the Queen for permission to form a government, July 24, 2019

Left: Jump. Kinetic energy at the Africa Investment Summit, North Greenwich, January 20, 2020

Below: With 109 new MPs – some from places that had never been Tory in 100 years, December 16, 2019

Blue passports. On Brexit day, returning from Sunderland regional cabinet, January 31, 2020

Left: With Irish Taoiseach Leo Varadkar and Italian PM Mario Draghi at the European Council, October 2019

Right: Invisibly treading on the toes of Jean-Claude Juncker

Below: I told you it was oven ready! With David Frost and the withdrawal agreement, January 24, 2020

Addressing the nation to ask people to stay at home, March 23, 2020

Covid press conference, April 30, 2020

STAY HOME ▸ PROTECT THE NHS ▸ SAVE LIVES

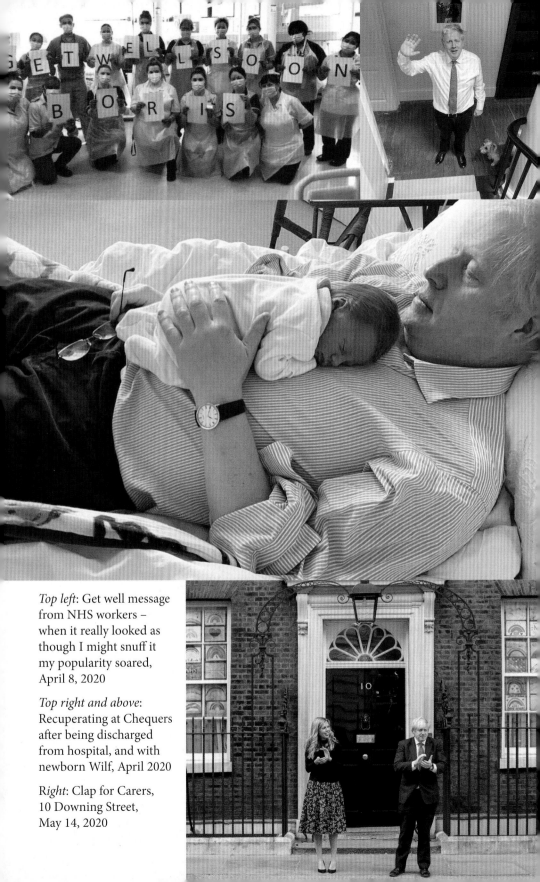

Top left: Get well message from NHS workers – when it really looked as though I might snuff it my popularity soared, April 8, 2020

Top right and above: Recuperating at Chequers after being discharged from hospital, and with newborn Wilf, April 2020

Right: Clap for Carers, 10 Downing Street, May 14, 2020

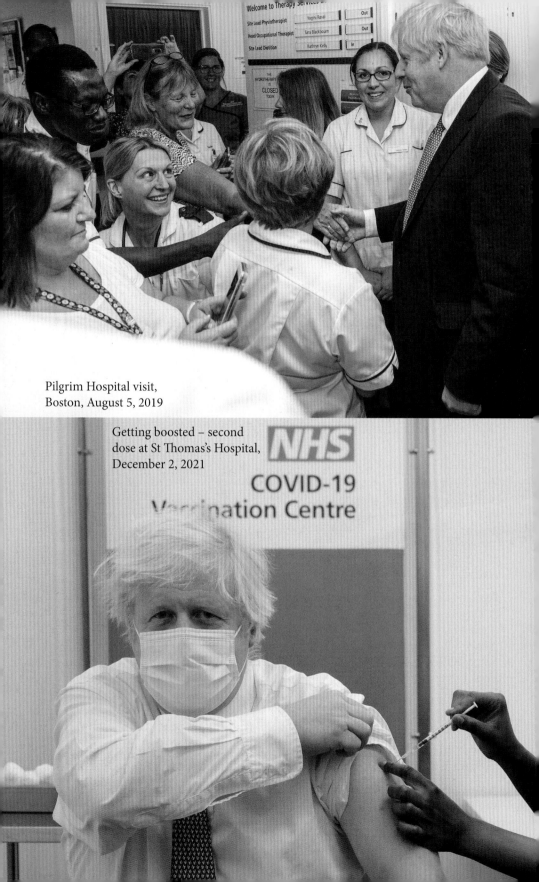

Pilgrim Hospital visit,
Boston, August 5, 2019

Getting boosted – second
dose at St Thomas's Hospital,
December 2, 2021

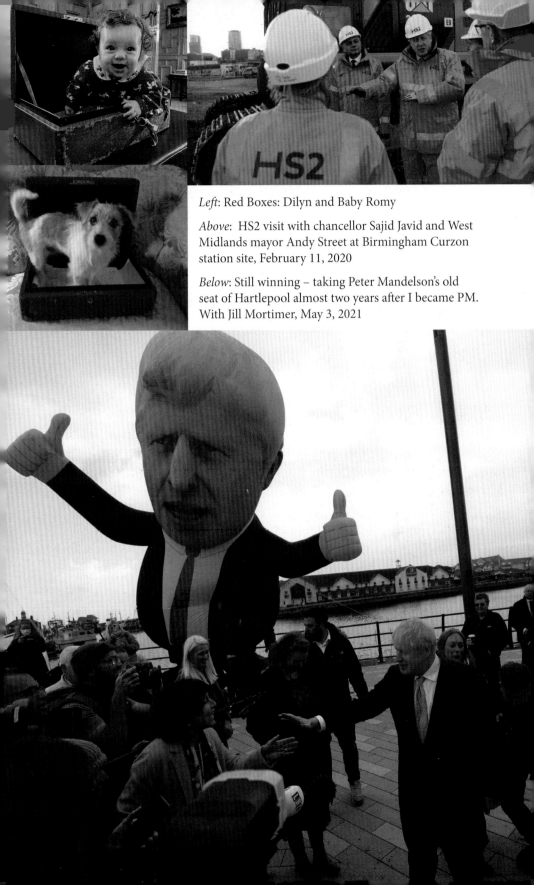

Left: Red Boxes: Dilyn and Baby Romy

Above: HS2 visit with chancellor Sajid Javid and West Midlands mayor Andy Street at Birmingham Curzon station site, February 11, 2020

Below: Still winning – taking Peter Mandelson's old seat of Hartlepool almost two years after I became PM. With Jill Mortimer, May 3, 2021

On the beach with Angela Merkel,
Carbis Bay, June 11, 2021

With David Attenborough at the
launch event for COP 26 in
the Science Museum,
February 4, 2020

Greeting the Bidens on arrival at the G7 Cornwall summit, Carbis Bay, on June 10, 2021

Below: Emmanuel Macron's visit to Downing Street, June 18, 2020

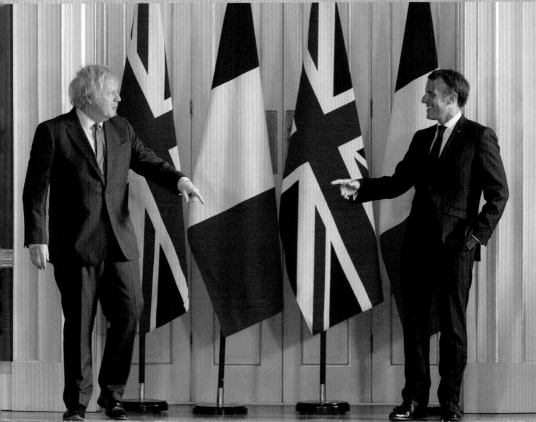

Ukrainian troops training in Yorkshire

With Zelensky in Kyiv on his first walkabout since the Russian attack, April 9, 2022

At Trump National Golf Club, Sterling, Virginia, May 25, 2023

With Putin, during the Berlin Conference on Libya, January 19, 2020

Top gun visit to RAF Coningsby, just after flying a typhoon, July 14, 2022

With Olaf Scholz who overcame his hesitations and backed Ukraine, June 26, 2022

Above: At Chequers with Carrie, Wilf and Romy, and at Downing Street, July 2022

Opposite top: Helicopter at Chequers with Wilf and Dilyn

Opposite middle: Christmas, 10 Downing Street

Opposite bottom: Great escape – with Carrie on my bike and camping in the wood behind Chequers where Churchill practised with his Tommy gun

Below: Wedding, May 30, 2021. Wilf and Romy in Downing Street flat

Trying to console Ann Sindall after my resignation, with Sarah Dines, Simone Finn, James Duddridge, Jacob Rees-Mogg, Alister Jack, Nadine Dorries, and Carrie in No. 10 lobby, July 7, 2022

Departing

He sent me email after email, warning that they were trying to box me in, trying to go back to austerity – the very policies that voters had rejected in 2016. We had the room for manoeuvre, he said; we had the space to cut taxes – and really unleash the animal spirits of the wealth creators. So I pinged his comments on to Rishi, who at that stage I took for a Lawsonian tax cutter by instinct. Come on, I would say: when are we going to do this?

After all, I said, there was plenty of public spending we could also cut. Lockdown had revealed an astonishing fact – that whole Whitehall departments seemed perfectly able to function with nobody in the office at all. Did we really need all these people?

Time and again I would remind the cabinet of the lesson I had learned in City Hall from sitting at the feet of Eddie Lister, the tax-slashing former leader of Wandsworth Council and my deputy mayor. In our eight years in power, we massively out-built Labour; we put in colossal quantities of infrastructure – but we also sacked thousands and thousands of public sector employees, all of whom immediately went on to get more productive jobs in the private sector.

We sold off dozens and dozens of TfL buildings and we culled about forty quangos – zap. We massively reduced headcount across London (and cut our share of the council tax by 20 per cent).

'Come on!' I exhorted the assembled secretaries of state, at least twice. 'It's time to slaughter the sacred cows.'

The second time I said it Rishi came up to me afterwards.

'That expression you keep using – slaughtering the sacred cows …' he said, slightly diffidently.

'Yes,' I said enthusiastically. 'I want a complete abattoir, a charnel-house, a total bovicide! It's the only way to do it,' I said.

'Yes, I know,' he said, 'but just remember that not everyone would choose to use that language.'

I gawped at him – and then I twigged. He was speaking to me as a convinced and practising Hindu, for whom cows are genuinely holy and their slaughter abhorrent.

I am not sure I have since then entirely purged the metaphor from my speech, since it must go back at least to Roman Britain. But you know what – I rather respected Rishi for sticking up for his religion, and for having the courage to raise it with me.

This was the stage when, of course, I both liked and trusted my chancellor, and warmed a great deal to him and his wife Akshata. If you had then put a gun to my head and asked who I wanted to be my successor, and carry on the work of levelling up – long after we had won again in 2024 – I probably would have said Rishi Sunak.

But for now, I just wanted him to cut Whitehall headcount, as we had done in London, cut pointless public spending – and cut taxes; and he exuded such charm and earnestness that I had the firm impression that he would, but perhaps not just yet.

We did in the end come up with a plan to trim the bureaucracy by 66,000, but I wish we had gone faster.

Chapter 41

Fighting the Tide

The grim inevitability of the second lockdown

I squinted at the shoreline and heaved harder on the plastic paddle. It was getting on for 5 p.m. The wind was freshening, and the swell was starting to rise. I was on the Kyle of Lochalsh, on the north-west coast of Scotland, in mid-August 2020.

There was no longer any doubt: the little whitewashed cottage on the shore was shrinking, the land was getting more distant, and things were going wronger by the minute.

By the end of July, Carrie and I had been desperate to get out of the Number Ten flat, now also occupied by a captivating baby Wilfred; and though I was getting my strength back after Covid, I was keen for a proper break, if only for a few days. But where?

Our first holiday, at New Year, had been to the Caribbean island of Mustique, playground to the super-rich, and though it was great fun our destination had inspired such slavering media comment that I re-baptised it the island of Mistake.

We needed somewhere simple but lovely, above all somewhere in Britain. I had blissful childhood memories of Skye, of swimming and kayaking and gathering mussels, and though Carrie was vaguely sceptical I scoured the web and found what looked like a total dream: a tiny, lonely cottage on a grassy clifftop overlooking the sea.

I goggled at it on my laptop. Even the name seemed lovely – Applecross. Ah, I said to myself in the hard weeks leading up to our holiday: Applecross. We'll get some peace there, put our feet up, look out at the sea. I could do some drawing. It'll be great, I told Carrie; and then, almost as soon as we arrived in Applecross, a huge row blew up back in London about the system for grading kids at GCSE and A-level when they hadn't been able to take exams in person.

Rather than trusting the assessment of the teachers – who we thought would be too generous to the pupils – we had used a rigid mathematical algorithm to distribute the marks, based on the school's previous performance. Many kids had clearly been unfairly treated, and for parents, exhausted by lockdown, it was all too much.

They were all over the media, shaking with rage, demanding the head of Gavin Williamson, the education secretary (who was, on this occasion, more or less innocent). People were starting to ask where I was, and why I was not returning to London.

There was no mobile signal in the cottage, so I would crouch by the landline under the stairs, trying to sort it out. As the exam crisis deepened, the media hunted us down and took photos of Applecross, and eventually we were forced to flee back to London.

Of course it was frustrating, after all those months of effort, to have our principal annual holiday truncated to three and a half days – but there was at least one reason why I was not devastated. There is a detail about Scotland in August that we never seem to talk about, a phenomenon that nature seems to wipe from our memories – and that is the midges.

What I could not see on those promotional computer images of Applecross is that somehow its marshy turf breeds huge grey clouds of insects. They bang on the windows at dusk, some of them seemingly the size of daddy long legs, and when you go outside you discover that there is no inch of flesh they cannot bite.

One night we tried moving to a tent we erected on the clifftop and lighting a fire. It was no better: they still descended in lung-fuls, and the media later took great delight in pointing out that both tent and fire were on the land of a farmer who, not unreason-ably, objected to our presence.

So that is why I now came to be on the open water in an inflat-able kayak from Argos: I was trying to get away from the goddamn midges – only to find a more serious problem. No matter how hard I gouged that paddle in the brine, I was going in the wrong direction. I was being tugged by wind and wave into the fast-flow-ing channel between the mainland and the Isle of Skye, and thence to the Atlantic, where the rolling black gulfs of ocean were waiting to wash me down.

It looked as though our short summer holiday was about to climax in disaster, and though my sinews were now popping with effort there seemed to be nothing I could do. This blue plastic Argos inflatable kayak was in theory a two-seater; but after briefly subjecting herself to my nautical expertise, Carrie had decided to sit this one out on shore.

The result was that I was weighing down the stern, while the bow of this fatal barque had reared up and was taking the wind like a sail – and soon I was scooting in the wrong direction, away from safety, away from the shore, away from the detectives that I had last seen a few minutes ago, stick-like figures waving despond-ently at my departing form.

My breath came in rasps as I asked myself what would happen. Would I be able to wrestle the kayak back on course – or would nature prove too strong? The events of the next twenty or thirty minutes were to be an excellent lesson in human folly, and a warn-ing – if only I had spotted it – about the struggle I was to wage that autumn with the ineluctable waves of disease.

As with the plastic kayak, there were moments when we believed that we were in command, that we had a way of beating the elements and steering things in the right direction. As with the kayak, we were almost right; but in the end we were wrong.

When we lifted the lockdown in July, we always knew that Covid would return in the autumn, as the weather turned cooler and people started to meet again indoors. So it did. On Saturday September 5, 2020, we had 2,576 new cases, the highest daily total since April. This time, however, I felt that we had some advantages. We had worked out that the steroids were good at stopping a violent immune reaction (such as the one I suffered). We had learned to avoid intubating people, unless it was absolutely necessary.

We were by now much, much better at tracking the virus. The UK had begun the pandemic with a very weak diagnostic capacity, and our initial efforts at testing and tracing had suffered badly by comparison with Germany. Now, though, we had caught up – more than caught up. The government labs at Porton Down had approved a variety of lateral flow tests, of a kind that most veterans of the pandemic will know all too well (you probably have a shelf at home bulging with blue boxes of things to stick up your nose or down your throat); and testing was now so widespread and the results were delivered so fast that my morning dashboard meetings were becoming more and more accurate in pinpointing the spread of the disease.

There were some places where it had never really gone away, but there were also places where Covid was very much in abeyance, if not quite extinct. In the West Country or rural Lincolnshire, for instance, the 'R' – or rate of reproduction – was close to zero. (Remember: if the R is higher than one, then the disease is doubling; if it is lower than one then it is halving.)

Everyone could see that Covid was gaining ground in some places – the West Midlands, Manchester, Leicester, etc. But they could also see that it was a very asymmetrical phenomenon; and so naturally people started to object to a one-size-fits-all solution.

Why should they close pubs in rural Devon and Cornwall, they said, in the hope of stopping the spread of Covid in the terraced streets of Old Trafford? It seemed to me that on the face of it they had a point – and so was born a fatal but ostensibly reasonable notion: that the country could be divided up into zones of infection, or tiers, according to the state of the pandemic in each zone.

In Tier 1 areas – on so-called medium alert – the pubs and restaurants remained open until 10 p.m., but the 'rule of six' applied, which meant that you could not socialise with more than six people either indoors or outdoors. In Tier 2, or areas of high alert, there were tighter restrictions, so that you could not socialise indoors at all, even with fewer than six people.

In Tier 3, where people were supposed to be on very high alert, you could not socialise indoors or outdoors at all – unless you were in a public park, in which case the gathering could be up to six people.

Did you get all that? Or shall I repeat it?

There were yards of such rules. Looking back on these restrictions, I can hardly believe the gall, the audacity of the government in trying to micromanage humanity. We told people that they could meet in the grounds of a National Trust castle (up to six) but not in a fairground or funfair.

We told them that they could have childcare indoors in Tier 1, but not in Tier 2, where they had to use childcare outdoors. We told them they could have a drink in a pub in Tier 2, but not in Tier 3, where alcohol was only allowed if it was part of a main meal, or room service. I think of those long discussions around the green baize of the cabinet table, well into the night, as brilliant young officials like Henry Cook came up with ever more elaborate schemes for modulating human behaviour – and I want to scream.

It's bonkers, really. It's like those weird bans in Leviticus on the types of four-legged animal you can eat, or the ban on trimming your sideburns. Actually, it was more bonkers than Leviticus – because unlike Yahweh or Moses, we kept changing the rules; indeed the whole point of the tiering system was that we would keep changing the rules.

The Covid-19 Taskforce under James Bowler (a very nice and able civil servant) would sit in their room in the Cabinet Office, night after night, somehow believing that they could magically orchestrate the nation – Slough into Tier 2, Windsor into Tier 1 – without any regard for the reality of people's lives, let alone for the virus.

How could I, Johnson, have conceivably authorised these super-complicated codes of behaviour? How could we ever have thought the tiering system was realistic?

The answer is partly that we hoped it would work. We thought we could play whack-a-mole. If Covid flared up in one area, then we would apply more restrictive measures until the R went down again in that area – and then we would open up.

So it would go on for months, we imagined, as we symphonically opened and closed the zones of the UK, like cuckoo clocks or sea anemones, until we had got through the second wave without the horror of a full national lockdown, closing the schools and sending the economy again into freefall.

The sheer complexity of the rules was a function of our attempt to differentiate between the tiers, and to apply (or so we fondly imagined) judiciously varied degrees of pressure on the Covid-19 virus. The real question, I suppose, is why on earth the public so avidly craved these rules – and why they were so willing to have their doings circumscribed in such rabbinical detail.

The answer is that for many months the rules were partly sensible, since it was obviously true that you could in general restrict transmission by restricting human contact; but in their rococo complexity they were also like a kind of religion – detailed rituals you just obeyed, Leviticus-like, in the hope of salvation – because science was so slow to help us.

People were frightened; they wanted something to believe in, something officially sanctioned that they could do to stop the spread of the disease; rules they could collectively obey. Like the children of Israel in the desert, we turned to highly regimented systems of behaviour, as part of our response to the horror and mystery of invisibly transmitted infection.

Of course we all knew that each individual rule or guideline might sound odd; but that wasn't the point. The point was the collective and public adherence to the new Mosaic law – because in the face of the wrath of the Almighty, that was all we had.

And we in officialdom were, of course, appalled by our own scientific impotence, and we also wanted to believe in the rules. They were the best we could provide, because as yet we had no cure. All summer long I had been hoping that we might find another way out, beyond the non-pharmaceutical interventions (the rules on lockdown and social distancing, etc.).

I was starting to think about the possibility of mass testing – on a scale that might make lockdown unnecessary. It was Dido Harding, a workaholic NHS executive, who led the expansion of our diagnostic capacity. Labour liked to beat her up (for the crime of being married to a Tory MP) and she had a difficult start. But the numbers began to climb. By October 16, 2020 she was testing 300,000 people per day – more than any other European country.

Then she got up to half a million, then a million. Together with Matt Hancock, the health secretary and one of nature's optimists, we conceived a 'moonshot' – a massive scheme of 'test-and-release'.

We tried it first in Liverpool, with the help of the mayor, Steve Rotheram, and the initial results seemed promising. The idea was that you would test yourself in the morning and if you were negative you could go to work as normal; and if all your colleagues did the same, then your workplace would be effectively Covid-free; and so maybe, just maybe, the UK economy could test its way out of the problem, and we could recapture some semblance of normality.

As the shades lengthened and the autumn drew in, I became deeply preoccupied with Christmas. As a former mayor of London, I knew how utterly crucial it was to the retail, hospitality and entertainment sectors to have a good November and December. For some businesses the Christmas season represents a huge proportion of their annual takings, and I dared to hope: could we – by a combination of tiering and testing – deliver something like a normal Christmas?

Well, perhaps, if we had been lucky. But Mother Nature was too fast for us, too fertile in her powers of invention.

The trouble with tiering was that it was intrinsically invidious: that is to say, the process of dividing the country inevitably involved a lot of arbitrary geographical decisions. One local authority area might be placed in Tier 3, and another in Tier 2, so that there could be different rules for pubs in the same rural area, even though the R was uniformly low.

MPs began to berate us for placing their area, unfairly as they saw it, in lockdown. Such is the natural paranoia of politicians that some of them – I am told – even started to believe that the whips were punishing them for some nameless misdeed. Resentments festered. People felt that by imposing sterner measures on their neighbourhoods, we were making some sort of statement about their hygiene, their discipline, their very morality. They started to feel that they were being judged adversely by comparison with their neighbours over the Covid border.

As a lifelong student of British politics and society, I recognised this as a very powerful emotion, and thought that it would perhaps galvanise people to keep up with the Joneses and stamp out Covid in their patch. Well, I was wrong. People didn't feel a healthy rivalry; they just felt outraged, and they ranted, understandably, about the social and economic cost of the restrictions.

Mayors like Andy Burnham of Manchester would demand compensation for the suffering of local businesses; and as soon as we had agreed a package with him, another town or city would demand the same, or more. Eddie Lister did an outstanding job of handling these negotiations – there is no one to touch him on a problem like this – but the result was that tiering was not simple.

It was not a question of opening or closing an area like an organ stop. It was laborious, and therefore slow; and in spite of our arduous and expensive efforts at whack-a-mole, the disease started to rise, more or less everywhere. By late October, the R was rising, even in Devon and Cornwall.

'RRRR,' I would say in the morning meetings. 'I see the RRR is strong in the West Country'; and if you ask why we sometimes said stupid, inane, pointless things – in an attempt at humour – it was because that is what British people generally do when things are unutterably grim.

As October wore on, I could tell that we were heading for another full national lockdown: the only question was when. For several days we debated the notion of a 'circuit-breaker', whereby you could lock down savagely for a couple of weeks, send the R back down below one, and then open up again. Some of the scientists had changed their tune since the first lockdown in March and were now saying that it was better to 'go hard and go early'. That was the logic of the circuit-breaker. I was unsure.

I felt that the warnings I had first been given about lockdowns were still valid – that if you went at the wrong time, you might end up doing them again and again; and in the general chaos you would lose public support and compliance. I hoped against hope that mass testing would rescue us, or that the tiering would come good, so that we could avoid locking down again – but by October 28 we had run out of road.

James Bowler came to see me, to say the tiers had ended in tears and that the disease was now rising quite quickly across the whole country – even in Liverpool, where the test-and-release scheme hadn't been enough to stop the virus.

Once again I was faced with two appalling choices. I could baseball-bat the UK economy in the chops, just as it was getting back on its feet, with untold damage to life chances; or else I could trust to the tiers (and there are some who still believe they could have worked, with a bit more time), and risk the lives of many, many thousands of people.

It was utterly agonising – and it was so lonely. Many of my natural political allies were by now actively hostile to lockdown; the cabinet was becoming more and more divided and agnostic.

There was absolutely no one else who could take the decision. But it was clear to me then – and it still is – that my fundamental duty as prime minister was to protect the lives of British citizens, and that whatever the many evils of Covid, saving life comes first.

In the words of Cicero, *salus populi suprema lex*. So on November 5 we went back into lockdown, though we kept schools and universities open. It was miserable, but by the end of the month it seemed to be working, and Matt Hancock reported that the R was falling across the board.

On December 2, we opened up again – in time, I hoped, for Christmas – and then, disaster.

For several days we had noticed a blob around Dartford in Kent, where the virus seemed to be spreading unnaturally fast. By the middle of December we had the dreadful news from the lab: that this wasn't some problem engendered by riotous Kentish nightclubs. This was a new variant, about 30 or 40 per cent more contagious than the original strain, and it was a catastrophe for the entire human race.

It was called the delta variant, and in other countries it was, I am afraid, called the English or Kent variant – though frankly, given where it pitched up on our shores, I suspect that you might just as well have called it the Belgian or Dutch variant.

Delta was to go on to kill millions of people around the world; and in almost every country, not just Britain, it greatly intensified the second spike. By December 18, it was obvious that we were beaten, and that my dreams were dashed.

London was going into full lockdown – which we called 'Tier 4' – at what should have been the happiest time of the year. I had told the British people that we would shift heaven and earth to give them some kind of Christmas – and now I had snatched it away.

It was way back in May that I had first announced – vainly, as it turned out – that we 'were turning the tide'. Month in, month out, I had thanked and congratulated the British people and assured them that by their heroic patience and forbearance they would rout the armies of disease and return to doing the things they loved.

Here I was, this supposed libertarian and lover of freedom – the first prime minister in history to cancel Christmas. Some people told me, sardonically, that they were actually perfectly happy about the decision – since it meant they didn't have to see their in-laws or other relatives.

I didn't feel that way at all. I felt deeply and unexpectedly emotional. I think I knew subconsciously that this was my mother's last Christmas, and we had a plan to spend it with her in the Number Ten flat. She had suffered a nasty scare at the very outset of the pandemic – though not from Covid – and I had hardly seen her in the last year; and like every other family in the country, I felt the separation.

I can see now that it was probably always unrealistic to think we could get things open for Christmas. Almost everywhere else sustained a big second wave – and as with the influenza pandemic of 1918–19, the second wave was bigger and more deadly than the first.

I should have learned the lesson of the kayak, back in August – that nature is sometimes irresistible.

As the wind got stronger and pulled me further from shore, I had to choose between two bad options. I could either get swept out to sea and drown, or at least trigger a ludicrous coastguard helicopter rescue; or else I could ship the oar, abandon the kayak and swim for it, while the coast was still just about within swimming distance.

So that, I am afraid, is what I did. I had a life jacket. The water wasn't too cold. It was only about six hundred yards from shore, and when I was quite close one of the detectives – a rugged, kite-surfing man called Mick – heroically stripped off and struck out in my general direction, though I wish to stress that at no stage did I need his assistance.

As for the kayak, it was instantly and completely lost to view, and I suppose it drifted on like the *Mary Celeste*, and who knows where it went, beyond the stormy Hebrides, perhaps, to wash up enigmatically in some Norwegian fjord. It actually belonged to Ollie, one of the Number Ten front of house staff, and though it took some time to find him a replacement, he never complained.

It is a testament to the amazing discretion of the detectives that the story of my aquatic humiliation never got out. Perhaps I should have stuck it out. Perhaps I could have paddled on for five hours, in the dark, until I made landfall on Skye.

Perhaps – by the same token – we could have trusted to tiering and avoided a second lockdown. Well, perhaps.

But sometimes you have to respect the power of the natural world – and cut your losses. As we headed into that bleak, atomised Christmas, there was one cold comfort: the Covid crisis was so bad, and the economic damage so huge, that it almost completely eclipsed the general anxiety about Brexit.

It remained the case that we had officially left the EU on January 31, 2020. We had got Brexit done. But after a year of negotiations, we still did not have a new trading relationship with the European continent. We still did not have the thoroughgoing free-trade deal I had promised, and it was getting very tense.

At the end of the month, December 31, the transition period would be over; the guillotine would come down – and the UK would be completely out, trading with the EU on World Trade Organization terms, like any other country: an outcome still referred to apocalyptically as a 'no deal' Brexit.

There had been a time when people had raved about the horror of this outcome: the potential cost to business, the damage to confidence, the barriers to freedom of movement of people and goods.

Well, all those warnings were always exaggerated – and the imagined disruption of Brexit had now been blown away by the very real nightmare of Covid. Far from making us weaker in the negotiations, I decided that the pandemic had made us stronger.

The only way to get a good deal was to be ready for no-deal, and Covid had showed that we could sustain immense logistical disruption and survive. It was time to play hardball.

So at the end of 2020 we were engaged in a life-and-death combat with Covid, and a brutal final negotiation with the EU. Just at the moment I needed everyone to stick together and keep their nerve, we had, I am afraid, an outbreak of what I can only call handbags – and I had to say goodbye to two of my longest-standing advisers.

Chapter 42

Dilyn Sniffs a Mole

Some overdue exits from Number Ten

It was what a previous prime minister would have called 'a little local difficulty'; and whatever the dispute was actually about, it now seems irresponsibly trivial. Consider what we were up against. We had Covid raging around us, and people still dying in large numbers – and sometimes in ghastly and lonely circumstances.

We faced the real possibility of tariffs and quotas and other barriers to trade with the EU; and on the evening of Friday November 13, I had to ask two of my most trusted advisers – Dom Cummings and Lee Cain – to leave the building forthwith.

It had finally become clear to me that they were systematically trying to undermine both me and the government, and, I now had no doubt, had been doing so for about a year.

Almost as soon as we got into Number Ten, I became aware of a weird and slowly gathering phenomenon. Odd little briefings would appear in the papers, snippets of information or gossip which – even if wrong or half-true – looked overwhelmingly likely to have come from someone in the building. It began with snide stuff about Carrie, but gradually widened.

In March there was what seemed to be a well-sourced attack on the morals and habits of Dilyn the dog – a doubtless irritating hound if you don't like dogs. He was guilty of sometimes charging into the Cabinet Room and running over the table, or sniffing away at senior advisers, including Cummings.

Perhaps, I grant you, he yapped a bit in the garden. But he is a very sweet dog – never bitten me once – and loyal to his core (perhaps that was his crime); and he certainly didn't deserve the off-the-record take-down he got one morning in *The Times*, and which was loudly played up by the *Today* programme, BBC, Sky News etc.

I discovered to my amazement that Cummings, my senior adviser, and Cain, the media spokesman, had actually been to see the editorial staff of *The Times* the previous day.

Hmmm, I thought. Fishy.

So that morning I asked Cummings directly – in front of the entire private office – as he sat at his desk.

'Dom,' I said, 'I don't suppose you were responsible for that stuff on Dilyn in this morning's *Times*?'

There was a pregnant pause. Cummings' jaw clenched.

'No,' he said, loudly and clearly.

Funny, I thought; it must be a coincidence – and because I of course believed him, and because we had about a billion more important things to do, and because it was just so childish, I let it slide.

By the summer of 2020, these briefers had got bolder, and I found that I was also being lightly peppered with anonymous attacks. One weekend the *Sunday Times* was full of behind-the-hand whisperings about my alleged forgetfulness, my habit of having a nap in the afternoons on the office sofa (true, for a few weeks after Covid; but also true of many great men and women), and when I read that the serious management of government was being left to others such as Rishi Sunak – which wasn't true – I started to have my suspicions about the possible origins of this nonsense.

These suspicions seemed to be all but confirmed on August 25 when a genial fox-hunting baronet called Sir Humphry Wakefield told a random visitor to his home – Chillingham Castle in Northumberland – that I was too knackered to do the job and would be stepping down in six months.

'If you put a horse back to work when it is injured, it will never recover,' Sir Humph is alleged to have said to the visitor, who then reported his comments to *Tatler* magazine. I don't blame the baronet at all, because he is a good and kind man, and he was surely only repeating what he thought he had been told, on good authority, by his son-in-law, viz. my adviser Dom Cummings.

Again, I taxed Cummings with this, and though he denied it fiercely, I should have realised then that his denials were false. We all know that if you do a big job, of any kind, there are always people around you who may be ready to put a stealthy boot in, given the chance; but I had never seen anything quite like this, certainly not in City Hall.

About a year after leaving Number Ten, Cummings gave an interview to the BBC in which he said that he first started conspiring with others, presumably Lee Cain, to get rid of me in January 2020 – only a few weeks after we had won a record general election victory. I mean – WTF?

You might have thought that the honourable thing to do would have been to resign, if that was how he really felt.

What was it all about? What was the point of surreptitiously trying to rubbish the government you are meant to be serving?

Was it some ancient or imaginary grudge that went back to the days of my *Spectator* editorship, when Cummings was briefly running our website?

Who knows? I fear we may be at risk, as S.T. Coleridge said of Iago, of the motive-hunting of motiveless malignity. Whatever the origins of the resentment against me, or Dilyn, I think – looking back – I may have made things worse by my handling of the Barnard Castle affair.

Back in early May, when the world was in lockdown, Cummings and his wife and child had been spotted on what appeared to be a day out at a nature spot near Barnard Castle in County Durham. Whoever had seen them was not a well-wisher, because the story had become the subject of a big *Guardian* investigation – and the allegation was that he was breaking lockdown rules.

The story broke on a Saturday night, in the *Observer*, so I rang Dom and he agreed to come in the following day to explain. We sat in the Downing Street flat, with Lee and another adviser called Dougie Smith, and Dom told us what he had been up to.

His story was so odd, and so complicated, that I decided it must be true. He had suffered badly from Covid and found afterwards, as I had, that his eyes seemed to be playing up. He was going to drive back to London from County Durham the following day, and he was worried that his eyes might fail on the motorway – so he decided to go on a drive to test them, and that was why he made the thirty-mile round trip to Barnard Castle.

He and Mary just happened to be out of the car, at the nature spot, because their child needed a break – and that was the moment, unfortunately, when they were spotted by the Guardianista.

I know, I know: it sounds pretty thin, put like that – but at the time I really believed it. I believed the bit about testing the eyes because I knew that he was devoted to his family, and I could imagine that he did not want to risk their safety. So, having been initially puzzled, I became indignant on his behalf.

In fact, I had a blazing row, over the phone, with my old friend and colleague Will Walden from City Hall. 'You have got to sack him, you have got to sack him,' shouted Will.

'Rubbish!' I shouted back. 'The whole thing is a put-up job. It's just a load of lefty journalists who want payback for Brexit.'

And so that Sunday afternoon I went out to do the regular Covid press conference – and threw myself bodily in front of Cummings and took an absolute hail of bullets from the media, like Kevin Costner protecting Whitney Houston in *The Bodyguard*.

What Cummings had done, I said, was reasonable, and responsible, and above all it was within the law. If I thought that would settle the matter, I was wrong.

The MPs were freaking out; their constituents were furious. Why should they obey lockdown rules, they demanded, when top people in Number Ten were apparently going on day trips to look at the countryside? The whole thing was becoming very, very poisonous.

Damn it, I thought: they can hear it from Cummings himself – and I was so convinced of his innocence, and so keen to knock it all on the head, that the following day we organised a press briefing in the Number Ten garden, for Cummings to explain. I am afraid it was not a success.

I wouldn't say that Dom was in any way wrong-footed, or caught out. He stuck to his story. But somehow his demeanour was so truculent that he failed to capture much sympathy, and as the press conference wore on the whole thing just sounded thinner and thinner.

We got through it, just about. A Scottish Tory MP resigned from his position, but the Durham Constabulary found that Cummings had broken no laws – confirming my view of what had happened; and gradually the story died away.

But it was bad for the government – we took our first big knock in the polls; and it can't have been much fun for Dom.

So I suspect, looking back, that he didn't thank me for trying heroically to defend him, as I had. He blamed me for the press conference – for pushing him out there, as he saw it, to become the object of public anger and ridicule.

Looking back, I now reckon the so-called 'Partygate' affair – the allegations of rule-breaking in government that he and Lee Cain were to orchestrate, much later – was a kind of payback for the indignities he believed he had suffered over Barnard Castle.

Cummings had certainly learned one thing: that any question of Covid rule-breaking by people in Number Ten can be politically toxic.

Dom and Lee were in one way great colleagues and friends. We had extraordinary success on the Vote Leave campaign, where Dom's role was pivotal, and he had good ideas about science and many other things. I was a bit sad to see them go, but by now I knew incontrovertibly what they had been doing.

I had discovered much later, by a circuitous route, that Cummings had lied to my face about the attacks on Dilyn. He WAS guilty. He was the author of the Jack Russell-bashing briefing. Perhaps he was somehow nervous of Dilyn, and his doggy nose for the truth.

Perhaps he had caught Dilyn staring at him, with his soulful brown eyes, and seen that the dog knew his guilty secret. Who knows?

But I am afraid that for far too long I was way too trusting, way too optimistic about my general powers of charm. Then their behaviour got weirder and weirder. First it was pretty clear that Lee and Dom were behind the so-called 'Chatty Rat' briefings on October 30, when for some reason they decided to leak the details of the November lockdown to the press, before I could announce it.

Then on November 9 it was revealed to me – by another minister – that they were behind some peculiar and spiteful briefing against Kate Bingham, who was doing vital and outstanding work on vaccines.

To leak lockdown details; to brief against our own Vaccine Taskforce. This was getting insane. I felt like the crew of the

Nostromo, the spaceship in *Alien*, when they discover that their colleague Ash is a homicidal robot – on a completely different mission.

They had to go. On November 13, Dom and Lee left Number Ten, both taking with them boxes of material, emails, etc. they were to use to confect their future attacks.

But from that moment on, for more than a year, I felt as if a great weight had been lifted – and for the government as a whole, things began to get dramatically better.

Part Eight
2021: A Vaccine-Led Resurgence

Chapter 43

If I Had a Hammer

How we did that final EU deal

For the first hour of the dinner with Ursula von der Leyen, I really thought it was going to be OK. We were high on the thirteenth floor of the star-shaped Berlaymont building in Brussels. I was gazing up in supplication at the Commission president from some sofa, where she had plonked us – David Frost, aka Frosty, our chief negotiator, and me.

She was beaming down at us from a straight-backed chair. She was blonde, coiffed, *soignée*, with a charming white-toothed smile. Of all my EU counterparts, Ursula was the pragmatist, and with seven children, umpteen horses and a long stint as the German defence minister, she had a reputation for getting things done.

Surely to goodness, I thought, this is the time for compromise. Come on, Ursula, I said: this can't be so hard. Our citizens depend on it. The world depends on us.

It was December 7, 2020 and in a few short weeks we faced the calamity of a so-called 'hard Brexit'. Yes, we had technically come out of the European Union eleven months before – but we were still in what we called the 'Transition Period'. We were a kind of non-voting member of the EU: out, but still part of the legal empire of Brussels. On December 31, all that was going to change.

Unless we did a deal, unless we agreed the terms of our future relationship, the EU and the UK would become total economic strangers. At midnight, a palisade of tariffs would spring up around the EU like a ring of sharpened stakes. Every British product could in theory be eyeballed and dismantled at the border, every traveller subject to body-cavity probes – and the result would be a total disaster, or so people had been prophesying for years.

Our supply chains would seize up; planes would choose to fall from the sky rather than disobey EU directives. The queue of honking juggernauts would coil from Kent to London, and from Calais to Paris, with lorry drivers forced to sleep for weeks in their cabs.

Still reeling from Covid, the global economy would fall flat on its face. We can't let it happen, I said to Ursula, who was accompanied by her chief Brexit adviser – a very smart young French woman called Stéphanie Riso. We have been negotiating for long enough, I said – and the fact is that the UK and the EU don't really have anything to negotiate.

After forty-five years of EU membership, we are fully congruent with every jot and tittle of Brussels legislation. We are two peas in a pod!

Let's get this done.

You know what – she seemed to agree, and for a surging moment I thought that this was going to be the decisive dinner, the moment of statecraft, of hope.

Then I became aware of a commotion at the door, and voices outside. At length a flustered-looking official came in and handed a piece of paper to the president of the European Commission.

She grimaced and handed it on to Steph Riso. Then Ursula rose and switched her beaming smile back on.

'I think we must now go into dinner,' she said. 'M. Barnier is here.'

It was then, of course, that matters decisively took a turn for the worse. As we discovered later, Michel Barnier, the EU's chief negotiator, had been outside the whole time, getting more and more agitated. He suspected that he was being deliberately cold-shouldered. He feared that Ursula was selling him out – doing some sweetheart deal with the dreaded Johnson. Finally he could take it no more.

As Frosty later discovered, the note he had written was an ultimatum to Ursula von der Leyen.

'If you do not let me join the meeting now, I will resign'!

Now he marched in: tall, white-haired, the red florette of the Légion d'honneur on the lapel of his perfectly cut dove-grey suit and a hectic flush on his cheek. The former French finance minister took over the conversation, and the result, as UK officials later described it, was the dinner from hell.

Ursula had been emollient and fun, and as a former student of LSE she was one of life's natural Anglophiles. Indeed, we had actually been at the same school – the European School in Uccle, Brussels; and though we disagreed about Brexit, we both wanted to get it done and rebuild as fast as possible.

Barnier was the opposite; prickly, Cartesian and suspicious. We sat down in the commissioners' dining room, with a fine view over night-time Brussels, and as Barnier glared at Ursula it occurred to me that he might not want a deal at all.

There is a long tradition, going back to de Gaulle in 1963, of French negotiators deciding that Britain can *ficher-moi le camp*; and if Barnier was thinking about the interests of Barnier, and the interests of France, as he assuredly was, then he might not be averse to some kind of bust-up in which *les Britanniques* were punished. The French, after all, had beaten us up on the way in, and it felt as though Barnier was determined to ensure that we were beaten up on the way out.

With just over three weeks to go until doomsday, our negotiating position was not, on the face of it, very strong. It was one of the many sad mistakes of the May government that we had begun the whole Brexit process, in 2016, by agreeing to the timetable set by Brussels. That is, we would first agree the terms of the withdrawal, and only then the terms of the future relationship.

Thanks to this elementary goof, we had already been forced to play most of our high cards. We had agreed to look after the interests of the three million EU citizens in the UK (five million, as it turned out), even though the EU only grudgingly – and often imperfectly – reciprocated our guarantees for UK citizens in the EU.

We had agreed the Northern Irish protocol, which, though better than the previous sell-out, was still suboptimal. And we had already agreed to pay tens of billions of pounds in alimony – cash for future EU budgets to which, so Brussels claimed, we were committed, so that UK taxpayers were coughing up (in ever-diminishing quantities) to the EU for a decade to come.

We agreed all this, with a gun to our head, because we desperately had to do a deal to get out – and now, with only twenty-one days left, we had to complete the all-singing, all-dancing Canada-style free-trade deal of which I had so often boasted.

It should have been technically easy, given that our economies and our legal system were in perfect alignment; but Barnier was determined not to make it easy. There were two big stumbling blocks. The first, and by the far the most constitutionally important, was the whole dynamic of the relationship.

We had to decide the terms of trade. I was absolutely adamant that it had to be a proper Brexit: that is, that the UK would in future be able to make its own laws, set its own tariffs, run its own subsidy regime, decide its own procurement rules – in a spirit of complete independence – and still have free and unfettered access to the EU market.

'*Mais non,*' said Barnier, pursing his fine features into a moue of disapproval. '*Ca c'est du cake, quoi.*'

Cake, or cake-ism, had become a shorthand in the EU for what they alleged was the incorrigible and impractical desire of the British prime minister to have his cake and eat it – or as they say in France, *avoir du beurre et l'argent du beurre.*

According to Barnier, we could have one or the other. We could have freedom to diverge from the EU; OR we could have tariff-free access – not both.

For month after month the Commission had insisted on a 'level playing field mechanism'; rules enshrined in the new Trade and Cooperation Agreement, which would give Brussels the eternal right to punish us by unilaterally imposing tariffs or other compensatory measures – if we dared to give a subsidy they didn't like, or if we dared to deviate from the Brussels rulebook.

I thought this was outrageous. It was also completely inconsistent with deals that the EU had already offered to third countries – notably Canada. The Canadians had gained more or less unfettered access to EU markets, and no one said that they had to comply with EU rules or consult Brussels about state aids.

Look here, I said to Michel, as the dinner began: this deal is meant to be a partnership, yes?

'*Bien sur,*' said Barnier, who liked to speak French if he possibly could.

'It's a relationship between sovereign equals, yes?'

'*Bien sur.*'

'Well, in that case, what is sauce for the goose is sauce for the gander' ...

There was a break while we tried to render this phrase into colloquial French.

I resumed. So if the EU could punish Britain for diverging from the existing acquis – the corpus of EU law – then it must follow that Britain had a symmetrical right to punish the EU.

I meant that if Brussels made a regulation we didn't like, or if Brussels allowed a state aid that we thought was unfair – then we would be able to slap punitive tariffs on goods from the entire EU.

I think you will agree that this was reasonable and logical. But a silence fell at the table, and the Commission officials all stared at their plates. It was as if they couldn't compute what I was saying – because it was outside their experience, and because the truth was that Barnier neither wanted nor expected a relationship of sovereign equals.

He didn't want mutual respect, or the mutual right to impose punishments for deviation; he wanted the UK – like the Swiss – to be outside the EU but locked in the gravitational field of Brussels. So by the first course we had reached a total impasse, and like Barnier I toyed with my scallops, because fish was on the menu both literally and figuratively.

Fish was the second big area of disagreement, and so Ursula had decided, with heavy irony, that we would all feast on scallops and monkfish – as if to remind us of the EU's rapacious demands. Their lust for fish was also, as we both knew, the EU's greatest area of vulnerability.

It is one of the many strategic advantages of the British Isles that they command some of the richest fishing grounds in the world, and for us Brexiteers it had been one of the added excitements of the great project that we would take back control of our waters and our fish.

We would undo the betrayal of the Heath government in 1972. Desperate to gain admission, desperate to buy off the French – and reverse de Gaulle's rebuff of 1963 – the Heath government had first betrayed Commonwealth agricultural exporters – with the result that some Australian farmers actually shot themselves in despair at the loss of access to UK markets.

Then, in the final rubber of the talks, the government betrayed British fishing as well. They agreed to the EU quota system, and under successive judgments of the European Court of Justice, EU-flagged trawlers expanded their rights to plunder British waters. Gigantic floating EU-flagged fish factories would lure our cod and haddock into their greedy nets, and hoover up the flounder and the sole from the seabed; and boats would come from Brittany and Normandy and take all the lobster and the crabs they could find.

Unfortunately, British fishermen found themselves unable to compete with mega-boats that fished British quota, and were registered in Britain, but were in fact owned and crewed by foreigners. In British ports and among British coastal communities there was a deep and burning sense of injustice.

They felt abandoned by the UK government, as though their interests counted for nothing. I am afraid that as long as we were in the EU, they were right.

I recall the incredulous curl on the lip of Philip Hammond in 2016 when we argued about fish, how he would scoff that it comprised about 0.01 per cent of UK GDP. It always enraged me, this attitude – this tendency to dismiss an industry that was so much a part of our culture and history. It was also a political mistake.

There was an extraordinary moment in the 2016 referendum campaign when Kate Hoey and Nigel Farage and others decided to highlight the plight of Scottish fishermen by bringing a flotilla of boats up the Thames to Parliament. With exquisite lack of good sense, the Remain campaign sent a counter-flotilla of pleasure craft to make fun of them, including a boat crewed by Sir Bob Geldof, the pop star, and (inevitably) my sister Rachel.

The sight of the multimillionaire rock star taunting and mocking these fishermen – flicking V-signs at them and shouting 'fook off' (not to mention Rachel laughing gaily beside him) was almost as big a boost for the Leave campaign, in retrospect, as Barack

Obama's pledge that Brexit Britain would have to get to 'the back of the queue'.

Now we had won, and having Got Brexit Done, we had to get our fish back. Time and again, during the Leave campaign or the election, I had been to some fish market in Grimsby or Peterhead. I had put on a white coat and a white pork pie hat and picked up some huge, cold, slimy monster of the deep and pointed its gaping fat lips at the camera; and I had promised that we would take back control of our fish. We needed full legal control of British waters, and Emmanuel Macron of France was determined to stop us. His fishing communities had been trawling UK waters since the Middle Ages; he needed their votes.

He wanted some way of ensuring that even after we had restored full control of UK territorial waters, he could force us to comply with French demands. So he came up with the same sort of mechanism they hoped to use to keep us aligned to the single market: a punishment – like the tariffs that the EU wanted to impose on us for diverging from the EU rulebook.

He wanted the right, backed by treaty, to impose tariffs – on anything and everything – unless the UK agreed that in future French trawlers would still have their quota of British fish.

It had to be in the treaty for Trade and Cooperation, he told Ursula. There had to be an instant and immediate way of punishing the UK if we refused to give France what it wanted.

She was quite open about it. She called it 'the Hammer'.

'I must have the Hammer,' she would say.

I said it was absurd: there was no way the UK could accept a treaty that allowed UK car manufacturers, or UK financial services, to be suddenly and arbitrarily punished – because of a dispute with France over fish.

Unless she dropped the Hammer clause, I said, we wouldn't have a deal at all. '*Kein Hammer, kein Hummer,*' I said – which was my way of saying, in German, no hammer and no lobster, either.

So the dinner ended in total deadlock; and we all went back grimly to the UK ambassador's residence in Rue Ducale and tried to calm our nerves with crisps and beer. Sir Tim Barrow, at the time our ambassador to the EU, is a generally optimistic soul, but I could tell he was worried.

We were miles apart. Over the next few days, I noted that people in Number Ten were starting to get really rattled by the prospect of a no-deal exit. That and the resurgence of Covid with the Kent variant: it was all too much.

Trusted aides stuck their heads round the door of my office and sidled in. 'We've got to do a deal,' said James Slack, the government's chief spokesman, and Allegra Stratton – then another key adviser – seemed concerned by my attitude.

'We have to compromise, PM,' said Allegra. 'It's time for statesmanship.'

As the deadline ticked closer, the business voices on the *Today* programme got ever more apocalyptic. We put the Royal Navy on standby – four warships – to guard UK waters against the incursion of the French fleet; and though I of course took James and Allegra seriously, I did not see how we could give in.

In Brussels, Frosty and Oliver Lewis and the other negotiators were starting to get cabin fever. Covid had locked Brussels down. They hadn't seen their families for weeks, and they gazed longingly at a picture they had stuck on the wall – of the Union Jack-liveried RAF plane that, I had promised them, would take them home in time for Christmas.

Now they instead faced the real prospect of spending Christmas with Ursula, rowing about demersal and pelagic fish. But though they sometimes betrayed signs of exhaustion, the British team were as implacable as I was. After all we had done, all the grind of the last three years – we couldn't settle for anything less than full economic and legal control of our country.

I was not only calm about our prospects. I was also completely

– and perhaps, in retrospect, excessively – confident that we would prevail.

Yes, I could see that Barnier was difficult, and that Macron wanted to use Brexit as a punishment beating. But I felt instinctively – you could tell it from Ursula's manner – that the EU wanted a deal.

It was still fundamentally true, as we had pointed out so often during the 2016 referendum campaign, that the EU had a big trade surplus with us. In fact, the UK buys more German cars (or did) than any other country in Europe; and I sensed that after all the nightmare and dislocation of Covid, they didn't want any more hassle from Brexit; indeed we all felt – on both sides of the negotiating table – that Covid had been so horrific that it made Brexit feel relatively trivial; and that gave me a sort of Zen calm.

Above all, I had a new and all-powerful weapon in the talks – a piece of legislation, which, though not yet passed into law, would utterly transform the UK negotiating position.

When I took over as PM I had no majority, no time and no popular electoral mandate, with the result that I was going naked into the conference chamber. By the end of 2020, not only did I have a powerful majority in Parliament, I was also busily using that majority, as the voters had doubtless intended, to equip the UK with the thermonuclear negotiating capital that we needed.

You will recall from earlier pages the central constitutional struggle of the last four years: to deliver a version of Brexit in which the UK would have genuine independence. You will recall that the Remain establishment, in collaboration with Brussels, came up with an ingenious ruse to frustrate this.

Their trick was to claim that in order to avoid a 'hard border' between Northern Ireland and Ireland, Northern Ireland had to remain effectively in the EU single market, a manoeuvre that in turn put pressure on the whole of the UK to remain in the single market, the tail wagging the dog, because otherwise we would have to accept barriers to trade between GB and NI.

The trouble with the Northern Ireland protocol – even the improved version that I eventually signed – was that it gave the EU Commission far too much control over that question: whether or not to have barriers to trade within the United Kingdom. The protocol handed the Commission the power to create a de facto border where there had been no border before. It was a crafty piece of work, in that it seemed to say two things at once.

On the one hand, I consoled myself that Article 6 of the protocol said that Northern Ireland was an 'integral part' of the UK internal market; on the other hand, it gave the Commission the power to check goods coming into Northern Ireland (on the theory that they might be 'at risk of circulating' in the Republic).

I was warned, I admit. Geoffrey Cox, the attorney general, came barrelling into my office on that fateful Wednesday in December 2019, just as I was about to go out to Brussels and do the deal.

'Prime Minister,' he boomed in his melodious baritone, wagging his finger like Rumpole of the Bailey, 'it is my solemn duty to inform you that under these arrangements Northern Ireland will be part of the UK customs union, but it will be the customs territory of the EU!'

Beneath the paint and plaster, in other words, was the hard reality of EU power.

How could I have signed it? Was I blind? On the contrary. I knew Geoffrey was right, in principle.

I did the deal because it was far better than before, in that we – the whole UK – were properly out of the EU; I did it because we were out of time; we were out of Tory MPs, in the sense that Theresa had blown our majority; and I did it because I didn't believe that the EU Commission would be so foolish and so pettifogging as to block trade WITHIN the UK.

I also signed because I calculated that if I could get a deal, I had a good chance of forcing and winning a general election, and winning a working majority; and that if the EU was still causing difficulties we would ultimately be able to use the might of primary UK legislation to fix the problem because we would be OUT, a free, sovereign and independent country, and it would be up to us to decide what happened in our own borders.

As 2020 went on it became clear, sadly, that the EU was determined to be unreasonable and to leverage their powers under the protocol, with no regard for the actual objectives of the agreement. 'Not a kilo of butter will go to Northern Ireland,' said one EU negotiator – and they had the power to stop it.

Bacon could no longer get through. Same for Cornish pasties. Same for Marks and Spencer biscuits. It was vicious, and bullying, and totally unnecessary. They didn't need these checks. There was no difference between English bacon and Irish bacon.

It was about power, about showing who was boss – and reminding Britain of the cost of a no-deal Brexit. The EU was reminding Britain that under the existing withdrawal agreement they had the right – if Britain diverged from the EU – to exercise a growing economic control over a part of the UK. It was another piece of leverage, like the level playing field clauses, like the fisheries 'Hammer', designed to keep us aligned and in our place.

Well, I thought, we can't be having this, and so was born the UK Internal Market Bill, or UKIM, which we had introduced into the House of Commons on September 7, 2020. It was, and remains, an essential piece of legislation.

Under the leadership of Theresa May we had decided, slightly bonelessly, that a lot of EU powers and responsibilities would be handed straight down to the devolved administrations in Scotland, Wales and Northern Ireland – without seeing that this would risk the break-up of the UK's own internal market. Suddenly there was a risk that the DAs would do their own thing, on food standards, or toy safety, or whatever – and you could have the insane situation in which goods could be placed on the market for sale in England and be banned in Wales, and vice versa.

Already the Welsh Labour government was trying to make its own provisions, I was told, about the sale of 'spreadable fats'. Give me a break, I said.

Are you trying to tell me the Welsh could start banning types of English spreadable fats? We needed a bill to ensure that any fats that could be legally spread on your bread in England could be spread across the UK.

The UK Internal Market Bill did exactly what we needed. With splendid clarity, it asserted the logic – previously implicit in EU membership – that the UK is one indivisible economic unit; and it gave back to the UK government powers the EU had taken over state aids and regional funding.

Seldom have I been more convinced that a legal measure was necessary, proportionate and right, and that conviction only grew as my opponents freaked out. Senior civil servants resigned; so did a rather nice Scottish law officer called Lord Keen. Five previous UK prime ministers denounced me as a renegade. The *FT* went spare, and Amal Clooney, wife of coffee ad man George, decided that she could no longer continue to serve as the UK government's envoy for media freedom. Why?

Because the UKIM Bill checkmated the EU. Under clauses 40–45, it gave a minister of the Crown the power to ensure that goods could move freely from GB to NI, and vice versa, and by effectively overriding the Northern Ireland protocol I was said to be in breach of international law.

I thought the whole fuss was ridiculous, and said so. We didn't want to break international law. If the EU was going to abuse the protocol, so as to create an unnecessary border WITHIN our own country, we needed to be able to fight back. We needed to show the EU that we could prevent them from controlling that border in a way that was unreasonable or offensive to those who cherished the Union between Britain and Northern Ireland.

In other words, what we were doing was extremely modest and sensible, and no more than any other self-respecting country would do. We were simply asserting the primacy, within the UK, of UK law.

I mean, seriously: can you imagine France, the US or any other country, large or small, allowing a foreign jurisdiction to manage trade between different regions of their own territory? Of course not.

The hysteria was yet another manifestation of the deep, ingrained and defeatist belief of the liberal establishment that Britain is somehow uniquely incompetent to run its own affairs. I loved that UKIM Bill, and it also had strong and widespread support from businesses – even from the CBI – because of the certainty it provided.

Our new attorney general, Suella Braverman, was exceedingly robust in defence of its legality. It sailed through the Commons, and the EU could see we had a hammer of our own.

And that, in conclusion, is how we did the deal. In the end, we both disarmed. The EU got rid of its ludicrous level playing field clauses, so that we had free and unfettered access to EU markets AND the perfect right to diverge from EU law in whatever way we chose.

They also dropped the fisheries hammer, so that by the middle of 2025 every sprat and mackerel in British waters would be His Majesty's Fish, with deep-blue UK passports forever.

In exchange we dropped the so-called notwithstanding clauses in the UKIM Bill, so that we no longer asserted our right to override the protocol. I was wary of this because I didn't trust the EU Commission, and I worried that they would still make difficulties for our bacon and our sausages (and I was right).

But it seemed unquestionably worth it at the time, on what was otherwise a pretty miserable Covid-bound Xmas, to get a deal and to set us free. On December 17, the UK Internal Market Bill was finally passed; and on Christmas Eve we did the deal.

I hailed Frosty in Parliament as the Great Frost, the greatest Frost in fact since the Great Frost of 1709, and he and Oliver Lewis and others came back to a hero's welcome.

Within weeks our new freedoms became useful, as Brexit came to our aid in the fight against Covid in a way I don't think anyone had imagined.

Chapter 44

Vaccination Miracle

Kate Bingham and the taskforce of hope

Britain is unique among major western democracies in that health care is fully and sometimes toxically politicised.

Since the NHS is entirely funded by the state, and controlled by the state, it is as true today as it was in 1948 – when Nye Bevan allegedly made the remark – that the sound of a dropped bedpan in Tredegar Hospital reverberates around the Palace of Westminster. In spite of all our efforts to insulate ourselves from blame – with NHS chief executives and other unelected and brilliantly evasive magnificoes – it is we politicians who are held responsible, and rightly so.

We carry the can, if not actually the bedpan, when something goes wrong. It is we who are exposed to the wrath of the public. Which means that it is always a bit of a crapshoot, for any PM, to visit a hospital.

As you go through the revolving doors, you feel your pulse quicken, your eyes darting around the gullies of the corridors, looking for the ambush. The staff are magnificent, the nurses wonderful, the equipment state-of-the-art, the patients generally models of good-humoured forbearance.

But let's face it: there is still a pretty good chance that someone will give you a piece of their mind, live on camera, in one of those ritual humiliations that are always so good for the soul. In the face of their suffering, you have no choice but to nod dumbly before their wagging finger, while your agony is lovingly captured by the cameras and replayed on the news bulletins until the joy of the broadcast executives is exhausted.

There were, moreover, good reasons for any member of the Tory government to feel apprehensive on the morning of December 8, 2020, round about breakfast time, when I visited Guy's Hospital in Southwark. In so far as we had made mistakes in the fight against Covid, they were my mistakes, since I had ultimate authority over every decision.

In so far as there had been unnecessary death and suffering, it was my responsibility – and so there was something remarkable about this visit. No one swore at me under their breath, or catcalled from the coffee shop.

No one even gave me the hairy eyeball. Perhaps it was because everybody knew – it was all over the news – that on this day our country was making history.

We stood at a respectful distance, sleeves rolled up, ties tucked into our shirt buttons, as we watched eighty-one-year-old Lyn Wheeler get her Covid vaccine. She wasn't the very first in the world: that had been a ninety-one-year-old at a hospital in Coventry, at 6.31 on the same morning. But she was one of the first.

This church-going school assistant was getting a vaccination that was both licensed and effective. 'I am doing it for Britain,' she said.

I was overwhelmed with excitement, as I then told the camera, my mask slipping down off my nose as if in anticipation of the freedom to come. I was also, frankly, amazed.

As far as I knew, it took about ten to fifteen years to bring a vaccine to market, and even then the chances were that it might not really work.

I couldn't see why we would have a vaccine in five years, let alone in one.

One day in April, I was sitting reading in Chequers, not long after getting out of hospital, when I heard from my private office that a team at Oxford had made some sort of breakthrough. It appeared that they were using chimpanzee flu, or adenovirus, to mimic the Covid virus, so that if your body were exposed to this bug via a vaccine, you would develop antibodies against Covid.

It all sounded promising, but still a long way off. It was like being Lt. Col. George Armstrong Custer at the Battle of Little Bighorn, with the Indian arrows whistling through your hat, and hearing that the cavalry had been spotted in Wyoming and might be coming sometime in the next few days. It was better than nothing – but it hardly amounted to a rescue.

When I got back to the office at the end of the month, I found some people – like my health adviser Will Warr – full of enthusiasm for the Oxford project. But they were worried. We had committed £65 million to support the creation of the vaccine, yet the IP belonged to Oxford. Now that the scientists, led by Sarah Gilbert, had made their breakthrough, they needed a commercial partner to bring it to market.

They were about to do a deal with Merck, the pharmaceutical giant. Which was great, except that Merck was American. That was a worry.

It wasn't about nationalism, or chauvinism, or some political desire to have a Union Jack on a British breakthrough. We had a hard-nosed, practical concern that in these desperate times any government – our own included – would do whatever it took to ensure that their own people had a supply of vaccines, if and when they became available. I knew that the US would have no hesitation in using the law – the Defense Supply Act, for instance – to sequester supplies of US-made vaccines and to ensure that they were consecrated for the saving of American life.

It was clearly essential to scupper the Oxford-Merck deal and to find a UK partner for Oxford. With the encouragement of Will Warr and Patrick Vallance, I wrote a letter addressed to both Oxford chancellor Chris Patten and the vice-chancellor, Louise Richardson.

I delicately reminded them of the situation: of the long-standing UK government support for the Oxford researches into vaccines, and expressed the strong preference that they should seek another suitor. They took the hint.

It wasn't long before Pascal Soriot and AstraZeneca stepped forward; a contract was signed, and the Oxford AstraZeneca vaccine was born. Even if AstraZeneca is partly Swedish, it is the direct lineal descendant of the pharmaceutical arm of Imperial Chemical Industries (ICI) and has its headquarters in Cambridge. Provided we did the right deal, no other government could expropriate its output.

That step – securing the vaccine supply before it even existed – was crucial. It is a very sad thing, but the whole experience of Covid so far had taught me that when national politicians panic, international cooperation goes out of the window.

Stuff the brotherhood of man; what mattered was the desperate, clamorous need of your own electorate.

When the storm broke over our heads in 2020, we had all suddenly recognised the vital importance of personal protective equipment (PPE), and there was an undignified flap to secure enough gowns, masks and gloves, most of which were made in China. One consignment of gloves was stranded for days on the tarmac at a Turkish airport as we wrangled with another government about where it was supposed to go.

I was so spooked by the PPE shortages, and so horrified at the idea of asking health and social care workers to do their jobs unprotected in a mist of Covid exhalations, that I decided I could not just leave this to the NHS procurement teams – admirable though they were. We needed a supremo, a man or woman with a genius for getting things done, and so I thought immediately of Lord (Paul) Deighton, who had triumphantly led the London Organising Committee of the Olympic Games in 2012.

It was some time before he could solve all the problems, but with Paul you sensed immediately that he had a plan, and that he would turn things around. Soon he had done so many deals, and set up such a prodigious domestic supply chain, that we were producing billions of items – indeed, we still have a mountain of stock. But we suffered, in those first few weeks and months, from being underprepared and were vulnerable to some opportunist 'suppliers' because we had failed to anticipate the scale of the demand.

When it came to vaccines, we would have no such excuse. We could see exactly what the demand was going to be and we needed someone, a tsar or tsarina, who could do in advance for vaccines what Paul Deighton was now scrambling belatedly to do for protective equipment.

Thanks to Patrick Vallance, we already had a committee of experts who were charged with assessing the vaccine experiments underway and considering the options for the UK. As we talked it over, it was clear to both of us that we needed a more attacking and dynamic approach, a group or a person who would be out in the market – hustling, negotiating, talking to Big Pharma.

We needed someone who could place the orders now, on behalf of the British public – in readiness for the day when the miracle occurred and we actually had that viable vaccine. We needed someone to do for vaccines what Beaverbrook had done for Spitfires – but who?

I thought of giving the job to Deighton; but he was reluctant. He was already flat out, and it wasn't his area of expertise. I looked down Patrick's list of the scientific great and good, the experts he had already co-opted.

There she was. We had her all along. I had known her for ages.

Of course governments make mistakes in times of national emergency; and so, sometimes, do oppositions. It was one of Keir Starmer's biggest goofs in 2020 that he and the Labour Party decided – as a way of getting at me – to attack Kate Bingham and the Vaccine Taskforce.

They sniffed derisively when I appointed her, and as the year went on they became progressively more caustic about Kate. They said that she only got the job because she was a chum of mine – and there was a limited sense in which they were right.

Yes, it was true that I had known her since I was about eighteen, because she was one of a bevy of brilliant and energetic Paulinas (alumnae of the Girls' School in Hammersmith) who went around Oxford in the mid-1980s, terrorising and breaking the hearts of their male counterparts and vindicating the maxim of their cigar-smoking headmistress, Dame Heather Brigstocke, who had told them that they were as good as or better than any man they came across.

It was true I had known Kate's younger brother at Balliol, and as an undergraduate I had even made a speech in honour of her father, top judge Tom Bingham (master of the rolls, lord chief justice, etc., etc.), on the occasion of his election as 'Visitor' of the College.

True, she had married an old school friend of mine, Jesse Norman, and yes, we had been friendly, if not exactly close friends, for a very long time, and oh yes, whoops, I forgot to mention that she had also been at school with my sister, the ubiquitous Rachel.

Some people will read all these facts with indignation because they seem to confirm that getting on these days is not about what you know, but about who you know; and that the whole thing is therefore an establishment stitch-up, and *passez-moi le sac de vomissement.*

To all these critics I would say that it was precisely because I knew her, and for such a long time, that I knew she was superabundantly qualified for the job. Kate Bingham is a force of nature. I can have a pretty powerful personality when stirred, and when confident of my facts; but you need to gird your loins, I can tell you, when you go up against Kate Bingham.

The first time I met her, in 1984, I was trying to get elected to some position in the Oxford Union.

'You!' she said. 'Why are you standing against my friend Neil Sherlock? How dare you?'

Well, I said, it was a free country, and the whole point of the society was that any member could stand in these elections.

'Huh,' said Kate. 'You are going to lose.' I crawled off, crushed – and duly lost to her friend.

Years later we were all on holiday in Scotland and were wondering somnolently what to do after breakfast. I had read in the paper that some kind of rocket was being launched from the moor, and since I love that kind of thing I tried to persuade everyone to come with me to witness this great moment in the otherwise underwhelming annals of British space flight.

I had managed to get some apathetic adolescent support when – to my dismay – Kate made a counter-proposal. 'Come on, everyone,' she said, sounding like a character from Enid Blyton. 'Never mind that boring old rocket, let's go to the beach – and cook sausages!'

At once it was clear to me that this was zero-sum. It was Kate or me, beach or rocket.

There could only be one winner; and for about an hour we slugged it out, like mastodons butting heads – and again, I was crushed.

In the end I drove on my own in search of the rocket launch – fruitlessly: I think they cancelled it, as usual. Meanwhile Kate led a party of about twenty of all ages to a beautiful, rainy Scottish beach, foraged a driftwood fire and soon had the sausages and some fresh-caught mackerel cooking nicely, plus a kettle for tea, followed by rounders. I had to agree that she had the winning proposition.

The point I am making is that her paper qualifications were perfect, because she had built a career and reputation by investing in new medicines; and there is no doubt that her appointment process – as some ridiculous litigation revealed – was also perfectly proper. But all this was of secondary importance.

I knew from my direct and frankly invaluable personal experience that – like Paul Deighton – she had exactly the right leadership qualities to do the job.

'It's got to be Kate Bingham,' I told Matt Hancock. 'I promise you. I just know.'

On May 6, 2020, I briefed Kate for the task and gave her three objectives: to get the vaccines we needed to protect the British public and to save life; to spread vaccines around the world, and to help global supply; and to make the UK better prepared for the future.

She succeeded in all three, but she succeeded heroically in the first. She procured a prodigious quantity of life-saving drugs and helped – finally – to turn the tide in the fight against Covid.

There were several reasons why she – and Britain – ended up having the edge over other countries.

Kate started early. She knew all the players in the life sciences sector. She did deals as fast as she could, and – with my explicit approval – she was pretty lavish in placing her bets. That is to say, she was like a slightly tipsy billionaire at the Grand National. She didn't just bet on one horse, or her favourite. She placed bets of varying sizes on about fourteen horses, and by the end she had procured six different vaccines and a total of about 350 million doses – far more than would be needed by the entire UK population.

She did watertight deals, under British law, and if necessary she paid over the odds to get delivery in 2020 rather than 2021. She bought large quantities of the adenovirus or whole virus vaccines such as Oxford AstraZeneca and Johnson and Johnson, and from Pfizer and Moderna she bought the rights to a new and exciting type of vaccine called messenger ribonucleic acid or mRNA vaccines, which ingeniously persuade your body to create antibodies to Covid without making use of the Covid virus itself.

She certainly spent public money, and thank goodness for her decisiveness in doing so; because, as an outlay, it was utterly dwarfed by the costs of the disease. As the summer months went by and the trials went on, and the results got better and better, it became clear that an effective vaccine was not only possible but likely – by the autumn!

Was that a distant toot from a bugle? Was that the drumming of hooves? Just as I was daring to dream that this was indeed the cavalry coming over the brow of the hill; just as it looked, kerchingeroo, as if Kate's bets might actually pay off, and spectacularly; just as she was about to be hailed as superwoman – the left decided to lay into Kate Bingham again.

For two weeks running there were bitchy pieces in the Sunday papers, on November 1 and then on November 8, 2020, some of it coming, sadly, as I now know, from my own fifth column in Number Ten – days before they were asked to leave the building.

The first was full of innuendo about her business connections, and seemed to imply that she might be somehow profiting personally from her work on vaccines – an absurd suggestion, not least since she was leading the taskforce pro bono. The second piece complained that she had spent £670,000 on PR consultants; which, again, was a travesty, because she was in fact trying to gauge public sentiment about vaccines – an absolutely crucial consideration given some of the challenges we were to face in the subsequent roll-out.

In fact, it was hard, at that stage, to think of a better use of public money. The BBC joined the hue and cry, with a programme asking whether Kate Bingham was an example of the new corruption in public life (a programme they later dropped from iPlayer); and Labour just couldn't resist it.

They piled in on Kate Bingham and her allegedly excessive expenditure – first Jon Ashworth, health spokesman, then Rachel Reeves, the shadow chancellor of the Duchy of Lancaster, then Keir Starmer himself.

I thought it was pitiful stuff, and a major error. It wasn't long before they had egg on their face; in fact, it was the following day that Pfizer caused the hearts of the world to leap with the news that its vaccine was 95 per cent effective in trials.

In less than a month the Bingham-bashers were looking like complete and absolute charlies, the whole lot of them.

On December 2, Britain became the first country in the world to approve an effective vaccine, in Pfizer BioNTech, and a few days later we were the first country to begin the roll-out – as I saw at Guy's in Southwark. By the end of the month, we had become the first country in the world to approve the use of Oxford AstraZeneca, and unlike Pfizer (which required quite cold refrigeration) Astra could be stored at room temperature.

The roll-out rolled on with ever-faster revolutions; because Kate had laid on the stocks, and because the approvals came faster than anywhere else in the world.

Much of this book has been about a struggle for legislative independence. I have tried to explain what I believe were the grave defects of the previous approach to Brexit, under the government of Theresa May. It is true that her 'deal' kept us 'closer' to the EU, but it also meant a kind of subordination to Brussels.

By effectively remaining in the EU single market, we were out of the EU but run by the EU. Under Theresa's deal, we remained as paid-up members of EU single market institutions, such as the European Medicines Agency.

Under my deal, we came out. We took back control. That meant that when it came to the approval of vaccines, we no longer had to go at the pace of the rest of the European Union. We had our own agency – the Medicines and Healthcare products Regulatory Agency – and we could do our own thing.

Thanks to the MHRA chief executive, June Raine, we had done just that. Working hand in glove with Kate and the Vaccine Taskforce, she had decided to be proactive, and to get to yes as fast as possible. I should stress that there was never the slightest political pressure on her to do this, either from me or from anyone else in government. Indeed, I had no idea what she was up to, and to this day I have not discussed it with her. She had simply decided that if we were going to do Brexit, then we might as well make use of the freedoms it brought.

So the UK MHRA behaved with the pharma companies like an air traffic controller, not a policeman. She engaged actively with them, to understand their vaccines and to assess their trials as they were happening; and so she was able to build up the data on Pfizer and Astra – and they were both very safe – faster than anywhere else. The result was that we approved these drugs weeks and weeks before anyone else.

That mattered. With more than a thousand people dying on some of our worst days, even as the roll-out began – 1,342 on January 19, 2021, the direst day of the pandemic – the exact speed of our roll-out, in those few weeks, mattered more than anything else in the life of our nation.

It meant, bluntly, that we were able to immunise huge numbers of elderly and vulnerable people who – if they had been living in an EU country, or in pre-Brexit Britain – would unquestionably have been forced to wait for EMA approval for their drugs, and who might therefore have died of Covid.

It wasn't long before some graffiti appeared on the wall in Portobello Road, west London.

'Brexit saves lives,' it said. It wasn't the sort of writing you expect on the wall in the largely Remain-backing Kensington and Chelsea, and I know that some of you will still find it a pretty indigestible assertion. But painful as it may be for some people, it's true.

If you want proof, look at the reaction of our continental friends and partners. It wasn't long before the success of the UK vaccine roll-out had started to drive them potty, first with irritation, then with rage.

Chapter 45

Roll-Out!

How British success inspired cross-Channel envy

Britain's top brass filed into my office in Number Ten, bearing with them hundreds of years of collective operational experience, from Afghanistan to Zimbabwe. It was about 6 p.m., at the very end of March 2021, and after several days of deliberation they had reached a verdict.

They had seen sieges, fire-fights, hostage rescues and hair-breadth 'scapes in the imminent deadly breach. It was clear from their manner, however, that they did not like the look of this one, Sarge. It fell to the deputy chief of the defence staff, military strategy and operational, Lt. Gen. Doug Chalmers, to act as their spokesman.

'Well, PM,' he coughed, 'it's certainly feasible.'

He explained how we could do it. We would send one team on a commercial flight to Amsterdam, while another team would use the cover of darkness to cross the Channel in ribs and navigate up the canals. They would then RV at the target; enter; secure the hostage goods; and then exfiltrate using an articulated lorry, and they would make their way to the Channel ports.

'But I have to warn you, PM' – and they all looked at me meaningfully – 'that it will not be possible to do this undetected.' He pointed out that there were lockdowns in place in Belgium and the Netherlands, and the local authorities might observe our movements.

I considered this. It did not seem an insuperable objection. OK, I said: so what if our movements are detected?

'Well, PM,' he said, 'if we are detected we will have to explain why we are effectively invading a long-standing Nato ally.'

Of course, I knew he was right, and I secretly agreed with what they all thought but did not want to say aloud: that the whole thing was nuts.

I beg you to forgive my desperation. It was in the best possible cause. I had commissioned some work on whether it might be technically feasible to launch an aquatic raid on a warehouse in Leiden, the Netherlands, and to take that which was legally ours and which the UK desperately needed.

We had the people who could do the job – special units that we had stood up in early 2020, as soon as it became clear that there was going to be a global contest for life-saving kit such as PPE and ventilators. We knew exactly where the target was: I could see it on Google Earth. It looked pretty easy to burgle, if you know what to do.

It was the plant where the EU had stowed five million doses of the AstraZeneca vaccine – doses that the company was trying, in vain, to export to the UK. As long as people in my country were dying of Covid, which I am afraid they still were in substantial numbers, I believed it was my paramount duty to secure those doses, which belonged to the UK, and use them to save UK lives.

I was angry enough to contemplate this clandestine operation, because after two months of futile negotiation I had come to the conclusion that the EU was treating us with malice and with spite; not because we had done anything wrong – we had not, far from it; but because we were vaccinating our population much faster than they were, and the European electorate had long since noticed.

Let me remind you that Oxford AstraZeneca was a vaccine that was pioneered in the UK, with UK government support. The only reason that five million doses had been waylaid at the Halix plant in the Netherlands was that Halix was a long-standing part of AstraZeneca's supply chain, and indeed the Dutch plant had been part-financed to the tune of £21 million by the UK government.

They had kidnapped our vaccines – but that wasn't the real outrage. That wasn't why I sat there in my office, Googling Leiden and shouting at my computer – so that Martin would rush in to check I was OK. The real cause of my pencil-snapping bin-kicking rage was that the EU was playing dog in the manger. They wanted to stop us getting the five million doses, and yet they showed no real sign of wanting to use the AstraZeneca doses themselves.

As a vaccine, Astra had several advantages. It was effective – almost as good as Pfizer – on the first dose, in warding off Covid. Unlike Pfizer, which required deep refrigeration, it could be transported at room temperature and stored in a normal fridge. We had been making it for months in the UK – bottling it in Wales at a plant called Wockhardt in Wrexham, in the hope that it would be approved by the MHRA.

I had been to inspect Wockhardt back in November, and was thrilled to discover that the plant's owners were an Indian family whose motto was 'Work Hard'. This they transliterated into Wockhardt, so as to make their company sound vaguely Teutonic and pharmaceutical.

They had been wocking so hardt in Wrexham that by the time we got approval for Astra, at the end of December 2020, we had millions of doses ready to go, and we were confident that supplies would hold up until the spring. So our roll-out had the advantage of an early start, and supplies on hand, and soon it was really humming along.

We worked our way through the UK population with a tightly organised plan. The Joint Committee for Vaccination and Immunisation announced a hierarchy, a sequence, so that we began by immediately protecting those most likely to die – those over ninety, then those over eighty, and so on; so that bit by bit, day by day, we were shrinking the numbers at risk.

People came forward in droves, rolling up their sleeves, taking off their shirts, fearlessly and proudly determined to protect themselves and everyone else. The British don't seem to have much fear of needles – it was Julius Caesar who noticed our love of tattoos – and soon the hypodermics were jabbing up and down across the country with the rapidity of a gigantic sewing machine.

By the end of January 2021 we had vaccinated about 10 per cent of the entire UK population, and a noticeable gap had opened up between the UK and the rest of Europe, who at this stage had done about 2 per cent. The pace of the continental roll-out was not exactly helped, on January 29, when Emmanuel Macron announced that in his view the British AstraZeneca vaccine was 'quasi-ineffective' for anyone over sixty-five.

I don't know where he got this idea, but it simply wasn't true – as the European Medicines Agency confirmed. Like Pfizer, Astra was about 80 per cent effective on dose one, and two doses gave you a very high degree of protection. I was flabbergasted by Macron's outburst.

Why was he knocking confidence in our vaccine, when vaccine confidence was so precious and so vital across all our countries? At the same time, out of the blue, the EU Commission launched a kind of legal war against AstraZeneca, claiming that the company was failing to honour its contract with the EU.

Why, asked Brussels, are you giving priority to the Brits? Why are you giving them so many vaccines?

Well, said Pascal Soriot, the chief executive of AstraZeneca, it's very simple. It's because Kate Bingham signed a bomb-proof contract with us, and that contract makes it very clear that we have to supply the UK with the first 100 million doses.

In saying this, Soriot was entirely correct. After some initial confusion, the EU countries had decided to procure vaccines jointly, in an effort led by the Commission. Through no fault of her own, Ursula von der Leyen and her team had failed to do the same sort of deals as Kate Bingham, and failed to do them as fast.

The EU officials spent too long wrangling about producer liability; their deals don't seem to have been as secure; and let's face it, Kate spent almost as much for one country of sixty-seven million people as the whole of the EU put together. So I knew that the EU's complaints were nonsense, and that their real anxiety was political.

The problem was that after their initial slowness in approving both vaccines – they were about a month behind us on both – their roll-out was further hampered by the hesitancy of their public. I don't know why this was (I think I heard someone say that in general the French prefer suppositories, hence Macron's attitude), but whatever the cause of the delay, the frustration of EU governments was, of course, being aggravated by the success of Brexit Britain.

So they announced that until AstraZeneca gave them more doses – of a vaccine they themselves disparaged as 'quasi-ineffective' for the people who needed it – they were going to stop the company from shipping its supplies to Britain. Their purpose was not to use the vaccine themselves; clearly not, since they continually disparaged it.

Their purpose was to stop us from using it and driving forward our roll-out. On January 30, having already announced their blockade on the export of Astra vaccines to the UK, they went further. The Commission had noticed a chink in their perimeter fence. Under the terms of the Northern Ireland protocol there was, of course, no barrier to trade between Northern Ireland and the Republic. This was essential, as we all agreed, so that communities on both sides could continue to move and trade freely, with no new impediment as a result of Brexit.

Mindful of sensitivities in Northern Ireland, we in the UK government had made it clear that we would NEVER impose checks in Northern Ireland. So on the evening of January 30, there was complete astonishment when the Commission invoked Article 16 of the protocol – an emergency clause designed for use in case of disaster or civil unrest – to impose a border in Northern Ireland. They were going to impose checks at the border, to stop AstraZeneca from using the Northern Irish loophole to send us our drugs.

In other words, they were making a mockery of the Anglo-Irish peace process and violating the sanctity of a border-free island of Ireland – over which they had themselves chanted such endless, balls-aching pieties – in order to try to stop elderly and vulnerable people in Britain from getting hold of life-saving medicines: NOT because they really wanted those Halix doses themselves (I am not sure they ever got round to using them, not when they were in real demand), but because they wanted to do something, no matter how egregious, to put a spanner in the works of the British vaccine roll-out. Why did they do it?

They did it because they (and above all, I suspect, Macron) could not abide the impression in the continental media that the UK was doing better than them, not in spite of Brexit but because of Brexit.

It was only a matter of hours after the Commission had announced this odious measure – banning medicines from crossing from one side of the Northern Irish border to the other, during a lethal pandemic – that they saw that they had overreached. The reaction in Ireland, from both Unionists and Nationalists, was furious; and the message from EU capitals to Brussels was that Ursula had gone too far.

When I rang her to remonstrate, she was deeply embarrassed, and it was clear that she was acting under orders from the major member states.

'Why are you stopping us from using our own vaccines?' I asked. 'It's not our fault that the UK public is very keen to get vaccinated, and that our roll-out is going so fast.'

'Yes,' she said, 'but you must not say that this is because of Brexit.'

'Why not?' I replied. 'Everyone can see that Brexit has at least been helpful. Why can't I say it?'

We both knew the answer to that. It was because for the last five years continental leaders, mainly Macron, had said that Brexit was a disaster, that it was based on lies, that I was a liar, that the British should be punished for Brexit, and that it should be made clear to the insolent Brits, over and over again, that they were worse off outside the EU than within – and then what happened?

Almost as soon as we were outside the EU, we were able to do something a little bit different in the regulation of medicines – a variation which, in that particular context, was able to make a huge difference to the survival prospects of a significant number of people in Britain. The German population was so fed up with their glacial vaccine roll-out that *Bild Zeitung* had run a front-page splash saying, 'Dear British, we envy you'.

That was why Macron, Merkel and co. were freaking out; that was the politics of the row. It wasn't about the Halix doses. It was about the prospect – so noisome to the EU – that we might actually be able to make a go of Brexit.

The following day I talked to Macron, in the hope of trying to find a way through and to calm everyone down. If I couldn't use *force majeure*, I didn't want a public row about vaccines, because I didn't want anything to rattle public confidence. I assumed that the EU would be embarrassed by their shameful attempt to impose a border in Northern Ireland, and that they would be in a mood to compromise. But Macron was evasive.

The EU might have lifted the ban on movement across the Irish border, yet they were using other laws to stop the vaccines leaving the Netherlands, and Macron wasn't helping. As we talked, I had the eerie sensation that he was looking down the schedule of our vaccine roll-out.

The French president seemed to know exactly how many doses we had, how many we expected to have, both of Pfizer and Astra. So in the end I gave up.

We had enough for two months. We could vaccinate all those who needed it most. We had no alternative but to get on with it.

In the middle of February, Angela Merkel also cast doubt on Astra, saying that it was not recommended for people in her age group (over sixty-five). I ground my teeth silently, because I didn't want to call attention to her foolishness.

The British public were happily oblivious, and vaccinating each other like crazy. In recreation centres, town halls, school gyms, GP surgeries the people of the UK were jab-jab-jabbing their way to freedom. I went to Wales, Northern Ireland, Scotland, constantly knocking elbows like the Birdie Song (by now the approved Covid-friendly form of greeting).

I could feel the mood of the country start to lift, the glorious serotonin of a collective endeavour – and the feeling of pride that, after all we had been through, we were starting to do rather well. I hadn't felt such a golden glow of positive national energy since the Olympic and Paralympic Games almost ten years earlier.

On February 18, 2021, I went to a vast vaccination centre in Cwmbran, Wales, where they were doing 1,400 jabs a day, and found myself singing an adapted version of the lyric by the great Welsh band Goldie Lookin Chain:

I've been all around the world, from LA to Japan,
but I've never found a place for vaccines like Cwmbran.

By the end of February, we had vaccinated 30 per cent of the UK population – as against 8 per cent in the EU. By the end of March, we had done 45 per cent, as against 10 per cent in the EU.

I knew that if we could keep this up, we would have built up so much immunity in our population that we would be one of the first major countries to make a safe exit from lockdown – which is another reason why I was so frustrated by the EU's behaviour.

I am, of course, glad that we did not violently seize the Halix supplies, even though they were ours. The EU are our friends, and it would hardly have improved relations. But it still enraged me – in fact it still does – that they were actually willing to let British people die rather than acknowledge the possibility that there might be an upside to Brexit. Their conduct was cynical, shameful and dangerous to human health. I said as much to Angela Merkel, who seemed to take the point. She then had the decency to get an Astra jab herself.

But they never gave us those Halix doses, and in the end we had to make do without. Thanks to Emily Lawson and the vaccine roll-out team – ably supported by vaccine minister Nadhim Zahawi – we more or less made up for the loss.

We decided to lengthen the interval between the first and second dose – so that we had more people with 80 per cent protection, rather than a smaller number with even higher protection. That expedient unquestionably saved lives. We also found artful ways to get more doses out of our vials, five rather than four, and to avoid dead space in our syringes.

The EU kept sniping away – trying to obscure its perfidy by accusing the UK of selfishly refusing to 'export' its vaccines. That was totally absurd. Unlike the EU, we never tried to interrupt supply chains – and there were British factories making substances such as lipids that were indispensable for the vaccine roll-out across Europe.

We would not have dreamed of blockading them. As for exports – we had done more than any other country. Unlike the EU or anyone else, we had done a deal with AstraZeneca so that the Oxford vaccine was sold at cost around the world. Contrary to the absurd claims of the Commission, we in fact helped to disseminate over two billion doses of AZ to more than 170 countries, saving an estimated six million lives.

By May it was clear that in the UK, at least, we had succeeded far beyond my dreams, and that we were on course to lift restrictions in the summer. On May 6 we held local elections, and a by-election in Hartlepool, where the Labour member had been accused of sexual harassment.

Isaac Levido had told me when Covid began that voters tended to be grown up about the handling of a pandemic. They would cut you some slack if you made mistakes at the beginning, provided you got them out of it.

'It's not the way in that matters,' he said. 'It's the way out.'

So it proved. There are limits, in a freedom-loving country, to the ability of government to contain the spread of a highly contagious disease. We Brits are elderly; we are by global standards very fat; we live in one of the most densely populated countries in Europe. The voters understood that the spread of Covid was not entirely the fault of the government.

But when it came to vaccination – well, that was something governments were supposed to do; in fact, vaccination was something that could only be really driven and delivered by government, and by that metric they obviously believed that the government had performed very creditably. By the week of the elections, we were already doing well in the polls – well ahead of Keir Starmer's Labour Party – when fortune decided to blow another great puff of wind into our sails.

For some reason the French Channel fishing fleet chose that week to invade the waters of the Channel Islands, in protest at what they saw as the iniquities of the Brexit deal. Since the Channel Islands are protected by the UK, I sent two chunky patrol boats armed with cannon and machine guns – and the French scarpered.

A tip to my successors: if you want to do well in mid-term elections, try having an eve-of-poll naval victory over the French. I couldn't believe my luck.

After eleven years of Tory-led government, we did not cede ground to the opposition; on the contrary, we once again defied expectations and made gains of 235 seats across the country, picking up control of thirteen councils. To cap it all, we won the Hartlepool by-election, with a 16 per cent swing from Labour to Conservative.

I had been up there to campaign and I can tell you, it wasn't just the vaccine roll-out that won it for Jill Mortimer. It was the case she was able to make about levelling up, the work that was being done by Tories across the north-east, especially Teesside mayor Ben Houchen, to bring jobs and growth to an area that had been neglected by Labour for decades.

Labour had held Hartlepool since the year I was born (1964). In fact, it had been the seat of Blair's guru, Peter Mandelson, now Lord Mandelson of Foy and Hartlepool. We took Blair's seat in 2019; now we had taken Mandelson's as well.

For the first time in more than a year I was really enjoying the job. My health was almost completely restored. My internal enemies had long since evaporated. My external foes, so it seemed, were in confusion and rout.

Chapter 46

Surviving the Bear-Pit

A few tips on handling
Prime Minister's Questions

When the mayoralty was going well, people used to talk about me one day becoming PM, and of course I was flattered. But as Clint Eastwood says in one of his movies, a man has got to know his limitations – and there was one part of the job that looked really intimidating.

I had held all sorts of leadership positions over many years, been a pretty successful editor and mayor of London, and had served in a major office of state. I was a far more experienced administrator, for instance, than Tony Blair before he became PM. I had seen more of the world than, say, Margaret Thatcher when she first entered Number Ten.

But there was one thing – though I never admitted it to anyone else – that really spooked me. I didn't like the look of this PMQ business. I mean Prime Minister's Questions, the weekly ordeal in which you go to the despatch box and answer any question, from any one of the 650 MPs, on any subject they like.

It is supposed to last only thirty minutes, from noon on Wednesday; but over recent years the speakers have let it drag on for forty-five minutes or even an hour. Since the sessions began in 1961, PMQs has become ever more adversarial, and now attracts audiences from around the world – because there is truly nothing like it in any other political system.

There is no other western democracy, with the possible exception of Ireland, where prime ministers are subjected to such a merciless catechism. When a PM has been brought to bay, it can be harrowing to watch.

It doesn't look like it from the TV, but the Chamber of the Commons is quite snug. When you stand up at that brass-plated despatch box (what does it contain? a minibar? a shoeshine kit? I never actually found out), you clutch the damn thing to mask the trembling of your fingers; because on a bad day it is like standing in front of angry, drunken football fans.

The opposition front bench is only a few feet away. You can hear every snicker, and when they give vent to collective indignation – which is often – their faces gurn with what looks like genuine hatred, and the cries of 'Shame' and 'Resign' are so loud that you can hardly think.

When things are going badly, you feel like some toothless bear in Elizabethan Southwark, feebly cuffing the hounds as they take great gumps of your flesh. For that fifty minutes you are on your own, with nothing except your file of briefing notes – and it is difficult to consult documents at the speed required in the Commons.

If you take more than a second to find a fact, an ecstatic cry will go up of 'It says here! It says here!' – because the theory is that you should have it all in your head. You have to show that you are in command of the detail, that you have a plan to fix things, and above all that you understand the anger and the pain of millions of people that our parliamentary system is effectively funnelling towards you, across the floor of the Commons, in a hairdryer blast.

As a young backbencher, I used to sit and watch Tony Blair as he was bathed in the noise from our benches. How could he do it, I used to wonder. How did he know so much about it all?

How was he so confident and so mellifluous in his put-downs? I had certainly done plenty of debating as a student, and I could sometimes hit some heavy returns of serve. But for an hour?

I had a terror of that sudden moment of silence when the question has been put and you get to your feet – because like many people, I expect, I have a slight defect in my processes of thought and speech. As I open my mouth, I find there is a sudden jam, as though too many bits of luggage have been loaded on the reclaim carousel.

The words get stuck. I can think of so many different things to say that I halt, and then stammer and gabble. It was all right, as mayor, because although I had Mayor's Question Time once a month, it was a Paris–Dakar rally by comparison with PMQs. It went on for almost three hours, and there was never the same pressure for instantaneous fluency. What if I froze? What if I simply couldn't remember the answer? What if I just stood there going ah-ah-ah while they all yammered with delight?

I was so worried about making an ass of myself that I wondered seriously whether I wanted the job. So I am really writing this for all the would-be prime ministers out there – by way of encouragement.

Yes, it can sometimes be brutal. But it is also a tribute to our democracy that we put our leaders through this weekly mauling. I mean, think how much tax we take; think how intensively and how clumsily we try to order the lives of the British people. It is quite right that the leader of the government should demonstrate that he or she has at least a vague idea of what the state is doing, and should be able to defend it.

Let me reassure all you would-be prime ministers – you will feel purer and nobler for having put yourself through the crucible of PMQs. You will get through it, and you will get better at it.

Over my three years plus, I spent more time, pro rata, at the despatch box, being accountable to Parliament, than all other recent PMs including Thatcher. I was never a brilliant parliamentary performer, but I became a fairly dependable middle-order slogger, and sometimes had my moments.

So here you are – my top-ten tips for how to survive the bear-pit. It helps to:

1 – Be lucky in your opponent

I certainly was – at first. When I became PM, my opponent was the member for Islington North, Jeremy Corbyn, a veteran fire-brand of the London left. He had given Theresa May a hell of a scare in the 2017 election, all but wiping out our majority.

On his day Jeremy could be an excellent speaker, specialising in a kind of white-faced fury at the iniquities of capitalism. He still had a cult status with the Labour grassroots. For some reason, however, he decided that he would bring a new super-democratic earnestness to PMQs, so that instead of asking questions himself, he would literally read out a question from a member of the public.

'I have here a letter from Jenny in Carlisle,' he would begin, and then relay Jenny's horrific experience at the hands of government. The whole House would fall silent, because all MPs naturally defer to the electorate. But after a while the technique started to stale. Provided you were suitably respectful of Jenny's suffering, you could normally answer the question in a sensible way – by reference to the forty hospitals we were building, the 60,000 nurses we were hiring, the 20,000 police officers, and so on – and the heat would be gone from the exchange.

It didn't help Jeremy that on the big issues of the hour – Brexit, and the parliamentary blockade on getting it done – he was in a bit of a muddle. He said he wanted another referendum on EU membership but refused to say which way he would vote, and after a few months he was in the ludicrous position, as leader of the opposition, of refusing my demands for a general election.

I never felt seriously under pressure from Jeremy – but

2 – You can never be complacent

By the spring of 2020, Corbyn was gone, and I knew that Starmer would be more difficult. Boxy-headed, privately educated Oxford graduate Sir Keir was, on the face of it, a serious customer – a former director of public prosecutions.

An acquaintance of his at the Bar had told me he was a bit of a 'dull dog', but I could see how dully and doggedly he would gnaw away at things and cause me problems. So he did, at first.

In one of his early outings, Keir asked me a series of simple questions about rape prosecutions. Why were so few rapists brought to trial, let alone convicted? Why was the criminal justice system letting down so many female victims? What was I doing about it?

As it happened, it was a subject I knew about and cared about, and had done ever since my days as mayor. With Kit Malthouse and Priti Patel, we were engaged in a big cross-government exercise to fix the problem – to make sure that there was far better coordination between police and prosecutors, and to speed up the courts.

We had put a lot of money into rape and domestic violence advisers – to make sure that women had the courage to come forward and the fortitude to stick with it until their assailants were punished. I was passionate about the subject, and had a good story to tell, or at least a reasonable defence of our position.

That day, I just couldn't get it out. I rambled and bloviated, and Starmer came off best. I got some pretty poor notices and went, I am afraid, into a bit of a black funk. Why didn't I have the facts on the tip of my tongue? I resolved to

3 – Read and re-read the brief

and to learn the basic data of government; because the truth is that the PM should prevail in PMQs.

You are the one driving the agenda. You have the initiative and the policies. You also have a great many wonderful civil servants who are only too happy to help.

Like all PMs since Tony Blair, I had the benefit of the advice of Nicholas Howard, who ran the civil service team and lovingly collated the ammo I needed. If you have ever watched PMQs on TV, you will know who I mean: a small, gnome-like, balding Welshman, sitting in that box for officials – on the left behind the speaker – watching the exchanges with the rapt intensity of a Wimbledon umpire.

It was the job of Nicholas and the team to prepare your big red file, which is a thesaurus of points to make in favour of the government – and ways of whacking the opposition. You may ask yourself how supposedly impartial civil servants can prime you in this way; and the answer is that it is their job: to help you explain government in the best possible way; and, of course, that also means helping you to biff aside the opposition attacks.

I have no idea about his real political sympathies; and it didn't matter. If you were doing well at the despatch box, then he and his team were doing well. That was what counted. It was also Nicholas's job to make sure that you never said anything to mislead the House, and that any inadvertent mistakes were speedily cleared up. I learned to trust him and to respect his judgement. In fact, the way to win at PMQs is to

4 – Have a great team behind you

And I did. I not only had some cracking civil servants; I had some ace political operatives, who served as my seconds and coaches and all-round horse-whisperers.

I have read that some PMs spend most of the previous day getting ready for PMQs; and frankly I don't believe that. There just isn't time. I would begin to get my thoughts together at about 5 p.m. on the Tuesday, and for about forty-five minutes I would sit down at the table and chat to my chief PMQ adviser, Declan Lyons: good-humoured, bearded, and with an extraordinary knack – I think he comes from a family of Irish horse-fanciers – of picking the topics that Labour would use as their lines of attack.

'Right, PM,' Dekkers (or Double-dekkers as he was known, in deference to his build) would say, as he barged into my office with a sheaf of printed notes. 'I think he will do three on x and three on y'; and six or seven times out of ten, Declan was completely right. It was eerie.

I sometimes wondered if he had some secret back-channel to the Labour Party, whereby he traded information and got the scoop on Keir. So I would go to bed vaguely mulling the likely punches and counter-punches.

But I tended to leave the bulk of the work to Wednesday morning, when the key thing is to

5 – Have a routine for match day

There was a period in my teens when I took rugby quite seriously, and before any big match I would actually polish my Elmer Cotton boots, boil the kettle to re-mould my gumshield and meditate on the combat ahead. I recommend something like that for PMQs.

I would get up in the dark, go through the file, and start making notes – on blank A4 sheets – on the politics of the week. What were the key events? Where were we vulnerable – and how could I turn it around? By 7.15 a.m. I was out in the park, running with Dilyn and doing physical jerks.

You need that dopamine; you need to have done some exercise at the beginning of the day. Then it was back to Number Ten, for 8.45 or 9 a.m., and after the first general meeting of the day it was time to face some bowling. By this stage Declan would have worked out what the lead question was going to be.

I don't know how he did it – watching Twitter, listening to Labour spokespeople on the media. He just seemed to know. He was also ruthless in formulating the attack in the most caustic and bruising way. Sometimes, frankly, he verged on the impertinent. I would hit the ball back over the net as smartly as I could, and try out any lines I had come up with overnight.

It is at this point – as you genuinely try to answer the question – that you start to see your real vulnerabilities. This is the moment when you ask your team to scour the armouries for better ammo. The facts seem terrible, I would complain. Get better facts!

But by now it was getting on for 10 a.m. I was going to be on my feet in two hours, and through the double doors of the office I could hear the murmur of conversation in the Cabinet Room. It was the wider team assembling for the rehearsal. Now was the moment to

6 – Lock down the answers

Because I cannot stress enough: this is not the moment for extempore brilliance.

Before you stand up in the Chamber, you need to know almost exactly what you are going to say. You are the PM; you are being examined, in public, on issues that matter hugely to your voters.

You must do the Commons and the electorate the elementary courtesy of preparing and testing your answers, and testing them to destruction. This is what happens now.

You walk through the blue baize double doors into the Cabinet Room, where the PM's seat is conventionally turned slightly to the right so that you can sit down in a hurry. Everyone falls silent.

It is a big group. You have your media spads, and you have the PMQs civil servants. You have your political team from Number Ten, including your political secretary, and you also have at least four parliamentary colleagues.

You have your parliamentary private secretary, possibly both of them; you have the chief whip, sitting some way down table; and you have a couple of experienced MPs who are there to reflect the mood of the House, to tell you what you can and can't get away with.

In my case I was lucky to have Michael Gove and Oliver Dowden, both of them political junkies and addicts of the theatre of Parliament.

'OK, folks,' you say. 'This is where we think it will go today.' And you explain how you reckon the leader of the opposition will mount his attack. There then follows about an hour of pretty rumbustious exchanges, in which they take it in turns to pretend to be Starmer and fire their attacks, and you counter-attack; and then they offer better or more effective counter-attacks, and all the while you note down the best lines and ideas.

Then, at about 10.55, you thank them all profusely, and as they leave you take some fresh sheets of paper and divide them into six blocks: each sheet representing a subject, with six possible lines of attack and defence.

At about 11.45, Jo the Number Ten events manager sticks her head round the door. 'You really must go now, PM,' she says.

Now you walk down the thirty-yard ochre corridor towards the door; and they swing it open just as you reach the black and white paved vestibule and you can see the cameras outside in Downing Street, and the great cacophony begins.

'Are you going to resign?' shouts someone with a mic (they started shouting that almost as soon as I became PM). 'Is your government in chaos?' and so on.

I would advise you to beam and say nothing and, making sure you cover all your notes, you get in the back of the car, which sets off fast towards the big black gates. From now on in, the only thing that really matters is to

7 – Look as though you are in command

The time for swotting is over. It is time to exude confidence – to everyone. You will go past crazed protesters, screaming abuse at your car and sometimes even hurling themselves in the road.

Your motorcycle escort, as ever, will deal with them with consummate skill. You enter the Commons through a small side door behind the speaker's chair, and you bound up the dimly lit oaken stairwell and cheerfully hail your parliamentary staff.

With the five minutes or so remaining, you hit an exhibition rally with Declan, rehearsing what you hope will be your zingers, and perhaps keeping your staff on their toes by saying a couple of really outlandish things – just to see if they are paying attention.

'No, PM,' they respond, screwing up their eyes, 'you can't say that!'

At one minute to go, the word comes back from the whips on the bench: Scottish questions is almost over. It's time for one last straightening of the tie, and then down the green corridor to where you are briefly held by the whip in the outer lobby, behind the speaker's chair. By this stage some of the gallery sketch writers will already be able to look down and see you in the gloom.

Your heart will be thumping, I promise. Look cool. Don't skulk. Don't be riffling frantically through the file. It's too late. You are on.

'Hear HEAR,' yells the whip as he or she shoves you forward; and the trusties (and not so trusties) take up the acclamation.

As you find your place on the front bench and squeeze in, I recommend that in all the confusion and noise you keep your finger on the first page of the file, so that you don't forget the first answer.

Someone has been chosen by ballot to shout, 'Question number one, Mr Speaker!' And though question number one is never actually articulated, it is to ask the PM to name their engagements of the day. This is to allow you to give an answer so general that any subsequent question would be relevant and admissible, or 'in order'. Since the House of Commons loves ritual, you have to get it right.

It is surprisingly easy to forget. So they print it out for you every time.

'Mr Speaker,' you say, 'this morning I had meetings with ministerial colleagues and others. In addition to my duties in this House, I shall have further such meetings later today.'

With that last clutch of the banister rail, you are on your own. In all the mayhem that follows, I strongly advise you to

8 – Observe the courtesies of the house

Don't get angry, or only in a fine show of righteous indignation. Don't get rattled. I would urge you not to shout or swear under your breath – and I am afraid I did, a lot – because even if the cameras don't pick it up, and the speaker misses it, the Labour front bench will note that you are under stress.

You can afford to switch your tone, depending on the type of question and the person asking. You can be genuinely interested and grateful. You can be savagely indignant, on the right issue.

Every so often – and you can't play this card much – you can admit to complete ignorance, and offer to write to the Member concerned. When you are asked something by your own back-benchers, remember how crucial this is for them. They need the right clip for their social media. So lay it on with a trowel. Show knowledge of their campaigns. Point out how lucky their constit-uency is to have such a helmsman. If asked to come for a visit, make clear that wild horses would not keep you away.

When it is the turn of the SNP and the Lib Dems, remember that about 80 per cent of the House view them with some measure of hostility if not contempt. So the best course, where possible, is to make gentle fun of them, because their questions don't really matter.

There are only six questions that matter in PMQs, and they come from the leader of the opposition. As you rise to your feet, you have to remember that for many people watching this will be a big moment – the moment when the PM is forced to explain some of the biggest problems in their lives: their cancer delays, their household bills, their kids' inability to buy a home, whatever.

You cannot be glib. But provided you show that you at least understand and empathise, you are entitled to blast back as hard as you like. You need to keep it short, but the ideal answer has three parts.

1 – Much as I sympathise with the sufferings of x or y, the Rt. Hon. Gent is wrong.

2 – We are in fact doing x, y, z and have invested x billions.

3 – None of these solutions would be possible under Labour – because (and here you hope your benches will be baying assent, as you pick at least one of the following generally

credible assertions) they are weak on defence, they hate wealth creation, they generally hate home ownership while living in stuccoed Islington mansions themselves, they kowtow to Brussels, they would release prisoners early, they would get rid of immigration controls completely and return to free movement, they are riddled with antisemitism, they bankrupted the economy last time they were in and, Mr Speaker, remember this, Labour always leave unemployment higher at the end of their time in office than it was when they came in! Cue Tory cheers – or so you hope.

You have to be quick, as I say, because otherwise the speaker will shut you up. But you must keep going, and keep attacking; because PMQs is your occasion. It's your chance to frame the debate and

9 – Frame your opponent

The first few months against Starmer were tough – from his election in the spring of 2020 right through to the end of the year. Covid was a nightmare, and he generally had an easier hand to play.

Most voters agreed with Labour in wanting the government to impose tighter restrictions, while Tory MPs were growing increasingly antsy about lockdown. It was hard, at times, to carry my party with me. But after a while I worked out that Starmer's persona – the north London lawyer – could be turned against him. Not only was he basically a rapist-releasing Remoaner. He was a barrister.

What is a barrister? Someone who is paid to have one opinion – and then another one! He was a human weathervane, I decided, swinging with the wind. First he announced he was a republican and wanted to get rid of the Queen – now he draped himself in the Union flag.

He had told the world that Jeremy Corbyn would be a great PM – now he was trying to purge him from the Labour Party.

He had repeatedly called for a new referendum on the EU – now he was embarrassed even to mention the subject.

As for Covid, he wobbled around all over the place. Was it safe for kids to go back to school, in the summer of 2020? What was the Labour view of the Vaccine Taskforce?

First he said one thing, then another. First he took one brief, then another. To the public, there seemed to be something opportunistic about the way he carped, but without offering any real programme himself.

He was 'Captain Hindsight', I said; and by the spring of 2021 I had noticed something else. There was something slightly stolid about his handling of PMQs. I mean that in spite of his credentials as a prosecutor, he could be a bit slow on the turn. He would ask a question and I would answer it, and then he would simply ask it again. I started to call him 'the human bollard', and 'Sir Crasheroonie Snoozefest' – and I think it began to get under his skin.

In 2021, as we started to race ahead again in the polls and won in Hartlepool, I am told that he even considered resigning. I am not sure whether to believe that, and if he had asked me I would certainly have told him to snap out of it. Politics is fickle.

In the end

10 – PMQs does not make the weather

It is a barometer. It tells you how you are doing overall. But it does not shape or determine the course of political events.

Most people agree that William Hague is a brilliant debater, the Michael Gove of his time. When he was leader of the opposition, from 1997 to 2001, he regularly bested Blair at PMQs. The trouble was that very few people noticed and even fewer cared. We were then at a stage when the public had formed a broad view of

Blair, and a broad view of the Tories, and it didn't matter much what happened at PMQs.

It was Punch and Judy, knockabout stuff. If Blair got knocked down occasionally, it didn't matter. He got up again, and in 2021 I felt that I was on the same long-term mission, to level up, to change Britain, and that I was more or less unassailable.

That was, of course, a complete delusion. But there was a long period when PMQs got easier, when the cheers behind me seemed genuine and fervent, and when poor Starmer seemed genuinely discombobulated by my primitive attacks. That wasn't because I was getting any better at PMQs. It was because the government, on the whole, was starting to get things right.

Chapter 47

Triumph at Carbis Bay

A good G7 – and the secret birth
of the Aukus agreement

Enid Blyton fans will know that her girls' school stories tend to begin with the pupils converging on their beloved Malory Towers – a picturesque establishment on the Cornish Riviera. The sun is out, the sky is blue, the sea the colour of forget-me-nots, and I say, golly gosh: it's a new summer term!

After the enforced idleness of the holidays, the gels are all overjoyed to renew their friendships, and the excitement is so intense that they clap each other on the back and shriek each other's names.

That was pretty much the mood of the G7 world leaders as we assembled in Cornwall, for June 11 to June 13, 2021. After eighteen months of lockdowns and Zoom calls, we were just elated to see each other in person; and soon the West Country air was buzzing with post-pandemic camaraderie.

We may have stayed socially distanced for the family photo – but we all felt sufficiently immunised to have meetings without masks, and to shake hands. In fact, we positively pawed each other.

As a backdrop to the three-day diplomatic schmoozathon, Cornwall did us proud. The Carbis Bay Hotel rose magnificently to the occasion; and as we feasted on the biscuit-coloured beach – with lashings of everything – I was reminded of one of Blyton's female characters who always insists that food tastes better in the open air.

It is in this crucial opening scene, as we Blyton fiends know, that the stock schoolgirl characters are briefly but powerfully delineated. There is always a sharp-tongued girl, famous for her catty sense of humour, called something like Alicia.

This was the role of Angela Merkel, chancellor of Germany, who is actually much funnier than people imagine and an excellent pricker of pomposity. Then there is generally a French exchange girl, who tends to be petite, delicate, and worried about getting a freckle on her nose. No prizes for guessing that this part was played by Emmanuel Macron, president of France.

Enid Blyton schoolgirl stories often feature a highly competitive pair of twins – and at Carbis Bay we had the delightful rivalry of the Euro-presidents. There was Ursula von der Leyen, president of the European Commission, jostling for primacy with Charles Michel, president of the European Council.

Their staffs would bicker heroically about which was entitled to the better chair at meetings, and which should be nearer the heart of the family photo. I honestly can't remember the right answer, and we happily shoved them both in.

There is always a sporty girl who insists on going swimming in the bracing Atlantic – and Justin Trudeau, PM of Canada, was game for an early morning plunge. But the greatest schoolgirl sensation always tends to be about a New Girl, whose father is so rich and so powerful that she arrives in a car bigger and swankier than anyone else's.

She has monogrammed luggage and a tennis racket from Harrods, and a ginormous tuck box. She is so rich in fact that it is quite embarrassing to watch as the other schoolgirls compete shamelessly to suck up. Starring in the role of New Richest Girl in the school was, of course, Joe Biden, the president of the United States, whose cavalcade was so vast – featuring the ten-tonne Cadillac 'Beast', with five-inch-thick armour-plated windows – that the queue of black machines almost choked the Cornish lanes. It must be wonderful to be president of the United States, though also rather exhausting, because wherever you go, whatever summit you are at, you will tend to be the centre of attention.

At any such meeting you can see the way the lesser world powers cluster round in simian acts of homage, presenting their bottoms like baboons. At Carbis Bay the competition was particularly keen, because this was the new president's first trip outside the United States. For the first six months of his presidency he had been confined at home – like the rest of us – and now we were all consumed with curiosity. Was he really as elderly-seeming as his detractors sometimes said?

His staff told us that he would not in fact be boarding our vast aircraft carrier – which we had proudly stationed in the bay – because it had so many steps; and we wondered what that meant about his physical fitness. And what about his mental acuity?

What if he fell asleep during meetings? Well, all I can say is that from the moment Joe and Jill Biden got out of their enormous car, they were charm personified. The president was wearing his aviator shades and a genial grin of dazzling whiteness. And he knew our names!

'I can see that Boris and I both married above ourselves,' he said as I introduced him to Carrie. In fact, he seemed to take a bit of a shine to her.

'Why don't you and I go down to the beach,' he said to Carrie a bit later, while Jill Biden rolled her eyes, 'and leave this guy here?'

The Bidens had brought presents: a little bike for Wilfred and a custom-made bike for me, decorated with British and American flags and silver facsimiles of our signatures. It was so valuable that in order to retain it, under our very proper rules, I later had to buy it, at considerable expense, from the British state.

Meanwhile Carrie got all sorts of clothes and goodies from Jill Biden – and what do you think we gave them in return? No one in Number Ten had a clue what to give the president. Perhaps a portrait of someone? Could we think of any British people that he admired? But Biden made a big thing of being Irish by extraction, not British. Hmmm.

Then someone mentioned a nineteenth-century anti-slavery campaigner called Frederick Douglass, who had apparently once travelled to Scotland. Could we find a picture of Douglass? I am not sure how much effort we made, but we couldn't find a print or a portrait of Douglass anywhere – and in the end I am afraid we simply printed off a picture from Wikipedia.

The Bidens had spent thousands on us. I doubt that we spent as much as a penny on them. It was fabulously mean; which I suppose will draw the approval of the UK taxpayer. At the time, I kicked myself, because these tokens can be oddly important – and in offering their tributes to Biden, I knew that the other leaders would not hold back.

Yes, here was Emmanuel Macron, toadying up with a pretty flash-looking crate of wine, a gift from the people of France to the American president.

'It is named in honour of Lafayette,' he said, showing me the label and reminding us that Lafayette was the French revolution-ary general who had fought for George Washington against, *bien sur*, the British!

I ground my teeth. It may all sound a bit teenage, this vying for Biden's affection, but it mattered. Which was going to prevail, in the Biden White House – his strong support for the EU or his instinctive belief in the relationship with Britain?

It was well known that I had been on excellent terms with Trump, but the media were somehow convinced the Biden White

House would be different; more aloof, more sceptical about Brexit. As an Irish-American, they said, he was surely going to back the EU over Northern Ireland.

Well, now was the moment of truth. I badly needed to make common cause with Joe Biden and, more particularly, I had to do a deal.

I needed at Carbis Bay to persuade him to agree, in secret, to a brilliant and ambitious geo-strategic proposal, whose only downside – sad but unavoidable – was that it was going to put French noses badly out of joint. In an ideal world we would have done this deal somewhere else, when we didn't have Macron and hundreds of French diplomats wandering around. But we had no choice.

Carbis Bay was the first time we had been able to meet, and it had to be done now. The G7 summit was significant because it was the first time that the leaders of the western economies had a chance to regroup, to look out at the blasted post-Covid landscape and discuss the way ahead.

So I had deliberately invited some additional guests, leaders of great industrialised democracies that were not in the G7: President Moon Jae-in of South Korea, President Cyril Ramaphosa of South Africa, Prime Minister Scott Morrison of Australia and Prime Minister Narendra Modi of India (who had to Zoom in, because the plague was still raging in his own country). These eleven delegations – plus the EU presidents – converged on this charming beach hotel, parts of which had to be more or less rebuilt to accommodate the requirements of the US Secret Service; and soon all the hotels of Cornwall were rammed, and some camp-followers ended up staying as far away as Wales.

I know that readers may be sceptical about the value of these summits – and if you looked at the pictures of Carbis Bay, bathed in sunshine, you might think it was a bunch of politicos living it up at taxpayers' expense. As the driftwood barbecues crackled beneath the fresh-caught Cornish lobster, you might say that the principal output was hot air. I would say that was not just harsh, but wrong.

The world had just been knocked sideways. Covid had hit us like a truck – and by many measures it was the world's poorest who had been hit hardest. We needed to show that it was us – the world's democracies – who had the answers; that we were the ones with the right plan to Build Back Better.

The first lesson of the Covid pandemic was staring us in the face. Why were we able to meet at all? Why this scene of in-person reunion?

Why did seventy-eight-year-old Joe Biden feel safe to attend what would otherwise have been classified as a superspreader event? Because we had all been jabbed, and the most interesting feature of the effective vaccines was that they were the product of – wait for it – the advanced western industrialised democracies.

Who among us had used the Chinese-made monkey gland vaccines, Sinovac or Sinopharm? Who had been jabbed with Sputnik, the Russian potion? Exactly.

There was a difference between the vaccines produced by the western capitalist democracies and the vaccines produced by the autocracies, and the difference was that our vaccines actually worked. They were the product of multinational pharmaceutical giants and of multinational scientific collaboration.

So the first conclusion of the pandemic was obvious, at least to me. We needed more capitalism, and more democracy, not less, and we needed more technological cooperation between capitalist democracies. Look at Pfizer – a Turkish-German-American concoction. Look at AstraZeneca – a British-Swedish company with a French chief executive that did its trials in Brazil and manufactured many of its doses (including mine) in India.

It seems to me that the vaccines are a crucial proof point in the big argument of our times. They show that western capitalist democracies – where companies are answerable to consumers and to shareholders – are far more likely to produce innovations that benefit humanity than companies that are answerable to party cadres and politburos.

We democratic leaders had been sent to Carbis Bay to bear witness by our punctured skin to this living truth: that intellectual freedom, commercial freedom and political freedom are in the end crucial for addressing the needs of humanity. So the whole spirit of the summit was about how to strengthen and develop that cooperation.

On the first day, Joe Biden and I met, and all my anxieties melted away. He defied the urgings of the EU and, I believe, of some of his own officials – and pointedly refused to weigh in on the row over Northern Ireland.

'I would not dream,' he said, 'of telling a friend and ally how to run his own country.'

In fact, he disarmed me completely by saying that his family origins were not really Irish at all, and that the Bidens were an old seafaring family from Kent (which seems plausible, since -den is a common Kentish termination).

I suppose that he may say something subtly different when in Dublin. But never mind! He was up for almost anything to take the relationship forwards.

We agreed a new Atlantic Charter. This set the framework for intensified US–UK cooperation in many important technologies, on climate change, on development – and it underscored the US commitment to European security: not a trivial statement, by Biden, when you consider what was to happen to Ukraine the following year.

We discussed at some length an idea – originating from Number Ten but seized upon by the White House – for a western democratic free-market alternative to China's Belt and Road policy. Covid had not just hit the poorest hardest; many of those countries were already groaning under the yoke of Chinese debt.

What they needed was western, market-led investment. If they were to have any hope of greening their economies; if they were really going to achieve economic growth, and tackle climate change, then they needed far more investment than any government could give. They needed the global financial institutions (World Bank, IMF, development banks) to trigger the trillions of the market.

Surely that was better than leaving the field to the Chinese loan sharks. We needed a plan to make it happen, to make sure that green technology was spread around the world with western finance. We began by calling this idea the 'Clean Green Initiative', but Biden's people preferred 'Build Back Better World' – and I was happy either way. The idea was to become the basis for a lot of the work we did at the COP 26 summit in Glasgow six months later. Then there was one more idea that was brought to birth at Carbis Bay, one concrete proposal to widen and deepen our collective security through the sharing of technology.

The only difference with the other proposals was that it was not in the communiqué, and hardly anyone knew about it at the time.

It was called Aukus. It was, at first, a nuts-and-bolts programme to equip Australia with the right submarines. Within a few months it had become a new and thoroughgoing defence pact, spanning three continents, between three countries that trusted each other so deeply that they were willing to share the most precious secrets; not just in nuclear propulsion, but in many of the key defence technologies of the twenty-first century.

When the Australian PM Scott Morrison arrived at Carbis Bay he was in a quandary, and he needed UK help. Under a deal done by his predecessor, Malcolm Turnbull, Australia had commissioned the French to supply the next-generation submarine. As is the way with all such contracts, things were taking longer, and proving more expensive, than the Australians had hoped. But there was a more basic problem. Without going into the details, the French diesel engines were too noisy.

The boats would be detected, and with Chinese technology improving the whole time, the Australians feared they were buying an obsolete vessel. So their admirals were in a state of some anxiety and had privately talked to our admirals.

What about the UK's Rolls-Royce nuclear propulsion units, they said. Could we perhaps collaborate? Britain would soon need a new submarine as well. If they whacked the French contract, could Britain and Australia perhaps find a way to build the next generation of submarine together?

Well, yes, said our first sea lord, Tony Radakin, who was highly creative in advancing this whole project; but this is big politics.

So he and my national security adviser, Sir Stephen Lovegrove, came to see me – and we discussed the complexities. The nuclear propulsion units for our subs are indeed made by Rolls-Royce, and we have great expertise in this country in making such engines.

But it is also true that we have the technology under licence from the Americans – because you will recall that in an act of typical generosity, the UK was the first country to split the atom and then, in the middle of the war, handed our nuclear secrets entirely to the US, under Operation Tube Alloys, and they went on to make the Bomb. Ever since then we have been very much the junior partner.

These weren't, strictly speaking, our secrets to share. They were joint US–UK secrets, and we would need US approval for any partnership with Australia. We thought that the Americans might agree, but that they would be wary.

The Anglo-American nuclear relationship is unique. We trust each other. We have systems and protocols to prevent proliferation and the theft of the technology we share. Would the Americans be willing to widen the partnership, to include the

Aussies? For weeks we beavered away at the project, and the early signs were positive. Jake Sullivan, Biden's NSA, seemed to like the idea – but it all depended on Biden.

When Scott Morrison explained the idea of Aukus to me (Aukus standing for Australia, UK, US), it was clear that there was one big problem: it meant that Australia must begin by breaking off a massively lucrative submarine deal for the French and going with the Anglosphere.

We could all see that this would go down exceedingly badly with the Élysée. It would cause Emmanuel to *jeter ses jouets dehors de la poussette*, and then *manger le tapis*. So the big question was: would Biden be willing to collaborate on a project – no matter how ultimately beneficial to America and the world – if at first it meant pretty massively cheesing off the French?

I should say that by this stage I had, myself, not the slightest inhibitions. I love France, and the French. My beloved grandmother, known as 'Grannybutter', was French, and I am trying to read ten pages of a novel in French every day. I also liked (and like) Emmanuel Macron, and for two solid years I had tried to ingratiate myself with the young French leader and to build a new post-Brexit Anglo-French partnership. I have to be honest with you – I was rejected at more or less every turn.

You may recall from an earlier chapter how one of the first trips I made as PM was to Paris, to see Macron, and how I tried to interest him in all sorts of new Anglo-French partnerships; and failed. Macron smiled enigmatically, but it was clear that post-Brexit Britain – and especially its leader – was *dans le frigo*.

A year later, I tried again. He came to London after the first lockdown, in June 2020, and we essayed another reset. We commemorated de Gaulle's famous June 18, 1940 broadcast to the Free French. We put on a flypast and a guard of honour in Horse Guards – which was only spoiled by Dilyn having hysterics in the Downing Street garden.

'Is zat your deurg?' said Macron incredulously. I offered him the honour of holding Dilyn himself, which he mysteriously declined. Again, at that meeting, I gushed with ideas for intensified Anglo-French technological cooperation. How about cyber? How about hypersonic transport – how about a new Anglo-French Concorde for the twenty-first century?

Surely it was absurd that two of the world's greatest economies, barely twenty miles apart, were connected by only one railway line. Wasn't it time, I said (slightly improvising), for a new road link across the Channel?

'*Non*,' said Macron; rather abruptly, I thought, as though he was suddenly appalled at the idea of all those rapacious Brits swarming across a bridge to his relatively underpopulated country – like the villagers of Oxfordshire protesting at the notion of a bridge over the Thames from Reading.

As time went by, it became clear that although Macron was personally charming, and although we often agreed on important issues, he really meant it when he said that Brexit Britain must be punished. On some issues I am afraid I therefore suspected him of being a positive nuisance.

Take the 'small boats', the endless stream of rubber dinghies and other unseaworthy vessels that cross the Channel to Britain from the beaches of France, risking the lives of tens of thousands of migrants every year – and infuriating the British public. The French won't let us patrol the beaches of Calais. They haven't been British for a long time.

They insist on doing it themselves – and so we give them hundreds of millions of pounds a year to monitor the beaches and stamp out the trade. As the months went by, and the boats kept coming, I am afraid I started to wonder. Were the French really doing all they could? Was the Élysée really giving the signal that this was a top priority?

It seemed at least possible to me that Macron was weaponising the problem, and discreetly allowing the migrants to come across in sufficient numbers to drive the British public nuts and undermine one of the most important facts of Brexit – that we had taken back control of our borders. Then, over the last few months, there had been his frankly dangerous dog-in-the-manger behaviour over the AstraZeneca vaccine, and the kidnapping of the five million British doses.

Now we were having yet another argument with the Commission over Northern Ireland. It seemed I had been too trusting, in the final negotiations of December 2020, in getting rid of our sledgehammer – the notwithstanding clauses in the UK Internal Market Bill that allowed the government of the UK to insist on free trade *within the UK's own borders*.

I had assumed that the Commission would be moderate and sensible in the operation of the agreement. They were not. They were blocking the movement of everyday goods – bacon, sausages, potted plants, packets of shortbread – from the island of Britain to Northern Ireland.

It was demented. Sausages made in England, Wales or Scotland are not only produced to the highest possible standards. They are also – or at least they certainly were in 2021 – in perfect conformity with all EU law on sausages. So why was Brussels insisting on checks on entry into Northern Ireland? It was driving Ulster Unionists potty; and I was pretty cross, too. So on the second day of the Carbis Bay summit, I had my bilateral with Macron and gently raised the matter.

He frowned in puzzlement. 'But Northern Ireland is a different country,' he said. 'It is reasonable to have checks.'

At that point, as you might expect, I almost lost it. The whole point about Northern Ireland is that it is NOT a different country; it is part of the United Kingdom, I said.

How would you feel, I asked, if a foreign power told the French people that they could no longer transport sausages from Toulon to Paris, or from Paris to Strasbourg? At that moment I couldn't work out whether he was genuinely muddled or whether he was winding me up. After the summit, I discussed Macron with HM the Queen. She had met all the leaders and their wives at a splendid dinner, on the first evening, in the Eden Project.

She observed that there seemed to be an interesting age gap between M. and Mme Macron.

'Yes', I said, 'he married his teacher.'

'Well,' said the Queen, 'she didn't teach him much history.'

In retrospect, I think that of course he knew. He knew the sensitivities about Northern Ireland, just as he knew how neuralgic it was to see people flout the law and come illegally across the Channel in inflatable boats.

I say all this, really, to explain why – after a long and determined attempt to build bridges (even literally) – I had more or less despaired of Macron, because even if we personally got on, and even if there were questions where we strongly agreed, there was also a host of issues where, given the chance, he would not hesitate to put his Cuban-heeled bootee into Brexit Britain.

Which explains, I hope, why I felt not the slightest compunction about advancing the Aukus plan; nor, in spite of all his later complaints, did I feel the slightest moral obligation to tell Macron what was afoot. It would have been quite wrong to do so. It wasn't our sub deal with France; it was Australia's. If Macron had got wind of Aukus at Carbis Bay he would have freaked out badly, and used all the leverage he had – in Washington and Canberra and London – to scupper the plan.

And until Morrison had Biden's agreement on Aukus, there was no way that he could level with Macron, because he risked falling between two stools.

So my most important job at Carbis Bay was to organise a discreet three-way meeting – Biden, Morrison and me – without being rumbled by the French; and on the evening of the second day, just before the display by the Red Arrows, we pulled it off.

The three of us sat in little armchairs in the rather sultry plywood hutch, looking out over the sea, which had been specially built for such meetings. I acted as a kind of matchmaker. I explained the Australian submarine problem, and how Britain wanted to help. Joe had been well briefed, and he was immediately positive. The idea worked for all of us.

We were all pondering the challenge of the Indo-Pacific region, and how we could work together more effectively. Aukus isn't meant to be directly anti-Chinese. It isn't meant to be anti-anyone. It is about strengthening the west. It is about much more than building new submarines together; it is about collaboration in hypersonics, AI, quantum – and, frankly, it is the sort of project the French should be involved in. Maybe, one day, they will join.

As we had predicted, they all went tonto in Paris when we finally announced the deal in September. I was accused of being a shameless opportunist, and other things, which I thought was a bit much, and referred later to the raucous squawkus from the anti-Aukus caucus.

Most people strongly welcomed the new Aukus pact. As Keir Starmer said to me as we stood in the Lobby, waiting for the statement, 'This is all really good. I can't see anything to object to here.'

I am not sure that all his MPs agreed, but he was right. That night in Carbis Bay we sat up late drinking, looking out over the sea – Scott Morrison, Cyril Ramaphosa, Angela Merkel, Charles Michel, their partners, and others. I was in a pretty good mood.

I know that some of you will think this is confirmation bias, after the huge emotional and political strain of delivering a proper Brexit, but it did seem clear to me that neither the vaccine roll-out nor Aukus could have happened – certainly not in that way – without Brexit.

Yes, I was certainly looking for things to show I was right, just as anti-Brexiteers are constantly looking for evidence the other way. On at least these points, I was sure. I was proud of the summit, and thought that the Downing Street ops team – Shelley Williams-Walker and co. – had done a bang-up job. I was also proud to have taken the world's leaders to Carbis Bay, where my great-grandfather Stanley Williams had spent his retirement, picking out the name of the station with seashells he gathered from the beach.

You could say it was his modest contribution to the transport infrastructure of Cornwall, and I was proud that the government was doing more in this respect than in any generation since Victoria. We were determined to modernise the rail and the roads of the West Country – the A303, the A38; we were putting in the broadband.

We were levelling up. Only a month previously, our agenda had helped us to a pretty thumping victory in the local elections in Cornwall, and as the sun set over the bay we raised our glasses like the Olympus-dwelling immortals to the ideals of democracy and intensified technological cooperation.

Oho, I thought, as I knocked back the red, this is pretty good stuff.

I consulted the label. It was Macron's Lafayette, which Biden had kindly donated for the general weal. Whatever his Irish antecedents, the US president never touches alcohol.

I thought the summit was great. The pictures looked great. Cornwall looked so ravishing that you wondered why anyone ever went on holiday anywhere else. The great British electorate are not so easily delighted.

They tend not to award their leaders many points for summiteering and junketing and global back-slapping. A few days later, on June 17, I was chagrined to lose the Chesham and

Amersham by-election, caused by the death of Cheryl Gillan, a much-missed former whip of mine.

It was, pure and simple, a Nimby-driven protest vote. They already hated HS2, which was now, admittedly, being driven in a huge scar of construction work across the landscape; and they hated the idea, sedulously peddled by the Lib Dems, that our new planning bill would mean boxy new brick homes all over Buckinghamshire.

I found the whole thing infuriating. Didn't people see that one of the key advantages of levelling up was that it would actually reduce the pressure for housing in the rural south-east? By enabling much more brownfield development, we would help families to find great new housing in the increasingly prosperous towns and cities of the whole UK, and we wouldn't have to carve up the countryside.

That was why HS2 and the infrastructure revolution were so important. That was why Rob Jenrick's planning bill was right. Come on, I told my backbenchers: we won't get anywhere without being the party of aspiration and home ownership.

We will not get elected, and we won't deserve to get elected, if we think we can rely on an ever-diminishing minority of elderly Nimby voters. We can protect the countryside, but we must offer hope.

Chesham and Amersham was a surprise, and an irritation. We slightly changed the bill, to show that we were 'listening', but kept the thrust of it and forged on (I am afraid the big cop-out came later, under Rishi); and we kept build-build-building new homes.

In spite of Covid, we were adding about a quarter of a million new homes a year (248,000 in 2019–20, then back up to 235,000 in 2022–23) – which was the fastest rate of building new homes for more than twenty years, and I was confident that with levelling up we would do even more.

Eddie Lister and I had long experience of getting things built. We knew that if the homes looked good, and were in the right place, local people – including Tory councillors – will come to like them, even love them. Especially their kids.

There was one event that summer which far eclipsed the Carbis Bay summit, or any by-election result, and helped explain the remarkable overall buoyancy of the government and our sense of forward momentum. On July 19 we celebrated Freedom Day.

By that date we had given more than sixty-eight million vaccinations, and about 60 per cent of the entire adult population now had some measure of protection. In the case of the more vulnerable groups – such as those over seventy – vaccination rates were running at almost 100 per cent. Yes, people were still getting Covid – but not fatal Covid. The fatality rate had plummeted.

We had created a huge pharmacological force field around the population, and it was time to open up.

I announced that we were removing all Covid restrictions: no more rule of six, no more mandatory masks, no curfews or other prohibitions on human contact. We restored freedom to the British people about eight to ten months ahead of most other European governments.

Labour's Keir Starmer called the decision 'reckless', and I was of course widely denounced by the left-wing media. If we had listened to them, we would have kept restrictions going for months longer than necessary with all the consequent social and economic damage.

We celebrated Freedom Day earlier than others, not because we were reckless but because we had been so efficient in vaccinating our population.

Which meant that people could go back to work and to the pub and to restaurants, in the normal way; and which meant that our economic recovery was faster than most of our comparators; in fact, the fastest in the G7. Forgive me if I seem to be belabouring this point, but it was all at least partly thanks to Brexit.

My opponents were wrong about Freedom Day, and proved to be wrong, and among them was the first minister of Scotland, Nicola Sturgeon. The sainted leader of the Scottish National Party had adopted a highly successful strategy for most of the pandemic of always appearing to be slightly more risk-averse than the government in London.

Since a majority of the British public tended to be on the cautious side, this generally went down well. So Nicola would use her devolved freedoms to keep schools closed, to keep masks on and to keep people locked down for that little bit longer than in England and Wales.

We made a huge effort to involve her in the committees and to try to move forward in identical steps – but it was never quite enough. If we decided, after agonising debate, that it was time for people to go back to work, she would immediately appear on the TV, lips pursed, brow furrowed, to say that Scotland wasn't ready for this yet; and some Scottish people seemed only too happy to spend a little longer at home at the general expense.

She had a strategy of gratuitous differentiation. It was deeply frustrating partly because it was confusing for the public, partly because it made me look like a brutal English Tory while she was an unco guid Princess Twinkletoes.

As things turned out, her Scotland-only measures were probably useless. There is no perceptible difference, at the end of the pandemic, in the overall mortality rate between England and Scotland. If she hoped the pandemic would in any way promote the notion of breaking up the UK, well, those hopes were crushed.

Covid demonstrated the vast and immanent strength of the United Kingdom. It was British Army helicopters that ferried sick patients from remote Scottish islands. It was the huge firepower of the Treasury that made furlough possible throughout the country. From test and trace to the vaccine roll-out, we were engaged in a gigantic national project, in which the four nations of the UK were strenuously and intimately involved.

Never outside wartime has that political and economic union proved so valuable. When I became PM in 2019 my opponents were only too keen to suggest that Brexit was about to shatter the UK, and that the Scots would shortly tell the English it was all over. Week after week I was challenged in Parliament to offer a new referendum on Scottish independence.

Every time I made the point that we had only just had such a referendum in 2014, but the pressure was real. As a lover and admirer of Scotland and a passionate Unionist, I viewed the whole thing with horror.

So I am happy to say that by the end of my time the campaign was more or less dead, and I believe that Covid has actually helped us to settle the question for a generation at least. As for Nicola, her halo slipped, and it turned out she and her husband had some questions to answer about how SNP funds were spent.

The Scottish Nationalist dog barked during the pandemic, but by the end the great United Kingdom caravan had moved on. Except, of course, for the deluxe £110,000 motorhome unceremoniously seized and impounded by Police Scotland.

The SNP have duly imploded and the Union is safe. For keeping up the pressure on the Nationalists, much credit goes to our highly effective and long-serving Scottish secretary, Alister Jack.

Chapter 48

Collapse in Kabul

And the Saigon-like scenes that followed

We were all so elated by Carbis Bay and the general success of the G7 presidency that we failed to notice one sign of impending disaster. It was a story that Biden told us about Afghanistan. In fact, he told it twice in my hearing, which I put down to the forgivable repetition of the elder statesman. It did not occur to me, alas, that he was just trying to ram the point home.

Back when he was vice-president, said Biden, he had gone on a fact-finding trip. For some reason he had taken a helicopter out of Kabul to a remote mountain fastness. This was the December of 2009, and the blizzard was so bad that the chopper had trouble putting down. The local tribe was, of course, thrilled to welcome such an important guest. Casting around for a suitable way to honour his arrival, they spotted some distant people on the far side of the valley – tiny, but conveniently silhouetted by the snow.

Taking out their six-foot jezzails, they announced that they would shoot these stick-like figures as a mark of respect; rather like a guard of honour firing off a salute.

No, no, said Joe, appalled.

Why on earth not? said the tribesmen, as though some do-gooder had told them not to pot the grouse on their moors.

'You can't just shoot people,' said the US vice-president.

'But they are our enemy!' responded the Afghans.

Biden concluded from this experience, he told us, that Afghanistan was basically ungovernable, that it was not a proper country but a collection of warring tribes, and that the US was wasting its time, blood and treasure in trying to keep order. He told that story twice, and yet somehow we failed to twig.

The whole of the UK defence, foreign policy and security establishment was therefore mightily taken aback in July 2021, a month after the G7 summit, by the sudden finality of Biden's confirmation that after twenty years the US really was pulling out of Afghanistan: no ifs, no buts; irrespective of whether the Taliban were fulfilling their side of the deal. Even as he said it, we did not think he could be entirely serious.

It had been twelve years since Biden had encountered those trigger-happy badmashes on the mountain; twelve years since he had been vouchsafed that not entirely startling insight about the ungovernability of Afghanistan. Obama had pledged to get out. Trump had pledged to get out. But the US was still there; because the standing advice of the US military was basically the same.

Their view – like ours – was that Afghanistan was never going to be a model of Jeffersonian democracy, but if you wanted to avoid a total collapse, and the return of the Taliban, then it would be sensible to keep at least a modest US presence. We agreed with that analysis, and so, it seemed, did Tony Blinken, the US secretary of state.

So we were simply not psychologically ready for the idea that this time Biden really meant it, that he was literally on the point of pulling out every last American soldier.

Years before, I had gone to Afghanistan, as foreign secretary. I had visited the Sherpur Cantonment – one of the saddest, spookiest places I have ever been. On a dilapidated perimeter wall, a wonky sign announces that this is the 'British Cemetery'.

You go through weathered wooden gates to a garden of graves, a sepulchral narrative of British imperial overreach; and a lesson, had I chosen at the time to see it, of what was fated to happen again. The British have invaded Afghanistan four times in the last two hundred years. In that garden of remembrance lie the remains of some of those who lost their lives in the first great massacre, in 1842.

As I looked at their memorials on that chilly November morning in 2016, I thought of the deathless prose of George MacDonald Fraser whose account of the retreat from Kabul, in the very first Flashman novel, was seared on my eleven-year-old mind. I remembered his description of the elderly Victorian catastrophist William Elphinstone, his skinny pale feet still in his slippers as he gave the order to retreat; still pathetically trusting his Afghan counterparts, still somehow believing that his allies among the Afghan tribes would honour their word and protect his fleeing army as they tried to make their way back to India through the snowy wastes of the Khyber Pass.

I brooded on the doom of those 4,500 soldiers, British and sepoys, and their 12,000 camp-followers; how the snows turned red as they were steadily butchered, and how only one man escaped to tell the tale (if you exclude the fictional Flashman).

In spite of that experience, we Brits had gone back again in 1872, and then again in 1919; and after each incursion we had been more or less ignominiously ejected. I looked at the most recent memorials, fresh marble slabs erected to those British troops who had given their lives since 2001, when Bush and Blair – with my support – had launched the 'War on Terror'.

There had been 457 fatalities in all. Some had been shot by snipers. Some had trodden on mines. Some had been riding in thin-skinned Land Rovers that had been ripped apart, all too easily, by improvised explosive devices.

They had been told that their cause was noble and just. So it was, in the sense that the Taliban government was incubating terrorism. The Islamists had given a home and a headquarters to Osama bin Laden, the mass-murdering mastermind of 9/11, and it was right that we had gone there to root him out.

Since then these British troops had been involved in many dangerous but valuable projects – such as the transport of turbines to the Kajaki Dam in Helmand Province, trying to bring electricity to some of the poorest people on earth; or ensuring the education of hundreds of thousands if not millions of girls and young women who would otherwise have gone without.

In the end, the operation became just too dangerous. Too many Union-Jacked coffins were being flown back to Britain, to be paraded though the silent, tearful crowds of Wootton Bassett. Far too many young men – and women – were suffering life-changing injuries.

In October 2014, the Tory-led coalition government pulled out of Helmand Province, the southerly slice of the country that had been assigned us by the Americans. Two years after that withdrawal, I stood by those graves and I knew the reality of what was happening across the country.

It was an overcast day, and the wind was whipping through Kabul from the ring of grey mountains. I knew that the Taliban were out there somewhere; and that slowly they were closing in. The situation in the capital was by now so tricky, even in 2016, that our diplomats and aid workers rarely dared to venture beyond their fortified compound (or cantonment, as their predecessors would have called it); and yet time after time, both as foreign secretary and prime minister, I had been called upon to deliver an identical message to the Afghan government

Again and again I had reassured Ashraf Ghani, the Afghan prime minister, that we would stick with him. Ghani is a slightly nervy former New York professor with a reedy voice, and his brown eyes would gaze searchingly at me as I repeated my lines.

'We are here for the long term,' I would say, as the FCO wallahs looked on approvingly. 'You can count on the British.'

As Ghani poured out his thanks, I did not doubt what I was saying. I believed it even now, in the summer of 2021, after Biden had made his sudden announcement. In spite of two hundred years of direct experience, and in spite of plenty of evidence to the contrary, the British military were convinced that this time we had done enough to change Afghanistan for the better.

We knew exactly what it was like to be forced to retreat from Kabul. We had done it three times. We were the world record holders. We weren't going to have a fourth evacuation, not this time. In the last twenty years the US had spent more than $2 trillion on Afghanistan – not least on training and equipping the Afghan army to protect the democratic government in Kabul and to fight off the Islamists.

British expenditure was only a tiny fraction – not much more than 1 per cent of what the Pentagon had spent; and yet it was still more than £22 billion – a tidy sum, by our standards.

I had seen some of our efforts. I had been to the UK-sponsored military academy, the Sandhurst-in-the-Sand as it was optimistically known, and been impressed by the bravery – considering the reprisals they were risking – of the Afghan recruits.

I had choppered out to a UK base, way south of Kabul. I had toted giant machine guns and met some of those lethal UK operatives so nut-brown and so densely bearded that they could pass for natives, which they did. Here at this facility we had helped to train a special detachment of Afghan commandos, in addition to the many thousands of UK-trained Afghan soldiers and police and intelligence officers.

I was persuaded of the permanence of our contribution. Even though we were near the ruins of a camp once made by Alexander the Great (which might perhaps have suggested something to me about the transience of western invasion forces), I believed General

Nick Carter, the chief of the defence staff, who stoutly insisted – even after Biden's announcement – that the Afghan army would hang on and fight.

From July 18 on, we met repeatedly in the National Security Council – a collection of senior ministers, with the defence and security chiefs – to consider the implications of what Biden was doing. We were apprehensive about the fate of Kabul and our £300 million per annum embassy, but the balance of opinion was that after two decades of exertion and sacrifice, the legacy of the west would endure. Our Afghan trainees would show the stuff of battle, we thought.

Well, we were wrong. I don't blame Nick, the CDS, at all. He was a good and wise counsellor. He had tried so hard to change that country, tried so hard with that Afghan army, that I don't think he could believe it would all unravel so fast.

You could blame the Trump administration for the debacle, in the sense that they did the Doha deal in 2020 which set the conditions for the US and Nato withdrawal. But Trump would argue, I expect, that those conditions had not been met. The US had fulfilled its side of the bargain – ending the air campaign against the Taliban, for instance. The Taliban certainly had not.

They made no effort to negotiate, no effort to bring peace. They kept up their attacks on the Ghani government and its soldiers. So when Biden confirmed that he would pull out anyway, regardless of the conditions, in July 2021, the stage was set for disaster. He had imposed a deadline of September 11 for a total withdrawal, and there followed what we should have predicted, a complete collapse of confidence.

Biden's statement snuffed out the last remaining Afghan faith in the US and the west. It abruptly became clear that without American support, and American logistics, there was no way we Brits could hang on in Kabul, no way any Nato country could safely remain – not even the Turks, who had been pretty gung-ho.

The Afghans could see that they were being left to the mercy of the Taliban, and they didn't like the look of it. Surrendering government troops were being shot, in defiance of the laws of war. As in 1842, and since time immemorial, there were terrible penalties exacted upon those Afghans who fought on and continued to side – as the Taliban put it – with the invader.

On August 15, Kabul fell, and Ashraf Ghani was streaking for the exit. He took a private jet to the Gulf, with barely a goodbye. Given how badly he had been let down by the west, and given that the general fate of puppet rulers in Kabul is to be shot and dragged through the streets by a truck, you can't really blame him.

A general panic took hold in western capitals. Biden had brought forward the deadline for total withdrawal to the end of August, and it was clear that we were facing an implosion, a fall of Saigon. It did not help that, as usual in August, many of the key people were away on holiday. After our truncated Scottish midge-fest of the previous year, Carrie and I were in Chequers, but poor old Dom Raab, the foreign secretary, was in Crete on a two-week break with his family.

Dom was actually back at his desk pretty fast, but there is nothing that delights the media more than the spectacle of a politician blatantly torn between his duty to the country and his duty to his wife and kids. They were very cruel. When the *Today* programme accused him of paddle-boarding during the crisis, he replied that he had been in constant contact with me and his officials, and able to join the Cobra meetings on a secure line (which was a good defence), and that anyway he could not have been paddle-boarding because the water was too rough that day, or, as he immortally put it, 'the sea was closed' (perhaps a less robust argument).

If there was a general sense that we were caught on the hop, or that there was an initial chaos in our response, then I am afraid that was true, and it reflected the reality of what was happening in Kabul. Soon the US, the UK and all Nato allies had been pushed

out to Hamid Karzai Airport, where a gigantic airlift was underway.

Thousands of utterly terrified people thronged the perimeter
fence and occasionally broke through to the runways. They were
people who had helped us in the previous two decades of our
mission: interpreters, guides, drivers, embassy staff, babysitters,
aid workers – anyone who was remotely associated with the western effort of running Afghanistan, and for whom that association
might now mean death.

There were heart-breaking scenes as babies were passed up
from the crowd and over the perimeter fence into the hands of the
American troops, in the desperate hope, I suppose, that they
might be borne aloft in some cargo-plane crèche, away to a better
life. In the same delusion, people clung pitifully to the undercar-
riage of the C-130s, falling to their deaths as the planes took off.

On August 26, a suicide bomb killed thirteen US soldiers and
over a hundred Afghans. Together with a handful of MOD officials, our ambassador Lawrie Bristow did a heroic job, staying on
at the airport and trying to process some of the thousands of
applications for asylum in the UK. As for the embassy, it was of
course ransacked, and the Taliban paraded pictures of the Queen
and what could have been oil paintings from the rooms where I
had stayed.

It was what it looked like: a total moral, political and strategic
defeat for the west. The mantle of old Elphinstone, the Victorian
catastrophist, had fallen on our collective shoulders. It was clear
almost immediately that the Taliban were going to take the country back to the dark ages. It wasn't long before women and gay
people were being executed once again, for the crime of having
sexual relations of a kind that offended against the new government's barbaric code.

Soon the ban had come down again on female education. It was
enough, frankly, to make you weep. I am sure that there are many

British families who weep today when they think of the lives our soldiers lost, the grievous injuries they sustained, and when they look at the way we were forced out of Afghanistan.

What was it all for? What did we achieve? It is hard to comfort such families; but it was my job to do so, and I repeat what I said at the time. I still believe that the loss of those soldiers was in a just cause, and that it was not in vain.

The war in Afghanistan was unlike the war in Iraq, in that we really did need to flush out the murderers of 9/11 and stop them from plotting more mayhem. In that twenty-year period of the Nato mission, it is also true that millions of Afghans grew up to have better life chances, not least the huge number of girls who got an education. There were great achievements in Afghanistan, and the families of those who died can take legitimate pride in what they did.

Even if 2021 marked the fourth British retreat from Kabul, that very operation was – in its way – a triumph of logistics. Under Op Pitting, as it was called, we airlifted 15,000 people to safety, and helped thirty-six other countries to protect their nationals, all in about two weeks. As with Dunkirk in 1940, the public imagination was caught by the energy and bravery of those involved in the evacuation.

The UK has the biggest heavy-lift capacity in Europe, and the sight of those British transports taking off from the airport, day after day, night after night, started to raise people's spirits – to the point where a fiasco actually began to feel like a success. I did my best to thank everyone involved, from the troops of 16 Air Assault Brigade, when they got back to Colchester, to the top brass at headquarters in Northwood.

I won't pretend that we extracted everyone who needed or deserved our help. I am sure there were people who had risked a great deal to assist the UK, and yet who did not get out, not in that first wave.

Indeed there were some we did get out who appeared to be a bit disappointed by life in Britain. A few months later, a group of about a dozen were brought to see me in Number Ten.

Where are you based? I asked them cheerily.

'Swansea,' they said.

Terrific, I said, and how are things in Swansea?

Well, said one of them, it was hard to get their kids into the right school.

'And the crime,' said another. 'The crime is bad.'

'And the drugs gangs,' said a third. 'There are too many drugs gangs.'

I almost got impatient with them, and was about to ask whether Swansea was really more crime- and drugs-ridden than Afghanistan. But I thought the better of it.

The overall result, politically, was that no one much blamed the UK government for the fall of Kabul – which was plainly precipitated by the US decision to withdraw – and overall they gave us credit for the daring and despatch of the evacuation.

The general view was that we had made the best of a bad job, and Op Pitting paradoxically confirmed the impression of the vaccine roll-out: that this was – at its best – a highly active, can-do government, capable of dealing with whatever fate might throw our way.

On September 18, I had a cabinet reshuffle, promoting the likes of Nadhim Zahawi, Simon Clarke, Kit Malthouse, Nadine Dorries, Michelle Donelan and others. The changes were pretty well received, and *The Times* even wrote a laudatory leader, saying that I was clearly gaining in prime ministerial skill (which was high praise from that quarter).

So I am afraid it was in a mood of some self-confidence, if not big-headedness, that I headed into party conference. We were getting on with all our plans for levelling up, and I was energised by discussions with Andy Haldane, the former deputy governor of the Bank of England, who had come on board as an adviser on the project. Michael Gove, the levelling-up secretary, was getting into his stride, and coming forward with more plans to give power and responsibility to local leaders – because you can't level up without local champions, who can tell the story of what their city or town is achieving.

The message at conference was simple – a sermon beautifully illuminated by Britain's vaccine triumph. I pointed out (not for the first or last time) that there was a reason why the UK vaccines had actually worked, and that was because they were made by western pharmaceutical giants, with their roots in liberal capitalist free market democracies.

I drew the contrast with Sinovac and Sinopharm, from China, and Sputnik from Russia. You were more likely to get genuine breakthroughs, and efficacious vaccines, from companies that answered to consumers and shareholders, I said, than you were from companies that answered to politburos and party cadres.

But, as with the vaccines, you needed government to lead, to set the pace, to create the conditions for capitalism to flourish. That's how we were levelling up, using the billions of our budgets to trigger the trillions of global investment. That's how we would tackle the problem of climate change, making the market so that the private sector could drive the technologies that would cut CO_2 emissions.

It was my third party conference as leader, and by far the most successful. The *Sunday Times* (again, not really prominent in my fan club) observed that I seemed to dominate the political land-scape, squatting over proceedings like a giant Buddha. Of course, I knew with one lobe of my brain that there were probably many people in my party who wanted me gone. I had sacked some dangerous people and failed to promote many others. In the course of writing about politics for more than thirty years, I had deliberately or inadvertently caused a great deal of outrage and offence. Above all, I had delivered Brexit – a project opposed at the time, remember, by a clear majority of Tory MPs.

So I can see, in retrospect, that my position was much more fragile than I thought. I assumed that we had a winning formula, and a great national project in levelling up, and that on the whole people would want to stick with it.

I was so confident about life, and the government, that in September 2021 I made a fiscal mistake. In the 2019 manifesto we had promised to fix social care – to end the terrifying costs of caring for dementia. The plan was expensive, and we also needed to raise funds for the Covid-battered NHS.

Rishi persuaded me that there was only one way to do it all: we had to put up National Insurance contributions by 1.25 per cent. Which was a breach of another manifesto promise, not to raise tax. I didn't like it, but assumed he was right.

Well, I now think he wasn't. We had the fiscal space. We didn't need to raise the tax. In fact, Rishi went on to cancel the NIC rises when he took over. But it didn't help me with colleagues.

I was utterly sure that we would be cutting taxes overall by the end of the parliament, probably quite substantially ... but that depended on getting to the end of the parliament.

Chapter 49

Saving the Planet

In which the UK stages a successful
COP summit

WAIT A mo, I said to myself as I was walking back to the UK delegation room, I know that face. It was the blond tresses and pouting lips of Hollywood's number-one heart-throb megastar.

Shining the light of his countenance upon us in gritty, gusty Glasgow on November 2, 2021 was none other than Leonardo DiCaprio. He was ten yards away, striding towards me down the prefab corridor, right here in the convention centre where the world's leaders had come together to stop the world from being fried.

He was getting closer. Yes, he seemed to have some business with us, little old us – the UK presidency of the UN conference on climate change, known as COP 26. What could he want?

Perhaps the *Titanic* star was here to sound the alarm about the iceberg ahead – the coming cataclysm that could whelm us all beneath the waves. Or perhaps it was the other way round, and he was actually pro-berg, like *Jaws* director Steven Spielberg, who now campaigned for the conservation of sharks; perhaps he was here to warn of the horrors of a world without icebergs, where even monsters like the one that sunk his ship had been dissolved by the warming oceans.

Maybe he had come to wish us all luck as we tried to bring 197 cacophonous and irresponsible nations to agreement and keep 1.5 alive: that is, to keep alive the pledge made at the Paris COP in 2015, six years previously, that even if we could not halt the rise in the temperature of the planet, we could at least restrain that increase to no more than 1.5 degrees.

As he drew closer, the real-life DiCaprio seemed taller and bulkier than the screen idol. Wha-wha-what can we do to help? we asked his phalanx of advisers. Someone came briefly to the point.

Mr DiCaprio was in need of the gentlemen's conveniences. They understood that this was the Presidency Suite. Did we possess the necessary amenities?

It would be an honour, we said, and without further ado the megastar marched past us in search of the bogs.

He seemed to be detained for some time, and in the hiatus Dan Rosenfield, my chief of staff, had an idea. The adjoining room was our nerve centre, full of overworked and brilliant young women. They had heard that DiCaprio was in the vicinity and were excited.

The COP negotiations were like trying to lead a giant group therapy session in which 197 addicts have theoretically pledged to give up hydrocarbons, while in reality remaining deeply dependent, with all the lies and cheats and finger-crossings involved. It was exhausting stuff.

Could Mr DiCaprio perhaps say hi to the team? Just share a few photons of his astral radiance? So I tried him out, as he eventually emerged and hastened past. Fans of DiCaprio will know that he is equally proficient at playing both the goodie and the baddie. Today, I am afraid, we didn't get the generous-hearted young romantic from *Titanic*. He was channelling a different persona: brusque, cynical ... Wait! I knew this role.

It was Danny Archer, the hard-bitten white Rhodesian gunrunner and gem smuggler from the 2007 hit *Blood Diamond* – which had been such a cult movie in my family that we all knew the dialogue off by heart.

As he quickened his pace, I found myself speaking in a thick South African accent and quoting some of his greatest lines.

At the sound of the UK PM impersonating DiCaprio impersonating a South African gunrunner, the film star checked his stride. He looked at me appraisingly.

'I will see you later, my friend,' he said, and stalked off.

It is a comment on the way the world works that if I had asked Biden, Macron, Modi, Merkel or any one of the 120 global leaders in Glasgow, they would of course have said yes, at the drop of a hat. That is just what we politicians do; because we are here today, gone tomorrow glow-worms by comparison with a supernova like DiCaprio.

Never mind, said Anouka and Tara and Sam and Dan and all the rest of the presidency team, and carried on hitting the phones. We would survive without DiCaprio's encouragement, though we decided that in view of his substantial spell in the presidency bogs we would rename him Leonardo DiCrapio.

Maybe he just couldn't be bothered, or maybe the view from team DiCaprio was that they didn't want his brand to be contaminated by the UK presidency, when at that particular juncture – the launch of the summit in November 2021 – there was every chance that COP would flop, and that the result would be somewhere on the scale between disappointment and disaster.

The climate summit in Glasgow was the world's biggest official meeting since the pandemic began, and the anxiety was very far from over. Some countries – like Russia and China – were still dealing with bad bouts of Covid, and neither Putin nor Xi was there. We had social distancing. Many people wore masks, though pretty intermittently.

We still had 40,000 delegates – and that was nothing, of course, next to the hordes of ravening eco-warriors who had gathered outside. Already the Glasgow COP 26 summit was under siege from the climate protesters. Whipped up by Greta Thunberg, their whey-faced teenage Joan of Arc, they boiled and seethed with reproach at the besuited buffoons within. They damned us for our complacency, our sluggishness, our endless blah-blah-blah, as Greta put it; so witheringly and – let's face it – so accurately.

What had we actually DONE, we world leaders, since Paris in 2015? We had told the world – I was there, as mayor of London – that we would deliver an astonishing change in human habits. We had said that we would give up burning fossil fuels, and do it so abruptly that we would actually slow the process of global warming.

You only had to look around to see the evidence of our failure. Every year seemed to be hotter than the last. The ice floes were melting. The defrosting mammoths were yawning from the tundra.

The deserts were encroaching, the species were dying and the lapping waves were besieging the small island nations – and all the while humanity was actually pumping more and more CO_2 into the atmosphere, swaddling the planet with an ever-thicker tea cosy.

The Chinese seemed to be building a new coal-fired power station virtually every week. How could they be restrained? How could we tell the developing world that they were now forbidden from burning fossil fuels – when the vast bulk of the problem has been caused by the historic emissions of the richest and most developed nations; above all by us, the Brits, who had been the first to industrialise at scale?

It was actually here in Glasgow that James Watt had come up with the world's first coal-fired steam engine; and now it felt as though we had to redeem ourselves, to atone for centuries of incontinent CO_2 flatulence.

We needed a global carminative for these appalling farts. We, the Brits, had to tame the carbon genie we had unleashed.

Every speaker in that opening ceremony competed to offer the most blood-curdling jeremiad. Time was running out. It was one minute to midnight. The mercury in the great global thermometer was about to boil and unless we acted, now, together, the entire planet and all of Creation was going to be sizzled up like a sausage.

Wait a minute ...

You mean to say you still don't believe it? You still need convincing about the central propositions of global warming?

Well, as I said a bit earlier on, I understand how you feel, because I once shared your anxieties. I just wish you could have been there, in the opening ceremony; because there was one speech that really stood out.

Never mind the flummery, the Polynesian drumming, the vatic recitations by African poetesses. Forget the political bombast – such as my own effort, in which I compared the summiteers to a tuxedoed James Bond (another famous son of Scotland), trying to defuse a ticking doomsday device.

There was one speech that really gripped the issue and spoke to the depths of my sceptical soul; and it was from a man who actually excited our female staffers far more than Leonardo DiCaprio, and that was the ninety-five-year-old David Attenborough, the great BBC naturalist. He only spoke for about six minutes (far shorter than me, I am afraid), but it was all gold. He flashed a number on the screen behind him: 414.

Focus on that number, he said. It is the current concentration of CO_2 in the atmosphere, measured in parts per million (ppm). It isn't a lot, but it is up by 50 per cent since naughty Britain ate from the tree of knowledge and led the world from our pre-industrial Eden.

That number was significant, he said, because if you looked at the last few hundred thousand years, it was clear that the atmospheric CO_2 concentration had been driving events – not just in meteorology, but in human history. Up until 10,000 years ago,

Attenborough explained, this number had been bouncing around all over the place – lurching from about 180ppm to about 300ppm.

For the evolving human race it had been a pretty wretched time as the world yo-yoed between extreme warmth and cold. Early humankind was constantly buffeted by climate change, reeling from drought to flood, from forest fires to Ice Age. It was hard to settle down, invent the wheel, double-entry bookkeeping and so on when every day was a fight for survival.

Then about 10,000 years ago all that changed, said Attenborough. Things calmed down. The atmospheric concentrations of CO_2 stabilised at about 280ppm. It was the long subsequent epoch of climate tranquillity that allowed the spectacular rise of modern humanity: survivable winters, reliable rainfall, reliable harvests; and so forth.

And now, with that CO_2 concentration shooting up vertiginously to 414 (I think at the time of writing it is about 420) – far higher than at any time in the history or even the prehistory of our species – that precious climate stability was starting to break down.

Attenborough described his own personal observation of the changes in a way that seemed unforced and wholly believable. It struck me that, at the age of ninety-five, he had seen an appreciable percentage of the historical epoch.

How far back do our human records go? Forty centuries? Attenborough had spent almost an entire century travelling the world and looking at the changes himself. He had recorded the data with his own eyes, and it was there in his head – and if he said that the climate was changing, he had authority in the matter, a credibility that perhaps went beyond the scientists and the statistics.

But what really enthused me, and had me trumpeting my approval through my Covid mask, was his absolute refusal to be negative. He didn't berate us for our failings. He didn't stand up like some Savonarola and denounce the weakness and short-termism of politicians, whatever he may have felt.

We have the fixes, he told us. We human beings were the greatest problem-solvers the world had ever seen. We would fix anthropogenic climate change, he said, and we would fix it in our lifetimes.

That really made me sit up and cheer – because that is exactly how I see it. I can see the possibility – the probability – of an impending disaster. But I can also see a way that humanity can ju-jitsu this problem, and with our Promethean ingenuity we can turn it into an almighty stimulus for global growth: a new kind of growth that does not automatically damage the planet; a type of growth that can release posterity from jeopardy.

As soon as I became PM I had a series of green teach-ins, first about the basic science, in which Patrick Vallance and others took me through a more detailed version of the Attenborough thesis – the hideous upward kink in CO_2 concentrations; then about all the technical remedies: from carbon capture to guilt-free flying.

Throughout that plague year of 2020, I was thinking about the economic recovery – we called it project bounceback – and how we could use this inflection point to switch to new green technology. I tried to get Tesla to build a vast factory in the UK; and then again with another start-up called Rivian.

I urged Rolls-Royce to get on with building small modular nuclear reactors; I went to Orkney to look at wind power, and how to use surplus electricity to make green hydrogen. By the end of the year my head was full of plans for a green industrial revolution.

People later said that I had become too messianical about this agenda – but my Tory friends can't have been surprised. I had said it many times during the campaign for the Tory leadership in 2019.

If eighteenth-century Britain could lead the world in burning hydrocarbons, twenty-first-century Britain could lead the next industrial revolution. I saw (and see) the green industrial revolution as a beautiful clean machine for driving levelling up.

As a small kid I had a lovely old jigsaw map of the counties of Britain, with each piece showing little pictures of the products identified with that county: steel cutlery from Yorkshire, hops and apples from Kent, and so on. In my mind's eye, I started to see how the benefits of these amazing green technologies were already being distributed across the UK – batteries in the West Midlands, carbon capture in Teesside, new nuclear in Somerset, fusion in Oxfordshire, wind power off the coast, etc.

Of course, it all sounds ridiculously over-schematic; and I hasten to say that I had no mad Soviet or 1970s-style industrial plan. But I was certain that if we were going to have a change as big as this, away from burning carbon, then government would have to give a lead – to show business where the country was going, so that the market could make investments with confidence.

So on December 17, 2020 – almost a year before the COP summit – I published a boiled-down version in the *Financial Times*, and called it a ten-point plan for a green recovery.

It was simple.

1 – RENEWABLE POWER GENERATION. We were going to be the Saudi Arabia of wind power, with enough offshore capacity to power every UK home by 2030. We were already one of the biggest producers of offshore wind in the world – perhaps number one or number two. But we had huge potential in the Dogger Bank and elsewhere. Plus solar, where there were sharp falls in the price of panels.

2 – HYDROGEN. We would make big investments in hydrogen for all purposes, including transport and perhaps even domestic heating. Angela Merkel was putting goodly sums into hydrogen trains, and I was determined that we should not be beaten.

3 – NUCLEAR. We would encourage nuclear power of all kinds, from the big reactors like Sizewell and Hinkley to the SMRs, which Rolls-Royce said they could make using the designs for their submarine propulsion units. We also continued to bet on fusion. As soon as I became PM – even before the 2019 election – I went out to the labs at Culham in Oxfordshire, where they told me that the secret of fusion – limitless clean green nuclear energy – was only twenty years away. Which was exactly what they had told me about twenty years previously, when I first became the local MP. Still: if fusion was going to happen, I wanted it to happen here.

4 – ELECTRIC VEHICLES. We were going to encourage not just gigafactories for the batteries in the UK, but also the building of EVs. I could see that electric vehicles were going to become ever more commonplace, and that pretty soon they would take over from combustion engines. Would British manufacturing seize this opportunity? Or would we just buy a load of EVs from China? I wanted us to get going and make our own. That's why I decided we should set such an aggressive timetable for the switchover from petrol and diesel to electric – 2030 – even ahead of the EU. I wanted the UK to have first-mover advantage; and later I put Dan Rosenfield in charge of the project of working with the car firms. I fear the foot came off the electric throttle after 2022.

5 – GREEN TRANSPORT NETWORKS. We were going to get people travelling on clean, green British-made buses, coupled with a big push on cycling. Good mass-transit systems drive levelling up, enabling people to reach the jobs they need. As we used to say on TfL, there are very few transport problems that can't be solved with a single-decker bus. I had championed cleaner, British-built buses in London; now was the time to do the same across the country. We promised 4,000 new green buses, made in the UK.

6 – JET ZERO. Almost exactly a century ago, the British duo Alcock and Brown had made the first transatlantic flight in a plane, and used a prodigious amount of fossil fuel. I pledged that the UK would make the first big London–NY flight – with passengers – using zero-emission fuel, and that we would do the same for ships, possibly by using ammonia.

7 – LOWER EMISSIONS FROM BUILDINGS. We were going to invest a billion a year on making schools and other public buildings greener, especially their heating systems. I had a teach-in on heat pumps, and a series of outsize machines was brought into the Cabinet Room. One day, when they are made at scale, these heat-exchange devices will be genuinely effective and affordable. I know they are slow to take off in this country, but is our climate really so different from those other European countries – like France – where they have been so popular?

8 – CARBON CAPTURE AND STORAGE. This is the process by which you can actually sequester CO_2 in the seabed and other places. You can use CCS to clean up industries like steelmaking, or you can use it to make green hydrogen. You take the hydrogen out of the hydrocarbons and put the carbon

deep underground. There is already a big BP project in Teesside. One day CCS will be a major part of the solution.

9 – NATURE. We were going to green up the entire country, with 30,000 more trees planted every year, to improve climate resilience and our general ability to absorb CO_2. And we were going to re-wild large tracts (this was much less popular with farmers) in order to improve biodiversity and restore lost habitats. We are a great nation of animal lovers, but we have fewer species of wild animal than any other country in Europe (look at our amphibians – tragic; a total of fifteen UK species compared to forty-three in France). As I said in my conference speech, it was time to build back greener, build back better, build back beaver.

10 – INNOVATION. We were going to put substantial investment into the new technologies that I believe can solve the problem, as well as develop new instruments of green finance.

That was the plan, and it went down well. The greenies liked it. The media liked it, and, somewhat to my surprise, business REALLY liked it.

I know it looks simplistic – but people need a basic statement of national intent, a flag to rally behind, a tune they can whistle as they march.

I merely observe that attempts by my successors as PM to move on from the green agenda, or to sneer at net zero, have not, to put it mildly, been crowned with electoral success; nor, frankly, do I even see much polling evidence that this strategy is popular.

The British people overwhelmingly want to cut pollution and to protect the environment. If you can explain to them clearly how you can do that while creating jobs 'n' growth AND ultimately cutting their energy costs – then you are on to a winner.

So I went to that COP as a hot-gospelling holy roller, a Moses armed with my green Decalogue; and the key difference between me and Greta Thunberg was that I wasn't preaching hellfire and damnation for humanity; I had all my proof points about the potential of green technology.

You say you can't do it, I told delegates at COP. You say you are hooked on coal. Well, how many people here were alive in 1970? That's right – a lot of us were.

When I was a child in 1970, six years old, bouncing around on my orange space hopper, guess how much of Britain's electricity came from coal-fired power stations?

It was 70 per cent. And guess how much of our electricity comes from coal today?

It's less than 1 per cent. That's how fast this can be done.

There are some days, I said, when more than half our domestic electricity is produced by wind power alone. That is how the UK has cut CO_2 emissions by 45 per cent on 1990 levels, while the British people, on the whole, have got steadily richer.

It was a persuasive message, I think, but the credit for making the arguments belongs not to me but to the whole presidency team, led by Alok Sharma, my former business secretary and MP for Reading, who did an outstanding job.

Slowly the negotiations began to come together. By the end of COP 26, after two weeks of talks, we had far exceeded expectations. I had been at the Paris summit in 2015 and found the whole thing too abstract, too lost in the physics.

It wasn't good enough to pledge to restrain the growth in world temperatures. We needed to explain HOW we were going to do that – in ways that everyone could understand. For months we had wrestled with this problem.

What does success look like? I kept asking Alok, and the director of COP, my former private secretary Peter Hill. I needed simple, almost cartoonish ideas.

Allegra Stratton, the COP communications director, was also an experienced TV journalist. Like me, she was passionate about the whole campaign – but she also understood the need to express our results in concrete ways.

She came up with a mantra: 'Coal, Cars, Cash, Trees'. We delivered on all four.

So: COAL.

We persuaded sixty-five countries that the time had come to move away from burning coal. There was some last-minute disappointment when the Chinese and the Indians changed the text from 'phase out coal' to 'phase down coal' – but I wasn't too fussed.

Whatever 'phase down' means, the direction was still the same.

CARS.

We got thirty-five countries to join us, and the EU, in pledging to get rid of petrol or diesel internal combustion engines by 2035 at the latest. Again, you can say we were going too fast. But then some European countries – like Norway – are already way ahead.

CASH.

We found more money to help the most vulnerable countries to adapt and protect themselves, and even if the world fell short of the target set at Paris – a transfer of $100 billion a year – that was no surprise. The target was always unrealistic.

We did much better at mobilising private funds. Under the leadership of Mark Carney, former governor of the Bank of England, we set up GFANZ – the Glasgow Financial Alliance for Net Zero. Even if Carney was exaggerating the private sector funds now committed to funding net zero ($130 trillion, he said!), the direction, again, was right.

Perhaps the most important innovation at Glasgow was the idea of the 'Just Energy Transition Partnership'. This was about helping countries such as South Africa to de-carbonise by using government investment – whether national funds, or funds from the global financial institutions – to stimulate the market to invest.

I had been deeply impressed by the success of the UK wind power sector, which was based on collaboration between government and the private sector. Under the 'contracts for difference' system, the government set the strike price for wind power – the minimum price at which it would buy the energy.

That has given the market more and more confidence to invest. The windmills have got ever vaster, the costs of production have come down, and the market has become entirely self-sustaining.

This was the basic idea – using government and GFI (global financial institutions) funding to trigger private investment – that Biden and I had first discussed at Carbis Bay, and which we eventually called Build Back Better World.

I suppose we conceived it as an alternative to the Chinese Belt and Road, but I see no real reason why the Chinese couldn't be involved. If we are going to pull it off in our lifetimes, as Attenborough suggested we can, and equip the developing world with the right green technology, then this is the way to do it.

Glasgow took a big step in the right direction.

TREES.

Ever since I had been foreign secretary, I had wanted the world to focus more on habitats, and nature, and the loss of species. Where do these endangered creatures generally hang out? In forests.

The Glasgow COP summit was remarkable for its focus on nature – much of the work led by Zac Goldsmith, the environment minister. In the end 130 countries signed the leaders' declaration on forests and land use, which committed their countries to 'halt and reverse' the loss of forests and woodland habitat.

This was backed up by $19.2 billion in public and private funding for the protection of trees, with a good chunk going specifically to the Congo basin. We made the argument successfully that tackling climate change and protecting nature are two sides of the same campaign.

You need that vast canopy of carbon-absorbing leaves to help you tackle carbon emissions; and you need to tackle carbon emissions to prevent the droughts and the fires that destroy the forests.

On coal, cars, cash, trees we had a good story to tell, and above all we had enough pledges to cut emissions to be able to say, at the end of Glasgow, that the goal was still attainable. If everybody stuck to their commitments – and by now 90 per cent of the world was committed to net zero, as opposed to 30 per cent when we started – then humanity was in with a chance.

If we fulfilled this programme we might, just might, restrict global warming to 1.5 degrees by 2100.

Looking back, I think we were probably fated to succeed, or at least to overachieve, at the Glasgow COP. The world wanted an agreement – partly because the whole experience of Covid had been so deeply disheartening. Faced with a new plague, the nations of the earth had spent months in a *sauve-qui-peut* competition for PPE and for vaccines. It had not been edifying. Now we all wanted to pull together, and we did.

At the end of it all, Alok was so overcome by his exertions that he wept – which slightly panicked me as I watched. I feared his tears would encourage the media to say it was all a failure; but they didn't, far from it.

Alok wept because he knew that there was more we could have done – but also because he knew we had made tangible progress. They were tears of relief as well as regret.

After a few days at the summit, I went back to London – feeling that things were going pretty well. In fact, I had got to the stage where you are impervious to the warning signals.

A few days before the COP summit in Glasgow we had been at the G20 in Rome, where some of my actions were causing tension with our EU friends.

We in the UK had been getting very fed up with the way Brussels was making life difficult for Northern Ireland, pointlessly interrupting the movement of bacon and sausages and shortbread and whatnot – even though the vast bulk of NI trade is with the rest of the UK.

So we were pushing on with the development of a new bill – later to be called the Northern Ireland Protocol Bill – which would stop this nonsense and make it clear once and for all that Northern Ireland was part of the UK economy.

It was, admittedly, a big bazooka, and arguably a breach of our international obligations under the Northern Ireland protocol. But I felt we had to tool up, to be in a stronger position, and get the EU to be more reasonable and less pettifogging.

I had been sitting at my place in the G20 chamber in Rome when I noticed Macron and Merkel and others in a knot, having a conversation. Then Merkel came and stood behind me.

She bent over. 'You must give up this plan in Northern Ireland,' she said, 'or else there will be a Shakespearean tragedy.'

What did she mean? What did she know? I now wonder.

It wasn't just the EU who disliked my legal blunderbuss. There were a lot of pro-EU Tory MPs whose long-suppressed feelings were now being triggered.

I was feeling generally so bullish that I did something no PM should ever do. I went out to a boozy dinner, that very evening, with some journalists.

I had for many years been a leader writer (among other things) for the *Daily Telegraph*, and ages ago one of my contemporaries – the affable Neil Darbyshire – had invited me to a reunion. I said yes, since my time at the *Telegraph* was full of happy memories. I was keen to catch up with old friends, and it looked as though we could just about squeeze it into the diary.

So I pitched up at the Garrick and made a little speech, drank a few glasses of wine and chin-wagged with my former colleagues – when frankly I should have been back in Number Ten, preparing for PMQs the following day and addressing myself to the problem of Owen Paterson.

This was the MP for North Shropshire, and former Northern Ireland secretary, who had got himself into hot water. According to the parliamentary commissioner for standards, Kathryn Stone, he had been lobbying in Parliament for some companies without properly declaring his interest.

I am ashamed to say that by the Tuesday evening I had not properly read her report, having been travelling for the last week – from the Rome G20 to Glasgow. But I knew that two of my closest allies – Mark Spencer, the chief whip, and Jacob Rees-Mogg, the leader of the House – had read it all carefully and formed strong views.

Whatever Owen had done wrong, they told me, the process was deeply unfair. He had not been given a proper chance to defend himself, and his wife Rose had been so heart-sickened by the whole business that she had gone down to the woods near their house in Shropshire and taken her own life.

Rose was a much-loved figure. Owen was popular, especially on the right and Eurosceptic wing of the party. Feelings, I was told, were running high.

We couldn't just accept the findings of Kathryn Stone, when she had effectively been judge and jury in her own cause. On top of his personal misery, Owen now faced a motion of censure that would see him effectively forced to step down as an MP. It was very cruel.

So my cabinet colleagues had come up with a compromise. That Wednesday morning we sat at the glass-topped dining table in my office. The minutes were ticking by until PMQs, and I tried to get my head round the proposed solution. I was instinctively inclined to be sympathetic to Owen. I had met him over thirty years previously, in Prague, just as communism was collapsing in eastern Europe. He was then a tanner, a seller of leather goods, and already a brave and principled sceptic on the EU.

I had him down as a good and kindly man, and I thought it most unlikely that he could deliberately have been engaged in some kind of financial misdemeanour. My feelings had been reinforced over dinner at the Garrick (where I should perhaps stress that there were women present) by talking to Charles Moore – my venerated friend and former editor.

Charles is a close friend of Owen, and had written fiercely in his defence.

Was I going to defend Owen Paterson? he asked me.

'You bet,' I said airily.

Now, with a slight hangover, I was discovering that this was more difficult than I had assumed.

Jacob and the chief were explaining that we could somehow acknowledge that Owen had been foolish, and yet reject the severity of Kathryn Stone's findings. That is, we could ask a specially convened cross-party committee of MPs to look again at the case and give him a proper hearing.

This approach was strongly supported by at least some of my political staffers, and as everyone was talking I was flipping quickly through the Kathryn Stone report.

Hmmm, I thought, as some of Owen's emails leaped out at me. I don't like the look of this.

He had definitely been interceding on behalf of these companies – and in quite an assertive way. But by now we were barely ninety minutes from PMQs, and it was too late to change tack.

I was going to have to make a go of it in the House. It was not easy.

I tried to make the distinction between the substance – on which the government conceded that Owen had at least a case to answer – and the process, which we said was flawed. I tried to arouse the sympathy of the House, usually in ready supply, for Owen's personal tragedy, but I could tell that it wasn't really working.

Tory MPs were muttering, and later, when we voted, a good few of them rebelled against the whip.

Still, we did it. We quashed the report against Owen, and I felt so queasy about it that I went up to him in the Lobby and begged him. He had to be contrite, I said; he had to apologise, because this was not, repeat not, an exoneration.

I am afraid he failed to heed my advice. He felt exonerated, and that, of course, was how it looked.

It looked as though I had tyrannically used my eighty-seat majority to crush the findings of the independent parliamentary commissioner for standards to protect a Tory colleague.

As the evening wore on, I sat in the flat with Carrie, phoning colleagues, feeling worse and worse. After all the idealism of the COP summit it felt awful, squalid. Worst of all, the plan didn't even work – and never could have worked. There was no way we could empanel a cross-party group of MPs to look again at Owen, because by this stage most MPs had read some of the details of the report, and we had no cross-party cooperation on the matter.

We were stuck, and there was a clear risk that the whole thing would drag on and hang round our necks like a putrefying albatross. So I decided overnight that there was nothing for it. I had to do the most painful thing of all, and execute a U-turn – and if there is one thing that colleagues hate, it is being marched up the hill and marched back down again.

Since the government could not give effect to its amendment, and since there was no chance of getting cross-party agreement on a new process, we had little choice but to back down and vote through the original report. Owen was duly cashiered and stood down; now we were facing a very nasty-looking by-election in

December, and the mood was already very different from the spring.

The world economy was in a state of post-Covid paralysis; supply chains were bunged up; inflation was on the horizon; supermarket shelves were empty of basic goods, and people's tempers were frayed.

Our voters were getting especially angry at the spectacle of the boats crossing the Channel, heavily laden with illegal immigrants, and the apparent inability of the government to fix it. I thought I had a solution, a really bold and beautiful one.

But we had to work on it in secret, and it was taking months longer than I wanted. I did not quite realise how much of my political capital I had already burned up with my parliamentary colleagues (if not the wider electorate), or how fast I was burning through the remainder.

Chapter 50

Omigod It's Omicron

After the fear comes the anger

You what? I said to my team in Number Ten. I could hardly believe our bad luck. We had worked wonders to vaccinate the British public. By a gigantic collective effort, we had succeeded faster than virtually any other country in administering two jabs against Covid – and certainly faster than any other country of comparable size.

By August 2021, 75 per cent of adults had been fully vaccinated, and that meant that we had been able to ease restrictions, and stage an economic recovery, faster than any country in the G7. In my imagination the vaccine now coursed in our veins like some immortal ichor. We had created a massive sea-wall of immunity, a rampart big and tall enough to repel the next wave of Covid, because there was no variant – no mutation of the disease – that could defeat two jabs. Or was there?

Er, well, PM, said my officials, it seemed we had bad news.

There was a variant that had cropped up in South Africa, called B.1.1.529, that was spreading with amazing speed; and it looked as though you could indeed contract it if you had been vaccinated.

Even with two jabs? I asked.

They looked at me, stricken, and nodded.

It was called omicron, the Greek letter meaning a small o, and the fifteenth in the Greek alphabet. They had missed out nu because it sounds like new; and as for xi, the WHO was heavily dependent on Beijing, and they weren't keen on a variant that seemed to be named after Xi Jinping – not when the Chinese were already so sensitive about their role in bringing Covid to the world.

Is it here, this omicron? I said. Is it in the UK? It was.

On November 27 there were two cases identified, but by early December there were hundreds. I could tell that the system was getting ready for another assault on personal liberty. The Covid Taskforce was preparing the legal instruments – and once again I was going to be passed the great jangling keyring and asked to lock up the nation.

On Monday December 6 they all filed back in, led for some reason by Munira Mirza, the head of the policy unit. I had always taken Munira for a staunch libertarian, ever since she had worked as my deputy mayor at City Hall. She was a friend and an ally, and I was surprised to see her at the head of a pro-lockdown delegation.

Their argument was simple. It was the old argument, the one that had proved repeatedly irresistible over the last couple of years. Yes, we had built up a wall against the invading virus; we had protected millions of people. But what about the unprotected? What about the immuno-compromised, what about the cancer patients? What about all those who couldn't or wouldn't be vaccinated?

As Munira saw it, a tidal wave of infection was about to burst on our battlements. Huge numbers would catch it; and even if the new omicron variant proved fatal in only a small percentage of cases, we all knew the mantra: a small percentage of a very large number is still a very large number.

I can't remember exactly if I ground my teeth, or swore, or held my head in my hands, but it's highly likely. It just seemed so insane, so wrong – after all we had suffered – that we were going to be forced to do the same goddamn thing all over again. It was now only a couple of weeks until Christmas, and inch by inch I was being sucked into the same political killing ground.

With every passing day, the number of infections was growing, and that meant – if omicron was as dangerous as previous variants – that every day on which I now failed to lock down would add exponentially to the eventual death toll. Already about 160,000 people had died on my watch. In fact, British mortality has never risen so fast at any time since the Second World War.

By this stage, furthermore, the scientists had thrown away all their previous hesitations about lockdown. They began the pandemic by arguing, you will recall, that governments had to be careful not to be premature, because of the risk of taxing public patience. Well, all that was now over.

My scientific and medical advisers had been scalded by suggestions (probably unfair) that we had been too slow the first time round. Now their advice was emphatic. If you think you have a problem, said Patrick Vallance, then you should probably go a bit harder and a bit earlier than the position seems to warrant.

'Go hard, go early,' he muttered. His view – the scientific view – was that we should strike now, and that we couldn't go wrong by doing so.

Couldn't go wrong, eh? I said to myself.

It was obvious what would happen if we locked down now. We would kiss goodbye to Christmas – again – with all the destruction that entailed for the hospitality and retail sectors. We probably wouldn't get the kids back into school in January, with yet more irremediable damage to the life chances of those kids; and what drove us to despair is that we were being forced, yet again, to act on the basis of inadequate information.

We knew that omicron was infectious, and that people were going to contract Covid, yet again, in huge numbers. We just didn't know one statistic – the infection fatality rate (IFR). We didn't know how many people the disease would kill as a proportion of those who caught it. We could, of course, wait to find out, but by the time we knew the IFR it might well be too late, and the level of infection would be such as to doom us to huge numbers of deaths.

As decisions go, it was appalling, and lonely. As I sat at my chair in the Cabinet Room, mulling it over, I sometimes wondered whether in future we will be able to use some artificial intelligence program – to feed in all the mathematical considerations involved in this devilish balance between the damage done by a pandemic and the damage done by lockdown – and somehow get the correct solution: moral, medical, economic, educational.

You only have to pose the question in that way to see that it will never happen. We won't be able to rely on machines to make our minds up because these decisions are so quintessentially political. They depend on dozens of separate value judgements and priorities, instinctual judgements that you can't just type into a machine. You have to be able to explain them to the public, to take people with you. You have to keep campaigning and explaining; and though people had been – on the whole – miraculously supportive so far, I could tell that by the autumn of 2021 the political mood was changing.

Yes, people had been impressed by the vaccine roll-out, proud of UK scientists and of the NHS, and that mood had been reflected by our buoyancy in the polls – which was pretty creditable for a mid-term government, and after eleven years of Tory-led rule.

But no plant withers faster than political laurels, and any post-vaccination glow had long since dissipated. Covid, the horror of Covid, had driven us together; and as the threat of Covid seemed to recede that sense of national unity was inevitably fractured and the public became prone, as ever, to a natural and forgivable grumpiness about more or less everything.

On September 30, we had finally axed the furlough payments – the extremely generous system whereby the Treasury paid you 80 per cent of your salary, up to £2,500 a month, to stay at home. With a fully vaccinated population, more or less everyone (except the Labour Party) could see that this was the right thing to do. The furlough programme – or Coronavirus Job Retention Scheme – was right; and Rishi and his team deserve great credit for the speed with which they acted to roll it out. But that scheme alone had by now cost about £70 billion, and as every politician knows it is much easier to hand out benefits than to take them away.

So by the autumn there were a great many people feeling the financial cold turkey of coming off furlough, and as they went grumpily back to work, and the economy came out of hibernation, the resurgent demand brought even more problems – like the sudden thawing of winter pipes. The world wanted things fast – gas, or microprocessors, or fresh vegetables – and at once our supply chains seized up.

We were dependent on vast container ships, all of which seemed to be stuck on the wrong side of the world, and one of which got spectacularly wedged in the Suez Canal. We had a fuel shortage; we had empty shelves in the supermarkets – and the nation started to ask itself furiously: where are all the truck drivers? Where are the shelf-stackers?

The voice of business was raised in panic. It was Brexit! they squawked. Brexit and Covid had sent them all home, all those diligent east Europeans with their allegedly superior work ethic. No wonder they couldn't find anyone to fill the pumps or staff the supermarkets. It turned out – as so often – that the problem wasn't really Brexit, or some EU exodus.

If anything, it seemed we had massively underestimated the number of EU nationals living in Britain. It wasn't three million – the figure bandied about by both sides in the 2016 referendum. It was more than five million. The problem in the labour force wasn't really a shortage of migrant workers; but more the Covid and furlough-induced discovery that working from home was generally pretty agreeable – given that you could always conceal your boxer shorts and chilled sauvignon from the Zoom call. Huge numbers of British people – especially men in their fifties – were quietly fading from the workforce; and this no-show caused such a panic across Whitehall that the Home Office and the Migration Advisory Committee understandably overreacted and turned on the taps, especially for social care workers, so that we were to have a record influx the following year, 2022.

By then, of course, it was too late. With a shortage of goods and a shortage of labour, we had the inevitable result. The most important political event in the autumn of 2021 was the reappearance, for the first time in a long time, of serious inflation.

It was no use explaining that this was a global problem. People could see that their household bills had gone up, and that makes everyone grumpy.

Above all, people were getting tetchy and scratchy because they were no longer afraid. As long as people were generally frightened of Covid, frightened of what it could do to them or their loved ones, they were willing us on, willing us to get it right, and they were at least temporarily willing to forgive our mistakes. The paradox of the vaccine roll-out was that the government's very triumph had made us vulnerable, because we had removed that overwhelming and pervasive anxiety that had inclined people, for so long, to give us the benefit of the doubt.

As Chris Whitty observed, it is a universal feature of all pandemics that after the fear there always comes the anger. As the summer of 2021 turned into autumn it became clearer to the British public that this dreadful and frankly monotonous business of Covid was finally drawing to an end.

Even if we had not been hit by fuel shortages, and inflation, and other inconveniences, I think people's pent-up frustrations would have come geysering to the surface – as soon as the fear was over. They were just fed up with it all. Fed up with being scared. Fed up with the whole next-slide-please portentousness of the Covid press conferences, fed up with seeing me on their screens saying 'alas' this or 'alas' that; and in this general climate of grumpiness and irritation, the media responded – quite properly – to the mood of the nation and became pretty unforgiving.

I found that the political going became much more difficult. It was harder to score runs, and things that should have gone well began to misfire. I first noticed the problem on about November 18, a few days after the fiasco of Opats (as Owen Paterson was known for some reason), when we launched the Integrated Rail Plan. This was a big old programme – a key part of levelling up and we had been working on it for months.

Among other things, the plan involved building three new high-speed lines. We were finally confirming that HS2 would go all the way to Manchester; we were sending a new high-speed spur from Birmingham to the East Midlands, in preparation for a new route to Leeds and the north-east; and we were beginning Northern Powerhouse Rail, the high-speed link from Liverpool via Warrington to Manchester and then on across the Pennines. We were also electrifying hundreds of miles of line, making services faster, greener, more reliable.

It was levelling up in this crucial sense, that we were at last trying to give the Midlands and the north the kind of fast and dependable commuter services that for 150 years had been part of the magic formula of London and the south-east. It was unbelievable, shameful, how long it took to get thirty miles by train from Liverpool to Manchester. As for the trans-Pennine service, it was clankingly slow and awful. Some of the rolling stock was made of converted single-decker buses.

It was a disgrace that Leeds was just about the largest city in Europe not to have a metro. Well, we were going to fix all that.

We were going to hook up London and the Midlands and the great cities of the north with high-speed rail – and bear in mind the 25,000 miles of completed high-speed rail track that the Chinese have built since 2008.

Compare the UK, the home of the railways, the place where the first train ever moved. Remember how many miles of high-speed rail track we have completed in the same period. That's right – a big fat zero.

And we were going to deliver to the north and the Midlands the productivity-boosting agglomeration effects of decent commuter rail. As far as I could see, it was an unadulterated good news announcement, and I spent a happy day on trains, touring the country and explaining to passengers how their journey times were going to be sliced by gleaming new British-built trains, with new track and state-of-the-art signalling.

It was big potatoes: £96 billion, and a thirty-year timetable of work. In trying to spread opportunity around the country, it was exactly the vision I had offered the Tory Party when I stood for the leadership in 2019. It was what we had proposed in our manifesto; and yet that day – it was as if the media didn't want to know.

We had trailed the announcement so extensively that Labour, for once, had got their act together, and they did a pretty good job of trashing what should have been an untrashable plan. It was the biggest thing to happen to the national railways since Victorian times, but instead of being hailed for our vision I found that the plan was being pooh-poohed.

It didn't go far enough, was the verdict, and I think that Labour even claimed it was a 'betrayal of the north'; which was pretty infuriating when you consider that Labour did not lift a finger to sort out the problem – in what they conceitedly believed were their heartlands – during their entire thirteen years in office (HS2 was just shoved in Gordon Brown's 2010 manifesto as a desperate eye-catching detail, with no plan or budget attached; Labour never actually DID anything).

I felt the indignation of one who suddenly believes that he is not being given a fair hearing. Next week, that feeling intensified.

I went to a kind of tent on a building site in Tyneside to give a speech to the CBI. This was the Confederation of British Industry, the lobby group for the biggest firms in the country. Our relationship had been a little choppy since Brexit, which the officers of the organisation (though by no means all its members) had fervently opposed.

But today I wanted to build bridges, figuratively and literally. I wanted to thank everyone for their work during Covid, and I liked the new secretary-general, a Northern Irish man called Tony Danker.

To adapt Elton John, Hold me closer, Tony Danker – that was our watchword today.

It wasn't a bad speech, on paper. It brought together a lot of the key themes of levelling up: skills, broadband, infrastructure, the ten-point plan for a green industrial revolution. In fact, it was going down pretty well, and might have been a great success, except that I chucked in a long riff about Peppa Pig, a peculiar hairdryer-faced cartoon animal who exercises such a mesmeric fascination upon young children, our own included.

Peppa is so culturally powerful around the world that she has – if you recall – taught American three-year-olds to mystify their parents by saying tomarto rather than tomayto. I was using the story of Peppa to explain the magic of British creativity, how a Picassoid doodle of a pig with two eyes in the side of her face had become a £6 billion global industry – when I completely lost my place.

I stared down at my text and realised that the pages had been irretrievably jumbled. They had no numbers. I looked up at the audience and tried to extemporise. But it was no use. I couldn't just ramble on about Peppa Pig, fascinating though she doubtless was.

I corpsed, and corpsed, and the speech turned into a nightmare. I would suddenly spot a page that seemed to fit with my argument and read out a few snatches. But the trouble was that there were about forty pages, since it had been printed out in very large type. As soon as I got to the end of one page, I had to find the next.

But which was it? None of it seemed to make any sense. It was like trying to solve a jigsaw puzzle live on air, and every time I thought I had got through the Peppa Pig bit she would suddenly crop up again, and a flop sweat broke out as I repeated bits of whimsical guff about this pestilent porker.

It was awful, a shambles, and instead of just making light of it and breezing on – as I would normally have done – I was rattled. I kept stammering 'Forgive me, forgive me', as I got more and more lost.

The media decided that I was having some sort of meltdown. 'Are you all right, Prime Minister?' was the first question the TV news asked afterwards.

So a good speech was turned into a Peppa Pig psychodrama, and a great announcement about rail had gone off at half-cock. I could see what was happening.

I was no longer being cut any slack. With a population feeling less fearful of Covid, it was safer, if not a positive joy, to give the government the kicking we had avoided for so long. What was true of the public, and the media, was of course doubly true of Tory MPs.

Many of them had become fretful during their long periods of absence from Westminster – far more fretful than I realised. The public broadly approved of our handling of Covid, and they generally wanted us if anything to be tougher and more restrictive. But there was a large and vocal minority who were appalled at the loss of liberty and who believed that the suppression of the disease should be a matter for individual judgement and responsibility.

This was also the view of the broadly Tory media, not least because lockdown, and the consequent collapse in travelling to work, had led to a vertiginous fall in the sales of newspapers. I knew where they were coming from.

I had sat in those self-same leader conferences, where we had competed with boss-eyed indignation to denounce the slightest infringement of a Briton's ancient liberties; and here I was, actually thinking – yet again – of ordering the entire population to be confined at home.

What had happened to me? Was I drunk on power? Not at all.

I just thought that my friends were wrong, and that they knew in their hearts they were wrong. We couldn't let Covid rip, and kill tens of thousands more people.

Some of their arguments I found baffling. The anti-lockdown brigade complained vociferously about the pressure that Covid was putting on the NHS. They said that cancer patients were being squeezed out, that people were missing out on vital appointments for diabetes or cardiovascular disease. All that was true – but the whole point was that a big wave of disease, and hospitalisations, would be even worse. It would mean scrubbing cancer appointments throughout the country; it would mean purging the wards of everyone except those who were literally about to die of Covid.

They weren't making an argument against lockdown – they were making an argument in favour of it – and yet they didn't seem to get it.

What I hadn't realised was that this anti-lockdown stuff had taken root with my colleagues in Parliament (if not with the general public); and the problem with Covid was that I did not have my finger on the pulse of backbenchers. For eighteen months, if not longer, I could not really engage with my MPs face to face, as I should have done if I was to make my case. Resentments were starting to fester – and not just with the many who felt they had been overlooked, or who were generally ill-disposed.

There were 109 new Tory MPs elected in 2019, some of them very young and inexperienced, and for the crucial period of my premiership they were forced by my edicts to sit at home and stare at their laptops. They were anxious; they were reading Twitter. They were easy prey for those who wanted to stir up trouble.

There is a sense in which their anxieties were absurd. Even now, in spite of everything, we were still ahead in the polls, and Starmer wasn't exactly setting the world on fire. But sometimes the very strength of your position can work against you.

People were thinking – well, we've got an eighty-seat majority. We've got a long time until the next election. What's the harm in rebelling? It will make those idiots in Number Ten appreciate me more.

There were plenty of people, moreover, who had long since decided that the circumstances were in fact propitious for the Tories to indulge their traditional tribal habit of regicide. The received wisdom – it seems hard to believe now – was that it was mathematically impossible for Labour to obliterate our majority since the swing required was too big, and that with the extra help of boundary changes in our favour the next election was a nailed-on certainty.

It followed not that they should keep with a winning formula; no, no, that was not how they thought.

It followed that the Tory parliamentary party could comfortably dispense with Johnson, the irritating mountebank, with his zeal for Brexit and levelling up and net zero, and other relative novelties to Tory thought; and that there was plenty of time to install someone new and shiny; someone who seemed to listen to them more – someone under whose regime their genius (I mean Tory

MPs' genius) could properly flower and who would accord them the promotion and preferment they deserved.

That is how it works in the Tory Party, and how it has always worked; and in a Darwinian way, perhaps it is not a bad thing that the leadership should be in perpetual peril.

I suppose that I was increasingly aware of the danger; and occasionally I may have dimly wondered why some people seemed to break off their conversation when I approached.

I may have glimpsed the monster in the rearview mirror, and forgotten that these things may be closer than they appear. But frankly I had no time to think about it; believe me a PM just has no time to worry about this stuff because of the sheer quantity of work you must do every day.

By December 8, 2021, it was clear we were going to have to take a decision on omicron. Over the previous few days I had gradually made up my mind.

The data, on the face of it, was ominous. On that day we had 568 cases, and the variant was clearly beginning to crackle through the undergrowth. But over the last two years I had spent many hours looking at epidemiological graphs, and – off a low base – my expertise had grown.

Every day for the last couple of weeks we had been monitoring the data from South Africa, where omicron began. We could see its near-vertical rate of climb. But I was, of course, interested in what happened next. How many went to hospital? How many died?

The data was so fresh that it was hard to make out, but I became obsessed with the graphs from Gauteng Province in South Africa. Look, I said, the infection rates were growing, and hospitalisations rising a bit – but the deaths; the deaths were flat!

When I said this I made a point of confessing what my advisers well knew: that my scientific training had consisted of cutting up cows' eyes and drawing pictures of buttercups for O-level biology. Were we really going to take a massive life-and-death decision on the basis of my amateurish understanding of the Gauteng graphs?

The professors came up with all sorts of plausible explanations for the low South African death rates, all sorts of reasons why that might not be the case in the UK. But by the morning of December 8, I'd had enough. I was sure we had enough of a vaccine wall. Like us, the South Africans had been largely vaccinated with AstraZeneca. If they were getting through it, so would we.

That afternoon we had a long and extremely argumentative cabinet. I set out the case for confidence – for staying open until Christmas and beyond, and for relying on the vaccines. Most colleagues either agreed or hedged.

But I was surprised by the level of disagreement, and how – even in this Tory cabinet – there were some who were passionately in favour of locking down.

I remember especially Michael Gove. 'When your plane is on fire, you have to land the plane,' he said. 'Prime Minister, the plane is on fire.'

I listened to him, and others, with great respect. Was he right? I really didn't know, but on balance, after almost two years of trying to juggle with the disease, my judgement was that he wasn't.

We rejected the lockdown and went for what we called 'Plan B'. This was more symbolic, and involved the wearing of face masks in public places such as churches and cinemas, coupled with some pretty baleful warnings from Chris Whitty about the need to remain cautious.

Instead of shutting people up in their homes and closing down the economy, I decided to rely on the vaccines. There was good evidence that a third dose – a booster – would protect you against omicron. So we launched a campaign to 'Get Boosted Now', and brought forward the date by which all adults could get a booster from the end of January 2022 to the end of 2021.

Once again the public and the NHS rose to the challenge; we achieved our target; and I was vastly happier to be vaccinating than locking down.

I suppose your view on this decision will depend where you are in the debate. Some will say that I gambled and got lucky; others that I should have gone with the scientists and been cautious.

I think it was not only completely right to resist lockdown for omicron, but also completely medically and scientifically justified – and it shows, to my mind, why these decisions can only be made by democratically elected politicians.

I didn't get much chance to preen. I may have got omicron right, but the trouble about being PM is that you have to keep an eye on every ball that bounces your way. On the very day that I was first learning about omicron, Jack Doyle, my comms supremo, came to see me.

I was in the middle of scribbling a speech about an exhibition of British food then taking place in Downing Street.

'Sorry to disturb you, PM,' said Jack. 'Have you got a tick?'

Of course, I said, scribbling away – since I was expected to give the speech in the next few minutes.

Jack explained that the *Daily Mirror* had a story about a breach of lockdown rules in Number Ten during the pandemic. They were accusing the press department of having a party on December 18, 2020 – almost exactly a year previously.

Jack said that the story was nonsense, because it was traditional for the press department to have a glass of wine at their desks on a Friday evening.

I looked at him blankly. 'So no rules were broken?'

'No, PM,' he said firmly, 'no rules were broken.'

'Fine,' I said, and carried on.

It sounded like a load of old cobblers – probably some desperate nonsense being peddled by embittered former advisers whom the reader may dimly remember – and I forgot about it. I was most surprised when it was raised at PMQs the next day – as Labour's main line of attack.

The other day I saw Ian Hislop – my old sparring partner from *Have I Got News for You* – being interviewed on TV. He was talking about the so-called Partygate scandal, or rather a dramatised reconstruction produced by Channel 4.

He was red-faced with fury. His jowls quivered. It was the first time, he said, that he had actually seen what went on – Boris Johnson, dancing drunkenly with his advisers.

I was amazed – because of course nothing of the kind actually happened: drunkenness, dancing – all completely untrue; but you know what they say – a lie goes halfway round the world before the truth has got its boots on.

Here is what actually happened, all you really need to know about this miserable and wildly inflated affair. Over the course of about two years of fighting Covid, there were about fifteen occasions when officials briefly slackened the tempo of their work and raised a glass to a departing colleague, or held a quiz, or marked a birthday – in the way that all offices do.

Most of them then got on with trying to get the country through Covid. At the time we believed that these events were in accordance with the rules – and I still think they were.

I only went to a handful – almost always to make a quick speech of thanks. Even in the brief time I was there I saw enough to say 'parties' is simply too festive a word for what went on.

These events were not common, but then again they were not thought to be odd, or unusual, let alone reprehensible. Remember, we are talking about thousands of Whitehall officials meeting in hundreds of rooms over a period of about six hundred days, in a country where it is still acceptable in the workplace to break off, very occasionally, for a glass of alcoholic drink of some kind.

Without belabouring this weary business, I think I made several catastrophic mistakes in the handling of the story.

1 – I should have been far more robust at the outset. I tried to defuse public anger by a series of rather pathetic apologies, even when I knew zero about the events for which I was apologising. My grovelling just made people even angrier – and made it look as though we were far more culpable than we were.

2 – I should not have sanctioned a ridiculous and unfair witch-hunt led by a woman who was to become – unbelievably – chief of staff to Keir Starmer, and whose evidence collation was overseen by a Labour-supporting QC who had publicly called on Twitter for me to be removed from office. I should simply have asked anyone with evidence of wrongdoing to go to the police.

3 – I should have realised that my old amigo Cummings – still scorched by Barnard Castle – was behind it all, and that he and Lee Cain actually had a 'grid' of grossly exaggerated stories that they were feeding to the media.

Ah well – never mind.

You know what, I was so confident of our fundamental innocence that never once did I think that the story would really endanger the government. And actually, I think we could and should have got through it far better if I had been less naive and less trusting.

Soon we had far, far bigger things to worry about – because for the first time since the end of the Second World War, we were about to see the brutal invasion of a sovereign and independent European country.

Part Nine
War in Europe

Chapter 51

An Unprovoked Invasion

And the reasons for Putin's appalling miscalculation

The iPhone went shortly after 4 a.m. on February 24, 2022, the silent screen flash enough to jolt me from my slumbers. As soon as I saw that the Number Ten switchboard was calling, I knew exactly what must be going on.

'Morning, PM,' said the switchboard operator in the same cheerful tones she would probably use to announce one of the Four Horsemen of the Apocalypse. 'I have the NSA on the line.'

As I stumbled for the bedroom door, she put me through to Sir Stephen Lovegrove, the national security adviser.

'He's done it, I am afraid,' said Stephen. 'Putin's invading Ukraine.'

I replied with Anglo-Saxon expletives intended to convey my general distaste for the invader.

The tanks were crossing the border as we spoke. There were reports of gunfire and bombing in cities across Ukraine. The gist of it was that all hell was being let loose – for absolutely no good reason whatever – on an entirely peaceful and innocent European democracy.

Within about twenty minutes I was downstairs at my desk in the flat, talking to President Volodymyr Zelensky of Ukraine. He described an all-out invasion. 'They are coming from the north, from the east, from the south,' he said. It seemed there was shooting in Kyiv itself.

As we later discovered, Russian sleepers and Spetsnaz agents were emerging from their cover and stirring up civilian terror. Already assassins despatched by Putin were trying to find Zelensky and kill him.

I stared through the bulletproof panes of my window at the dark, quiet trees and lake of St James's Park. 'Are you safe?' I asked Volodymyr.

'I am safe, I am safe,' he said. His voice was urgent. We had to sanction Putin now, he said. We had to cut Russia off from the world financial system. In particular, we had to kick him out of the Swift global payments system.

I was on it, I told him. I knew that there were people on the call who were already trying to corral the world's finance ministers and impose the heaviest sanctions ever devised.

We all know the limits of sanctions, however, against a man like Putin. We know how they can be evaded, how they degrade over time. What else can we do, I asked Volodymyr. What weapons could we provide?

I got the obvious answer. Everything, frankly, was welcome, he said, because the position of the Ukrainian forces was desperate. They were facing a blitzkrieg attack by a military superpower.

In their ability to project extreme violence abroad, the Russian armed forces were probably second only to the United States. There were already tens of thousands of enemy troops in his country, and their objective was clear: to capture Kyiv, to overthrow the elected government, to remove (preferably liquidate) Zelensky and install a puppet regime. They were already well down the road – literally – towards destroying Ukraine as a sovereign and independent country and turning that country into a satrapy of a reborn Russian empire.

I told Volodymyr what I had told him before, and what I was to tell him many times in the months and years ahead: that he and the Ukrainian people would have the complete support of the British government, and that we would do whatever we could to keep his country free.

As our conversation came to an end – he had many other calls to make to world leaders – I went back to the subject of his personal safety.

Volodymyr and I already had a good relationship. We had both been elected leaders of our countries in 2019, and had met shortly afterwards. I liked him and admired him. We were both in some sense outsiders who had first come to public notice on TV comedy shows – his efforts, it must be said, much more successful than mine.

At this pivotal moment, I could see that the survival of an independent Ukraine depended to a large extent on the survival of Zelensky, and by the sounds of things he was in imminent danger. Since we were already making plans to move our embassy out of Kyiv – it was by now getting on for 5 a.m. – I wondered if Zelensky should do the same.

If it came to it, I said, he could form a government in exile in London. As ever, Volodymyr was polite. He was grateful for the offer, and for the support of the UK government, but he had no intention of leaving the Ukrainian capital.

He didn't need a ride, as he later put it, he needed weapons. He needed all the help we could give: military, economic, political. I reassured him again that we would do everything we could, and we hung up.

I felt vaguely embarrassed, in the face of Zelensky's bravery, to have made that offer of sanctuary – to have even suggested that he might want to flee. It was perhaps forgivable in view of the advice I had been given over the last few weeks.

The overwhelming expert view was that Ukraine would be

crushed – and in a matter of days. That was the view of defence intelligence in Washington and in London. It was also, of course, the advice that was being given to Vladimir Putin.

In the previous few weeks the shadow of impending war had loomed ever darker over Europe, and I had been meeting our best military minds, together with the security and intelligence services – sometimes in Number Ten, sometimes in the Ministry of Defence. We discussed the coming attack – which seemed both inevitable and unbelievable – and what we would do to support the Ukrainians.

Throughout these discussions our assumption was that we would no longer be helping a Ukrainian government in Kyiv. We would be helping the resistance. We took it that the scattered Ukrainian forces would be out there in the maquis, trying to make Ukraine ungovernable by the occupying power, blowing up Russian supply lines, ambushing the gauleiters as they lolled in the bars and shooting them in the back of the head.

We discussed the ways in which we might supply and fortify the rebels – but the Russians, we assumed, would shortly be in charge of Ukraine. In our basic pessimism, I am afraid we were unconsciously infected by the arrogance of Putin's mindset. It was a fundamental mistake that was to bedevil our thinking for months to come – a superstitious and wholly unmerited awe of Russian military prowess, and a boneheaded reluctance to see that not only were Zelensky and the Ukrainians determined to resist, but they had the drive and the sheer patriotic fervour to beat the Russians.

All they needed, as Volodymyr had insisted to me on that first morning, was the right support, the right kit, the right tools – and they would finish the job.

We couldn't see it like that in those suspense-filled days of January and early February, as we sat in that windowless ultra-hush-hush room in the MOD. We could see the sheer weight of Russian armour gathering on the border, eventually mounting to

115 battalion tactical groups. We could hear their chatter and the revving of their tanks as they moved to their forward positions. We could see the deployment of their field hospitals and their blood supplies. We could see the maps – and how short a distance it was down the motorway from the Belorussian border to Kyiv.

No matter how plucky the Ukrainians were, we didn't think Zelensky would have the men or *matériel* to hold out. That was the military view. How could I contradict them?

I couldn't, and didn't. But niggling away at the back of my mind, from the very beginning, was the thought that Putin might well have miscalculated. I had already been to Ukraine, twice, and had taken a keen interest in the country.

I stayed at the UK embassy, up on an ancient acropolis over-looking the Dnieper. I talked to Ukrainians – lawyers, politicians, journalists – and ate real chicken Kyiv: a most peculiar dish, completely different from the Marks and Spencer butterbombs, each with its own chicken drumstick which – I gagged when I discovered this – they actually put in the dishwasher, so that they could wash this grey little bone for the next diner.

On my morning runs I had passed the beautiful golden domes of Ukrainian churches, and then found myself chugging back through a vast memorial to Ukrainian sacrifice in the Great Patriotic War (for a Ukrainian, and a Russian, from June 1941 to May 1945). This is one of those tributes that are more literalist than symbolic. There are huge bronze bas-relief friezes depicting actual battles, with hundreds of figures – life-size or bigger – engaged in acts of war: stabbing with bayonets or hurling grenades, their limbs and torsos arranged in what art historians would call the heroic diagonal.

You look at the violence of that iconography and you remember that when Hitler was defeated in the Soviet Union, there were perhaps ten million Ukrainian soldiers under arms. They played a decisive part in the most savage and important conflict of the entire Second World War. To put it bluntly, they killed a lot of Germans, those Ukrainians.

Of course, that World War Two memorial was a Soviet-era construct. It was designed to reinforce the idea of joint sacrifice, and of the fundamental unity between Ukraine and Russia. Which was the very point that Putin was trying to make in his rambling essay, published in the summer of 2021, in which he set out in advance the ideology of his war.

Ukraine wasn't really a country, he said. It was indissolubly linked to the Russian motherland, and he supported his case with all sorts of semi-mystic guff about Kievan Rus and the Ukrainian origins of the Russian Orthodox faith. He poured scorn on the very notion of Ukrainian identity; he thoroughly rubbished Ukrainian nationhood. By 2022 I knew enough about Ukraine to suspect that he had made a grievous mistake.

Any official visitor to Kyiv is taken to see the memorials to those who have died fighting the Russians since Putin's 2014 invasion of the Donbas and Crimea. On both visits, as foreign secretary, I had walked down the Wall of the Martyrs – about 15,000 haunting black and white photos of young men and women who gave their lives for freedom in the grim mud trenches of the Donbas. Even back then they were dying, day after day.

One lunchtime I went to a pub run by veterans, some of them wounded, in the middle of Kyiv. Their bulging arms were tattooed, the wooden walls studded with thousands of brass ammo casings. It occurred to me that I had come across folk like this before, almost twenty years before. They reminded me of another group of Slav soldiers, the steel-toothed glass-eating militias of the former Yugoslavia.

If anything, the Ukrainians struck me as even tougher, and more passionate in their patriotic feeling.

At one point I stood with our then ambassador, Judith Gough, looking out at Kyiv in the sunshine. It was bustling, cheerful, the shop windows bursting with western brands, the cafés full of life. We both knew that this seemingly peaceful and prosperous country was already at war with Putin – in the Donbas. We knew that Ukraine was chronically vulnerable, because its status was so uncertain.

It was clear to me that after thirty years of independent existence, the Ukrainians were choosing their own path – away from Moscow towards a pluralist, open, western European model of society. We in the UK were firmly in their corner. As foreign secretary, I had set up a 'Ukrainian Reform Conference' to help haul them down the right track: to tackle the endemic corruption (still pretty bad, I am sad to say), and to support such elements of a free society as an independent judiciary.

We also knew that it was this very choice that enraged Putin and scared him – because of the example it might set to the Russian people themselves. If the Ukrainians chose democracy and freedom – and made a success of it – then that was an existential threat to Putin, and a huge boost for his struggling domestic opponents.

He wanted to crush this pro-western, pro-European Ukraine, and to fold the place forcibly back into the bosom of Mother Russia. There was therefore an arm-wrestle for influence taking place; and the matter was far from decided. We in the west were crooking our finger at the Ukrainians. We were assuring them of their place in the comity of democratic European countries. But since the end of the Cold War, we had signally failed to give them the one thing they needed to make that choice with confidence.

We had refused, in spite of all our promises, to guarantee their security. When, in 1994 the US and the UK had joined Russia and Ukraine in signing the infamous Budapest Memorandum, under the terms of this document the Ukrainians gave up their substantial arsenal of Soviet-era nuclear weapons and transferred them to

Russia. The fledgling Ukrainian state thereby placed itself at the permanent mercy of the Russians and their nuclear blackmail.

So President Bill Clinton and Prime Minister John Major gave them solemn assurances, at Budapest, that in the event of an attack on Ukraine both the United States and the United Kingdom would come to their aid; and the Russians, with heavy irony, made the same pledge. Well, we all know what happened when Putin first invaded in 2014. There is a difference, it turns out, between 'assurances' and a full Nato security guarantee. Until Ukraine is in Nato, the Budapest Memorandum must rank for bog-roll worthlessness with the piece of paper once waved by Neville Chamberlain.

So as Judith Gough and I looked out at Kyiv, domes twinkling above the mighty river, we knew we were looking at a giant enigma. Which way would the Ukrainians turn? It was 2018, and already Ukraine was like a child at the centre of some ghastly custody dispute, with the Russians brutally asserting their dynastic rights over a country that increasingly wanted to make its home elsewhere.

This is not some minor state. It is vast, the second-biggest in Europe by surface area, with forty-five million people, a highly advanced technological and industrial sector, an abundance of minerals and such rich, black soil that a large proportion of the world's calories are derived from its crops. It is the kind of country that produces free and original spirits – from the winners of the Eurovision song contest to heavyweight boxing champs to a president whose rise to power was not impeded by his decision, in 2016, to go on TV and pretend to play the piano with his genitals.

Let me try to sum up the difference between the Russian and the Ukrainian systems of government. In Russia, supreme power belongs to a man who shoots journalists and who jails and murders his opponents. His elections are a foregone conclusion. In Ukraine, the president is a man who – among other distinctions – was once the voice of *Paddington Bear the Movie*, in Ukrainian. He wins his elections fair and square. I know what sort of government I prefer.

As I looked at the city, it seemed so beautiful and yet so fragile – completely unprotected by any serious western treaty. Back then in 2018, I remember asking Judith Gough what already seemed to me to be the key question.

Suppose Putin decided to invade the whole place, I said. Would they fight?

Judith paused. She really knew Ukraine, and was one of the few in the Foreign Office who could speak both Russian and Ukrainian.

'Oh, they'll fight,' she said. 'They'll fight, all right.'

So as the crisis brewed at the end of 2021 and the beginning of 2022, I thought I had at least some sort of insight into Ukraine. I thought the Ukrainians were fiercely patriotic, and accomplished fighters; and that if Putin thought he could just waltz in and capture Kyiv, I believed he was severely mistaken.

From New Year 2022 onwards, the intelligence chatter got louder and louder. I should stress that this was 'Five Eyes' intelligence. It was the view from Washington and London, and though extremely well-founded it was hard to substantiate without giving away its provenance.

Other countries, notably the French and Germans, were more dubious. They were wedded to the morally bankrupt 'Minsk Process', the pathetic attempt at negotiations that had been set up after the first Putin invasion of Ukraine in 2014. Under this 'process', the war was treated as a kind of marital tiff between Russia and Ukraine, with France and Germany acting as therapists.

In reality, the conflict was nothing of the kind. Putin was the aggressor, and he was just pretending to negotiate – until such time as he decided to strike again. In its moral equivocation between Russia and Ukraine, the 'Minsk Process' was frankly obscene. But the result was that our key European allies were deeply committed to this rigmarole – and far more trusting of Putin than they should have been.

Towards the end of January 2022, I talked again to Putin. I had already called him, before Christmas, to say that we were aware of his preparations for war and that any attack on Ukraine was insane. Now we thought it was worth having a last shot. It was a peculiar and ambiguous conversation.

It was a Wednesday, and we did it from my parliamentary office, after PMQs – so that keen Kremlin ears would have caught the ravings of the anti-Brexit protesters in the background. Putin seemed notably relaxed, using – said the interpreter afterwards – a familiar form of address.

Was he just bluffing? Or had he made up his mind to attack, irrespective of what we said? We went over familiar ground.

No, he wasn't going to invade, he said (big fat steaming lie number one). But he had to think about Russia's security.

There was a risk that Nato strategic weapons would be deployed in Ukraine (big fat steaming lie number two).

I was exasperated. Yes, it was true that Nato had expanded since the end of the Cold War. Most of central and eastern Europe had joined, and so had the Baltic states – former Soviet republics. It was, in my view, a wonderful transformation, even if it greatly cheesed off the Russians (my sympathies were limited, to put it mildly).

But Ukraine? In Nato? Now? I personally thought it was a good and reasonable idea, but he knew as well as I did that there was not a snowball's chance in Hades of Ukraine joining Nato – or at least not for a very long time.

There was a queue of Nato members who would veto the move, led by the French and the Germans, and in any case it was not what the Ukrainian population themselves said they wanted. (Not then, at least – all that has, of course, changed since the invasion.) As for the missiles – it was pure science fiction.

No one was proposing Nato missiles on Ukrainian soil. But Putin kept going back to it. It would take hardly any time, he said, for a missile launched from Ukraine to hit Moscow. At one point he made a kind of spooky-jocular remark about the risk of miscalculation – an unintended nuclear exchange between Russia and Nato. 'I would not want to hurt you, Boris,' he said (a remark the Kremlin later denied. Never believe anything Moscow says until it has been officially denied).

I said it was all completely unreal, this talk of confrontation with Nato. I repeated what I believe – that Nato is fundamentally a peaceful alliance, whose objective is the mutual protection of its members.

I am afraid we were basically talking past each other.

According to Putin, Russia had been cheated and betrayed since the end of the Cold War. He harped on about western promises that had allegedly been made about not expanding Nato, and how they had been broken. He claimed to believe that Ukraine was somehow about to join and to station Nato weapons pointing at Moscow.

I said it was up to free and independent countries to decide which alliances or clubs they belonged to. It was wrong in principle for us to rule out Ukrainian membership – but as a matter of practical politics I didn't think it was going to happen any time soon. Putin's fears were groundless, and he was risking a disaster for Russia.

We parried back and forth for a while, but that was the gist of it. We ended with some guff about all the mistakes that both sides had made since the end of the Cold War, and how sad it was that relations had decayed so badly.

Some of my officials were heartened by Putin's tone, and what they believed was his interest in future strategic discussions.

Frankly I was none the wiser from the call. Was he really going to invade? Or was he just trying to make our flesh creep?

On February 1, just a few days later, I was on a plane to Kyiv to see Zelensky. What did he think was going to happen? How was he going to resist, and what more could we do to help? By now there was a general ferment of diplomatic activity, and a horrible 1914 feeling that we were locked on train tracks to war.

It was a pretty eerie trip. You couldn't tell, looking at the street life of the Ukrainian capital, that the population was under imminent threat of the most violent invasion since Hitler hurled the Wehrmacht at the rest of Europe. And you couldn't tell from Zelensky's demeanour that he was in such grave personal peril. Of the pair of us, in fact, I seemed more alarmed than he did.

We sat in the blue and white wedding cake plasterwork of the Tsarist Mariinsky Palace, and I told him what we knew: my weird conversation with Putin; the sigint and humint from the border. He listened carefully, but fairly inscrutably.

He wanted more weapons, and in particular Stinger anti-aircraft missiles. He wanted a big pre-emptive package of sanctions – something the Germans in particular were resisting. But on the whole I found his sangfroid remarkable. As I drove back to Boryspil Airport with Melinda Simmons, our new ambassador, we struggled to understand what was going on.

Perhaps Zelensky thought Putin was bluffing? Perhaps – in spite of all the evidence we had laid before him – the Ukrainian president still did not believe that his country was about to be invaded.

It was only later that we worked out the real explanation for his calm. He couldn't afford to panic, or to sound the alarm – because that was playing Putin's game. The Ukrainian currency, the hryvnia, was already collapsing. The economy was under massive strain.

If he stood up and announced that Russian troops were about to pour down from the north, then he might actually terrify the population into fleeing, and in the ensuing chaos all resistance might collapse. If Ukraine was to have the slightest chance of resisting, Zelensky had to hold it together for as long as possible. Still – it wasn't entirely obvious, and a couple of days later I held a seminar of experts in the Cabinet Room to try and work out what the hell was going on.

This was February 17, and though of course we didn't know it we had only a week until the catastrophe.

At the end, I asked them all to stick their necks out. Would Putin actually do it? Yes or no?

There was Mark Galeotti, the expert on Putin and Russia; there was Lawrence Freedman, the noted military historian and strategic thinker; there was Rod Lyne, the former UK ambassador to Moscow; and Shashank Joshi, the defence editor of the *Economist*. Three of the four – all except Joshi – said that Putin was bluffing, that he might be trying to destabilise Ukraine but that he would not actually invade. Shashank proved to be right; but the remark that really got my brain whirring was from Lawrence Freedman.

He said that Putin probably wouldn't invade, but that if he did, 'It would be a disaster, a disaster for Putin.' That sounded right to me.

The following day – February 18 – I flew to Germany for the annual Munich Security Conference, full of think tankers and analysts, and German generals floating about in their pale-grey tunics. By this time the mood was getting surreal. The 'Five Eyes' – US, UK, Canada, Australia, New Zealand – were all convinced that Putin would invade. Others were still, even now, not so sure. Emmanuel Macron had been engaged in some last-ditch diplomacy – flying off to see Putin in Moscow, sitting opposite him at some preposterously long white marble table, like some bickering Hollywood couple, and generally grandstanding. He genuinely seemed to think he could talk Putin out of it.

That day in Munich – with only six days to go – I had a long bilateral with Olaf Scholz of Germany, in which I explained that we thought an invasion was now all but inevitable. The Germans were miserable. They had become hugely dependent on Russian gas – having unwisely junked nuclear power – and they could already see that the war would entail massive economic disruption.

At one point one of Olaf's most senior aides looked at us and said, almost wistfully, 'What if the Ukrainians don't resist? What if they collapse quickly?'

I could see what he was thinking. Might it not be better for the world – even if it was a tragedy for Ukraine – if this whole thing was over quickly? Might we not save many thousands of lives, as well as avoiding agonising economic pain? I understood why he said it, but I passionately disagreed.

What he was proposing was nauseating – just abandoning a sovereign European country, allowing a democracy to be engulfed by a tyranny. It was wrong in principle. It was also wrong in practice, even on a utilitarian calculus.

Far from minimising global disruption, a swift Putin victory in Ukraine might be the prelude to further violence – in Georgia, the Baltics, across the whole periphery of the former Soviet Union. If Ukraine were toppled, it would be a general disaster for the rule of law and the integrity of borders around the world.

What would it mean for any other country threatened by an expansionist neighbour? What would it mean for Taiwan?

I gave the Munich conference what was by my standards a pretty fiery and trenchant speech, calling for us all to stand shoulder to shoulder with Ukraine. I announced various military gestures, intended to show Putin our engagement in the crisis – beefing up our troop numbers in Estonia and Poland, some more naval manoeuvres in Norway and the high north, air patrols in Cyprus and Romania. I mobilised a thousand troops to go to

Poland, to help with what would surely be a huge humanitarian crisis.

What I did not and could not do was prepare British troops to go to war in Ukraine; because as Putin knew full well, there was no constituency for that option, either in Parliament or in the country – or in any EU country, come to that.

The whole point, the whole disaster, was that Ukraine was NOT a member of Nato; we owed the poor Ukrainians no Article 5 security guarantee; and that was precisely why Ukraine was at risk. If Putin invaded Ukraine, the only blood that would be shed in the defence of that country would be Ukrainian blood.

We Brits would do what we could to help, militarily, politically – and we were already doing quite a lot. But in the end the fate of the Ukrainians would depend on the world's greatest power.

I cornered Senator Lindsey Graham, a long-standing friend, by a lift in the Munich hotel. What would America do? I asked the Republican from South Carolina. What will they think in Congress?

Lindsey is highly influential and experienced. He reflected.

'It depends,' he said. 'If they fight, we will help them.'

I could understand that. Congressmen would want to know that Putin was wrong about Ukraine, and that the Ukrainians were real patriots, real lovers of liberty, as J.S. Mill puts it, who were willing to fight and die for their country.

How long have they got to fight for? I asked.

'Two weeks or so,' said Lindsey – which was about a week longer than they were expected to hold on.

PUTIN DID NOT INVADE UKRAINE because he was really worried about Nato or Nato expansion.

He did it because he was an authoritarian ruler who had been in power for two decades, and with a pretty patchy economic record he needed something – something big – to rally domestic opinion behind him.

He did it because there is nothing better, when it comes to rallying domestic opinion, than a short, sharp, successful foreign war.

He did it because he had thought through the post-Covid global economic position, and he could see that an invasion of Ukraine would cause a sharp spike in the price of oil and gas – which would be excellent news for Russia.

He did it because he had foreseen, with chess-like cunning, that the very chaos he unleashed would therefore help to fund his war machine.

He did it because he knew that China would back him, and continue to buy his oil; indeed, he had been to the Beijing Winter Olympics on February 4 to get the explicit approval of President Xi Jinping.

He did it because he was a former KGB man whose very soul had been seared by the unbundling of the Soviet Union, an event he described as one of the great catastrophes of the twentieth century.

He did it because he thought the re-amalgamation of Russia with Ukraine would be a giant step towards avenging that hurt and rebuilding the Soviet empire.

He did it because he had seen the feebleness of the west in the face of his aggression – in Syria, Ukraine, Libya and elsewhere – over the previous ten years.

He did it because he had seen what looked like the undignified and precipitate flight of the western powers from Afghanistan.

He did it because he thought we were soft, and that he would get away with it.

He did it because he had come to believe his own chauvinist propaganda about Ukraine – that it was not a proper country, with no really strong national sentiment.

He did it because he therefore believed that the Ukrainians would crumple before his onslaught.

It was on that last point that I had long believed him to be wrong; and, together with defence secretary Ben Wallace, I was determined to help the Ukrainians prove him wrong.

Chapter 52

The Battle for Kyiv

How Belfast-made weapons were crucial for Ukrainian victory

So Putin attacked Ukraine and immediately began to disprove his own ridiculous thesis about that country's psychic status. With every hour that went by, his cruelty was intensifying a patriotism – a desire to protect the independence of Ukraine – that was stronger than any national feeling I have ever seen in Europe.

The Russian president genuinely seemed to believe that the Ukrainians would fold themselves into his embrace. Someone had convinced him that the crowds would stick red roses into the barrels of his tanks.

He must have been stunned, as the days began to tick by, to see that the Ukrainians were actually fighting like wildcats for their freedom. The fiercer the Ukrainian resistance, the more ruthless Putin became. In his desperation to reach Kyiv, he started to shell apartment blocks; even schools and hospitals. The death toll of women and children began to climb.

It was not long before we heard whispers of the methods – the torture, the summary executions – that Putin was prepared to use in order to terrorise the population. As our horror mounted, so did the flush of shame: the gnawing guilt that a European nation was being dismembered before our eyes, a democracy that Britain had solemnly pledged to protect.

I felt that it was my job – since the UK was a Budapest signatory – to rally global support; and I was fortunate in that it seemed to me so obvious what needed to be done. Never in my experience of international affairs had I seen a question of such Manichean simplicity.

The choice between Ukraine and Putin was a choice between right and wrong, good and evil, and if I was vociferous in those crucial early meetings – of the G7, Nato and other bodies – it was because I had no doubt that I was right, and that the cause was desperate.

In every meeting, from February 24 on, my mantra was always the same. Putin must fail and Ukraine must succeed. Putin must be defeated and Ukraine must be free.

Not everyone, I am sad to say, agreed. In some of my phone conversations with other world leaders – even friends of ours – I realised that Putin's tentacles were everywhere. China was actively pro-Putin (which was and is a disaster), while India was ambivalent to say the least.

I remember talking to a distinguished leader of a Gulf country, with whom I had the best possible personal relations.

'Why should I care about Ukraine?' he said.

But our very closest allies were sound from the beginning. I launched 'Putin must fail' in the first call between the 'Quint' – US, UK, France, Germany, Italy – and Joe Biden picked it up almost at once, followed by Emmanuel Macron. We put together the most stringent sanctions we could; we sent humanitarian aid to the region. But the Ukrainians were desperate for serious military help. What we gave was so limited – at first – and so cruelly slow in arriving.

On March 1, five days after the invasion, I went to Poland in what was becoming a rhythm of shuttle diplomacy, drumming up support for Ukraine. By this stage Putin's armour was seemingly poised to engulf the three-million-strong Ukrainian capital. His column of tanks and armoured personnel carriers was fifteen miles long, and as it ground towards Kyiv it felt like a snake about to engulf its prey.

I gave a passionate speech, in a modern British Council building outside Warsaw. I talked up sanctions, our humanitarian assistance, and everything we were doing to fortify Nato's eastern frontier. I warned Putin (again) that he faced disaster, and urged him to turn back that column of tanks.

It all sounded cogent, and seemed to go down well with my largely Polish audience. But we all knew that the position was dire, and that we weren't doing enough, and that there was something a bit reedy in my note of defiance.

Then I was blown out of the water.

A woman got up. I eyed her warily. I wasn't sure I was expecting questions. She said she was called Daria Kaleniuk and she was a Ukrainian who had just made it over the border to safety. She wanted me to know that as we spoke, civilians were dying; that her family were utterly terrified. Did I not realise, she asked, that under the terms of the 1994 Budapest Memorandum, Britain had vowed to come to the defence of Ukraine?

Why was I here in Poland, when I should be in Ukraine? As I looked on dumbly, she began to sob. People were being bombed, she said, and yet I was not there because I was afraid. The whole of Nato was afraid, she said.

At this stage a British embassy person in a Covid mask moved towards her, as if to try to persuade her that she had said enough. But she carried on.

Why could we not have a no-fly zone, she asked, to stop the bombs and missiles?

There are times when you have to be blunt, even when what you are saying will be unwelcome to your audience. Ben Wallace and I had already discussed the concept of a no-fly zone – whether we could use Nato air power to clear the skies above Ukraine and stop Putin's aerial torment of the population. As I told Daria, it just was not possible.

It would mean that I was issuing orders to UK pilots, for instance, to shoot down Russian fast jets. It would mean that Nato was effectively at war with Russia; and never mind our Nato allies, that was not something the UK government was contemplating. It was terrible to tell the Ukrainians this wretched truth, that we could not use our planes to shelter them from the bombs and missiles; and I felt that Daria had been right, frankly, to give me a drubbing.

What I did not know, as we spoke, was that there was one significant way in which British military technology was already providing crucial assistance to Ukraine, and even beginning to turn the tide of war.

Way back in the summer of the previous year, 2021, Ben Wallace started lobbying me about sending weapons to Ukraine. He had grasped the message of Putin's mad essay, with its implicit threat, and become convinced that the Russian leader was serious. By September 2021 he had come up with a proposal to send anti-tank weapons, and I have to admit that I was initially sceptical.

I noted the wariness of the Foreign Office experts and some on the security side. What if it just provoked Putin? they asked. What if it just gave him an extra pretext to cause trouble – even to invade?

Ben rolled his eyes. 'Look,' said the ex-Guards officer, 'he's going to do it anyway. He's gonna invade, believe me. We have got to help them.'

OK, I said, let's go ahead with your plan – provided that we are in step with the Americans. So began what proved to be an infuriatingly slow business of changing UK policy.

The UK had been giving some assistance to Ukraine since 2014, the first Putin invasion. We had a small number of troops out under Operation Orbital. They were providing 'training' and tactical advice (though after their years of hand-to-hand combat in the trenches of the Donbas, I wasn't sure there was much we could teach the Ukrainians about fighting).

Now, though, Ben and I were determined that the UK should go a big step further. We should go outside the EU consensus and become the first major European country to supply the Ukrainians with significant quantities of lethal weapons. Liz Truss, the foreign secretary, was also enthusiastic.

The system continued to push back. UK officials sucked their teeth and talked of the risk of 'escalation'. I thought this was nonsense. It was Putin who was threatening to escalate. It wasn't as if the Ukrainians were thinking of attacking Russia; it was Putin who was unsubtly signalling his willingness to use further violence. If we couldn't actually come to the defence of the Ukrainians, surely to goodness we could give them the kit to defend themselves? What was the problem?

Much to our frustration, Wallace and I kept finding the proposal popping up on the agenda of the National Security Council, even though we thought it had been agreed. I found myself scribbling impatiently in the margin of submissions, urging officials to get on with it. I think I had to give the instruction four times before the plan was finally activated.

As it was, the 2,000 NLAW anti-tank missiles got there in mid-January 2022 – the very nick of time. When historians study that Battle for Kyiv in March 2022, I reckon they will find all sorts of reasons why the military experts turned out to be so staggeringly wrong.

There was the heroism of the Ukrainians, and the incompetence of the Russians. There was the inspirational leadership of Volodymyr Zelensky – whose communications were starting to inspire audiences around the world (pretty amazing, when you consider that he could barely speak English when I first met him).

There were also two ways in which we, the Brits, were able to supply what I think was some pretty valuable military assistance. Since we knew a great deal about the Russian battle plans, we were able to help the Ukrainians anticipate what might happen at Hostomel Airport, and to prepare its defence.

Hostomel is a big cargo airport, about thirty-five kilometres from Kyiv, where the Soviets used to make the vast Antonov cargo planes. We knew that the airport was critical to Putin's plans. He was going to use airborne troops to capture the place, and then airlift in thousands and thousands of reinforcements. These would be joined by the great procession of tanks coming down from Belarus, and – *pow* – he would have overwhelming force, men and tanks, to deliver a knock-out blow to Kyiv.

Putin's first problem was that Hostomel proved impossible to capture. Every time Putin sent in a big helicopter, the Ukrainians seemed to know where it was going to land, and it would get shot down. When the Russians did finally capture the place a few days later, they found that they were out on their own.

They controlled the blitzed-out airfield – but they couldn't bring up their reinforcements. It was a bit like the 1944 Operation Market Garden, the Second World War disaster in which Allied Parachutists took the bridge at Arnhem on the Rhine, but got stranded and surrounded by Germans.

It became increasingly clear that the Russian armour – that terrifying convoy of tanks – was motionless not because it was poised to strike but because it was stuck, blocked; and the reason it was stuck was that across the whole of the theatre of conflict the Ukrainians were discovering the joys of asymmetric warfare, using NLAWs and other devices against the Russian tanks.

The NLAW – or next-generation light anti-tank weapon – is made in Belfast by what used to be Short Brothers (now Thales) and is a deceptively simple bit of kit. It is basically a giant tube that you sling over your shoulder. You get the tank in your sights, you push a button, and *whoosh-bang*. It is remarkably effective.

The NLAW can blow the turret off a tank, or set it on fire, or knock the tread off its wheels. So the tank just sits there in the road, blocking the traffic. The US-made Javelins – previously supplied by Trump – had a longer range. But the NLAWs were apparently a cinch to operate, and excellent at close quarters.

The Ukrainians started to swear by them. 'I'm in love with NLAW,' they said – a word play that works if, like Ukrainians, you say the 'w' as a 'v'.

The upshot was that after a few weeks the great crocodile of Russian armour was starting to look positively inert. It wasn't a crocodile; it was a log. The Russian tanks were log-jammed in, as the Ukrainians learned to pick off the front and rear tanks, immobilise that section of the convoy, and then target the rest at their leisure.

It didn't help the Russians that they had air superiority. They had to get their tanks to the rendezvous at Hostomel Airport, and to their fury they couldn't. Their tanks were getting plinked by the NLAWs and the Javelins, time and again.

As the war went on, drones were to become more important, but in those early weeks shoulder-launched anti-tank missiles were crucial for the defence of Kyiv. I am as proud of getting those NLAWs to the Ukrainians as I am of anything in my career.

By the end of March, the Russian position at Hostomel had become untenable. They were surrounded by Ukrainian forces; and the casualties in the Russian tank columns were so bad that the men were proving reluctant to advance, so that senior officers – colonels – had to go to the front to put some lead in their pencil; with the result that the casualties among the senior officers were also high.

Finally the pantomime tank crocodile was forced to disperse and retreat, and the threat to the capital evaporated. Against the odds and in defiance of every military prognosis, the Ukrainians had put the boot into Putin and sent him flying.

They had fulfilled the first and most important condition for further western support – as identified by Senator Lindsey Graham in Munich, just before the invasion. They had shown they were willing to fight in defence of their nation, that they truly loved their own liberty.

Even more important and more attractive to the American mind, they had shown that they were winners; and people do love it when they can back the winning side. So the arms began to flow. Other countries followed our lead in sending lethal equipment, including France and Germany, and most of Nato, and many others around the world. By the following month, April, Ben Wallace and his counterparts were running a huge conference of military donors at the Ramstein air base in Germany.

In the months and years that followed, I felt we were always too slow with this military aid, always too hesitant and worried about 'escalation' – when the person who really feared escalation was Putin. But the sending of the NLAWs was significant in that it helped break the ice and banish the general qualms about being seen to give arms that would be used, immediately, to kill Putin's troops.

By using those borrowed weapons so effectively, the Ukrainians showed that not only did they have right on their side, not only did they deserve to win, but with the right kit they could and would win. Unlike Putin's miserable conscripts, they were fighting for their country, their hearths and homes.

Chapter 53

The Cost of War

Inflation and a growing battle
with Treasury inertia

The war in Ukraine moved the sympathies of the British in a way that it moved no other European population. It wasn't long before blue and yellow Ukrainian flags started to appear in windows, on lapel pins, on the spires of churches up and down the country. We led Europe in the quantity of aid we sent, especially military kit. We welcomed 210,000 fleeing Ukrainians into our homes.

We saw things with a particularly vivid moral clarity. According to opinion polls, 87 per cent of the British people blamed Putin, and Putin alone, for the invasion: a higher proportion even than Estonia. Fervent pro-Ukrainian feeling united political parties and all socio-economic groups.

Perhaps it was the instinctive British tendency to side with the underdog; perhaps it was a continuing outrage at Putin's behaviour over the Salisbury poisonings.

They backed the Ukrainians, even though the war was driving up the price of oil – to $110 per barrel and beyond – and fanning the flames of the inflationary bushfire that was now spreading across the world.

By January 2022 inflation in the UK was running at 5.5 per cent, and was expected to rise above 7 per cent that year. It was the worst spike since my childhood in the 1970s. People's fuel bills were spiralling, and the media were soon talking about a 'cost of living crisis'.

All Tories hate inflation, not just for the damage it does to household budgets but also to savings and investment. As chancellor, Rishi was right to focus on stamping it out (and probably right to think that the Bank of England had been slow, the previous autumn, to put up rates).

But was this the limit of our economic ambitions? Surely we needed a post-Covid, post-Brexit strategy for growth, I argued.

I had been nettled, talking to some global investors, by their view that Brexit Britain had yet to differentiate itself from the sputtering European model. I could see what they were driving at, so one morning I stumped down the red carpet, without warning, to see Rishi in his office in Number Eleven.

He was sitting there under a portrait of Hugh Gaitskell – another Wykehamist chancellor, though not fabled for his tax-cutting or deregulation.

Come on, Rishi, I said, how about some dramatic fiscal gesture – to show that we are different now? How about cutting corporation tax right down below Irish levels? 10 per cent? That would show them.

Rishi was polite, as he always is, but he reminded me that he had just signed up to a G7 agreement not to cut corporation tax below a certain level.

Well, what, then? I asked. We needed to show global business that we had a new and different approach. He was always going on about California and tech. What could we do?

He said he got my point, and he would take it away and think, but week after week went by and I was getting nowhere.

I wanted us to launch a growth strategy for Brexit Britain, and I was getting fobbed off. I now think of course that he was temporising.

He could see my political embarrassment over the Sue Gray inquiry, and then the police inquiry, and I expect he had people in his ear foolishly encouraging him to get ready to replace me. Come to think of it, he had registered a website, called 'Ready for Rishi', back in January.

It now occurs to me that he was saving his growth strategy, and his new fiscal approach, for the moment he took over. Oh well!

In those days I assumed that he was still on my side, and waited, and in my frustration I turned my attention to the long-term solutions to our problems. It wouldn't help much now, since the cost of lighting and heating was a function of global markets.

In the long term, though, I wanted to make us less dependent on imported energy and more capable of producing our own.

We were too dependent on gas, and Putin's war had caught us out badly. We had once been self-sufficient in energy; now we were not only importing huge quantities of gas, we were even importing electricity from France. We needed to drive towards green self-sufficiency – as I had set out in the ten-point plan. We were doing well with offshore wind, but we needed to do more.

I set a new target of 50 gigawatts (about half the daily UK electricity needs) from offshore wind by 2030. But we needed baseload – power that is not dependent on the vagaries of the wind gods. We were the home of civilian nuclear power, and yet our nuclear industry was collapsing; so I set up a new mission – Great British Nuclear – to champion both big reactors such as Hinkley and Sizewell and the small modular reactors, and to produce at least 24 gigawatts from nuclear by 2030.

Across the country, British nuclear reactors were on the verge of being wound down. I went to see some of them and they had a slightly alarming air of antiquity, with throbbing machinery that had evidently been painted and repainted many times over the decades, like the walls of a Victorian primary school.

I also went to see the vast new development at Hinkley in Somerset – the biggest engineering project in Europe. Hinkley has already taken years, and has been brain-achingly expensive to build. It has been designed to withstand a direct hit from a fully laden 747 jumbo jet. It will be just as expensive to run, with the government guaranteeing a pretty fruity strike price for the electricity.

I can see why the Treasury has been so reluctant to maintain the nuclear lead we enjoyed in the 1950s; but that short-termism has been disastrous for consumers today. One of the reasons the French were better placed, at the outset of the energy crisis, was that they had fifty-six nuclear reactors. At Hinkley I announced the British Energy Security Strategy (BESS), so that in future – if not now – we could be better insulated from the craziness of men like Putin, with more renewables and more nuclear.

Crucially, I didn't exclude the use of UK oil and gas; indeed, I could see that we would need more hydrocarbons to tide us over. But by 2030, on my plans, the vast bulk of our energy would be clean and green and from the UK.

To help me I appointed Champions for Wind – Tim Pick – and Nuclear – Simon Bowen – to help me campaign for the infrastructure, and am very grateful to them both.

I was sitting at my desk in Chequers one Sunday, working on BESS, when I heard a really mind-boggling piece of news. The Metropolitan Police had for some reason decided to fine me for a breach of lockdown rules.

My first reaction was that this must be some form of practical joke.

Then I heard they fined Rishi too. It really must be a joke, I thought.

I know there may be some readers who have been sufficiently influenced by the media coverage as to believe that I was indeed 'partying' during lockdown: spending my evenings in wassail with my cronies from the Covid Taskforce and the Cabinet Office. It simply wasn't true.

I didn't 'party' with anyone. In fact, given how hard we were all working, and how desperately we were trying to stop a pandemic, I find the whole suggestion nauseating. Nor was I aware of any illicit socialising by anybody else.

As for this 'event' on June 19, 2020 – almost two years before – it had never occurred to me or Rishi, either then or since, that it was in some way against the rules.

Here is what actually happened. I stood briefly at my place in the Cabinet Room, where I have meetings throughout the day, while the chancellor and assorted members of staff said happy birthday. I saw no cake. I ate no blooming cake. If this was a party, it was the feeblest event in the history of human festivity.

I had only just got over Covid. I did not sing. I did not dance. I ate a salad – but then it was lunchtime, and I do normally eat at my desk. I did not meet anyone that I don't meet in the course of the working day.

We then got on with another meeting. I do not for one moment believe that this so-called birthday gathering in any way constituted a breach of the rules. The event was thought to be so innocent that it was actually briefed out to the media at the time.

It says a lot about the change in mood, and the desire for revenge, that when the event actually took place – almost two years previously – people read about it in *The Times* (actually a slightly exaggerated version) without batting an eyelid.

Of course I have no idea what version of events other people gave the police. I was obviously vulnerable to the testimony of some who were determined to bring me down.

And I relied upon Sue Gray, who (though I did not know this) had already been approached to be the chief of staff to Ed Miliband, former Labour leader, and who was to go on to be the chief of staff to Keir Starmer – my number-one political foe.

I have no idea what these people said to the Metropolitan Police. But I very much doubt that it was fair.

As for all the other fines that were issued – more than 120 – the answer is of course that I don't know. I wasn't there, or didn't see anything that looked illegal.

If the fines were like mine, they must have been a bit puzzling. Some of the allegations in Sue Gray's report – vomiting, fights, and so on – turned out to be untrue, and had to be withdrawn.

But what could I do? I paid the fine and got on with the job.

I had a lot on. Europe was now in the grip of its biggest war in eighty years, and the British were seen as the biggest champions – politically, diplomatically, militarily – of Ukraine.

Chapter 54

Night Train to Ukraine

And the total myth of the thwarted peace deal

Whoa, I thought. What the hell was that? As I came to my senses, I found that there was something very peculiar about my bed. It seemed to be quivering, and bouncing up and down.

In fact, the whole room was lurching from side to side. Then there was another bang, like the one that must have woken me up.

What the hell time was it, anyway? I couldn't read my watch and, oh yes, I had no mobile phone – because I was travelling with only a couple of companions through a war zone.

I was taking a train through Ukraine, without my police protection officers and in conditions of what we hoped were total secrecy.

I lay back down and opened the curtains behind my head. I tried to calm myself by staring at the mile after mile of ghostly birch forests slowly passing outside, the nameless rivers and darkened farms with rickety wooden barns.

The banging, I realised, was not some missile slamming into the side of the carriage. It was just the clanging of the commie-era train over the points.

Look, I said to myself: he wouldn't do anything so stupid. We had decided not to tell the Russian invaders that I was making the trip, but even if Putin found out, he wouldn't take out a G7 leader – would he?

We weren't entirely sure what he might do. He'd used chemical weapons on British soil. He'd invaded a sovereign European country.

He might easily try to shrug off a stray railway derailment, and the accidental loss of a western leader. The UK's security establishment are a wonderful body of men and women but they were nervous about the trip, to put it mildly. They took weeks to 'sign it off', refused to allow any civilian staff to come with me, and in the end Ben Wallace, defence secretary, had to intervene to make it happen.

The only people with me were a small handful of soldiers from HM Armed Forces – and pretty extraordinary soldiers they were. Before turning in, I had sat up late with my two companions – my Number Ten military advisor, Col. Jaimie Norman, a Marine commando of great distinction, and Gen. Gwyn Jenkins, who had overall command of special operations.

Convention rightly forbids me from describing what these men did, or do. But I can safely say they had both been involved in some pretty hair-raising scrapes around the world; and as they sat there capping each other's stories I began to hold my manhood cheap.

So now I lay there in the clattering Ukrainian train, thinking about what they had said, and my confidence began to return. I was being a wuss, I decided.

It was – so they told me – surprisingly difficult for the Russians to hit a moving train. It was, furthermore, a magnificently fortified train, hundreds of tonnes of steel; tall, stately, with a presidential suite that included a gold and brown mosaic bathroom, a carpeted conference/TV room full of shaggy sofas, and the bedroom where I lay – whose bucking king-size bed had been most recently occupied by the Hollywood movie star Sean Penn.

Yes, of course it was a risk to make this journey – but probably about the same as cycling in London (itself very safe, *vide supra*); and it was a risk that simply had to be run. I needed to see Ukrainian president Volodymyr Zelensky, and I needed to see him in person.

By the time I set off for Kyiv on April 8, 2022, the war was entering a new and very dangerous period. By their sheer heroism, and with the assistance of the first tranche of western weaponry, the Ukrainians had repelled the Russian advance on their capital. The sinister forty-kilometre crocodile of Russian armour had eventually given up and turned tail.

The Ukrainians had scored a stunning military success against what was supposed to be the second-greatest military power on earth. But they still had not won; far from it. Putin had already bitten off a large chunk of Ukraine, and with great savagery. A few very brave Ukrainians were still fighting in Mariupol, on the Black Sea, but by now he had captured most of the land-bridge between Russia and Crimea, including the cities of Berdyansk and Melitopol.

He had begun a brutal programme of Russification: castrating Ukrainian men and taking hundreds of children for forced re-education in Russia. His methods were essentially the same as he had used in Grozny, against the Chechens – mercilessly bombing civilian areas, shredding apartment blocks with his artillery, not caring how many innocents died.

The Ukrainians had enraged Putin, they had unnerved him; and it was obvious that he was willing to fight for as long as it took. As the rest of the world looked on, there were many – understandably – who prayed for another way out. The economic consequences of the war had already been appalling. Inflation was taking root. There had to be a way of bringing peace to Ukraine, by providing an 'off-ramp' for Putin, some face-saving solution.

The French and Germans were clearly hoping that there could be some kind of deal, maybe involving land for peace. Negotiations of a kind had already been taking place, first in Belarus and then in Turkey. I was deeply suspicious of these talks.

Did we really have to save Putin's face? Couldn't he do that himself? The Russian proposals basically involved the humiliation of Ukraine, turning an independent country once more into a vassal state of Russia.

The plans were plainly a disaster for Zelensky and for Ukrainians – to say nothing of the catastrophic message they would send to the rest of the world about the rewards for aggression and the lassitude of the west. But I could imagine that the shell-shocked Ukrainians might contemplate the long-term prospect of standing up to Putin, and feel so exhausted, and so alone, that they simply felt obliged to capitulate; and I could imagine that if the Ukrainians decided to surrender – or to reach a terrible and unequal agreement with Russia – then the west would be so weak and divided that the Russians would get away with it, just as they had got away with it in 2014.

So I wanted to reach out to Zelensky and give him the most vivid reassurance possible. It was not my job to tell him how to conduct the negotiations, or to prevent him from coming to an agreement, if he thought that a deal was really in the interests of his country. Passionately though I supported Ukraine, I could not be more Ukrainian than the Ukrainians.

All I wished to say to him was that IF he continued to fight, and if the Ukrainians decided that they wanted to continue to purge their country of the invader, as I was 99 per cent sure that they would, then I wanted him to know that he could count on the wholehearted support of the United Kingdom. The Ukrainians knew that the UK had played a significant role, in the last six weeks, in mobilising western opinion: against Putin's aggression and in favour of Ukraine.

I wanted to be clear with Zelensky – that as far as we were concerned, this was just the beginning, and that we were there for the long haul; and the way to do that was to be there in person. We had to stand shoulder to shoulder, physically as well as metaphorically.

I also felt it was important to show that we agreed with their own assessment – that they had vanquished the Russians, that they had saved Kyiv from a terrible fate, and that Ukraine was going to be free.

They said that the city was safe from Putin – even though the Russian forces were still less than thirty kilometres away. The obvious thing for a Ukraine-backer was to go there and prove it. I was strongly supported in this by Prof. John Bew, the brilliant Number Ten defence and security adviser, as well as by Jaimie Norman. That was the case we made to the security establishment, and after a fair bit of teeth-sucking they'd signed the necessary permissions.

That was how I came to be clunking slowly, steppe by steppe, on the eleven-hour trip from Poland to Kyiv. I would be amazed if anyone had wind of it, so tight was our operational security. We had left the previous evening, after dark, when an RAF Wildcat helicopter landed without lights on the lawn at Chequers. Everything was blacked out, and they gave me some *Silence of the Lambs*-style night-vision goggles so that I could read my brief one last time: we would have to abandon my notes in the UK.

From a base in Britain we took a transport plane to a town in eastern Poland, and then drove about an hour or so to a town on the border. Here we had arranged to pick up the train. After waiting for about half an hour in some spooky and deserted crossing, we realised we were in the wrong place. So we just drove on to the main station.

This was much busier, and brightly lit. There were trestle tables with fruit and nappies and bedding – things a fleeing family might need – because Ukrainians were still pouring over the border to the west. Considering how late it was, there were plenty of people about. Someone might just recognise this odd detachment of Brits, heading in the other direction.

I shoved my TfL bobble hat lower on my head and avoided people's eyes. We walked through a gap in the fence and over the tracks to our train. I hoisted myself up the steel steps and was welcomed aboard by a pale, thin, humorous young man called Oleksandr Shevchenko, who revealed himself to be the corporate communications director of Ukrzaliznytsia, or Ukrainian state railways.

It was to be the first of many happy journeys with his company, and I should record that the railway men and women are also heroes of the war. They have lost hundreds of employees, and on the very day I arrived there had been an appalling and cynical missile attack on the station at Kramatorsk, killing sixty-three civilians, including nine children. All told, the Russians hit four Ukrainian railway stations that day alone.

Dawn banished the terrors of the night. The Ukrzaliznytsia staff were in good spirits, and insisted on giving us a breakfast of kings: cottage cheese pancakes and a kind of potato rosti, with coffee and all manner of ham and cheese and fresh vegetables.

As we started to get closer to Kyiv, I saw signs of the fighting: a few blackened and bombed-out buildings. At Irpin, in the suburbs of the capital, we clanked over a new-built bridge, which had replaced the one destroyed by the Russians only a few weeks before. Oleksandr was very proud of his company's achievement.

By mid-morning we were in the capital, slinking unobtrusively off the train. Melinda Simmons, our ambassador, met us at a side-exit from the platform. The Ukrainians spirited us into the presidential compound. We went through anti-tank roadblocks and past gun emplacements covered with webbing, then through a darkened and dusty corridor to a stone plaza with a bizarre

Victor Horta-style building called the House of the Chimaeras. This 1902 masterpiece of art nouveau is also known as the House of the Mad Architect, and is decorated with concrete kitsch sculptures of exotic beasts.

I suppose if Putin had succeeded it would now be part of the Russian colonial administration of Ukraine. Today it is still the place where Ukrainian presidents welcome foreign guests.

Zelensky was standing outside, wearing his khaki fleece and surrounded by a familiar cast of ministers and advisers. He looked pale and tired (so did we, I expect). But he beamed to see us.

We had two long meetings, one tête-à-tête and the next with our teams. The essence of the meetings was the same. I told him how much we admired his achievements and the heroism of the Ukrainians. I said what I believed, and still believe.

'You are going to win,' I told him.

To underline our support, we had put together another package of military funding, worth £100 million. Zelensky was grateful, and stressed that he intended to recapture all the territory currently held by the Russians.

He asked for more weaponry, in particular more armoured vehicles, so that the Ukrainians could counter-attack and rescue the troops stranded in Mariupol. We agreed that we would do whatever we could: eventually the British were the first major European country to deliver not just anti-tank weapons but actual western tanks.

The UK Challengers eventually broke the taboo and paved the way for the American Abrams and the German Leopards; though again it all took months longer than I hoped. We discussed the longer term, and how to ensure that once Putin was finally expelled he would never come back.

Perhaps we wouldn't be able to get Ukraine immediately into Nato, but we could supply the Ukrainians with such an abundance of western kit, training and intelligence support that no one would attack them again. The idea was to turn Ukraine into a steel-quilled porcupine, indigestible to predators. It was no real substitute for Nato membership, but it would have to do for the time being.

We then did a slightly surreal event: a press conference without press – because the trip was still meant to be secret. So Volodymyr and I made statements to the cameras, for release the following day; and then, according to the agenda, we were due to have lunch.

I was certainly keen to have lunch. It was getting on for 5 p.m. Ukrainian time, and we were all bushed. But there was a key target still unattained. I felt I still needed to show full, public and unmistakable confidence in Ukraine.

My media statement had hailed the Ukrainian victory in the battle for Kyiv. I had assured them that they were going to win. But my actions, so far, did not quite back up my claims. I had arrived in secret; I had sat in heavily guarded meeting rooms; I had refused even to talk to journalists. I obviously needed to get out there and show that I believed Kyiv was a free city, and that here, at least, the Russians were no longer to be feared.

'Volodymyr,' I said, 'I think we need to go for a walk.'

The president's head of security was sitting behind him, and I could see his eyebrows shoot up his high domed forehead, but Zelensky agreed immediately.

'Let's do it,' he said.

'I would love to see the city.'

'I will show you.'

We hadn't recce'd the route. We didn't know exactly what we would find, or whom we would meet. It would be the first proper walkabout by Zelensky since the Russian invasion had begun. It was only six weeks ago that the city had been full of explosions and shots, and Russian special forces operatives apparently trying to assassinate him. But we both knew that it was dramatically essential for us to appear together in a city that was now safe and at peace.

So that dull grey afternoon, damp underfoot, we walked through the centre of Kyiv for about forty-five minutes, and I must confess that I kept my eyes peeled for snipers on the roofs of the art deco mansion blocks. We were completely untroubled. One man came up to us as we walked down the cobbled street and poured out his thanks to the UK.

Yup, I thought – I was definitely more popular in Kyiv than in some parts of Kensington.

A woman also spotted us, and rushed off to get two traditional Ukrainian earthenware jugs, shaped like cockerels, one for me and one for the Ukrainian president. She explained that they had become symbols of resistance – because of a now-famous photo of the aftermath of Putin's attack on Borodyanka, a town near Kyiv.

The photo showed a kitchen smashed to smithereens, except for a cockerel jug still standing intact on the shelf. You look at that cockerel jug, and you think about the family whose home was destroyed, and you wonder how many of them died and how many of them will live to see a completely free Ukraine.

A little over a year later, I was an ex-PM having lunch at a restaurant in Greece. At the next table I could see a German family, and one of the women appeared to be eyeing me grimly. She had very short grey hair and a downturned mouth. She didn't look like one of my natural supporters.

As they left the restaurant she came over and suddenly slapped a Post-it note in my hand, like Blind Pew delivering the Black Spot. In tiny handwriting it said, 'Mr Johnson, how can you live with yourself when hundreds of thousands of people have died after you went to Kiev and stopped a peace agreement in April 2022?'

I was amazed, and then did some research and found that this view was being widely peddled in Germany and has since gained ground elsewhere. Putin himself repeated the allegation, in the course of his utterly mendacious interview with the US journalist Tucker Carlson in February 2024.

It is complete tripe. The Ukrainians were never going to agree to Putin's terms – nothing like them. By the time I arrived in Kyiv, the world could see the atrocities the Russians had already committed in Bucha and elsewhere. I don't think any Ukrainian leader, Zelensky or otherwise, could have agreed to a peace deal and survived for more than five minutes in office.

My function was not to avert a deal, or to scupper Putin's beautiful 'peace plan'. My job was just to reassure Zelensky of western support, and above all of UK support. Given the horrors endured by the Ukrainians in what is not just a fight for the independence of their country but a universal fight for western values, it was the least I could do.

After a long lunch in the House of Chimaeras we went straight back to the station, and, jug in hand, I began the journey back.

Chapter 55

Welcome to Kent,
Twinned with Kigali

A viable deterrent to the gangs

I felt that what we were doing in Ukraine was important – vital – but I always knew the reality: the voters want you to focus on their immediate concerns; and for months the number-one issue had been those damned people smugglers and the cross-Channel dinghies.

It drove our voters wild to see how they flouted the law, coming across in their homemade coracles – on one occasion in a kiddies' paddling pool. It was dangerous: people were regularly drowning at sea, and by coming here illegally they were of course making a mockery of all those who did the right thing and made proper applications to come.

The 'small boats' seemed unstoppable; they were on the news every night; there were hundreds of people coming every day – and tens of thousands every year: from 10,000 in 2020 to 30,000 in 2021. In 2022 it looked as if we would hit 45,000. The whole exercise was a daily humiliation of the UK state.

How could we claim to have 'taken back control' of our borders when they were being visibly overwhelmed on television by a tide of humanity? We were spending a fortune supporting the French gendarmerie, in the hope that they would intercept them on the beaches of Calais and elsewhere; and though they did stop some, many were getting through.

We had tried all kinds of crackers and probably inhumane ideas: wave machines, ramming the boats, physically picking them up with giant trawlers and taking them back to France. They were all too dangerous. Any such project would collapse, quite rightly, with the first drowning.

So there was only one other option – and I knew from my conversations with the great former Australian prime minister, John Howard, that it would work. When Australia was suffering from a similar problem – illegal immigrants landing in boats – he came up with the radical idea of taking them immediately to be processed elsewhere, in fact 4,500 miles from Australia on the guano-rich island of Nauru. Of course the policy was not perfect, but the Australians found that the prospect of ending up on Nauru was a massive deterrent, and the flood became a trickle.

We needed to find an equivalent destination, an offshore processing centre. That would destroy the confidence of the gangs, undermine their pitch to their potential customers and seriously disrupt the trade. We looked at all sorts of places, from Ascension Island to the Falklands, and I talked to all kinds of governments.

Priti Patel, the home secretary, worked incredibly hard. Then, one day, she hit the jackpot. I was thrilled. We had found a place to process the illegal arrivals, and it was ideal. So on April 14, not long after getting back from Ukraine, I went down to Dover to announce it.

I began by reminding everyone of the fundamental humanity and decency of the British people in welcoming those fleeing persecution. Just since 2015 we had taken 185,000 people fleeing conflict or oppression: 100,000 Hong Kong Chinese, 20,000 Syrians, 13,000 Afghans and now 50,000 Ukrainians. I believed the public overwhelmingly supported this, and I added that several members of the cabinet were immediately descended from those arriving here in fear of persecution in another country: Dominic Raab, Priti Patel, Nadhim Zahawi – and myself, if you think about great-grandfather Ali Kemal fleeing to Wimbledon in 1912.

I emphasised the cruelty of the cross-Channel trade, the damage it was doing to the cause of those who came here legally. So we were going to have a Migration and Economic Development Partnership with Rwanda. We would send the illegals to be processed in Kigali, and though it would take time, and though the plan would of course face fierce opposition, I was confident that eventually it would work.

Finally – whatever you said about it – we had a plan. Now we could get on with the careful and painstaking business of making it legally invulnerable.

We had taken back control of legal migration; and even if the numbers had been high post-Covid, that was readily explicable: we had what looked like a frightening shortage of workers, and we had to beat inflation.

Everyone was panicking – about shelves not getting stacked, about the Brussels sprouts not being picked for Christmas. So yes, in that post-Covid year I can see that the Migration Advisory Committee overcompensated.

But that didn't change the fundamental point: that thanks to Brexit we could fix that mistake, and cut the numbers radically next year. And thanks to Brexit, we now had a radical – if contro-versial – plan to deal with the illegals on the sea.

Could I have really pulled it off?

If you look at what we did with Brexit, or with vaccines, to say nothing of the sheer public appetite to get it done, I think there are good grounds for thinking that we would have succeeded. But would my party give me time?

Chapter 56

Dear Sir Graham

How the letter writers were really thinking

When the whole Partygate hoo-ha began, I am afraid I suffered from what they call cognitive dissonance. I tended to dismiss the notion that it might be seriously politically dangerous, let alone fatal.

Come off it, I said to myself. I was certain that I had done nothing wrong. From the reports I heard, the so-called parties seemed to consist almost entirely of people sitting at their desks in the evening and continuing to discuss, over a glass of warm white wine, the same miserable subject that had occupied them for the previous twelve hours – viz. Covid.

The media clamour being so intense, my advisers were a bit less confident. When we got back after the Christmas break, I found that my colleagues in Parliament were being brought in to see me, so that I could feel their pulse and be sure of their support. To my slight amazement, people were already talking about 'the letters' going in. By this they meant the Tory Party's peculiar method of epistolary assassination.

If 15 per cent of the parliamentary party – in this case fifty-four Tory MPs – decide to write to Sir Graham Brady, chairman of the 1922 Committee of backbenchers, expressing no confidence in the prime minister, then a vote must be held on whether the PM can remain in office. History shows that most PMs survive these votes, more or less comfortably. But they are invariably wounded so badly that they do not survive for long.

It was important to sort things out, and to anticipate any grievances colleagues might have. My intelligence network suggested that all was still well.

The House of Commons hairdresser, Kelly Dodge, sees all and knows all. As she snips and twirls the locks of the MPs and polishes their pates with her hot towels, she hears the things the whips don't pick up. She also had a contact in Sir Graham Brady's office.

'It's OK,' she told me one morning as she gave me a trim. 'We think there are only about a dozen.'

But what if Kelly was wrong? What if Sir Graham's drawer was already bulging? My backbench colleagues were generally ushered in to see me after PMQs on a Wednesday, with the meetings kept to time by Declan Lyons and Ben Gascoigne.

I was startled by the MPs' mood. Covid lockdowns meant that I was badly out of touch with them. It was clear that the Partygate allegations had triggered a hail of anti-Tory abuse, both on their emails and via social media; and they blamed me. It was the handling of the crisis that enraged them more than the substance of the issue.

It was the constant drip-drip-drip of allegations (much of them totally untrue) that were being fed to the media, and the misery of having to wait, first for Sue Gray and then for the police. At the same time, of course, the sheer ferocity of the media storm was making it more difficult for Sue Gray, and then the Met, to look at things dispassionately and recognise that the vast majority, if not all, of these allegations concerned reasonable workplace events, and that no one had set out to break the law.

Even if they had been minded to give officials the benefit of the doubt (which Sue was not), it was becoming politically and optically more difficult. Which was, of course, what my enemies intended. I tried pleading with colleagues that it was very largely nonsense, a media-driven campaign being fed by some former advisers, whose identities they knew well.

Look, I said: why on earth is all this stuff coming out now, more than a year after the so-called gatherings took place? If any of the hundreds of officials involved had thought there was anything awry, surely we would have heard about it much, much earlier. These people working in Number Ten and the Cabinet Office were not all my supporters.

If someone had thought that the rules were being broken, they would have leaked it months ago. But we had heard nothing.

Many of my MP colleagues got it and could see that it was unfair. Many of them decided that this was the moment to bargain with me. They could see I was getting into a fix, and if they were going to back me, then they wanted something in return. Let us take the case of a former minister, a banker by trade, who had been sacked under a previous administration for some misdemeanour or other.

This chap had given me voluble support in the past, but I suspected that this was not because he was a great enthusiast for Brexit, or for levelling up, or indeed for me, but because he saw me as a route to political redemption. In the course of my campaign to become leader of the Conservative Party, he had formed the impression that I had promised I would restore him to the cabinet, and now he had come to see me – to remind me of my alleged obligation.

I was a bit confused by this. I racked my memory. It was true that I had made soothing noises about the indignity of his dismissal (in the hope, I admit, of securing his support), but I was pretty sure I had not made any concrete promise about a post in cabinet, since such promises are a very bad idea.

Look, I said, as we sat on the green sofas in my parliamentary office beneath the beaky-nosed marble bust of Pitt, I am not ruling anything out for the future, but now is not the time.

He took it badly. 'What you don't understand,' he said, 'is that the Tory parliamentary party is a cuntocracy. The bigger the cunt you are, the more successful you are.'

Just then someone stuck their head round the door to say that time was up.

My companion's face, already pretty vinous, flushed deeper. 'These people are going to get you,' he said, and stalked out.

As I gazed at his furious back, I knew exactly who he meant by 'these people'. He meant himself, and all who felt as he did, and I am afraid there were far more of them than I had realised. If you add together my natural enemies in the parliamentary party – the Remainers, the Cameroons, the Mayites, the sacked, the over-looked, the obscurely jealous – you had a lot of people, in fact way over 50 per cent of the Tory MPs.

Too many of them regarded me with the outrage of Chief Inspector Dreyfus as he beholds the triumphs of Clouseau. They were the competent, diligent ones, and here was this buffoon who seemed to shrug off all disasters and absurdities and rise from success to success and from one position of prestige to the next.

It got their goat. It made them homicidal. I often used to sense this problem, but I am afraid I didn't do enough about it. Looking back, I am absolutely sure that with enough love and attention I could have restored relations with the party in Parliament.

But I was just complacent. I bitterly regret it. I was used to being mayor, with supreme monarchical power and no back-benchers to worry about. I also believed that they would not be so foolish as to get rid of me.

I had won a big majority, had a clear vision for the country, and even after months of being hammered by the media over these so-called parties we weren't far behind in the polls, a handful of points.

Surely they wouldn't be so dumb? I mean, would they?

Chapter 57

Britain and India

A relationship as good as it has ever been

I suppose it is always tempting for a politician in domestic trouble to seek the consolations of international travel. Somehow the people of other countries seem kinder, gentler, more impressed by your achievements and altogether more brilliantly perceptive of your good qualities.

If I wanted my morale lifted by April 21, 2022 – and I did, a bit – then the Indian governments, regional and national, applied themselves to the task with almost hysterical enthusiasm. From the moment we touched down in Ahmedabad, Gujarat, it felt like an orchestrated orgy of state-sponsored Beatlemania.

First there was the fanfare at the airport: the dancing, the garlands, the general riot of 10,000 decapitated orange chrysanthemums. Then we drove for mile after mile past crowds behind barriers – as though to restrain their otherwise boundless enthusiasm – waving plastic British and Indian flags. At every street corner there seemed to be a new folkloric troupe of dancers or pipers or drummers, and on billboard after billboard there were giant images of my face, like a big red squashed tomato, glowering down on the apathetic multitudes.

Well, I thought to myself as I waved graciously back through the window of the HMG Range Rover: this is more like it. This, in fact, is uncommonly civil.

After the misery of the Commons, the ghastly confected outrage of Starmer, the ululations of the Labour MPs, the scorn with which they greeted my stammering and (in retrospect) slightly ill-judged apologies, it was balm for the soul. I defy any politician not to feel a bit cheered by the full glory of a proper Indian welcome, even if you have been feeling as blue as Krishna himself.

The media seized on the contrast – abused at home, adored (apparently) abroad – and thrashed around with it joyfully, like a dog with a new toy.

I was a cowardy custard, fleeing my foes, they suggested. I was dodging the flak in foreign fleshpots, they said, as though the whole trip had been devised for the purpose of media management. Which was, of course, absurdly unfair.

To do a big and proper India trip had been a key objective of mine ever since I had become PM almost three years earlier. Much to my frustration, it had been cancelled twice because of the pandemic. So I was thrilled to be there at last. I had a major problem to solve, and a big Global Britain objective in mind.

I love India, and have four children who trace their origins via Marina to the subcontinent. Over the years I have become a veteran of Indian weddings. I have dressed up in the full Sikh wedding fig, with kurta pajama and chapal sandals, and a turban tied, in the approved manner, with the help of a doorknob (I once appeared so attired at a reception to find all the other chaps wearing suits).

I have spent many happy hours doing Indian dancing, where the secret is to rotate your hands twice as though changing a light bulb and then twice as though revving a motorbike, so it goes light bulb, light bulb, motorbike, motorbike. My politics has also involved a lot of happy Anglo-Indian syncresis. I am proud to have run the most ethnically diverse cabinet in UK history, partly because we had at least four senior ministers of Indian origin: Rishi, Priti, Alok and Suella. There are deep ties of history, kinship and culture between our two countries, and many extraordinary examples of Anglo-Indian cooperation, not least during the battle against Covid.

One of the reasons we had the AstraZeneca vaccine in such plenty – and were able to help inoculate about two billion people around the world, at cost – is that we did a deal with the dynamic Mr Poonawalla of the Serum Institute of India. It was the Indians who actually fabricated the drug that eventually protected me from further infection, and millions of others in the UK alone.

We in the UK have no other relationship quite like our friendship with India. And yet we must be frank. For decades this relationship has underperformed its potential, both commercially and strategically.

In the last thirty years our trade with China has mounted a vertiginous forty-five-degree climb, to the point where it is now worth about £100 billion a year. Trade with India has grown much more slowly, and now stands at about £40 billion – though the population of India is even bigger than China's. According to my brother Jo, a former *FT* Delhi wallah who has written whole books on the subject, there are all kinds of reasons for this relative tepidity in our economic relations.

Partly it is because we no longer make enough of the kind of things that the Indians have needed in their path to industrial development. I am afraid that when it comes to machine tools and locomotives, modern Britain has long since ceased – with some noble exceptions – to be the obvious source.

In the areas where we are highly competitive, Britain faces unnecessary barriers to trade. There are, for instance, the infamous 150 per cent tariffs on Scotch whisky. These I denounced during the course of some impromptu remarks to the congregation of a Sikh gurdwara in Bristol during the 2017 election campaign, prompting much outrage because I seemed to be preaching the consumption of alcohol in a holy place.

As ever, the frenzy was overdone. Anyone who has been to a Sikh wedding will acknowledge the vital lubricating role of Johnnie Walker Black Label (or indeed Blue, Purple, or even White label, such is the sophistication of Indian taste).

How long, I asked, and still ask, must visitors to India go clinking in with duty-free booze for friends and family because the 1.4 billion Indians are still being starved of Scotch at decent prices?

More significantly, the Indians place all kinds of restrictions on UK services exports – where our country truly excels. According to Jo, and I am sure he is right, the Indian economy will never reach its full potential, and the people of India will never achieve a western standard of living, unless they end these restrictive practices and open up – in the law, banking, insurance, accountancy and so on. It is the right thing for both sides.

So I wanted a proper free-trade deal, and in Narendra Modi I believed I had found exactly the partner and friend that we needed. Yes, he was controversial, and in 2012 – on my first trade trip to India, as mayor – the FCO was distinctly sniffy. They even said I should not meet him. He was a Hindu nationalist, they said. Well, they soon dropped all that.

A few years later he was electioneering in London, and we met outside City Hall. For some reason we went down to stand in the dark in the plaza by Tower Bridge, in front of a crowd of his supporters. He raised my arm and chanted something or other in Hindi, and though I couldn't follow it I felt his curious astral energy.

I have enjoyed his company ever since – because I reckon he is the change-maker our relationship needs. With Modi, I felt sure, we could not only do a great free-trade deal but also build a long-term partnership, as friends and equals. We have so much in common: both democracies, both English-speaking, and with many shared anxieties, not least on terrorism and climate change. Modi has done a storming job in building India's solar power, and played an important role in making the Glasgow COP a success.

There is also the rise of China. We are both – the UK and India – conflicted on this subject. We want the best possible relations with China, but we are wary. We are wary of Chinese expansionism in the Pacific, wary of being pushed around. That was why I had launched the new post-Brexit foreign policy and defence review with what we then called the Indo-Pacific Tilt, opening embassies in the region, and in May 2021 sending a huge flotilla of ships, led by the *Queen Elizabeth*, our aircraft carrier, with a complement of 800 men and 65,000 sausages (work it out) on a forty-country round trip to the South China Sea, exercising with the Indian Navy in the Bay of Bengal.

I also wanted to make a gentle point to Narendra and his superb advisers, such as his foreign secretary Subrahmanyam Jaishankar and national security adviser Ajit Doval, because it struck me that we were at a global inflection point. Putin's invasion of Ukraine had broken all norms of civilised behaviour. His appalling decision had obviously been enabled and approved by China.

I knew all the history and the sensitivities, the reasons for India's post-war non-alignment with the west, the seemingly unbreakable relationship with Moscow. I understand the Indian dependence – like China's – on Russian hydrocarbons. But I wondered if it was not time for a modulation, a rethink.

The relationship between Russia and China was different from the days of the Cold War. Putin was now very much the junior partner, the client if not the punk of China. Did India really want to be aligned with this pair of autocracies?

Putin's military blunders had also highlighted the unexpected deficiencies in the Russian war machine. As I was to put it to the Indians, Russian missiles were turning out to be less accurate, statistically, than my first serve at tennis. Did they really want to keep Russia as their main supplier of military hardware?

Now was the time, I reasoned, to go further – way beyond trade and climate change and educational partnerships – and embark on a whole programme of military and technological collaboration. Well, as these things go, the trip was a tremendous success. After nearly two years of work on the agenda, we had a huge amount ready to be signed off.

We gave our trade negotiators a fresh kick in the pants and vowed to get it all done 'by Diwali' (inevitably prompting the question, which Diwali?). Overcoming the qualms of the MOD, who are always worried about India's closeness to Russia, we agreed to work together on all kinds of military technology, from submarines to helicopters to marine propulsion units.

I was so engrossed in this happy work that I almost forgot about my problems at home.

I was in the process of opening a giant new JCB factory in Gujarat, and about to make a speech hailing JCB as the great custard-yellow counter-example to the suggestion that Britain cannot make and export the most beautiful state-of-the-art machines to the rest of the world, when I was told that I had a phone call from London.

The JCB employees started to form up in the cavernous machine assembly hall. My speech was due. Slightly cheesed off, I went into a small office to get some privacy.

It was the chief whip, Chris Heaton-Harris, and he had news of some Labour motion that had gone down that day. They were trying to refer me to the Privileges Committee for allegedly misleading Parliament about rule-breaking in Number Ten.

It sounded like absolute twaddle, a typical Labour stunt, and the chief wanted to vote it down.

Then I thought about it some more. I didn't want to look as though I was evading scrutiny. I didn't want to be accused of using my majority to ride roughshod over Parliament – a repeat of my Owen Paterson goof. Since I was absolutely confident that I had nothing to hide and nothing to fear, and since I knew that I hadn't misled Parliament, certainly not intentionally, I told the chief whip to let it go through.

Once again, I was making the elementary mistake of trusting my fate to people who might turn out to be my enemies.

I look back at that decision and I groan inwardly.

Ah well. Such are the perils of making decisions whole thousands of miles from home. Big international trips are great, but all politics is local.

Part Ten
Last Months

Chapter 58

A Torrid Sort of Summer

My enemies make their move

You might call it complacency, or conceit, or just stark insensibility. But if you had asked me in June 2022 whether I was likely to continue as leader of the Conservative Party, I would have blinked in surprise and replied that not only was I confident of leading my party into the next general election, but that I was sure we were going to win.

On any objective view, the position, all things considered, was pretty darn good. In spite of the battering we had received in the previous six months, we were at times still only a handful of points behind the Labour Party, sometimes only two or three, sometimes (at least once) even level-pegging. Bear in mind that the Tories under Cameron were more than ten points behind Labour for most of the 2010–15 period, before going on to win. For all the indignation of my detractors, the signs were that the public was getting a bit fed up with Partygate – and wondering whether the media was just slightly over-egging it.

When it came to the local elections on May 5, 2022, the predictions had been ghoulish: that Tory councils would be slaughtered. The last time these seats were contested, it was pointed out, was during the brief moment of Theresa May's *Gloriana Imperatrix* twenty-point ascendancy over Corbyn – so logically we were due a drubbing.

As it happened, the Labour attack fizzled. We lost a few hundred good councillors – and that is always very painful – but the swing to Starmer was only about 5 per cent: nothing like enough for Labour to win a general election majority. In fact, he only picked up a handful of councils, while in some parts of the country – where Tories had never traditionally been strong – we were actually winning seats. If you looked beneath the surface of the results, you could see the realignment still going on.

For a government that had entered mid-term, and for a party that had been in power for twelve years, it wasn't half bad. Yes, of course I could feel the pressure and the tension – but then what is life without pressure?

In politics you are always going through cycles of pressure and relaxation, compression and decompression. The trick of it is to suck up the punishment while it lasts, in the knowledge that your enemies can't keep firing forever. In all the orc-like smithies of my foes, I was confident they had not yet made the bullet that could take me out.

We had between two and three years before the next election – a political aeon – and by then, I calculated, there would be so much that we would have completed or delivered. We were fixing the nation's infrastructure, from energy to broadband to high-speed rail. We were fixing housing and planning. We were building forty new hospitals and fixing social care, so as to relieve one of the main pressures on the NHS. We were building a whole new agenda for skills, and lifelong learning, and by 2024 I reckoned there would be scarcely a left-behind town in the country that was not somehow feeling the benefits of levelling up.

The fruits of Brexit had begun to show and would show more – provided we kept our nerve. We were fixing the Channel crossings with the Rwanda plan. It was hard, but we would get there.

We had a Labour leader who had absolutely no plan to fix the problem himself, mainly because he was so clearly part of the problem: a human rights lawyer who had championed complete free movement of people – Brownian motion of human beings across the world – and who recoiled, with every fibre of his being, at the idea of sending illegals back. David Blunkett he most certainly was not.

And remember – when I was PM the Reform Party, which was to do such catastrophic damage to the Tory Party in 2024, was on zero per cent in the polls. Zero.

So yes: if you ask me the counterfactual question, would I have won again if the Tories had kept me on, the answer is yes, absolutely. (Remember: Starmer ended up with a 10 per cent smaller vote share than we won in 2019. He actually got about half a million fewer votes than Jeremy Corbyn.)

As we came to the end of the first term, I was confident that we would be able to explain to the electorate that we had begun building a bridge to the future – a glorious and beautiful bridge – and that we needed to keep going in order to make landfall on the other side.

Sure, I was impatient to hear Rishi Sunak's growth strategy, and I yearned for that Lawsonian vision of tax-cutting and simplification. But we had time; we had discussed it. I believed that the combination of our skills, his and mine, was very powerful and that we would get there in the end.

It all seemed logical to me. The trouble was (soft wheezing sigh) that too many members of the Tory parliamentary party just did not see it that way.

When things are febrile, a tiny episode can make a sudden difference for the worse. At the beginning of June 2022, my colleagues were spooked, like a herd of cows by a barking dog. It was enough to push them, or at least 15 per cent of them, over the edge. At the beginning of that long, hot summer, the nation was celebrating the unique achievement of the Queen in spending seventy years on the throne – the longest reign in British history.

There was a huge outpouring of love for Her Majesty, and she did her best to respond. She appeared and waved at the balcony; she was filmed, in a lovely cameo, taking tea with Paddington Bear; but the truth was that by now she had to conserve her energies. As I had known for about a year or more, she had a form of bone cancer, and her doctors were worried that at any time she could enter a sharp decline.

She was too infirm to go in person, for instance, to a great service of Thanksgiving that was held in St Paul's Cathedral on Saturday June 3, 2022. The crowd outside was large, and in boisterous spirits. It is a long way up those steps, for any politician, and as Carrie and I went up – she in a seemingly precarious red and white hat, me in morning dress – I could feel those thousands of eyes on our backs. So I was relieved to hear what sounded like a very favourable reception – loads of cheers and claps, and then, uh-oh, just as we got to the top, I heard another noise cut through.

Carrie didn't even notice it, but I picked it up all right. It sounded as though there had been a couple of boos, or jeers, down there to the left. Of course that was enough.

It didn't matter that the general mood was positive, or that some reporters didn't even detect the disapproving noise. In her Sky News commentary Kay Burley simply observed that we were cheered.

The good old Beeb had the boo-ers on their soundtrack, and were of course so enchanted by their contribution that they sought one out for interview (he turned out to be a French resident of London, who didn't much like *le Brexit*); and they churned, churned, churned the story, as you can with twenty-four-hour news.

Now my political instincts are not always bad, and something told me that for skittish Tory MPs this was going to be a difficult moment. Every day for the last six months the poor things had been pelted with ordure intended for me: social media messages saying what a prat I was, and worse. Now here, to their jangled imaginations, was the proof of what some of my colleagues were whispering in the shadows.

They said I was losing my grip on our public. They said that the voters would be glad I was gone, and look here – across the Astons of every TV screen – booed, by God, at a moment of national unity and rejoicing. So when the phone went the following day, just as we were getting ready for some climactic Jubilee pageant, I looked down with a liverish eye and was not surprised to see the name of Graham Brady on the screen.

I had a feeling I knew what Sir Graham was going to say. He didn't sound particularly gloaty, or chuffed – but unquestionably pleased to be in on the action. 'Prime Minister,' said the chairman of the 1922 Committee, 'the fifty-four letters are in.'

Well, from then on in I can now see that events were moving ineluctably towards their grisly conclusion; but what strikes me today is my blithering refusal, at the time, to give in to despair. You can be taking an active part in your own decline and fall without realising that it is going on.

On the morning of the vote – June 5 – I sat at the cabinet table, topping and tailing about 365 letters, one for every Tory MP, setting out what I believed was a powerful case for my remaining in office. As I wrote out each Christian name and urged their support, I began to see the full difficulty of my position.

For every Tory MP that I felt I could call my friend there was at least one, I am afraid, who was most definitely not on my side.

'This is terrible,' I groaned to Nigel Adams MP, an old friend and colleague who was organising the fightback – an operation called, for some reason, 'Save Big Dog'.

'These people hate me,' I muttered.

'Don't worry,' said Charlotte Owen, one of my political advisers who was helping with the whipping operation. 'We are going to win!'

Well, of course, we did – and pretty comfortably. I felt I had won a reprieve, and that if I could just get past the summer all would be well.

With a sense of almost cockroach-like invincibility, I got on with the job – because June was a very busy month, and among other things I had to keep up my campaign for the Ukrainians.

When Putin launched his invasion on February 24, 2022, there was very wide global support for Ukraine. In the UN vote condemning the attack, 141 countries expressed their distaste, with only 5 actively siding with Russia and 35 abstentions. Sadly, though, the vote masked the reality that there were far too many countries where support for Ukraine was lukewarm, or where there was a more than sneaking sympathy for Putin.

It was monstrous, and it mattered, because we needed to do everything we could to tighten the global sanctions on the Russians. On June 23, 2022 I flew (plus Carrie plus Romy, then a babe in arms) to Kigali in Rwanda for the long-delayed Commonwealth heads of government meeting, or CHOGM.

This was fortuitous because it gave me a chance to show the media what a safe, clean, green country Rwanda now is – and the ideal place to process illegal immigrants. They struggled to deny the point.

It was also another chance to rally support for Ukraine. I had memories of the last CHOGM, four years earlier in London, when as foreign secretary I had shoved some language into the communiqué denouncing the Russians for the Salisbury poison-ings, only to find that it had been whipped out again by the Commonwealth secretary-general, Baroness Scotland. This time, I thought, the case is overwhelming.

We are talking about an invasion, the murder of thousands of civilians – we must be able to get them to agree.

Hah!

In the first plenary session, I made what I thought was a reasonable argument against the invasion, only to find that my old friend Yoweri Museveni, the president of Uganda, was raising his hand.

'I do not agree with what Boris Johnson has said.' Generally I got on famously with this merry-faced old fighter, who had helped overthrow the dictator Idi Amin. No one would pretend that Uganda under his rule is a perfect model of democratic pluralism – but it is a lot better than it was under Amin (who kept the heads of his opponents in the freezer).

Over the years Museveni and I had happy discussions of Land Rovers and cattle farming, and he always seemed to me to have a sentimental interest in – if not quite allegiance to – the old colonial power. As he once explained to me, his very name is a reminder that his father had fought for the 7th Battalion of the King's African Rifles: hence Mu-seveni.

When it came to Putin and Ukraine, however, we were miles apart. He trotted out some of the Kremlin talking points: the nonsense about Nazis and terrorists in Ukraine, for instance.

I tried my ace. Museveni is about eighty years old. He is one of the post-war generation of African rulers who took part in the unbundling of the British Empire. Surely he could see what was happening. Putin's attack was a neo-colonialist assault on a newly independent state. It was naked imperialism. Surely he was anti-imperialist?

It didn't wash. 'Putin gives us weapons,' he said simply – and there, I am afraid, he has a point.

Look around sub-Saharan Africa and you will find that Russia is the biggest supplier of weapons, with about 25 per cent of the market. Unlike some of us western countries, Putin believes in a no-questions-asked approach. You got a problem with Islamists?

says Moscow: we'll send the Wagner group! They will blow them away.

There is none of that onerous but necessary stuff about following the rules on international humanitarian law. The Russians don't preach about democracy, or press freedom, let alone the protection of LGBTQI communities. I am afraid that in many countries our delicious disputations on these subjects are viewed with bemusement, if not outright hostility – not just by the leaders, but by many of the people themselves.

Putin doesn't give a damn about these complexities. On the contrary, he presents himself as the champion of old-fashioned family (or Christian) values. It is no wonder that his dark charisma proves so compelling with some audiences; and the result is that in Africa today there are far too many governments that are at best ambiguous on Ukraine, and plenty of places where – incredibly – you will see crowds of young men waving the Russian flag, as if to cock a snook at the west in general.

So after Yoweri Museveni and I had argued each other to a standstill, I gave up, and the fifty-six countries of the Commonwealth contrived in their long communiqué to say nothing about Ukraine at all. Oh, except for a brief reference to the food shortages and price inflation, which Russian propaganda was blaming – in a demonic inversion of the truth – on the western embargoes on Russia rather than on the Russian invasion of Ukraine.

It was infuriating. Let's face it – Britain is, or ought to be, a FAR more important partner, for these countries, than Russia. The UK economy is much bigger and more diverse than the Russian economy; we trade more with most of them; we invest more.

Do they speak Russian? No. They speak English. Do they send their children to university in Russia? No – on the whole they vastly prefer universities in the UK, and quite rightly. Why are we so meekly allowing Russia – never mind China – to acquire this hold over Africa, and why don't we make better use of the Commonwealth?

This grouping has amazing potential – so much of the youth and future economic growth of the world. There are too many people in the Foreign and Commonwealth Office who treat their eponymous institution as a post-colonial embarrassment. I enjoyed the summit, but left Kigali feeling strongly that the whole thing needed more oomph.

Imagine if the French had an institution so naturally pregnant with possibility as the Commonwealth. Think what they would do with it.

When we got to the next global jamboree – the G7 in Schloss Elmau, Bavaria – I found myself up against yet more Russian propaganda. Olaf Scholz, the German chancellor, had moved a long way since the first discussions on Ukraine. He comes from the SPD, the social democrats, the party of Ostpolitik – of reaching out and engaging with Russia. So he had been almost incredulous, to begin with, at the idea that German armour should be sent into Ukraine to fight Russians. The idea of German panzers thundering eastwards: well, it carries some pretty heavy historical associations.

To begin with, the Germans had sent things like helmets and a field hospital. But then – much to his credit – Olaf gripped it and turned things around, and now the Germans are sending huge quantities of stuff, from Leopard tanks to Patriot missiles; in fact, I believe they have overtaken the UK as donors.

At every stage, however, we have all been too slow, too nervous of the Russian response – too worried that we might 'poke the bear' and provoke an escalation in the conflict. At Schloss Elmau – a hyper-luxurious *Sound of Music*-type place in the Bavarian alps – we were being told that Putin 'must not be humiliated' (Macron), and that there was a risk of nuclear conflict. Gah, I said, and became impatient.

At one stage there was a bizarre meeting of the P3 – the three nuclear-armed democracies in the UN Security Council, viz. the US, UK and France – to discuss how to handle the nuke problem. What would we actually do if Putin used a nuclear weapon on the battlefield – for the first time since 1945?

Look, I said, Putin wants us to talk about nuclear weapons. He wants to frame this war as a stand-off between a nuclear-armed Nato and a nuclear-armed Russia. He wants to scare our populations and make our flesh creep.

In reality the war in Ukraine is nothing of the kind. It is the brutal and criminal invasion of a sovereign European country by conventional means, and we should give the Ukrainians the maximum support until they win. There were all sorts of reasons, I suggested, why Putin would not dream of using a battlefield tactical or any other type of nuclear weapon.

He would terrify his own population, who would assume there would be reprisals; he would lose Chinese support; he would turn his country into a global leper; and he would not even win. The Ukrainians would just fight on.

So my view was that we should drop the subject – and we did.

By the Nato summit in Madrid on June 29, everyone seemed much more confident – about backing Ukraine and standing up to Russia. I suppose that's the thing about Nato. It has a coagulating effect. As the most successful military alliance in history, it has a way of getting everyone to focus on the collective foe – and this time absolutely every one of the twenty-eight members was willing to denounce Russia, and in the strongest terms.

It was only a couple of years earlier that Macron had called Nato 'brain-dead'. Now the alliance was not just plainly vital, but expanding – in a way that no one had foreseen. It is a proof of how catastrophically Putin has miscalculated that he has managed, by invading Ukraine, to overturn seventy-five years of Finnish and

Swedish neutrality. He wanted less Nato on his borders, and he has ended up doubling his border with the alliance.

In both countries the change of heart has been prompted not just by the political classes but by bottom-up popular demand. After decades in which they maintained the chaste purity of their non-aligned status, two great Scandinavian countries have said stuff this, so to speak, for a game of soldiers. We want the security that goes with a Nato guarantee.

I was proud of the role that Britain had played in bringing this about. Both countries were worried about the period between the application for Nato membership and their actual accession. They would be effectively aligning themselves with Nato, and courting Russian wrath, before they had the precious Article 5 security guarantee – by which in 1949 the founders of the alliance decreed that an attack on one was an attack on all. What if Russia chose the interval to threaten or bully them, even attack them?

It was a small risk. But that was what we used to say about a Russian invasion of Ukraine. It needed an answer. So we in the UK made a formal offer that British forces would come to their aid in the event of aggression. On May 11, the previous month, I had been out to Sweden and Finland to sign the relevant agreements.

In Sweden the prime minister, Magdalena Andersson, welcomed us to her equivalent of Chequers, a country estate called Harpsund. I rowed her out on the lake to show the photographers that we were all now in the same boat.

In Finland I met the president, Sauli Niinistö, in his waterfront palace in Helsinki – not that far, across the Gulf of Finland, from St Petersburg. Nato was so popular that there was a small knot of pro-Johnson demonstrators at the gate: sadly lacking these days from the gates of Downing Street.

Both countries applied to join a couple of days after my visit, and now, by the end of June, it was clear that they were going to succeed. The most difficult objections had been from the Turks, but I was sitting next to my old friend Tayyip Erdoğan, and I was sure that his reservations were melting away.

The summit ended well, and among other things I announced that we in the UK would hit 2.5 per cent of GDP as our defence spend by 2030; indeed we can hardly fail if we do what is necessary for the subs, FCAS (Tempest) and so on.

My blood was still coursing with the dopamine of my final Nato press conference when I came back to the UK delegation room to find that Ben Gascoigne, my political secretary, needed to talk to me. There was another problem at home, it seemed. The deputy chief whip, Chris Pincher MP, was in trouble for allegedly groping a man's bottom, while drunk, in the Carlton Club.

I could imagine the hilarity and scorn in the Kremlin: that this was (a) the kind of thing that British MPs got up to and (b) the kind of thing that required the attention of the prime minister.

'These MPs will be the death of me,' I said to Gascoigne. At the time I meant it to be satirical.

I am told that after I announced my resignation a week later, on July 7, 2022, there was a fair bit of confusion on Tory doorsteps. Some voters seemed mystified by what had happened. They had voted me in with a large majority three years before.

They had high hopes, and now I was being removed – without consulting the electorate. Why exactly had I gone? What was my crime?

What was it really all about? I hope the reader will forgive me if I say I find it all pretty painful to describe, and I am sure there are plenty of other blow-by-blow accounts. But I feel people are entitled to know – after all this – precisely why I ceased to be PM, or at least what I think happened. Let me rule out some of the ostensible causes.

It was nothing to do with Chris Pincher, though I certainly handled that one badly. The weekend after I got back from Nato (feeling fairly chipper), my mind was on other things, and I was paying no attention to the media. For some reason Number Ten had decided to respond to a media question by saying that I knew of no previous allegations against Chris.

That wasn't right, since it was widely known that he had a reputation for acting badly – sometimes – when drunk. His reputation was known to the previous PM, Theresa May, who promoted him after he had first become the subject of rumours. I knew the rumours, certainly. Pincher by name, Pincher by nature, was the joke.

But as far as I had previously understood it, Pincher's behaviour could be sometimes embarrassing, or unbecoming – rather than bullying or inexcusable. The tragic reality is that if you excluded everyone from governmental office, just because they had at one time faced allegations of unbecoming or embarrassing behaviour, you would have precious few Tory MPs to choose from.

What we should have said was that I knew of nothing – so far – that was fatal to a ministerial career. That would have done the job. It was just a muddle, and under normal circumstances we would have breezed through it.

So what went wrong? Why did so many of my colleagues have a fit of the vapours? It wasn't even Partygate, which by then was feeling pretty stale. It certainly wasn't the polls, since – as I say – even in my final week some polls put us less than five points behind, one poll as little as two points, certainly nothing like the vast gulf that opened up after I was gone.

The fundamental problem was that too many Tory MPs just wanted me out of their hair. Some had certainly been rattled (unnecessarily, I think) by the hate storms of Twitter. Some disliked me, some of them for personal reasons, some of them because they thought they could do better under someone else.

Quite a lot of them, of course, still secretly opposed me over Brexit. Many of them weren't worried about the next election; or at least they weren't worried that I would lose. They were worried I would win, and that they still wouldn't get the preferment they thought they deserved.

So they wanted CHANGE. They thought they could painlessly switch horses, and with an eighty-seat majority, and the boundary changes coming, they thought they could still canter to victory. They also had an obvious replacement in view, and had done for months if not years.

'Rishi will win my seat,' said a bumptious young MP back in January, in my office in Parliament. In 2019 he had won one of those north-eastern seats that had scarcely ever been Tory before, and he came to explain, with magnificent condescension, that as far as he was concerned I might as well disintegrate.

I was of course far too polite to disagree, but as I looked at him I wondered …

Really? I thought (he was vaporised, of course). I liked Rishi, I considered him my friend and partner. But I had not seen the evidence that he knew how to cope with the scale of the job, how to mount a truly massive campaign, how to project a vision of the future that really resonated with the voters. I thought Rishi's best bet would be to hang on, help get us through 2024, and then take over in due course.

We had discussed it several times, and he assured me of his complete support 'for as long as you want', and it goes without saying that I was pretty fervent in my support for him. He had run into some difficulties in April over his wife's tax affairs, and I can tell you that we were all full-throated in our defence of Rishi and his family. I just assumed he would reciprocate.

So when Sajid Javid resigned over the Pincher business on Tuesday July 5, I was fairly phlegmatic. I loved old Saj, but he was finding it very hard to reform the NHS and fix waiting lists, and I suspected that he was paranoid about his own position as health secretary. But when Rishi resigned later that day, at 6 p.m., I was sad.

It was worse than a crime, I thought, it was a mistake – both for Rishi and for the party, never mind the country. So it proved.

As I read his resignation letter, with its leaden phrases, I murmured (at least internally) the dying words of Julius Caesar, *kai su, teknon*. If Caesar had twenty-three stab wounds I ended up with sixty-two, in the sense that a grand total of sixty ministers decided to follow Saj and Rishi out of the door – and if you want to know the formal reason why I resigned two days later, it was because in this absurd situation I really didn't feel I could go to the Queen and say that I was able to appoint her ministers from the very best of the governing party, and that it was therefore time for someone else to have a go.

Was it a plot? You bet it was a plot, in the sense that a lot of them were at it for ages, some of them from the very moment I took over. Was the plot enough, on its own, to bring me down?

Well, I don't think you should underestimate the many goofs I made. I made too many duff appointments, some of which turned out to be homicidal maniacs. I badly mishandled our response to some of the crises.

Above all, and partly because of Covid, I did nothing like enough to explain myself to the parliamentary party and keep them onside. Too often I would go back to the Number Ten flat, tired out, and work into the evening, when I should have been talking to colleagues and keeping them cheerful. That was my failing, and not the only one.

In retrospect I should have done more to protect myself, and the rest of Whitehall, against Partygate-type allegations. I should have said something to the entire staff – perhaps in a letter – about the vital importance of not only obeying the rules, but being seen to obey them, and reminding everyone that people were angry and wanting to find fault.

In retrospect that is an obvious thing to do, and I greatly regret it; and I only didn't do it because I assumed it was understood.

I was complacent and thought I could just charm people into sticking with me, when actually I should have taken more time with them, and if necessary had a row.

I am afraid I was also sometimes arrogant. I should have realised how different being prime minister is from being mayor, in that you serve not just at the pleasure of the people but of your colleagues.

I don't blame Rishi for prematurely wanting to be PM; in fact I don't blame any of them, really, for trying to turf me out. It's just what Tory MPs do. As Frank Johnson once said to me, they are a rabble. They must be constantly reassured – and Covid made it much more difficult.

Rather than blaming my colleagues for kicking me out, I should actually thank the majority who stuck by me, and who believed in me, and what we were doing, and in many cases still do.

They were right. They were the heroes. We had a great agenda for the country. We would have gone on in the next two and a half years to defeat inflation, as we had defeated Covid. We would have been in the throes of delivering the infrastructure revolution, and helping young people to own beautiful new homes.

We would have delivered on the 2019 manifesto: police, doctors, nurses, and we would have been visibly getting on with levelling up, and even if that process had been slowed by Covid, the direction of travel was clear.

By cutting taxes and simplifying regulations – thanks to Brexit – we would have been making Britain the greatest place in the world to live and invest and start a family.

It goes without saying that if we had all stuck together I have no doubt that we would have gone on to win in 2024, and a lot more of my friends would now have their seats.

How did it feel, then, getting assassinated? Well, I have never been shot (only in the stomach by my brother Leo, with an airgun) but I am told that sometimes you hardly feel the wound, at first.

Then after a while, like all big human rejections, it hurts a lot. Then you start to think about the future, and it gets better.

Chapter 59

Some Pointers
for the Future

Good things done, but a lot left to do

'Hasta la vista, baby,' I bellowed at the speaker at the end of my last session of Prime Minister's Questions. To my surprise I found the benches behind me rising in a standing ovation. It might have been almost tear-jerking, I thought, as I brushed past my smiling and clapping colleagues on the way out of the Chamber – if so many of them had not been actively trying to remove me from office.

Oh, well! It was very generous of my friends, and on the whole I thought they were right to be proud of what we had done together. A few days later I gave the House my perspective on what we had achieved in three years.

I beg readers to forgive the tone of what follows, since it falls firmly in the category of blowing your own trumpet. But so much of what we did and tried to do has now been sadly forgotten; and if you want your laurels burnished these days, you better do it yourself.

I reminded them that we had won the biggest Conservative majority since 1987, and had won the biggest share of the vote since Margaret Thatcher's landslide in 1979. We had won from Wrexham to Workington, from Bishop Auckland to Barrow-in-Furness.

We had sent the great blue ferret of One Nation Toryism so far up their left trouser leg that the Labour Party went rigid with shock. We had then blasted Brexit through even though it had previously seemed impossible – and by the way, I said, in no fewer than forty-eight divisions on the matter, Keir Starmer, that human bollard, had tried again and again to block the will of the people.

It was that proper, fully liberating form of Brexit which enabled us to license a Covid vaccine faster than any other European country, and Brexit had therefore helped to deliver not just the fastest vaccine roll-out of any comparable country – and thereby save many lives – but also the fastest exit from lockdown, and thus the fastest economic recovery in the G7.

The result was that, contrary to all the predictions of doom, we had come through the pandemic with unemployment at or near a fifty-year low, with 620,000 more people in paid jobs than before Covid hit us, and we had youth unemployment at a forty-five-year low.

We were fulfilling our bargain with those millions who had come over to us from Labour – lifting the living wage by record sums, forcing boardrooms to invest more in their staff, cutting the tax on universal credit, cutting National Insurance, so that people even in the poorest households had the satisfaction of knowing that most of their income was coming from their own earnings, and not – as was the case under Labour – from benefits.

Never forget, I told the House (which was, as you can imagine, fairly noisy), that none of this would have happened if we had simply listened to Keir Starmer, the pointless traffic cone, because at every stage he had wanted more lockdown, more delay and expense, and had even been so boneheaded as to attack the very Vaccine Taskforce that had helped to set us free.

In spite of the hurricane headwinds of the pandemic, we had fought to deliver the 2019 agenda. We were on track to recruit 20,000 more police, as promised, with 13,500 already signed up;

we had taken thousands of knives off the streets in a renewed campaign of stop and search; we had rounded up 1,500 county lines drug gangs; we were engaged in a big cross-government campaign to make Britain safer for women and girls, and to make sure that the men who were responsible for rape and violence were actually taken to court and then sent to prison for their crimes.

Our efforts, after only three years, were paying off. By trusting the police, by allowing them more freedom to exercise their powers and by putting more officers out on the streets, we had cut neighbourhood crime by 31 per cent; and that in my view was a great thing, since crime falls hardest on the poorest, and getting crime down is the absolute precondition of investment and growth.

We had promised that we would put billions more into the NHS – and we certainly had, even before Covid struck. Yes, whatever the defeatist moanings of the opposition, we were building those forty more hospitals by 2030. We had recruited 10,000 more nurses in the last year alone, we were on track to hit our target of 50,000 more, and as I spoke the NHS had more doctors and nurses in its employment than ever before.

After decades of dither by all parties, we had launched a plan to stop bed-blocking – the absurdity that in any big British hospital, on any given day, you could find that about 30 per cent of the beds were occupied by people who frankly did not need to be there, but whose families did not know where to put them because they were worried about the expense of their care.

We had tackled social care, and gripped the most painful nettle in the political undergrowth. We had agreed that for those facing unexpected and catastrophic costs – such as dementia, for which people could not reasonably be expected to provide – the state would step in, above a reasonable cap in costs. Everyone else, however, would be expected to insure themselves.

We had invested massively in schools, in teachers' pay, in tutoring. We were not only tackling the perennial problem of post-sixteen skills, with the LifeTime Skills guarantee. We had launched a campaign to tackle the root of the skills shortage, and to insist that 90 per cent of eleven-year-olds in the UK must be both literate and numerate – rather than the current 65 per cent.

It wasn't that these 35 per cent of kids were thick; it was that they were being pointlessly left behind. I reminded the House of what levelling up, my creed, was all about. We Conservatives believe there is genius and talent everywhere, and that you will find natural energy and imagination distributed in every corner of the country.

You could not say the same for opportunity. That was why we needed to keep spreading that infrastructure revolution, the biggest programme of rail and road investment since Victorian times, not just HS2 but also Northern Powerhouse Rail, and above all the electronic connectivity that was now indispensable to the modern economy.

When I became PM in July 2019, only 7 per cent of households had so-called gigabit broadband. That was now running at 69 per cent and climbing, and every day, thanks to the efforts of government-backed schemes, the fibre-optic vermicelli were sprouting through new wainscots.

We were making Britain a technological and science superpower, with £22 billion going to science, a new Advanced Research and Innovation Agency, and literally hundreds of low-earth-orbit satellites that I had bought in the hope of rivalling Elon Musk, which we later sold at a profit. We had two new space centres, at Newquay and Shetland, and plans to launch from them in the coming year.

The whole point of all these exertions was to lay the foundations, manure the flowerbed – make the UK, in the eyes of the world, the best place to live, work and invest.

You could see it paying off, I boasted. We had tech unicorns, or start-ups now worth more than $1 billion, emerging virtually every fortnight, not just in the golden triangle of Oxford, Cambridge and London but across the whole country. We had just overtaken China as the centre of tech venture capital, with £16 billion rolling in during the last year.

The investment in public services, in safe streets, in infrastructure was paying off in the sense that the builders were producing record numbers of homes. Last year there had been 400,000 first-time buyers, I said, and dwelt on the divide between the parties – the Tories always the party of home ownership, Labour the party of state-owned housing and government-controlled rents, notwithstanding the fact that people like Starmer invariably dwell in stuccoed Islington palazzos.

I concluded by lifting my eyes to the horizon, and explaining how we had helped to deliver the vision of a Global Britain and to restore our country's mojo on the world stage. I might as well quote the whole peroration, and though it is inevitably bombastic, it gives the flavour of how I felt that day.

On this sweltering day, let me remind the House that there are very few governments in the world who could have organised a COP 26 summit so far-reaching in its impacts. I thank my Right Hon. friend the Member for Reading West [Alok Sharma] for what he did: committing 90 per cent of the world to net zero by 2050, moving the world beyond the use of coal, moving from fossil-fuelled cars to electric vehicles, planting billions of trees around the world and launching the clean green initiative as we did at Carbis Bay, by which G7 governments will now leverage the trillions of the private sector to help the developing world to use the clean, green technologies that offer economic as well as environmental salvation.

I think that people around the world can see more clearly than ever before that we have in this country – and, I think, in this House – a renewed willingness as Global Britain to stand up for freedom and democracy. There could be no better proof of that than our campaign to help the Ukrainians. If it is true that I am more popular on the streets of Kyiv right now than I am in Kensington, that is because of the foresight and boldness of this government in becoming the first European country to send the Ukrainians weapons – a decision that was made possible by the biggest investment in defence since the Cold War. Although I think that that conflict will continue to be very hard, and our thoughts and prayers must continue to be with the people of Ukraine, I do believe that they must win and that they will win.

That will be not merely of massive strategic importance, in the face of Putin's adventurism and aggression. When the people of Ukraine have won it will also be a victory of right over wrong and of good over evil. I think that this government saw that clearly, saw it whole and saw it faster than many other parts of the world. That is why I have confidence in this government.

By the way, I have absolutely zero confidence in the Opposition. Eight of them – I never tire of saying this, and everyone must be saying it right up until the general election – eight of them, including the shadow foreign secretary, voted to discard this country's independent nuclear weapon. I do not believe they would have done the same thing in standing up to Putin in a month of Sundays.

Last week I went up in one of our 148 Typhoon fighters, and I flew out over the North Sea, over Doggerland. The drowned prairies are now being harvested again with tens of gigawatts of clean green energy. We will have 50 GW of offshore wind by 2050, and thanks to this government's activism I am proud to say that offshore wind is now cheaper than onshore wind.

I looked down at that ghostly white forest of windmills in the sea, financed with ever-growing sums from international investors, and I thought, This is how we will fix our energy problems; this is how Europe should be ending its dependence on Putin's gas. I am proud of the way we have responded to the challenge, with a nuclear reactor every year rather than one every ten years – or none at all, as was the ridiculous and catastrophic policy of the last Labour government.

And then the wing commander interrupted me, and for a glorious period I was at the controls of the Typhoon. I did a loop the loop and an aileron roll and a barrel roll, and then – I am coming to the point, Mr Speaker – I handed back the controls. In a few weeks' time, that is exactly what I will do with this great party of ours.

After three dynamic and exhilarating years in the cockpit, we will find a new leader, and we will coalesce in loyalty around him or her, and the vast twin Rolls-Royce engines of our Tory message, our Conservative values, will roar on: strong public services on the left and a dynamic free-market enterprise economy on the right, each boosting the other and developing trillions of pounds of thrust. The reason we will keep winning is that we are the only party that understands the need for both.

Whatever happens in this [coming leadership] contest, we will continue to fight for the lowest possible taxes and the lightest possible regulation. The Opposition's problem is that they would try to fly on one engine, kowtowing to the union barons, endlessly inflicting more tax and more spending, endlessly giving in to the temptation to regulate us back into the orbit of the European Union, and flying round in circles.

Some people will say, as I leave office, that this is the end of Brexit. Listen to the deathly hush on the Opposition Benches! The Leader of the Opposition and the deep state will prevail in their plot to haul us back into alignment with the EU as a prelude to our eventual return. We on this side of the House will prove them wrong, won't we? [Hon. Members: 'Hear, hear!']

Some people will say that this is the end of our support for Ukraine. [*Interruption.*] That is exactly the analysis. The champanskoye corks have allegedly been popping in the Kremlin, just as the Islington lefties are toasting each other with their favourite 'Keir Royale'. But I have no doubt that whoever takes over in a few weeks' time will make sure that we keep together the global coalition in support of our Ukrainian friends.

Some people will say – and I think it was the Leader of the Opposition himself who said it – that my departure means the eventual victory of the Labour Party. I believe that those on this side of the House will prove the Leader of the Opposition totally wrong, and that in due course we will walk the Right Hon. and learned Member for Holborn and St Pancras into the capsule at Newquay that I mentioned earlier and send him into orbit, where he belongs.

And I tell the Right Hon. Member for Ross, Skye and Lochaber [Ian Blackford], who speaks for the Scottish nationalists, that it is time for him to take his protein pill and put his helmet on, because I hear it will not be long before his own party is taking him to Shetland and propelling him to the heavens.

This government have fought some of the hardest yards in modern political history. We have had to take some of the bleakest decisions since the war, and I believe that we got the big calls right. At the end of three years, this country is visibly using its newfound independence to turbocharge our natural advantage as the best place in the world not just to live and to invest but to bring up a family.

With a new and incontrovertible spirit of global leadership, I believe that we can look to the future with rock-solid confidence not just in what this government have done but in what they will do and will continue to do. I commend this motion to the House.

Two years later I look back at those words, and you know what, I fervently agree with them; and yet (as Labour members were not slow to point out) there was also something melancholy about the speech.

So much had been done, but so much was only half done. We had the time – more than two years of the parliament left. But I was relying on my successor – whoever he or she might be – to continue on the path I had laid out, and of course it was miserably frustrating not to be able to do it myself.

Government is hard. Change is hard. For a lot of the time I felt as if I was pulling a jumbo jet single-handedly down the tarmac with a leather bit between my teeth. I worried that without constant forward grunting we would now wallow and lose momentum.

Well, there is no point going over whatever I may think were the mistakes of my successors. Both Liz Truss and Rishi Sunak have very good qualities, and each was handed some bad luck. Like many ex-PMs, I am afraid I have found it impossible to disengage emotionally, and sometimes I have found myself tearing my hair out at some of the decisions.

Like what? I hear you ask. I really didn't want to go into this – but feel I have to for the sake of completeness.

Why did we do so badly in 2024? It is surely pretty obvious. We junked the agenda on which we were elected, and turned our backs on many of the people who put us in power. We ingeniously managed to alienate both sides of the coalition that gave us fourteen million votes in 2019 (over four million more than Starmer got in 2024), and a 44 per cent share of the vote.

Among other things it was madness to use a Tory conference in Manchester to announce the cancellation of HS2 to the north of the country, and the consequent scaling back of Northern Powerhouse Rail and much besides. Whatever the difficulties of HS2 (all UK infrastructure is hellish to build), the decision sent a message to communities across the north and the Midlands, that no, contrary to our promises, we were not that interested in levelling up.

We weren't determined to give them the same quality of transport infrastructure as the south-east; we weren't interested in their commuter networks and their journey times; and we weren't interested in the long-term growth of the whole country.

Did we really expect to cancel HS2 and go up in the polls? How many times can I say it: you don't win an election unless you own the future, and it felt like we were cancelling the future.

For the same reason, it was bonkers to water down the planning bill, so that we went into the 2024 election with no big housing offer for young people – only a cowardly capitulation to the alleged prejudices of their Nimby grandparents.

We gave enormous prominence to the Rwanda policy (even though Rishi had actually been against it, as chancellor), but for reasons I simply don't understand we called the election before it had been given a chance to work. So we mightily cheesed off all those who were worried about our borders, and – in a massive unforced error – created a surge of votes for Reform.

At the same time we shot ourselves smartly in the other foot, by sneering at net zero and rowing back on environmental commitments I had made, helping to send another large group of Tory voters into the arms of the Lib Dems (who now control the whole of what was Tory Oxfordshire, which I once represented).

For whatever reason, we never mentioned any of the good things that had been done in the period 2019–2022, when I was PM. Brexit was taboo. The fastest vaccine roll-out in Europe was not mentioned. We were all but silent on Ukraine and Russia. The advantages and potential of constitutional independence – it was all but forgotten.

Instead we had a few zany ideas like making maths compulsory for all eighteen-year-olds, when we should have been focusing on basic numeracy at eleven.

We were no longer talking to the people who elected us; we no longer seemed to share their ambitions; and we didn't seem to be offering any hope or vision for the country.

That, frankly, was how we plummeted from the biggest victory in forty years to the biggest Tory defeat since 1821. So now I have at last got that off my chest, here is what we – or anyone interested in politics – should be doing.

1 – FIX HOUSING. You can't hope to appeal to the younger generation if you have no plan to help them buy a home. We built a lot of homes, more than Labour – just as I out-built both Livingstone and Khan in London. But we should do more. We need to fix the planning system, and we need to use Brexit freedoms to address some of the mind-boggling delay and expense in getting one brick legally placed upon another. Starmer has begun very badly, by seeming to ignore the development opportunities in London.

2 – FIX IMMIGRATION. Labour people like Starmer basically want to get back to free movement of EU nationals; in other words, a total surrender of control. That won't wash with modern Britain. The present Labour government have no plan whatsoever to deal with illegal arrivals. The Rwanda plan was always going to be difficult, always going to be

contested, but it remains by far the best long-term deterrent to the cross-Channel gangs.

3 – FIX SKILLS. We need a national campaign for proper literacy and numeracy at eleven, and a thoroughgoing effort – which we attempted – to exalt practical skills and to integrate those qualifications into tertiary education. For decades now we have failed to invest in our human capital – with the result that British business has become addicted to migrant labour, pushing up the population and adding to the pressure on housing and services.

4 – FIX THE NHS. With an ageing population, the costs of caring for the elderly are out of control. We must fix the interface between the NHS and social care, which is responsible for all manner of delay, misery and expense. We must strike a new bargain with the public. The state will step in to help those facing catastrophic costs of dementia, but only IF people begin to insure themselves against the general cost of old age. We need to start that now.

5 – FIX OUR INFRASTRUCTURE. We need to revive the vision for High-Speed Rail across the country, including HS2. We need a solution for London's airports, and we need Crossrail 2. To be truly productive and creative and competitive you need to meet other people, and working from home is not enough.

6 – FIX GOVERNMENT. The state is taking and spending far too much money. It is insane, after the massive Covid-driven expansion in the state, that Labour is determined to go further and tax and spend more, with endless above-inflation pay rises and no productivity gain. This will pre-empt private

investment and choke the economy. Since such a large proportion of public spending is inevitably on the salaries of public servants, we must find ways of using technology to perform at least some of their functions, and help them to find new and probably better-paid careers in the private sector – where their skills are desperately needed.

7 – FIX THE TAX SYSTEM. It was one of my biggest regrets that we didn't use Brexit to put a big 'Invest Here' sign over Britain, by cutting corporation tax or some other such incentive. Rishi and I had always intended to cut both inheritance tax and income tax at the end of the parliament, once we had dealt with inflation; and we obviously need to get back, at the very least, to the rates under Tony Blair. If you can cut the cost of government, and you can, then you can certainly cut taxation.

8 – FIX CLIMATE CHANGE. You can't expect to win over middle Britain if you seem to dismiss people's concerns over the environment. Yes, of course there is a place for transitional fossil fuels, but we in Britain are world leaders in many green technologies and the net zero agenda is already driving the creation of many tens of thousands of good jobs. The answer is not to abandon net zero, or to sneer at it, but to explain the difficulties and to keep going. Contrary to the belief of many of my Tory friends, there just aren't enough votes in being anti-net zero. Look at the polls. Look at the election results.

9 – FIX CAPITALISM. One of the reasons people voted for Brexit was that they felt the system wasn't working for them. Quantitative easing was pushing up asset values for the very people who triggered the 2008 crisis, and yet most people saw

no increase in their incomes. The gap between boardroom and shopfloor pay has continued to grow. We can't be indifferent to this – which is why we began with a record increase in the Living Wage: the definition of levelling up. If we want to defend our capitalist system, we have to be aware of its failings – including those of water companies that pay huge dividends and salaries while pumping rivers full of sewage.

and finally

10 – FIX THE NATIONAL OBSESSION WITH RUNNING OURSELVES DOWN. When the people of this country voted for Brexit, it was a fantastic statement of self-belief. They thought that their country was more than capable of self-government. They wanted to take back control.

They were right, in the sense that our new-found national autonomy is already delivering results.

We are using Brexit freedoms to regulate differently, on everything from vaccines to wine production to slot allocation at airports. We have been able to cut VAT on everything from solar panels to tampons.

We have taken complete control of our fisheries and coastal waters, and we are able to promote agricultural policies that suit the needs of British farmers rather than central France. We have been able to drive regional growth and levelling up by inaugurating seven low-tax freeports.

We have become the number-one global champion of free trade, with more free-trade agreements than any other independent country, and we are opening up markets across the world for UK goods, selling pork to Mexico, beauty products to China, under agreements that would not have been possible before because our trade was run from Brussels.

We have completely exploded some of the more shameless lies that were peddled during the 2016 referendum campaign. There was no great post-Brexit spike in unemployment – quite the reverse. There was no collapse in exports; indeed we are now the fourth-biggest exporter in the world, the second-biggest exporter of financial services, at £200 billion a year, and the third country in the world, after the US and China, to have a tech sector worth $1 trillion.

Oh – I almost forgot to mention: as the great red bus of truth foretold, we have taken back £15 billion a year to spend on our own priorities, in this country, rather than handing it over to Brussels to be spaffed up *le mur*.

I don't want to be unnecessarily provocative, but I might as well say it here: Brexit is never going to be overturned.

Whatever the polls may say now, you have to imagine that the British people could be persuaded to vote to pay £15 billion a year (and rising) for the privilege of abandoning control of their laws and their borders – and scrapping the pound sterling in favour of the euro, since membership of the monetary union is a condition of joining the EU.

Why would they? What is the case, when we have already grown faster, since leaving the transition period, than France and Germany and Italy? Amigos, it ain't gonna happen.

We can love and support our EU friends in so many other ways, without rejoining an EU whose teleology we never accepted.

We are unleashed, and we will never be leashed again. After the Brexit vote, Henry Kissinger was asked how Britain should now conduct itself on the world stage. 'Supreme self-confidence,' he replied, and he was right.

No one can seriously doubt this country's systemic and habitual faults and weaknesses. We see them in the headlines every day, and quite a few of them could be fixed by some of the remedies I have set out.

But I wish that sometimes (without abandoning our gift for self-deprecation) we could remember our strengths, because they are colossal; and they would be even more colossal for being manifest, as they should and I hope will be, in every part of the UK.

Which is why it will be the job of the next Tory government to unite, to stop the feuds, to rebuild the great coalition of 2019 – and get back to levelling up.

As for whether I will ever stand in the Commons again, to call the speaker 'baby' or anything else, I have no idea. I used to claim that my chances of becoming PM were about the same as my being reincarnated as an olive or decapitated by a frisbee. The longer I spend away from Westminster, the stronger my belief that you should only get involved if you really think you can be useful.

Chapter 60

Balmoral

My last conversation with
Her Majesty Queen Elizabeth II

It was one of those dreich days in Aberdeenshire with the leaves just beginning to turn, and the mist coming off the wide brown river. A solitary cagoule-clad cameraman recorded our entry through the castle gates.

Like all my thirteen predecessors, I had come to spend the last hour of my premiership in the company of Queen Elizabeth II. The date was September 6, 2022, more than two months after I had resigned, and under our system I had, of course, been required to stay on and mind the shop while the Conservative Party got on with choosing a new leader.

As you can guess, it had been a rather frustrating summer. Shelley Williams-Walker had tried valiantly to keep me occupied: visiting nuclear power plants, and thanking some of the unsung heroes of government, such as the motorcycle Special Escort Group: the leathered and goggled Steve McQueens who hurl themselves into the traffic with astonishing bravery and skill and help the PM to get about.

But authority forgets a dying king. I couldn't drive things through, not in the way I wanted. Now I was in the spacy mood of someone who just wants to get it over.

When Carrie and I got to Balmoral, we were shown into a library with a fire going. We stood around for quite a while and had coffee. I noticed something in the mood of her courtiers. I tried a few jolly remarks, about the kind of advice I might give to Her Majesty, about who she might really send for to be PM; that kind of thing.

They smiled. But they looked tired. Edward Young, her private secretary, tried to prepare me.

'She's gone down quite a bit over the summer,' he said, and then the footman knocked and showed me into Her Majesty's drawing room.

'Good morning, Prime Minister,' said the Queen, and as we sat down opposite one another on the greeny-blue sofas I could see at once what Edward meant.

She seemed pale and more stooped, and she had dark bruising on her hands and wrists, probably from drips or injections. But her mind – as Edward had also said – was completely unimpaired by her illness, and from time to time in our conversation she still flashed that great white smile in its sudden mood-lifting beauty.

To go and see the Queen, for an hour a week, and to pour out your heart was more than a privilege. It was a balm. It was a form of free psychotherapy. It was like being at school and getting taken out to tea by a much-loved grandmother.

I felt there was nothing I could not tell her, and her genius – as I gave her my descriptions of government infighting or foreign chicanery – was to sound both understanding and sympathetic, and then, at just the right moment, to give the tiniest nudge of advice. Whatever crisis you laid before her – like one of her dogs finding something revolting on the moor and putting it on the carpet – she had seen worse.

On one occasion I was belly-aching about the miseries of Covid; the human toll, and the awful economic consequences. 'Oh well,' she said briskly, 'I suppose we will all just have to start again.'

I realised that she spoke with the historical knowledge of someone whose first PM was Winston Churchill, and who had actually served, in uniform, in the Second World War. She knew that her kingdom was infinitely capable of rebounding and recovering. We just needed to get a grip, and get on with it.

She radiated such an ethic of service, and patience, and leadership that you really felt you would, if necessary, die for her. That may sound barmy to some people (and totally obvious to many more), but that loyalty, primitive as it may appear, is still at the heart of our system.

You need someone kind and wise, and above politics, to personify what is good about our country. She did that job brilliantly.

That is why I can't, of course, say anything about her political views, though some of them were pretty clear. What I can say is that she had a deep personal knowledge, not just of history but of history-makers.

Of the people who really made the modern world, in her seventy-year reign, she had met them all: from Charles de Gaulle to Emmanuel Macron, from Harry Truman to Joe Biden, from Chairman Mao to Xi Jinping (whose security goons, much to her indignation, had once tried to infiltrate her royal coach).

So if I forgot the name of George II's battle, or the late prime minister of Zambia, she would immediately snap 'Dettingen' or 'Kenneth Kaunda', like a pub quiz winner. Sometimes she even seemed to know things before I had been briefed.

It was she who broke it to me that a very expensive RAF F-35 plane had blown a gasket and dropped off its aircraft carrier and into the drink because someone had left a plastic tray over the air intake. Doubly embarrassing to hear it from the Queen.

Today we talked, among other things, about Ukraine. I mentioned our well-known difficulties in persuading our Indian friends to take a tougher line with the Russians. She remembered something the former Indian prime minister Jawaharlal Nehru had told her in the 1950s.

'He told me that India will always side with Russia, and that some things will never change. They just are.' I cite that as an illustration of her amazing ability to reassure and to contextualise.

Two days later she died. As Edward Young explained to me later, she had known all summer that she was going, but was determined to hang on and do her last duty: to oversee the peaceful and orderly transition from one government to the next – and, I expect, to add another departing PM to her record-breaking tally.

She gave me at least two bits of crucial advice. Without offending convention, I think I can pass them on.

At the end of the last meeting, Carrie was sent in, by tradition, to join us, and the Queen repeated something she had said earlier. She was surprised by my general lack of bitterness, given what had happened in Westminster, but she approved.

'There's no point in bitterness,' she said, and amen to that. If everyone in politics – and life – could see that as clearly as she did, the world would be a much, much happier place.

The other piece of advice concerned magpies, because in the course of one of our meandering conversations – at Windsor this time – I admitted that I was neurotic about seeing single magpies. I was sure they brought bad luck.

Ah yes, said the Queen. She was exactly the same. But she had an apotropaic ritual for banishing the curse.

'If you see a single magpie, you just say, good morning Mr Magpie, today is the Monday the 12th of March – or whatever the date is. That sorts it out.'

There, in case anyone else is in need of similar comfort. How to make your own luck. A tip from the absolute top.

Afterword

How to cope with it all

I sincerely hope that in the course of this occasionally turbulent narrative I haven't put anyone off going into politics. It is a great and noble profession. Looking back even on my three and a bit years as PM, I am proud of many things we did. In case you haven't been paying attention …

We routed a semi-Marxist Labour Party, many of whom thought they were finally about to win power.

We gave the UK back its constitutional and legal independence.

We vaccinated our population faster than any comparable country and so helped to protect the population from a deadly disease.

We helped to protect the liberty of the Ukrainian people. And more.

I am conscious that many people will disagree with this assessment, often furiously. You will see and hear them all over the media when this book comes out, eyes bulging, voices sometimes hoarse with rage.

If you are on the receiving end, the criticism can feel particularly sharp these days, particularly personal. Perhaps it is a function of social media and the sudden firestorms of hate that seem to consume the internet.

So I may not be alone in thinking that a lot of good people are currently discouraged from entering politics, just because they can't face the aggro.

Am I right? Are you perhaps one of them?

If so, here is the key thing to remember. It's not about you, baby. It's about them.

It's about the frustrations, the pain, the doubt, the anxiety of people you are elected to represent. It's not about your dreams and your ambitions. It's about theirs.

You represent the system. You represent the law. You personify everything that is going wrong with their lives. For better or worse, you are the expression of the democratic will, you take the decisions, you levy the taxes, and therefore you are the person who perfectly properly gets to be shouted at.

As for the media, they are doing something absolutely essential: giving a voice to those who would otherwise have no voice. So you mustn't be hurt. You can of course take the necessary steps if the criticism seems justified.

But you mustn't be downcast.

And then there is the symmetrical point that you will also get a lot of love, and a lot of praise, and a lot of applause. I am afraid that to adapt Kipling, you have to treat the love in the same way that you treat the hate. They are both impostors.

Don't be fooled into thinking that any of it is personal. It's part of the job. As Her Majesty the Queen once said to me in one of our sessions, 'It's not about being popular, it's about being useful.'

I reckon that in the last fifteen years at or near the top of UK politics I have built and done or set in train a lot of things that are useful, from hire bikes to new nuclear reactors to new bridges and colossal new railways. We launched a programme of levelling up to unleash the full potential of the UK – and it remains the right way ahead for the entire country.

Thanks

In writing this book I have been helped above all by Ross Kempsell, who was a masterly head of the Conservative Research Department during my time in Number Ten. He has supplied the endnotes, though any mistakes are of course my own.

I have been conscious throughout that I have failed repeatedly to pay tribute to all the people who really delivered so much of what I claim to have achieved.

That is because every time I tried, I found that one acknowledgement inevitably triggered another, and the story became a bit congested.

I apologise to anyone who may feel that their efforts have not been properly recognised in the course of the narrative, but here are SOME of those to whom I will always be indebted.

For their work in London, my thanks go to: Ann Sindall, my executive assistant, who has given loyalty and kindness for almost thirty years; Wayne Lawley, who came with me from the Henley constituency; Simon Milton; Eddie Lister; Lynton and Dawn Crosby; Roisha Hughes; Ben Gascoigne; Daniel Moylan; Guto Harri; Isabel Dedring; James Cleverly, fire and emergency chief; Will Walden; Munira Mirza; Ray Lewis; Richard Barnes; Kulveer

Ranger; Andrew Gilligan, cycling supremo; Kit Malthouse; Stephen Greenhalgh; Victoria Borwick; Bernard Hogan-Howe; Paul Stephenson; Peter Hendy and the TfL team; Ron Dobson; Veronica Wadley; Harvey McGrath; Simon Reuben and David Reuben and the Reuben family for their heroic support for volunteering in London; Daniel Ritterband; Neale Coleman; Katie Perrior; Jo Tanner; Gerard Lyons, Brexiteer economist; Anthony Browne; Ian Clement; Nimco Ali; Matthew Pencharz; Lance Forman, salmon king; Mark Florman; Lord Marland; David Ross; Stanley Fink; Nick Candy; Clare Foges; Rachel Wolf; Jonathan Dobson; Camilla Groom; Sara Cadisch; Amy Selman; Lizzie Noel; Richard Sharp; Anita and Poju Zabludowicz; Jim and Fitri Hay; Lakshmi and Usha Mittal; Bob Diamond; Evgeny Lebedev; Mervyn Davies for bravely championing the Garden Bridge; and many more.

It was a huge honour next to represent the people of Uxbridge and South Ruislip, and my thanks go above all to Sir Ray Puddifoot and the illustrious tax-cutting Conservatives of Hillingdon Council. Andrea Laybourne did a wonderful job in my parliamentary office. For her indefatigable constituency work, I am particularly grateful to Catherine Rostron; and to Alice Robinson; Alex Simpson; Richard Mark; Greg Munro.

When it came to Voting Leave in 2016, I was one of the figureheads of a great and happy campaign. My thanks to Matthew Elliott, Rob Oxley and all involved; and to Chris Harborne for backing Brexit.

As I explain in the text, my life in the Foreign and Commonwealth Office was enriched by the many brilliant minds in that department. I was particularly lucky to work with Martin Reynolds, Serena Stone, Nick Wareham, among the officials, and I will always be grateful to Ben Gascoigne; David Blair, peerless speechwriter and foreign policy analyst; David Frost; Liam Parker, our spokesman who adroitly sandpapered a few stray phrases.

I would never have become prime minister without the friendship and support of a very large number of people. There are too many to thank here, but I should record my debt to:

Ben Wallace MP, the first person to suggest that I should have a crack at it, and who went on to become an outstanding defence secretary;

Nadine Dorries, who did a first-rate job both at health and then in rolling out gigabit broadband as culture secretary, and who was with me from the beginning;

Jacob Rees-Mogg, who has always showed great personal kindness and generosity, and whose advice on the economy I should probably have followed earlier;

Nigel Adams, who helped me get the job and then mounted a Rorke's Drift-like defence of our position in the last few months;

Ben Elliot, the soul of charm and tact, who raised the funds and went on to be a great party chairman;

Anthony and Carole Bamford, for their unstinting support in good times and bad.

I should thank the MPs who became early adopters of the cause, including Jake Berry, Amanda Milling, Anne-Marie Trevelyan, Simon Clarke, Conor Burns, James Duddridge, Andrew Griffith, Ranil Jayawardena, Ross Thomson, John Whittingdale, Iain Duncan Smith; and other far-sighted colleagues. Among the peers I should mention Zac Goldsmith and Dan Hannan. Thanks especially to Steve Barclay, who selflessly helped out in Number Ten.

The election victory of 2019 was the work of many hands, but I would single out Isaac Levido, the campaign director, for his patience and creativity, and the great Brett O'Donnell for preparing our debates.

As for my time in Downing Street, I cannot possibly thank everyone, but among the heroes were: Eddie Lister, who should have been chief of staff from the election onwards; Simone Finn, deputy chief of staff, wonderfully loyal and a great public servant; Ben Gascoigne (third mention); Jack Doyle, media spokesman; James Slack, author of Slacky's sex ban; Rosie Bate-Williams; Henry Newman; Henry Cook, inventor of the rule of six; Meg Powell-Chandler; Declan Lyons; Charlotte Owen, who worked tirelessly to pacify the Tory backbenches; Sophia True; Martin Reynolds, a hugely talented diplomat who came across from the FCO to be my PPS; Stuart Glassborow; Steve Higham; Shelley Williams-Walker; Dan Rosenfield, who stepped in at a key moment; Sam Cohen; Sam Richards; Allegra Stratton; Ed Oldfield; Will Lewis; Peter Cruddas; David Frost; Oliver Lewis; Kate Bingham; Paul Deighton, Mark Sedwill; Sarah Vaughan-Brown; Josh Grimstone; Ush Patel, the brilliant diary secretary; Harry Jameson, who tried to keep me fit; the dynamic double-O certificate men and women of Protforce, who strike fear into our foes; Peter Wilson; Jack Airey; Sheridan Westlake; Emily Maister; Alex Hickman; Will Gelling; Nikki da Costa; James Phillips; James Webb; the front of house team and all who helped exercise Dilyn; Mark McInnes, who did great work keeping the UK united; Martha Gutierrez Vetez who drove our son Wilf to school; all the officials; Maggie Betts, Alison Kay and all the front of house staff; Garden Room staff, correspondence teams who made everything work so well.

In helping to forge the UK's robust response to Putin's invasion of Ukraine, I thank especially Prof. John Bew, my strategic adviser, and Col. Jaimie Norman, my military advisor.

Some may have formed the impression from this account that by the end the entire Tory parliamentary party had turned their backs on me. That wasn't true. Under the (crazy) rules, I had just too many foes; but there were many who were more or less loyal to the end. I want to thank them now. They included: Adam Afriyie; Lucy Allan; Stuart Anderson; Sarah Atherton; Gareth Bacon; Shaun Bailey; Stephen Barclay; Simon Baynes; Scott

Benton; Bob Blackman; Peter Bone; Ben Bradley; Paul Bristow; Sara Britcliffe; Conor Burns; Bill Cash; Maria Caulfield; Christopher Chope; Simon Clarke; Brendan Clarke-Smith; Chris Clarkson; James Cleverly; Thérèse Coffey; Robert Courts; David TC Davies; Sarah Dines; Leo Docherty; Richard Drax; James Duddridge; Mark Eastwood; Michael Ellis; Nigel Evans; David Evennett; Ben Everitt; Michael Fabricant; Nick Fletcher; Richard Fuller; Andrew Griffith; Kate Griffiths; James Grundy; Jonathan Gullis; Rebecca Harris; Trudy Harrison; John Hayes; Chris Heaton-Harris; Gordon Henderson; Darren Henry MP; Antony Higginbotham; Philip Hollobone; Adam Holloway; Paul Howell; Eddie Hughes; Jane Hunt; Alister Jack; Ranil Jayawardena; Mark Jenkinson; Andrea Jenkyns; Caroline Johnson; Gareth Johnson; David Jones; Marcus Jones; Kwasi Kwarteng; Edward Leigh; Ian Levy; Brandon Lewis; Ian Liddell-Grainger; Marco Longhi; Craig Mackinlay; Cherilyn Mackrory; Kit Malthouse; Scott Mann; Julie Marson; Karl McCartney; Stephen McPartland; Mark Menzies; Amanda Milling; David Morris MP; Joy Morrissey; Jill Mortimer; Wendy Morton; Holly Mumby-Croft; Sheryll Murray; Lia Nici; Matthew Offord; Priti Patel MP; Mike Penning; Mark Pritchard; Tom Pursglove; Dominic Raab; Jacob Rees-Mogg; Andrew Rosindell; Dean Russell; Paul Scully; Grant Shapps; Alok Sharma; Greg Smith; Henry Smith; Royston Smith; Amanda Solloway; Mark Spencer; Alexander Stafford; Andrew Stephenson; Jane Stevenson; Bob Stewart; Graham Stuart; James Sunderland; Kelly Tolhurst; Justin Tomlinson; Michael Tomlinson; Anne-Marie Trevelyan; Liz Truss; Shailesh Vara; Matt Warman; Suzanne Webb; Craig Whittaker; John Whittingdale; Nadhim Zahawi.

OK, so some of them may have occasionally strayed off message but by and large they were solid. Carve their names with pride.

This book would not have been written but for the wisdom and encouragement of Arabella Pike at HarperCollins and my wonderful agent Natasha Fairweather. One of the pleasures of writing it has been trying to explain everything to a pair of avowed and passionate Remainers. Thanks also to Guglielmo Verdirame KC who kindly read the text in draft; and my cousin Sam Blyth in whose dining room much of this was written.

Finally I should thank my whole family. The medal has not been struck that can do justice to their heroism and forbearance. Thanks to all my siblings, to my late mother, to my father and stepmother; thanks to Marina, who was with me for much of this journey.

Thanks to all my children, for putting up with it all more or less without complaint, and above all thanks to Carrie, my beloved wife and inspiration.

Brightwell-cum-Sotwell, August 2024

Notes

Chapter 1: The Curse of Spiderwoman

4 *I was on my feet in the House when one of my colleagues* Bracknell MP Dr Phillip Lee quit the Conservatives on September 3, 2019. 'Phillip Lee quits Tories, leaving government without a majority', *Guardian*, Sep 3, 2019.

6 *It was the longest since the English civil war of the seventeenth century* The parliamentary session had begun on June 13, 2017. 'Brexit impasse leads to longest UK parliament session since civil war', *Guardian*, May 13, 2019.

7 *colleagues such as Dominic Grieve* Dominic Grieve had, in fact, already committed to resign if I became Conservative Party leader. 'Dominic Grieve: I will leave party if Boris Johnson becomes leader', *Guardian*, Aug 8, 2018.

11 *But what really enraged my opponents* I faced criticism in the House of Commons on September 25, 2019 over my use of the term 'surrender'. 'MPs' fury at Boris Johnson's "dangerous language"', BBC News, Sep 25, 2019.

Chapter 2: Poisoned Chalice

13 *'his political career is over'* Michael Portillo, 'Laughing Boris is gone: Now for a serious Tory contender', *Sunday Times*, Nov 21, 2004.

14 *not forgetting Wales, which heroically voted Leave by 52 per cent* Results given for the EU referendum as published by the BBC. Available at 'EU referendum: Welsh voters back Brexit', BBC News, Jun 24, 2016.

15 *George Osborne's emergency tax-raising budget* Osborne said an emergency budget would be needed to address a '£30bn "black hole"' if the UK voted to leave the European Union. 'EU referendum: Osborne warns of Brexit budget cuts', BBC News, Jun 15, 2016.

16 *on May 2, 2019 … On Thursday May 23 we managed to get only 9 per cent of the vote in the Euro-elections* Results in full for the May 2019 local elections published by the House of Commons Library (2019). Results in full for the May 2019 European Parliament elections as published by BBC News, May 27, 2019.

25 *As the Sutton Trust continually informs us* For example, see *Elitist Britain 2019: The Educational Backgrounds of Britain's Leading People*, Sutton Trust (2019).

30 *UK's secondary cities* As Professor Michael Parkinson found: 'British second-tier cities have long lagged behind their European peers – from Munich and Amsterdam to Lyon, Barcelona, Milan and Copenhagen. The most comprehensive and up-to-date survey of the international evidence on city performance is the 2020 study

by the OECD. This report found that gross value added per worker in the UK's core cities is just 86% of the national average in 2016: that's a 14% gap, the biggest, in terms of domestic productivity, amid the larger OECD countries. And the productivity gap between second-tier cities in the UK and elsewhere is even greater. Productivity per worker was 30% higher in Australia and Germany, 26% in the Netherlands, 22% in France and 17% in Italy than in Britain.' *The Conversation*, Mar 15, 2022.

30 *Andy Haldane* For more on this see, for example, 'Unleashing the Potential of the UK's Cities: Report of the UK's Urban Futures Commission', Royal Society of Arts, Sep 2023.

Chapter 3: Locked-in Syndrome

34 *a state of emergency had been declared* The sudden partial collapse of the Whaley Bridge Dam prompted fears of a total failure. 'Whaley Bridge dam collapse: Evacuation over Toddbrook Reservoir fears', BBC News, Aug 1, 2019.

37 *Angela's words at the beginning of the 2015 refugee crisis* 'Flüchtlingskrise: Angela Merkel will "Wir schaffen das" nicht wiederholen', Wiwo.de, Sep 17, 2016.

41 *half the cabinet was flown … to Florence* 'PM's Florence speech: A new era of cooperation and partnership between the UK and the EU', Sep 22, 2017.

44 *On September 4, 2019, they passed the Surrender Act* Eurosceptics frequently referred to the law as the 'Surrender Act'.

Chapter 4: The Madder Hulk Gets

48 *We sacked more Tory MPs, in one go, than had been sacked in the previous four decades* All in all, twenty-one rebels had the Conservative whip withdrawn.

49 *my brother Jo resigned from the cabinet* When asked about the resignation of my brother, I said: 'Look, people disagree about the EU. The way to unite the country, I'm afraid, is to get this thing done. That is the reality.' 'Jo Johnson quits as MP and minister, citing "national interest"', *Guardian*, Sep 5, 2019.

53 *no 'selfish strategic or economic interest' in Northern Ireland* Peter Brooke, former Northern Ireland secretary, included the phrase in speech in London on November 9, 1990.

53 *'the loss of Northern Ireland is the price the British must pay for Brexit'* Selmayr repeatedly denied making such a remark.

56 *A special Saturday session of Parliament, for the first time since the Falklands War* The House of Commons sat on Saturday April 3, 1982.

57 *Danny Finkelstein … John Curtice* 'Jeremy Corbyn doesn't need to win to become PM', *The Times*, Nov 5, 2019; '"Remain alliance" involving Labour could cost Conservatives up to 50 seats, analysis finds', *Independent*, Aug 29, 2019.

Chapter 5: Earthquake

62 *Ashworth said my refusal … The Lib Dem guy* Jon Ashworth continued: 'It's clear he (Johnson) could not care less.' The Lib Dem guy was Tim Farron.

Chapter Six: The Greatest City on Earth

76 *Who the hell put that thing on the road?* Ken Livingstone said on introducing the 'bendy bus': 'Just like on the continent, all the doors can be used for getting on or off the bus, providing hassle-free, comfortable and reliable travel for everyone.'

79 *He had championed the IRA* On the IRA Ken Livingstone said: 'That is how the IRA saw themselves. They were prepared to die – ten starved themselves to death. That's not what a criminal or godfather of crime does; it's someone who believes they're fighting for the freedom of their country and you've got to deal with them on that basis.' *Guardian*, Apr 12, 2000.

81 *Which was the world's greatest city in 1900? Still London … By 1939 … the population of London had reached 8.6 million* 'Population changes over the decades', Trust for London: trustforlondon.org.uk/data/population-over-time/

87 *combed my back articles* I said in April 2008: 'No one candidate has the right to assume any community will automatically vote for them – every vote must be earned. The current Labour mayor has run out of ideas and has concentrated on the politics of division rather than uniting people.'

Chapter 7: Crisis in London

93 *cover of Time magazine showed a tidal wave Time*, Oct 20, 2008.

Chapter 8: The Cult of the Knife

104 *In one twenty-four-hour period in July, six people were stabbed to death* 'The scourge of knife crime gripping Britain has reached new depths with six murders across the country in less than 24 hours.' *London Evening Standard*, Apr 13, 2012.

107 *called 'Time for Action'* The report, published in November 2008, was subtitled: 'Equipping Young People for the Future and Preventing Violence – the Mayor's proposals and call to partners'.

108 *More important, it worked* By May 2009, it had emerged that the Metropolitan Police were using stop and search powers in London to stop someone every three minutes.

Chapter 9: The Cycling Revolution

120 *Colin Buchanan's famous 1963 report, 'Traffic in Towns'* 'The Buchanan Report: Traffic in Towns' was published in November 1963.

123 *Trixi mirrors on the poles* Reuters explained: 'A new roadside mirror, designed to reduce accidents involving lorries and cyclists, is being installed in London as part of a major safety initiative.' Reuters, Jul 6, 2010.

125 *By 2016 ... 20 per cent of all vehicles in central London were bicycles* I wrote in my foreword to City Hall report 'Human Streets: The Mayor's Vision for Cycling Three Years On' in March 2016: 'Exactly three years ago, I unveiled my vision to make cycling in London safer, more popular and more normal. My single biggest regret as Mayor is that I did not do it sooner. Our original painted lanes were revolutionary at the time. But knowing what I do now, we would have blasted ahead with our new segregated cycle lanes from the beginning.'

Chapter 10: Hop On, Hop Off

137 *The new Routemaster* The *Daily Mail* reported: 'They're back. Well, sort of. A 21st century version of the old hop-on, hop-off bus was unveiled yesterday. The successor to the London Routemaster, which was withdrawn from all but a few tourist routes in 2005, will enter service on February 20.' *MailOnline*, Dec 17, 2011.

Chapter 11: London Burning

139 *Reeves Corner, a furniture store* Iconic Croydon furniture store House of Reeves was founded in 1867, just after the end of the Crimean War.

140 *more fires burning in London that night than on any evening since the Blitz Time* magazine reported: 'Not since the blitz during World War II have so many fires raged in London so intensely at one time.' *Time*, Aug 9, 2011.

146 *In Ealing a sixty-eight-year-old man* Richard Mannington Bowes died after he suffered head injuries in an attack in Ealing as he tried to put out a fire during the riots.

Chapter 12: A Summer Like No Other

154 *unveiled our Olympic logo* The *New York Times* reported: 'It was said to provoke epileptic seizures. Someone compared it to a broken swastika or "some sort of comical sex act between 'The Simpsons.'" The mayor was not amused.' *New York Times*, Jun 7, 2007.

156 *G4S had received* 'London 2012: G4S "only knew eight days ago" of shortage', BBC News, Jul 14, 2012.

Chapter 14: Copping Out in Copenhagen

177 *TfL controllers at Centre Comm had thrown in the towel* TfL's David Brown told the BBC: 'We haven't had a circumstance like this for over two decades. We were prepared in the sense that all our cold weather plans on the underground were put into place. But I think that actually the volume of the snow falling during the middle of the night was very difficult for us.'

182 *I announced that London would have at least 100,000 electric vehicles* City Hall paid for a third of the £60m plan, with Gordon committing to fund the rest in the budget.

182 *I ... did a deal with Geely Business Green* reported: Geely invested £250m in a new Coventry factory, creating up to 1,000 jobs.

Chapter 15: Some More Radical Solutions

187 *wreck of the SS Richard Montgomery* Liberal Democrat MP Julian Huppert said: 'Just last month the Royal Navy had to destroy a wartime mine found in the Thames Estuary because of the "significant risk to public safety". If this cargo ship was disrupted by construction the explosion would be 2,000 times larger, it would blow out every window in Sheerness, and create a 16ft wave just outside the capital. The last time we tried to move a similar wreck it exploded.' BBC News, May 30, 2012.

192 *in 2015 I fought the general election in Uxbridge* I was elected as MP for Uxbridge and South Ruislip on May 7, 2015 with a 50.2 per cent share of the vote and a majority of 10,695.

Chapter 16: Prawn Cocktail Flavour Crisps

201 *picnic was staged at the border of Austria and Hungary* According to the German federal government: 'The Hungarian Democratic Forum and the Paneuropean Union issued an invitation to a "Pan-European Picnic". They wanted to demonstrate for open borders and a reunited Europe.'

Chapter 17: Voting Leave

211 *build a cable car with an £8 million contribution from the EU's 'regional funds'* According to City Hall: 'The significant majority of the construction cost has been covered by the Emirates sponsorship contract. The European Commission has also approved TfL's application for £8m from London's European Regional Development Fund (ERDF) programme which will make up much of the remainder.'

213 *the Remain campaign was ahead* On June 14, 2016 Bloomberg reported: 'While polls show the UK's Brexit vote poised on a knife's edge, bookies remain fairly confident the nation will stay in the European Union.'

214 *the piece was done* It was published on March 16, 2016 on the *Daily Telegraph*'s website as 'Boris Johnson exclusive: There is only one way to get the change we want – vote to leave the EU'.

215 *like an ancient suasoria* According to the *Oxford Encyclopaedia of Rhetoric*, the *suasoria* and the *controversia* are 'exercises in the composition and delivery of speeches on a given theme.'

Chapter 18: Inside the Bus

226 *'at the back of the queue'* Obama said: 'The UK is at its best when it's helping to lead a strong European Union. It leverages UK power to be part of the EU. I don't think the EU moderates British influence in the world, it magnifies it. America wants Britain's influence to grow, including within Europe.'

226 *a whole seventy-page paper, with a preface by George* The document was published in May 2016 by Osborne's Treasury as 'HM Treasury analysis: The immediate economic impact of leaving the EU'.

226 *send a pro-Remain leaflet to every household* The leaflet drop was later criticised as an unfair advantage for Remain, for example by UCL's Independent Commission on Referendums.

228 *like an incoming tide, up every creek and inlet in Britain* Lord Denning wrote in his judgment to HP Bulmer Ltd and another v J Bollinger SA and others – [1974] 2 All ER 1226 at 1232-3: 'But when we come to matters with a European element, the treaty is like an incoming tide. It flows into the estuaries and up the rivers. It cannot be held back.'

230 *'The strain of the campaign'* Asked if I could lead the Conservative Party, Lord Heseltine told the BBC: 'I'd be very surprised ... I think that every time he makes one of these extraordinary utterances, people in the Conservative Party will question whether he now has the judgement for that role.'

230 *2011 regulation 'on the presentation of bananas'* Text from: 'COMMISSION IMPLEMENTING REGULATION (EU) No 1333/2011 of 19 December 2011 laying down marketing standards for bananas, rules on the verification of compliance with those marketing standards and requirements for notifications in the banana sector.'

Chapter 19: Triumph – and Disaster

235 *John Major was there* Major said on *The Andrew Marr Show*: 'The NHS is about as safe with them as a pet hamster would be with a hungry python.'

236 *for some reason had conceded defeat* Farage said it 'looks like Remain will edge it' in the early hours.

236 *G.K. Chesterton* Lines from Chesterton's poem 'The Secret People' (1907).

Chapter 21: Brexit in America

256 *'You guys threw our tea into the sea'* The Boston Tea Party saw American colonists hurl 340 chests of East India Company tea into Boston Harbour.

262 *Compare the growth rates* According to *Le Monde*: 'In 2008, the eurozone and the US had equivalent gross domestic products (GDP) at current prices of $14.2 trillion and $14.8 trillion respectively (€13.1 trillion and €13.6 trillion). Fifteen years on, the eurozone's GDP is just over $15 trillion, while US GDP has soared to $26.9 trillion.'

262 *poorest people in America ... are now richer* As the European Centre for International Political Economy puts it: 'The US economy has clearly outperformed the EU. This disparity in economic outputs has been sustained over a long period of time and, thanks to the power of compound interest, resulted in an 82 percent GDP per capita gap in favour of the US in 2021.'

267 *doctrine of 'liberal interventionism'* Blair spoke in April 1999 at the Chicago Economic Club: 'We are all internationals now, whether we like it or not ... We cannot turn our backs on conflicts and the violation of human rights within other countries if we want still to be secure.'

Chapter 22: Britain Abroad

272 *The British and their armed forces have invaded, conquered, or at least partly governed* Historian Stuart Laycock's *All the Countries We've Ever Invaded: And the Few We Never Got Round To* finds in a survey of 200 of the world's countries that Great Britain has invaded all of them except 22.

Chapter 23: Mayhem in Mesopotamia

284 *Estimates vary* For figures, see for example Iraq Body Count which 'maintains the world's largest public database of violent civilian deaths since the 2003 invasion'.

285 *a company called Sheffield Forgemasters had been making* According to the BBC, 'Components for the Big Babylon gun were manufactured in Great Britain ... The enormous steel pipes on display at Fort Nelson were manufactured in the UK by Sheffield Forgemasters – known for manufacturing high quality steel.'

286 *Another company, Matrix Churchill* 'The arms for Iraq scandal: Firm claims pounds 4m from taxpayer to cover Saddam bill', *Independent*, Dec 12, 1992.

Chapter 24: Killing Gaddafi

289 *Blair himself went to Tripoli* As the *Guardian* reported: 'Tony Blair today shook hands with Colonel Muammar Gadafy, in a symbolic end to three decades of the west's isolation of Libya … Mr Blair met the Libyan leader in an elaborate Bedouin tent on farmland near the Libyan capital, Tripoli, for the historic talks. "You look good, you are still young," Col Gadafy told him.' *Guardian*, Mar 25, 2004.

289 *a former Libyan Airlines official called Abdelbaset al-Megrahi* US president Barack Obama said the decision was 'a mistake' and victims' families reacted with fury.

290 *engaged from on high by an RAF Batavia Tornado* As a Nato statement at the time put it: 'We later learned from open sources and Allied intelligence that Qadhafi was in the convoy and that the strike likely contributed to his capture.'

Chapter 26: Going Global

308 *the Gambian leader* The *Guardian* reported: 'The Gambia's new president, Adama Barrow … is proud of an experience that included working as a security guard in an Argos store in Holloway Road, north London.'

310 *ban on British tourists travelling* The *Guardian* reported: 'British holidaymakers could be soon returning to Sharm el-Sheikh after the UK government lifted restrictions on flights to the Egyptian resort.' *Guardian*, Oct 22, 2019.

Chapter 27: Selling the Same Camel Twice

321 *time to do justice to the second half of that sentence* Boris Johnson, 'My vision for Middle East peace between Israel and a new Palestinian state', *Telegraph*, Oct 29, 2017.

Chapter 28: Freeing Nazanin

329 *I then made a mistake* The BBC reported: 'A charity fears a British-Iranian woman held in Iran could have her prison sentence doubled following remarks made by the foreign secretary. Boris Johnson told a Commons committee that Nazanin Zaghari-Ratcliffe, who was arrested at Tehran Airport in 2016, was "teaching people journalism". The Thomson Reuters Foundation said she was seeing family and urged Mr Johnson to correct his "serious mistake".'

330 *Thomson Reuters decided to go public* A statement from Monique Villa, Thomson Reuters Foundation CEO, issued on November 6, 2017, read: 'I see a direct correlation between this statement by Boris Johnson, who rightly condemned the treatment that Nazanin has received in Iran, and the fact that Nazanin was brought once again into Court on Saturday 4 November and accused of "spreading propaganda against the regime".'

331 *called for me to be sacked* Corbyn's statement read: 'We've put up with Johnson embarrassing and undermining our country with his incompetence and colonial throwback views and putting our citizens at risk for long enough.'

333 *the Iranians had paid the British* As *The Week* put it in November 2021: 'There is a simple solution: ministers could settle the UK's debt of some £400m to Iran. In 1971, the UK agreed to sell 1,500 tanks to the Iranians. After the Shah fell in 1979, however, "we refused to deliver the tanks but kept the cash" – a bone of contention ever since.'

Chapter 29: Putin the Poisoner

341 *we wanted to see the famous cathedral* Boshirov claimed in the interview on Russian state TV: 'There's a famous cathedral there, the Salisbury cathedral … It's famous not just all over Europe, it's famous all over the world, I think. It's famous for its 123-metre spire, it's famous for its clock, the first clock made in the world that still runs.'

342 *biggest expulsion of Russian diplomats* 'More than 20 western allies have ordered the expulsion of dozens of Russian diplomats in response to the nerve agent attack in the UK, in a show of solidarity that represents the biggest concerted blow to Russian intelligence networks in the west since the cold war.' *Guardian*, Mar 27, 2018.

Chapter 30: Golden No More

354 *Xi's state visit* From October 20 to 23, 2015 the UK welcomed President Xi Jinping to London for the first state visit from China in ten years.

356 *I went back in 2013* In a joint press conference with George Osborne at Peking University in October 2013, I said: 'I'm here to let students know that if they would like to study internationally, London's world-class higher education institutions will welcome them with open arms.'

358 *destroying the Summer Palace* The BBC reported: 'There is a deep, unhealed historical wound in the UK's relations with China – a wound that most British people know nothing about, but which causes China great pain. It stems from the destruction in 1860 of the country's most beautiful palace. It's been described as China's ground zero – a place that tells a story of cultural destruction that everyone in China knows about, but hardly anyone outside.'

366 *Channel 4 recorded me* Reports read: 'UK Foreign Secretary Boris Johnson was prevented from reciting an "inappropriate" colonial-era poem by Rudyard Kipling by the British ambassador to Myanmar while on an official visit there in January, according to footage to be aired for the first time Sunday.'

Chapter 31: Teach Her to Read

374 *more than a hundred missing Chibok girls* The *Guardian* reported: 'Ten years on, many of the Chibok abductees, now women, have been freed or escaped, but about 100 are still missing.'

376 *only 26 per cent of Somali women can read* According to the UN-backed survey 'in 2006, the adult literacy rate for women in Somalia was estimated to be 26 per cent, up from 19 per cent in 2001. For the same time period, the literacy rate was 36 per cent for men, up from 25 per cent in 2001, and 31 per cent for both men and women.'

381 *We did an event* I launched the Platform for Girls' Education at a reception attended by Meghan Markle and Prince Harry on April 20, 2018.

Chapter 32: The Road to Serfdom

388 *A lot of plaster came off the ceiling over that one* I told the Med 2 conference in Rome in December 2016: 'There are politicians who are twisting and abusing religion and different strains of the same religion in order to further their own political objectives. That's one of the biggest political problems in the whole region. And the tragedy for me – and that's why you have these proxy wars being fought the whole time in that area – is that there is not strong enough leadership in the countries themselves.'

389 *we disagreed on stop and search, and the use of water cannon* 'Boris Johnson reportedly openly challenged Theresa May over her decision to reduce the use of stop and search powers in a heated Cabinet exchange earlier this week.' PoliticsHome, Mar 22, 2018.

392 *Lancaster House* Theresa May set out '12 priorities' for negotiating Britain's exit from the EU in a speech on January 17, 2017 at Lancaster House.

Chapter 33: Chucking Chequers

396 *going nose to nose* The interviewer pleaded during one exchange (on June 2, 2017): 'Boris, just a second. Please, just a bit of peace.' I hit back, pointing at Ian Lavery: 'He's just been shouting in my ear!' Later, I can be seen standing uncomfortably close to Lavery, causing the then Labour chairman to say: 'Do you mind? Stop being so rude!'

Chapter 34: Infrastructure Revolution

407 *£14 billion we were putting into education* Committing to the education spending uplift, I said: 'The effect is – I hope – not just to give every school an increase, both primary and secondary, but to make sure the schools allowed to fall furthest behind are seeing the biggest uplift. I can't think of anything more fundamental for society than education spending.'

411 *Saj sent me the plan* Sajid Javid said prior to the 2020 budget: 'There will be an infrastructure revolution in our great country.'

413 *tunnel would cost* My administration published the Union Connectivity Review in November 2021. A feasibility study – 'A Fixed Link between Great Britain and Northern Ireland: Technical Feasibility' – found 'the physical challenges of the Irish Sea and the North Channel must not be underestimated. Both a tunnel and bridge option are technically feasible to construct, but they would be the longest undersea tunnel or the longest span bridge ever built. A combination of tunnel and bridge incorporating artificial islands as employed in Scandinavia and China is not possible due to the great depth of the Irish Sea and other inhibiting factors. It is also important to note that the road and rail infrastructure required to connect the fixed link crossing to the main transport networks in Northern Ireland and Great Britain are in themselves major construction works.'

415 *when I became PM it was less than 2 per cent* The government said at the time: 'The UK has cut its emissions by 43 per cent since 1990 while growing the economy by more than two-thirds – the best performance of any G7 nation.'

419 *I told them all to go through their budget lines* The *Sun* reported the contents of a memo to ministers from myself and chancellor Sajid Javid: 'We have been elected with a clear fiscal mandate to keep control of day to day spending. This means there will need to be savings made across government to free up money to invest in our priorities.'

419 *In London, Eddie Lister and I had abolished* The *Evening Standard* reported – presciently – in 2012: 'The Mayor plans to cut £5 billion over nine years by cutting "back office" costs, restructuring and more efficient working … Sources close to the Mayor insist that alleged tensions between him and David Cameron and Mr Osborne are overblown, suggesting he is given special leeway to depart from the party line to speak up for London. But some around the leadership are nervous about Mr Johnson's future leadership ambitions.'

Chapter 35: Zoonotic Nightmare

423 *'You must stay at home'* My address to the nation was broadcast on March 23, 2020.

424 *presence of salmonella in UK eggs* The BBC reported: 'Health minister Edwina Currie has provoked outrage by saying most of Britain's egg production is infected with the salmonella bacteria.'

425 *great slaughter of cattle* As the *Daily Telegraph* later reported: 'In December 1984, cow number 133 fell ill at Pitsham Farm, near Midhurst, West Sussex. It was unsteady on its legs, suffered from tremors and loss of appetite and displayed erratic behaviour. When it died in 1985 laboratory tests on its brain showed the strange, tell-tale pattern that is the hallmark of BSE. But the Ministry of Agriculture failed to recognise this, the first known case of mad cow disease, for what it was until nearly two years later, when other cases were cropping up.'

Chapter 36: How the Crisis Began

430 *Matt made a statement to the House* The *Daily Telegraph* reported on January 27, 2020: 'Britain will put people airlifted from China into quarantine amid concerns that around 1,500 people who arrived in the UK since the new year have not undergone checks. Matt Hancock, the Health Secretary, ordered a "belt and braces" approach to the coronavirus amid concerns that the virus is far more contagious than was thought.'

430 *We had come to Brexit city* As the *Daily Mail* reported: 'Boris Johnson insisted it will be "full steam ahead" after Brexit today as he gathered his Cabinet in Leave-backing Sunderland hours before the historic moment. After three-and-a-half years of turmoil, the UK's legal membership of the EU will come to an end on the stroke of 11pm – opening a new era for the country.'

431 *one of the first doctors to raise the alarm* The BBC reported on February 7: 'Li Wenliang contracted the virus while working at Wuhan Central Hospital. He had sent out a warning to fellow medics on 30 December but police told him to stop "making false comments". There had been contradictory reports about his death, but the *People's Daily* now says he died at 02:58 on Friday (18:58 GMT Thursday).'

432 *Saj had resigned* Sajid Javid resigned on February 13, 2020. As the *MailOnline* reported: 'Furious Sajid Javid today insisted no "self-respecting" minister would have obeyed Dominic Cummings' order to sack his aides – after he quit as Chancellor throwing the reshuffle into chaos.'

434 *no evidence that the virus was circulating* Public Health England released a statement on February 26, 2020: 'A new surveillance system to detect cases of COVID-19 in England has been established by Public Health England (PHE) and the NHS to strengthen existing systems and to prepare for and prevent wider transmission of the virus. There is no current evidence to show that the virus is circulating in the community in England.'

437 *we had put another £34 billion into the NHS* The *Daily Telegraph* had reported in December 2019: 'Boris Johnson will put the NHS at the heart of his domestic agenda as he sets out his programme for Government in the Queen's Speech on Thursday. In a statement of intent to the nation, the Prime Minister will enshrine in law a £33.9 billion increase in annual NHS spending by 2023/24 as soon as MPs have voted through his Brexit bill.'

Chapter 37: Intensive Care Unit

445 *As soon as I was diagnosed* In the video message, on March 27, 2020, I said: 'I'm self-isolating. And that's entirely the right thing to do. But be in no doubt that I can continue, thanks to the wizardry of modern technology, to communicate with all my top team to lead the national fightback against coronavirus.'

445 *I was deeply grateful to everyone* The *MailOnline* reported: 'A sickly-looking Boris Johnson took to his doorstep on Thursday evening amid his coronavirus quarantine in Downing Street to applaud NHS staff and other key workers such as supermarket employees and delivery drivers up and down the country.'

447 *I had read my J.G. Frazer* cf. *The Golden Bough: A Study of Magic and Religion* by Sir James George Frazer (1890).

453 *my popularity figures were the highest they had ever been* For example Ipsos's Political Pulse for April 2020 found: 'Boris Johnson's favourability rating increases sharply, with the Conservative Party's image also showing some improvement. The majority of Britons (51%) now have a favourable opinion of Boris Johnson (up 17 points from early March), with three in ten (31%) saying they have an unfavourable opinion of him (down 16 points).'

Chapter 38: Silent Streets

455 *On the day I was released* BBC News reported: 'The UK has recorded 737 new coronavirus-related hospital deaths, taking the total number to 10,612.'

459 *total bill for government support* The House of Commons Library found: 'The Covid-19 pandemic resulted in very high levels of public spending. Current estimates of the total cost of government Covid-19 measures range from about £310 billion to £410 billion. This is the equivalent of about £4,600 to £6,100 per person in the UK.'

Chapter 39: Closing Schools

464 *began to get kids back into school* On June 1, 2020 the *Guardian* reported: 'Thousands of children returned to schools across England for the first time since the coronavirus lockdown began in March, but many others remained at home because of parental concerns and warnings from some councils that it is still too early to reopen more widely.'

467 *education is something universal* As the UK Parliament puts it: 'The 1870 Education Act stands as the very first piece of legislation to deal specifically with the provision of education in England and Wales. Most importantly, it demonstrated a commitment to provision on a national scale.'

Chapter 40: Build Back Better

475 *surveyed the economic damage* As BBC News reported: 'UK government debt has risen above £2 trillion for the first time amid heavy spending to support the economy amid the coronavirus pandemic. Spending on measures such as the furlough scheme means the debt figure now equals the value of everything the UK produces in a year. Total debt hit £2.004tn in July, £227.6bn more than last year, said the Office for National Statistics.'

479 *I went to Dudley* I said in Dudley: 'It may seem a bit premature to make a speech now about Britain after Covid – when that deceptively nasty disease is still rampant in other countries, when global case numbers are growing fast and when many in this country are nervous – rightly – about more outbreaks – whether national or local – like the flare-up in Leicester … and yet we cannot continue simply to be prisoners of this crisis.'

479 *The polls said* According to a KCL/Ipsos MORI survey published in April 2020: 'Half of people (49%) say they have felt more anxious or depressed than normal as a result of coronavirus, 38% have slept less or less well than normal.'

Chapter 41: Fighting the Tide

493 *the possibility of mass testing* I said in a TV press conference on October 16: 'We've created a huge diagnostics industry from scratch, scaling up the ability to test from 2,000 in February to more than 300,000.'

496 *a blob around Dartford* The so-called Kent variant, 'VUI – 202012/01', was associated with 1,108 cases by December 13, 2020, predominantly in the south and east of England.

Chapter 43: If I Had a Hammer

515 *multimillionaire rock star taunting* The *Sun* reported: 'Referendum diehards clashed on the Thames yesterday, as Nigel Farage led a flotilla of 30 fishing boats to Westminster – prompting the smug Irish singer to try drown out the protest.'

520 *UKIM* Brandon Lewis told the House of Commons that the Internal Market Bill breaks international law, but only in a 'specific and limited way'.

520 *an essential piece of legislation* The UK Internal Market Act received royal assent on Thursday December 17, 2020.

522 *we did the deal* At a press conference in London on December 24 – wearing a tie with a fish pattern – I said: 'We have also today resolved a question that has bedeviled our politics for decades and it is up to all of us together as a newly and truly independent nation to realise the immensity of this moment and to make the most of it.'

Chapter 44: Vaccination Miracle

525 *Lyn Wheeler* ITV News reported: 'One of the first people to receive a Covid-19 jab as part of the national vaccination programme in the UK told Prime Minister Boris Johnson it was "all for Britain". Lyn Wheeler, 81, from Bromley, south-east London, was the first to receive the Pfizer vaccine at Guy's Hospital on Tuesday morning.'

529 *one of Keir Starmer's biggest goofs* Starmer claimed that money spent on PR consultants by the vaccine programme 'can't be justified'.

533 *the first country* As BBC News reported on December 2, 2020: 'The UK has become the first country in the world to approve the Pfizer/BioNTech coronavirus vaccine, paving the way for mass vaccination. Britain's medicines regulator, the MHRA, says the jab, which offers up to 95% protection against Covid-19 illness, is safe to be rolled out.'

Chapter 45: Roll-Out!

538 *waylaid at the Halix plant* The *Telegraph* reported on April 1, 2021: 'The Halix factory in Leiden, the Netherlands, is caught in a cross-Channel tug of war. Stung by a 200 million shortfall in its own contracted AstraZeneca deliveries, the European Union has vowed to block the export of every single dose made in the 6,700 square metre Halix factory to the UK. Yet it can now be revealed that the UK taxpayer spent millions of pounds to build up capacity at the state-of-the-art plant before the Oxford vaccine had been proven to work.'

539 *'quasi-ineffective'* Macron said on January 29, 2021: 'The real problem on AstraZeneca is that it doesn't work the way we were expecting it to … We're waiting for the EMA [European Medicines Agency] results, but today everything points to thinking it is quasi-ineffective on people older than sixty-five, some say those sixty years or older.'

542 *'we envy you'* As *Sky News* reported on February 24, 2021: 'Germany's top-selling newspaper has hailed the UK's COVID vaccine rollout success and its plans to lift lockdown, announcing on its front page: "Dear British, we envy you." The article in the tabloid paper *Bild* says Brits "are reacting with overwhelming euphoria" after Boris Johnson revealed plans to gradually lift all restrictions by 21 June.'

545 *sold at cost around the world* In July 2022, Oxford University said: 'The University believes that this has been – and continues to be – achieved through our partnership with AstraZeneca, with over 3 billion doses made available for use in 183 countries. As a result of this commitment to ensuring global and equitable access, the Oxford-AstraZeneca vaccine saved 6.3 million lives in the first year of the global vaccine rollout – the most out of all the vaccines in circulation at the time.'

Chapter 47: Triumph at Carbis Bay

569 *It was called Aukus* As BBC News reported: 'China has condemned the agreement as "extremely irresponsible". Foreign ministry spokesman Zhao Lijian said it "seriously undermines regional peace and stability and intensifies the arms race". China's embassy in Washington accused the countries of a "Cold War mentality and ideological prejudice". The pact also created a row with France, which has now lost a deal with Australia to build 12 submarines. "It's really a stab in the back," France's Foreign Minister Jean-Yves Le Drian told France Info radio.'

Chapter 48: Collapse in Kabul

582 *sudden finality of Biden's confirmation*: Remarks by President Biden on the drawdown of US forces in Afghanistan, Jul 8, 2021.

582 *We agreed with that analysis* As the *Daily Telegraph* reported in April: 'The UK wanted US troops to stay in Afghanistan, the head of the Armed Forces has revealed. General Sir Nick Carter said President Biden's decision to pull out all 2,500 US troops by September 11 was "not the decision" the UK wanted.'

585 *a tidy sum, by our standards* As a parliamentary answer revealed: 'As at May 2021, the total cost of Operation HERRICK to Her Majesty's Treasury Special Reserve is £22.2 billion.'

Chapter 49: Saving the Planet

600 *ten-point plan for a green recovery* I wrote in the *FT*: 'Now is the time to plan for a green recovery with high-skilled jobs that give people the satisfaction of knowing they are helping to make the country cleaner, greener and more beautiful. Imagine Britain when a Green Industrial Revolution has helped to level up the country. You cook breakfast using hydrogen power before getting in your electric car, having charged it overnight from batteries made in the Midlands. Around you the air is cleaner; trucks, trains, ships and planes run on hydrogen or synthetic fuel. British towns and regions – Teesside, Port Talbot, Merseyside and Mansfield – are now synonymous with green technology and jobs. This is where Britain's ability to make hydrogen and capture carbon pioneered the decarbonisation of transport, industry and power.'

604 *UK has cut CO$_2$ emissions* According to the UK government (February 6, 2024): 'The UK is the first major economy to halve its emissions – having cut them by 50% between 1990 and 2022, while also growing its economy by 79% – new official statistics released today confirm. This compares to a 23% reduction in France and no change in the USA between 1990 and 2021.'

Chapter 50: Omigod It's Omicron

613 *75 per cent of adults had been fully vaccinated* 3 in 4 UK adults receive both doses of a COVID-19 vaccine. UK Government, Aug 10, 2021: https://www.gov.uk/government/news/3-in-4-uk-adults-receive-both-doses-of-a-covid-19-vaccine

615 *British mortality has never risen so fast* Oxford University found: 'The COVID-19 pandemic triggered life expectancy losses not seen since World War II in Western Europe and exceeded those observed around the dissolution of the Eastern Bloc in central and Eastern European countries.'

Chapter 51: An Unprovoked Invasion

642 *a familiar form of address* The readout of the call issued by Downing Street on February 2, 2022: 'The Prime Minister spoke to Russian President Putin this afternoon. The Prime Minister expressed his deep concern about Russia's current hostile activity on the Ukrainian border. He emphasised the need to find a way forward which respects both Ukraine's territorial integrity and right to self-defence. The Prime Minister stressed that any further Russian incursion into Ukrainian territory would be a tragic miscalculation.'

646 *bilateral with Olaf Scholz* The readout of the meeting issued by Downing Street February 19, 2022 read: 'The Prime Minister met German Chancellor Olaf Scholz today in Munich. The leaders discussed the tensions in Ukraine and agreed on the need for NATO unity in response to current threats. The Prime Minister said that we are currently in the most dangerous phase in the crisis with a Russian invasion possible at any moment. The Prime Minister and Chancellor Scholz resolved to redouble efforts to reach a diplomatic resolution to prevent unnecessary bloodshed.'

646 *trenchant speech* I said in the speech at the Munich Security Conference on February 19, 2022: 'I believe that Russia would have absolutely nothing to gain from this catastrophic venture and everything to lose, and while there is still time, I urge the Kremlin to de-escalate, to disengage its forces from the frontier and to renew our dialogue. Every nation at this conference shares a vision of a secure and prosperous Europe of sovereign states, deciding their own destiny and living without fear or threat. And that vision of course extends to Russia, a nation whose cultural patrimony we revere, and whose sacrifice in the struggle against fascism was immeasurable.'

Chapter 52: The Battle for Kyiv

651 *stringent sanctions* As BBC News reported: 'The UK has announced a series of sanctions against Russia after it ordered troops into two rebel-held regions of eastern Ukraine. Five banks have had their assets frozen, along with three Russian

billionaires – who will also be hit with UK travel bans. Boris Johnson said Russia's actions amounted to a "renewed invasion" and the sanctions were a "first barrage". He stressed these could be extended – but faced calls for tougher action now.'

652 *I gave a passionate speech* I said in Poland on March 1, 2022: 'I will not waver in my conviction that, however long it takes, a sovereign and independent Ukraine will emerge once again, because Putin has stubbed his toe and tripped on a giant and immovable fact: Which is no matter how many troops and tanks he sends, the Ukrainians desire to live in freedom in an independent country – which is something that Poles will immediately understand – and in this desire the UK will always give them our wholehearted support.'

Chapter 53: The Cost of War

658 *welcomed 210,000 fleeing Ukrainians* According to the Migration Observatory at Oxford University: 'Around 210,000 people had arrived in the UK by 16 July 2024 using one of the two bespoke entry visa schemes for Ukrainians.'

658 *By January 2022 inflation in the UK* BBC News reported in February 2022: 'The cost of living hit a fresh 30-year high last month as energy, fuel and food prices continued to soar and retailers reined in seasonal discounts. Prices surged by 5.5% in the 12 months to January, up from 5.4% in December, increasing the squeeze on household budgets. Inflation is now rising faster than wages and is expected to climb above 7% this year.'

660 *I set a new target* The government published its British Energy Security Strategy in April 2022.

662 *people read about it in* The Times … *without batting an eyelid* See 'Rishi Sunak settles in as Downing St's Captain Sensible', *The Times*, Jun 20, 2020.

Chapter 54: Night Train to Ukraine

670 *another package of military funding* The announcement included more than 800 more NLAW anti-tank missiles and additional Javelin anti-tank systems.

Chapter 57: Britain and India

684 *deal with the dynamic Mr Poonawalla* According to Reuters (March 3, 2021): 'The UK will receive 10 million AstraZeneca COVID-19 vaccine doses made by the Serum Institute of India (SII), the UK government said on Tuesday. SII, the world's largest vaccine manufacturer by volume, is mass producing the AstraZeneca vaccine, developed with Oxford University, for dozens of poor and middle-income countries.'

685 *prompting much outrage* As the *Guardian* reported on May 17, 2017: 'Boris Johnson has apologised after he caused a "livid" reaction in a worshipper in a Sikh temple by discussing his enthusiasm for a boost in the whisky trade, apparently without realising that alcohol is forbidden under some Sikh teaching.'

Chapter 58: A Torrid Sort of Summer

693 *Starmer ended up with* As Fraser Nelson wrote in the *Spectator*: 'Something pretty big is missing from Labour's historic landslide: the voters. Keir Starmer has won 63 per cent of the seats on just 33.8 per cent of the votes, the smallest vote share of any modern PM. Lower than any of the (many) pollsters predicted. So Labour in 2024 managed just 1.6 percentage points higher than the Jeremy Corbyn calamity in 2019 – and less than Corbyn managed in 2017.'

702 *UK would hit 2.5 per cent* Reuters reported: 'Britain will boost defence spending to 2.5% of its gross domestic product (GDP) by the end of this decade, Prime Minister Boris Johnson said on Thursday, making a new commitment to bolster the military budget after Russia's invasion of Ukraine.'

Chapter 59: Some Pointers for the Future

709 *unemployment at or near a fifty-year low* As the *FT* reported: 'UK unemployment fell to its lowest rate in nearly half a century in the first quarter of 2022, as the number of job vacancies rose to a new high of 1.3mn.'

709 *lifting the living wage* The UK government said on March 31, 2022: 'Millions of UK workers will receive a pay rise from Friday 1 April 2022, as the National Minimum Wage and National Living Wage rise comes into effect. The uplift in wages, which will benefit around 2.5 million people, includes the largest ever increase to the National Living Wage. It will put £1,000 a year more into full-time workers' pay packets, helping to ease cost of living pressures.'

718 *just as I out-built* According to a *CityA.M.* report in May 2021: 'Sadiq Khan has completed just over half the amount of affordable housing in his first five years that Boris Johnson did when he was mayor of London. Numbers from the Greater London Authority show Johnson completed 62,387 affordable homes in his first five years, while Khan has completed 34,659 in that same time period.' *CityA.M.*, May 20, 2021.

718 *want to get back to free movement* As reported in *The Times*: 'Free movement curbs could be relaxed under EU reset', *The Times*, Aug 21, 2024.

Chapter 60: Balmoral

726 *dropped off its aircraft carrier* As BBC News later reported: 'The pilot of a British fighter jet that rolled off a Royal Navy aircraft carrier has spoken of his relief at managing to eject from the £100m F-35. Speaking soon after the incident in November 2021, the pilot, known as Hux, recalled having only seconds to react. An official investigation concluded the sudden loss of power on take-off was probably caused by a cover being left on one of the aircraft's jet intakes.'

Illustrations

Winning the Tory leadership *(Andrew Parsons/Parsons Media)*
I wasn't exactly sure how *(Andrew Parsons/Parsons Media)*

Section Two
Bulldozing to victory *(Andrew Parsons/Parsons Media)*
A kiss *(Andrew Parsons/Parsons Media)*
Cry Haddock! *(Andrew Parsons/Parsons Media)*
Cornering some Tory voters *(Andrew Parsons/Parsons Media)*
Undignified exit poll ecstasy *(Andrew Parsons/Parsons Media)*
Asking HM the Queen for permission *(WPA Pool/Getty Images)*
Jump *(WPA Pool/Getty Images)*
109 new MPs *(PAUL GROVER/Alamy Stock Photo)*
With Irish Taoiseach Leo Varadkar *(Associated Press/Alamy Stock Photo)*
Blue passports *(Andrew Parsons/Parsons Media)*
Invisibly treading on the toes *(PA Images/Alamy Stock Photo)*
I told you it was oven ready! *(Leon Neal/Getty Images)*
Addressing the nation *(Andrew Parsons/Parsons Media)*
Covid press conference *(Andrew Parsons/Parsons Media)*
Get well message *(Courtesy of author)*
Bottom of stairs *(Courtesy of author)*
Recuperating *(Courtesy of author)*
Clap for Carers *(Mark Thomas/Alamy Stock Photo)*
Pilgrim Hospital visit *(Andrew Parsons/Parsons Media)*
Getting boosted *(Andrew Parsons/Parsons Media)*
Red boxes *(Courtesy of author)*
HS2 visit *(PA Images/Alamy Stock Photo)*
Still winning *(Associated Press/Alamy Stock Photo)*
On the beach with Angela Merkel *(WPA Pool/Getty Images)*
With David Attenborough *(Chris J Ratcliffe/Getty Images)*
Greeting the Bidens on arrival *(Imago/Alamy Stock Photo)*
Emmanuel Macron *(Andrew Parsons/Parsons Media)*
Ukrainian troops *(Andrew Parsons/Parsons Media)*
With Zelensky *(Anadolu/Alamy Stock Photo)*
At Trump National Golf Club *(Courtesy of author)*
Top gun *(Andrew Parsons/Parsons Media)*
With Putin *(ALEXEY NIKOLSKY/Getty Images)*
With Olaf Scholz *(Andrew Parsons/Parsons Media)*
Helicopter at Chequers *(Courtesy of author)*
Christmas *(Andrew Parsons/Parsons Media)*
Great escape *(Courtesy of author)*
A camping holiday *(Courtesy of author)*
Family portraits at Downing Street and Chequers *(Andrew Parsons/Parsons Media)*
At Chequers *(Andrew Parsons/Parsons Media)*
Wedding *(Fulton Photography, www.fultonphotography.co.uk)*
Wilf and Romy *(Courtesy of author)*
In No. 10 lobby *(Andrew Parsons/Parsons Media)*
Departing *(Andrew Parsons/Parsons Media)*

Index